THE BUKE OF THE SEVYNE SAGIS

Germanic and Anglistic Studies of the University of Leiden

Editors: Professor A.G.H. Bachrach, Professor C. Soeteman, Professor J.G. Kooy.

volume XX

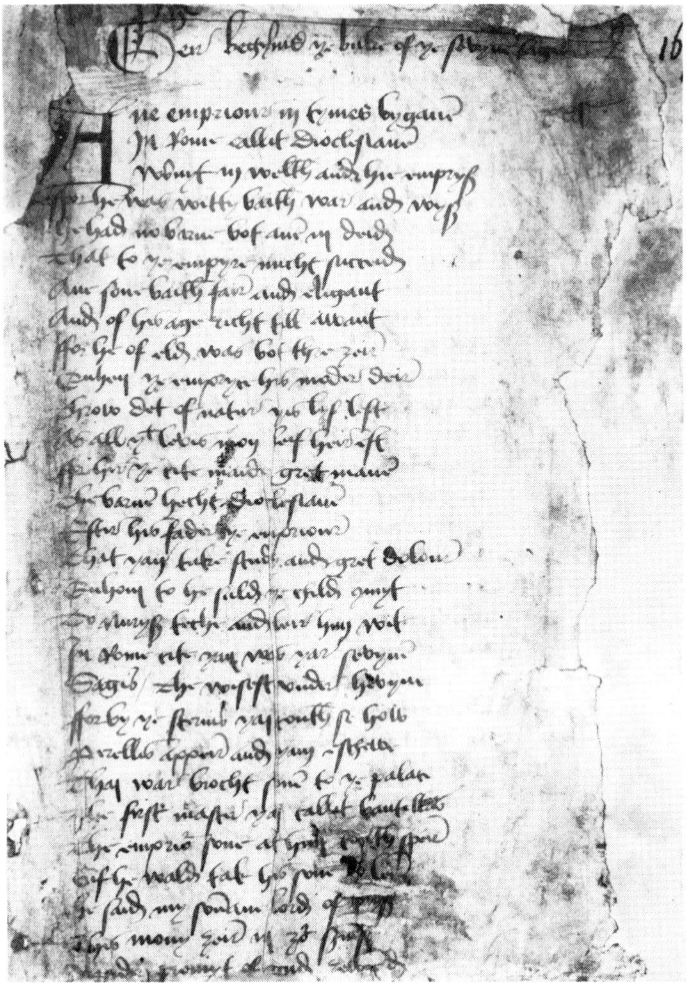

Opening page of the *Buke of the Sevyne Sagis*
Asloan Manuscript folio 167r

THE BUKE OF THE SEVYNE SAGIS

A Middle Scots Version of
THE SEVEN SAGES OF ROME

Edited from
the Asloan Manuscript
(NLS Acc. 4233), c. 1515

by

CATHERINE VAN BUUREN

LEIDEN UNIVERSITY PRESS
1982

Distributor:

E. J. Brill Publishers
P.O. Box 9000
2300 PA Leiden

Library of Congress Cataloging in Publication Data

Seven sages of Rome.
The buke of the sevyne sagis.

(Germanic and Anglistic studies of the University of Leiden; v. 20)

Bibliography: p.
Includes index.
1. Asloan, John, fl. 1515. I. Buuren, Catherine van. II. Title. III. Series.
PR2065.S3 1982 821'.1 81-23667
AACR2

ISBN 90-6021-498-6

PRINTED IN THE NETHERLANDS

TABLE OF CONTENTS

LIST OF ILLUSTRATIONS

LIST OF ABBREVIATIONS

For the abbreviations referring to manuscripts used in section XIII see pp. 131-33 and 194-95.

a., adj.	adjective
a.	*ante*, before
AN	Anglo-Norman
Ang	Anglian
BM	British Museum, London
BN	Bibliothèque Nationale, Paris
BSS	*Buke of the Sevyne Sagis*
Campbell 1898	Killis Campbell, *A Study*, see Bibliography
Campbell 1907	- - *The SSR*, - -
CF	Central French
Da	Danish
DNB	*Dictionary of National Biography*, see Bibliogr.
DOST	*Dictionary of the Older Scottish Tongue*, see Bibliography
Du	Dutch
EETS	Early English Text Society
EME	Early Middle English
ESc	Early Scots
F	French
Faer	Faeroese
Gael	Gaelic
Gmc	Germanic
Go	Gothic
Harl	Harleian
Icel	Icelandic
Ir	Irish
Jord	R.Jordan, *Handbuch der mittelenglischen Grammatik*, see Bibliography
L(at)	Latin
LME	Late Middle English
LOE	Late Old English
Luick	K.Luick, *Historische Grammatik*,see Bibliography
MDu	Middle Dutch
ME	Middle English
MED	*Middle English Dictionary*, see Bibliography
Merc	Mercian
MF	Middle French
Mi(dl)	Midland
MiS	*Mishle Sindbad*, see Bibliography, s.v. Epstein
ML	Medieval Latin
MLG	Middle Low German

MoE	Modern English
MoSc	Modern Scots
MS(S)	Manuscript(s). For the abbreviations concerning MSS, see pp. 131-33 and 194-95
MSc	Middle Scots
MSw	Middle Swedish
NED, OED	*New (Oxford) English Dictionary*, see Bibliography
NED + date	First occurrence of a word, according to *NED*
Nhb	Northumbrian
NLS	National Library of Scotland, Edinburgh
NME	Northern Middle English
NMiME	Northern Midland Middle English
N(o)	Northern
n.rh.	not rhymed
NS	New Series
NWS	Non-West Saxon
ODEE	*Oxford Dictionary of English Etymology*, see Bibliography, s.v. C.T.Onions
OE	Old English
OF	Old French
OFris	Old Frisian
OHG	Old High German
OIc	Old Icelandic
OMerc	Old Mercian
ON	Old Norse
ONF	Old Northern French
ONhb	Old Northumbrian
OS	Old Saxon
OSc	Older Scots
PGmc	Primitive Germanic
p.p.	Past participle
pr.p.	Present participle
pt.	Preterite
SATF	Société des anciens textes français
Sc	Scots
Scand	Scandinavian
SND	*Scottish National Dictionary*, see Bibliography
SSR	*Seven Sages of Rome*
STS	Scottish Text Society
WGmc	West Germanic
WS	West Saxon
>	developed into
<	originated from
*	not recorded, hypothetical form
:, rh.w.	rhyming with

UT SCOTIA SERVETUR

To the memory of
W.M.C. and J.S.V.

PREFACE

The work here edited is part of the so-called Asloan manuscript, an important Scottish miscellany, dated about 1515, which since December 1966 has been the property of the National Library of Scotland in Edinburgh (press-mark Acc. 4233). The book bears the name of Asloan because John Asloan was its scribe, signing himself as such in the explicits of most of the items of which it consists. The whole Asloan manuscript was edited by Sir William Craigie for the Scottish Text Society (NS 14 & 16, 1923 & 1925). In this edition Craigie printed the full contents of the manuscript with short descriptions of the various items, some corrections and a few notes, but without glossary or any other kind of apparatus.

In the present work my aim has been to offer a new transcription of one of the most important items found in the manuscript, the anonymous Middle Scots poem *The Buke of the Sevyne Sagis*, and to provide an adequate apparatus, a detailed description of the language and a full glossary. I have wished to facilitate the work of others and so I have tried to present the material in such a way that it can be easily compared with related studies, especially those that have to do with Middle Scots. As a result some information may appear twice, but this will make reference easier and help the specialist to find what he is looking for.

The Buke of the Sevyne Sagis is a Scottish version of the widely known medieval collection of tales within a framework narrative, usually called *The Seven Sages of Rome*. This version is independent of the Middle English rendering which is preserved in eight manuscripts, dating from between c.1320 and c.1530. For a full description of these manuscripts the reader is referred to pp. ix ff. of Karl Brunner's edition (EETS OS 191, 1933) and to Section XIV, pp. 194-95 below. There are no other known copies of *The Büke of the Sevyne Sagis* as presented here. A later Scots version is the poem *The Seuin Seages* by John Rolland of Dalkeith, which is dated about 1560 and which is not directly related to the present version; in fact, it is said on the title-page to be

'Translatit out of prois in Scottis metre' (STS III 3, 1931).

In 1898 Hermann Varnhagen in an article (*Englische Studien*, XXV, pp. 321-25) announced that he was preparing an edition of *The Buke of the Sevyne Sagis* for the Scottish Text Society. Evidently nothing ever came of it, and in 1933 Brunner in the preface to his above-mentioned edition said that the Scottish version in the Asloan manuscript deserved of a special edition as soon as the manuscript itself and not merely Laing's transcript was made accessible to scholars. It is rather surprising that Brunner apparently did not know about Craigie's edition of 1923-25.

It was Mr A.J.Aitken M.A., Senior Lecturer in English Language at the University of Edinburgh, and Editor of the *Dictionary of the Older Scottish Tongue*, who suggested to me the editing of this texts as a suitable subject for a doctoral thesis, and for this I wish to express my sincerest thanks to him; also he allowed me again and again to use unpublished material of his, and generally the present book owes a very great deal to his help, advice, support and supervision during the many years over which the work was extended.

The initial part of the labour was executed under the encouraging tutelage of my former teacher and head of department Professor Dr A.A.Prins when he occupied the chair of English Language at Leiden till 1968. It gives me pleasure to acknowledge my gratitude and indebtedness to him. It is largely due to the educational innovations since then and the ensuing time-consuming but fascinating new methods of university teaching in our department that it has taken me so long to get this edition ready for the press. I wish to express here my appreciation of the patience of my younger colleagues who bore with me and took over part of my teaching when, through the kindness of the Faculty of Letters, I was given a semester's leave of absence.

I also wish to acknowledge my great gratitude for the inspiring guidance of my promotor, Professor N.E.Osselton, the stimulating lessons of Professor Dr G.I.Lieftinck and his successor, Professor Dr J.P.Gumbert, in the field of palaeography, and for the latter's willingness to go over the palaeographical items of my edition and suggest several improvements.

Thanks are also due to Lady Joyce Talbot de Malahide who during her ownership of the Asloan manuscript allowed me to have photographs made of it and who gave me valuable information about its history; to Dr N.R.Ker for his kindness in comparing the handwriting of the *Scottish Troy Book* fragments in MS. Douce 148 (Bodleian Library, Oxford) with that of the Asloan MS. and confirming my assumption that they are identical; to Mr D.D. Murison M.A. (Aberdeen), B.A. (Cantab.), Editor of the *Scottish National Dictionary*, for his unfailing willingness to answer questions on points of language and history, and for allowing me to go over the then unpublished material of the *Dictionary*; to Miss Helen Armet, one-time Keeper of the Burgh Records of the City of Edinburgh, for kind assistance in the research concerning Edinburgh notaries; to Mme M. Berne *née* Aïache, who readily lent me her unpublished thesis of the Ecole des Chartes, Paris, on the French prose versions of the *Roman des Sept Sages*; to Mr H. Voorn of the Museum Meermanno-Westrenianum at The Hague for help in the matter of the watermarks; to the Staffs of the National Library of Scotland, the Public Library of Edinburgh, the Scottish Record Office in Her Britannic Majesty's Register House, Edinburgh, the University Library of St. Andrews, the British Library, the Bodleian Library, St.John's College, Oxford, the Cambridge University Library, the Bibliothèque Nationale and the Bibliothèque de l'Arsenal in Paris, to Captain and Lady M.H.Erskine-Wemyss of Wemyss Castle, Fifeshire, and the Staffs of Leiden University Library and the Royal Library at The Hague, for allowing me to consult manuscripts and books in their keeping.

I gratefully acknowledge grants from the Netherlands Organisation for the Advancement of Pure Research (Z.W.O.) and from the Curators of Leiden University, which made possible the photographing of some manuscripts and enabled me to consult manuscripts in Edinburgh, Oxford, Cambridge and London in 1964.

Finally I wish to express here my gratitude to Mrs Drs G.G.J. Duijfjes-Vellekoop, Miss M.Gentevoort and Dr J.Kerling for their willingness to assist me in the creation of this edition.

INTRODUCTION

I. DESCRIPTION OF MANUSCRIPT AND WATERMARKS

The Asloan Manuscript is now in the National Library of Scotland in Edinburgh; the press-mark is Acc. 4233. It derives its name from the scribe who signs himself at the ends of several items as Io(.), Ihōīs, Iohānis or Ihōn. Asloan or Sloane. It consists of 304 paper leaves. For its history see Section IV, for its contents the lists in Appendix I.

BINDING AND MENDING

In its present form it is a large handsome volume, bound in boards covered with pale-brown leather, gold-tooled, marked on the back, stamped in gold, 'SCOTTISH TRACTS IN PROSE & VERSE' and below this 'MS.TEMP.JAC.V '. A small printed label stuck on the *verso* of the flyleaf at the beginning of the book states that it was 'Bound by Thomson, Edinburgh' (see Section IV). The paper of the manuscript is early sixteenth-century French as has been ascertained by the evidence of the watermarks, on which see the relevant section below.

The manuscript-leaves have been very carefully mounted on frame sheets of rather heavy yellowish paper, watermarked J.Whatman, with several dates, all early nineteenth-century (1804, 1808, 1810, 1812, 1822). Each page has a very wide margin, so that the student is able to handle the work without fear of damaging the original paper. The missing leaves have been replaced by blank sheets of the heavy paper mentioned above. Owing to these rebinding operations the original quiring cannot be commented on, but see under Foliation below. There are no catchwords and there is no numbering of quires. The mounting has been carried out so carefully that there is hardly any cropping. The following list gives all the instances of cropping in *BSS* that have been noticed:

f. 167^r: Top of capital H; of 167^r and ^{v} the bottom lines had been lost before the mounting was done.

f. 182^r and ^{v}: Top and bottom lines had suffered from damage done to the MS before it was repaired; two words in the *recto* bottom lines had been practically lost; the same applies to the *verso*, where some letters had been traced by a later hand with darker ink. The outer margin of the leaf, before being mounted, had been restored to a width of approx. 5 cm, which only just affected the *verso* initial letters.

f. 198^{r}: The tops of flourishes are slightly covered by the surrounding yellow paper.

f. 202^{r}: Top of initial H has been cut off.

f. 205^{r} and ^{v}: Tops have been slightly damaged and mended with paper; the text has hardly suffered.

f. 207^{r}: The top has been slightly cut, involving loss of the flourish of the capital H.

Tears and other damage have been carefully mended. Here and there partially obliterated letters have been traced with a later and darker kind of ink in order to make them more legible. Several pages of the MS show tears which have been mended at a fairly early date, as is obvious from the paper used and from the fact that the folios have been numbered after the mending, in the hand which did the numbering of Alexander Boswell's index (see Appendix I).

Folio 167, the first page of *BSS*, may at one time have been the first page of the second volume before it was bound, since it shows considerable wear and soiling of the paper. This folio and ff. 175, 182, 205 and 206 have been skilfully mended with paper strips, sometimes between the lines and at both sides of the page. There is a very good example of meticulous mending outside the text of *BSS* on folio 64.

MEASUREMENTS

The measurements of the book are: 41.2 cm in height, 30 cm in breadth, and 5.5 cm in thickness (roughly $16\frac{1}{8}$" x $11\frac{3}{4}$" x $2\frac{1}{2}$"). The size of the leaves is 39.8 x 29 cm ($15\frac{3}{4}$" x $11\frac{1}{4}$"), and the thickness without the boards is 4.5 cm ($1\frac{3}{4}$"), whereas the actual manuscript-pages are 23 x 16.5 - 16.8 cm (9" x $6\frac{1}{2}$"). The size of the written part of the page is 20 - 21 x 9.5 - 10 xm (roughly 8" x 4") for poetry, 20 - 21.5 x 12.5 - 15 cm (roughly 8" x 5 - 6") for prose. Nowhere in the manuscript does the scribe use bounding lines.

HANDWRITING

The opening leaf, of which the *verso* is blank and the paper different from that of the manuscript, bears the names of several successive owners of the book, on which see Section IV, pp. 32-33. On the next leaf, also of later paper than that of the manuscript, we find a table of contents in the hand of Alexander Boswell, later Lord Auchinleck[1], containing the items actually found in the book[2]. After this we find a table of contents in Asloan's hand[3], which is much longer than Alexander Boswell's table and mentions a great many items that must have been lost between the time of writing and the date at which the later index was made; of the sixty items in Asloan's index thirty-four are now missing, among which are several pieces by Dunbar, Henryson and Walter Kennedy, and also tales such as *Rauf Coilȝear, Colkelbie's Sow* and *Golagros and Gawane,* which fortunately have come down to us elsewhere. Asloan's numbering as in the index is also found in the margin of the manuscript pages at the beginning of each item.

Asloan's handwriting is a Scottish secretary book hand, fairly regular, consistently executed in a rather steady fluent cursive script and therefore pleasant to read. Both N.Denholm-Young[4] and L.C.Hector[5] refrain from giving the name of 'Secretary' to any writing before the sixteenth century, presumably because, as Denholm-Young observes, 'the secretary hand is the name applied by the writing-masters of the sixteenth century to the formal business hand which developed out of the free small hands of Henry VII's reign'. Grant Simpson[6], when dealing with several hands of the same style as Asloan's handwriting and contemporary with it (Plates 11 - 14), calls them 'pre-secretary' cursive hands, in which he demonstrates typical secretary-hand features. He declares, however, that the name 'pre-secretary' is 'not fully satisfactory since it describes only a limited selection of characteristics. It may be that, as in England, the emergence of secretary as a recognisable script can be dated in Scotland to about the 1520s' (p.15). I have called Asloan's hand secretary, because I agree with M.B. Parkes[7], who identifies secretary features in English cursive handwriting from the third quarter of the fourteenth century. It is his opinion that in the Archiepiscopal registers at Lambeth it

PLATE I

I a

Yester Instrument (see Section II)
9.3.1517/8

Register House Charter 958A (see Section II)

Asloan MS. f. 150^{v}

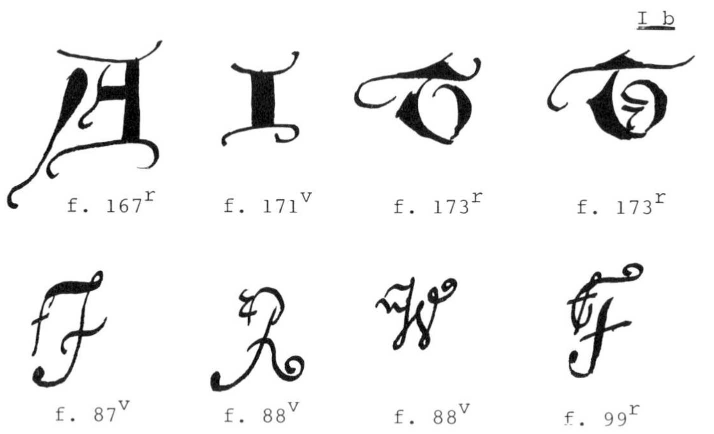

I b

f. 167^{r} f. 171^{v} f. 173^{r} f. 173^{r}

f. 87^{v} f. 88^{v} f. 88^{v} f. 99^{r}

I c

GD 28 (Yester) 381 Register House Charter 958A

9.3.1517/8 14.7.1524

first occurs in some entries in Archbishop Sudbury's Register (1375-81) and remains the normal hand of the clerks until the late seventeenth century. As to its use as a book hand he states that the script 'appears in a manuscript of Rolle's "Emendatio Vitae", dated 1384, and from a comparison of hands of undated manuscripts and dated hands in documents it is clear that it was well established as a book hand by 1400' (p.xx).

Asloan's hand is clearly related to that shown in Parkes's Plate 13 (ii), where we find a specimen of the handwriting of MS.Arch.Selden B.24, Bodleian Library, Oxford, the manuscript that contains among other items *The Kingis Quair* and Chaucer's *Troilus and Criseyde*. Parkes states that this manuscript was written in Scotland, most probably by James Gray shortly after 1488.

M.P.McDiarmid in his edition of *The Kingis Quair*[8] also discusses the Selden manuscript and states that its *terminus ante quo* must be 1513 because in that year in the Battle of Flodden Lord Sinclair, James Gray's employer for whom the manuscript was made, met his death. McDiarmid concludes, however, that Gray in 1504 must have been approaching his seventieth year and 'that we should not look much beyond 1505 for his part in the copying of the *Quair*.'

For Asloan's dates and his activities as a scribe the reader is referred to the relevant sections below.

The entire manuscript is in Asloan's hand, except for two items: f. 53^r and ^{v} is in a much smaller, probably seventeenth-century, secretary handwriting; it was evidently inserted later to replace a lost leaf; it has no watermark.

The Spektakle of Luf, ff. 137^r - 150^v, is written in a somewhat darker ink than the preceding and following items and also much less neatly than these. Its word-initial *c* has the shape of a **<**, a form seldom seen in Asloan's script. The minuscule *a* is somewhat different too. The *E* of the word *Explicit* is totally different from that of f. 40^v and the capital *E*'s of Asloan's notarial instruments (see Plate I a). The text leaves narrower margins and it has many slants at the end of lines, more than we find in Asloan's prose pieces. The general impression is that the handwriting of this item is much less bold and more hurried and unstable than that of the rest of the manuscript. These differences probably warrant the assumption that this is not Asloan's own script, but perhaps that of a clerk of his. The watermarks in this item are the same as those in the preceding and following pages, viz. no. 1, see Plate III. *The Spektakle of Luf* is not signed with the name of Asloan but with G. Myll, which is the name of the translator[9].

There are a few corrections in the text of *BSS* in Asloan's hand; e.g. on f. 172^{v} between lines 356 and 357 a line has been deleted which is identical with line 350. The scribe was evidently led astray when he read the word *nobilité* in line 356, mistaking it for *noble trè* of line 349. This is the sort of mistake that proves that the manuscript is a copy, for only in copying could a misreading of this kind take place. It also suggests that the foliation of the copied manuscript was different from Asloan's because lines 349 and 356 are on different pages in the Asloan MS. Minor mistakes or corrections will be mentioned in footnotes to the text.

There are no real marginal notes in *BSS* nor elsewhere in the Asloan MS., only scribblings and squiggles, which for the greater part have been erased, e.g. ff. 168, 171, 172^{v}, 174, 189, 189^{2v}, 190^{v}, 194^{v} , 195^{v}, 198. Outside *BSS* on f. 76^{v} some writing has been removed by the application of some liquid, not by rubbing or scratching as in other places throughout the manuscript. On f. 98^{v} under the colophon eight lines of script have been made illegible in the same way. Something resembling a signature in the last line that looked very promising for evidence of ownership appeared when viewed under ultra-violet light to be like the final words of a stanza, and not legible at that.

Some writing has also been removed in the margin of f. 101^{v}, the beginning of which shows the words 'Quhen I am seik and lyik to die ...'; the first three words are found also on f. 299^{r} where a scribbler probably meant to write the same clause as on f. 101^{v}; the script in the margin of f. 252^{v} has become illegible[10].

FOLIATION

The numbering of the leaves of the manuscript is in a later hand, not that of Asloan, most probably that of Alexander Boswell, who also wrote the folio-numbers after each item of Boswell's index already mentioned. Here and there mistakes are found; for instance, in *BSS* no. 189 occurs twice. The binding is inaccurate in several places; the *Schort Memoriale* (ff. 109-23) is incorrectly numbered and there are irregularities in the 240s. The case of *The Buke of the Chess* is particularly interesting; on the framing paper of the manuscript-leaves remarks in pencil are found, commenting on the correct order of the folios. On f. 54 there is a remark saying 'This comes after fol. 63', and on f. 59 'This comes after fol. 53', but more re-arranging is needed to arrive at the correct sequence of the pages, which is: 53, 59, 60, 61, 62, 63,| 54, 55, 56, 57, 58, 64,|| 65, 75, 70, 72, 68, 67,| 74, 73, 69, 71, 66, 76 ||. From this the original quiring can be concluded. *The Buke of the Chess* begins with f. 41 and ends with f. 76. It was probably gathered in twelves: 41-52, 53-64, 65-76. The first twelve does not present any irregularities, but the other two do; f. 53, as has been mentioned above, is in a later handwriting than that of Asloan, so this is probably a case of mending; its counterpart, f. 64, is still in the manuscript in its original form, and, as seen above, the misbinding starts from f. 53. The binder must have turned over the next five double folios, so that 54-58 changed places with 59-63. The next quire was bound completely our of order, but by re-arrangement of the double pages the correct sequence can be arrived at.

In the *Schort Memoriale* the numbering is as follows: 108 (no watermark) is blank, probably not later than Asloan's paper, the preceding item being unfinished, broken off at the bottom of the page; 109; 110; 111; 114; 115; 116; a blank yellow sheet, inserted because somebody wrote at the bottom of 116^{v} 'I suspect there is a blank here' since the text breaks off there; 117; 118; 112; 113; 119; 120; 121; 122; 123; 124, the beginning of *The Scottis Cronikle*, which should have been bound before the *Schort Memoriale* as the numbering in Asloan's index shows, where the two items have nos. xviij and xvij respectively; 125; 126; &c. This should be: 109; 110; 111; 117; 118; 112; 113; 119; 120; 121; 122; 123; 114; 115; 116; 124; 125; 126; &c.[11]

Before f. 243, starting 'The which pilleris bene far beȝond ynd ...', there is a note on a blank page of the yellow paper, saying

'The next four leaves are misplaced. They should follow folio 298, as they form part of the Complaynt of the Black Knight by Chaucer'; this title is written in the margin in a neat hand, possibly that of Thomas Thomson (1768-1852) who worked with the manuscript (see Section IV); in Asloan's table of contents it is called the 'Maying and Disport of Chaucer', but it is in fact Lydgate's 'Complaynt of the Black Knight'[12]. Ff. 243, 245 and 246 have the same watermark as ff. 296, 297, 298 and 302 (no. VII, Plate III below, a small shield with one fleur-de-lis, crowned by a cross, which does not occur elsewhere in the manuscript), whereas ff. 248 ff. have a different watermark (no. VI below, a large shield with three fleurs-de-lis).

As has been mentioned above, a blank leaf of the yellowish paper was usually inserted where gaps were suspected at the time of rebinding. Throughout the book we find remarks such as 'Here there is a part wanting', 'Here is a want', 'Imperfect', 'I suspect there is a blank here', &c., in part done probably by Alexander Boswell, Lord Auchinleck, on the original paper, and in part later, perhaps by Thomson, perhaps by Sir Alexander Boswell[13], on the marginal nineteenth-century paper. At the bottom of f. 212^{v} one of the later hands has written 'Cetera desunt'. Since f. 213, beginning *The Buke of the Howlat,* is very soiled, some pages may have been lost at an early date, before the several parts of the manuscript were collected and bound together. The initial page of *Orpheus and Erudices* (f. 247^{r}) is also more soiled than the preceding and following pages, and the previous item (no. 17, see Appendix I) is imperfect.

Soiled pages in the manuscript are: the first page of Asloan's index, 1^{r}, 17^{r}, where the seventh chapter of the *Treatises* begins, 76^{v}, 77^{r}, 123^{v}, 124^{r}, 137^{r}, 167^{r} (much damaged at the edges), 182^{r} and ^{v} (greatly damaged at the edges), 213^{r}, 247^{r}, 257^{r}, 304^{v}. Slightly soiled are 16^{v}, 109^{r}, 136^{v}, 166^{v},242^{v}(this ought to precede f. 247; ff. 243, 244, 245, 246 should follow f. 298), 256^{v}. The much-soiled pages coincide with first pages of new items. The manuscript parts may have lain about unbound for some time, hence the soiling. There would then have been ten parts.

PLATE II

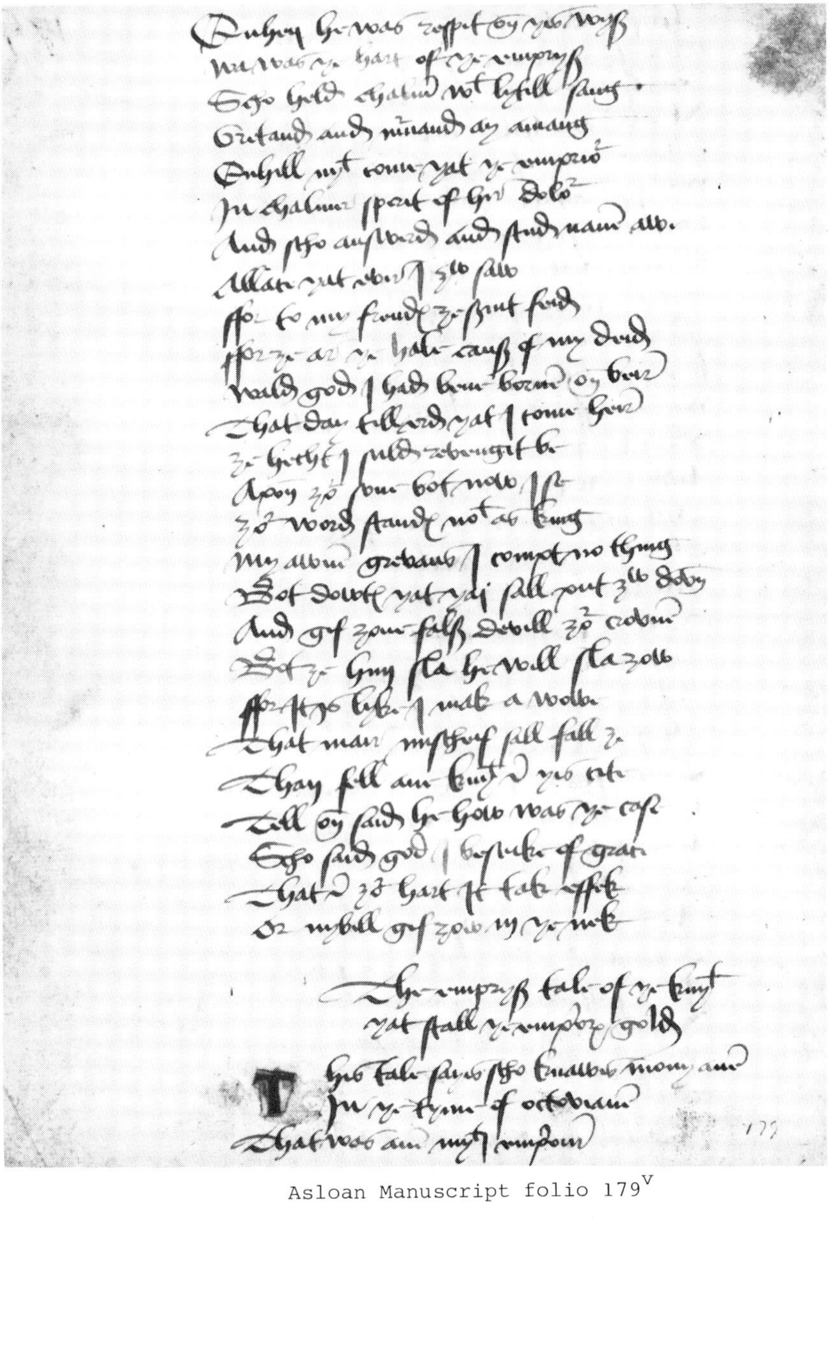

Asloan Manuscript folio 179v

THE BUKE OF THE SEVYNE SAGIS

The *BSS* consists of forty-four leaves; the number of lines to the page is between thirty-one and thirty-four; the verse is written in single columns. The lines often begin with capital letters, sometimes with larger varieties of minuscules.

In the *BSS*-part of the manuscript there are no blank leaves of the original paper, but between ff. 167 and 168 a leaf of the yellow paper has been inserted; apparently Sir Alexander Boswell or Thomas Thomson thought that something was missing here. In this he is followed by Craigie, but I do not agree[14]. F. 167 is the first leaf of *BSS* and it was mended on three edges with paper, right up to the letters of what is now the last line, so that it cannot be established whether there may have been any lines underneath. The handwriting on most pages of *BSS* covers approx. 21 cm, whereas on this folio it is only approx. 20 cm.

INITIALS

In *BSS* we find red initials on the first few folios only, see Plate I b. Sometimes we find spaces left open or provided with small guide-letters in which evidently the capitals should have been inserted later. The lack of these was apparently felt keenly by some one-time owner of the manuscript, for in many places the guide-letters have been more or less skilfully used or covered in making large capitals in a blacker ink in a rather late script, e.g. on ff. 87^v, 88^v and 99^r, see Plate I b.

Here and there initials written on small pieces of parchment have been used, pasted into their places. These were probably cut out of an older manuscript. We find red capitals *T* on f. 175^r and f. 179^v, and a red capital *I* on f. 195^v. Elsewhere in the manuscript we find a green *E* (f. 4^r), a blue *T* (f. 52^r), a red *I* (f. 77^r), and a blue *I* stuck on in a very untidy way on f. 93^r. It is to be noted that the parchment capital *I* in red, beginning the name of *Iulius Cesar* on f. 77^r, has been pasted over a later darker capital *I* as referred to above. In the same way the blue *I* on f. 93 covers a later *I*. At first sight one would think that Alexander Boswell, whose script in his index is also blacker than Asloan's, had filled in the capitals. The mystery is that the black capitals

PLATE III a

I. Asl.MS. f. 107

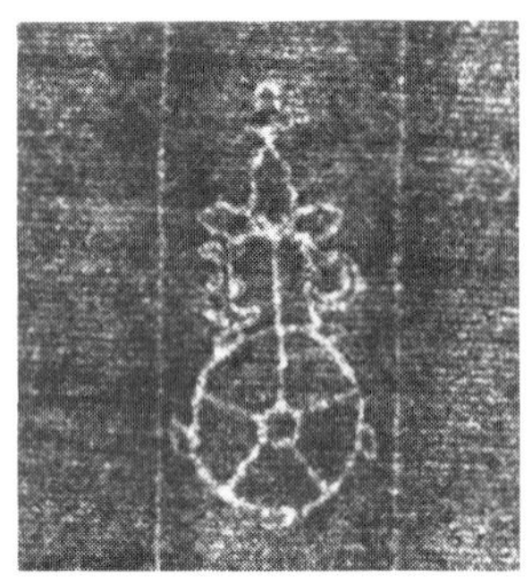

II. Asl.MS. f. 26

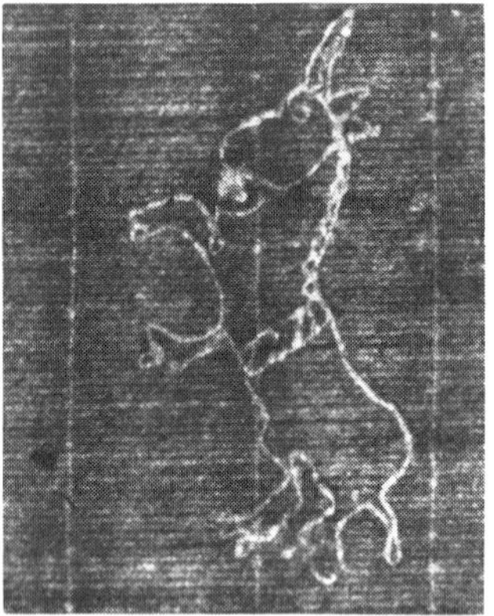

III. Asl.MS. f. 39

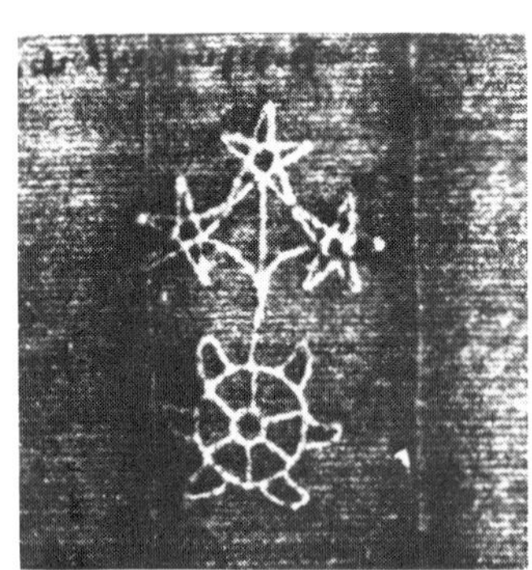

IV. Asl.MS. f. 66

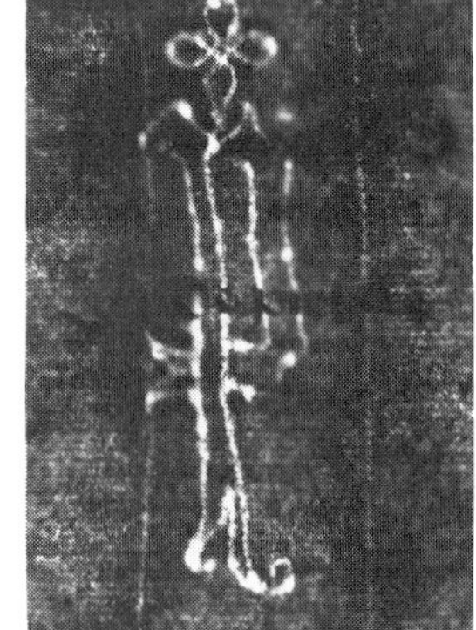

V.Asl.MS. f. 56

are in a rather late, somtimes rather clumsy, script, probably dating from the second half of the eighteenth or the beginning of the nineteenth century; also it seems out of character to think of either of the Alexander Boswells (see Section IV) as sticking parchment fragments into a paper manuscript, let alone cutting up an old parchment manuscript or document to use its coloured capitals. It may be surmised, therefore, that this was done after Sir Alexander Boswell's death, either before or after the removal of the manuscript to Ireland[15].

WATERMARKS (See Plates III a and b)

In the manuscript ten different watermarks are found, distributed as follows:

Watermark	Folios	Items
I	on ff. 4-10, 52, 77-166	Item I[16], *Treatises upon Divinity*, comprises Watermarks I, II, III; Waterm. I is also used in Items III up to and including X
II	on ff. 3, 15-26	
III	on ff. 29-39	
IV	on ff. 42-50, 66-67	Item II, *Book of Chess* (f.52 Watermark I)
V	on ff. 54-60	
VI	on ff. 167-242, 247-262	Items XI up to and incl. XIX
VII	on ff. 243-246, 293-300, 302	Item XXIII 'Chaucer' (f.302 contains Item XXIVa)
VIII	on ff. 263-291	Items XX, XXI, (XXII)
IX	on ff. 303	Item XXIVc
X	on ff. 304	Item "

Watermark I is nearest to Briquet[17] 8987, in which, however, the letter *R* is still entire. Briquet's findings date this watermark between 1493 and 1523.

II is rather similar to Briquet 13519, for which the dates 1521-27 are given.

III: Briquet 10445 is the only unicorn-watermark with a double band across the body with similar oblique strokes. The tail, however, is different, and the chainlines are more closely together than in Briquet's example. The date of 10445 is 1508.

IV is somewhere between Briquet 13367 and 13370. The first is dated between 1512 and 1548, the second 1518-1525.

V is identical with Briquet 8702 for ff. 54, 59 and 60. On ff. 55 and 56 the left-hand chainline is nearer to the letter *P* and

PLATE III b

VI. Asl.MS. f. 251

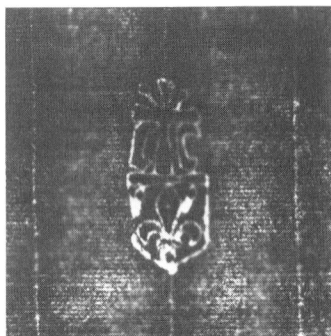

VII. Asl.MS. f. 245

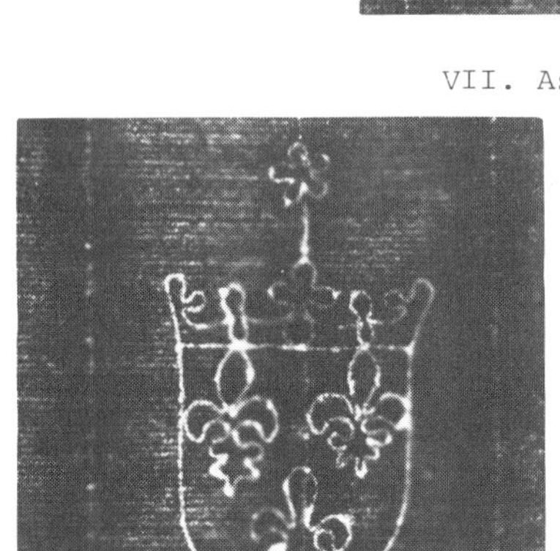

VIII. Asl.MS. f. 273

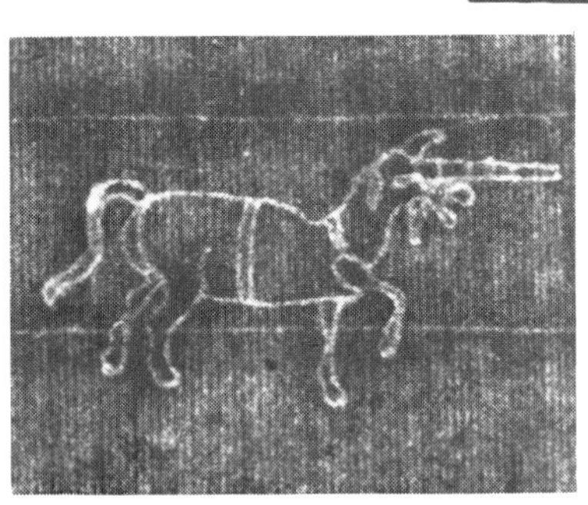

IX. Asl.MS. f. 303

X. Asl.MS. f. 304

somewhat bent. The dates of 8702 are between 1508 and 1514.
VI is Briquet 1748 with slight variations but practically identical. Dates: 1509-22.
VII is in between Briquet's 1612 and 1613, which, however, do not have a chainline in the middle of the shield but toward either side. In the Asloan-variety the letters to the left and right of the cross are more like those in 1613, but the lines between the fleurs-de-lis and the 'drops' on the top-line of the shield are not in evidence. Dates of 1612: 1513-29, of 1613: 1515-23.
VIII is like Briquet 1774, though this has the chainline not through the middle, is wider and higher, and without the wedge at the lower end. Perhaps the mark in the Asloan MS. is a more careful execution than 1774, and therefore possible a somewhat older form[18]. Dates of Briquet 1774 are 1519 and 1520.
IX seems like a variation of X, but for the angle of the unicorn's head; here the horn is parallel to the chainlines, but the face givesthe impression of being mutilated, so this may be a damaged variety of X[19]. The width of the chainlines is the same in the two.
X is a variation of Briquet 10449, without its crown but with the band across the body. The attitude is similar, the tail does not differ greatly. The size from head to tail is not much different, the height from the horn to the ground is almost the same. The dates of Briquet 10449 are between 1521 and 1528.

The above data about the paper used do not give any grounds for disagreement with the former conjectural estimates[20] of the approximate date of copying of the Asloan MS., *viz*. c. 1515.

Notes to Section I

1. This has been ascertained by comparison with the table of contents in MS. Adv. 25.4.15 of the National Library of Scotland, which is prefaced by a notice, dated 6 December 1776, in this Alexander Boswell's hand and signed with his name. See Section IV.
2. Appendix I, pp. 414-15.
3. Appendix I, pp. 416-17.
4. N.Denholm-Young, *Handwriting in England and Wales,* Cardiff, (1954) 1964, p. 71.
5. L.C.Hector, *The Handwriting of English Documents,*London, (1958) 1966, p. 61.
6. Grant G.Simpson, *Scottish Handwriting 1150-1650,* Edinburgh, 1973.
7. M.B.Parkes, *English Cursive Book Hands, 1250-1500,* Oxford, 1969.
8. *The Kingis Quair of James Stewart,* London, 1973, pp. 2 ff.
9. For further particulars see the introduction to *The Spectakle of Luf* in the *Bannatyne Miscellany,* Vol. II, ed. D.Laing, Edinburgh, 1836, pp. 121 ff.
10. For the names written on f. 40^{v} and f. 166^{v} see Section IV.
11. Cf. Craigie, Vol. I, pp. 105 ff. and 109 ff.
12. Cf. Craigie, Vol. II, p. ix.
13. See Section IV.
14. See explanatory notes to lines 30 and 62, pp.327-28.
15. See Section IV.
16. The numbers as given to the items by the present editor are shown in Appendix I, the first table of contents, pp. 414-15.
17. C.M.Briquet, *Les Filigranes,* 4 vols., Paris, 1907, and the new edition, Amsterdam, 1968.
18. For extremely interesting explanations of the work of the watermark maker and the deterioration of marks see Allan Stevenson, *The Problem of the Missale Speciale,* London, The Bibliographical Society, 1967, pp. 245-52.
19. Plate III.
20. See e.g. J.H.Millar, *A Literary History of Scotland,* London, 1903, p. 5 n., and G.Gregory Smith, *Specimens of Middle Scots,* Edinburgh, 1902, p. 14.

II. THE IDENTITY OF JOHN ASLOAN[1]

At the end of several of the items in the manuscript we find the name of the scribe, eight times as Iohānis, Ihōn or Io(.) Asloan, once as Ihōīs Sloane[2]. By research, done mainly in Edinburgh, I have been able to ascertain that John Asloan was a notary public[3] in that town.

The earliest reference to a John (A)Sloane is found in William Robertson's *Parliamentary Records of Scotland*[4], where we read that on 5 February 1494/5 John Sloane appeared at Linlithgow as Procurator for George Herris of Terrauchty and others, having been summoned at the instance of Herbert Lord Herris of Terreglis. In *Acts of the Lords of Council in Civil Causes*[5] he occurs as procurator together with James Young, notary public, on 24-26 January 1498/99, again for George Herris of Terrauchty. Asloan's name occurs several times in James Young's *Protocol Book 1485-1515*[6]: 22 May 1497 as John Sloane, a witness, 1 July 1500 as John Slowan, a witness, 3 July 1500 as John Aslowan, a witness, and 6 March 1505/6 as John Asloane, mentioned as cousin of 'Robert Asloane, cordiner' (shoemaker).

In August 1512 we find him named as a witness in the 'Carta Alexandri Rynde' in the *Registrum Cartarum Eccl.S.Egidii de Edinburgh*[7], and from 23 July 1512 his name occurs six times in the *Protocol Book of John Foular 1514-1528*[8], three times as a witness in 1512, 1513 and in 1525/6, three times as a notary public and witness in 1518, 1520 and 1522. In Foular's books his name is written as John Sloan(e) and John (A)Slowan(e).

In the *Protocol Book of Vincent Strathauchin, Vol. I, 7 December 1507 to 4 February 1524-5,* transcribed in manuscript by Miss Helen Armet, former Keeper of the Burgh Records of the City of Edinburgh, we find John Slowane mentioned three times as a witness, *viz.* 23 October 1511, 16 June 1512, and 14 June 1513. (There are three more volumes which, however, have not yet been transcribed and indexed: Vol. II, 14 February 1524 to 19 March 1533; Vol. III, 21 March 1533 to 5 January 1547; Vol IV, 10 January 1547 to 16 September 1553, of which especially Vols. II and III might have given us clues as to John Asloan's possible further activities.)

The earliest mention of Asloan in the capacity of a notary public is dated 9 March 1517/8. It is found in an instrument among the writs preserved at Yester House (the seat of the Marquis of Tweeddale), now in the Scottish Record Office, in Her Britannic Majesty's Register House in Edinburgh. This instrument is in his own hand and shows his notarial sign: an *I* and an *S* interlaced, and his signature (see Plate I c). He signs himself as John Asloan, clerk of the diocese of St.Andrews, Notary Public. A second instrument, also from Yester House and dated 29 March 1524, mentions John Asloan as a notary public[9]. Another instrument in his own hand is also in Register House, Edinburgh. It is dated 14 July 1524, and bears his notarial sign and his signature with the qualifications: clerk of the diocese of St.Andrews and notary public[10]. There is no doubt whatever that this handwriting is the same as that of the Asloan MS.

Finally we find two references to John Asloan, notary public, in the *Register of the Great Seal of Scotland, 1513-46*[11], *viz.* of the dates 23 March 1527/8 and 3 March 1529/30. After this we hear no more of him[12].

It has been suggested by George Chalmers in his transcription of the Asloan MS.[13] that the scribe of the manuscript was a Procurator or Advocate in the reign of James IV (1488-1513). He quotes from Robertson's *Parliamentary Records*[14] and adds that John Sloane was probably a Galloway man, who appears to have either inherited or acquired a small landed property named Garreach in the Stewartry of Kirkcudbright (Galloway). I do not agree; there are indeed several records of a John Aslon(e), Ascloane, Slowane, Sloane, the owner of a property called Garhauch, Gareach, Garroche, Gariauch, Garoch, or Garaith, situated in the Stewartry of Kirkcudbright, but to my mind this can hardly be the scribe and notary of Edinburgh.

In 1473/4 a Herbert Sloone figures in the *Accounts of the Lord High Treasurer 1473-1566*[15] in connection with his lands in Garveauch. In 1477 Herbert Ascloane de Garehauch and his son Joh. Ascloane are among the witnesses of the sale of the lands of Trarachty 'infra dominium Galwidie et Senesc. de Kirkcudbrycht' to 'Georgeo Heris filio et heredi apparenti Roberto Heris de Kirkpatrick-Irnegray et heredibus ejus'[16]. We also find Herbert Asloan of Gawrawch mentioned[17] on 29 May 1485 as a witness for an instrument of resignation by George Heris of Terawchtie. One of the other witnesses was master Robert Heris, vicar of Tereglis[18]. In 1503 John Asloane of Gareach, Drumfreis (*sic*) is found in the *Exchequer Rolls of Scotland*[19], and from this item it must be concluded that his father, Herbert Asloan, must have died between 1485 and 1503. In 1508 Johne Slowane of Garroche was juror on assize at Kirkcudbright[20]. In 1510 the King granted a charter of confirmation of a Charter by John Sloane of Gariauch, to John Sloane, of the lands of Gariauch[21]. It appears that there were a father and a son, both called John Sloane; the father must have died between 1510 and 1520, for in 1520 Johnne Asloane of Garoch is referred to as 'umquhile Johne Asloane' and wardship of Garoch is given to a 'David Anderson', so that we must conclude that 'Johne Asloane the son and aire of the said umquhile Johne' referred to was presumably under age in 1520[22]. For the year 1531 we find entries concerning him in the *Exchequer Rolls*, in the *Register of the Great Seal* and in the *Accounts of the Lord High Treasurer*. In 1542 John Asloane of Garroch is heard of for the last time; he appears as a witness in the *Protocol Book (1541-1550) of Herbert Anderson, Notary in Dumfries*[23].

Though the names of the notary public and of the owner of Garroch are identical it seems highly unlikely for a landowner in south-west Scotland to have a notarial practice in Edinburgh, and to busy himself with the transcription of manuscripts.

It might perhaps be suggested that John Asloan the notary was a relation of the Asloans of Garroch, recommended to George Herris who lived in the same district, Kirkcudbright, for the transaction of his affairs at Linlithgow and Edinburgh in the 1490s.

Notes to Section II

1. See my article in *English Studies,* XLVII, 1966, pp. 365-72.
2. The prefix *A-*, an equivalent of Irish *O'*, was a common feature of many south-west Scottish surnames, see G.F.Black, *The Surnames of Scotland,* New York, 1946, s.v. *Sloan.*
3. For particulars on the function and activities of notaries public see Grant G.Simpson, op.cit., p. 7, Richard F.Dell, 'Some Differences Between Scottish and English Archives', *Journal of the Society of Archivists,* III, 1965-68, pp. 386-97, and David Murray, *Legal Practices in Ayr and the West of Scotland, a study in economic history,* Glasgow, 1910, pp. 7 ff.
4. Vol. I, Edinburgh, 1804, p. 455.
5. Vol. II, *Scotland 1496-1501,* eds G.Neilson and H.Paton, Edinburgh, 1918, p. 316.
6. *Protocol Book of James Young, 1485-1515,* ed. Gordon Donaldson, Scottish Record Society No. 74, Edinburgh, 1952.
7. Ed. D.Laing, Bannatyne Club, 1859, p. 196.
8. *Protocol Book of John Foular,* Vol. I, 1500-03, eds Walter Macleod and Marguerite Wood; Vol. II, 1503-13, and Vol. III, 1514-28, ed. Marguerite Wood; Scott.Rec.Soc. Nos. 64, 72, 75, Edinburgh, 1930, 1941, 1944.
9. *Calendar of Writs preserved at Yester House 1166-1625,* eds Charles C. Harvey and John Macleod, Scott.Rec.Soc. No. 55, Edinburgh, 1930.
10. For transcription see the handwritten *Calendar of Charters and other Original Documents preserved in H.M.General Register House,* Vol. V, 1513-50, No. 958A (available in the said Register House, Edinburgh).
11. Eds Sir James Balfour Paul, J.M.Thomson, J.H.Stevenson, W.K. Dickson, Edinburgh, 1882-1914.
12. A John Asloan mentioned under 1552 in *Records of the Burgh of Edinburgh,* Vol. II, 1528-57, ed. J.D.Marwick, Scottish Burgh Record Society, Edinburgh, 1871, and in *City of Edinburgh Old Accounts,* Vol. I, 1544-67, ed. Robert Adam, Edinburgh, 1899, was clearly a merchant. There appears to be no means of telling whether he was related to our notary public or not.

13. Chalmers MS. Collections, Edinburgh University Library.
14. Loc.cit., note 4 above.
15. Ed. Thomas Dickson and Sir James Balfour Paul, Edinburgh, 1877-1916.
16. *Register of the Great Seal,* see note 11 above.
17. *The Lag Charters, 1400-1720, Sir Philip J.Hamilton-Grierson's Calendar,* ed. Athol L.Murray, Scott.Rec.Soc. No. 88, Edinburgh, 1958.
18. See p. 21.
19. Ed. G.Burnett and others, Edinburgh, 1878-1908.
20. *Ancient Criminal Trials of Scotland 1487-1624,* ed. Robert Pitcairn, Edinburgh, 1833.
21. *Register of the Privy Seal,* Vol. IV, f. 129, as quoted by Chalmers in his transcript of the Asloan MS., see note 13 above.
22. *Registrum Secreti Sigilli Regum Scotorum,* ed. M.Livingstone and others, Edinburgh, 1908-
23. *Dumfriesshire and Galloway Natural History and Antiquarian Society Transactions,* 3.ser.ii, Dumfries, 1914, pp. 176-224.

III. ASLOAN'S ACTIVITIES AS A COPYIST

In my article in *English Studies*[1] mentioned above I have identified Asloan as the man who, in the Colophon of MS. Douce 148 (Lydgate's *Troy Book*, with the *Scottish Troy Book Fragments*, in the Bodleian Library Oxford) said that he had 'written and mendit' this manuscript 'at the Instance of ane honourable chaplane Schir Thomas ewyn in Edinburgh'. He did not give his own name there as he does in the Asloan MS., but the handwriting of the two manuscripts is identical as is shown in Plate IV . The white-on-black fragments are from MS. Douce 148, the black-on-white ones from the Asloan MS. The writing in the Douce MS. is more careful, it seems, and done with a steadier hand. It does not seem too bold to conjecture that it was done earlier.

In the above-mentioned article I also expressed the opinion that Asloan had likewise 'mendit' the First Edinburgh MS. of Wyntoun's *Chronicle* (NLS Adv.MS. No.19.2.3) on the evidence of the handwriting, the fact that the folios written by Asloan do not have the bounding lines consistently used in the rest of the MS, and on the fact that the watermarks of the leaves written by Asloan are different from those of the leaves done by the other scribe or scribes. Eleven folios in all have been done by Asloan; he uses paper with a watermark like no. VI, depicted in Section I, Plate III, and with one showing an upright hand with a trefoil above the fingers, whereas the leaves before and after those written by Asloan have watermarks in the shape of a very inelegant pot-bellied unicorn, a crown above a six-pointed star, and a letter *P*.

Another difference between Asloan and the other copyist of the First Edinburgh MS. of Wyntoun's *Chronicle* is that Asloan hardly ever uses the letter *y* (for *th*) at the beginning of a line, whereas the other man does this often.

The divergence of watermarks also applies to the leaves written by Asloan in the *Troy Book* MS. Douce 148: ff. 1-44 and 302-312 show a watermark very much like no. VIII, see Section I, Plate III); ff. 46-138, done by the other scribe, have a different watermark, a shield with two illegible letters (perhaps *be* or *hc*) with a fleur-de-lis on top; f. 139 written by Asloan has a unicorn; f. 63 by the other scribe has a letter *P*; ff. 317-336 by Asloan show a hand with a flower held between the index and middle finger; ff. 141-255, 258-299 by the other scribe have a wheel with six hooks, with a crozier-like object above.

The Wemyss MS. of Wyntoun's *Chronicle*, which I was very kindly given the opportunity of seeing by Captain M.J.Erskine-Wemyss at Wemyss Castle, Fife, in December 1966, is written throughout by one scribe, whose handwriting is very much like that of Asloan. There are some differences, however. The capital *A* used regularly in this MS is of a kind not commonly used by Asloan; also there are bounding lines on three sides of the writing area, a feature not found in the MSS that can be safely attributed to John Asloan; furthermore the writing gives the impression that it was done more hurriedly and less neatly than that of the other MSS discussed.

The watermarks of the paper of the Wemyss MS. very often show a hand held vertically with the palm visible, a cuff surrounding the wrist; very often a trotting unicorn is found or a letter *P* with a split shaft; once only do we find a shield with three fleurs-de-lis, very similar to Nos. VI and VIII of the Asloan MS. watermarks. Since I was not able to obtain permission to have the Wemyss MS. photographed I cannot reach any further conclusions concerning it, for lack of sufficient material for comparison.

To the evidence that notaries public often did copying work[2], adduced by me in the above-mentioned article in *English Studies*, I might add that they also figured as authors: Richard Holland, the author of the *Buke of the Howlat* was a notary public[3], as was John Rolland, the author of the later *Seuin Seages* and of the *Court of Venus*[4]; John Reid alias Stobo, mentioned by Dunbar in his *Lament for the Makaris* and the possible author of *The Thre Prestis of Peblis*, was a notary besides being a churchman and secretary to James II, James III and James IV[5], and 'Robert Henryson is possibly the notary witnessing deeds in Dunfermline in 1477 and 1478'[6].

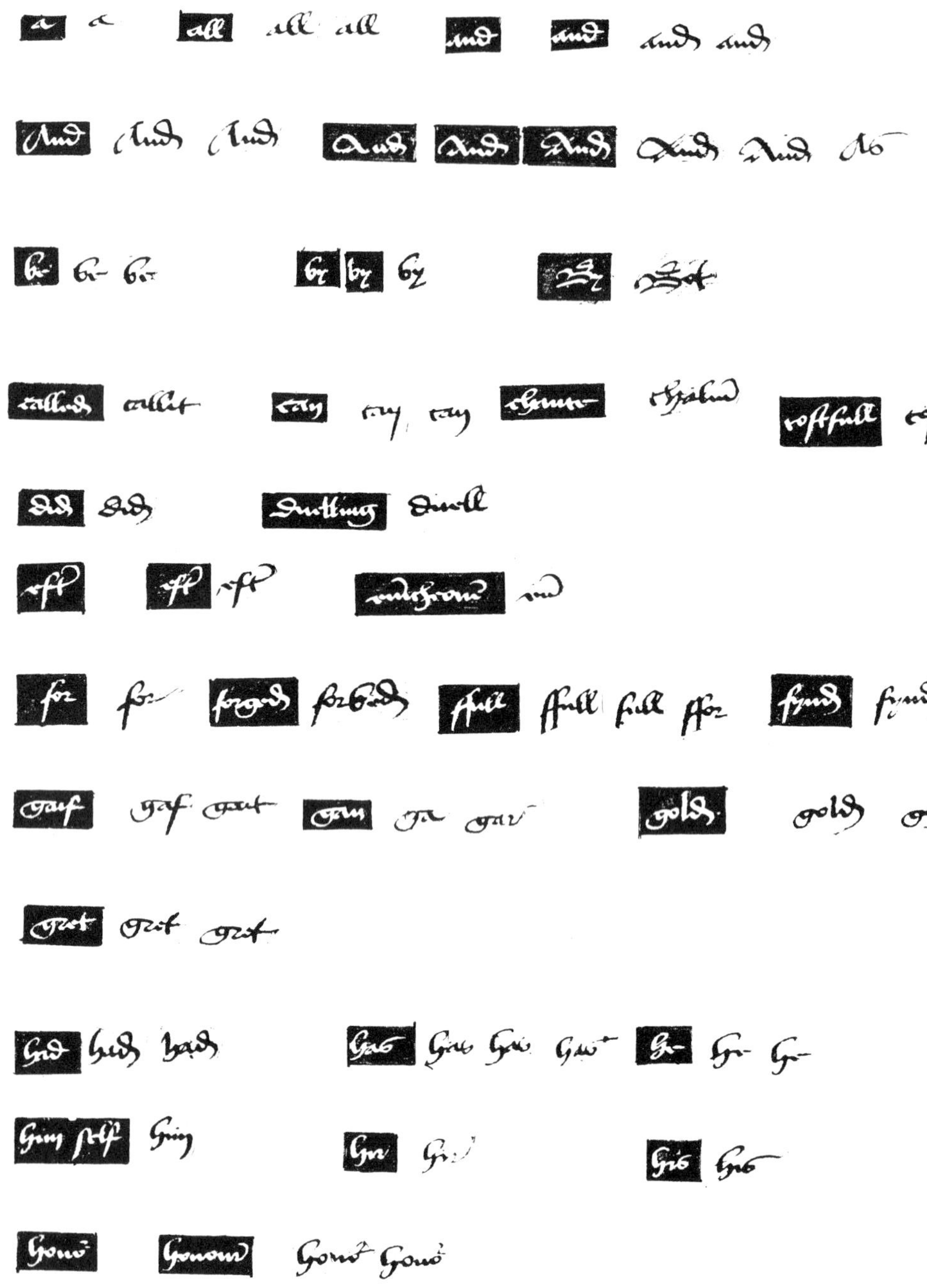

Plate IV b

Notes to Section III

1. See Section II, note 1.
2. In a recent article 'The literature of fifteenth-century Scotland' Professor John MacQueen mentions two more notaries public who copied out vernacular manuscripts, viz. James Gray, who wrote part of the well-known MS. Bodleian, Arch.Selden B.24, in which we find several of Chaucer's works, *The Kingis Quair,* &c. (see Section I, p. 9); and Richard Striveling, who copied part of the *Scotichronicon* (MS. BL Harl. 4764). See *Scottish Society in the Fifteenth Century,* ed. Jennifer M.Brown, London, 1977, pp. 201-202.
3. See *Scottish Alliterative Poems,* ed. F.J.Amours, STS I. 27 and 38, Edinburgh, 1897, pp. xxiii-xxv; the *Buke of the Howlat* also occurs in *The Asloan Manuscript,* ed. W.A.Craigie, Vol. II, STS NS 16, Edinburgh, 1925, pp. 95-126.
4. See John Rolland's *Ane Treatise Callit The Court of Venus,* ed. Walter Gregor, STS I.3, Edinburgh, 1884, pp. vii-ix, and *The Seuin Seages,* ed. Geo.F.Black, STS III.3, Edinburgh, 1932, pp. xi-xii.
5. *The Thre Prestis of Peblis,* ed. T.D.Robb, STS NS 8, 1920, pp. xvi ff., quoting Dr. Renwick's 'Historical Notes on Peeblesshire Localities', p. 119.
6. Marion M.Stewart, 'The Makars' Scotland: Some Facts from the Records', *Scottish Literary News,* Vol. 3, No. 2, July 1973, p. 16. See also Denton Fox, ed., *Robert Henryson , Testament of Cresseid,* London, 1968, pp. 16-17 on Henryson being a schoolmaster and a notary public, and Fox's note 1 on p. 17.

IV. HISTORY AND OWNERSHIP OF THE ASLOAN MANUSCRIPT

From the fact that Asloan wrote and mended 'The Sege of Troye' for Sir Thomas Ewen (see Section III and my above-mentioned article in *English Studies*), and that he evidently mended the First Edinburgh MS. of Wyntoun's *Chronicle* - though it is not known for whom this second work was done - we might surmise that the copying of the Asloan MS. was also done to order.

Hermann Varnhagen in the introduction to his short work *Eine italienische Prosaversion der sieben Weisen*[1] quotes David Laing's introduction to his edition of Rolland's *Seuin Seages* on the subject of the Asloan MS. and adds that the manuscript was 'formerly in the possession of Mr. Asloan in Edinburgh'[2]. The use of the word Mr. makes it clear that Varnhagen looked upon Asloan as one of the later successive owners of the manuscript. Though it is obvious that a man who copies a book 'possesses' the copy for some time while he is working on it, even if it is done to order for someone else, the fact that he may have been just the copyist does not become clear from the words used by Varnhagen. On the other hand there is nothing to prove that Asloan might not have compiled the manuscript for his own pleasure. The circumstance that the several parts of the manuscript must have lain unbound for a long time (see Section I, p.12) might point to this.

The earliest indication of ownership is found in the Asloan Manuscript on f. 40^v, at the end of the first item after 'Explicit *per manum*:Johannis Asloan. Finis', where we find the following words: *per me Gulielmum Murray Manu Mea et ...* These words must have been covered with paper for some time. Craigie does not print them nor does he mention them; perhaps he thought them irrelevant, since he did not concern himself with the history of the manuscript. The paper has now been for the greater part removed and, as elsewhere in the book, someone seems to have tried to remove the handwriting, probably by applying some liquid; however that may be, the two or three letters after *Manu Mea et* cannot be deciphered. The words are written in italic script, most likely of the first half of the seventeenth century. The name mentioned, Murray, is a common one, and Scottish documents of the sixteenth and seventeenth centuries mention a great number of individuals called William Murray. The name is not found in Durkan and Ross[3], either among the bishops or among the private owners. Helena Shire[4] speaks of several men named William Murray, one a court servant at the time of the Ruthven Raiders (1582-3), another, Sir William Murray of Dysart, a poet still alive when Sir Robert Aytoun died in 1638. Caroline Bingham[5] mentions Sir William Murray of Abercairney, connnected with the House of Mar, as one of the small group of boys who were educated with young James VI by George Buchanan and Peter Young. Maurice Lindsay[6] states that one William Murray seems to have been the only poet in the retinue of the King when he was in the hands of the Ruthven Raiders. He also mentions William Murray of Dysart[7]. However regrettable, it does not seem possible to identify anyone of the above as the potential one-time owners of the Asloan MS.

Another possible indication of ownership is on f. 166^v in the margin where we find a fragmentary clause, reading as follows: 'I William Leslye off Bowquhan grantis me to haff rasavit fre ye haiye(?)' and below: 'Ffader'. This may be just meaningless scribbling, perhaps copying of a receipt which happened to be lying before the scribbler, but the name mentioned may be a reference to the family of Leslie of Balquhain. According to Col. Charles Leslie, *Pedigree of the Leslies of Balquhain*, Bakewell, 1861, there were two members of this family of the name of William:
1. William Leslie, 9th Laird of Balquhain, who died in 1571;
2. William Leslie, 13th Laird, who died c.1660. Of the two the first must from the language and the handwriting be the man mentioned. This seems to point to the possibility of the presence of the manuscript at the house of or in the neighbourhood of Balquhain, an ancient seat of the Leslies which is near Inverurie in Aberdeenshire.

For further indication as to ownership the flyleaf of the manuscript is conclusive. Three of the owners have written their names there:

1. Alexander Boswel. March. 1730.
2. R.W.Talbot from J.J.Boswell, June 29th, 1882.

3. Talbot de Malahide, James Boswell, March 1921. According to the first entry the book was in 1730 in the possession of Alexander Boswell of Auchinleck, who lived from 1706 to 1782; he was the eldest son of James Boswell of Auchinleck, advocate, and Lady Elizabeth Bruce, a daughter of Alexander, second Earl of Kincardine[8].

The estate of Auchinleck in Ayrshire had been given to one of his ancestors, Thomas Boswell, by King James IV in 1504 as a token of royal favour[9], and Alexander was the 8th Laird of Auchinleck. Like his father and many others preparing for the Scottish bar he had gone to Leiden; he matriculated at Leiden University on 29 December 1727, and stayed for about two years[10]. He was admitted advocate at Edinburgh on 29 December 1729. In 1754 he was elevated to the Bench as one of the fifteen judges of the Court of Session, the supreme Court of Scotland for civil cases; he took his seat as Lord Auchinleck[11]. The following year he was also nominated a Lord Justiciary, one of the five judges of the High Court of Justiciary, the supreme Court for criminal cases in Scotland. He was a man of strong religious and political convictions, with a love of Presbyterianism and a loyal attachment to the House of Hanover[12] and according to one of his friends 'one of those great beams which are placed here and there to support the edifice of Society'[13]. He donated several manuscripts to the Advocates' Library in Edinburgh, for example the well-known Auchinleck MS, (NLS, Press-mark Adv.MS. 19.2.1, No. 155) and two manuscripts of the *Regiam Majestatem* and other Scots law treatises (NLS, Adv.MSS. 25.4.14 and 25.4.15). The Auchinleck MS. had been acquired by him in 1740 and he gave it to the library in 1744 or 1745; the other two manuscripts he had acquired in 1731 and 1750 respectively and he presented them to the library on 6 December 1776, each with a note in his own handwriting on the flyleaf. That of MS. 25.4.14 reads: 'I Alex^r Boswel of Auchinleck, one of the Senators of the College of Justice considering that this manuscript which I have possesst long may be of great Use to any man who shall incline to publish the Antient Laws of Scotland And that it is fit such a manuscript shoud be deposited in the Library of the Learned Faculty of Advocates Hereby make the same over to that learned society. Alex^r Boswel.'

The next owner of the Asloan MS. was his grandson[14], Alexander Boswell (1775-1822), who was created first Baronet of Auchinleck in 1821. He was an antiquary, wrote Scottish songs and established a private printing-press at Auchinleck where many rare books in both English and Scots were printed and also a series of old poems, which were afterwards collected under the title 'Frondes Caducae'[15]. Two of the products from this press were items of the Asloan MS.: Item 6, *Ane Tractat of a Part of the Ynglis Cronikle ...,* and Item 2, *The Buke of the Chess,* dedicated to Thomas Thomson, both done in 1818. Another item, No. 7, had also been printed before 1819, by Thomas Thomson (see below), but it was not published until 1877, when T.G.Stevenson issued it under the title 'The Auchinleck Chronicle' with an introduction from his hand[16].

It was through the latter Alexander Boswell's care that the Asloan MS. was so expertly treated and made into the beautiful volume which it now is. He had the leaves mounted, and the binding was done in the General Register House, Edinburgh, under the supervision of Thomas Thomson, Deputy Clerk Register. 'Mr. Thomson was an authority in historical matters, very judicious and very intelligent and learned, but it was thought rather dilatory in getting work through his hands' according to David Laing as quoted by T.G.Stevenson[17]; this is borne out by Cosmo Innes in his *Memoir*[18]: ' ... his grand defect was a morbid reluctance to commit his opinions to paper. ... Even the excellent books which he employed his leisure in preparing for the press - the Accounts of the Lord Chamberlain, the little Auchinleck Chronicle, ... he allowed to go forth without any worthy preface. Each of these correct, tasteful books he turned out upon the world with the slenderest introduction'. Therefore it need not surprise us that he was slow in returning the private records and documents that had been placed at his disposal by various owners for the purpose of compiling an edition of the Acts of Parliament of Scotland, among which records was the Asloan MS.[19]

Innes also tells us: 'From 1805 downwards, Sir Alexander Boswell of Auchinleck was a frequent correspondent of Mr. Thomson's. He consulted him about the arrangement and completing of his library, and was always ready to communicate whatever of books or MSS. his grandfather old Lord Auchinleck's curious collection afforded'. In a letter of 14 May 1810 from Alexander Boswell to Mr. Thomson the former mentions his copy of 'Winton' and says: 'I hope the printing of the "Chronicle" goes well'[20]. This referred to Item 7 of the Asloan MS. (see Appendix I, p.414), which Thomson 'valued as one of the few contemporary authorities of the reign of James II. It was the first of his publications'[21]. From other items of correspondence[22], dating from 1817 and 1819, it is clear that Boswell and Thomson were in regular contact about books and manuscripts, and that Sir Alexander was taking much trouble over his library; in the letter of August 1819 he says, for instance: 'If I live I shall certainly endeavour to increase it; but in that department, viz., books relating to Scotland, I have unfortunately started too late, as they now bear a most exorbitant price. ... It is much to be lamented that the Advocates' Library did not see the value of such a collection long ago. Even now as a national library they ought to direct their attention to such books as relate to the history and progress of the literature of Scotland, for there should not be a book in existence connected with either that is not to be found in that collection'. In the same letter he says that he only removes books from his grandfather's collection when he purchases better copies: '... but unless I supply a better, I keep all my grandfather's, out of respect to his exertions, which I regret were not greater at so favourable a time'.

A number of manuscripts from the Auchinleck library, together with the Asloan MS., remained in Mr. Thomson's hands for many years until they were reclaimed after Sir Alexander's death in 1822[23] by Mr. James A.Maconochie, Advocate[24], one of the trustees of his son James. Mr. Maconochie died in Edinburgh in February 1845, without having returned the books to Auchinleck. His library was sold about three months later by Mr. Peter Scott Fraser, who in his catalogue did not mention any manuscripts. He must have kept them back, for in 1876 it appeared that he had sold the Asloan MS. in 1867 to William Paterson, an Edinburgh bookseller, who had it in his possession on the occasion of evidence adduced to the House of Lords in the claim of Sir Frederic John William Johnstone, Bart., to the Earldom of Annandale[25].

It is not known how and when the manuscript was returned to Auchinleck; Sir Alexander's son James, second and last baronet, died in 1857[26], leaving two daughters. One of these, Emily Harriet, married in 1873 Richard Wogan, 5th Baron Talbot de Malahide (1846-1921) whose name we find as the second entry on the flyleaf of the Asloan MS., with the date 1882[27]. According to Lady Joyce Talbot de Malahide in a letter to me dated 27 June 1967 it was Sir James Boswell's widow who had given him the manuscript. She is the J.J. Boswell mentioned after the name of R.W.Talbot in the second entry. She was Jessie Jane, daughter of Sir James Montgomery Cunninghame, and mother-in-law to R.W.Talbot[28]. In 1917 Lord Talbot granted access to the manuscript and gave to Sir William Craigie permission for its publication[29], thus putting an end to the complaints of scholars who had not been able to consult it[30].

At his death in 1921 Lord Talbot was succeeded by his son James Boswell Talbot, 6th Baron (1874-1948), and the third inscription on the flyleaf was inserted by the latter. He left the book to his wife, Lady Talbot just mentioned, who was so kind as to grant it on loan to the British Museum, where it was kept for a number of years. In December 1966 it was purchased from Lady Talbot by the National Library of Scotland and was moved there shortly before Christmas 1966, so that this product of Scottish culture has now happily returned to Scotland.

Notes to Section IV.

1. London, 1881, pp. x--xi.
2. The German original has: *ehemals im besitze des Mr. Asloan in Edinburgh.*
3. John Durkan and Anthony Ross, *Early Scottish Libraries,* Glasgow, 1961.
4. Helena Mennie Shire, *Song, Dance and Poetry of the Court of Scotland under James IV,* Cambridge University Press, 1969, pp. 91, 214 and 227.
5. Caroline Bingham, *The Making of a King,* Collins, London, 1968, pp. 83-4.
6. Maurice Lindsay, *History of Scottish Literature,* Robert Hale, London, 1977, p. 94.
7. From Donaldson & Morpeth's *Dictionary of Scottish History* (see note 19 below) we learn that William Murray of Dysart (c.1600-51) was educated with Charles I.
8. *DNB,* Vol. II, s.v. Alexander Boswell, 1706-82.
9. James Paterson, *History of the Counties of Ayr and Wigton,* Edinburgh, 1863, Vol. I, Part I, pp. 190-91. Thomas Boswell was killed at Flodden in 1513, see David Buchanan, *The Treasure of Auchinleck, The Story of the Boswell Papers,* London, 1975, p. 310.
10. He lived first in the *Rapenburg* in the house of the widow of Steven Boenen, later at 'Philip Ramacq's'; he paid his enrolment fee twice. See *Album Studiosorum Academiae Lugduno Batavae MDLXXV - MDCCCLXXV,* Hagae Comitum, 1875, Inscript. 1727-1755.
11. G.Brunton and D.Haig, *An Historical Account of the Senators of the College of Justice,* Edinburgh, 1832, p. 518.
12. *Boswelliana, The Commonplace Book of James Boswell.* With a memoir and annotations by Rev. Charles Rogers LL.D., London, 1876, p. 6.
13. Ibid., p. 238.
14. The father of this Alexander was James Boswell, Samuel Johnson's biographer, of whose interest in the library of Auchinleck there is no evidence here. But David Buchanan, op.cit., p. 5, tells us that the 'transmission of his papers was governed by his will, made ten years (before his death). To Alexander, his elder son and heir to the entailed estate of Auchinleck, he bequeathed "greek and latin Books, as also all Manuscripts of whatever kind lying in the House of Auchinleck."'

15. *DNB,* s.v. Alexander Boswell, 1775-1822.
16. Thomas Thomson (ed.), *The Auchinleck Chronicle- Ane Schort Memoriale of the Scottis Corniklis for Addicioun, ... Printed from the Asloan Manuscript in the Library at Auchinleck, Ayrshire ...* , 1819. With an introductory note by T.G.Stevenson, Edinburgh, 1877. See note 20 below.
17. Ibid., p. ix.
18. Cosmo Innes, *Memoir of Thomas Thomson, Advocate,* Bannatyne Club No. 99, Edinburgh, 1854, pp. 184 f.
19. In this connection we find in *DNB* s.v. Thomas Thomson, 1768-1852: 'Devoted as he was to legal and antiquarian research, Thomson was remarkably neglectful in regard to matters of finance, and careless in the expenditure of money. After an inquiry into the accounts of the register office in 1839, they were found so unsatisfactory that he was removed from the office of deputy clerk-register.' For a recent short appraisal see Gordon Donaldson and Robert S. Morpeth, *Who's Who in Scottish History,* Oxford, 1973, and the same authors' *Dictionary of Scottish History,* John Donald, Edinburgh, 1977.
20. Cosmo Innes, op.cit., p. 127; this is evidence that the printing of the *Auchinleck Chronicle*(see note 16 above) was in progress in May 1810; in fact, some copies were distributed shortly after this without title-page; this printing was published, with title-page and preface and dated 1819, in 1877 by T.G.Stevenson. It seems that David Laing was responsible for the mistaken date of 1819 which he gave in *Proceedings of the Society of Antiquaries of Scotland,* Vol. XII, 1876-78, in an article 'Inquiries respecting some of the Early Historical Writers of Scotland', pp. 72-87, *viz.* No. 5: 'A Short Chronicle of the Reign of James II, King of Scots', pp. 84-86.
21. Cosmo Innes, op.cit., p. 128.
22. Ibid., pp. 159, 163-65.
23. The latest date in the watermarks of the framing paper of the Asloan MS. is 1822 (see Section I, p. 5). This seems to warrant the assumption that when Sir Alexander's books were taken out of Mr. Thomson's hands, the Asloan MS. was still undergoing its framing operations. It may have been handed over to

Maconochie after the binding had been done. This may have been at any time between 1822 and 1845. Thomson died in 1852.

24. 'A letter from Sir Alexander to his friend Robert Maconochie dated 24 March 1822 is preserved in the Signet Library, Edinburgh. Sir Alexander asks Maconochie to be his second (at his duel with James Stuart of Dunearn) and suggests the duel might take place at Calais.' (David Buchanan, op.cit., p. 16, n.81.)
25. T.G.Stevenson, op.cit. in note 16 above, pp. vii ff.
26. For interesting data on the vicissitudes of the Auchinleck Library see David Buchanan, op.cit., pp. 204-05 and 211.
27. In his above-mentioned edition of an Italian *SSR*-version, which must have been written in or before 1880 - it was his *Weihnachtsgabe* of that year to his father - Varnhagen says (p. xi) that the Asloan MS. was then in Edinburgh. He was evidently sure of its whereabouts and was carrying on negotiations with the owner about an edition of the Middle Scots version of the *SSR* in the Asloan MS. Who this owner was we do not know; perhaps it was William Paterson who had the MS in 1876 when it was produced as evidence in the proceedings over the Earldom of Annandale; perhaps, since on that occasion it turned out that it should have been returned to the Boswells half a century earlier, it had been given back to them shortly after.

    In an article on this MSc version in *Englische Studien*, XXV, 1898, Varnhagen again spoke of his intention to edit the *Buke of the Sevyne Sagis*, but this time he mentioned a transcription with which he was going to work. We know now that the MS went to Lord Talbot in Ireland in 1882, and also that the latter did not grant scholars access to the MS until 1917, when Craigie was finally allowed to edit it for the STS. Varnhagen must have felt considerably frustrated over all this. He died in 1924 without having been able to execute his long-planned edition; see *Englische Studien*, LVIII, 1924, pp. 473-79 for his obituary.
28. See *DNB* s.v. Alexander Boswell, 1775-1822; Charles Rogers, op. cit., pp. 194-95; James Balfour Paul, *The Scots Peerage*, 9 vols., Edinburgh, 1904-14.

29. See Craigie's preface to his edition of the Asloan MS., p. x.
30. Cf. Killis Campbell, *A Study of the Romance of the Seven Sages with special reference to the Middle English Version,* Baltimore, 1898, p. 83, n.1.

V. THE DATE OF THE ASLOAN MANUSCRIPT

On the spine the volume is marked: 'SCOTTISH TRACTS IN PROSE & VERSE' and 'MS. TEMP. JAC. V'. Though most of the items in the manuscript are of earlier dates and might just as well have been composed in the reign of James IV or even earlier, we find a reference to King James in item 5, *The Scottis Originale,* about which Craigie says in his preface[1]: 'An earlier copy of this, from a manuscript belonging to Lord Panmure and apparently written about 1460, is printed in Vol. III of the *Miscellany of the Bannatyne Club,* pp. 35-42. The differences in wording between the two copies suggest that they were independent versions from a Latin original. On p. 189 (f. 95^r) after the words "our souerane lord" Asloan has inserted "Iames the fyft" which has nothing corresponding to it in the earlier copy.' This is then sufficient proof that when Asloan was copying this part of the text James V was king of Scotland, and therefore the manuscript may be said to date from about 1515[2]. Most of those who have written about it agree to this. The *terminus a quo,* therefore, is 1513, as is also clear from item 8, *The Scottis Cronikle,* the text of which ends about one third of the way down f. 136^v [3] with the capture of Norham by James IV, which took place on 28 or 29 August 1513[4]. The tragedy of the Scottish defeat at Flodden on 9 September of the same year is not described. As the narrative ends in mid-page the possible loss of a continuation cannot be attributed to a later loss of leaves of the Asloan MS. such as we find elsewhere in the book[5]. It is therefore possible that Asloan or his model ended there, and this would put the date of this item in or not much later than 1513[6]. Perhaps Asloan did not care to bring it up to date, or he was not asked to do so.

In Section III it has been shown that the latest known record of the life of John Asloan, notary public in Edinburgh, dates from March 1529/30. The evidence at present at our disposal does not therefore allow of any more specific dating for the Asloan MS. than between 1513 and 1530, though if it was composed much later than 1513 the reason why the chronicle of item 8 was not brought up to date remains obscure.

Notes to Section V.

1. Op.cit., vol. I, p. vii.
2. James V became king in 1513, when he was not quite eighteen months old, after his father's death on the battlefield of Flodden on 9 September.
3. Craigie, op.cit., vol. I, p. 270.
4. R.L.Mackie, *King James IV of Scotland,* Edinburgh and London, 1958, p. 249.
5. The fact that there is no continuation about Flodden links up with R.L.Mackie's statement (op.cit., p. 261): 'The Scots who escaped wanted only to forget; no account of the battle by a Scottish soldier is known to exist.'
6. For completeness' sake a list of all the items of the manuscript with their dates of origin is given in Appendix II.

VI. PHONOLOGY OF STRESSED VOWELS[1)]

In this section a survey is given of the phonemic system of Middle Scots vowels, i.e. in this case Scots of around 1500, and the sources of the various Middle Scots vowels are enumerated, based on the evidence of the rhymes in *BSS*.

The editor of the *Dictionary of the Older Scottish Tongue*, Mr A.J. Aitken M.A., at an early date very kindly placed at my disposal his then unpublished notes on a great number of subjects concerning Middle Scots. It is from his 'Vowel Systems of Scots' and his 'Notes on Some Characteristic Features of the Phonology of Scots'[2)] that the vowel-table and the numbering of the phonemes used below are taken, corroborated with the latest data. Mr Aitken's system derives from the evidence of (1) older related languages, (2) modern Scots and English dialect reflexes, (3) former rhyming practices, (4) Older Scots orthographic practice, in that order of predominance; the system was also used on Mr Aitken's advice by Fr C.H. Kuipers in his Nijmegen doctoral thesis[3)].

Long Vowels

	ESc		MSc
1.	ī	→	ei
2.	ẹ̄	→	ī
3.	ę̄	→ (ī / ẹ̄)	
4.	ā	→	ẹ̄
5.	ō	→	ō
6.	ū	> ū —	ū
6a.	ul	↗	
7.	ǖ	— (< ō) →	ǖ

Short Vowels

	ESc		MSc
15.	i	→	i
16.	ę	→	ę
17.	a	→	a
18.	ɔ	→	ɔ
19.	u	→	u

Diphthongs in -i

	ESc		MSc
8.	ai	→ (and > ā)	ęi
8a.	ai#	> ā → ę̄; →	ęi#
9.	oi	—	oi
10.	ui	—	ui
11.	ei#	→ ē# →	ī#

Diphthongs in -u

	ESc		MSc
12.	au	> au →	ā
12a.	al	↗	
13.	ou	> ǫu →	ǫu
13a.	ol	↗	
14.	eu	> iu →	iu
	iu	↗	

PHONEME 1 ESc /ī/ > MSc /ei/

ESc /ī/, from OE and Scandinavian /ī/ and /ȳ/, and OF /i/ if it had remained stressed, had been diphthongised to /ei/ in the Great Vowel Shift.

The diphthong derives from OE ī in *besyde, byid, quhy, ryde, wyf,* &c.; from OE *i* before lengthening groups in *child*; from OE ȳ in *fyre, hyre, kyth, litill,* &c.; from OE *y* before lengthening groups in *kynd, mynd* (see *DOST* s.v. *Kind*); from Scand ī in *knyf, ryf(e), tyte*; from Scand ȳ in *tyne*; from OF *i* in *cry, cryme, delyte, dyne, gyde, senȝeory, seruis, syne* 'sign' n., 'make a sign' v., *virgine,* &c.

In *hyne* and *syne* advs. the development was probably *-eþen > ein > īn > ein*. In *huntyne*, rh.w. *syne* adv., we find the ending OE, ME *-ing*; see section IX.10.f.

MSc spellings in *BSS*: *i, y(/e)* [4] *,yi*.

PHONEME 2 ESc /ē/ > MSc /ī/

ESc /ē/ derived mainly from OE ē, Anglian ē, OE ēo, Scand ē and œ, OF ẹ, AN ē if it retained the stress, OE, Scand, OF *i(y)* if lengthened in open syllables. In MSc it was shifted to /ī/.

BSS rhyme-words belonging to this group, derived from OE, Ang ē (WS $\bar{æ}_1$, WGmc ā) or OE, Ang ē (PGmc $\bar{e}_1$), are e.g. *beir* 'bier', *brer, deid* 'deed', *dreid, leche, reid* n., v., *speche, streit, weit, ȝe(i)r*; from OE ē (Gmc $\bar{e}_2$) : *he(i)r* adv., *meid*; from OE ē (ō + *i/j*): *bleid, feir* 'equal', *feit, grene, hed* 'heed', *meit* v., *quene, sweit* a.; from OE ēo: *be, devill, erd, fleyt* v., *kne, se* v., *thee* 'thigh', *thre, tre,* &c.; from Ang ē (WS īe, ēa + *i/j*): *heir* v., *scheit, schete* rh.w. *feit* (or from OE *scēat*), *ȝit, ȝet* (rh.w. *sweit* a.); from Scand ē: *lete* pt., Scand œ : *feir* a., *sle*; from OF ẹ: *cité, cle(i)r, succeid,* &c.; from AN ē: *beif, cheir, gref, grevit, pre(i)f, releif*; from OE *i* + *g* in the ending *-ig*: *witté* (rh.w. *cité*), *ryple* (not in rh.); from OF *i*: *pleseir, peté* (first syll.); from OE and Scand *i* or *y* in open syll.: *ewill, levit, speir, steir, unsterd* (rh.w. *erd*). For *clene, leir, lerd, me(y)ne, se* n. and *spreid* see phon. 3.

The rhyme *says* : *extremiteis* (651) most probably points to the meaning 'sees' for *says*, and not 'assays', since that would imply an *ei/i*-rhyme, which otherwise is not found in this text. (Cf.

grace; I. 349-50 *lychtlynes* : *place*; II. 293 ff. *cas* : *rychtwisnes* : *grace*. *Ner* (: *cheir*) is probably the reflex of Ang *neor*.

Spellings in *BSS*: *e*, *e(i)* [4)], *ei*, *e(y)* [4)], *ei/e*, *e/e*.

PHONEME 4 ESc /ā/ > MSc /ē̮/ ESc /ā/ from earlier /ā/ of whatever derivation was fronted to /ē̮/, except when it was the result of the monophthongisation of /au/, and in those cases where a labial consonant in the neighbourhood inhibited the shifting.

The sound occurs in the following rhyme-words in *BSS*, derived from OE ā in *aith*, *baid* n., *bair*, *clath*, *ga*, *hait*, *hame*, *laif*, *ma*, *ma(i)r*, *nane*, *rais*, *sa*, *sair*, *schane*, *stane*, *straike*, *twa*, *wa*, &c.; from OE *a* lengthened in open syllables in *baile*, *cair*, *maid* pt., *name*, *raith*, *schame*, *spard(e)* (rhyming with *reward*), *tale*; from OE *a* before a lenghtening group in *wame* (OE *wamb*); from OE *ea* in open syllable or before a lengthening group in *barn(e)*, *scare*, *scair* (rh.w. *bair* n., *mar*); from OE æ in open syllable in *bair* a. (rh.w. *mair*, *fair* [OE *faran*]); from Scand ā in *baith*, *hair*, *sla*, *stra*, *thra*, *war* 'were'; from Scand *a* in *ga(i)f*, *gait*, *ha(i)f*, *(our)tane*, *(wnder)ta*; from OF *a* in *age*, *-age*, *blame*, *cage*, *cas(e)*, *cais(e)*, *decla(i)r(e)*, *face*, *fame*, *grace*, *sage*, *space*, *wage*, *wary*; from OF *a* + *st* in *ha(i)st*, *taist*, *waist*; from L ā in *pynula*, *Pollema*, *Dioclesiane*, *Octoviane*; from MLG *a* in *traide*. For doublets of *ăr* + cons., *ār* + cons., see Phoneme 17.

Several rhymes in *BSS* indicate that the reflex of OF /ai/, AN /ē̮/ was MSc /ē̮/; the only instances occur before liquids and nasals: *barane* : *nane* (OF *ai(gn)* : OE ā), *thar* : *contrar* (ONhb ā : OF *ai*, L ā); *haile* : *counsall*, *haile* : *avale*, *hale* : *faile*, *all hale* : *counsall* (OE ā, perh. ON *ei* : OF *ai*, *ei*).

Note rhymes like *consaif* : *haf* (ME ā : ON *a*), whereas *gaf* and *ha(i)f* are also found rhyming with *laif* n. (OE ā) and with *saif* v. (AN *sa(u)ver*, ME *saven*). The spelling probably reflects one variant in /ă/ (*haf*, *gaf*), and the rhyme the other variant with ESc /ā/ > MSc /ē̮/.

In rhymes like *knawlege* : *heretage*, *wisage*, there is post-tonic reduction of the NME *a*, ME *a*, in *knawlege*, and the vowel is obscured.

also *sene* and *se* in ll. 653 and 657.)

The rhyme *gif* v. : *leif* n. 'leave', 2509, can be accounted for, since in MSc there are doublets *gif* and *geve, geif*.

The rhymes *tuk hed* : *leid* inf., *deid* a.: *leid* inf., *hed* 'head' : *leid* inf., *dreid* n. : *reid* inf., and *forbed* inf. : *reid* inf., make it highly probable that *reid* and *leid* had two pronunciations in the present text, as in the works investigated by Heuser, *Anglia* XVIII and XIX[5].

The rhymes *wele* : *devill, dele* 'devil', *deile* 'deal' n., *fele* n. 'feeling', *fele* v. 'to feel', as against the rhymes *wele* : *perell, damysele,* suggest that *wele* had two pronunciations, cf. Heuser, *Anglia* XIX, p. 330, where he suggests that the substantivised ME adverb /wḗl/ and the ME noun /wē̆l/ existed side by side.

Note such rhymes as *prevḗ* : *ladye* and *citḗ* : *wittḗ* 'witty', which are also found elsewhere. By the second half of the fifteenth century rhymes of orig. OE *-ig* (e.g. in the adverbial ending *-ly*) also rhymed with orig. OF *-ḗ*.

Note the rhymes 1. *ferd* : *lerd* (OE *ēō* : OE *ǣ*)
2. *erd* : *vnsterd* (OE *eo* (*ea*) : OE *y*)
3. *erd* : *ferd* 'fourth' (OE *eo* (*ea*) : OE *eo*)

For 1. cf. *leir* : *ȝer, speir*; for 2. cf. *steir* : *heir* adv. In connection with this I would rather derive *erd* from *eorþe* than from *eard*. Cf. Heuser, *Anglia* XVIII, p. 126, where we also find under /ẹrd/: *eird, steird, leirt* (Henryson); and under /ḗr/: p. 116, *ster, ler* (*Wallace*); *Anglia* XIX, p. 321, *lere* (R. Rolle), p. 328, *lere* (*OE Legends*), p. 339, *steir* (G. Douglas).

Heuser's conclusions, op. cit., that the $æ_1/æ_2$-division did not apply regularly in MSc, and that before *-r* and *-d* Phonemes 2 and 3 fell together by the time of Dunbar, holds good for the present text.

It is clear from the spellings in the manuscript that the scribe could write *ē* and *ā* either with or without *i*. Cf. K.J. Kohler, 'Aspects of Middle Scots Phonemics and Graphemics: the Phonological Implications of the sign<I>', *Transactions of the Philological Society*, 1967, pp. 32-62.

Spellings in *BSS*: *e(i)*[4], *e(y)*[4], *e/e*.

PHONEME 3 ESc /ę̄/ > MSc /ī/, /ē/

ESc /ę/ from OE $\bar{æ}$, $\bar{ea}$, Scand *ae*, and earlier /e/ lengthened in open syllables, often coalesced with earlier /ẹ̄/ and, like it, could be raised to /i/. Before dentals and in final positions ę̄ > ẹ̄ in the ME period in the North and NE Midlands, cf. Sisam[6], § 8, p. 283, and Dobson[7] II.108, n.2. This ẹ̄ subsequently became MSc /ī/. This raising occurred with ever greater frequency as the sixteenth century progressed (see J. Craigie's study of the language in *The Works of William Fowler*, vol. iii, STS, 3rd ser., No. 13, 1940, pp. lvi ff.). In *BSS*, however, the rhymes show that the two phonemes were usually kept apart there; impure rhymes are not numerous.

The phoneme derives from OE $\bar{æ}_2$, (Gmc *ai* + *i/j*) in *leid*, v., *euer*, *womanhed*, &c., where it usually is ę̄; from the same, figuring as ē̥ in *clene*, *leir*, *lerd*, *me(y)ne*, *se* n., *spreid*; from OE $\bar{ea}$ (Gmc *au*) > ę̄ in *deid* a., n., *he(i)d* 'head', *leis* 'falsehood'; from OE *eo* in open syllables > ę̄ in *hevyn*, *sevyn*; from ME *e* in open syllables > ę̄ in *deir* v., *meit(e)*, *mete* n., *speike*, *steike*, *swer* v., *weir*; from Scand *æ* in *rad* (rh.w. *maid* p.p.; although the spelling suggests a shortened vowel this is probably a correct rhyme, as *maid* is found elsewhere in *BSS* in rhyme with *baid* 4x, *slaide* 1x and *traide*1x; it is found twice spelled *made*); from OF *e* in *allege*, *ces*, *deces*, *disseuer*, *fest*, *remeid*, *replege*; from OF *ai*, *ei* > AN ę̄ in *burges*, *courtas*, *eis*, *feid* 'feud', *peis*, *pes*, *pece*, *pledis* (: *hedis* 'heads'), *pleis*.

The ending -*nes* rhymes with (*mair or*) *les*, (*na*)*les*, *neuertheles*, *distres*, *leis* 'falsehood'; cf. Phoneme 16.

For the rhyme *feile* (OE *fela*) : *heile* (OE *hǣlan*) cf. Heuser, *Anglia*, XIX, p. 330 (*OE Legends*) and p. 338 (Gavin Douglas).

Sometimes long and short vowels more or less coincided or formed inaccurate rhymes. Note the rhyme *space* : *seknes* 631. Heuser records one case of rhyme ĕ : ę̄ in Henryson: *liknes* : *incres*; in Gavin Douglas *incres* v. rhymes with ĕ; in *OE Legends riches* (-ess) : *disses* (èèz) is found; -*nes* is often rhymed with -*ace* and -*as* in MSc, cf. e.g. *Buke of the Howlat*[8] 106 ff.: *face* : *case* : *halynes* : *space*; 235 ff. *cas* : *was* : *richnes* : *place*; Henryson *Fox and Wolf*[9]: st. 10 *grace* : *face* : *halines*; st. 14 *wickitnes* : *allace*; st. 16 *tendernes* : *grace* : *Pasche*; *Wallace*[10] I. 39-40 *falsness* :

In rhymes like *vrinale* : *tell*, *coronale* : *kell*, where OF *a* rh.w. OE, ME *e*, the same explanation applies; cf. *Buke of the Howlat*, ed. cit., 119 ff. *perell* : *counsall* : *sall* : *apparale*.

The rhyme *hale* : *castale* in ll. 2595-96 is the only case where we find the latter word in rhyme. Elsewhere in the text we find the forms *castall* and *castell*. We might therefore derive *castale* from ON *kastali*, whereas the other forms may be due to OF and OE. Wyntoun, too, uses this form *castale*.

Spellings in *BSS*: *a*, *a(i)* [4], *a/e*.

PHONEME 5 ESc /ō/ > MSc /ō/ — ESc /ō/, which remained unchanged in MSc, derived from earlier /o/ lengthened in open syllables. It is found in the rhyme-words *befor*, *forlor*, *schore* and *restore*. The spelling is *o*, *o/e*.

In ll. 2537-38 we find the rhyme *ioye* : *hoye* 'stop'. The phoneme in *ioye* is the diphthong /oi/, which late in the fourteenth century was levelled with Phoneme 5 and could still be pronounced and written either *oi* or *o* in the present text. The word *hoye* is found elsewhere as *ho* (Gower) and as *ho(o)*, see *NED* s.v. *ho* for several instances of fifteenth-century usage. In MSc it usually figures as *ho*, see *DOST* s.v. *ho*, which does not mention the spelling *hoye*. It is therefore likely that the spelling *hoye* is due to *ioye* and that it represents the monophthongised /ō/-pronunciation of these words, with the *y* marking the length of the sound. There are no other rhymes of this kind in *BSS*. See also Kohler, p. 58[11].

For the English form *so* see section VIII on Anglicisation.

PHONEME 6 ESc /ū/ > MSc /ū/ — Esc /ū/ remained unchanged in MSc, whether it was derived from OE *ū*, Scand *ū* or Of/AN *u*. The source is OE *ū* in *about*, *dovne*, *found*, *grewhound*, *how*, *lowde*, *lowte*, *now*, *out*, *tovne*, &c.; earlier *og*, *ow* in *swoun*, where it is due to the preceding /w/; Scand *ū* in *almous*, *bovn*, *schout*, *trow*; OF/AN *u* in *crovne*, *dowt*, *hour(is)*, *stout*, *towre*, *wowe* 'vow', and the endings *-oun*,

-our, -ous. In *ȝow* the sound goes back to OE *éow* with the stress changed to *eów*, but instead of /ou/ it has /ū/, rhyming 13x with the words *how*, *now* and *fow* 'full', which have indubitable /ū/; in *crovde* it may be derived from ME *u* due to Celtic (Welsh *crwth*, Ir *cruit*); in the forms *eschewe*, *eschow*, rh.w. *how* and *now*, the sound is due to OF *eu*, *iu* and the influence of /ʃ/, see Phoneme 14.

The rhyme *owr*, *our* 'over': *four* occurs three times; once we find the rhyme *empriour* : *four*, which is an impure one in MSc, but correct in ME, where /*our*/ became /*ūr*/; Chaucer-rhymes prove the pronunciation /fūr/. But *owr* has Phoneme 13 /ou/, and so has *four*.

We find the word *mesour* rhyming with *empriour* (3x) and *tresour* (1x). This indicates the Northern form /ūr/ for /ǖr/ in *mesour* [OF *mesure*].

Note the rhyme *spur(e)* (OE *u* in open syllable) : *empriour*; the regular development of OE *spura* to MSc *spur(e)* would result in /ǖ/, see Phoneme 7, but in the present text *empriour* rhymes most often (18x) with an *-our*-ending (from OF /u/) in the following words: *colour, dolour, honour, hour, myrrour, retour, towre*, and so it seems most probable that in the case of *spur(e)* we have the Northern form /ūr/ instead of /ǖr/.

On the other hand there is a good deal of fluctuation between *-ure* and *-our* endings, cf. *DOST*, e.g. s.v. *creatour, creature*, and cf. Buss[12], p. 10, for the existence of *u* : *ou* rhymes (/ǖ/ : /ū/).

OF *-ous* endings are found in rhyme with *almous*, *plentuos* and *Oulumpos*, but see also Phoneme 19.

Spellings in *BSS*: *ou, ov, ow*, (*ew* in *eschew*); for the *o*-spelling in *plentuos, effectuoslye*, see section VII on Orthography, pp.60-1.

PHONEME 6a
ESc /ul/>
MSc /ū/

ESc /ul/ could be vocalised to /ū/ in MSc. OE *ul(l)* is found in *fow(e)* twice, rhyming with *ȝow*. When not in rhyme the form *full* is used in *BSS*.

PHONEME 7 ESc /ō/ > MSc /ǖ/ — In ESc OE /ǭ/ had become /ǖ/, levelled with OF /ü/ and not affected by the Great Vowel Shift. Other sources of MSc /ǖ/ were earlier /u/ in open syllables, Scand /ō/, OF /ọ/, OF /ü/ and monophthongised OF /üi/, which was already /ü/ in AN.

The sound derives from OE ō in *behude, blud(e), buke, bute, do, dome, done, flud, flure, fude, fut(e), gud, lo, moder, nother, scho, sone* 'soon', *to, (wnder)stude, wisdome, wod, ȝud*; from OE *u* in open syllable in *abone, dure, luf(it)*, (for *spur(e)* see Phoneme 6); from ME ō in *bure, hone, nuke*; from Scand ō in *rute, tuke*; from OF /o/ in *contruf, dule* (*pace* Jord. 228), *fule, movit, pruf, pure*; from OF /ü/ in *assure, conclude, cure, huge, iuge, mixture, nature, presome*; from OF /üi/ in *frute* rh.w. *rute, conȝe* (AN *coigne*, OF *cuigne*) and *sonȝe* (OF *essoigne*).

Rome rhymes with *presome* and with words in *-dome*.

Beside *ȝud*, which went out of use early in the sixteenth century, *ȝeid* is found twice, rh.w. *speid* and *bleid*. These doublets result from variation in the stress on the two elements of the diphthong of the OE *ēode* .

Spellings in *BSS* rhyme-words: *o, o/e, u, u/e*.

PHONEME 8 ESc /ai/ > MSc /ē/ or /ei/ — In all dialects ESc /ai/ developed into /ȩi/ in most words in final position, but merged with Phoneme 4 in a few common words, viz. *day, lay, may, say*, and, in some dialects, *away* and *thay*. In many dialects it developed, without merging, into /ȩi/ in non-final position also, but in the Central Scots dialects mostly merged with Phon. 4, i.e. as /ē/, in this case.

The sound derives from OE *æġ* in *agane, (a)way(e), day(e), fa(i)r, fa(y)ne, lair, may* aux., *may* n., *say*; from OE *eġ* in *play(e)*; from Scand *ei* in *ay(e), bane, rasit, thai* pers. pron.; from OF *ai* in *abasit, air, assay, aval(ȝ)e, consaif, consauit, delay(d), fa(i)le, falȝe, payd, plane, trane, wane* 'vain', &c.; from OF *ei* in *air* 'heir', *counsall, pane, pray, resauit, vane* 'vein'.

The word-final merging with Phon. 4 in *day*, etc. is not found in *BSS*, but is evident in the following rhymes, e.g. Barbour's *Bruce* II. 235 and VI. 509 *thai* : *alsua*; IV. 77, VI. 587, X. 179 *thai* : *twa*; VII. 211 *swa* : *thai*; IX. 462 *ga* : *thai*; X. 147 *ta* : *thai*; Wyntoun I. 759 *twa* : *þai*; *Bk. Alex.* 8846 *alsua* : *sa* 'say'; *Bk. Chess* 67 *Seneca* : *pa* 'pay', 533 *anima* : *pa* 'pay', but in these earlier texts these cases are infrequent, and some of the *thai*-forms can be explained as deriving from *tha* 'those'.

An investigation of the /ā/- and /ai/-rhymes in ESc and MSc verse has made it clear to me that the phenomenon of 'impure' rhymes (/ā/ rhyming with etymological /ai/) became more and more frequent in the course of the fifteenth century, though one must allow for an author's idiosyncrasies in this matter. An equal number of lines (approx. 2785) checked of several poems gave the following number of 'impure' ā/ai-rhymes: *Bruce* 5, *Leg. Sts.* 1, *STB* 4, Wyntoun 6, *Bk. Alex.* 11, *Wallace* 35, *Thre Pr. Pebles* 48, *Lancelot of the Laik* 30, *Bk. Chess* 24, *Bk. Howlat* 73, *Gol. & Gaw.* 2, *Rauf Coilȝ.* 13, *King Hart* 15, *Kingis Quair* 1, Henryson 6, Dunbar 26, Gavin Douglas 1501 39, Gavin Douglas 1513 62. For bibliographical data on the works mentioned see Section XIa, n. 1, and Section XVII, Editions of Middle Scots texts.

Spellings: *a*, *ai*, *a(i)*, *ay(e)*[4], *a/e*, *ay/e*.

PHONEME 9
ESc /oi/>
MSc /oi/

See Phoneme 5: *ioye*.

PHONEME 10
ESc /ui/>
MSc /ui/

ESc /ui/ remained /ui/ in MSc. Derivations in *BSS* are from OF *oi*, *ui* in *anoyit*, *distroyit*, *ioynt*, *poynt*.

Spellings in *BSS*: *oy*.

PHONEME 11
ESc /ei/#>
MSc /i/#

ESc /ei/# was monophthongised to /ē/# and then was levelled with Phon. 2 in the second half of the fourteenth century, sharing its subsequent history.

The sound derives from LOE *eġ* in *de* 'to die', *e* 'eye', *eyne* 'eyes', *he* (*hie*, *hye*), *le* v. 'tell lies'; by the time of *BSS* (a. 1500) this phoneme had entirely coalesced with Phon. 2; it is here given for completeness' sake.

Spellings: *e*, *ey*, *ie*, *ye*.

PHONEME 12
ESc /au/>
MSc /ā/

ESc /au/ before the third quarter of the fifteenth century became MSc /ā/.

The sound derives from OE *āg* in *awn*(*e*) a.; from OE *ag* in *draw*(*e*), *drawin*, *fawne*, *saw* pt., *sawe* n.; from OE *āw* in *blaw* n., *crawe* v., n., *knawe*, *ourthrawe*, *wnknawin*; *saull*; from OE *ēāw* with shifting of the stress in *schawe*, *schawin*; from Scand *ag* in *aw*(*e*) n., *law*(*e*) n.; from OF *au* in *caus*, *paus*, *pavs*, and from L *au* in (*St*.) *Paule*.

Spellings: *au*, *av*, *aw*(*e*); *al* is also found, but not in rhymed words, see Section VII, Phon. 12.

PHONEME 12a
ESc /al/>
MSc /au/

Esc /al/ became MSc /au/ and shared its monophthongisation to /ā/ (Phon. 12).

l-vocalisation. In the first quarter of the fifteenth century the characteristic Scottish sound-change known as *l*-vocalisation took place; it affected the consonant /l/ when preceded by a short back vowel, viz. Phonemes 17, 18 and 19. In this position /l/ was evidently pronounced with a velar or /u/-modification; /l/ ceased to be pronounced as a lateral consonant, but was simply realised as /u/ (section 11 of A.J. Aitken's 'Notes on Some Characteristic Features of the Phonology of Scots').

The sound in *BSS* rhymes is derived from OE (*e*)*al* in *all*, *fall*, *hall*, *sall*, *wall*; from OE æ< L *a* in *pall*; from Scand *al* in *call*, *cald* p.p. (*all*, *fall* and *sall* might be from Scand as well); from OF -*ald* in *cukkald* (AN, OF **cucuald*); Ang -*ald* is represented in *cald* 'cold', *fald*, *hald*, *wald* and in *ald* (*auld*), *sauld*, *tald* (*tauld*). During the fourteenth century *ald* in stressed forms had become /auld/, spelled *auld* or *ald*, i.e. Phoneme 12 +

/ld/. Thus the conditions for *l*-vocalisation (Phon. 17, 18 or 19, + /l/) no longer existed and the later history of this combination, e.g. in *auld, sauld, tauld*, is of Phon. 12 + /ld/.

PHONEME 13
ESc /ou/ >
MSc /ou/

ESc /ou/ remained MSc /ou/. It had its origin in the vocalisation of intervocalic /v/ and /g/ and of post-vocalic /w/.

The diphthong is derived from OE *ōw* in *growe*; from OE *ēow* (with shifting of stress) in *four* (OE *fēower*); from OE *o* + /*v*/ in *owr, attour* (OE *ofer*); from ME /*əw*/ from EME /*əg*/ in *borowe, sorowe*; from OF *ou* in *how* n. In ll. 2105-6 we find the impure rhyme *four* : *empriour*.

Spellings: *ou, ow, ow/e*.

PHONEME 13a
ESc /ol/ >
MSc /ou/

This phoneme does not occur among *BSS* rhyme-words, but in ll. 2615 and 2679 (not in rhyme) the converse spellings *rolpand* and *rolpit* are found (OE *hrōpan*, ON *raupa*). For the anglicised rhyme *behold* : *gold* see Section VIII.

PHONEME 14
ESc /eu/, /iu/ >
MSc /iu/

ESc /eu/ and /iu/ coalesced into MSc /iu/; its sources in *BSS* rhyme-words are OE *ēow*, OE *ōg*, OE *ō* before /χ/, OE *īw* < *iġ* + *w*, OF *eu, iv*.

It occurs in *blewe, hewe* v., *knew(e)* pt., *newe, trewe, reuth, treuth*; *drewe, slewe* pt., *ynewe*; *sleuch, yneuch*; *stewart*.

From OF *iv, eu* is *eschewe, eschow*, rhyming with phon. 6 in word-final position after liquids and /ʃ/.

Spellings: *ew(e), eu*.

PHONEME 15
ESc /ĭ/ >
MSc /ĭ/

ESc /ĭ/ remained unchanged in MSc. The main sources of this sound are OE *i* and *y* in closed syllables, Angl *e* (+*ht*); Scand, OF/L *i* in closed syllables and shortened OE *ī* and *ȳ*.

The phoneme is derived from OE *i* in *begyn, bid, bill, blyn, blynd, bring, bynd, dicht, drink, fynd, hiddir, hir, iwis, mys* v., *pik, sit, stik, wist, wit*; from OE *y* in *did, fulfill, syn, thyn* a.; from OE ī shortened in *betid, gryst*; from OE ȳ shortened in *kid, hid*; from Scand *i* in *ill, kirk, myn, mys* adv., *skill, till*; from OE/Scand *y* in *byr, kyn, myrk*; from Scand ī in *wicht* a., Scand ȳ in *tynt*; from Scand *œ* in *slicht*; from OE *i* + *ht* in *knycht, nicht, nycht, sicht, wicht* n.; from OE (Ang) *e* + *ht*, *y* + *ht* in *bricht* a.; from OMerc ē + *ht* in *hicht* n.; from OE *æ* , *e* in *togiddir*; from OE *e* (+ /ŋk/) > *i* in *think*, see Dobson, op. cit., II. 77, n. 2; from OF *i* in *gyn*; from L *i* in *commyt, promis* n., *Virgil*.

The words *blynd, bynd* and *fynd* have ǐ since in MSc the combination *i* + *nd* did not produce a lengthened *i* (cf. Jordan[13], § 36.2). OE -ǐ*nd*-types did not rhyme with OE -y̆*nd*-types in MSc. In the present text *blynd, bynd* and *fynd* rhyme among themselves, while *kynd* and *mynd* rhyme only with each other.

In the rhymes *frist* : *list* 1503 and *best* : *frist* 1590 *frist* in the first case seems to be derived from OE **firstan*, in the second from ON *fresta*.

The rhyme as found in *drinkyn* : *thing* 1623 occurs also in Barbour's *Bruce*, see Mühleisen[14], pp. 202 ff.

Spellings in *BSS*: *i, y*.

PHONEME 16 ESc /ĕ/ > MSc /ĕ/

ESc /e/ remained unchanged in MSc. The main sources of the sound are OE *e* and *eo* in closed syllables, shortened OE ǣ , ēa, ēo, Scand *ae* and Scand, OF and L *e* in closed syllables.

The phoneme derives from OE *e* in *bed, bell, duell, eft, ellis, end, fed, fedder, forȝet, hell, let, men, nest, send, tell, west*, &c.; from OE *eo*/Ang *e* in *fer* 'far', *werk*; from OE ǣ shortened in *left*, (*mair or*) *les, lest* (note the rhyme 2403 *eftir : left hir*); from OE ēa shortened in *reft, ȝet* 'poured'; from OE ēo shortened in *fell* pt.; from Scand *ae* in *uncled*; from Scand *e* in *clek, get, ken, kend, wer* 'worse'; *frist* (rh.w. *best*); from OF *e* in *cruell, defend, dese, det, distres*, (*ef*)*fek, fell* 'cruel', *forest, honest, mend, mese* 'food', *pen, pres, sciens, serpent*, &c.; from OF *ei*, *e* in *plet*; from L *e* in *proces, degest*.

In line 1185 we find *rak* rh.w. *effek*, in l. 2238 *led* pp. rh.w.

bad pt. *Rak* and *led* are cases of spelling-doublets, due to the different developments of OE $\bar{æ}$: 1. $\bar{æ}_2$ > OE $\breve{æ}$ > ME *a*; 2. $\bar{æ}_2$ > EME ę̄ > ME *e*. In the cases of *rak* and *led* the spelling reflexes one form, the rhyme the other.

In *kest* pt. (rh.w. *degest*) the *e* had probably arisen from some analogy, cf. de Vries[15], p. 13.

For rhymes in *-nes*, see the rhyme-words, Phon. 3; cf. Heuser, *Anglia*, XVIII, p. 127.

Spellings in *BSS*: *e*, *i*.

PHONEME 17 ESc /ă/ > MSc /ă/ ESc /ă/ remained /ă/ in Msc. The sources of the sound are mainly OE *æ* , *ea* and *a* in closed syllables, Scand, OF and L *a* in closed syllables.

The sound derives from OE *æ* in *bad*, *bak*, *brak*, *bras*, *fader*, *fast*, *glad*, *last*, *mast* n., *sat*, *spak*, *was*, &c.; from OE *ea* in *efterwart*, *harme*, *hart* (ONhb *ea*), *instewart*, *orchart*, *scharpe*, *warme*, &c.; OE *a* in *amang*, *can*, *fand*, *hand*, *hang*, *land*, *mak*, *man*, *rang*, *wan* pt., &c.; from OE/Scand *a* in *fang*, *gang*,*wrang*; from Scand *a* in *anger*, *band*, *carpe*, *cast*, *gat*, *lak*, &c.; from Scand *e* in *quert* (rh.w. *instewart*); from OF *a* in *art*, *awant*, *discharge*, *eligant*, *large*, *part*, *past*, *perchance*, (*re*)*gard*, *taxt*, &c.; from OF *e* in *powert* (rh.w. *instewart*), *expart* (rh.w. *hart*). The spelling *expert* is also found but not in rhyme; in the fourteenth century *er* + consonant might become *ar* + consonant:

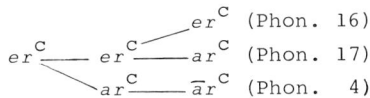

er^C — er^C — er^C (Phon. 16)
er^C — er^C — ar^C (Phon. 17)
er^C — ar^C — $\bar{a}r^C$ (Phon. 4)

The form *was* had two types, /was/ and /wes/, the former rhyming with *bras*, the latter with *space*, *grace* affected by the Great Vowel Shift. All the words rhyming with *Bantillas* and *Ypocras*, such as *palace*, *pas* v., *allace*, *trespas* contained /a/.

Spellings: *a*, *e*.

PHONEME 18
ESc /ŏ/ >
MSc /ŏ/

ESc /ŏ/ remained unchanged in MSc; the sources of the phoneme are mainly OE /ŏ/ in closed syllables, OF/L /ŏ/ and OE /ō/ shortened before consonant clusters.

The sound derives from OE *o* in *born, drope, ford* 'for it', *forlorne, lord, morne, stop, sworne, wrocht*; from OE ō shortened in *nocht, soft, thocht*; from Scand *o* in *slokin*; from OE/Scand *o* in *knokit, lokit* 'locked'; from OF *o* in *cors, fors, record, remord, sport*; from MDu *o* in *coft*.

Ourthort shows Scand *e* becoming *o* under the influence of *w* (ON *þvert*).

Behold (Ang *a*) rh.w. *gold* is an anglicised rhyme, see Section VIII on Anglicisation.

Spelling: *o, o/e*.

PHONEME 19
ESc /ŭ/ >
MSc /ŭ/

ESc /ŭ/ remained /ŭ/ in MSc, the main sources being OE /ŭ/ in closed syllables, also before *-nd*, and Scand and OF /u/ in closed syllables.

The sound derives from OE *u* in *bundin, con(e), cum, dvm, fundin, foundyn, hunder, murn, son* 'son', *thus, tuskis, wnder, won* p.p., *wounder, worth*; from OE *o* in *furth, hurdis, wordis*, cf. Jordan, op. cit., § 35 A2; from Scand *u* in *ruskis, tunder*; from OF *u* in *merwalus* rh.w. *thus* (for other *-ous, -us* rhymes see Phoneme 6); from OF *u/o* in *sudiorn* (both vowels).

Before *nd* the reflex of OE *u* seems to have regularly had doublet results, as spellings and modern dialects indicate, i.e. *ground* (Phon. 6) beside *grund* (Phon. 19). *BSS* has one example of this in *fundin* beside *foundyn*.

The reflex of OE *sweord* is found as *swerd* (rh.w. *word* 2x) and as *sword* (rh.w. *word* 2x).

Spellings: *o, o/e, ou, u, v, w*.

Notes to Section VI

1) Only words in rhyme are used for this purpose, for with rare exceptions the rhymes are very accurate and constitute, therefore, on their own a reliable source of information about phoneme distribution, though rhymes containing the reflexes of identical OE, OF or Scandinavian vowels prove nothing about the quality of the MSc phonemes. For unstressed vowels and consonants the reader is referred to Cornelis H. Kuipers, *Quintin Kennedy (1520-1564):Two Eucharistic Tracts, A Critical Edition*, diss. Nijmegen, 1964, and to indications in the transcriptions in A.J.Aitken's article in *Bards and Makars, Scottish Language and Literature:Medieval and Renaissance*, eds Adam J. Aitken, Matthew P. McDiarmid, Derick S. Thomson, University of Glasgow Press, 1977, pp. 1-21. I am confining myself to stressed vowels because here my edition can offer useful additions to and corroboration of the systematic information presented by Aitken and Kuipers; for the other aspects no suitable basis exists.
2) More recently Mr Aitken's views on this have become available in print, see the article mentioned above.
3) See pp. 76-91 of the work mentioned above.
4) Notations with brackets indicate spelling variations in the same word.
5) W. Heuser, 'Offenes und geschlossenes *EE* im Schottischen und Nordenglischen', *Anglia*, XVIII, pp. 114-28, and XIX, pp. 319-40, (1896 and 1896/7), for which he investigated the *Wallace*, Henryson's *Fables*, Gavin Douglas's works, Richard Rolle of Hampole's (!) *The Pricke of Conscience*, and the *OE Legends* as from MS. Harl. 4196.
6) Kenneth Sisam, *Fourteenth Century Verse & Prose*, Oxford, 1950.
7) E.J.Dobson, *English Pronunciation 1500-1700*, 2 vols, Oxford, 1957.
8) W.A.Craigie, *The Asloan Manuscript*, STS NS 16, Edinburgh, 1924, pp. 98 and 102.
9) 'The Taill how this foirsaid Tod Maid his Cōfessioun to Freir Wolf Waitskaith', H. Harvey Wood, ed., *The Poems and Fables of Robert Henryson*, Edinburgh & London, (1933) 1958, pp. 24 ff.

10) Hary's *Wallace*, ed. Matthew P. McDiarmid, 2 vols, STS 4th Ser. 4 & 5, 1968-9.

11) Op.cit., see Phoneme 2 above.

12) Paul Buss, *Sind die von Horstmann herausgegebenen schottischen Legenden ein Werk Barberes?*, diss. Göttingen, 1886; also Halle, 1886.

13) Richard Jordan, *Handbuch der mittelenglischen Grammatik, Lautlehre*, Heidelberg, (1925) 1968.

14) Fr. Wilhelm Mühleisen, *Textkritische, metrische und grammatische Untersuchungen von Barbour's Bruce*, Bonn, 1913.

15) F.C. de Vries, *Floris and Blauncheflur, a Middle English Romance edited with Introduction, Notes and Glossary*, diss. Utrecht, 1966.

VII. ASLOAN'S ORTHOGRAPHY[1)]

In the previous section some general indications as to spelling were given with each phoneme, but it seems useful to go further into the matter in order to provide more material for comparison with other texts on this point. Whereas in Section VI only rhyme-words were used, attention will here be devoted to the vocabulary in its entirety, in so far as we will mainly deal with spelling-variations, since the prevailing spelling of any word can be found in the glossary.

The spelling of *BSS* is fairly consistent, as compared with that of many other writings of the period. Some of the variants are caused by the spelling of the rhyme-words concerned. It must also be borne in mind that *BSS* is a copy, so that the scribe may have felt the influence of the spelling of his model, while applying his own orthographic standard.

PHONEME 1 ESc /ī/ > MSc / ei/ — Beside the spellings *i*, *y*(*/e*), *yi* used in *BSS* rhyme-words (see section VI), we find the variations *aspyd*, *espyid*, *byde*, *byid*; *empryce*, *emprice*, *emprys*, *empris* 'empress'; *inclinit*, *inclynit*; *liand*, *lyand*; *ly*, *lye*; *lyk*, *lyke*; *price*, *prys*; *quhilom*, *quhylom*; *strik*(*e*), *strykis*; *thy*, *thi*; *time*, *tyme*; *wisest*, *wysest*.

PHONEMES 2 & 3 ESc /ẹ̄/ ESc /ę̄/ > MSc /ī/ — Beside the various spellings found in the rhyme-words, *e*, *e/e*, *ei*, *ey*, there are spelling-alternations in *appe*(*i*)*r*; *bleid*, *bledis*; *cle*(*i*)*r*; *cle*(*i*)*th*; *de*(*i*)*r*; *dredand*, *dreid*; *fe*(*i*)*st*; *gre*(*i*)*f*, *grevit*; *he*(*i*)*d* 'head'; *he*(*i*)*le* v.; *he*(*i*)*r* adv.; *heir*, *heris* v.; *leif*, *levis*, *levit* 'live' v.; *me*(*i*)*kly*; *meit*(*e*), *mete* 'food'; *mische*(*i*)*f*; *ne*(*i*)*r*; *pece*, *pe*(*i*)*s* 'peace'; *ple*(*i*)*s*, *plesis*; *pre*(*i*)*f*; *scheit*, *schete*; *se*(*i*)*knes*; *speke*, *speik*(*e*); *spe*(*i*)*r* n.; *speir*, *sperit*, *sperand* v.; *sweit*, *swet*(*e*); *we*(*i*)*le* 'well' adv.; *ʒe*(*i*)*d*; *ʒe*(*i*)*r*. *Hed* 'heed' has *e*-spelling only.

E/*ey* alternation occurs in *e*, *eyne*; *le*, *leyis* v.; *me*(*y*)*ne* 'mean' v.; *meyne*, *menit* 'moan' v.; *se*(*y*)*ne* 'seen'; *se*(*y*) 'sea'.

Alternation of *e* with *y* occurs in *requerit*, *requyrit*.

Note the frequent spelling *ȝit* (26x), as against one single example of *ȝet*, both rhyming with *sweit* (*ȝit* 1x).

PHONEME 4 ESc /ā/ > MSc /ē/ The usual spellings in *BSS* are *ai*, *a*/(*e*). Alternation *a*/*ai* is found frequently with or without additional -*e*: *airly*, *arlye*; *aith*, *athis*; *cas*(*e*), *cais*(*e*); *cla*(*i*)*th*, *clathis*; *decla*(*i*)*r*; *fair*, *faris*, *farandly* v.; *gaf* (18x rh.w. *laif*, *haif*, *persaif*), *gaif* (4x n.rh.); *ha*(*i*)*f*, *haue*; *ha*(*i*)*le* 'sound' beside *hele* a.; *ha*(*i*)*st*, *hastely*; *made*, *maid*; *ma*(*i*)*r*; *ma*(*i*)*st*; *saif*, *savit*; *sca*(*i*)*r*; *spair*, *sparand*, *sparit*, *spard*(*e*); *straik*(*e*), *strake*; *ta*(*i*)*le* 'tale'; *tha*(*i*)*m*.

Note the alternation in *consaif*, -*sauit*; *dissaif*, -*sauit*; *persaif*, -*sauit*, -*savit*; apparently the *i*-digraph option is blocked when a minim letter follows.

Alternation *a*/*ay* occurs in *ma*(*y*)*ne* 'moan' n., and *quha*(*y*); instead of the usual *a*-spelling in *sage*, *sagis*, we once find *sege*.

PHONEME 5 ESc /ō/ > MSc /ō/ The spelling in *BSS* is *o*/(*e*); there are no alternate spellings, except in the rhyme *hoye* : *Ioye*. Beside the words mentioned in section VI we find e.g. *astronomy*, *cloke*, *copy*, *dolour*, *impotent*, *innocent*, *opinioun*, *swor* pt., *thole*, *towall*. Monophthongised *oi* is represented in *reiosit*, *voce*, *woce*, and *wodas*.

PHONEME 6 ESc /ū/ > MSc /ū/ The spellings in *BSS* are *u*, *ou*, *ov*, *ow*. Alternation of *u* and *ou* is found in *cuth*, *couth*; other spelling-variations show themselves in *foule*, *fowlely*; *out*, *owt*; *thou*, *thow*; *ȝou*, *ȝow*(*e*); *sound*, *sovnde*; *bovnit*, *bowned*; *dovn*(*e*), *downe*; *drovne*, *drownit*; *provdly*, *prowdly*; *tovne*, *towne*; *tovr*, *towr*(*e*) beside *torris*.

o/*ou* variation is found in *commonly*, *commoun*; *preso*(*u*)*n*; *questio*(*u*)*n*; *masoun*, *masonnis*. The alternative spelling -*oun* for -*ioun* which is commonly met in MSc texts is found once in *BSS* in *obligacoun* (and perhaps in *clarioun*, *claroun*). The prefix *con*- takes the form with *o* in the majority of cases, but is invariably *coun*- in *counsall*, n. & v., and in *countenans*. Most *ous*-endings take this form, but the spelling -*os* in *effectuoslye*, *petuoslye*, *plentuos* is evidently due to the preceding *u*. *U/ou* variation occurs in *covatus*, *cowatousnes*; *merwalus*, *merwalous*; *misaventour*, *misawentur*.

For the alternations *curtas*, *courtas* and *fundin*, *fundyn*, *foundyn* see Phon. 19 below.

PHONEME 6a
ESc /ul/ >
MSc /ū/

The spelling *fow(e)*, due to *l*-vocalisation, is found twice, both cases in rhyme with *ȝow*. *Full* adj. & adv. is found 71x in *BSS*, never in rhyme.

PHONEME 7
ESc /ō/ >
MSc /ǖ/

The spellings in *BSS* are *o/(e)*, *u/(e)*, *v/(e)*; spelling alternation *o/u* occurs in *other*, *vther*; *behovit*, *behufit*; *remuf*, *movis*, *movit*. Beside the examples of this phoneme in rhyme-words, mentioned in section VI, we also meet *brother*, *burd(e)*, *conȝe*, *cule*, *froit*, *frut(e)*; *fure*, *fussoun*, *hony*, *hurdome*, *luke*, *pur(e)tê* (beside *powert*), *rudlye*, *schupe*, *schut*, *scule*, *sonȝe*, *suth*, *tvme*, *vs* 'to use', &c.

Sche (6x n.rh.) is found by the side of *scho* (227x, 5x rh.w. *tharto*, *do*, *to*); on this variant see Section VIII on Anglicisation and Section IX on Accidence.

PHONEME 8
ESc /ai/ >
MSc /ęi/
and /ē̜/

This phoneme is variously spelled *a*, *ai*, *ay/(e)*, *a/e*; alternation *a/ai* occurs in *agane* (36x), *again* (1x); *fa(i)le*; *fa(i)r* 'fair'; *strait*, *stratlie*; *tra(i)st*; alternation *a/ay* in *day(e)*, *daly*; *fa(y)ne* 'glad'; *na(y)* interjection; *ra(y)ne* 'rain'; alternation *ay/aye* in *away(e)*; *ay(e)*; *gay(e)*; *play(e)*; *way(e)*; alternation *ai/ay* in *iornay*, *iornais*; *say(e)*, *said*, *sayd*, *sais*, *sayis*, *says*, though it must be borne in mind that in the latter cases the *is*-endings may be (syllabic) inflectional endings.

PHONEME 9
ESc /oi/ >
MSc /oi/

In *BSS* this phoneme is spelled *oi*, *oy/(e)*, e.g. *iois*; *ioy(e)*; *noy*, *noys*. For a remark about the word *ioye* see Section VI, Phon. 5.

PHONEME 10
ESc /ui/ >
MSc /ui/

The spelling found is *oy*; it occurs in *anoyit*, *distroyit*, *ioynt*, *poynt*.

PHONEME 11
ESc /ei/# >
MSc /ē/# >
/ī/#

For examples of the spellings *e*, *ey*, *ie*, *ye*, see Section VI, Phon. 11. Examples with inflectional endings are *de*, *deit*; *le*, *leyis*.

PHONEME 12
ESc /au/ >
MSc /ā/

The spellings of this phoneme are *au*, *av*, *aw*/(*e*); for examples in rhyme see Section VI, Phon. 12. In non-rhymed positions we find *aucht* 'ought', *auchtand* 'eighth', *fyre-flaucht*.

Converse spellings in *BSS* are *chalmer*; *palpis*; *salf* beside *saif*, *savit*; *talburn*; *walkinnit*, *walkand* vb. 'to wake'; note the spelling *mawlisoun* (beside *malice* and *malicious*), which also has the same history as *wawter*, viz. /*wātir*/ with unshifted /ā/ in labial environment. See Aitken's article 'Variation and Variety', p. 187 and note 31.

PHONEME 12a
ESc /al/ >
MSc /au/ >
/ā/

This phoneme is spelled *al*, *au*, *aw*; for examples in rhyme see Section VI, Phon. 12a. *Al*/*aw* alternation is found in *stall* (4x) and *staw* (1x), none in rhyme; *a*/*au* alternation occurs in *ald* (12x, 1x rh.w. *cald* 'called'), *auld* (2x, 1x rh.w. *cald* 'cold'); *tald* (21x, 5x rh.w. *wald*, *cukkald*, *sauld*, *hald*), *tauld* (3x, 2x rh.w. *wald* 'would'); *sauld* (1x, rh.w. *tald*). Of twenty rhyme-words only three are spelled with *au*. For the history of the combination /ald/ see Section VI, Phon. 12a.

PHONEME 13
ESc /ou/ >
MSc /ou/

The spellings in *BSS* are *o*, *ou*, *ow*/(*e*); beside the examples occurring in rhyme we find *bow* n., *fallows*, *fallous*, *lownar*, *wyndo*(*w*), *wyndois*, and in *our*, prep. and prefix, beside *owr* adv. *Four* is also spelled *fowre*.

Converse spellings are present in *rolpand*, *rolpit*. The spelling *o* is confined to post-tonic syllables as in *wyndo*, *newo*.

PHONEME 13a
ESc /ol/ >
MSc /ou/

This phoneme is found in the word *gold* which occurs 25 times, once rhyming with *behold*.

PHONEME 14
ESc /eu/, /iu/ >
MSc /iu/

The spellings of this phoneme are *eu*, *ew(e)*. Beside the examples mentioned in Section VI, Phon. 14, we find *chewe*, *rewe*, *rewlis*, *schewe*, *trewly(e)*, *threwe*.

PHONEME 15
ESc /ĭ/ >
MSc /ĭ/

The spellings are mostly *i*, *y*. In stressed syllables *i/y* alternation occurs in *bir*, *byr*; *bring*, *bryng*; *drink*, *drynkand*; *king*, *kyng*; *kinrik(e)*, *kynrik*; *lichtly*, *lychtly*; *litill*, *lytill*; *micht*, *mycht*; *michti*, *mychti*; *middis*, *myddis*; *promis*, *promys* n.; *richt*, *rycht*; *siclyk*, *syklyk*; *wit*, *wyte* (OE *witan*); in unstressed syllables in *borit*, *boryt*; *bundin*, *bundyn*; *castin*, *cassyn*; *drawin*, *drawyn*; *evyn(e)*, *ewin*, *ewyn*; *gardiner*, *gardyner*; *lattin*, *lattyn*; *madinnis*, *madynnis*; *madinhed*, *madynhed*; *opinly*, *opynly*; *ravinnis*, *ravynnis*; *takinnis*, *takynnis*.

The ending *-ing* is variously realised: *covering* unrh.; *cunnyng* n. & adj. (1x rh.w. *syngyng*); *dremyng* unrh.; *drinkyn* (rh.w. *thing*); *ending* unrh.; *gnawyn* unrh.; *greting* unrh.; *gudding* unrh.; *hame-cummyn* unrh.; *hunting* (2x unrh.), *huntyne* (1x, rh.w. *syne* adv.); *iusting* unrh.; *lesingis* unrh.; *lesyng* (1x, rh.w. *thing*); *menyng* unrh.; *meting* unrh.; *purgyn* unrh.; *syngyng* (rh.w. *cunnyng*); *warnyng* unrh. Note the converse spellings of the nouns *basyng* 'basin', *courting* 'curtain', *garding* 'garden'; see Section IX, 10,f.

The ending of some past participles of strong verbs (OE *-en*) is variously spelled *-in* or *-yn*: *bundin*, *bundyn*; *etyn*; *fallyn*; *for-gevin*, *forgevyn*; *foundyn*, *fundin*, *fundyn*; *lattin*, *lattyn*; *moltin*; *schawin*. See Section IX, Accidence, 10, g.1.

Note that *dremyt*, *menyt*, *murnyt*, *wonnyt* have *-yt* spellings only; once *BSS* has a plural ending *-ys* (*banys*) instead of the usual *-is*. In these cases the preceding *m* or *n* is probably the reason for the use of *y*. For *is/es* variation in noun-endings see Section IX, 1,a.

Of the verbs *mary* and *tary* the pt. and p.p. show the spellings *marijt* (9x, 1x rh.w. *miscarijt*), *taryit* (1x) and *tarijt* (1x).

Spelling variations *i/e* are found in *citeȝouris, ceteȝener; studyit, studyet,* the latter paralleled by *iustifyet; subtilté, subtelté; y/e* occur in *myrk, merk; witty, witté.* For other *i/e* variations see Phon. 16 below.

In the various forms of the verb 'live' we find the spellings *liffit, liffand* beside *leif, levis, levit* mentioned above.

For the different meanings of *be* and *by,* both ultimately derived from OE *bĭ̄*, see Glossary and *DOST.*

PHONEME 16 ESc /ĕ/> MSc /ĕ/ The normal spelling is *e*; for examples see Section VI, Phon. 16.

A certain group of words displays spellings in either *er,ar* or an abbreviation which may be represented as *Vr,* where *V* may be realised as *a* or *e, viz.* before final *r*: *chyer,* 2x, *chyar* 2x; *dyner* 2x, *dynar* 1x; *fer* 17x, *far* 2x; *gardiner* 2x, *-ar* 4x; *gardyner* 3x, *-ar* 1x; *gerris* 2x, *garris* 7x; *mediciner* 2x, *-ar* 2x; *sqwyer* 1x, *-ar* 1x; *wer* 1x, *war* 3x; *thar/yar* is written approx. fifty times, beside over sixty of the *Vr* version, including cases of both adv. 'there' and the pers. pron.; *ther* is found only once, in unstressed position, unabbreviated in the MS;[2)]

before *r* + cons.: *ernist* 1x, *arnistlye* 1x; *expert* 1x, *expart* 1x; *herd* 5x pt., *hard* 8x pt., 1x p.p., none conditioned by rhyme; *hert* 2x, *hart* 18x, 2x in rh., 'heart', *hertlie* 1x, *hartlie* 2x, *hartfully* 5x;

before final *l*: *bar(r)ell* 3x, *barrall* 1x, *barrellis* 2x; *castell* 1x, *castall* 9x, *castale* 1x; *iowell* 3x, *iowall* 1x; *merwell* pres. ind. 3x, *merwalit* pt. 3x, *merwell* n. 2x, *merwale* n. 1x, *merwal(o)us* 3x.

A second group has *er,ir* and the same *Vr* abbreviation (where *V* may stand for either *e* or *i*) in unstressed syllables, *viz. hidder* 1x, *hiddir* 3x, *hidd<u>er</u>* 1x; *never* 1x, *nevir* 1x, *neu<u>er</u>* 32x; *quhidder* 1x, *quhiddir* 1x, *quhidd<u>er</u>* 1x.

A third group has *er* beside *ir, viz. efter* 18x, *eftir* 5x; *euer* 9x, *evir* 7x; *nother* 10x, *nothir* 1x; *tother* 3x, *tothir* 2x; *lever* 3x, *levir* 1x, whereas *other* 2x and *vther* 13x are only present in the *Vr* variety.

In stressed syllables the alternation *e/i* is also found: *herd* n. 8x, unrh., *hird* 1x, rh.w. *bird*; *mesalry* 1x, *missalry* 1x; *ȝestrene* 1x, *ȝisterday* 2x.

One can interpret these facts as follows: three spellings occur, *er*, *ir* and the abbreviation for *Vr*, where *V* may, it seems, be realised when spelled out as *a*, *e* or *i*. The stressed alternations no doubt are phonemic doublets. In many cases the alternation with *a* may represent Phon. 17, see Section VI, Phon. 17. Before *l* and perhaps in *lykest* 1x, *lykast* 1x, there may be variants between /i/ and /ʌ/ as found in MoSc., two fully reduced unstressed vowels, corresponding to the vowels which are always fully short when stressed. The first of these is Phon. 15, the second occurs e.g. in -*ar* and -*and*. The ambiguous spelling of /ɪ/ is *i*, *y*, of unstressed /ʌ/ *a*. Ambiguous between these is *e*.

PHONEME 17 The normal spelling is *a*; for examples see Phon. 17
ESc /ǎ/ > in Section VI.
MSc /ǎ/ Note the variants *cast* (2x, rh.w. *fast*, *lykast*) and *kest* (10x, 1x rh.w. *degest*). For other *a/e* alternations see Phon. 16 above.

PHONEME 18 The normal spelling is *o*; for examples see Phon. 18
ESc /ǒ/ > in Section VI.
MSc /ǒ/ Spelling-variation *o/ou* is found in *dochter*, *douchter(is)*. Note *drope*, 1x n.rh., 1x rh.w. *stop*.

PHONEME 19 The spelling very frequently is *u*, but *o*, *ou*, *v* and
ESc /ŭ/ > *w* are also found.
MSc /ŭ/ *o/u* variation occurs in *bot*, *but* prep; *sodan(e)ly*, *sudanlye*, *sudand*; *ou* alternates with *w* in *toun*, *twn* 'tun'; the word for 'dumb' is variously spelled *dum*, *dvm*, *dwm*. The alternations *curtas*, *courtas*, and *fundin*, *fundyn*, *foundyn* are probably doublets in Phon. 6 alongside forms in Phon. 19.

A survey of the use of vowel + *i* or *y*[3)] by John Asloan in *BSS* gives the following results:

Of about 175 types with an original (Early Scots) tonic /a/ or /ai/ we find[4]

65 occurrences of	/a/ spelled	*a* only, e.g. *able, banys, cage, dame, fra, ga, haly;*
26	/a/	*ai* only, e.g. *baid* n., *baith, forsaike, laite, raif* pt., *traide;*
24	/a/	*a, ai, ay,* e.g. *airly, arlye, cla(i)th, ma(y)ne, na(y);*
22	/ai/	*ai, ay* only, e.g. *air, aye, assay, hair, palfray, way(e);*
33	/ai/	*a* only, e.g. *abasit, danté, grath(lỳ), madin, nalis;*
8	/ai/	*a, ai, ay,* e.g. *consaif, -sauit, fa(y)ne, tra(i)st.*

Of about 175 types with an original (Early Scots) tonic /e/ or /ei/ we find[4]

77 occurrences of	/e/ spelled	*e* only, e.g. *betwene, brer, brest, ches, fre, gredy;*
50	/e/	*ei, ey* only, e.g. *beif, breid, cheir, deile, leip, succeid;*
38	/e/	*e, ei, ey,* e.g. *appe(i)r, cle(i)th, de(i)r, gre(i)f, me(y)ne, se(y)* n.
4	/ei/	*ei, ey* only: *eis, key, obeys, wey;*
3	/ei/	*e* only: *de, dese, sustene;*
4	/ei/	*e, ei, ey*: *e, eyne; le, leyis; pece, peis, pes; pleis, plesis.*

With original tonic *o* we never find *i* or *y* added to the vowel, except in the rhyme *hoye* : *Ioye*, where *hoye* is from OF *ho* , ME *ho(o)*. The form *io* for 'joy' was already found at a fairly early date, though the other example in the Asloan MS, (Vol. II, p. 273, line 22) may be a case of rhyme for convenience: *io* : *nescio*.

With original tonic *u* Alsoan never used *i*-digraph spellings in *BSS*.

Of about fifty types[4] with *u* representing phoneme 7 about twenty-five are due to OF /u/, e.g. *assure, cure, dule, excusit, huge, iugement, remuf*; the rest are all original /o/, e.g. *buke, cule, dure, flude, scule, tume; other, vther; behovit, behufit.*

The use of *i*-, *y*-digraphs was already common in the fifteenth century, but scribes had a free choice whether to apply them or not. In the present text the use of *i*-,*y*-digraph spellings instead of the formerly regular simplex vowel spellings of phonemes 2, 3, 4, 5, and 7 is not general practice. We also find cases where the final -*e* as well as the *i*-, *y*-digraph spelling are present, e.g. *bair(e)* n. & a., *laite, maid(e)*v., *meit(e)* n., *speik(e), straik(e); ma(y)ne* 'moan' n.

Final -*e* occurs in several situations in MSc:

1. corresponding to (O)F final -*é*, in *BSS* e.g. in *cite, cuntre, dignite, entre, plente, preve, werite*, and in such words as *he* 'high', *the* 'thee', *tre* 'tree'. It represents original *i* in *hardear* and in *witte*[5];
2. purely graphically under the following conditions,
   a. after a simple vowel-spelling representing one of the long monophthongs 1 - 7 of Aitken's vowel system, and, less consistently phonemes 8 - 14, followed by a single consonant-spelling, e.g. 1. *delyte, fyre, ryf(e)*; 2. *grene, mete/meit(e), quene*; 3. *me(y)ne, spe(i)ke*; 4. *stane, straike*; 5. *cloke, restore, schore*; 6. *fowle, how(e), lowde*; 7. *buke, fude, rute*; 8. *day(e), fa(i)le, fa(y)ne, play(e)*; 9. *ioy(e)*; 11. *hie/hye*; 12. *aw(e), crawe, draw(e), law(e)*; 13. *fowre, growe*; 14. *hew(e), newe, trewe*;
   b. after certain consonant-groups, e.g. *mp, nd, nk, rd, rk, rm, rn, rp, sch*; examples: *arm(e), ask(e), attempe, awn(e), barn(e), born(e), burd(e), carpe, clerk(e), crovde, crovne, defowle, dovn(e)/downe, dranke, drovne, erle, fand(e), fawne, fende, fetche, forfarne, fische, fravde, freschenes, harme, harpe, herbe, hurd(e), innes, lowde, morn(e), port(e), renowne, rowme, rusche, scharpe, scurge, sovnd(e), speche, stanche, sterne, sworn(e), teche, tempe, tovne/towne, tovr/towr(e), trumpe, warme, warn(e), ȝarne*;

c. after root-final *y* in *ay(e)*, *ioy(e)*, *key(e)*, *lady(e)*;

d. in a few words in which a simple vowel-spelling representing one of the ESc short monophthongs (in an unstressed syllable only) is followed by a single consonant-spelling, e.g. *follow(e)*, *kinrik(e)*, *pyot(e)*, *sevyn(e)*, *worschip(e)*.

Where it seems clearly necessary final *-e* is sometimes left off, e.g. *blud(e)*, *com(e)* pt., *frut(e)*, *fut(e)*, *kep(e)*, *now(e)*, *son(e)* 'soon'. After *g* /dʒ/ it is sometimes omitted, too, e.g. in *larg(e)nes*, *ymag(e)*. We also find this practice in other fifteenth-century Scots texts, cf. e.g. *Ratis Raving*[6] 435 *knawleg* : *outrage*, 1544 *lynag* : *outrag*, beside 795 *rage* : *knawlege*; and *Thewis off Gud Women* 291 *age* : *mareag*, beside 221 *ȝouthege* : *knawlege*; root-final *g* can be seen as an abbreviation of *-ge*, see Petti, p. 23[7].

The spelling of /θ,ð/ (*th*).

In *BSS* the scribe uses the symbol *y* for *th* initially in the following words and their compounds if any: *yai* 'those' 9x; *yai* pers. pron. 144x, of which 1x line-initially, 2285; *yam* pers. pron. 61x, never with *th*; *yan* adv. 100x, of which 1x line-initially, 1460; *yan* conj. 9x, all within the line; *yar* in *all yar maist*, *all yar lest*, *all yar werst*; *yar* adv. 58x, all within the line; *yar* poss. pron. 43x, all within the line; *yarabone* 1x, *yarat* 1x, *yarby* 1x, *yarefter* 3x, *yarfor* 8x, *yarin* 3x, *yarof* 4x, *yaron* 3x, *yartill* 1x, *yarto* 6x, *yarwith* 2x, *yarwithall* 3x, *yarwnder* 1x, all within the line; *yaris* poss. pron. 1x; *yat* conj. 85x, *yat* dem. pron. 95x, *yat* rel. pron. 91x; *ye* def. art. 773x, *ye* pers. pron. 33x, *yi* in *for yi* 14x, *yi* poss. pron. 38x, *yiddir* adv. 1x; *yin* adv. 'thence' 1x, *yin* poss. pron. 3x, *yir* dem. adj. 6x, *yis* dem. pron. 119x; *yocht* adv. 6x, 1x line-initially 965; *you* pers. pron. 2x, *yow* id. 60x, *yus* adv. 15x, *yusgatis* adv. 2x, *yusway* adv. 1x. All these words have a voiced initial sound in Modern English. When they stand at the beginning of a line the scribe uses *th*, except in the three cases mentioned: *yai* 2285, *yan* 1460, *yocht* 965. Once we find *the* within the line, after a slant, in line 20, and once *thus* 229. *Thy* occurs 5x, all line-initially.

Most of the words mentioned above are found line-initially as follows: *Thai* pers. pron. 43x, *Than* adv. 134x, *Than* conj. 8x, *Thar* adv. 13x, *Tharby* 1x, *Tharefter* 1x, *Tharfor* 6x, *Tharof* 7x, *Tharon* 1x, *Tharto* 2x, *Tharwith* 1x, *That* conj. 89x, *That* dem. pron. 11x, *That* rel. pron. 66x, *The* def. art. 216x (1x within the line, see above), *The* instrum. 1x, *Ther* adv. 1x, *Thir* dem. adj. 2x, *This* dem. pron. 34 x, *Thow* pers. pron. 8x, *Thus* 16x, 1x within the line, see above.

Other words with initial *th* occurring in the text are *thak* 2x, *thank(it)* 13x, *thee* n. 'thigh' 1x, *thing(is)* 25x, *think(and)* 6x, *thocht* n. 3x, *thocht* pt. 13x, *thole* 1x, *thousand* 1x, *thra* 3x, *thrang* 1x, *thre* 8x, *threwe* 1x, *thrid* 3x, *thrist(it)* 2x, *throu* 2x, *throw* 8x, *throwe* 1x, *thyn* a. 1x; these are never written with *y*. They have a voiceless initial sound in so far as they occur in Modern English.

Within the word we usually find *th*, viz. *athis* 1x, *birthy* 1x, *blythar* 1x, *-est* 1x, *-ly*, *-lie* 6x, *-nes* 1x, *hethinnes* 1x, *ourthort* 1x, *ourthrawe* 1x, *sumthing* 4x, *tything* 1x, *vmbethocht* 1x, *with* and its compounds 221x, *worthy* 9x, *worthit* 1x, *ȝouthhed* 2x, *ythandly* 1x. Exceptions are the cases of *broyer* 1x, *noyer* 10x, *oyer* 2x, *toyer* 3x, *-ir* 2x, *vyer(is)* 10x, *vyerwayis* 1x, where only *y* is used. Once we find *nothir* rhyming with *toyir* (731).

The symbol *y* for *th* is never used word or stem-finally: *aith* 1x, *baith* 24x, *blyth* 11x, *bedclathis* 1x, *cla(i)th* 7x, *cle(i)th* 2x, *c(o)uth* 62x, *eith* 1x, *faith* 1x, *forsuth* 6x, *freth* 1x, *furth* 21x, *furthwith* 1x, *girth* 2x, *grath(ly)* 2x, *hundreth* 4x, *kyth* 1x, *laith* 1x, *pith* 1x, *raith* 1x, *reuth* 1x, *scaith* 8x, *suth(-fast, -ly, -nes)* 15x, *swyth* 4x, *treuth* 2x, *welth* 1x, *(in-, out-)with* 6x, *worth* 5x.

In the present edition only *th* has been printed, because it did not seem necessary to use two distinct symbols: Craigie's edition can be consulted for the scribe's use of *y* and *th*, as it prints the text diplomatically. See Sections XV and XVI for editorial method and abbreviations, and Section XIX for misreadings in Craigie's text.

Notes to Section VII

1. See also the sections on Accidence, Anglicisation and Phonology, the Glossary, Sir William Craigie's 'Older Scottish and English, A Study in Contrast', *Transactions of the Philological Society*, London, 1935, pp. 1 ff., and A.J. Aitken's 'Variation and variety in written Middle Scots', *Edinburgh Studies in English and Scots*, eds A.J. Aitken, Angus McIntosh and Hermann Pálsson, London, 1971, pp. 177-209.
2. For *thar* see Section XVI, Abbreviations, p.204 s.v. *-ar*.
3. See James A.H. Murray, *The Dialects of the Southern Counties of Scotland*, London, 1873, pp. 35 and 51-53, but cf. K.J. Kohler, 'Aspects of Middle Scots Phonemics and Graphemics: The Phonological Implications of the Sign <I>', *Transactions of the Philological Society*, Oxford, 1967, publ. 1968, pp. 32-61.
4. Full lists of examples are presented in Appendix IV.
5. For the editorial placing of accents see Section XV.
6. For other examples: *Ratis Raving* (c. 1420) *misknawleg* : *rage* (l. 1630),
Consail (c. 1460) *ȝouthage* : *knawleg* (l. 1),
knawlege : *wysage* (l.401),
Foly of Fulis (c. 1460) *knawleg* : *age* (l. 19),
cusinage : *knawlege* (l. 329),
see R. Girvan, *Ratis Raving, and Other Moral and Religious Pieces, in Prose and Verse*, EETS OS 43 and STS III 11.
7. Anthony G. Petti, *English Literary Hands from Chaucer to Dryden*, London, 1977.

VIII. ANGLICISATION IN THE MANUSCRIPT

In connection with the present text we can hardly speak of anglicisation[1], because examples of this phenomenon, which is common in most fifteenth-century Scottish texts, are very rare in *BSS*. It is among the least anglicised narrative pieces in Middle Scots, comparable with *The Buik of Alexander*[2], *Rauf Coilȝear*[3], and the *Thre Prestis of Peblis*[4], but with less anglicisation than *Lancelot of the Laik*[5], *Lufaris Complaynt*[6], *Quare of Jelusy*[7], *Wallace*[8], *Buke of the Howlat*[9], and *Golagros and Gawane*[10], all dating from before 1500. The few cases which are found in *BSS*, almost none of them occurring in rhymes, are more probably due to the scribe(s) than to the author. They are:

go 4 x, not in rhyme; cf. *gang*, 6 x, in rhyme 4 x: with *hang*, *sang*, *fang*, *wrang*; *ga*, 13 x, in rhyme 10 x: with *sa* 5 x, *ma* 2 x, *twa*, *ta* and *stra*, once each;

more once, not in rhyme, cf. *ma(i)r*, 45 x, in rhyme 19 x: with *decla(i)r* 5 x, *thar* 'there' 5 x, *bair* 'bare', *cair* 'care', *scair* 'share', *war* 'were' once each, and with *sair* 'sore' 3 x, *lair* 'lore' 2 x;

sche 6 x, not in rhyme; *scho* occurs some 220 x, rhyming with *do* and *to*, twice each;

also 2 x, not in rhyme; *alsa* occurs 2 x, not in rhyme, while *sa* is found in rhyme 11 x: with *ga* 5 x, *twa* 2 x, *ma* 'more', *wa* 'woe' once each, and with *sla* 'slay', *ta* 'take' once each;

no adj. is found 3 x, not in rhyme;

no adv. with comparatives, is found 5 x, not in rhyme; *na* in several functions is used frequently;

no thing is found 2 x, whereas *na thing* is usual;

quhom occurs once as relative pronoun, once in the compound relative pronoun *quhomevir*; *quham* does not occur in *BSS*.

There are two examples of anglicisation for convenience:

1. *so : in verbo regio*; *so* is elsewhere in *BSS* found 18 x unrhymed, as against *sa* 110 x unrhymed, 9 x rhymed. This rhyming example of

so, therefore, must be due to the author, whereas the other cases are most probably the scribe's work. Indeed, the use of *so* to rhyme with Latin *o*-endings is common practice, cf. Dunbar's *Of the Resurrection of Christ* (first line: *Done is a battell on the dragon blak*)[11] which consists of five stanzas, ecah ending in the line *Surrexit dominus de sepulchro*, and where the words rhyming with *sepulchro* are *go, so, Appollo, so, fo*.

In Henryson's poems we also find evidence that he could use some words at will either with an *o* or with an *a*-rhyme; we see e.g. in the *Testament of Cresseid*[12] in ll. 100 ff. the rhyming words *soir : moir : thairfoir*, as against 407 ff. *cair : euermair : bair* adj. *: sair*; ll. 163 ff. *hoir* adj.*: woir* pret. *: boir* pret., as against 177 ff. *hair* n. *: gair* n.*: bair* pret. In his *Orpheus and Erudices*[13] the following oppositions occur: ll. 127 ff. *sore : more*, 409 ff. *sore : tharfor : forlore*, but 445 ff. *sair : misfair* (where the Bannatyne MS. has *soir : misfair*) and 162 ff. *sair : hair* n. *: bair* n.; 128 ff. *wo : go : fro*, 395 ff. *wo : fro : go*, but 308-9 *Proserpine : ga*.

In Henryson's short poems, too, examples of this phenomenon can be observed. Some of these spellings could indeed be due to scribes, but not all, as is evident from examples mentioned above.

2. 1651-2 *behold : gold;* this is the only example of an *-old*-rhyme in the present text, whereas *-ald-* rhymes are fairly common, cf. ll. 395, 1027, 1057, 1369, 1971, 2507, 2557, 2585, 2597, 2635.

   Examples of similar rhymes are found e.g. in Sir Richard Holland's *Buke of the Howlat*[9]:
   321 ff. *fold (OE fold) : behold;* 340 ff. *gold : behold;* 360 ff. *gold : bold (OE bald)*, whereas in the same poem we also find *behald : cald* ('called') in 87 ff., *behald : ald : cald* 543 ff., and *behald : pundfald : wald : bald* 782 ff.

Notes to Section VIII

1. See Marjory A.Bald's articles in *The Scottish Historical Review,* Glasgow, 1926-28: 'Anglicisation of Scottish Printing', Vol 23, pp. 107 ff.; 'The Pioneers of Anglicised Speech in Scotland', Vol. 24, pp. 179 ff., and 'Contemporary References to the Scottish Speech of the Sixteenth Century', Vol. 25, pp. 163 ff., and A.J.Aitken's article 'Variation and Variety in Written Middle Scots', *Edinburgh Studies in English and Scots,* eds. A.J. Aitken, Angus McIntosh and Hermann Pálsson, London, 1971, pp. 177-209.
2. *The Buik of Alexander,* ed. R.L.Graeme Ritchie, STS II 12, 17, 21 & 25, 1921-29.
3. *The Taill of Rauf Coilȝear,* ed. S.J.H.Herrtage, EETS ES 39, London, 1882.
4. *The Asloan Manuscript,* Vol. 2, ed. W.A.Craigie, STS NS 16, pp. 175 ff.
5. *Lancelot of the Laik,* ed. M.M.Gray, STS NS 2, Edinburgh, 1912.
6. *The Lufaris Complaynt,* ed. Kenneth G.Wilson, from Bodleian MS. Arch.Selden B 24 (the *Kingis Quair* MS.), in *Speculum,* XXIX, 1954, pp. 719-23.
7. *The Quare of Jelusy,* ed. J.T.T.Brown, STS III 4, Miscellany Vol., 1933, pp. 191-212.
8. *Hary's Wallace,* ed. Matthew P.McDiarmid, 2 vols., STS IV 4 & 5, 1968 & 1969.
9. *The Asloan Manuscript,* Vol. 2, pp. 95-126.
10. *Scottish Alliterative Poems in Riming Stanzas,* ed. F.J.Amours, STS I 27 & 38, 1891 & 1897.
11. *The Poems of William Dunbar,* ed. W.Mackay Mackenzie, London, (1932) 1970, pp. 159 f.
12. Ed. Denton Fox, London, 1968.
13. *The Asloan Manuscript,* Vol. 2, pp. 155-74.

IX. ACCIDENCE

1. NOUNS.

a. Number.

In the majority of the plural nouns in *BSS* the ending is spelled *-is*:

antaris, barnis, bellis, cuntréis, dayis, erandis, houndis, landis, partis, wyfis, &c.

Once it is written *-ys*: *banys*.

The plural ending is spelled *-es* in the following cases:

armes, bewes, dremes, expenses, heres, innes, tymes.

This may sometimes be due to the consonants preceding the ending, cf. Section VII, sub Phoneme 15, for *-yt/-it* endings.

From the metre in this text it is apparent that the *-is*(*-es*)-ending is sometimes syllabic (e.g. 59, 65, 80), sometimes non-syllabic (e.g. 21, 22, 42).

There is doubling of the final consonant in the spellings

dettis, doggis, madynnis, masonnis, spurris, takinnis, torris, wittis, ȝettis.

Doubling is optional in

durris, castall duris, baronis, baronnis.

There is no doubling of the consonant in *cokis, mattokis.*

The plural ends in *-s* in

fallous, fallows; gallous, gallhous[1]; *iornais* (sg. *iornay*); *enemys.*

Words ending in accented *e* /i (:)/, either of English or French origin, have their plural forms in *-is*:

extremiteis, cuntreis, danteis, kneis, treis.

The ending *-en* is not found, *-ne* only in the case of *eyne* (sg. *E*).

The plural of *lyf* occurs as *lyfis* and as *lyvis.*

The following plurals reflect OE *i*-mutation:

feit, men, women.

The nouns *barrell* 1694, *ȝe*(*i*)*r* and *thing* occur in uninflected form with plural meaning:

he of eld was bot thre ȝeir (: *deir*) 9; cf. *tuelf ȝeris of age* 2566; *he sall be techit in five ȝer* (: *leir*) 46; cf. *within sex ȝeris* 42; *befor all thing* 304; *our all vther thing* 407; for pl. see 1703, 2179.

The word *hors* has only this one form, for sg. and pl.; see also Genitive below.

b. Genitive.

The genitive singular ending is *-is*:

barnis, bodyis, faderis, kingis, ladyis, treis, wyfis.

Doubling of the final consonant occurs in *sonnis, womannis.*

Some genitives have no ending:

burges, emprys, empryce, hors, sister in the phrase *his sister son.*

The genitive plural ends in *-is*: *birdis.*

A relic of the old genitive plural in *-er* is found in

all thar lest, all thar werst, all thar maist,

in forms with epenthesis of *th* (OE *alra* > ME *aller* > *alþer* > *all thar*).

For nouns ending in *-ing* and *-and* see under VERB.

2. ADJECTIVES.

There are no traces of any declensional endings.

a. The comparative ends in

-er: *farer* 'fairer';

-ar: *blythar, gretar, hardéar, honestar, lelar, lownar, waar.*

The periphrastic comparative occurs only once: *mar reiosit.*

b. The superlative ends in

-est: *blythest, farest, lykest, nerrest, wisest;*

-ast: *derrast, lykast.*

The periphrastic superlative occurs only once: *mast leif* (in rhyme).

c. The following irregular degrees of comparison occur:

gud	*better*	*best*
ill	*war*	*werst*
laite	---	*last*
litill,	*les*	*lest*
lytill	*myn*	---
mekle	*mair, mar*	*mast*
mony	*ma*	---

feile	---	---
		nerrest
		nixt

d, *nane* is used seven times as adj. before a vowel or with *nother; nane vther, nane othir* are also found.
na adj. is used sixty-one times before consonants, four times before a vowel.

3. ADVERBS.

a. The majority of the adverbs in *BSS* is formed by adding *-ly*, e.g. *amorusly, bitterly, clenly, dulfully, grathly, halely, habundantly, prevely, wysly, ythandly*, &c.
In some cases the ending is spelled *-lye*, in a few *-lie*:
arnistlye, fraitlye, nakitlye, petuoslye &c;
blythlie, hartlie, pertlie, &c.
Once the suffix is spelled *-lé*: *ryplé*.
The original genitive-ending *-is, -es* is found in the adverbs *anys, ellis, ofttymes, quhylis, thusgatis, vtherwayis, ȝongatis*, cf. Campbell[2], 668.
A number of adverbs in *BSS* have no distinctive endings, e.g. *bane, bedene, dowtles, evyn, fast, half, lowde, mys, odious, quyk, raith*, &c.
Some words occur in both adverbial and adjectival functions: *best, better, clene, fair, fane, hale, hie, newe, sweit, thra, wele*, &c.

b. The comparative of adverbs ends in *-ar*: *erar, hiear, langar*; in *-er*: *lever*, and in *-ir*: *levir*.
The periphrastic comparative is not found.

c. The superlative occurs only in the case of irregular degrees of comparison, q.v. below.

d. Irregular degrees of comparison:

wele, weile	*better*	*best*
---	---	*lest*
ill	*wer, war*	---
mekle	*mair, mar, more*	*maist, mast*
neir	---	---

Note. The adverbial constructions *the day, the morn* and the older equivalents *to-day, to-morne* and *to-nycht* all occur in *BSS*.

4. NUMERALS.

a. Cardinal numerals: *a, ane; twa; thre; four, fowre; five; sex; sevyn(e); ten; tuelf; twenty; forty; hunder, hundreth; thousand.*

b. Ordinal numerals: *first; secound; thrid; ferd; fyft; sext; sevynt; auchtand.*

c. Multiplicative: *anys.*

d. Distributives: *ilk, ilka* 'each'; *euerilk. ilk* is used three times in *BSS*, in each case before a consonant; *ilka* is found four times, equally before consonants only.

e. Indefinite numerals: *all; baith; ha(i)le; nother, ony, sic; sum; vther; yneugh, ynewe.*
The original inflectional difference between sg. and pl. is still observed in *BSS* in the case of the last two words: *yneugh* is used with sg. nouns, *ynewe* with plural nouns.

5. ARTICLES.

a. Indefinite articles:

the form *a* is used: before consonants: *passim* (151x);
before *h*: 6x;
before a vowel once, in l. 1625, but this is evidently a mistake, since *arow and* are metrically redundant in this line;

the form *ane* is used: before consonants: *passim* (91x);
before *h*: 9x;
before vowels: 16x.

The fact that *a* before consonants occurs more often than *ane* before consonants is in accordance with the date of the original of *BSS* (1460-80, see Section X), since the latter usage was not established till the second half of the fifteenth century. Cf. *DOST* s.v. *ane* indef. art.

ane nothir n. & adj., and *ane nother* n. & adj. show the results of wrong division.

b. Definite article:

it is found written *the* and *ye* (see Craigie's edition). *The tane, the tother* and *the tothir* show the results of wrong division and retention of the old neuter article *þæt* which in due course became *thet*.

6. PRONOUNS.

The following forms are found in *BSS*:

a. Personal pronouns.

Nominative sg.	1.	*I*
	2.	*thou, thow*
	3.	*he; sche*[3]*, scho*[4]*; it*[5]
pl.	1.	*we*
	2.	*ȝe, ȝhe*[6]
	3.	*thai*
Objective sg.	1.	*me*
	2.	*thē*
	3.	*him; hir; it*
pl.	1.	*ws*
	2.	*ȝou, ȝow(e)*
	3.	*tha(i)m*

A NOTE ON THE USE OF *ȜE* AND *THOU*.

In his edition *Complete Works of Geoffrey Chaucer*, Oxford, 1894, Vol. V, p. 175, W.W. Skeat gave the following much quoted guidance as to how the use of the pronouns of address should be interpreted in earlier English: '*Thou* is the language of a lord to a servant, of an equal to an equal, and expresses also companionship, love, permission, defiance, scorn, threatening; whilst *ye* is the language of a servant to a lord, and of compliment, and further expresses honour, submission, or entreaty.' Subsequent scholarship in this field has entirely agreed with him, gratefully elaborating his findings, and discovering that, even if at first glance a text might seem to contain inconsistencies, careful examination would show that in the greater number of instances 'usage was in accord with the pattern given by Skeat'[7], and that 'seeming errors often disappear upon further analysis'[8].

The usage in *BSS* is no exception and shows very few cases of the use of pronouns *ȝe* and *thou* not in keeping with Skeat's rule. In addressing a plural audience *ȝe*, *ȝow* and *ȝour* are used invariably, e.g. when the emperor is speaking to the sages, 201, 984, 1308, &c.; a man to his wife and her mother, 1954; the author to his readers, 374, 505; a doctor to his pupils, 764.

In normal polite address *ȝe*, *ȝow* and *ȝour* are used, e.g. when barons are speaking to their emperor, 115, 117, 265; a doctor to a queen, 655, 658, &c.; a gardener to his master, 306; a youth to an emperor or a king, 2176 ff., 2670 ff.; also in the relation stepmother/youth, emperor/youth, mother-in-law/son-in-law, and lovers among themselves (1926 ff.) who are not speaking of love but of the dangers of detection of their adulterous behaviour.

A son addressing his father always uses the polite form, e.g. 858, 2544, 2730, whereas the father uses *thê*, *thou* and *thi* invariably to the son, e.g. 196, 853, 901, 2555, &c. A daughter speaking to her mother uses the polite forms, 1359, 1436, &c.; the mother commonly uses the familiar forms, e.g. 1351, 1484, 1501, but there are two exceptions to this, *viz.* *ȝe* 1433 and *ȝow* 1576. L. 1433 is the final line of a six-line speech in which the mother has used *thow/thê* three times. She here 'is especially serious and is attempting to give (her) words unusual force and dignity'[9]. In l. 1576 we find the mother greeting her daughter with great concern about a serious situation.

A wife speaking to her husband generally addresses him in the polite form, the husband, however, calls his wife *thê* and *thou*. This was the general usage at the time; when in Sir David Lindsay's *Satyre of the Thrie Estaits* we find a husband calling his wife *ȝe* and she him *thou* this is meant to be comic[10]; similarly in the *Nun's Priest's Tale* Chauntecleer and Pertelote constantly address each other in the polite plural. Once in *BSS* (1553) a husband uses the polite possessive pronoun to his wife in an angry command, but given in front of a servant[11]. Four times in PUTEUS the wife addresses her husband as *thòu*, &c. but this is when she speaks in scorn[12] and has him totally at her mercy (ll. 1130 ff.).

There are several places in *BSS* where a person, after addressing someone in the polite plural form, switches to the singular. This is so in the case just mentioned and in three of the scenes when the empress explains her story to the emperor, wishing to impress on her husband the dangerous position he will find himself in if he allows his son to live, and to show how concerned she is for his welfare: 357 ff., 572 ff., 1830 ff. Towards the end (2745) when she sees that all is lost, she says: 'All ȝone I wrocht To tempe thi sone allanerly ...', again using the familiar form, this time possibly in defiance, though she goes on to implore mercy.

The emperor sometimes addresses his empress in the polite form, but three times in anger and contempt (2743, 2747-2748) and three times when complimenting her (363, 1278, 1842) he uses the familiar form. The latter three cases do not agree with Skeat's statement quoted above, for he groups compliment under the polite plural. Possibly we can explain these three cases as compliments lovingly given; moreover, these are cases of husband speaking to wife. He uses the polite form to her twice in a command (1172 f.), three times in a request (1184, 2109 f.) and once in a compliment (2235), but in the latter case we have to do with a possibly corrupt line.

One of the sages, who in all the other addresses to the emperor speak to him in the polite form, calls him *thou* in ll. 499-500, where he threatens him with future mischief if he listens to the false words of his wife. The emperor switches to *thow* three times in anger, reproaching one of the sages with the fact that they have brought his son back dumb (377, 1305, 1861). In one case, however, there is no question of anger or threat but rather of compliment or appreciation (2508). This is a case exactly parallel to 2235 just discussed: in both lines the emperor expresses his satisfaction at a tale told to him.

It is rather surprising that in SENESCALCUS the doctor prescribing treatment to the sick king addresses him with the familiar pronoun (1208 ff.), also in CANIS the nurse telling the lady that her child is dead (456 ff.); both statements, however, can be explained as expressive of concern. In MEDICUS 673 f. the queen switches from *ȝe* to *thy* in a threat, and in VIRGILIUS 1822 ff. the barons address the emperor in great anger with *thow* and *thi*. In the story AVIS the bird is addressed with *thow* as well by its loving master, whom it answers in the same way, as by its master's wife who threatens to kill it. In the same story the merchant in surprise at discovering in his own house a knight with a naked sword in his hand addresses him with *thow* (1942).

One final example must be mentioned where we find

> And all the peple cryit ȝarne
> 'Gud master, now defend thi barne!' (1855 ff.)

This may be a misreading for *the*, since the youth is not the master's child but the emperor's. On the other hand here again, as in most of the other cases discussed, an emotional feeling like concern is involved, which may explain the use of the informal address.

For further examples from MSc poetry cf. Robert Henryson's *Fable of the Fox, the Wolf and the Cadger*[13)], where the wolf addresses the fox with *thou*, the fox calls the wolf *ȝe* and *schir*, and the cadger, finding the 'dead' fox, says *ȝe* to it, but when the fox has taken his fish the cadger calls him *thou*; see also *The Flyting of Dunbar and Kennedy*[14)], a scolding-match, in which *thou* is in constant use, and the interesting passage in the *Wallace*, Bk. I, 398-99 (ed. John Jamieson, Edinburgh, 1820, Vol. II, p. 398):

> Wallace ansuerd, said: 'Thow art in the wrang.'
> 'Quham thowis thow, Scot? in faith thou serwis a blaw.'

See also *Hary's Wallace*, ed. Matthew P. McDiarmid, STS IV.4, p. 14, and 5, p. 144, note to line 399 for the variation *dowis*; and *DOST* s.v. *dow*, v.[4].

In conclusion we may state that *BSS* largely conforms to Skeat's explanation of the use of *thou* and *ye*; the category 'concern' should, however, be added to those mentioned by him for the use of *thou*.

b. Compound personal pronouns.

Nominative	sg.	1. *my-self*
		2. *thy-self, thi-sell*
		3. *him-self, he ... his-sell*
	pl.	1. ---
		2. *ȝour-self*
		3. ---
Objective	sg.	1. *my-self, my-sell*
		2. ---
		3. *him-self, him-sell; hir-self, hir-sell; the self* 'itself'
	pl.	1. ---
		2. *ȝour-self*
		3. ---

The forms with *sell* all occur in rhyme; Murray[15] dates the use of *sel(l)* at the end of the fifteenth century; *NED* dates it sixteenth century, but it is found quite commonly in Hary's *Wallace*, c. 1480.

Note the use of *hir awne self* (662) and *his awne self* (1508).

c. Possessive pronouns (adjectives).

sg. 1. *my*
2. *thi, thy; thin* (once before *h*, twice before *a*, but *thi, thy* are also used with following vowel or *h*)
3. *his; hir*

pl. 1. *our*
2. *ȝour*
3. *thar*

Of the substantive or absolute possessive pronouns we only find:

sg. 1. *myne*

pl. 2. *ȝouris*
3. *tharis*

Compound possessives occurring in *BSS* are: *for my awn* and *of my awn*.

d. Interrogative pronouns: *quha*,and *quhat* n. & adj.

e. Relative pronouns: *as* (after *the* + plur.n.), *quha(y), quhat, (the) quhilk, quhom, that.*

at as a rel.pron. is not found in *BSS*, but it is used four times as a conjunction after e.g. *quhill* and *quhen*.

The double form *quhilk that* occurs twice.

Compound relatives: *quhasa evir, quhat evir, quhom evir.*

f. Demonstrative pronouns: sg. *this* pl. *thir*
that *thai*
sg. and pl. *sic, ȝone.*

g. Indefinite pronouns: *all* 'everything', *all* 'all, everyone', *ane* 'someone', *ilkane, nane, ocht, na thing, no thing, vther, nother, nothir, (the) tane, (the) tother, tothir.*

Note: For *all thar* + superlative, see § 1.b above, on the genitive.

7. CONJUNCTIONS.

The following conjunctions are used in the present text:

als
alsa
also
and 'and' or 'if'
as adv. and conj.
at 'that'
becaus adv. and conj.
bot adv. and conj.
for
fra
gif
na adv. and conj.
nor
nother 'neither ... (nor)'
notherane 'neither'
oder (... or)
or 'or' and adv. 'before'
quhidder, quhiddir 'whether'
quhill 'until' and 'while'
sa, so adv. and conj.
sen 'since'
suppos 'although'
than
that
thocht 'although'
to 'also'
with-thi

8. PREPOSITIONS.

The following prepositions occur in *BSS*:
abone, agane, aganis, amang, apon, at, attour, be, befor, behynd, besyde, betwene, betuix, bot, but, by, eftir, for, foroutin, fra, in, intill, into, neir, ner, nerhand, of, on, our 'over', *outwith, per* 'by', perhaps Latin, *quhill* 'until', *saifand, till, to, towart, throu, throw, vnder, wnder, vnto, with, within, without, withoutin, wp.*

9. INTERJECTIONS.

We find the following interjections:

allace, alake, Amen, lo, na, nay, par de, quhat, ȝa, ȝeis, ȝis.

10. VERBS.

a. Present indicative.

Sg. 1. Stem only: *ask, bid, compt, dreid, fynd, grant, hecht, murn, sover, stand, tak, thank, wey, will,* &c.

Written with *-e*: *allege, beseike, fele, meyne, presome, rewe, ȝarne,* &c.

Note: In many cases throughout the text the final *e* is merely scribal and has no grammatical significance.

Ending *-is*, when placed in the sentence as second verb to the same subject, and so separated from its personal pron.: *bledis* 950, *dowtis* 811, *seis* 2135, *tornis* 110, cf. Sisam, § 13 (iii)b, p. 291, and G.G. Smith, p. xxxv [16].

Sg. 2. Ending *-is*: *answeris, chesis, heris, knawis, leyis, seis,* &c.

Sg. 3. Ending *-is*: *alis, beginnys, clymmis, countis, cummis, fylis, lestis, makis, proffettis, ruskis, sayis,* &c.

Ending *-s*: *obeys; sais, says* 'says'; *says* 'sees'.

Pl. 1. Stem only: *bynd, fynd, se, tak, trow, think, want.*

Spelled with *-e*: *knawe, mene, schape.*

Ending *-is*: *layis* (second verb to the same subject).

Pl. 2. Stem only: *consaif, fynd, heir, ken, knaw, ly, mak, say,* &c.

Spelled with *-e*: *knawe, ȝarne.*

Pl. 3. Stem only: *follow, trast.*

Spelled with *-e*: *begyle, schape.*

Ending *-is*: There are four different cases here: *followis* 2671 is the second verb to its subject[17]; *garris* 2203, *begylis* 1838, *bulleris* 2181, *clawis* 579, *cummis* 2183, *schapis* 1284 are dependent on *that* (rel.); *playis* 2181, *rewlis* 2204 are second verbs and dependent on *that* (rel.); and in the cases of 333 *The* *branchis lattis it to get air* and 948 *My sisteris gretis sa sair* the subject is a plural noun.

Note: The ending -(*i*)*s* in the 1st and 2nd p. sg. and in the plural is typically Northern; so is -*i*(*s*) in the second verb to the same subject, cf. Sisam, *loc.cit.*

b. Present subjunctive.

Sg. 1. Stem with or without -*e*: *de, heile.*

2. " " " " " : *begyn, byde, purge,* &c.

3. " " " " " : *cum, de, fund, mak, manteine, ples, pvnis, send, speke,* &c.

For 2068 *God ws levis* see expl. note, Section XX.

Pl. 1. Stem only : *de, dissever.*

2. Stem with or withour -*e*: *desyre, gif, hald, prent, put, rewe, sla, speike,* &c.

3. Stem only : *cum, fle, tak.*

Note: These subjunctives are found in clauses opening with: *and* 'if', *better is* (*that*), *bot* 'unless', *gif* 'if', *luke* (*to it that*), *for dreid* (*that*), *gif ʒe desire that*, *or* (*that*), *quhill*, *se* (*to it that*), *that* 'so that', *with thi* (*that*).

c. Imperative.

Sg. Stem with or without -*e*: *defend, defowle, fair, gref, hald, hewe, leif, tempe,* &c.

Pl. Stem with or without -*e*: *bannis, bring, declair, forgif, grant, kepe, luke, pas, remuf,*&c.

Stem with -*s*, only one example: *Says all Amen for cherité* 2782.

Stem with -*is* occurs with the verb *garris* (*gerris*) only:

263 *Schir, garris kepe him quhill the morne, that we ... may ryplé counsall ʒow ...*

999 *Bot garris ʒour sone be brocht agane, quhill I haf tauld, and heir remane ...*

1318 *'Schir', said he, 'garris the child retour, syne heir my tale...*

397 *Bot gerris the child be brocht ws till, syne heir my tale and gif gud skill.*

In the case of *garris* 1318 and in that of *gerris* 397 there is a second imperative without -*s*, but no such second imperative is found in 263, 999 and 2782.

On the other hand, we find two or more imperatives together in one clause several times without any of them having the *-is*-ending, e.g. 521, 1796, 2205, 2673, cf. G.G. Smith, op. cit., p. xxxvi.

Gar is found twice as imperative, 1995, 2645, but these may be singular forms.

Note: The ending *-es* (*-is*) in the imperative plural is a Northern feature, cf. Mossé, 94 [18].
-is imperatives went out in the sixteenth century.

d. Infinitive.

The majority of the infinitives have stem only; some are spelled with *-e*, e.g.: *absolue, attempe, bere, bruke, distroye, followe, myne, ourthrawe, smyle, tyne*, &c.

Note: *slokin* 1835, 2200, 'to slake' ending in *-in* is no doubt due to ON *slokna*.

e. Present participle.

The present participles in *BSS* end in *-and*:

birnand, chargeand, drynkand, fawnand, liffand, prekand, rolpand, sperand, wepand, &c.

A number of present participles are used as adjectives:

aperand, deand, ganand, liffand, plesand, &c.

Derived from a present participle is the form *ill-farandly* 1569.

Note: Notice the analogous ending in *sudand* 1530 with its excrescent *d*; the adverb *sudanlye* 2145 is also found (OF *sodain, sudain*, LLat. **subitanus*).

f. Verbal nouns.

The majority of the verbal nouns end in *-ing* and *-yng*:

asking, clething, blissing, grutching, gudding, mannasing; cummyng, dremyng, murnyng, redyng, warnyng, &c.

The MSc feature of the interchangeability of *-ing* and *-in* is evident in the following *-yn*(*e*)-endings:

drinkyn : *thing* 1623, *gnawyn* 555, (*hame*)*cummyn* 1077, *huntyne* : *syne* 1382, *purgyn* 1191.

The variation *-yn*(*e*)/*-yng* was mistakenly or by analogy introduced into words where the original *-in*(*e*) was not a verbal ending, *viz.*:

basyng 'basin' (OF *bacin*) 2585; *courting* 'curtain' (OF *co*(*u*)*rtine*) 1453; *garding* 'garden' (ONF *gardin*) 1366.

Note: Notice the nouns with -*and*-ending: *cunnand* 'covenant' 1716 and *seruandis* 'servants' 2693, 2697.

g. Past participles.

1. Of verbs which were strong in OE:

Ending -*in*: *biddin, bundin, drawin, forgevin, gottin, knawin, lattin, spokin, wittin, writtin*, &c.

Spelled -*yn*: *bundyn, cummyn, etyn, fallyn, forgevyn, foundyn, lattyn*, &c.

Ending -*ne*: *borne* 'carried', *forfarne, forlorne, sene*, &c.

Ending -*n*: *born* 'brought forth', *sworn, won*.

Note: *forȝet, hecht*.

2. Of verbs which were weak in OE:

Stem only : *frist, picht, put, set*.

Ending -*it*: *borit, cursit, erdit, fosterit, gadderit, levit, lokit, lovit, lufit*, &c.

Spelled -*yt*: *dremyt*.

Ending -*t*: *brocht, brynt, kist, left, schent, wont*, &c.

Note: *coft*.

Ending in -*d*: *cled, fed, forsàid, hard, kend, lerd, maid, send, sped*, &c.

-*de*: *made, maide, sparde*.

-*ed*: *schamed, warmed* (cf. pret. *warmit*). In Older Scots verbs with stems ending in liquids or nasals have doublet pt. and p.p. endings in -*it* and -*d*; -*ed* here is a variation of -*d*.

3. Of verbs of French or Latin origin:

Ending -*it*: *abasit, adornit, awisit, commandit, consauit, defendit, drest, ordanit, presonit, reiosit, suprisit , vsit*, &c.

Spelled -*et*: *iustifyet*.

Ending -*t*: *banist, ioynt, oblist, past, perist, pvnist*.

Stem only, sometimes original Lat p.p.: *degest, hurt, inflat, respit, rewest, suspect, torment*, a common contraction in Sc and NoE, cf. note to *Rauf C*. 344, *Scott. Allit. Poems*, ed. F.J. Amours, STS I, 27 & 38, 1891-97, p. 321.

Ending -*jt*: *marijt, miscarijt*.

Ending -*d*: *delayd, exild, payd.*
-*id*: *espyid.*
-*de*: *astonade* 161, cf. *astonait* 1992.

4. Of verbs of ON origin: *bovn, cald, callit, cassyn, castin, gart, slokinnit, (our)tane, takin, tynt.*

h. Preterite.

1. Of verbs which were strong in OE:
Endings: Sg. 1: no ending: *gaf, lay, saw, stall* 'stole', *(wnder)stud.*
-*e*: *come, slewe.*
-*it*: *chesit.*
2: -*it*: *sowkit.*
3: no ending: *bad, bait, began, brak, clam, fled, forgaf, grat, knew, leit, met, saw, slaid, spak, swor, wox,* &c.
-*e*: *baide, bure, dranke, ete, fure, grewe, lete, schane, strake,* &c.
-*it*: *bowit, helpit, lowtit, schowit,* &c. -*yt* in *murnyt.*
Pl. 1: no ending: *saw.*
2: no ending: *hecht, wnderstud.*
-*e*: *tuke.*
3: no ending: *bad, brak, bred, fell, forfur, gaf, leuch, met, sat, wan,* &c.
-*e*: *blewe, come, drewe, flawe, knewe,* &c.
-*it*: *chesit, delfit, delvit, slepit,* written -*yt* in *murnyt.*

2. Of verbs which were weak in OE:
Endings: Sg. 1: -*it*: *happinit, levit, lufit, trowit.*
-*d*: *herd, tald, ȝeid.*
-*t*: *thocht, wrocht.*
2: -*it*: *thristit,* written -*yt* in *dremyt.*
-*d*: *tald.*
3: -*it*: *askit, bannit, birlit, fessynnit, gaderit, halsit, kendillit, liftit, plukit, rasit, sperit, warnit,* &c., written -*yt* in *boryt, dremyt, menyt, wonnyt.*
-*de*: *behude.*

-d: *answerd, aspyd, cled, feld, herd, led, said, send, tald,* &c.

-t: *brocht, dicht, fet, kist, mist, put, reft, thocht,* &c.

...: *wryth,* see note to line 220.

Pl. 1: *wend.*

2: *send.*

3: -d: *answerd, hard, maid, said, sauld, spard, sped, tald.*

-de: *made.*

-it: *askit, dropit, erdit, playit,* &c.

-t: *brocht, duelt, went, wist,* &c.

3. Of verbs derived from French or Latin.

Endings: Sg. 1: no ending: *hurt.*

2: ---

3: -*it*: *assemblit, causit, chapit, chargit, culȝeit, denyit, discoverit, efferit, plenȝeit, studyit,* &c.

-*et*: *studyet.*

-*d*: *aspyd, begyld.*

-*t*: *menyst, past, salust.*

no ending: *degest, statut.*

Pl. 1: ---

2: -*it*: *seruit.*

3: -*it*: *assentit, begylit, cowerit, dissauit, ischit, pantit, persauit, semblit, spulȝeit, succurit, tursit, vsit,* &c.

-*t*: *past, salust.*

4. Of verbs of ON derivation.

Sg. 3: *biggit, buskit, callit, carpit, ettillit, slokinnit, tynt.*

Pl. 3: *biggit, bovnit, callit, slokinnit.*

Note on some preterite and past participle-endings:[19)]
Though the usual ending is -*it*[20)] the following special cases are found:

214 *exild,* rhyming with *child;* 2504, 2777 *begyld* rh.w. *child;* otherwise *begylit* is found, once (952) rh.w. *wylit,* further

unrhymed, 1073, 1758, 1821, &c.; 1027 *cald*, rh.w. *ald*, otherwise we find *callit*, unrhymed; 681 *espyid*, rh.w. *byid*; 172 *aspyd*, rh.w. *besyde*; 636, 1221, 2141, 2341 *spard(e)*, all rh.w. *reward*, cf. 875, 1067, 1450 *sparit*, unrhymed; 2564 *behude*, rh.w. *gud*, as against *behovit* 2551, unrhymed, and *behufit*, 890, 892, 1200, 1215, unrhymed.

i. Survey of the forms of OE strong verbs.

Infin. or related forms	Preterite	Past Participle	
<u>Class I</u>			
byde, *byid*	*bad*	---	
---	*bait*	---	
ryde	*raid*	---	
rys	*rais*, *(wp)ras*	*rissyn*	
---	*schane*	---	
---	*slaid*	---	
smyte	---	---	
strik	*straik*, *strake*	*strikin*	
wryte	---	---	
(OE *wrīðan*)	*wryth*[21]	---	
<u>Class II</u>			
(OE *būgan*)	*bowit*	*bowit*	
bruke	---	---	
ches	*chesit*	---	
fle (OE *flēogan*,	*flawe*	---	
fle (OE *flēon*)	*fled*	---	
fleyt (OE *flēotan*)	---	---	
forbed	---	---	
forlor	---	*forlorne*	
(OE *grēotan*)	*grat*, *gret*	---	*gretand*
le (OE *lēogan*)	---	---	
(OE *lūcan*)	*lok(k)it*	*lokit*	
lowte (OE *lūtan*)	*lowtit*	---	
(OE *scūfan*)	*schowit*	---	
schut (OE *scēotan*, or *scyttan*, caus. of *scēotan*)	---	---	
(OE *sūcan*)	*sowkit*	---	
(OE *gēotan*)	*ȝet*	---	

Class III

bynd	*band*	*bundin*	
---	*began*	---	
---	---	*brynt*	*birnand*
clymmis	*clam*	---	
---	*delfit, delvit*	---	
drink	*dranke*	*drunkin*	*drynkand*
fecht	---	---	
fynd	*fand*	*fundin, foundyn*	
help	*helpit*	*helpit*	
---	---	*moltin*	
murn	*murnyt*	---	*murnand*
ryn	---	---	
---	*sprang*	---	
syng	*sang*	---	
---	---	---	*stynkand*
wyn	*wan*	*won*	
---	*worthit*	---	

Class IV

bere	*bure*	*born, borne*	
cum	*come*	*cummyn*	
heile (OE *helan* 'conceal')	---	---	
---	*stall, staw*	---	

from OE *stelan, stæl, stǣlon, gestelen* or from ON *stela, stal, stálum, stolinn.*

Class V

brek, abrek	*brak*	---	
bid	*bad, baid*	*biddin*	
---	*ete*	*etyn*	*etand*
gif	*gaf, gaif*	---	
---	*forgaf*	*forgevin*	
---	*misgaf*	---	
---	*forȝet*	*forȝet*	
---	*lay*	---	*lyand, liand*
meit	*met*	---	
---	*quod*	---	
se	*saw*	*sene*	

sit	*sat*	---	*sittand*
speike, speke	*spak*	*spokin*	
steike (OE **stecan?*)	---	---	
stik	*stak*	---	
Class VI			
draw(e)	*drew(e)*	*drawin*	
fair	*fure*	---	
---	*forfur*	*forfarne*	
---	*leuch*	---	
---	*schupe*	---	
sla (ON *slá*, ONE *slá(n)*)	*sleuch, slewe*	*slane*	
stand	*stud*	---	
wnderstand	*wnder-, vnderstud*	---	
swer	*swor*	*sworn(e)*	
---	---	---	*walkand*
Class VII			
---	*blewe*	---	
crawe	---	---	
dreid	---	---	*dredand*
fald	---	---	
fall	*fell*	*fallyn*	
befall	---	---	
fang	---	---	
ga, go	---	*gane*, (*went*)	*ganand*
---	---	*bygane*	
gang	---	---	
get	*gat*	*gottin*	
grow(e)	*grewe*	---	*growand*
hald	*held*	---	
behold	*beheld*	---	
hang	---	*hangit*	
---	*hate*	---	
---	*hecht*	*hecht*	
hewe	*hewit*	*hewyn*	
knaw(e)	*knew(e)*	*knawin, wnknawin*	
leipe	*lap*	---	
lat	*leit, lete*	*lattin, lattyn*	

reid	*red*	---	
slepe	*slepit*	---	*slepand*
(*our*) *thrawe*	*threwe*	---	
---	---	---	*wepand*
---	*wox*	---	

From this list it is apparent that several originally strong verbs developed a new preterite with an *-it* ending, thus conforming to the pattern of the weak preterites.

j. Preterite Present verbs.

1. Infinitive: *wit, wyte* — Class I

Pres. indic.	sg.	2.	*wait*
		3.	*wait*
	pl.	2	*wait*
Pret.	sg.	1.	*wist* (subj.)
		3.	*wist*
	pl.	3.	*wist*

Imperat. *wit*

Past part. *wittin*

2. Infinitive: *con(e)* — Class III

Pres. indic.	sg.	1.	*can*
		2.	*can*
		3.	*can*
	pl.	1.	*can*
		2.	*can*
Pret.	sg.	3.	*couth*
	pl.	2.	*couth*

3. Pres. indic. sg. 1. *dar* — Class III

3. *dar*

4. Pres. indic. sg. 1. *sall* — Class IV

Pres. indic.	sg.	1.	*sall*
		2.	*sall*
		3.	*sall*
	pl.	1.	*sall*
		2.	*sall*
Pret.	sg.	1.	*suld*
		3.	*suld*
	pl.	1:	*suld*
		2.	*suld*

	3.	*suld*	
5. Pres. indic.	sg. 1.	*mon*	Class IV
	3.	*mon*	
6. Pres. subj.	sg. 3.	*mot* (optat.)	Class VI
7. Pres. indic.	sg. 1.	*may*	Class obscure
	2.	*may*	
	3.	*may*	
	pl. 1.	*may*	
	2.	*may*	
	3.	*may*	
Pret.	sg. 1.	*mycht, micht*	
	3.	*mycht, micht*	
	pl. 1.	*mycht*	
	3.	*mycht, micht*	

k. Anomalous verbs.

1. Infinitive: *be*

Pres. indic.	sg. 1.	*am*	Pres. subj.	sg. 1.	*be*
	2.	*art*		2.	---
	3.	*is, beis*		3.	*be*
	pl. 1.	*ar*		pl. 1.	*be*
	2.	*ar*		2.	*be*
	3.	*ar*		3.	*be*
Pret.	sg. 1.	---	Pret. subj.	sg. 1.	*war*
	2.	---		2.	---
	3.	*war, was*		3.	*war*
	pl. 1.	---		pl. 1.	---
	2.	*was* (1391)		2.	---
	3.	*war, was*		3.	*war*

Imperat. *be*

Past Part. *bene*

2. Infinitive: *do, fordo, vndo*

Pres. indic.	sg. 1.	*do*	Pres. subj.	sg. 1.	---
	3.	*dois*		2.	---
	pl. 1.	*do*		3.	---
	2.	*do*		pl. 1.	*do*
	3.	*do*		2.	*do*
Pret.	sg. 1.	*did*		3.	*do*

3. *did*
pl. 2. *did*
3. *did*

Imperat. *do*

Past part. *done, fordone*

3. Infinitive: *ga, go, gang*

Pres. indic. sg. 1. *ga* Pres. subj. sg. 1. *ga*
3. *gais*

Imperat. *go*

Past part. *gane, bygane, went*

Pres. part. *ganand*

Preterite sg. 1. *ȝeid*
3. *ȝeid, ȝed, went*
pl. 3. *ȝud, went*

4. Pres. indic. sg. 1, 2, 3. *will*
pl. 1, 2, 3. *will*

Pret. sg. 1, 2, 3. *wald* (sg. 3. optat. 523, 805; condit. 1232)
pl. 1, 2, 3. *wald* (pl. 2. condit. 1845)

5. Pres. indic. sg. 3. *aucht*

l. The verb *to have*.

Infinitive: *haue, haf, haif*

Pres. indic. sg. 1. *has*,[22] *haf* Pres. subj. sg. 1. *haf, haue*
2. *has* 3. *haf*
3. *has*
pl. 1. *has, haf, haif, haue*
2. *haf, haue*
3. *has, haf*

Pret. sg. 1. *had* Pret. subj. sg. 1. *had*
3. *had* 3. *had*
pl. 2. *had* pl. 3. *had*
3. *had*

Imperat. sg. *haf*
pl. *haf* (*ȝe*)

Past part. *had*

Notes to Section IX

1. The word *gallous* has a plural form, but is considered as a sg., as is also evident from the spelling *gallhous*.
2. A. Campbell, *Old English Grammar,* Oxford, 1959.
3. See Section VIII on anglicisation.
4. The young bird in ll. 2650 ff. is referred to by *scho, it, his* and *him*.
5. The change of the pers. pron. *it*, '*t* into '*d* after a voiced sound occurs in *BSS* in the phrase *I stand ford*, ll. 362 and 1739. *DOST* (s.v. '*D*) dates its earliest use c. 1420 in *Ratis Raving,* l. 1103. *It that,* or with ellipsis of relative *that* simply *It*, is used in the sense of 'that which' in ll. 1406, 1408, 1717, 1770, 2499.
6. The *ʒhe*-form was obsolescent at the end of the fifteenth century. Asloan may have modernised the spelling of the manuscript he was copying, but left some old forms standing.
7. Norman Nathan, 'Pronouns of Address in the "Friar's Tale"', *Modern Language Quarterly,* XVII, 1956, p. 39.
8. Norman Nathan, 'Pronouns of Address in the "Canterbury Tales"', *Mediaeval Studies,* XXI, 1959, p. 193. See also Muriel Kolinsky, 'Pronouns of Address and the Status of Pilgrims in the *Canterbury Tales*', *Papers in Language and Literature*, 3, 1967, pp. 40-48.
9. Charles Child Walcutt, 'The Pronoun of Address in *Troilus and Criseyde*', *Philological Quarterly*, XIV, 1935, p. 284. For various interesting examples see Roger Brown and Albert Gilman, 'The Pronouns of Power and Solidarity', *Style in Language,* ed. T.A. Sebeok, Massachusetts & London, 1960, pp. 253-76.
10. *Ane Satyre of the Thrie Estaits,* ed. James Kinsley, London, 1954, pp. 87 & 114.
11. Cf. Angus McIntosh, '"As You Like It": a grammatical clue to character', in *Patterns of Language,* eds M.A.K. Halliday and Angus McIntosh, Longman, 1966, p. 76.
12. Cf. *Sir Gawain and the Green Knight,* ll. 2140-51, ed. Sir Israel Gollancz, EETS OS 210, 1940, note to l. 1071.

13. *The Poems and Fables of Robert Henryson*, ed. H. Harvey Wood, Edinburgh, (1933) 1958, pp. 68-77.
14. *The Poems of William Dunbar,* ed. W. Mackay Mackenzie, London, (1932) 1970, pp. 5-20.
15. J.A.H. Murray, *The Dialects of the Southern Counties of Scotland*, London, 1873, p. 197.
16. K. Sisam, ed., *Fourteenth Century Verse & Prose*, Oxford, 1950; G.Gregory Smith, ed., *Specimens of Middle Scots,* Edinburgh, 1902. See also D.F.C. Coldwell., ed., *Selections from Gavin Douglas,* Oxford, 1964, p. 117, n. 112. The general rule is that the verb inflects when immediately adjacent to a personal-pronoun subject.
17. With *followis* (as with *tornis* 110) there is also the chance of confusion with the infinitive form, since an infinitive comes between first verb and second verb; cf. *scurge/scurgis* 253 and expl. note.
18. F. Mossé, *A Handbook of Middle English*, Baltimore, 1952.
19. Apparently the vowel in the ending could be either mute or pronounced, cf. Section XI.
20. Cf. G.G. Smith, *Specimens,* p. xxxvii; Jordan, op. cit., pp. 126, 145, 179, and C.H. Kuipers, *Quintin Kennedy (1520-1564)*: *Two Eucharistic Tracts,* Nijmegen, 1964, p. 77.
21. See expl. note to l. 220.
22. Used as second verb, first verb understood (782).

X. DATABLE WORDS AND USAGES

From the following criteria it may be concluded that the original of *BSS* must have dated from the second half of the fifteenth century, perhaps between 1460 and 1480, and that it is therefore more or less contemporary with Hary's *Wallace*, with some of Henryson's works, with *Contemplacioun of Synnaris*, *Thre Prestis of Peblis*, &c.

1. *ford* 'for it'.
   'd is a reduced and voiced variant of *it* which is used after vowels and certain consonants (like *l*, *m*, *n*, *r*), mainly in rhymes, e.g. *albeid*, *beid*, *dude* and *ford* (see *DOST* s.v. *'d*). The earliest example is c.1420 in *Ratis Raving* 1103: *feild* 'feel it'.[1]

   ford is found twice in *BSS* in the expression 'I stand ford'; in l. 362 it rhymes with *lord*; in l. 1739 it is used within the line. The earliest example in rhyme mentioned in *DOST* is from the *Consail and Teiching at the Vys Man gaif his Sone*, which dates from c. 1460[2]. It is also used in the same expression *I stand ford* in *Sum Practysis of Medecyne* 8, attributed by Bannatyne to Henryson.[3]
2. *sell* 'self' is found in *BSS* in the compounds *my-sell* 1100, *hir-sell* 1118, *him-sell* 1747, *thi-sell* 1830, *his-sell* 2534, all in rhyme. For *him-sell* the earliest example in *DOST* is in rhyme with *befell* from the *Wallace* (VIII.1348), dated 1478[4]; for *hir-sell* it is from Rolland's *Seuin Seages* of which the date is 1560[5]; for *my-sell* it is again from the *Wallace* (IV.411), rhyming with *tell*. *His-sell* is recorded in *DOST* only from the seventeenth century, see Vol. III, Additions and Corrections, s.v. *He*.
3. *fow(e)* 'full' adj., with vocalisation of *l* after a back vowel, suggests a date not earlier than c. 1450[6]. It is found twice in *BSS*, in both cases rhyming with *ȝow* (759, 1740). The earliest occurrence of the form (not in rhyme, used as an adv.) according to *DOST*, is in the *Legends of the Saints*, VII. 753[7], of which the extant manuscript is much later than the presumed date of composition, *a*. 1400. *Ratis Raving* (c. 1420) has *fow* within line 246[8], but again the manuscript is a good deal later than the

probable date of composition of the poem and this form might, therefore, be due to the copyist.

Beside the cases in *BSS*, the other earliest instance in *DOST* is from *King Hart*, *a.* 1500, in rhyme with *bow* vb.[9]; another instance is found in Gavin Douglas's Prologue VIII of the *Eneados* (*a.* 1513)[10]. The form *full* is used seventy-one times in *BSS*. We also find *staw*, 1055, beside four instances of *stall*, p.t. of 'steal', none of these forms in rhyme. An early example of *a + l*-vocalisation is indicated by A.J.Aitken in his article 'Variation and Variety in written Middle Scots'[11], p. 197: *kaw* for 'call', 1438 *Ayr B.Ct.*32b, *pace* Jordan[6].

3a. Reverse spellings in *al, ol, ul* in words originally containing the phonemes /au/, /ou/ and /u:/ respectively, date from the second half of the fifteenth century; see *DOST* s.vv. *chalmer* and *halk* for dating of this phenomenon, also 'Var. and Var.'[11], p. 182, the same author's article 'How to Pronounce Older Scots', *Bards and Makars*, Univ. of Glasgow Press, 1977, p. 4, item 6a, and p. 5, item 13, and *OED*, s.v. *powder* n.

BSS has examples of this use in *chalmer, palpis, talburn,* and in forms of the verb 'to cry': *rolpand, rolpit,* and of 'to wake': *walkand, walkinnit.*

Forms like *salf, saluiour* (beside *saif, savit, saifand*) and *dulce* may be due to Latin prototypes or to what Onions (*ODEE* s.v. *cauldron*) calls etymologising spellings; they do not have these shapes for the sake of rhyme.

4. *dele* 'devil'.

According to *DOST*, s.v. *deil(1)* n.1, the form *dele* does not appear earlier than in passages in the Asloan MS.: *Howlat* 799 within the line[12], and *BSS* 512 in rhyme with *wele* 'well' adv. *Deill* occurs first unrhymed in *The Cursing of Sir Iohine Rowlis vpoun the steilaris of his fowlis* 145 (c. 1500)[13], and in Kennedy's *Flyting* (*a.* 1508) in rhyme with *feill* 257/59[14].

Assuming that Asloan correctly represented Sir Richard Holland's intention in the *Buke of the Howlat* for the spelling of *dele*, this would give us an earliest date of c. 1450. The unreduced or uncontracted form is found in several spellings as from *Legends of the Saints*, *a.* 1400, see *DOST* s.v. *devil.* In *BSS devill* is found three times rhyming with *wele*: 248, 378, 1452; this indicates a reduced pronunciation of the unreduced spelling; *dele* unrhymed is not found in *BSS*; *devill/devile* unrhymed occurs six times, in four of which the scansion seems to demand a monosyllabic pronunciation: 357, 961, 1128, 1176. The spelling *dewill* occurs once in *BSS*, in rhyme with *ewill* (981-2), which may point to an uncontracted pronunciation, although several examples of *ewill/evill*, possibly representing one syllable, can be adduced from other metrical texts: Scottish *Troy Book* fragments II. 941 (c. 1400)[15], *Ratis Raving* 1738 (c. 1420)[16], *Buke of the Chess* 61, 76 (a. 1500)[17], and perhaps *Rauf Coilȝear* 95 (a. 1500)[18]. However, it must be borne in mind that there is no evidence for an **ēl* > **ĭl* form for *evil*, and *deill* and *ill* will not rhyme, so in the case of *ewill : dewill* the author of *BSS* may have been solving a rhyming difficulty.

Note: *ewill* is found only once in *BSS*, as against *ill* twelve times unrhymed, and twice rhyming with *Virgill* and *till* (1675, 2742); in *Troy Book*, too, *ewill* is found only once, whereas *ill* is used three times, once in rhyme with *skill*, which bears out *DOST*'s statements s.vv. *ill* and *ivil(1)*, that *ill* was often regarded as a variant or reduced form of *evil(1)* and that *evil(1)* and *ivil(1)* were sometimes written in place of *ill*[11]. Elision of a *v*-element between vowels is indeed fairly common, not only in MSc, cf. such forms as *antaris* (OF *auenture*) 'adventures' 1471, *cunnand* 'covenant' 1716, *courche* (earlier *coverchef*, mod. *kerchief*) 208, the numerous cases in Chaucer's works where the metre demands elision, and the frequent occurrence of forms like *e'en* and *e'er* in modern English poetry. See also G.Greg. Smith's note, *Specimens*, p. xxviii, § 23.

5. *ȝestrene (: quene)* 380 is another example of loss of intervocalic *v* in Older Scots, usually dated in the second half of the fifteenth century; cf. *Kynd Kittok* 13 (a. 1508), *wene : evin* n.[19] In the Bannatyne MS. the form is *ene*[20].

6. Another form with *v*-elision is *behude (: gud)* 2564, which also points to a date after the middle of the fifteenth century. Of this contraction of the preterite of the verb *behufe, behove* the first example in *DOST* is this one in *BSS*; the second recorded form is in Dunbar's *Tua Mariit Wemen and the Wedo* (c. 1500 - c. 1512).

The first recorded form of the present tense *behuse*, however, is in the *Liber Pluscardensis*, dated 1461[21], and a parallel form *behwys* is found in the *Craft of Deyng* 29[22] (c. 1450), in the *Ratis*

Raving MS. which is late fifteenth-century.

7. The loss of *t* after *k* and *p* is an early phenomenon. In *NED* s.v. *tempt* v. we find the first occurrence of the form *tempe* a.1340 in Rolle's *Psalter*. In *BSS* it occurs twice, 1425, 2745; *attempe, attempit* is found in 94, 1665, 2222; the forms with final *t* are not used in *BSS*.
   The other relevant example is *effect*, which we meet once (91) in its full form, not in rhyme, three times written *effek*, rhyming with *nek* and *rak* (673, 819, 1186), and once as *fek* rh.w. *clek* (2664). The earliest example in *DOST* of *effec* dates from 1415, whereas *fek* is first met in Hary's *Wallace* (c. 1475).
8. The use of *ȝud (: gud)* 2489 points to a possible early date of c. 1450[23].
9. *coft* p.p.[24] is found in rhyme with *soft* 728. *DOST* mentions as earliest occurrence of *coft* p.t. *The Buik of Alexander* (?1438 or ?*a.* 1400)[25] II. 4365; in Wyntoun (c. 1420) it is used figuratively[26]; *coft* p.p. is first found in *Peebles Burgh Records*[27], 1471; in *Accounts of the Lord High Treasurer of Scotland*[28], in the year 1473.
10. The rhyme *prevé : gay ladye* 135-6 indicates a date in the second half of the fifteenth century, because for an earlier date no rhymes of this kind are found; see A.J.Aitken's review, mentioned in note 23 below and also Girvan, *Ratis Raving*, p. lvi; cf. Jord. § 246, $\bar{e} > \bar{\imath}$. This kind of rhyme is rare in *BSS*; beside the example mentioned, we find only *witté : cité* 1707-8 (note the spelling *witty* in line 4, n.rh.).
   The word for 'high', adj. and adv., is spelled *he* once in the whole text, in rhyme with *be* vb., 307-8; it is once more found in rhyme, spelled *hie*, rh.w. *cité*, 2285-6; the latter is spelled thus throughout (33 x). In non-rhymed positions we usually find the spelling *hie(-ar), (-nes)*; once the spelling is *hye*, n.rh., 1197.

These features seem to point to a position in time for *BSS* intermediate between such texts as on the one hand *Ratis Raving* (c. 1420), *Foly of Fulys* (c. 1460), *The Consail & Teiching* (c. 1460), *The Thewis of Gudwomen* (c. 1460)[29], the *XV Ois* (*a.* 1450)[30], of which none has rhymes of original $\bar{e}$ with original $\bar{\imath}$, and on the other hand *Contemplacioun of Synnaris* (a. 1499)[31] and *The*

Passioun of Christ by Walter Kennedy (a. 1508)[32], which use the mixed rhymes frequently. Elsewhere in *BSS* *lady* rhymes only with words ending in *-y* (5 x).

11. Rhymes of Older Scots *ā* with original *ai* are comparatively rare in *BSS*.

While a number of scholars[33] voiced the conviction that *ā* and *ai* had coalesced in ESc in the second half of the fourteenth century, Girvan[34] made it clear, especially in connection with rhymes of final *ā* with final *ai* , that confusion was exceptional in the fifteenth century, though commoner as the century advanced. He was fully aware, however, that at the time *ā* and *ai* seemed clearly to have coalesced in one sound in normal speech, and not recently, either. As a possible reason for the consistent avoidance of mixed rhymes by some poets, Girvan says[35] that in 'a period of change poets may very well adhere to the old pronunciation and eschew the new, though perfectly familiar with both, maintaining with advancing years the habits of an earlier generation'. This, he shows, was certainly so in the cases of Barbour and Wyntoun.

Be that as it may, Kohler demonstrates that to-day in most modern Scots dialects the continuations of ESc *ā* and *ai* are still distinct and he suggests that the coalescence occurred after the MSc period[36].

A.J.Aitken in his recent study on the subject of Older Scots[37] believes, however, that the widespread Central Scots merger of non-final *ai* with *ā* must be more ancient than Kohler's theory allows.

At any rate, in *BSS* few examples of mixed rhymes are found. We never meet final *ā* in rhyme with final *ai*, the two being kept distinct consistently, *day* occurring in rhyme with *delay, (a-, all-)way, thai, say(e), lay; lay* with *day, allway; say(e)* with *ȝisterday, (a-, all-)way, day; may* v. with *ay, away, ȝisterday; (a)way* with *saye, play(e), day, pray, may, ay.*

Most of the mixed cases are rhymes in which the environment following the vowel is a nasal or a liquid. Of two cases of apparent *ā/ai*-rhymes the first is *thare* 'there': *contrare* 1103, where, however, ME already had *contrare,* and most of the early examples given in *DOST* s.v. *contrar(e), contrair* have the spelling without *i*, which may point to a pronunciation without the *i*-element; the second case is *sair : car(e)* 2071, where *care* is derived from ON *keyra;* see Aitken, op.cit., p. 8, on the merger of vowels 8 and 4.

The case of *barane* (OF *baraine, baraigne*) in the rhyme *barane : nane* 323 is similar in that practically all the examples in *DOST* s.v. *barrane, barane* have the spelling without *i*; the written forms in MSc do not usually show the shortening of the second syllable nor does MSc poetry have the shift of stress toward the first syllable that is rather common in ME poetry.

We find *ai/ā*-rhymes with following *l* in: 41 *liberale : fale* 'fail' n., and 725 *medicinale : faile* id., and four cases where *hale* is involved: 707 *hale : faile,* 1023 *haile : counsall,* 1919 *counsall : allhale,* 2107 *haile : avale* (beside 331 *avalȝe : falȝe*). Since *ha(i)le* could be derived from either OE *hāl* or ON *heill* it cannot be decided in which way the *ail/al(e)/all*-rhymes are pure or impure. For examples of some of Wyntoun's impure rhymes see Girvan, op.cit., p. lxi.

Finally three rhymes occur in *BSS* of *consaif, persaif* with *haf, gaf* (327, 1679, 2683), whereas we find the spelling without *i* in the rhyme *resauit : consauit* 151[38]. The reader is referred to Section VI, Phoneme 8, and Section VII.

In my tentative study of rhyme evidence in MSc poets (see Section XI Rhyme, and Appendix V) I found that *BSS* agrees with most of the older texts in the low number of impure *ai/ā*-rhymes, *viz.* with *Bruce, Legends of the Saints,* the Scottish *Troy-Book*-fragments, Wyntoun, *XV Ois, Ratis Raving, Golagros and Gawàne, Kingis Quair* and Henryson, all of these showing fewer than ten cases in 2782 lines (i.e. the length of *BSS*).

12. *The day* 'to-day' is found once in *BSS* 204, unrhymed; the alternative *this day* occurs four times, 986, 1162, 1595, 2089. From the unpublished material of *DOST* it appears that the first example of this usage is found in Henryson's writings (*a.* 1500). *The nicht,* not met in *BSS,* is first found in the *Wallace* (c. 1475), see *DOST* s.v. *nicht* 3 c; *the morn(e)* 'to-morrow' is found several times in *BSS;* the earlies usage recorded in *DOST* is in the *Taill*

of Rauf Coilȝear 288 (*a*. 1500)[39].

13. *at*, conjunction, after *sone be, quhill, quhen*, cf. *DOST*, s.v. *at*, rel. pron. and conj., B.b. The fact that *at* is used in *BSS* as a conjunction (225, 1599, 1812, 1990) may date the text in the second half of the fifteenth century. The examples adduced by *DOST* for this use are from dates between 1375 and 1489. Girvan[40] states that the disuse of *at*, both as relative pronoun and conjunction, 'was due to a conscious literary convention which regarded it as a reduced and colloquial form of *that* ... and accordingly abandoned it completely, especially in print. ... As we trace the disuse of the form in the fifteenth century (earliest in the pronoun) we find a notable decrease in the second half, and before the close it had disappeared, apart from isolated and exceptional instances which crop up even in the following century'. This is borne out by Sarah Caldwell in a later study[41] where she says (41*.9.3): '*At* becomes rare in texts after c.1500'. In *BSS* *at* may be, however, primarily scribal and not necessarily due to the author.

    In the Scottish *Troy-Book* fragments[42] (c. 1400) we still find *at* as relative pronoun used eight times, as conjunction ten times in about 3700 lines. In *BSS* *at* as a relative pronoun does not occur.

14. *quhilk, the quhilk*, 'which, who', relative pronouns.
    The way in which *BSS* uses *(the) quhilk*[43] confirms the suggested date in the second half of the fifteenth century.

    According to Girvan[44] both *(the) quhilk* and *(the) quhilkis* were in early use, as innovations which started in prose; *quhilk* and *quhilkis* without the definite article are later, of the fifteenth century, and not very early in the century at that. He gives a very useful survey of the use of *quhilk*, &c. in several texts, and states that *quhilk* grew in frequency while *the quhilk* receded, though it did not disappear entirely. No text of the second half of the fifteenth century was without examples of *quhilk* without the article, and texts with a distinct preference for *quhilk* alone are to be associated with the mid-century period at the earliest.

    We must of course bear in mind the relative importance of

the deductions to be made from the use of *quhilk* with the article, as we are dealing with poetry; the author, at a loss for an extra-syllable, may have had recourse to older *the quhilk,* where in prose he might by then have used *quhilk* alone. In *BSS* we also find *quhilk that* and even *the quhilk that.* Again we cannot be sure whether the choice of the relative forms is scribal or authorial.

As a last point it should be remarked that *BSS* in its present version does not contain certain older forms signalised by Girvan[45], such as *havis, selvyn, alswa, swilk* or *swik,* and *anerly,* where it has *has, self* and *sell, als, sic,* and *allanerly,* but on the other hand it has *euerilk,* never *euery*[46]. Such later forms as *not* and *fathir,* mentioned by Aitken in his review of 1957 (p.148, see note 23 below), are not used in *BSS;* we find *nocht, na* and *no,* and *fader* there.

The above data virtually all provide a *terminus a quo* for *BSS* of *post* 1470. The *terminus ad quem* is chiefly provided by the date of the MS (c. 1515), furthermore by points 8 and 13.

Notes to Section X.

1. *Ratis Raving and Other Early Scots Poems on Morals,* ed. R.Girvan, STS III.11, 1937-39, p. 31. In default of any other data I have accepted the dating in *DOST,* Part XXI, *Lokhol(e - Lyv(e)tennandry,* 'Combined Register of Titles or Works Quoted', pp. xiii - xxxii.
2. Ibid., p. 77, line 390.
3. *The Bannatyne Manuscript,* ed. W.Tod Ritchie, Vol. III, STS, 1928, pp. 28-31.
4. *Hary's Wallace,* ed. Matthew P.McDiarmid, STS IV. 4 & 5, 1968-69.
5. *The Seuin Seages by John Rolland of Dalkeith,* ed. George F.Black, STS III.3, 1931-2.
6. See R.Jordan, *Handbuch der mittelenglischen Grammatik,* 3. Auflage, Heidelberg, 1968, § 292B.
7. *Legends of the Saints,* ed. W.M.Metcalfe, STS 13, 18, 23, 25, 35, 37, 1887-96.
8. Op.cit., p. 8.
9. *The Shorter Poems of Gavin Douglas,* ed. Priscilla J.Bawcutt, STS IV. 3, 1967, p. 169, ll. 908-10.
10. *Virgil's Æneid, Translated into Scottish Verse by Gavin Douglas,* ed. David F.C.Coldwell, STS III. 27, 1950-57, p. 121, l. 138.
11. See A.J.Aitken, 'Variation and Variety in Written Middle Scots', in *Edinburgh Studies in English and Scots,* eds A.J.Aitken, Angus McIntosh and Hermann Pálsson, London, 1971, pp. 195 ff.
12. *The Asloan Manuscript,* ed. W.A.Craigie, STS NS 16, 1925, p. 120.
13. *Bannatyne MS.* 104b-107a and *Maitland Folio* xlvi, see *Early Popular Poetry of Scotland and the Northern Border,* ed. David Laing, rev. W.C.Hazlitt, London, 1895, Vol. I, pp. 289-99.
14. *The Poems of William Dunbar,* ed. W. Mackay Mackenzie, London, (1932) 1970, p. 12.
15. *Barbours des schottischen Nationaldichters Legendensammlung, nebst den Fragmenten seines Trojanerkrieges,* ed. C.Horstmann, Heilbronn, 1881-82, p. 254.
16. Op.cit., p. 49.
17. *The Asloan Manuscript,* ed. W.A.Craigie, STS NS 14, 1923, p. 83.

18. *The Taill of Rauf Coilyear,* ed. Sidney J.H.Herrtage, EETS ES XXXIX, 1882, p. 6.
19. *The Poems of William Dunbar,* see note 14 above, pp. 169 f.
20. A.J.Aitken, loc.cit.
21. Ed. Felix J.H.Skene, Vol. I, Edinburgh, 1877, p. 397, line 13.
22. See *Ratis Raving* (note 1 above), p. 167.
23. See A.J.Aitken's review of *Devotional Pieces in Verse and Prose from MS. Arundel 285 and MS. Harleian 6919,* ed. J.A.W.Bennett, STS III 23, 1955, in *The Scottish Historical Review,* No. 122, October 1957, pp. 147-50, where he mentions *ȝeid* (read *ȝude*) rhyming with *blud,* occurring in a piece called the *Fifteen Ois,* of which the date is *a.* 1450 *(DOST).*
24. Past part. of *cope,* [MDu *copen* 'to buy'].
25. Ed. R.L.Graeme Ritchie, STS NS 12, 17, 21, 25, 1920-28.
26. *The Original Chronicle of Scotland,* ed. F.J.Amours, STS 50, 53, 54, 56, 57, 63, 1902-09, IX. 1144.
27. Burgh Record Society, 2 vols, 1872, 1909.
28. Eds Thomas Dickson and Sir James Balfour Paul, 11 vols, Edinburgh, 1877-1916, I. 14.
29. All found in R.Girvan, op.cit.
30. Ed. J.A.W.Bennett, see note 22 above, pp. 170 ff.
31. Ed. W.A.Craigie, see note 12 above, pp. 187 ff.
32. Ed. J.A.W.Bennett, op.cit., pp. 7 ff.
33. Karl Luick, *Historische Grammatik der englischen Sprache,* Vol. I, 1, (Stuttgart 1914-21) repr. Basil Blackwell, Oxford, 1964, § 434. 1; Richard Jordan, op.cit., § 132.
34. Op.cit., p. lv.
35. Op.cit., p. lvi.
36. K.J.Kohler, 'Aspects of Middle Scots Phonemics and Graphemics: The Phonological Implications of the Sign<I>', *Transactions of the Philological Society 1967,* Oxford, 1968, pp. 32-61.
37. 'How to Pronounce Older Scots', *Bards and Makars, Scottish Language and Literature: Medieval and Renaissance,* eds A.J.Aitken, M.P.McDiarmid, D.S.Thomson, University of Glasgow Press, 1977, p. 8.
38. Cf. Girvan, op.cit., p. lix, and Kohler, op.cit., p. 49, who explains this kind of rhyme from the existence of monophthongal forms in the relevant French paradigms.

39. See p. 12 of ed. mentioned in note 18 above.
40. Op.cit., Introduction, pp. l-li.
41. Sarah J.G.Caldwell, *The Relative Pronoun in Early Scots, A Lexicographical and Syntactical Study,* Unpubl. Ph.D.Thesis, Edinburgh, 1967. In her monograph *The Relative Pronoun in Early Scots,* Helsinki, 1974, based on the above, we find this on p. 32.
42. C. Horstmann, ed., op.cit., pp. 218 ff.
43. *The quhilk* twice, *quhilk* eleven times, as against *that* rel.pron. 157 times; the plural forms *(the) quhilkis* do not occur.
44. Op.cit., Introduction, pp. li-liv. See also Sarah Caldwell, op.cit., relevant chapters.
45. Op.cit., p. xlv.
46. Ibid., p. lv.

XI. METRE AND VERSIFICATION

The *Buke of the Sevyne Sagis* is written in fairly regular octosyllabic couplets, a metre frequently used in Older Scots poetry, e.g. in Barbour's *Bruce*, in the *Legends of the Saints*, the *Scottish Troy Book Fragments*, Wyntoun's *Chronicles*, the *Buik of Alexander*. In the Asloan MS., however, there are no other pieces in this metre.

The octosyllabic couplets of *BSS* are no better and no worse than those in the other works just mentioned; there are irregularities here and there, most of which could be corrected in a simple way and may therefore be due to the copyist(s)[1]. The lines are mostly iambic, usually with masculine endings, though feminine endings also occur. Within the line anapaestic substitution is fairly frequent and in a number of cases it seems certain enough that there was initial trochaic subsitution. Final *-e* is usually silent, but it may be sounded here and there according to the needs of the metre. Run-on lines are frequent and the sentence often runs from one couplet into another, thus linking several numbers of couplets. The end of the first line of a couplet often coincides with the end of a sentence, e.g. twelve times in the first 288 lines.

In this way the reader is presented with verse that moves freely and smoothly, with fewer rhyme-tags, stop-gaps or paddings than in many other works in the same metre, and especially in the colloquial parts one finds occasion to admire the author's adroitness. The greater part of the lines scans naturally and most of those that seem to be faulty at first sight can be made metrical by applying syncopation, elision, or by making a final *-e* syllabic. It should, however, be noted that not all lines can be scanned according to the more or less strict octosyllabic pattern which the present writer assumes was what poets tried to achieve to delight their audiences.

An examination of the metrics of the text shows the following major characteristics:

1. Final -*e* usually has no syllabic value, but it may have been sounded for the sake of the metre in most of the following cases: *Catone* 47 (the name is usually stressed on the second syllable, except once, 1881, where it is given as *Cato*); *awne* 147; *courche* 208; *mischance* 391, 603; *pure* 539; *dule* 587; *stanche* 753; *tvme* 756; *large* 841, 893; *hamewart* 1360; *besyde* 1661; *hale* 1971; *strange* 2391. In some of these cases and some others like *byde* 181, *wache* 1146, *Ane* 1720 we may be dealing with silent stress or with single-syllable feet[2]. In line 406 *hie* is possibly disyllabic; the other possibility is a syllabic final -*e* in *worschipe*. In line 83, though *bed* is the written form, *bedde* seems to be called for. This feature is amply signalised by Friedman and Harrington[3]. See also *DOST*, s.v. *bed*.
2. The word *empriour*, which occurs eighty-four times in *BSS*, can be used in a number of ways to suit the demand of the metre:
   a. It is found as a trisyllabic word, e.g. in line 1: *ane ém-priőur in tŷmes bygâne*; 60, 185, 353, 506, &c. In all these cases the stresses are placed on the first and third syllables.
   b. It occurs very often in combination with the definite article, where the *e* of the article is elided, but where the word is still trisyllabic with stresses on first and third syllables, e.g. in ll. 1089: *and bê the crővne of the‿ém-priőur*, 1133, 2244, 2502, 2516, 2772. In all the other caese a choice between *the‿emprîour* and *the émpriour* with synizesis or anapaestic substitution seems possible, whatever the place of the word in the line:

      25 *The empriour sone at him couth speir*, 121, 136, 193, 199, 271, &c., all in combination with the definite article;

      110 *And to the empriour tornis my pen*, 112, 258, 781, 1302, &c.;

      351 *To the empriour than said the quene*, 494, 1752, 1773, 2094;

      2237 *Sone on the morne the empriour bad.*

   Though the form *emprîour* appears rather unnatural it seemed useful to consider it.

c. Sometimes the metre demands compression to a disyllabic form with syncope of the *i* or synizesis:

143 *Was to the empriour hir wikit thocht;*

502 *'Be my crovne!'said the empriour than;*

592 *And halsit the empriour foroutin hone;*

981 *The empriour said:'ȝe sall fynd all ewill;*

1003 *Ane empriour in our eldaris dayis.*

Syncope of the *i* in *empriour* can be accounted for by reference to the fact that in Middle Scots (*Bruce, Leg.S.*, Wyntoun) the form *emperour* also existed, a form which could easily be syncopated when the metre demanded this. Also in the present text the word *empriour* in the majority of cases is presented in a shortened form with an abbreviation for *ri* which is practically the same as the one for *er* and *ir* (see List of scribal abbreviations, p.204).

3. Beside the cases in which it is followed by the word *empriour* the definite article, followed by a word with initial vowel, shows elision in a number of cases, e.g.:
1313 *the‿empris*, unless one assumes an anapaest in the first part of the line; not elided in 205, 277, 506, 796, &c. In 525 it can be used either way, according as *blynnit* is made monosyllabic or disyllabic;
104 *the‿erd,* 1737, not elided in 443, 461, 861, 1703, 1755;
1280 *the‿instewart*, not elided in 1271;
2039 *the‿ill wedder*; *the‿ymag(e)* shows elision in 1636, 1786, 1829, not so in 1833.

4. After *ȝe, he, scho* and *thow* the vowel (and initial consonant) in a following auxiliary is often elided: 804, 1220 *ȝe‿ar*;1154 *ȝe‿haf*; 1498 *he‿will*; 1158, 2274 *scho‿had*; 1129 *thow‿art*.
In cases with *it*, it is probably the *i* in *it* which is elided: 1128 *is it,* 113, 1830 *it is,* 867 *for it*, cf. *ford* (Glossary).

5. Final *y* requires anapaestic substitution or synizesis in: 16 *study and*; 255, 2518 *worthy of*; 446 *wery yneuch*; 460 *lady as*; 1109 *allmychti I*; 2241 *tary and*; 2292 *study into*; 2372 *ladye and*; 2529 *dulfully and*; 2589 *crabitly or*; 2599 *courtly and*. Initial *y* in *ymagis* shows synizesis or anapaestic substitution in four out of five cases, 1646, 1667, 1673, 1680,

against 1689 where it has its full form; it is evident from the scansion that *ymag(e/is)* has variable stress.

6. The endings *-ioun, -iale* often show synizesis, e.g. 416, 2688 *regioun*; 994 *relacioun*; 1376 *speciale*; 114, 1025 *successioun*, not in 638; 670, 1602, 2187 *questio(u)n*, not in 511, 2144; 187 *clarioun*, the spelling *claroun* also being found, 2523. The *i* is syllabic in the endings of: 830 *condicioun*; 120, 1315, 1534, 1608 *confusioun*; 2339 *obligacoun* (sic); 762 *restrictioun*; 1804 *conclusioun*; 511, 2144 *questioun*; 2119 *porcioun*; 2719 *opinioun*; 2523 *symphion*, and in 35, 41, 49, 63, &c. *science*. The scansion of 119 *generacioun* depends on whether one takes *falȝeit* as monosyllabic or disyllabic. In 457 *falȝe* is monosyllabic, in 331 it rhymes with *avalȝe*; in 1536 *falȝeit* is dissyllabic, but *faile* in 708 and 726 are both monosyllabic, rhyming with *hale* and *medicinale*, and so *falȝeit* might have been pronounced as a monosyllable if necessary.

7. The *-it* endings of preterite and past participle are used either with or without syncopation, e.g. (examples taken mainly from the first five-hundred lines):

bovnit	66, its parallel *bowned* disyllabic in 682;		
bowit	223, disyllabic in 65;		
callit	2, 47, 54, 314, disyllabic in 55, 248, 512;		
forsit	379, 387	-	- 513;
kepit	236,	-	- 443;
plesit	194,	-	- 554;
savit	497,	-	- 475;
sperit	455,	-	- 101, 279, 303, 464;
techit	71,	-	- 46;

cryit 244, *cryid* 453 monosyllabic, *cryit* 508 disyllabic; *passit* 301 monosyllabic, cf. *past* 1437 which should be pronounced as a disyllabic word.

Wryth in 220 probably stands for *wrythit*. The absence of an *-it* ending here might suggest the reduction of final *-it* in pronunciation such as occurs after stems ending in a dental in forms like *erdit* 956, *grantit* 2323, *lichtit* 978, 2570, *liftit* 1635, 2001, *schoutit* 453, *stettit* 1941; in *studyet* 716, *studyit*

2313, and *lichtlyit* 715, the ending possibly shows elision, or there may be anapaestic substitution.

8. The *-is* ending of plural nouns and of verbal inflections can be pronounced as a separate syllable or not, as the metre demands, cf. Murray, p. 155: 'At the end of the 15th century and the beginning of the 16th, the *-is*, although still generally making an independent syllable in monosyllables, or after a final accent, had quite sunk into *-s* in other words of two or more syllables. Even in writing, *s* alone began to appear. Monosyllables ending in a *vowel* or *diphthong* made an additional syllable or not, of the inflectional *-is*, at the pleasure of the poet.'[4] The more modern view is that even before the literary Scots period *-is* was always syncopated after a secondary or unstressed syllable, but optionally syllabic after a stressed syllable. This is also found in Middle English poets. It seems that syncopation occurs the more frequently as the texts are later and/or written in a less grand style.

Verbal forms, monosyll. or syncopated:		unsyncopated:
	12 *levis*	125 *kepis*
	110 *tornis*	247 *schawis*
	304 *dois*	263 *garris*
	332, 500 *garris*	515 *standis*
	333 *lattis*	
	355 *comfortis*	
	383 *knawis*	
	397 *gerris*	

Plural and genitive forms, syncopated:		unsyncopated:
	21, 155, 169 *sternis*	80 *wallis*
	22, 382 *per(r)ellis*	83 *barnis*
	42, 49, 54 *ȝeris*	173 *dayis*
	77 *masonnis*	243 *nalis*
	78, 82 *middis*	278 *rutis*
	101, 107, 176, 194 *masteris*	282 *schamis*
	145, 153 *letteris*	442 *tornis*
	155 *planetis*	462 *handis*
	208 *madynnis*	501 *wordis*

The syncopated forms are more numerous than the unsyncopated forms in about five-hundred lines investigated.

In the case of the word *sagis* we find several examples of an elided syllable or anapaestic substitution, e.g. 146, 164, 2161, 2229, 2531, out of the twenty-six times that the word occurs in the whole poem. The word *burges* occurs eighteen times and is found with the second syllable possibly elided in 286, 301, 1874, 1903. There is contraction in *claithis (: rais)* 1442, 2466, and in 1541; also possibly in the word *athis* 203. Note that *nurys* n. 'nurse' is disyllabic in 431, but monosyllabic in 450.

9. Adverbs in *-is* show syncopation of the ending; 150, 400 *ellis* is monosyllabic, also in the seven cases where it occurs later in the text; 218 *anys* is monosyllabic, also the other examples, 1425 and 2020. *Ofttymes, quhylis, thusgatis, vtherwayis* and *ȝongatis* show syncopation whenever they occur in *BSS*.
10. Final syllables ending in a liquid often show syncope or slurring: e.g. 1502 *counsall*, 447 *credill*, 1269 *example*, 536 *gentill*, 1820 *iowell*, 827 *moble*, 1576 *perrell*, 327 *pynule*, 960 *sample*, 2704 *towall*; 253 *bundin*, 183 *cummyn*, 1061 *drunkin*, 2692 *fallyn*, 737 *fundin*, 270 *hethinnes*, 388 *madin*, 2615 *ravynnis*, 1550 *blude lattyng*, 1285 *lyking*; 938 *brother*, 79 *chalmer*, 127 *dochter*, 731 *efter*, 73 *erar*, 1473 *fader*, 298 *gardiner*, 92 *quhidder*, 1473 *togiddir*.[5]
11. Elision is often found in words with intervocalic *v* or *w*:[6] *euer, evir* occurs fourteen times in the text; ten times the metre seems to demand elision or anapaestic substitution, e.g. 160, 488, 846; *neuer, nevir* is found thirty-one times; it shows syncope in eleven cases, e.g. 377, 760, 900. *Evyn(e)* 1937, *ewin* 1112, *hevyn(e)* 105, 2781, *sevyn(e)* 36, 132, 173, &c., *sevynt* 55, 2240, show elision by the side of unelided forms of the same words.

The following words also show potential elision or syncope: 1098 *awentour*, 1873 *misawentur*, 517 *misaventour*, 1453 *covering*, 1542, 1711 *cowerit*, 2340, 2760 *discoverit*, 1420, 1466 *forgevin*, *forgevyn*, 1744 *gavillok*, 2226 *governans*, 2780 *governit*; 248, 378, 1452 *devill (: wele)*; 357, 961, 1128 *devile*, *devill*,

1176 *devillis*. Unsyncopated forms of the word occur in 812 and 1444. The word is spelled without *v* in 512 *dele (: wele)*.

Other cases of the loss of *v/w* in the spelling are found in 1471 *antaris* 'adventures', 1716 *cunnand* 'covenant', 208 *courche* 'kerchief', 545, 1711, 1829, &c. *abone* 'above', in *our, owre* 'over' *passim*, and in 2564 *behude (: gud)*, as against 2551 *behovit* (disyll.), 890, 892, 1200 *behufit* (disyll.) and 1215 *behufit* (trisyllabic).

Covatus has syncope or elision in all its four occurrences, 1265, 1618, 1714, 1731, but in *covatis* 1270, 1819, 2204 and in *cowatousnes* 1823 there is none.

12. A number of stems ending in *-ow* show occasional apocope of that syllable: 1830 *arrowe*, 1632 *fallows* 'fellows', 2617 *follow*, 424, 2529 *folowit*, 972 *gallous* 'gallows', 371, 2063 *sorrow*, 1039 *wyndo*, 1915 *wyndois*, by the side of fully syllabic forms of the same words.

VERSIFICATION

In an attempt to evaluate the skill of the poet of *BSS* and to discover possible relationships among Middle Scots poetic works, an investigation was carried out of the /ai/, /ā/ and /ă/-rhymes in a number of poems of more or less contemporary authors. For this purpose I used in the first place other works in octosyllabic or four-stress couplets: Barbour's *Bruce*, *Legends of the Saints*, the *Scottish Troy-Book Fragments*, the *Buik of Alexander* and Wyntoun's *Chronicle*; besides I inspected works in decasyllabic couplets: *Ratis Ravyng*, the *Wallace*, the *Thre Prestis of Peblis*, *Lancelot of the Laik* and the *Buke of the Chess*; poems in alliterative stanzas: the *Buke of the Howlat*, *Golagros and Gawain*, *Rauf Coilȝear*; in non-alliterative stanzas: the *Kingis Quair* and *King Hart*, and works in various metres by Henryson, Dunbar and Gavin Douglas[7]. Wherever possible I examined approximately 2780 lines of each item or poet since *BSS* has 2782; in cases where poems were shorter the number of lines and findings was multiplied so as to arrive at the number of 2780. Of some of the longer works longer fragments were consulted, the findings again arithmetically equalised to 2780.

The resulting overall statistical data are presented in Appendix V, pp. 428-38.

The outcome concerning *BSS* is as follows:
BSS has by far the greatest variety of /ă/ and /ai/-rhymes, *viz.* sixty-four different rhyme-endings, with Gavin Douglas second with about fifty-three, and *Bruce*, Wyntoun, *Buik of Alexander, Thre Prestis, Ratis Ravyng* and Dunbar all with just under fifty; the lowest number of such rhymes is found in the *Kingis Quair* and *Rauf Coilȝear* (about thirty-five). The high number in *BSS* proves, it seems to me, the poet's versatility and command of language.

BSS has very few impure or mixed /ai/ : /ā/ rhymes. This feature it shares with *Bruce, Legends of the Saints, Scottish Troy-Book Fragments*, Wyntoun, *Ratis Ravyng, Golagros and Gawain, Kingis Quair* and Henryson. In all the other works it is far more common, with Gavin Douglas 1513 and the *Buke of the Howlat* (c.1450 -52) having the highest number of impure rhymes. Evidently these authors did not feel any impurity in this usage, whereas the earlier poets and the *BSS*-poet did.

With reference to Kohler's relevant remark[8] it must be stated here that *BSS* has neither *tham, thaim,* nor *thar* 'their' in rhyme; it has the spelling *haile* rhyming with *counsall* and *avale,* and the spelling *hale* rhyming with *faile* and *counsall,* as well as with *taile* 'tale' and *castale* 'castle'. Where 'slay', 'again' and 'they' are concerned, *BSS* does not use the spelling *slay* at all, but it has *sla* four times in rhyme with words in /ā/; it has *slane* eight times in rhyme with /ai/, *agane* twenty times, always rhyming with /ai/, whereas we find *thay* 'they' six times in rhyme with /ai/, but no case of *tha*-spellings.

As demonstrated in Section VIII anglicisation is very rare in *BSS*; there are only two cases in rhyme, see pp. 71-72. Of the earlier works investigated only the *Scottish Troy Book*[9] and the *Kingis Quair* have a great deal of anglicisation in rhyme; later works like the *Buke of the Chess* and *Lancelot of the Laik,* both dated a.1500 (see *DOST*, 'Register of Titles of Works Quoted'), show frequent to very frequent anglicisation, while in Henryson's and Gavin Douglas's poems it is a common phenomenon.

The use of *sere* as a rhyme-word does not occur in *BSS*, nor in *Kingis Quair, Thre Prestis, Buke of the Chess*, nor in the works examined of Henryson and Dunbar. All the others use it more or less frequently, with *Legends of the Saints*, Wyntoun and *Ratis Ravyng* standing out with the highest rates of occurrence. The word *certane* is found in rhyme fairly frequently in the *Scottish Troy Book*, less often in the *Buik of Alexander*, *Golagros and Gawain*, once in the *Buke of the Howlat*, the *Kingis Quair*, and Gavin Douglas 1501, and not at all in *BSS* and the rest of the works scrutinised. In my opinion such an idiosyncrasy points to a poetic poverty that the author of *BSS* did not suffer from.

Notes to Section XI

1. Compare R.L.Graeme Ritchie, ed., *The Buik of Alexander,* STS NS 12, 17, 21, 25, 1920-28, Vol. I, p. cclxi: "The easy-going metre allows lines to remain with syllables too many or too few, in cases where it would have been the simplest thing in the world to regularise their number ... but though this apparent negligence offends the modern ear, it is universal in Middle English, and in no wise peculiar to the 'Buik' or the 'Bruce'".

   Kenneth G. Wilson in his edition of *The Lay of Sorrow* and *The Lufaris Complaynt (Speculum,* 29, 1954, pp. 708-26) also refers to these phenomena: 'Several ... lines can be made to fit the pattern only with special treatment of some unaccented syllables. Many such lines seem to fit the pattern, however, since the same words appear to have received consistent special syllabification throughout the poem (*Lay of Sorrow).* Some of these words, such as *euir* and *neuir,* which are always monosyllabic, are common in Scottish poetry of the period; *creature* consistently requires three syllables in these poems, and *sorow* gets only one syllable, while *sorouful* receives but two.'
2. David Abercrombie, *Elements of General Phonetics,* Edinburgh University Press, 1967, p. 36, and the same author's 'Some functions of silent stress' in *Edinburgh Studies in English and Scots,* eds A.J.Aitken, Angus McIntosh and Hermann Pálsson, London, 1971, pp. 147-56.
3. Albert B. Friedman and Norman T. Harrington, eds., *Ywain and Gawain,* EETS No. 254, 1964 (for 1963), p. xlix.
4. James A.H. Murray, *The Dialect of the Southern Counties of Scotland,* London, 1873.
5. Cf. Friedman and Harrington, op.cit., p. li, and R.L. Graeme Ritchie, op.cit., Vol. I, pp. cclxii f. for slurring of syllables.
6. On loss of *v* or *w* see the general rule mentioned by G. Gregory Smith, *Specimens of Middle Scots,* Edinburgh, 1902, p. xxviii, § 23, that intervocalic *v* disappears in pronunciation.
7. John Barbour, *The Bruce,* ed. W.W.Skeat, 3 vols., STS, 1893-94 *Legends of the Saints,* ed. W.M.Metcalfe, 6 vols., STS, 1887-96

Scottish Troy-Book Fragments, in *Barbour's ... Legendensammlung nebst den Fragmenten seines Trojanerkrieges*, ed. C.Horstmann, Heilbronn, 1881-82

The Buik of Alexander, ed. R.L. Graeme Ritchie, STS, 1920-28

Andrew of Wyntoun's *Oryginale Cronykil*, ed. F.J.Amours, STS, 1902-29

Ratis Ravyng and Other Early Scots Poems on Morals, ed. Ritchie Girvan, STS, 1937

Hary's *Wallace*, ed. Matthew P. McDiarmid, STS, 1968

Lancelot of the Laik, ed. M.M.Gray, STS, 1912

The Buke of the Chess
The Buke of the Howlat
The Thre Prestis of Peblis } *Asloan Manuscript*, ed. W.A.Craigie, STS, 1923-25

Golagros and Gawane
Rauf Coilȝear } *Scottish Alliterative Poems in Riming Stanzas*, ed. F.J.Amours, STS, 1891-96

King Hart, pp. 139-70 in *The Shorter Poems of Gavin Douglas*, ed. Priscilla J. Bawcutt, STS, 1967

The Kingis Quair of James Stewart, ed. M.P.McDiarmid, London, 1973

The Poems and Fables of Robert Henryson, ed. H. Harvey Wood, Edinburgh, (1933) 1958

The Poems of William Dunbar, ed. W. Mackay Mackenzie, London, (1932) 1970

Gavin Douglas 1501, i.e. *Palice of Honour*, in *The Shorter Poems of Gavin Douglas*, ed. P.J.Bawcutt, STS, 1967

Gavin Douglas 1513, i.e. several parts of the *Eneados*, in *Selections from Gavin Douglas*, ed. David F.C. Coldwell, Oxford, 1964

8. K.J.Kohler, 'Aspects of Middle Scots Phonemics and Graphemics: The Phonological Implications of the Sign<I>', *Transactions of the Philological Society*, 1967, pp. 32-61: 'We must exclude a number of rhymes straightaway because they contain words that existed in two etymologically justified forms, one with E.Sc. /a:/ from O.North. /a:/, and one with E.Sc. /ai/ from O.N. /ei/, e.g. *hale* (O.North. hal, O.N. heill), *tham, thaim* (O.North. þam, O.N. ðeim) 'them', and *thare, thair* (O.North. þara, O.N. ðeira) 'their'. There are also three words which had monophthongal and diphthongal variants because of differences in English: *sla*,

slay 'slay', *slane, slain* 'slain' and *agane, again* 'again'. *thay* (O.N. þeir) 'they' and *tha* (O.North. þa) 'those', on the other hand, were usually distinguished in spelling as well as in pronunciation and meaning' (pp. 46-47).

9. In the case of the *Scottish Troy-Book Fragments* it should be borne in mind, however, that the anglicisation consists solely in the purposive adoption of anglicised or quasi-anglicised spellings, in order to fit the fragments into defective copies of Lydgate's *Troy Book*.

XII. THE STYLE AND NARRATIVE ART OF THE *BUKE OF THE SEVYNE SAGIS* AND ITS PLACE IN THE SCOTTISH TRADITION OF THE DAY

It was long the custom of critics of Older Scots literary products to say that the language in which they were written was 'the special affair of literary habit, as distinguished from spoken dialect'[1], or words to much the same effect[2]. Some of the works in Middle Scots may indeed warrant verdicts like the above, e.g. Dunbar's *Goldyn Targe* and *The Thrissil and the Rois*, Henryson's *Testament of Cresseid*, and parts of Gavin Douglas's *Eneados*. C.S.Lewis, however, in his chapter on late medieval Scots literature[3], shows that Scots authors at the time were capable of handling five principal genres of poetry: forthright narrative in couplets, poems combining rhyme and alliteration in various patterns, comic poetry, pure lyric, and the full-blown high style. All these genres are well-represented in Middle Scots literature.

In the first category we have e.g. Barbour's *Bruce*, the present *Buke of the Sevyne Sagis*, David Lyndsay's *Squyer Meldrum* in octosyllabic couplets, and Blind Hary's *Wallace* in decasyllabic couplets, all in a simple, direct, unadorned vernacular style.

The second category contains such works as *Rauf Coilȝear*, *Golagros and Gawane*, and Richard Holland's *Buke of the Howlat*, of which the language is in a way similar to that of the narrative in couplets but with more and various elements of poetic diction.

Among the Middle Scots comic poetic pieces we find burlesques, flytings, lampoons and tales with a low-life background, such as Dunbar's *Dance of the Sevin Deidly Synnis* and large parts of his *Twa Mariit Wemen and the Wedo*, *Colkelbie Sow*, *the Wyf of Auchtermuchty*, *Peblis to the Play* and *Christis Kirk on the Grene*. C.S.Lewis called the language of this class 'broadly and exaggeratedly Scotch' (op.cit., p. 76). Aitken labels it more precisely and calls this the 'colloquial style of Older Scottish verse-writing'.

Lewis's fourth class, pure lyric, contains a number of very divergent genres, viz. lyric, personal, satirical, moralising and religious poems. Their styles are divergent, too; some share features with the courtly aureate style of Lewis's fifth category with its anglicisation and Latinate vocabulary, others share elements with the comic poetry.

The fifth class, that of poetry in the 'full-blown high style', comprises the courtly pieces for which the Scots poets have been given the label of 'Scottish Chaucerians', full of the colours of rhetoric and the just-mentioned Latinisation and anglicisation: Gavin Douglas's *Palice of Honour,* John Rolland's *Court of Venus,* the anonymous *Quare of Jelusy* and *Lufaris Complaint,* beside the works mentioned in the first paragraph above.

When Lewis is speaking of Dunbar (op.cit., pp. 90-98) he mentions the several styles in which his poems are written, and Kurt Wittig[4], agreeing with him, gives three fragments in illustration, showing that Dunbar handles his language on several levels, and uses the high, courtly, 'aureate' style, the normal educated language, and the broad vernacular; what is applicable to Dunbar also goes for a number of other writers in Middle Scots.

Aitken in his so-far unpublished 'Characteristics of the "Courtly Style" of Middle Scots Verse' and 'Notes on the "Colloquial Style" of Middle Scots Verse' goes further into the matter, and in conclusion presents 'the relations of the two extremes of Middle Scottish poetic style' in the following diagram:

'Colloquialisms'	The main stream of traditional literary and spoken usage	'Chaucerianisms'
Reduced forms		Anglicised forms
Many vernacular and abusive words found only in these poems	Many words and usages including 'form-words', common to both styles	Poetic adoptions from fifteen-century English: *lusty, schene,* etc. Aureate diction
lug *tyke*	*ere* *dog*	Avoidance of vernacular words

An examination of *BSS* will show that it belongs to the normal narrative middle style with excesses toward neither courtly nor colloquial styles; it has few 'Chaucerianisms', hardly any aureate diction[5], very little anglicisation (see Section VIII); it has no verbal inflections in *-ith* and *-n* (see Section IX, 10) and none of the poetic adoptions as mentioned by Aitken: *lusty, schene, morrow* 'morning', *twane, anone, tho* 'then', all found in *The Thrissil and the*

Rois.

The elisions analysed in the previous section (pp.114-15) also indicate a middle style, now and then fairly close to the colloquial.

Speaking of the colloquial style in his above-mentioned notes and in a more recent article[6] which once and for all refutes the former conceptions of Middle Scots as an artificially created language, Aitken signalises 'progressive' phonetic spellings and reduced forms, frequent only in some genres of verse: comic and satiric verse and certain narrative poems, such as Hary's *Wallace,* the Asloan *Sevyne Sagis,* Rolland's *Seuin Seages,* Douglas's *Eneados* and Stewart's *Chronicle,* while they are avoided in transcribing poems in other styles and in good literary prose.

A number of forms showing phonetic reduction by the loss or assimilation of intervocalic or final consonants are found in *BSS.* They are: *abone* 5x (2x in rh.); *behude* 'behoved', rhyming with *gud* (2564); *dele* 'devil' rhyming with *wele* adv. 'well' (512)[7]; *effek* 3x in rhyme beside *effect* not in rhyme; *fek* (2664, rhyming with *clek);* *ford* 362, 1739, (once rhyming with *lord)* where *-d* is the reduced and voiced variant of *it,* cf. *DOST* s.v. *'d; fow(e)* 'full', rhyming with *ȝow* (759, 1740); *sell* 'self' 5x, all in rhyme, as against *self* 15x, none in rhyme; *staw* 'stole' pret. 1055, not in rhyme, beside *stall* 4x not in rhyme; *ȝestrene* (380) rhyming with *quene.* Some words, though written in full, were pronounced in a contracted way as becomes clear from the metre (cf. Section XI) and the rhyme, e.g. *cla(i)this* rhyming with *(wp)rais* (1461, 2465). Aitken states (op.cit., p. 196) that *claithis, fow* and *abone* show no obvious tendency towards specialisation of distribution, nor does *behude* (see *DOST* s.v. *behufe* vb. 4b), but *dele, -sell, staw* and *zestrene* belong to the style of the genres mentioned in the previous paragraph.

The distribution of items of vocabulary also provided indications of style. Of the pair *tyke/dog* mentioned in Aitken's above diagram we only find *dog* in *BSS* ; in his 'Variation and Variety', p. 178, he moreover draws attention to the relation with the word *hound* which belongs to a higher level. This is borne out by the usage in *BSS* ; in the caption before line 405, in 481 and 497 the word *hound* is used for a knight's beloved greyhound; in ll. 1440,

1442 and 1451 the word again indicates a favourite dog (no breed specified) and in l. 1362 the plural *houndis* is spoken by servants about their master's pack. The word *dog,* however, is used in 1428 and 1434 by two women having evil designs on the creature, and in l. 1455 *doggis* are referred to with great disgust by one of the scheming females.

Other paired words signalised in Aitken's article, such as the verbs *knaw* and *ken, pass* and *ga, gang,* are distributed in *BSS* as follows: *knaw, knawis, knawin* are found twenty-three times, of which eight in rhyme; fourteen cases are used in direct speech, of which four in rhyme; *ken, kennit, kend* are used ten times, of which four in rhyme; five cases occur in direct speech, of which one in rhyme.

The distribution of the pair *pas/gang* is: *pas* 10x (1x in rh.), *passit* 15x (n.rh.), *past* 30x (12x in rh.), *passing* n. (1x in rh.); out of fifty-six cases *pas* is only used three times in direct speech, none rhyming; *gang* 6x (4x in rh.), *ga* 13x (10x in rh.), *gais* 1x (in rh.), *gane* 15x (10x in rh.); out of thirty-five occurrences we find *gang, ga, gane* fourteen times in direct speech, nine times in rhyme.

It is clear that the higher-style *knaw* and *pas* are used much more frequently in *BSS* than their colloquial counterparts. Proportionally, however, the colloquial words are more often used for rhyming purposes than the other forms.

The use of *can* and *couth* as auxiliaries of the preterite was limited to narrative verse, see *DOST* s.v. *can*, v. 2; *did* tended to supersede them in imitation of Chaucerian poetry, and began to appear in Scottish verse in the early sixteenth century.

Rupert Taylor's findings on the use of *can* and *couth* in this function by several Early and Middle Scots poets[8] led him to conclude that *can* from older *gan*, after having been in use for some time, 'began to lose ground to *couth.* By the middle of the fifteenth century *couth* was slightly the more preferable form. Both *can* and *couth* gave way at the close of the fifteenth and the beginning of the sixteenth centuries to *did.*'[9] *BSS* uses *can* 13x, *couth* 43x, as preteritive auxiliaries, their notional verbs all in rhyming positions. *Did* is not found in this function in *BSS,* nor is *gan. Can* is consistently used as a preterite; in all cases except one (2713) *can* and *couth* are used with the third person sg. or pl. By Taylor's standards this would place *BSS* in the latter half of the fifteenth centry. As to authorship the usage in *BSS* does not afford any clue: it does not tally with any of the other poems investigated by Taylor.

BSS consists for the greater part of conversations (about 1670 lines out of a total of 2782); these are all very well managed as to contents, and adroitly handled as to language, see ll. 327-33, 520-24, 764-72, 1587-90, 1613-16, 2377-8, 2391-8, 2581, &c. Lines 1486-7 also strike us as very natural; the fact that they possibly are in part a faithful translation of the Latin H-text[10]: '*O sancta Maria, cur presbyterum?*' does not detract greatly from the skill of the author. Other parts of *BSS* which are close parallels to known Latin texts (see e.g. section XIII, note 63, and section XX, notes to ll. 1934-60 and 1990-2012), also show this quality of excellent translation which is equally found in the *Scottish Troy-Book Fragments*[11], a very capable rendering of Guido delle Colonne's *Historia Troiana* by an unknown author (c.1400).

There are no outstanding poetic heights in *BSS*, though e.g. 'wnder the nychtis myrk scilens' (868) is admirable, but there are no great depths either; the poet manages his 2782 lines with only about twenty-five rhyme-tags occurring (see below). We often find enjambment, e.g. 19-22, 39-42, 90-92, 151-53, 193-96, and very flowingly rhymed parts, e.g. 531-35, 541-44, 597-600. The author does not seem to have been averse from alliteration here and there, cf. ll. 4, 404, 439, 548, 1434, 1453-54, 1540, 1707. There are hardly any superfluous details, no long-winded explanations or tedious repetitions. Though ll. 489-92 may be a seeming redundance at the end of the tale, they serve to stress the fact that it was because of his wife's words that the knight unreasonably killed his greyhound.

The poem speaks of God fairly frequently[12], always in a Christian sense, never using the word as a rhyme-tag or stopgap; once God is invoked rather amusingly, when one of the thieves planning to rob the emperor's treasury says to the other: 'God will ws saif, Becaus that we sic mister haif.' (865-6)

Several other humorous passages occur, such as the conversation between the queen and the physician in ll. 667-80, where the latter's flippant answers of ll. 672 and 675-77, and his ironic 'with Goddis blissing and myne' (678), as well as 'now sall I ȝarne Kepe your secretis and hele ȝour barne' (695-96) stand out. Sarcasm is found in the husband's answer of 1102-04 and in the author's mocking remarks in 1410, 1417 f., 1460 and 1988, and humour of the wriest in 2397-98; the repetition of the verb *fynd* in ll. 980-81 and of the verb *se* in ll. 1966-67 are significant. Very witty is the repetition of ll. 1089-90 spoken by the husband, in ll. 1133-34 when the wife uses them against him.

There are a few inelegancies, such as the use of the noun *hole* four times in ll. 885-90, the repetition of *ilk port(e)* of l. 1708 in the next line, the words *It that I did* of 1406 repeated in 1408, though the latter example might be defended as adducing emphasis by the repetition.

Of the twenty-five rhyme-tags[13] only four seem really objectionable, viz. *withoutin dreid* 1026, 1779, *but dreid* 2117, *forsuth indeid* 1887, and perhaps *blyth and glad* 293.

A feature of the narrative is the predominance of simple sentences linked by simple coordination with *and* (503 times in 2782 lines, i.e. somewhat more than once in every five lines, not counting *and* 'if', eight times).

Though some of the stories, or fragments of stories, are found in or go back to collections of *exempla, BSS* has nothing of the moralising tendency of this genre, but it rather shows the racy and economical way of tackling the material in hand that one finds in the better *fabliaux*.

In the giving of personal names to the protagonists in the tales *BSS* is original and departs from the usage in *exempla*, where the characters are as a rule referred to as 'a man', 'a certain knight', 'a burgess', 'a merchant', etc. There are no detailed descriptions of the circumstances in which the actions take place; a situation is usually indicated in a pithy adequate way. Sometimes, however, one feels that the simplicity has been carried too far, e.g. in PUTEUS and INCLUSA the absence of servants seems rather unlikely.

Several of the points mentioned above show that the language of *BSS* displays features which according to Aitken are characteristic of both the colloquial and the courtly style, and so does not fall clearly or unequivocally into either of these categories of his. But the apparent tendency of the author to prefer items characteristic of the first rather than the second category gives some support to these categorisations in that *BSS* proves to be a middle-style piece with greater preference to colloquial than to courtly items, as Aitken predicts for simple narrative poetry.

Notes to Section XII

1. G.Gregory Smith, *Specimens of Middle Scots,* Edinburgh, 1902, p. xi.
2. W.W.Skeat, ed., *The Kingis Quair,* STS NS 1, 1911, p. xxiv: 'a purely artificial dialect, such as probably was never spoken'; H.Harvey Wood, ed., *The Poems and Fables of Robert Henryson,* Edinburgh , (1933) 1958, p. xxxi: 'an artificial, created, "literary" language'; M.W.Stearns, *Robert Henryson,* New York, (1949) 1966, p. 6: 'a literary language which was probably never spoken'. Even in such a recent book as Maurice Lindsay's *History of Scottish Literature,* London, 1977, we find a remark about 'the curious mixture of Scots and Chaucerian English ... which, we are told, was never spoken'. He is referring to the *Kingis Quair* , it is true (p. 35). It is a pity that Mr Lindsay's reading on the early Scots literature has not been broad enough; he still ascribes *King Hart* to Gavin Douglas in spite of Priscilla Bawcutt (formerly Preston): 'Did Gavin Douglas write *King Hart*?', *Medium Aevum,* 28 (1959), 31-47, and Florence H.Ridley, "Did Gawin Douglas write *King Hart* ', *Speculum,* 34 (1959), 402-12; he also says that *Christis Kirk on the Grene* and *Peblis to the Play* are by James I though this attribution is no longer tenable (see C.S.Lewis, op. cit. below -n. 3-, pp. 105 f. and the datings in *DOST* , Part XXI, pp. xvi and xxvii). It would have been useful for Lindsay to have had this part of his history vetted by a specialist. See also the very perceptive review by R.D.S.Jack, 'The First since Millar', *Scottish Literary Journal,* Supplement No. 5, Winter 1977, pp. 12-20.
3. *English Literature in the Sixteenth Century,* Vol. III of the *Oxford History of English Literature,* Oxford, 1954, pp. 66-119.
4. *The Scottish Tradition in Literature,* Edinburgh and London, 1958, p.62.
5. By aureate diction I understand not just 'the use of polysyllabic coinages from Latin *(celsitude, jocundity, lachrymable)* as an ornament to style' (C.S.Lewis, op.cit., p. 75), for many Latin-derived words are polysyllabic which I should not like to call aureate, e.g. *conclusion, declaration, disposition, generation,* whereas there are short words like *curyale, dulce, inflat,* which are borrowings more or less straight from Latin. I would rather agree

with Baugh (*A Literary History of England*, 2nd edn, Vol. I, London, 1967, p. 291, n. 23), who defines aureate vocabulary as 'the excessive use of Latin derivatives, often slightly assimilated', though the best definition of 'aureate' seems to me 'floridly rhetorical' *(Chambers' Twentieth Century Dictionary*, New Edition 1972, Edinburgh, 1972, s.v. *aureate)*, as this stresses the overdecoratedness of the style.

In his study *The Latin Element in the Vocabulary of the Earlier Makars Henryson and Dunbar*, Lund, 1977, p. 14, Bengt Ellenberger says that 'when David Lindsay commended the "aureat termis" of Walter Kennedy he gave posterity a technical term for the phenomenon: "aureation" became the term for a Latinate poetic diction in late Middle and early Modern English.' On p. 21 he gives the following definition: 'a latinism is a lexical item of Latin origin that -- whether borrowed directly or through French -- betrays no sign of Gallo-Roman or Old French sound changes in its base, and so can be immediately related to its Latin counterpart.'

In my opinion a word, derived ultimately from Latin, but amply recorded in Old French and Middle English before it appeared in Middle Scots, should not be designated as a latinism, nor as aureate. Such words were part and parcel of the language and cannot be called 'floridly rhetorical', because they were not used for (over-)decoration. Reasoning from this point of view we can only specify as Latinate (i.e. newly or recently borrowed from Latin) the following neologisms or near-neologisms occurring in *BSS: absolve, attempe, curyale, dulce, eligant, inflat, inflature, mixture, producit, promyt* n., *replege, spekle*.

6. 'Variation and variety in written Middle Scots', *Edinburgh Studies in English and Scots*, eds A.J.Aitken, Angus McIntosh and Hermann Pálsson, London, 1971, pp. 177-209.
7. For *dele/devill* and several other of these reduced forms see also Section X.
8. Rupert Taylor, 'Some Notes on the Use of *Can* and *Couth* as Preterite Auxiliaries in Early and Middle Scottish Poetry', *Journal of English and Germanic Philology*, XVI, 1917, pp. 573-91.
9. Ibid., p. 591.

10. Georg Buchner, ed., *Die Historia Septem Sapientum nach der Innsbrucker Handschrift v.J.1342 nebst einer Untersuchung über die Quelle der Seuin Seages des Johne Rolland von Dalkeith,* Erlangen und Leipzig, 1889, p. 36.
11. Carl Horstmann, ed., *Barbour's des schottischen Nationaldichters Legendensammlung nebst den Fragmenten seines Trojanerkrieges,* Heilbronn, 1881, pp. 217-307.
12. *God* 31x, *God(d)is* (gen.) 4x; further *Ihesu sweit* 2592, *Cristis natiuité* 1658, *Sanct Mary* 1486, *Peteris kirk and Paule* 1110, *Cristin men* 956, *in hethinnes and in Cristindome* 270. The case in l. 1110 is the only one where a saint is called upon to help out with the rhyme; cf. Version D*, ed. Thomas Wright, where it is done 33x in about 3400 lines.
13. Other rhyme-tags used in *BSS* are: *but let* 409, *but faile* 726, *but weir* 1798, *but mair* 1122, *(at)anys* 2020, *at all* 1543, *tharwithal* 467, *in deid* 629, *on deid* 1421, *in plane* 756, *parde* 2177, *les na mair* 190, *yneugh and mar?* 1032, *mair or les* 832, *mar nor les* 227, *mar nor myn* 1943, *nycht and day* 5 times, *day and nycht* 2 times, *fair and bricht* 2491, *suth to saye?* 1837, *be this buke* 202, *I sover ȝow* 760, *I make a wowe* 814, *I ȝow assure* 2190, *or thai wald blyn* 79, *or he wald ces* 1858.

XIII. SUMMARY OF THE CONTENTS; THE *BUKE OF THE SEVYNE SAGIS* COMPARED WITH OTHER VERSIONS

A detailed summary is provided on the right-hand pages that follow, so as to allow easy comparison of salient points in this and other versions without requiring perusal of the whole Middle Scots text. The Latin names given here to the stories within the frame of *The Seven Sages of Rome* were first put forward by Karl Goedeke in his article on the *Liber de Septem Sapientibus*[1], and have been in general use in the literature of the Seven Sages since then. The simple style of *BSS* has been preserved as far as possible in this summary, so have the different spellings which some names show in the Asloan MS., and the indiscriminate denomination of the protagonists of the frame-story as emperor and empress, or king and queen. On the left-hand pages references are given to other versions; the notes in the text on the right-hand pages refer to the items on the left. Many of Campbell's notes[2] have been incorporated and throughout the present work Campbell's method of indicating the versions has largely been followed[3]. This originated for the greater part with Gaston Paris[4], who classified the different versions of *SSR* under ten heads:

1. A, a very large group of prose versions, named A by Gaston Paris after Alessandro d'Ancona, who published the Italian prose *Libro dei sette Savjdi Roma*, belonging to this group, in 1864
2. C, the version found in MS. Chartres 620, partly in verse[5]; this manuscript was burned during the 1939-45 war[6]
3. D, the 'Version Dérimée', edited by Gaston Paris, *Deux réd.*, pp. 1 ff.
4. H, *Historia Septem Sapientum*, a Latin prose version of which Gaston Paris published a French translation printed at Geneva in 1492, op.cit., pp. 55 ff. The oldest Latin prose text is found in an Innsbruck manuscript dating from 1342, which was published by Buchner[7].
5. I, the 'Versio Italica', a group of one Latin and two Italian versions, which Mussafia brought under this head[8]
6. K, the Old French poem (MS. BN.fr. 1553), edited by Keller[9] and

by Misrahi[10]

7. L, a French prose version of *SSR* (MS. BN.fr.19166), first edited by Leroux de Lincy[11], later by M. Aïache, op.cit.
8. M, *La Male Marastre*, an anomalous version which has only a few tales in common with the other versions[12]
9. S, the *Scala Celi*[13], a fourteenth-century Latin abridgment, made by Johannes Gobii Junior (1320-30)[14], of the lost *Liber de Septem Sapientibus*
10. V, the French versions in verse, comprising K, C and D

For the Middle English versions, too, I follow Campbell[15]:

A* Auchinleck MS., National Library of Scotland, Edinburgh, press-mark Adv.MS., 19.2.1, No. 155

Ar MS. Arundel 140, British Library

As Asloan MS., National Library of Scotland, Edinburgh, press-mark Acc. 4233 (the present version)

B MS. Balliol 354, Balliol College, Oxford

C* MS. Cotton Galba E IX, British Library

D* Cambridge University Library MS. Dd.I.17

E MS. Egerton 1995, British Library

F Cambridge University Library MS. Ff.II.38

R MS. Rawlinson Poet. 175, Bodleian Library, Oxford

I have introduced the following additional abbreviations:

BSS *The Buke of the Sevyne Sagis*

CR MSS. C* and R as edited by Campbell[16]

Br. the ME MSS as edited by Brunner[16]

HF the French variety of version H[17]

HL the Latin variety of version H[18]

BN 95 Bibliothèque Nationale fds.franç. 95, Paris[19], OF prose A/L-version

Gg.6.28 Cambridge University Library Gg.6.28, unedited, OF prose A/L-version

and the OF prose A-versions:

McCl.179 Fitzwilliam Museum MacClean MS. 179, Cambridge, unedited

St.J.CII St.John's College MS. CII, Oxford, unedited

Gg.I.1 Cambridge University Library MS. Gg.I.1., unedited

BN 1421 Bibliothèque Nationale fds.franç. 1421, Paris, unedited
BN 2137 " " " " 2137, " "
BN 13521 " " " " 13521, " "
Ars.3152 Bibliothèque de l'Arsenal 3152, Paris, unedited

An endeavour was made to establish a possible source of *BSS*; I compared it not only with the ME manuscripts but also with a number of Old French prose manuscripts of the A-version, especially those extant in Great Britain, *viz.* St.J.CII, Gg.I.1, Gg.6.28, and McCl.179; the latter is a thirteenth-century manuscript not mentioned by Karl Brunner in his EETS-edition of the *Seven Sages*, although it has been in the Fitzwilliam Museum from before 1912[20]. I did not incorporate Brit.Libr.Harl.MS. 3860, as this is a very much abbreviated rendering not comparable with full-length versions. I used BN 95 as it was accessible through Plomp's edition[19], and Ars. 3152 because some of the stories lacking there (VIDUA and ROMA) are also lacking in *BSS*, but this did not yield any specific similarities: Ars. 3152 is a normal A-type collection which has lost a quire[21].

In addition I compared *BSS* with versions K and D, and with HF and HL; the latter two versions especially yielded several interesting points, as can be seen in my conclusion (pp. 178-81).

Notes to Section XIII.

1. *Orient und Occident,* III, Göttingen, 1866, pp. 385-423.
2. Killis Campbell, ed., *The Seven Sages of Rome,* Boston USA, 1907.
3. Op.cit., pp. xxii f. I object, however, to Campbell's idea of starring the French versions A and D so as to differentiate them from the ME versions A and D; this seems rather inelegant to me since the French versions were edited earlier and consequently all the scholarship dealing with *SSR*-matter uses the older designations. I therefore asterisk the ME versions of which the sigla coincide with those indicating French versions.
4. *Deux rédactions du roman des sept sages de Rome,* Société des anciens textes français, Paris, 1876.
5. Ed. Hugh A.Smith, 'A Verse Version of the Sept Sages de Rome', *Romanic Review,* III (1912), pp. 1-68. The prose text ends in the middle of TENTAMINA, told by the fourth master; the rest is written in verse.
6. Mauricette Aïache, 'Les versions françaises en prose du Roman des Sept Sages', a thesis of the Ecole des Chartes, Paris, 1966, regrettably unpublished, a very thorough and useful study of the *SSR,* p. 48. Mademoiselle Aïache is now Madame Berne.
7. Georg Buchner, *Die Historia Septem Sapientum nach der Innsbrucker Handschrift v.J. 1342. Nebst einer Untersuchung über die Quelle der Seuin Sages des Johne Rolland von Dalkeith,* Erlangen und Leipzig, 1889.
8. Adolf Mussafia, 'Ueber eine italienische Bearbeitung der Sieben Weisen Meister', *Jahrbuch für rom.u.engl.Lit.,* IV (1862), pp. 166 ff.
9. Heinrich Adelbert Keller, ed., *Li Romans des sept Sages,* Tübingen, 1836.
10. Jean Misrahi, ed., *Le Roman des sept Sages,* Paris, 1933.
11. Auguste L.A.Loiseleur Deslongchamps, *Essai sur les fables indiennes,* followed by *Roman des Sept Sages de Rome en prose,* publié par Leroux de Lincy, Paris, 1838.
12. Hans R.Runte, ed., *Li Ystoire de la male marastre, Version M of the Roman des Sept Sages de Rome,* Tübingen, 1974. This recent book, dealing as it does with one of the versions of the *SSR*-

tradition, necessarily covers part of the ground I had been going over for a long time before I was in the position to learn of its contents. My own findings, therefore, may be allowed to stand. I was pleased to see that Mr Runte and myself are in agreement on all the points that matter in the common pursuit.

13. Ed. Karl Goedeke, *Orient und Occident*, III (1866), pp. 402-21.
14. Alfons Hilka, ed., *Historia Septem Sapientum, Die Fassung der Scala Celi des Johannes Gobii Junior, nach den Handschriften kritisch herausgegeben*. Sonderabdruck aus der Festschrift für Alfred Hillebrandt, 1913.
15. Op.cit., pp. xxxvi ff. For further details about these MSS see the more elaborate list in Section XIV, pp. 194-5.
16. Op.cit. See also Karl Brunner, ed., *The Seven Sages of Rome (Southern Version)*, EETS OS 191, London, 1933, pp. ix-xiii, and pp. 194-5 below.
17. Ed. Gaston Paris, op.cit., pp. 55 ff.
18. Ed. Georg Buchner, op.cit. above, n. 7.
19. Ed. Herman P.B.Plomp, *De Middelnederlandsche bewerking van het gedicht van den VII Vroeden van binnen Rome*, diss. Utrecht, 1899.
20. See Montague R.James, *A Descriptive Catalogue of the MacClean Collection of Manuscripts in the Fitzwilliam Museum*, Cambridge, 1912, p. 340.
21. Cf. Gaston Paris, op.cit., p. xx.

The *BSS* starts without the kind of introduction as found e.g. in CR, D, E(Br.) and K.

1. This is found nowhere else in *SSR*. In all the other versions the father and son have different names or the son's name is not mentioned at all. See explanatory note to line 2 (p. 327) and Appendix VI ; see also note to l. 9, p. 327.
2. See note to l. 24.
3. Each sage stipulates one year less than his predecessor, Bantillas starting with seven, and Cratone ending with one year. This consistent falling of the numbers seems to be logical and original; it is also found in most of the H-versions. In some MSS the sequence is disturbed; in most of the A-versions the last sage does not mention a term, cf. notes Campbell 1907 to ll. 115, 126, 139.
4. See expl.note to l. 55.
5. See expl.note to l. 74.
6. *Thai pantit all the science sevyn.* The seven arts are not enumerated here as they are in most of the MSS of the A-version. They are not mentioned either in G.Paris's HF-version, nor in Leroux de Lincy's L-version (MS.BN.fr.19166).
7. 89. Cato is mentioned as the master who suggests the testing of the prince; CR 215 has *his maisters,* Br. 183 *þei,* D*173 *Thay,* HF *les maistres,* HL *inter se magistri dixerunt.* D has no testing by leaves, whereas K 381 says *Baucillas le volt asaier.*
8. See expl.note to l. 97.
9. In *BSS,* K, D, A, L, CR, D* and Br. nothing is found about the first queen's request as mentioned in the H-versions, cf. HF p. 57, HL p. 7.
10. *BSS* 9 mentions three years; in all the other versions the boy is seven years old. See expl.note to l. 9.
11. In *BSS* the emperor remonstrates that he is too old to marry again; usually this is not the case. In Ars.3152 we read *Li empereres fu vieus. Si pensa. Quant il ot pense longement si dist Je le prenderoie volentiers...* BN 95 has *Li empereres pensa .i. poi et apres son pense si dist Iou le prenderoie uolentiers ...,* nor is there anything in the ME MSS of the emperor's dislike of marrying again. There is nothing similar in HL or L either, nor in I, K, M, or S.
12. In *BSS* she 'hears' that he has a son; in most of the French prose versions *on auoit dit a lempereis que ses sires auoit .i. fil;* in these and *BSS* she then takes up her evil plan for his death, but there is nothing so spectacular as the calling in of a witch as counsellor which we find in CR 300 and in D* 296.
13. *his letteris.* MSS A*, E, B have no mention of letters, but of an oral message by messenger(s). St.J.CII has two messengers, similarly Gg.6.28, Gg.I.1, BN 19166 and 95; version I has three messengers. The fact that the emperor seals the letters himself is also recorded in HF, not in A, K or D.
14. 149. *In the fest of the Trinitē,* to rhyme with *thai all suld de;* HF has *a celle prochayne fest de la penthecoste,* HL *in festo Penthecostes;* BN 95, Ars.3152, McCl.179 have no day specified, neither has Br., but in CR l. 359 we find *to morn by prime* and in D* l. 312 *withinne the thrydde day.*
15. In many of the versions the young man observes the stars *and* the moon, and he sees an *estoille clere qui sembloit estre a .ii. toises pres de la lune* (MSS. St.J.CII, Gg.I.1, McCl.179, L). BN 95 has *Li valles regarda et vit vne clere estoille a .ii. toises pres de la lune,* CR l. 422 *A litel stern þe mone bisyde,* Br. l. 342 *a ster ... whiche sat next þe mone,* D* l. 354 *in a stere;* HF *il vit clèrement en une petite estoile que sy se pouvoit abstenir de parler de celluy jour assigné sept jours suyvans il conserveroit sa vie,* HL *vidit in quadam parua stella quod, si per .vii. dies ab omni verbo abstineret quod non*

THE BUKE OF THE SEVYNE SAGIS

1 A Roman emperor of long ago, called Dioclesiane, had an
only son of the same name[1], whom he entrusted to seven sages
24 to be educated. The first sage, Bantillas[2], promised to teach
the boy 'all science ... within no more space than seven[3]
years'. The second sage, Amipullus, told the emperor that he
would teach him astronomy within six years. The third sage,
Lentalus, said he would teach him in five years. The fourth,
47 Catone[4], said he would need four years; the fifth, Malcome,
three years; the sixth, Ampustinus, asked for two years, and
the seventh, Cratone, said that in one year the youth would
know all that he and the other sages knew. They went to live
outside the city[5] with the boy 'for dreid he walk in wanyté'
and taught him there for seven years[6]. Then they[7] tested him
as to his 'science' by placing waterlily-leaves[8] under the
legs of his bed, but as soon as he awoke he noticed that his
bed had been 'raised' and so his masters were very pleased
about his perspicacity.

111 In the meantime the emperor, who had been widowed[9] when
the boy was three[10] years old (line 9), had been persuaded by
130 his counsellors to take a second wife[11]. As soon as she heard
that he had a son, she decided to contrive his death[12] and in
order to bring this about she asked the emperor very sweetly
to be allowed to see his son, for if she should not have one
herself, she would regard this boy as her own. The emperor
immediately sent letters[13] to the sages ordering them to
bring his son to him on the feast of the Trinity[14]; otherwise
they would all die. When they consulted the stars about the
outcome of their journey they saw that at the end of it the
youth would die at the first word he spoke, at which they were
greatly perplexed. The youth, on being told, also observed the
stars and discovered that if he might be silent for seven
days he would speak on the eighth day and overcome all his
enemies[15]. The masters promised to defend him, each taking one
day[16]. On coming before the emperor with Bantillas[17] the boy
greeted his father very civilly but did not speak a word[18].

loqueretur vitam suam haberet.

16. 175. *Ilkane a day tuke to defend.* In all the French prose MSS (A and L-versions) the *bois Saint Martin* is mentioned as the place where the masters will stay while the youth goes to court, in order to be able to come forth and defend him, each on his own day. The ME MSS also have this, cf. CR l. 482 *Boys Saynt Martine.* We do not find it, however, either in *BSS* or in HF and HL.
17. In *BSS* the youth when going to the emperor is accompanied by Bantillas, similarly in D*. In most of the French prose versions it is said expressly that he goes on alone or with the emperor's messengers.
18. 185. The prince is received by his father the emperor amidst musical rejoicings. This is original in *BSS*, and found nowhere else, as far as I can ascertain. In D we read *les menestreurs faisoient leur debvoir ...* In CR the emperor is not mentioned at all: it is the empress who goes to meet the prince and takes him to her room.
19. With *BSS* 213-24 cf. the French prose A-text, e.g. MS. McCl.179: *sire dist ele est cou chi uostres fiex que ie voi. dame oil. mais il ne puet parler. ce poise moi. Sire dist elle baillies le moi et se il onques parla ie le ferai parler se ia mais le doit faire. par ma foi ie le baillai bien parlant as .vii. sages. li emperes prist son fil par le main et le bailla a lempereis et li ualles ne dist mot. ales dist li emperes biaus fiex auoec li. cil ne losa contredire. Si sen ala apres li en sa cambre* and St.J.CII *Sire. fait elle.est ce vostre filz. dame fait il oil. mais il ne parole mie. ce poise moy. Sire fait lempereresse sil onques parla bailles le moy. et ie le feray parler sil doit iamais parler.*
20. 235 *to your swet youthhed ... I haf kepit my madinhed.* CR 511 reads *Vnto the, sir, so God me rede, Have I keped my maydenhed*; Br. 446 similarly, D* 467 *My body, maydenhod and alle, I haue tokyn hyt to thé*; Ars.3152 has *si vous ai gardé mon pucelage*; likewise other A and L-MSS; HF *pour l'amour de toy j'ai gardé ma virginité*, HF *propter amorem tuum me ipsum virginem custodiui.* In the H-version she offers him pen and ink and he writes down that he rejects her. This seems very illogical and foreign to the story; it is not found in the Hebrew version *Mishle Sendabar* either (see Section XIV).
21. 248 *Your callit son is bot a devill*; CR 553 *He was neuer cumen, sir, of thi blode*, Br. similar, D* 498 *For soth he nys nouȝt thy blode; Hit his a devel, and his wode*; St.J.CII *Il ne vous est riens ... cest ung deable*, BN 95 similar, Ars.3152 *Il ne vous es de noient Car il est fors dou sens*, L p. 11 *Il ne vos est riens, c'est un vif deable*; HL *Iste non est filius tuus, sed est dyabolus*, but HF *A devise cestuy ne fut jamais vostre filz, mais est ung ruffien et tresdesloyal ribaulx.*

ARBOR

22. In none of the other versions known to me is the burgess's name given; here it is used to rhyme with *wele*. In D* the owner of the tree is a knight.
23. In HF p. 72 the fruit of the tree has the property of healing even leprous patients. None of the other versions correspond to this, and HL p. 14 *quicumque infirmus excepto leproso de fructu commedit, sanitatem perfectam inuenit* seems quite the opposite; cf. *BSS* 315 f. In CR 626 the tree is called *a faire pine-appel tre*, in D* 598 *an appul-tre*.
24. In *BSS* the shoot starts to grow after the burgess's return from *merchandis*. In CR the shoot is there when the burgess returns. In the French A-versions the shoot has shown itself before he goes *en marcandise* (BN 95, also L, &c.) In H the *marchandise* is not mentioned.
25. 338. *The ȝoung tre na better sped*, but CR has *þe ymp ... wex ful fast*, similarly Br. 585.
26. Similarly in the ME MSS and the French A-versions. In L p. 14 the young tree

205 When the empress heard that he had arrived, she came into the hall to see him, and the emperor told her that the youth could not speak[19]. Then she took him with her to her room, promising to make him speak, and there offered herself to him, saying that she loved him[20]. When she saw that he refused her, she tore her face with her nails, shouted for help and when the emperor came and saw her injuries, she told him that the young man had tried to rape her[21]. At this the emperor ordered his son to be executed, but his councillors pleaded for a pro-
255 per trial of the boy, and the emperor promised them that he would let him live for the next night at least. The empress, on hearing this, showed great despair, and as a warning she told her husband the story of the tree (ARBOR).

ARBOR

291 A burgess, called Cornele[22], had an orchard, in which his favourite tree was a beautiful pine-tree[23], which he recommended to the special care of his gardener, particularly when from the root a new little pine-tree[24] started to grow. When it proved barren, his gardener advised him to have the branches of the big tree taken off to let the small one get more air. However, since this did not help either[25], he had the old tree hewn down completely[26] and his fellow-citizens greatly lamented his folly[27].

351 The empress then told the emperor that he was the noble tree, his son the young tree, and the false gardener the seven sages who wished to destroy him. The emperor was convinced and ordered his son to be hanged the following morning.

366 As the youth was being taken to the gallows, the first sage came riding by and went to the emperor to tell him that it was against the law for the boy to be put to death, and threatened him that if he had his son executed he would meet with as bad a misfortune as did a certain knight. The emperor wished to hear about this and the sage consented to tell him, provided that the youth were brought back to the court. When this had been done, Bantillas told the story of the dog that saved his master's son (CANIS).

grows very well and in the end the old tree is hewn down altogether. In H when the old tree has been hewn down the young one also dies, thus defeating the object of the story of the empress, viz. to show how a young tree (the prince) can cause the death and destruction of its parent (the emperor).

27. 347-8. The only parallel to this is in HF where people start to *mauldire* the owner of the tree (p. 73); in HL p. 15 we find something similar.

CANIS

28. The story is told of *a knycht of this cite* (392); in the French A-MSS we find *Il auint iadis en ceste ville* ... (Ars.3152, BN 95, McCl.179, &c.). In the ME MSS CR the events occur *in this same ceté*. In K 1165 the scene is laid in Rome, where it is, however, not a tournament but a bear-baiting which takes place; in D p. 6 it is a *chasse de l'ours*.
29. The day of the tournament is not specified in *BSS* and H, but cf. Ars.3152 *.i. jour com apelle le roi des diemences cest li iours de la trinite*, similarly McCl.179, Gg.I.1 and L; BN 95 has *un soir de la trinite*. CR, A*, E have *on a day of the Trinitė*, B *on the day of the Trinitė*, D* 745 *in May*. K 1199 has *a Pentecouste*, D p.6 *une feste solonnelle a Penthecostes*.
30. The knight, as in *BSS*, is usually indicated as the host; in CR he is just one of those taking part.
31. In most versions the baby has three nurses, each with her duties mentioned. In D* 754 there are *two* (rhyming with *goo*); in *BSS* there is only one nurse, in ll. 431 and 450.
32. In H there is moreover a favourite falcon, which, on seeing the snake, awakes the dog by flapping its wings. In H and *BSS* the cradle is not taken to the foot of the wall as in the other versions. Consequently the struggle of the dog and the snake takes place indoors.
33. 469 ff. *The grewhound quhen he saw the knycht/Waikly rais as he best micht. His lord full hartlie couth he fawne* ... HF p. 78 has *le levrier comme il avoit de coustume se leva contre son maistre et luy fit feste comme sy le vouloit saluer*; HL p. 18 *Leporarius, cum dominum suum vidisset, surrexit, sicut potuit, et applausum domino suo fecit*. In the French versions this is described very well and at greater length, cf. for instance BN 95 p. 9* *Li leuriers connut le cheual son singnour et sot bien que ses sires estoit uenus Quant il loi parler, si sailli em pies, si malade come il estoit, et en vint a lui et li mist ses .ij. pies deuant enmi les pies.*
34. 476. *Quhen he had strikin of his hed* as in all the French versions, cf. Ars.3152 *si li coupa la teste*, K 1384 *Si li a la teste colpee*, HF p. 78 *d'ung seul copt luy coupa la teste*, and HL p. 18 *caput leporarii vno ictu amputavit*. In the ME version the knight hits the dog on the back, cf. CR 885 f. *With his swerd on the rig he hittes And sone in sonder he him slittes*. For D* see next note.
35. D* is different from all other versions here, when it comes to looking at the cradle:

In towarde the halle he hym drowe,
And the lady with hym nam.
Into the halle sone he kam:
The grewhond hys lorde syghe,
And sete bothe hys fete on hyghe
Oppon hys brest to make solas;
And the more harme was.
The knyght drow out hys swerd anoon,
And smot out the rygge boon.
The knyght comanded anoon ryght,
Bere the cradyl out of hys syght.

CANIS

405 A certain knight[28], very fond of jousting and tournaments,
had set a day[29] for a great tournament near his castle[30], and
when the time for this had come all his family and house-
hold[31] went to see it, so that nobody stayed within the
castle to guard his baby son, except the knight's favourite
greyhound[32]. A snake, seeing the house empty, wanted to kill
the child but the greyhound fought with it and after a long
struggle killed it. The floor was covered with blood and the
444 cradle overturned, but the child had fallen in such a way
that it had not been harmed and it just slept on.

When the baby's nurse on her return saw the blood on the
floor she gave a shout and fled; the lady, meeting her, asked
her what the trouble was, and the nurse told her that the
greyhound had killed the baby. The lady fell to the ground
and lay there, tearing her hair. When the lord came in and
heard that his son had been killed by his favourite grey-
hound he went to the hall and was greeted kindly by the ex-
hausted dog[33], but he drew his sword and killed it[34]. Only
then did he look at the cradle[35], where he found first his
son safe and sound and afterwards the dead serpent.

480 Understanding that the dog had saved his son and greatly
regretting that he had listened to his wife's words, he broke
his spear in four pieces and vowed that he would go on a
pilgrimage to the Holy Land[36].

493 After this tale Bantillas said to the emperor that far
greater harm would come to him if he killed his son because
of the words of the false empress. The emperor promised that
the youth would not die that day, but the empress wept and
cried and told the emperor another warning story: the tale of
the boar and the herdsman (APER).

APER

525 There was a boar that killed practically everyone who came
into the wood[37] where it lived[38]. A herdsman[39], seeing that
he could not escape the beast, climbed into a tree. The boar

Ther stood a man that was glad
To do that the knyght bade,
And bare the credyl out in hys arme,
And sawe the childe hadde no harme.
In hys arme the childe he hent,
And into the halle he went,
And sayed, 'Alas, thy good grewhond!
869 Hire isti sone hole and sounde.'

D* is on the whole rather clumsy; it probably suffered a good deal at the hands of its copyist(s), but in this place it shows originality and contains an excellent description of the meeting of master and dog, and of the finding of the living child. It is original, too, in that the knight does not go into exile (see next note) but *Into hys horchard thay way he nome, And to a fische pole he come, And for dule of hys hounde He lepe in and sanke to gronde* (882).

36. Similarly in H. In the French A-MSS the knight goes into exile, it is not stated where. In CR, A, E and B he goes *into the woddes wilde And to the forest* (CR 920). CR also mentions that he goes *barfote*, cf. the French texts, e.g. Ars.3152 *Lors sassist & fist descauchier & caupa les auant pies de ses cauches Et se mist a la voie sans regarder feme ne enfans. Et sen ala en essil sans retour pour le duel de son leurier*. The fact that in the knight breaks his spear in *four* parts as against the *three* pieces mentioned in HL and HF may be due to the demand of the rhyme *four : owre*.

APER

37. 527. *In this cuntre nocht fer heir west, Sumtyme thar stude a fair forest.* Cf. CR 963 and some of the other ME MSS: *Sir, a litel here by west was sumtime a fair forest,* but after this there is a clear divergence. Campbell ascribes similarities like this to 'the sameness of the ME romancers' vocabulary' (p.lvii). In this case the authors were probably at a loss for a word to rhyme with *forest*. See also expl.note to line 527.
38. The forest where the boar lives does not belong, as it does in H, to an emperor who offers his daughter and the succession to his kingdom to anyone who will kill the boar, cf. VATICINIUM. In most versions the ownership of the forest is not mentioned.
39. No reason is given here why the herdsman should have gone into the wood. In the A-version he goes because he has lost one of his beasts, in H because he realises that by killing the boar he will not only advance himself by gaining the hand of the princess, but will also exalt his whole lineage. When he is attacked he climbs a tree on which he finds the fruit with which to assuage the boar.
40. 563-4. *And clawit him softly on the bak, Syne on the same, I wndertak.* In CR 1009-11, as in *BSS*, the boar is 'clawed' first on the back, then on the belly; in D* 978 the herdsman *clavde the bore under the syde* alone. In the A-version the place where the herdsman scratches the boar is not specified, neither is it in H.
41. The queen's explanation of the allegory as rendered in *BSS* is not unlike the one found in H. In CR 1021 we also find the queen saying *Thou ert the bare* &c., but there is no clear parallel. In the French A-versions there is no allegorical explanation.

MEDICUS

42. 639. *Bot Ypocras no way wald wend,* &c. In CR 1123 *Ypocras thoght lath to gane,* in D* 1062 Ypocras does not go himself because he *was ale olde And hys blode wax ale colde,* Br. 1025 *Ypocras wende ne miȝt*; in H Ypocras

with claws and tusks tried to uproot the tree, but the herdsman, as a last resource, threw to the animal some of the fruit of the tree so that it stopped to eat this. In the end it had eaten so much that it could only lie down. Thereupon the herdsman slid down from his perch, scratched the beast on its back[40], then on its belly, until it fell asleep and he then killed it with his knife.

569 The queen explained to her husband that he was the boar, his son the herdsman, the fruit the fair words of the sages[41]. The next morning at the emperor's command the hangmen took out the youth again, but the second sage, Maxillas, intercepted them and told them to wait. Going to the emperor he expressed his doubt as to the loyalty of the queen, and after the boy had been brought back to the palace the second master told the story of Ypocras and his disciple (MEDICUS).

excuses himself, but to test his nephew he sends him to the king. In A Ypocras says that he cannot go, without giving a reason for this. In K Ypocras is ill when summoned by the king: *Malades fu, n'i pot aler* (1714), similarly in D.

43. As in the A-version the doctor asks for the urine of the sick prince and both his parents. In CR the doctor asks only for that of the child, and in D* he sees that the child was *mysgettyne* (1076) merely by looking at him for a while. In K and D there is nothing about seeing the urine of the parents and the son. In HF Galliein visits the child, sees his urine, feels his pulse, then takes the queen aside. In HL Galienus asks for the parents' urine after he has seen that of the sick prince.

44. 673ff.'*Say ȝe that in effek, Thy hed sall gang than of thi nek!' 'Na hed haf I bot ane' said he, 'and gret misfortoune happinnit me, Gif I come hidder that hed to tyne...'* Cf. HF p. 122 *'Se je sçavoye que vous tenissiez pour chose certayne ce que vous dites, je vous fairoie couper la teste de sus les espales'. Et il luy respondist: 'Et je vous dis que cestuy roy n'est point le père de cestuy filz; mais je ne suis pas venus cy pour dire que je perde la teste ne que je soie ainsy guerdonné comme vous dites. A Dieu vous dis'*; HL p. 47 *'Si scirem quod talia ex corde diceres, caput tuum amputari facerem'. Et ille: 'Et ego tibi dico quod rex non est pater suus. Huc ad uos veni, ut premia reciperem, non, ut caput amitterem; et ex quo sic est, ad deum te recommendo. Provideatis de alio medico!'* There is a striking similarity here between HF, HL and *BSS*, none of the A-MSS available to me having anything like 'I have not come here to lose my head'.

45. *Artane* rhymes with *tane*; all the other versions have different names for the provenance of the queen's lover: HF p. 123 *ung roy de Bourgoigne*, HL p. 47 *dux de Burgundia*, K 1748 *signor de Frise*, D p. 13 *roy de Frise*; the L and A-versions have him come from *Namur*. In most of the ME versions he is the earl of *Nauern(e)*; in D* 1098 we find *a prince hire bysyde*.
The name *Artane* does not figure in either Flutre's or Langlois' tables of medieval proper names (see Bibliography under Reference Books), nor in any other related source. It is, however, found in James Joyce's *Ulysses*, Penguin edn, p. 103:32 and p. 218:11. In *Notes for Joyce, An Annotation of James Joyce's Ulysses*, Don Gifford with Robert J. Seidman, E.P. Dutton & Co., Inc., New York, 1974, p. 91, it is stated that Artane is a village 'three miles north of the center of Dublin'. To link the name of the earl in *BSS* with an Irish village seems very incongruous; we must therefore conclude that it was the wish for a word to rhyme with *tane* which made the author come out with this name, wherever he had found it.
In *Le Roman de Laurin, fils de Marques le Sénechal* (ed. Lewis Thorpe, 2 vols, Cambridge, 1950-58), one of the sequels of *Les Sept Sages de Rome*, we find *li duc de Athaines*, and *li roys de Sartaigne* (=Sardinia). Though faintly reminiscent of the form the *erle of Artane* there is nothing to suggest that these two might have any connection with the latter form.

46. 697 mentions beef and water; most of the ME versions have this (A*, Ar, E, B, F), also HF, HL, K. D has *char de beuf et pain bis moullié en eaue et aultres choses servans a garison selon la nature du pays de Frise.* The A-MSS available to me do not mention water. CR has *beres fless and bro with wine* (1200) to rhyme with *medicine*. D* does not mention at all how the child is cured.

47. 704. *The qwene in secret gaf fer mare*; a parallel to this is not found in A, L, K and D, but cf. HL p. 47 *Sed premia a regine occulte recepit* and HF p. 123 *il eust des dons de la royne secrètement assez et largement.*

48. In *BSS* the young doctor is killed after the finding of the *third* plant *into the bak* (740), in CR after the *second* stoop *in the rig-bane* (122);

MEDICUS

615 Ypocras, the famous doctor, had his nephew living with
him, but he never taught him anything because he was afraid
625 that the young man would exceed him in fame. Nevertheless the
nephew was in the meantime learning all he could, and when
the king sent for Ypocras because his son was ill, Ypocras
declined to go himself but sent the young man to test him[42].
The young physician went and examined the sick child and af-
terwards asked the queen, his mother, for specimens of her
own and her husband's urine[43]. Having examined these he asked
671 the queen who the father of the child was and she answered
'The king my lord'. 'No more than I', said the doctor, and af-
ter some bickering[44] she told him that the young earl of
Artane[45] had begotten the boy. When he knew this the doctor
695 fed the child with beef[46] and water and soon the boy was
cured. With great rewards[47] the nephew came back to Ypocras
and when the latter heard the way in which the patient had
been cured he concluded at once that the child had been con-
ceived in adultery.

713 From that day the uncle tried to find a way to kill his

in HF p. 124 after the second stoop Ypocras cuts his throat, while in HL p. 48 with a dagger after the third stoop *a parte posteriori ad cor percussit*. In McCl.179 and Ars.3152 the nephew is hit *parmi le cief*; no place is specified in L, BN 95, Br. In D the young man is killed at the first time he kneels down; no part of the body is specified. In K 1847 his heart is pierced with a knife at the first kneeling.
The A-versions tell us that Ypocras also burned his nephew's books; so does HF p. 124, but in HL, CR and *BSS* there is no mention of this.

49. In the A and L-versions Ypocras does not confess that he has murdered his nephew. In H he tells those who watch the performance with the barrel that his nephew might have cured him, but that he himself has killed him with his own hands. In K, which in point 42 is more logical than other versions, we find the illogical sequence of Ypocras first showing the barrel and later killing his nephew. In CR Ypocras knows his death is God's vengeance; not so in *BSS* nor any of the other versions I have seen.

GAZA

50. 822. *Octoviane*. Some form of this name is usual: HF *Octaviain*, HL *Octauianus*, St.J.CII *octouiens*, similarly Gg.I.1, Gg.6.28; Ars.3152 *oteuiiens*, McCl. 179 *octeuyens*, BN 95 *Octiuiens*, L *otheviens*, K *Octeviiens*, D* *Ottovien*, CR *octouian*, Br. *octouien* (B *octavian*); in D* no name is given.

51. 829. *twa knychtis*. Campbell in his note on CR 1319 says that A*, Ar, E and B add 'with the support of L(A) and D' that there had *formerly* been seven clerks, five of whom had gone to some other country (italics mine). This is inexact; in some MSS it is said that the five had gone *en conquest* and this is not equivalent to *formerly*. In some of the MSS the five are not mentioned; in BN 95 e.g. we read *Si* (i.e. *Octouiens) ot .ij. sages en celle uile remes*; L *Si ot .ii. sages remès en ceste ville. Li .v. en furent alez en conquest*, D* 1200 *Thorow the emperour comandement The five were out wente*. In K we equally find two sages; in D two wise men are the actors (p. 34). In *BSS* 829 we do not find any sages; the protagonists are two knights, just as in versions HF and HL.

52. In *BSS* the thriftless knight has one son and two daughters, no wife is mentioned; similarly in H, in Gg.6.28 and BN 95. In St.J.CII *il auoit .ii. fiex et .ii. filles*, as also in Ars.3152, Gg.I.1 and McCl.179, where it is stated that the elder son goes with the father, though we do not hear anything about the younger. In K *il auoit femme et biaus enfans Et bielles filles avenans* (2877-8). One son is mentioned; similarly in D. In CR there is mention of *ane of his sons*, and later of children and a wife. In D* 1204 he had *both childryn a(nd) wyf*. In Br. we hear of *his sone*, later of sisters.

53. In *BSS*, before they go, the father tells the son that he is hard up; similarly in HF p. 89, HL p. 25, K 2881, D p. 34, but not in A, L, CR, Br., D*. In many versions, as in *BSS*, the son remonstrates with the father when he first hears of the plan to break into the tower (Campbell: L(A), D, A*, Ar, E, B), not in CR, nor in D*. In K, too, the son protests (2885). In H the son approves at once of his father's plan.
In *BSS* they go in together, at least there is no specification as to who goes in, neither is there in D*, HF, K. In CR it is clear that the father goes in, while the son waits near the hole. In HL *ambo intrabant*. Campbell remarks: 'A*, Ar, E and B, in agreement with L(A) ... report that both father and son went in'.

54. The versions saying that lead and/or pitch is used in the cauldron do not mention how it is kept hot and fluid. K is the only one to do so, see 2935 ff.:

nephew and indeed a little later he bade him pick some herbs, and while the young man was stooping, he killed him with a
746 knife[48]. God punished him with a disease which neither he nor the doctors whom he had taught could cure; even a herb of such astringent properties that it kept water from running through holes made in the bottom of a barrel, could not staunch Ypocras's flux. After having made a clean breast of the murder of his nephew, Ypocras died[49].

780 The emperor, convinced by Ancillas's tale, promised that his son would not die that day. The empress, however, tried to make him see the necessity of killing the young man by telling him the story of the knight who stole the emperor's gold (GAZA).

GAZA

821 In the time of the emperor Octoviane (sic!)[50] there were two knights[51] who were greatly different; the one was miserly,
837 the other generous to such an extent that he spent all his money on feasts for his friends. The first knight was made governor of the king's treasury, the other became so indebted that he conceived the idea of stealing some of the riches from the king's treasury in order to be able to discharge his debts. Together with his son[52] he stole a great quantity of gold[53], but soon he had spent it all again, so that they had recourse to the same remedy.

884 In the meantime, however, the knight in charge of the treasury had noticed that there had been a theft, and he had devised a trap to catch the thieves if they should come again: a cauldron full of pitch near the hole through which the thieves had come in[54]. The father fell into this cauldron and could not get out. He told his son to strike off his head so as to prevent his identity from becoming known and his children from being dispossessed of their heritage[55]. The son obeyed and threw the head of his father into a bog[56].

921 The keeper of the treasury, on finding the headless body, had it dragged through the streets, ordering his men to enter

Quatre enclumes tres bien boillans
Bouterent ens bien roujoians
Pour tenir tiede longhement
Ne refroidast isnielement.

55. In *BSS* the idea of the beheading originates with the father and is carried out by the son without the slightest demur or remonstrance, as in H and D*. Campbell says: 'In D, p. 35, the father foretells the incidents of the following day, and instructs the son as to the course he is to pursue.' (Similarly in K 2954 ff.) 'In some of the variants of GAZA the idea of beheading the father originates with the son, who carries this idea into execution in the face of much remonstrance from the father'. In BN 95 the son remonstrates, as also in St.J.CII, Gg.I.1, Ars.3152, McCl.179, Br.; in L his protests are rather weak, similarly in CR.
56. The D*-version ends here with the son throwing the head *in a forme*; it states that he now had all his father's possessions and that he had *no sorow in hert* (1270).
57. *BSS*, A*, Ar, E, B, L, A, D and K say the son strikes himself in the thigh, F in the hand, CR in the cheek, HF *le visage*, HL *in crurem*.

PUTEUS

58. In most of the other versions the story first states that there was an old man who married a young wife whom he kept under lock and key, and only later mentions the custom of imprisoning anybody found outside after the ringing of a bell.
59. In version CR the man is called rich, not old, but in other versions, e.g. D, L, A and H, the fact is stressed that he is old, while his wife is young. Sometimes we also find that the young woman is of better standing than her old husband, but not so in *BSS*. In F the rich man had already been married twice, like the old husband in TENTAMINA in the CR-versions.
60. It is only in *BSS* that names are mentioned; this time they are not there for the sake of the rhyme.
61. *BSS* agrees with most of the known versions on the point that the young wife takes a lover later, but version CR tells us that the woman had a lover before she married, who came with her from the country where she lived before her marriage.
62. In CR, D*, L, A, D, K, there is no mention of the woman being locked in, nor of the keys under the pillow, nor of the old man being plied with wine, but cf. HF p. 82 *toutes les nuys de ses mains yl fermoit les portes et les clefz mestoit soubz sa teste au lyt*. HF p. 21 is similar.
63. Perhaps in *BSS* and H we may suppose contamination with INCLUSA (see p.169), but cf. *Disciplina Clericalis*, Exemplum XIV, *De Puteo*, (eds. Alfons Hilka and Werner Söderhjelm -Kleine Ausgabe-, Heidelberg, 1911, p. 20) which is much more like the tale of PUTEUS in the *BSS*-version than any other on the point of the woman falling in love with someone whom she sees passing the house, although *BSS* has the beginning of the A-version, while the curfew-part is not found in the *Disciplina Clericalis* version, see Appendix III and expl. notes to ll. 1934-60, 1990-2012.
64. The excuse that her mother was ill is found in *BSS* (1084) in common with H; HF p. 83 *j'ai esté demandée de la servente de ma mére pour aler a elle hactivement*; similarly in HL p. 21. In the ME versions no excuse is found. In A and L she argues that she had gone out of doors because she had been ill; in D because of an attack of toothache; in K she had been feigning illness the whole day (2139).
65. The testament is not mentioned in any version except *BSS* and H, cf. HL p. 22 and HF p. 84.

the house where they should hear the inmates making laments while they were passing with the body, and to arrest them.

The dead man's daughters indeed could not contain themselves when they saw what was happening to their dead father, and the brother, seeing he could not stop their outcry, made a large cut in his thigh[57] so that he bled abundantly. When the treasurer's servants entered the house he explained to them that his sisters cried because they feared he would bleed to death. The men believed him and went away. So the dead man's son lived on and forgot his father.

959 By means of this story the emperor was again persuaded to have his son killed and the next morning he ordered him to be taken to his execution. But Lentulus met the procession on its way to the gallows and went to intercede for the youth with the emperor. As before, the emperor reproached the sage angrily with the young man's dumbness, but was again prevailed upon to listen to a tale, this time about a perfidious woman who made her husband believe she had fallen into the well (PUTEUS).

PUTEUS

1003 No so long ago an emperor made a statute[58] that a bell should be rung at night, and that whoever was found outside after this, should be taken to prison and the next morning displayed publicly in the pillory, afterwards to be judged. An old citizen[59], Ysak[60], who had married a young wife called Ianot[61], lived with her in a house with but one window and one door which he kept locked, and the keys of which he hid under his pillow during the night[62]. The only pastime the young woman had, being thus kept under lock and key[63], was to sit and look out through the window. In this way she and a
1053 young man who happened to pass the house, fell in love with each other and in spite of all the difficulties they contrived to meet; she plied her old husband with wine and while he slept she stole the keys and joined her lover. After a long time Ysak wondered why she made him drunk so often and

66. 1146. *The chakwache has Ysak tane*, a very short statement; in H it is only slightly longer, but elsewhere we find a lengthy argument between the husband, the wife and the nightwatch; the guards even offer to allow the wife to take her husband into the house, so as to avoid his punishment, but she is adamant. In D* alone we find the husband telling the watchmen that he had a spaniel which had been lost for a week, and since he thought he heard it outside, he had gone out to call it in, but his wife said he was lying (1446) and that they must take him away.
67. The CR-version has (1669) *leuer war me oway be gane þan se þi landes fra þe tane*; D* 1500 has *I nylle no langer abide To se the wo that ye sal bytyde*. In A and L she says that she will go away in the morning. In HF p. 88 she says she would have gone home to her father, if she did not fear that in her absence evil would come to the emperor.

SENESCALCUS

68. The king's name is peculiar to *BSS*.
69. St.J.CII has *en puille*, similarly Gg.6.28, Ars.3152, McCl.179, Gg.I.1, BN 95; L has *Puile*, CR *Poyle and Calaber land*, Br. *Poile and Calabre lond*, D* *Pule*; K and D have *en Egypte*; H does not mention any country.
70. St.J.CII has *ung roy ... qui estoit sodomites*, similarly McCl.179, Ars.3152, Gg.6.28, Gg.I.1, BN 95, L; K *soldomite*, D *sodomite*. In Br. we find (1554) *(he) usede sodomiȝte*. In CR the king is not accused of sodomy, nor is he in D* and H. Ar l. 652 and E l. 1594 report illogically that he had great delight in women.
71. 1192. *His wame was rissyn with sic inflature ... that nane mycht se the wand of his wirilité*. The king's disease is rather diversified in the various versions: CR 1695, the king *on his members had bolnyng that the skin might nocht ouer it reche*, D* 1523 *Hys body al to-swal That hys body was al to-blaw, no man mycht his membris know*, Br. 1556 *A swele in his membres cam than. The skin miȝt hit nowt helde, Ne he miȝte him selue welde*.
In HF p. 127 the king's complaint is that he was *enflé merveilleusement et contreffays tellement que les femmes en avoient grant abhomination*; similarly HL p. 49.
A: St.J.CII ... *et enfla que tous ses membres furent en repost dedens lui*; McCl.179, Ars.3152 *il enfla & entra en grant maladie, si que tot si membre li retraioient*;
Gg.I.1 *e enfla si que tuit si menbre repristerent dedenz li*, similarly Gg.6.28, BN 95;
L *e anfla si que tuit li menbre li repostrent dedanz lui*;
K 1446 *si estoit il aussi cras Comme toriaus, et estoit gros, Dur le ventre comme le dos*;
D *il devint si gras que le ventre lui aloit jusques aux genoux, et si gros estoit comme ung tonnel*.
72. The sick king's diet is *breid of beir, made of a gryst, and (he) dranke bot water quhen he had thrist*, likewise in A*, Ar, E, A and L. No diet is mentioned in CR and D*. In K it is *Pain d'orge ... de l'eue sans del vin*. D, too, speaks of *pain d'orge et ... eaue*. In H no illness and no diet is mentioned; the king merely wants a woman for the night.
73. This remedy is mentioned in all the versions, except H (see above, 71, 72) and in some the seneschal says that he is afraid that he will not be able to find a woman, because it is universally known that the king is ill or too fat, but nowhere do we find that the king is *suspect of missalry* (leprosy), except in *BSS* 1220.
74. The nearest to this is found in version D *cent mars d'argent et plus*, and in K *cent mars d'argent*. HF has *mille florins*, HL likewise; L *xx mars*,

he decided to find out the reason. He feigned sleep and kept
1078 quiet when she stole the keys and left, but he locked the
door after her and waited for her to come back. When this
happened she found the door locked, so she knocked. Old
Ysak asked who was there, and she answered that she had been
summoned to her mother who was dying[64]. He, however, said
he knew that she had been with a young man and that he was
going to let her stay outside until the guards came and put
her into prison. Her protests he answered with the remark
'You are too hot and you will cool if you stand there!'
1105 She made her testament[65] there and then, leaving her soul
to God, her body to the church of Peter and Paul, and all
her goods to her husband, and said that she was going to
drown herself. She took a big stone and let it fall into the
well; when old Ysak heard the noise he rushed out of the
house to the well, naked as he was, but she, having stood
hidden behind the door, slipped in, locked it and remained
unmoved by his requests to be let in. So he himself was
caught by the guards[66] and put in the pillory next morning.

1153 Moved by this story the emperor promised that his son
would not die that day. When the empress heard of it she took
to her bed and said she would go back to her father[67], but
again tried to change the emperor's mind by the story of the
evil fate of a greedy steward (SENESCALCUS).

SENESCALCUS

1187 King Oulumpus[68] of Apillis[69] had a great hatred of women[70],
but when he fell ill[71], his physician, after having cured him
with barley bread and water[72], said that henceforward the
king should 'use women'[73], otherwise he would become a leper.
The king then ordered his steward to get him a woman, but the
1213 steward said he was afraid he would not be able to find one
since the king was suspected of leprosy. The king then pro-
mised a reward of a hundred marks[74] for the woman who was
willing to come, provided the steward got him a good and
fair lady. The steward, made greedy by this large sum,

St.J.CII *xx mars*, similarly Gg.I.1, Gg.6.28, BN 95; McCl.179 and Ars.3152 have *xx libres*. In the ME versions CR has *ten pownd of gold*. A*, Ar, B have *twenty marks*, E *twenty pounds*; D* mentions no sum, it says just *gold and silver*.

75. The wife remonstrates because of the sin she is ordered to commit, similarly in H. In the A-versions she says she will not do it and when her husband commands her she says *ie ne le feroie pour tere mangier* (BN 95) as in L; in D the word *pechié* is not found, only *faulte*. In K she only thinks of the *hontaige*. As to the ME versions, in CR the wife protests, not because of the sinful act, but because the king is *noght lufsom to lig by* (1740), Br. 1590 has *Hit is foul man to liggen bi, And þat wot euerich womman wel*. In D* the only reply of the lady is (1574) *Certis, syre ... Now thow lovest lytil my lyf,* after the seneschal has told her about the matter and said that she would *ben asolyd of (her) synne*.

76. In *BSS* there are three attempts to persuade the king to let the lady depart before he has the chance to recognise her as the steward's wife; similarly in H. In K and D there is a conversation between the king and his seneschal, who finally has to confess that the lady is his own wife. He does not come and go several times as in *BSS* and H. Neither in CR does the steward go away twice, but in a conversation with the king he informs him that the lady in the king's bed is his own wife. In the A-versions he opens the window when he comes into the king's bedroom for the second time so that the sunlight shines on the lady, and the king recognises her. In D* the steward comes to the king's bed once.

77. The steward is banished from the kingdom under threat of the most dire punishments should he ever return, in A and L. In *BSS* the king says *Thou sall hangit be*; in HF p. 129 *je te fairay morir de mort honteuse,* in HL p. 51 *morte turpissima eris condempnatus!* In D he is banished and sent away *sans riens emporter,* similarly in K 1641-2. In B the steward is ordered by the king to have molten silver and lead poured down his throat, a parallel to the end of the covetous emperor in VIRGILIUS.

78. 1274-5. *The king marijt this worthy woman For hir lawté with gret honour*. This may imply that he makes her his own wife, cf. l. 130; similarly in K and D the king marries the seneschal's wife himself. In H he keeps her with him as long as he lives and honours and rewards her greatly. In A and L *li rois maria la dame bien et bel en son pais.* In CR he keeps her for as long as he likes and then weds her to a baron of the land, likewise Br. *to a riche erl of that lond*. There is no mention of the wife's fate in D*.

TENTAMINA

79. The names are peculiar to *BSS*; they both occur in rhyme.

80. In some versions the man had been married before, in CR he had even been twice widowed, as also in L. K and D mention only one wife. F, D* and H do not mention previous wives. In some MSS the man even has children by the wife who later proceeds to make him a cuckold, viz. St.J.CII, Gg.6.28, BN 95. There are no children in McCl.179 and Ars.3152. Gg.I.1 says *li sage en od .ij.,* but it is not clear whether wives or children are meant.

81. The meeting of the mother and the daughter takes place soon after the wedding in *BSS* 1335, similarly in CR and Br. In HF this happens after *ung temps et qu'i n'avoient point d'enfans*; in HL p. 36 *Accidit quod per .iii. annos ad inuicem steterunt et nullam prolem habere potuerunt*.
In *BSS* the mother asks *at hir full tenderly ... how plesit scho hir lord*. In HF the mother greets the daughter *doulcement comme yl appertenoit et luy dit: 'O ma fille tres chiére, comme te va de mariage, et comme te plait ton bon mary?'* HL p. 36 has *Dic michi, quomodo de marito tuo tibi*

ordered his protesting[75] wife to spend the night with the king.

1247 In the early morning he wanted to conduct her discreetly away from the king's bedroom, but the latter said he was quite pleased with her and did not want to let her go. After two more attempts[76] the steward had to confess that the lady was his own wife. The king, disgusted by the steward's greediness, sent him away from his kingdom[77] and married the excellent lady[78].

1276 The queen at the end of this story urged the emperor to banish the seven sages, and he promised to have his son hanged in the morning. As the hangmen passed through the street with the young man, the fourth master, Maucundas, went to the emperor; the youth went back to prison and Maucundas told the story of the lady who was let blood (TENTAMINA).

placet! In D *Une fois entre les aultres, la jeune dame parla a sa mére;* no time is mentioned. In K mother and daughter meet on the occasion of an annual feast (2491) at the father's house, not in the church as in most of the other versions. L has *La dame fu environ son seingneur .i. an que onques folies ne fist ... Au chief de l'an, si vint au moustier, et s'asist joste sa mére.* In a number of the A-versions a period is not mentioned, only e.g. *lonctans* or *maint iour,* but in Gg.I.1 we find *vn ane,* as in St. J.CII.

82. 1344. *Als leif tharfor war me to lye By a stok of a widderit tré!* With this compare HL p. 36 *Tantum michi placeret iuxta truncum iacere, quam iuxta maritum meum,* whereas HF p. 105 has *j'aymeroie tant dormir, boyre, mangier avec ung porceau comme avec luy;* no such comparison is found in K, D, A, L, CR, Br., D*.

83. 1346. *Ane nother luf I will ches me;* CR 1916 *I most luf sum other man,* D* 1687 *I wyl have another love,* Br. 1743 *Ich moste haue som other loue.*
HF p. 105 *Je veulx aymer ung aultre,* HL p. 36 *alium volo diligere.*
D p. 25 *Je voeul faire ung amy,* K 2511 *Or n'i avra plus atendu Que je ne fache un cointe dru.*
A: St.J.CII *ie vueil amer,* similarly McCl.179, Ars.3152; Gg.I.1 *Ore sachez qe ioe voil amer;* L *Sachez que je veil amer;* Gg.6.28 *Je voel aillors amer,* BN 95 *ie uoil aillors amer.*

84. In *BSS* it is the mother who suggests the three tests, one after another, as also in CR and Br. In D* the mother merely suggests that the husband be tested, and does not in any case specify in what way; the young wife devises each of the tests. In H the three ideas come from the mother, as also in K; in D the first two means by which the tests are carried out are suggested by the daughter, but only in answer to questions asked by the mother, who then tells her daughter how to act. In the case of the third test she gives her instructions directly. In L the ideas all originate with the daughter, as also in Gg.6.28. In BN 95 the first test is the daughter's idea, the second the mother's, the third the daughter's again. In the A-versions the mother devises the three tests in St.J.CII, McCl.179, Ars. 3152 and Gg.I.1.

85. 1445. The woman strikes the dog on the head and *brak his harnis, sa was he deid,* after the dog has leapt on to the bed. In H she throws the dog against the wall, after he has leapt on to the bed (HF p. 109, HL p. 38). In A the dog lies down on the lady's furs; she snatches a knife from one of the servants, with which she kills the dog, striking him in the body, cf. BN 95, Gg.6.28, St.J.CII.
Ars.3152 and McCl.179 have: a servant *uint a la dame & dist dame que vous plaist. baille moi dist ele ton coutiel ameure. Cil le traist de sa gainne se li bailla & la dame le leua en haut al abaissier quelle fist del coutiel si feri le leurier el cors a mort.* In Gg.I.1 she strikes the dog with a knife *parmi les wiaus.* In L she strikes him with a knife she has at her girdle; no part of the dog's body is mentioned. In K 2652 the lady has borrowed a knife beforehand, even before the husband returns. The knife strikes the dog *ou cuel* (but this should probably be *cuer,* since the rhyme-word is *suer*). D p. 27 has ... *laquelle elle tua d'un coustel qu'elle lui bouta entre deux costes.* In CR 1983 she draws her knife when the dog lies in her lap and kills him; in Br. 1805 she is playing with the dog while he is in her lap, and when he hurts her, she draws her knife and kills him. In D* 1743 the dog lies in her lap and she kills him there.

86. In H she tells her mother that she wants a priest as her lover *before* the first suggestion of a test. Also the remark of the daughter that her parents married each other when they were both young *(BSS* 1479 ff.) comes before

TENTAMINA

1323 A rich old knight, called Gedeon[79], on the advice of his
friends married a young lady, called Pollema[79], in order to
beget children[80], but he was impotent; the wife went to the
church to have an interview with her mother[81] there, to make
1355 complaint[82] and to tell her that she intended to take a
lover[83]. The mother suggested that she should first test her
husband with some other offence, to see if he forgave her
easily[84]. When the daughter asked her how she was to do this,
the mother said that she might hew down a tree of which he
was very fond. The daughter did this and although the hus-
1410 band was greatly annoyed, he forgave her when she asked mer-
cy and 'let the tears fall'.

When she reported this to her mother, the latter advised
her to test him again, this time by killing his favourite
dog[85]. The daughter again carried out her mother's suggestion
1485 and again was forgiven when she wept at seeing her husband
aggrieved. She then told her mother that she intended to
take a priest as her lover[86], at which the mother was great-
ly shocked[87] and once more suggested a test[88]. The daughter

the tests. The remark is placed before the first test in K and D, but the mention of the priest after the second test. In the A and L-versions these two items come after the second test, as in *BSS*. In most of these versions the young wife wants to love the *provoire de ceste vile*, who has already begged for her love. In K 2684 and D p. 27 he is called *Guillaume, le chapelain*. The reason why she prefers a priest to a knight or squire as a lover in *BSS* 1494 ff. seems less logical than that in the other versions, where she says that the priest has as much ground as she has to keep a love-affair quiet, while a knight or squire might jest about it to others. Some MSS do indeed mention the fact that a secular lover would ask for clothes and jewels. D* is peculiar in the fact that though the mother suggests a third test, the daughter says she will test her husband no more and takes her leave. On her way home, however, she bethinks herself of a third test. F inserts another test before the final one: the killing of the husband's hawk (761-88).

87. 1486. *'Sanct Mary succour! quod the moder, 'Quhy a prest? ...'*; cf. HL p.36 *Que ait: 'O Sancta Maria, cur presbyterum? ...'*
There is nothing like this exclamation in K, D, HF, A or L.

88. With 1499-1504 cf. HF pp. 109 f.: *'Escoute moy', dit la mére, 'ceste foy, et jamais je ne t'empesche. Tu scés bien que tu es alectée du lac de mes mamelles, et quant je t'enfantay je souffriz grans douleurs et oppressions incredibles pour toy; par toutes ces passions je te ammonète que tu ne me dedies de ma damande. Et fais veul a Dieu que jamais je ne te empecheray ne ne toy devieray de ton vouloir'*, and HL p. 39, which is very similar; this is not found in K, D, A, L, D*, Br. or CR.

89. With 1571 ff. cf. HF pp. 112 f.: *Quant elle fut au lyt bien debilitée, elle dit comme elle peut a la chambriér: 'Va incontinent a ma mére et luy dis qu'elle viegne a moy avant que je meure'. Quant la mére seut, elle vint prestement a la fille, laquelle dit a sa mére quant elle l'entendit: 'O ma doulce et chiére mére, je suis quasi morte car j'ay tant perdu de mon sang que je croy qu'i m'en fauldra morir'. 'Ne te dis je pas', respont la mére, 'que les hommes vieux sont grandement cruaulx et fort subtilz pour ce vengier des injures que on leur fait? mais dis moy maintenant se tu veulx estre amoureuse du prestre'. La fille, qu'estoit de son premier propos bien refroydée, dit a sa mére: 'Le dyable puisse confondre le prestre! ne m'en parlés plus, car jamais aultre n'aymeray que mon mary.'*
In the A and L-versions we find this said very succinctly, e.g. BN 95, p. 24*, 5-9: *et elle comenche a crier et a braire et manda sa mere, et elle uint a li. Et ele le salua et dist a li: Bele mere, morte sui; il ma fait sainier. Dont dist la mere: Ore bele fille, as tu talent damer? Si mait Dieux, bele mere, ie namerai iamais. Certes, bele fille, tu feras que sages.*

90. In some versions, e.g. CR, the mother is presented as trying to 'mend' her daughter right at the beginning of the story. In *BSS* the impression given is that the mother has known from the start how matters would end, when she said that old men are often cruel and will take fierce vengeance.

VIRGILIUS

91. The emperor has no name in *BSS*, K and D. In the A and L-versions he is called Cras(s)us. In HF his name is *Octoviain Cesar*, in HL *Octauianus*. In the ME MSS he usually has a name, some variant form of Crassus.

92. The clerk is called Virgile in all the versions, except in D*, where his name is Merlin.

93. *BSS* 1627 *Quha strykis me trow weile that I sall me revenge richt hastely!*
HF p. 115 *Celluy qui cy me frappera De moy vengier tantost sera.*
HL p. 42 *Qui me percusserit, vindictam in continenti accipiat.*

was to upset the great table on the occasion of a dinner her old husband was giving, and if he forgave her then, the mother said she would not object anymore.

1530 Thus it happened; Gedeon was very angry and the next morning he appeared in his wife's bedroom with a barber and had her bled to such an extent that she was almost dead[89]. Only then did she promise her mother that she would forsake illicit love[90].

1587 The emperor was dissuaded from his son's execution by this story, and the empress in reply induced him to listen to her tale of the mirror of Rome (VIRGILIUS).

K 3945 *Ki me ferra, je trairai ja.*
D p. 40 *Se nul me fiert je trairay tost.*
L p. 50 *Qui me ferra, je tre(s)rai jà.*
A, e.g. *Ki me ferra ie (le) trairai; qui me ferra ke trairai ia.*
CR 2179 *Whoso smytes me, knight or swain, Sone I sal smyte him ogayn.*
" 2185 *If ani man me smyte, I sal shote at him ful tite.*
Br. 1971 *Ȝif me smitez ani man, I sschete him anon agan.*

94. The name of the student is peculiar to *BSS* and serves as a rhyme for *found* in the preceding line; his nationality is not given. In A and L MSS he is *uns clers de Lombardie*, e.g. in BN 95. In K and D the person who hits the statue is *uns vesque ... de Cartaige, ung evesque du pays de Cartage.* In HF p. 116 *ung clerc*, HL p. 43 *quidam clericus* hits the statue because he thinks a treasure is hidden underneath; his name and nationality are not given. In CR he is a Lombard, as also in B. In D* the incident is not found at all; the fire and the well are not mentioned either.
95. He gave the image a blow (1634), as also in H, L, BN 95, Gg.6.28, Gg.I.1, McCl.179 and Ars.3152. In K and D the bishop strikes the statue with a stick. In CR the Lombard shoots at the image with a crossbow bolt, in Br. he gives it a blow.
96. *BSS*: After the disaster Vergil makes a tower with ten statues, each with a bell; in the middle of the tower stands the fairest statue with apple and mirror. H: At the beginning of the story Vergil makes a tower with as many images as there are provinces in the world, each with a bell; in the middle a statue with an apple of gold; between the fire and the fountains the statue with the inscription; there is no mirror. A: After the falling of the statue, which extinguised the fire, Vergil made two images which threw a ball to each other, and a marble pillar with a mirror (BN 95). In some A-versions it is specified that the two statues throw the ball on Saturdays, e.g. McCl.179, Ars.3152, also in K and D. In CR and Br. Vergil makes two images, one on the East wall, one on the West wall of the town, and a ball with which *the childer* played (CR 2204; i.e. presumably the two images; Br. 1994 *Wiȝ þat bal to gider þai plaid)*. In the middle of Rome he placed the statue with the mirror. In D* it is Merlyn who makes just the pillar with the mirror. Brunner's statement about this on p. xvi of his EETS-edition is wrong. In the English versions there are two images, as also in A (BN 95). In L there are no images; there is only the mirror *sus les pilers de marbre* (p. 51).
97. *BSS* 1653-60. None of the other versions has anything like this forecast that the tower would stand till the day that a virgin should bear a son.
98. *BSS* and H have three kings; K 4003 has *en Hongrie estoit uns rois*, likewise D; in L it is *li rois de Puile*, A *Puille*, CR *Poyle*, Br. *Poile*, D* *Pule*.
99. *BSS* and HF p. 116 have four knights, HL p. 43 has *.iii. milites*, *.iii. bachelers qui frère estoient*, but later *li deus freres*; A (BN 95) *.ij. bacelers qui frere estoient*, similarly St.J.CII, Ars. 3152, McCl.179, Gg.6.28 and Gg.I.1; K 4007 *quatre serghans*, D p. 41 *quatre sages* CR 2227 *twa clerkes*, similarly Br. and D*.
100. *BSS* has four barrels of gold, HF p. 116 *quatre tonneaulx pleins d'or*, HL p.43 *.iv. dolia auro plena*, L p. 51 *.ii. costerez d'or*, A-versions St.J.CII *2 costeres dor*, McCl.179 *.iij. barius de fin or*, Ars.3152 *.iii. baris de bon or*, Gg.6.28 *deus costeres dor*, BN 95 *.ij. costeles dor*. K p. 108 mentions four casks, D p. 42 *douze, charettes d'or en tonneaulx* and four barrels; CR 2229 two coffers of gold and silver, Br. two coffers, D* 1913 *twa coffyns of golde and of preciouse stonnys*.
Consequently we see that *BSS* has four knights, four barrels, four finds plus the mirror, BN 95 two brothers, two barrels, two finds plus the mirror,

VIRGILIUS

1617 In the time of a rich and covetous emperor[91] there dwelt
here (*sic*) a clerk Virgile[92]. He made an ever-burning fire
for the poor to warm themselves by, and a well for them to
drink from. Above these there was a marvellous statue with
bow and arrow, bearing on its forhead an inscription: 'Who
strikes me trust that I shall revenge myself!'[93] A student,
called Edmound[94], struck[95] the statue to see what would hap-
1644 pen. It fell into the fire which was extinguished forthwith,
and the well dried up. When this had taken place, Virgilius
built a tower[96] with then statues, each of which had in its
hand a bell, that would be rung in times of peril to the ci-
ty. In the middle of the tower he put the fairest statue
holding in its left hand an apple of gold and in its right
hand a mirror. When asked how long the tower would last, he
said it would stand until a virgin should bear a son; and so
it stood till Christ's birth[97].

1661 Three kings[98] living near Rome were always considering
how they could destroy the city, but whenever they tried
anything the statues rang their bells and the middle statue
showed in its mirror what the city's enemies were planning
to do. These kings then held a conference, and four knights[99]
offered to destroy the tower for four[100] barrels of gold.
Parliament consented and they went to Rome, stealthily hid

whereas L, pp. 51-3, has three, later two brothers, three barrels (one was hidden at the third gate but there is no mention of its being found), two finds plus the mirror.

101. In L, p. 52, they do not go away to dream the third night, but after the second find they say that they have dreamed of a treasure so large that all the horses of the king's court will hardly be able to pull it away. Horses are not mentioned in HF p. 118: ... *sy grans et innumerables tresors que se vous permectés qu'on les serche vous serés sy tresriche et puissant qu'en ce monde n'aura point a vous semblable.* In HL p. 44 we find the horses mentioned: *tantum latet de auro purissimo, quod omnes equi romani non portarent;* L p. 52 has *.i. si grant que à poine le porroient trère li cheval de vostre cort,* A (BN 95) ... *un si grant que a painnes le trairoient tout li cheval de uotre court,* as also Gg.6.28, Gg.I.1. In D p. 43 we find *ung mervilleux tresor tel que onques Ottovien ne Nabugodonosor n'avoient eu le pareil,* K 4111 ff. ... *si grant avoir ... K'il n'est hons nés ki le nombrast Et si n'est nus qui l'espuisast.*

102. In D, p. 43, the undermining of the tower is done during the day; at evensong the 'dreamers' stop working, saying that they intend to continue the next morning; they flee the town at night and the tower falls down without fire being put to it, killing a thousand persons. In K there is no fire either, but thirty houses are destroyed when the tower falls (4147). In L, p. 53, they work during the day; at midnight they come and set fire to the tower; similarly in A: St.J.CII, McCl.179, Gg.6.28, BN 95.
In HF, p. 119, they wreck the foundations of the tower during the night; they mount their horses and flee, without setting fire to the tower; before they are out of Rome it falls down. In HL, p. 45, there is a fire, however. In CR they stop working at nightfall, make a fire during the night, and do not leave the town until the image and tower have fallen. In D* the miners (dreamers) make a hidden fire; then they take their leave of the emperor and go home: 2044. *Thay were bot a lytil withouten toun That the pyler fel a doun;* cf. *BSS* 1805.

103. When he is about to undergo his punishment, the emperor is told by his executioners:

BSS 1824 *Thow thristit gold and gold sall drink.*
HF p. 120 *D'avoir de l'or as heu grant soif, Pourtant de l'or maintenant boy.*
HL p. 45 is totally unlike.
K 4153 *Or avoies, or couvoitas, Et par plenté d'or remorras.*
D p. 44 *Or avoies, or convoitoies, et par planté d'or mourras.*
L p. 54 *Or vosis, or convoitas, or auras, et d'or morras.*
St.J.CII *Or voulas, or en aras, or couuoitas, or en as.*
McCl.179 *Or amas, or couuoitas, or aueras & par or morras.*
Gg.6.28 *Or vausis, or couoitas & or auras.*
Gg.I.1 *Or voulis & or amas. or vouetas & or perdras e par or morras.*
BN 95 *Or mangue, or convoitas, et or auras, et dor morras.*
CR 2335 *þou sal be fild now, or we go, of gold þat þou has couayt so.*
Br. 2133 *Sire, for godes loue, þou hast mad þral þat was aboue.*
Nou artou ful, nou make þe heit, nou wiltou nammore coueit.

In D* they do not address him when they fill him with gold. Incidentally, it is not molten gold they use in this version but powdered gold (2066).

104. After the sage has saluted the emperor the latter says *Never worth thé wele;* HF p. 93 has *Jamais bien ne te soit,* HL p. 27 *Nunquam tibi bene sit.* Nothing like this is found in A, L, K or D.

one of the barrels under each of the four gates of the city and went to the emperor. They told him that by dreaming they could find things hidden under the earth. The covetous emperor liked the idea very much and so the 'dreamers', after having heen promised half of what might be found, retired to their lodgings. The following morning the first dreamer declared that he had seen a barrel of gold under the first gate of the city. They dug it up and the emperor was very
1775 pleased. The second, third, and fourth days similar things happened[101]. Then all four of them came to the emperor telling him that there was more gold under the mirror than all the horses in Rome could draw. After having asked them to see that no harm should come to the mirror the emperor allowed them to go and dig under it. During the night they thoroughly wrecked the mirror by undermining it and putting fire under it; subsequently they fled[102]. The great men of the town were very angry with the emperor; they buried him and poured him full of molten gold[103]; thus he died miserably.

1828 The empress, concluding, said that the emperor was the statue with the bow and arrow. The youth who struck it down was his son, the treacherous 'dreamers' were the sages, and she herself was the mirror of warning. He thought this a good story and promised to have both his son and the sages killed, but when the execution of the youth was about to take place the fifth master, Catoun, intervened[104] by telling the tale of the magpie (AVIS).

AVIS

1883 A burgess, Annabill[105] by name, had a magpie[106] that could speak[107] and so was able to tell him all that had happened while he had been away from home. His wife loved a knight[108] who visited her when her husband was away, and in spite of the woman's threats the magpie told her master, the burgess, everything, thus causing a quarrel between him and his wife.

On the next occasion, in spite of the measures the wife

AVIS

105. In none of the other versions does the burgess have a name. In the present tale his name is given as *Annabill,* 1886, not in rhyme; *Balaine* rh.w. *than,* 1973; *Balan* rh.w. *lemman,* 1983; *Balan* 1991 and 2035, not in rhyme; *Balan* rh.w. *than,* 2005; *Balane* 2052, not in rhyme.
The form Annabill shows a curious likeness to Amabile (*L'Amabile di Continentia,* a fifteenth-century work, edited by A. Cesari, Bologna, 1896, Collezione di opere inedite o rare dei primi tre secoli della lingua 37) which Dr. Alfons Hilka ('Die Wanderung der Erzählung von der INCLUSA aus dem Volksbuch der Sieben Weisen Meister', *Mitteilungen der schlesischen Gesellschaft für Volkskunde,* Breslau, Band XIX, 1917, pp. 29-72) calls the most important representative of the Erasto-cycle, Erasto being part of the *Versio Italica,* see Table of Versions, p. 187. In *L'Amabile di Continentia* the names of the seven sages are totally different from those in the other versions, the sequence of the stories is different, too, and four stories (PUTEUS, SENESCALCUS, AVIS and VIDUA) have been replaced by four others, so that it seems highly unlikely that the likeness Annabill/ Amabile could be explained from any possible contact between the two versions.
The name Balan is fairly common in medieval literature, cf. *Le Morte d'Arthur,* Book II, where the hero Balin has a brother called Balan, as also in the source of this story, the thirteenth-century prose romance *Roman de Balain.* In the ME romance *The Sowdone of Babylone* of c.1400 we find the Sultan's name given as Balan and as Laban; in the *Legends of the Saints* (ed. W.M.Metcalfe, STS, I. 13, 18, 23, 25, 35, 37, Edinburgh and London, 1887-96) a Bala(a)n occurs in *St.Katherine* (Chapter L), lines 443 and 449. Both Flutre and Langlois are negative on *Annabill.*

106. *BSS* 1887 *ane pyot,* HF *une pique,* HL *pica,* K *une pie,* D *une pique,* L *une pie,* A *une pie,* CR *a py,* Br. *a pie;* D* has a *popynjay* as in the Oriental versions.

107. *BSS* 1888. The magpie spoke *in Romane leid,* in A and L-versions it has *la langue romainne, langaige de Rome;* in HF, p. 94) the bird is taught *latin et ebrieu,* in HL, p. 28 *linguam ebraycam;* CR 2419 has *in Frankis langwage,* Br. *in Romayns langage, of Rome, Freinch*; in D* no language in mentioned. K 3097 has *El parloit si apertement Et si tres entendablement Autressi comme che fust fame,* and D p. 31 *une pie ... qui si proprement et bien parloit comme se ce fust une femme.*

108. *BSS* 1893. The lover is *a knycht,* in CR 2424 *anoþer,* in F a priest. In K 3176, 3211 he is a knight called *Gerart li fils Tierri,* in D p. 32 a knight, *Girard le filz Thierry* (cf. note 141 below); in HF p. 94 *ung biaul jeune filz,* in HL p. 28 *alium,* later *amasium;* L p. 56 says *ele amoit en vile;* A (BN 95) mentions the woman *qui amoit par amors en la uile.*

109. In none of the other versions is a mother found. This insertion about the lover posing as a fugitive, speechless and sword in hand, is a parallel of *Exemplum XI: De gladio,* as found in the *Disciplina Clericalis,* see expl. note to ll. 1934-60.

110. This is another insertion derived from the *Disciplina Clericalis,* see expl. note to ll. 1990-2012.

111. Similarly in HF p. 95: *elle et sa chambrière firent ung partuys et par celluy partuys gectérent du sablon, de l'areyne et des petites pierres et de l'eau assez largement,* as also in HL p. 29; in the H-versions there are no lightning and thunder-effects. In D, pp. 31-2, she orders a man-servant to drop water and gravel on the magpie and also to make the noise of thunder and with a handful of candles to imitate lightning; similarly in K 3137 ff. In L p. 56 she equips her chambermaid with water, pebbles, a ham-

had taken to prevent the magpie from knowing that the knight
was visiting her again, the bird perceived what was going on
and hardly had the lovers been together for an hour when the
burgess called at the gate. The wife's mother[109] handed the
knight a naked sword and told him to stand by the door and
1941 not speak a word. When the burgess came in and wondered at
the presence of the silent knight, his mother-in-law said
that the knight had been the victim of an assault and that
he had fled into their house for safety. The burgess told
the women that they had done very well; he thanked them,
took the knight with him and entertained him. When the
knight had gone the burgess went to the magpie and asked her
why she did not sing. She said that she could neither sing
nor smile, seeing how foully he had been beguiled by his
wife and her mother. These denied everything and said that
the magpie was telling lies.

1982 When soon afterwards the burgess went on a pilgrimage, the wife sent for her lover and in the middle of their festive dinner the burgess came back. The knight was hidden forthwith and the burgess announced that he was very tired and wanted to go to bed. The wife was completely at a loss but her mother said that first they should show her husband the new sheets[110] they had made together. While they were holding up the sheet for the burgess to admire, the knight escaped; the burgess did not notice this and even thanked the women for making him such cloth.

2012 After he had gone to bed his wife got a ladder and a maid-servant[111] to help her, and through a hole in the roof they poured pitch, tar, water and small stones on the magpie's head, all night long. When in the morning the burgess went to see how his bird was, he found her almost dead; she complained of the bad weather of the past night, and even more of the deceit practised upon him. At this the burgess marvelled greatly, since the night had been very fine. His wife then said this just showed the falseness of the bird, and the burgess went and asked his neighbours[112], who all said they had never seen such a beautiful night. The burgess,

mer and a burning candle and orders her to go on to the roof and fake a thunderstorm. A is similar, except for the pebbles (McCl.179, BN 95, Gg. 6.28). In CR 2452 the woman and her lover put up the ladder and go up to the roof; in Br. 2227 she goes up with a maid; in D* 2162 she sends a boy up to the roof, who produces the noise of thunder by breaking great blown bladders.

112. In D p. 33 he does not inquire of the neighbours but kills the bird at once after his wife's words, as also in K, BN 95, Gg.6.28. In HF p. 96 he goes and asks the neighbours, similarly in HL p. 29, L p. 57, McCl.179 and Gg.I.1, in Br.2265 and D* 2240; in CR 2511 he asks his household.

113. HF p. 97: He breaks his lance in three, goes off to the Holy Land and never comes back;
HL p. 30: he breaks his lance in three, sells everything he has, and goes to the Holy Land, never to return to his wife;
D p. 53 : he draws his sword and kills his wife, as in K 3261;
L p. 58 : he chases his wife out of the house, as in the A-versions;
CR 2533 : he beats her and drives her off; in version B he sends her to her lover;
D* 2252 : he kills the bird and that is the end of the story; nothing is found about the punishment of the wife; in the Hebrew version of the Seven Sages, *Mishle Sendabar,* the wife is not punished either, she is sent gifts and brought back to the house.
In F the woman and her lover, a priest, kill the husband.

SAPIENTES

114. The emperor's name is *Herod*, as also in L and in the A-versions St.J.CII, McCl.179, Gg.6.28, Gg.I.1, BN 95, spelled either *Herode* or *Herodes*. No name is mentioned in HF, HL, K, D. CR has *Herod,* Br. *Herodes, Herowdes, Erodes, Harowde;* D* gives no name.

115. In H the king when outside his palace is made blind by means of the subtle practices of the seven sages, but after some time they cannot undo their sorcery. In D* there is a fat emperor who is blamed by his barons for always staying at home. When he tries to ride out, his horse balks and refuses to go through the gate, and this happens at every gate he tries to pass, even when he rides other horses. In A and L he has a disease which makes him blind as soon as he wants to pass the gates. In K and D his horse balks at the city-gate whenever he wants to go outside the city.

116. When he asks the seven sages the cause of his blindness they say they want time to find Merlin, but a term is not mentioned here, as distinct from other versions. In HF p. 100 they ask for ten days, as also in HL p. 32; Merlin is not mentioned. In K 3319 they want fifteen days, in D similarly, because the moon is not in the right position until then. In L p. 59 they are given eight days after they have declared four days too short a time. As to A, in St.J.CII they are given fifteen days, after eight days were thought too short, similarly in McCl.179 and BN 95; in Gg.I.1 seven days are changed into fifteen. In the ME versions the numbers vary a good deal: Ar, R, E and B have seven, A* has fourteen, F has twelve days. On C* 2611 Campbell says: 'The original reading of the MS. has been imperfectly erased, and the space has been filled in with what I take to be *four skore; four* is quite legible, as also the *re* of *skore*. This reading, however, is unique.'

117. *BSS*: *Merlyng (Merling)* is found, we are not told how and where. There is nothing about his having no father. In HF p. 100 the child is called *Mellin;* he is among children playing in a street. As in *BSS* he interprets the dream of a man who had come to ask the seven sages for an explanation of

2025 convinced that the bird had been lying, wrung its neck, but hardly had he done so when he espied the ladder. Climbing up he found the hole just above where the bird had been sitting and the mess that had been dropped on the magpie's head. Seeing the truth at last he renounced his wife[113], chasing her from his house, broke his spear in three, and went to the Holy Land.

2079 The emperor again postponed the death of his son, but when the empress heard of it she sat in her bed moaning until the emperor came. Then she told him the story of the seven sages who deceived the emperor Herod (SAPIENTES).

SAPIENTES

2113 The emperor Herod[114] had seven sages who counselled him
in everything, while they also interpreted dreams for anyone
who had had one and brought them gold. Herod always stayed
within the city, for as soon as he went out of it he became
blind[115]. When he complained about this to the queen, she
said she thought his seven sages were to blame. He summoned
them and told them he wanted to know the cause of his ail-
ment. They asked for time[116] to find Merlyng[117] the marvel-
lous, and when he had been found they promised him great
rewards if he could solve the problem. On going to the king
2150 with him they met a man who had a dream to be interpreted.
Merling forbade him to give gold to the sages and told the
man what he had dreamed and the meaning of it. The man went
away and found that it had come about as Merling had said.
The sages were glad at this and took Merlyng to the emperor.
When asked if he could tell the emperor why he was blind as
soon as he went out of the city, he said he could tell him
the cause and the remedy. He went to Herod's bedchamber and
showed him that under his bed there were seven wells. If
these could be stopped the emperor would be able to see
when outside the city, and the only things with which the
seven springs could be stopped were the heads of the seven
sages. The king had all the sages beheaded and indeed all

this dream. The boy refuses to be rewarded, similarly in HL p. 33, where his name is *Merlinus*. There is no mention of the fact that he had no father. In K 3345 ff. we find *Cil enfes molt sages estoit / Icil varlés ot non Jessé / ki onques ne fu engendré / Mais d'une porre* (=powder) *concheü*. In D pp. 21 f. the boy (no name given) is found by the dreamer before the latter meets the seven sages and he interprets the dream immediately. When the dreamer meets the seven sages afterwards he tells them about the boy and leads them to him. In L p. 60 the child is called *Mellin* and he was *uns enfès qui n'avoit eu point de père*. They find him because they hear his friends reproaching him with being fatherless. In A the sages hear *que uns enfes estoit nes en Engletere, qui onques not eu pere*. They find the boy and his name is *Merlins* (BN 95 and Gg.6.28). In St.J.CII *ung enfant estoit nes en la terre qui onques not eu pere*; its name is *Mellins;* McCl.179 and Gg.I.1 have the same combination of *tiere (tere)* and *pere*, probable evidence of an earlier rhymed version, cf. note 136; the name is *Merlins* in both MSS. In CR 2620 the seven wise masters meet an old man who tells them that only a fatherless child can advise them, and they find it finally, because in a town one boy is beating another, calling him a *faderles lurdan* (2641); similarly in Br. In D* the clerk is called *Merlyn*; the emperor hears about him and summons him.

118. Most of the versions end with the mention of Herod's happiness at finding that he can leave the city without being blind anymore; in *BSS* 2224, moreover, Herod *has ordanit Merling His stewart, and gaf him till his hyre The governans of his hale empyre*. HL p. 34 has: *Merlinum ad divicias et honores promouit*; this is not found in HF. Compare D* 2423 *Than hadde Merlyn grete honour And lafte with the emperour*.

119. Between ll. 2234 and 2235 Craigie in his notes to this place assumes that 'a considerable portion of the text is missing, containing the tale of the sixth sage and the empress's reply to it'. Though the writing is continued without any indication of an omisssion the exhortation starting in l. 2234 is left unfinished. This may be due to the loss of part of the manuscript that Asloan was copying. It is interesting, however, that in the L-version we also find a divergence after SAPIENTES, cf. G.Paris, *Deux réd.*, pp.xvii and xix, where he shows that the end of the L-version is AVIS, SAPIENTES, NOVERCA, FILIA, Conclusion, whereas A has AVIS, SAPIENTES, VIDUA, ROMA, INCLUSA, VATICINIUM, Conclusion; he proves, moreover, that after SAPIENTES A has been derived from K. If we take this into consideration it seems unwise to assume that there is a large omission in the Scots version, since in L, too, the sixth master does not tell a story, nor is the queen's sixth tale found there. For another possible solution of the question as to how the potential gap originated see explanatory note to l. 2234.

INCLUSA

120. In the present version the knight comes from *Mobrig* and finds his beloved in *Hungry, Vngary, Vngry*. In HF and HL no names are given; in HF rather illogically the story is told by the queen, but Gaston Paris, op.cit., p. xxxii, has something to say in favour of this. In K the names are *Monbergier*, later *Monbrison* (4354) and *Hongrie*; in D no names are found. L does not have INCLUSA. In the A-versions the following forms of the names are found: Gg.I.1 *Montbergier* and *Hungerie*; McCl.179 *Montberengier* and *Hongerie*; Ars.3152 *Montberengier* and *Hungrie*; BN 95 *Montogier* and *Hongerie*; Gg.6.28 *Montogier* and *Hongherie*; St.J.CII *Mōberg*[2] and *Hongrie*; it is quite conceivable that a copyist might not understand the abbreviations and so might read *Moberg* here. Such a case may have caused the name *Mobrig* found in *BSS*. In CR the knight comes from *Hungery* and finds his lady in *Hungeri*!

the springs stopped flowing. When he rode out of the city he could see clearly, so he promptly made Merling his steward[118].

2227 After this story the empress urged the emperor to slay the seven sages[119]. He said that his son should die the next morning but when the youth was led to the gallows the seventh master, Cratone, came riding, prayed the executioners to tarry and proceeded to the palace. He promised the emperor that the following day his son would speak and, to warn him against trusting his wife, he told him the story of the knight who gave his wife away (INCLUSA).

In Ar, B, E, F and D* the knight lives in *Hungary* and finds his love in *Poyle* (E and F), *Puyle*(D*), *Pletys* (Ar), while no name for the latter is given in B. See also expl. note to l. 2265.

121. We are not told how long they travel, similarly in H. K 4247 has *trois semainnes,* D *trois sepmaines,* A *trois semaines.* CR has three months, as also Ar, E and F; B has one month, D* *thre wykkys and more.*

122. We do not hear any more about the squire. In HF the knight takes with him *serviteurs, chevaulx, or et argent,* in A *.i. sommier dor et dargent;* in HL *Ascendit dextrarius;* in K *un bon sommier ... d'or et d'argent,* not mentioned in D; in CR *horses and hernays,* Ar *gold and siluer,* F *golde and syluyr and odur thynge,* D* 2798 *hors and armes anon.*

123. In H the lady's husband is a king; in K he is referred to as *li sires,* D *le seigneur,* A *le sire, le segnor, li quens;* CR *an erl,* as also in B, F, Ar. In D* he is spoken of as *the lord.*

124. In HL p.140 the lady drops a letter *before* the tower has been built; similarly in HL p. 59, where the building is called a house; in K she drops him a hollow reed or rush; in D he builds stables for his horses. In A a hollow reed or rush is dropped before the building of the tower. In CR it is a letter, as also in E and F. In Ar and B she throws a rush, in D* she makes out of rushes a *karole* or wreath, which reaches all the way from the window to the ground. The knight explains the hollow rush as a sign that he should try to get into the tower and gain admittance to the lady.

125. In HF pp. 141 f. she does what he asks *après aucunes deffenses gracieuses;* in HL pp. 59 f. alone the lady is not willing to be the knight's lover, when he suddenly enters her tower; he threatens her with his sword, and his will is granted. But she does give him the ring. The tale may have been changed in this way because in H it is told by the queen; cf. also A. Hilka's 1917 article (op.cit., p. 36).

126. In *BSS* the mason who makes the secret passage is killed by the amorous knight. He is *not* indicated as a foreigner, similarly in H. In K the mason is a foreigner and he is killed after the work has been done; there is no burgess who has seen the mason making the passage and who therefore is also killed by the knight (see sub A below); in D p. 45 the mason is not a foreigner, but he is killed. As for A, in BN 95 p. 39* and Gg.6.28 the mason is a foreigner; he is killed; the burgess is also found in this version; in St.J.CII the mason is a foreigner; he is killed, but there is no burgess; Gg.I.1, Ars.3152 and McCl.179 are similar. In CR the mason is a foreigner and he is killed; in E he is no foreigner but he is killed;in B he is *newe* from a far country and he is killed, as also in Ar and F; in D* a mason and his brother make the secret passage; neither is killed.

127. In HF p. 142 and HL p. 60 the incident with the ring is rather different. The king sees the ring on the knight's hand when the latter has fallen asleep near a well on a hunting expedition, but nothing is said; when the knight understands that the king must have seen the ring, he feigns illness and hurries back to his house whence he returns the ring to the lady. In K the lord sees the ring when he and the knight are sitting together, but he does not remark on it. D omits the incident of the ring altogether. In D* 2921 the action with the ring is premeditated by the lady. In CR the earl keeps quiet about the ring, as also in Br. In A the lord says nothing about the ring when he sees it on the knight's finger. Therefore *BSS* is the only version in which a conversation occurs between the knight and the earl, after the latter has noticed the ring. Still it is consistent with what follows in connection with the lady's appearance.

128. In K 4475 the lady, on appearing at the dinner, wears new clothes and a wimple of silk: *si ot guimple ensafrenee de soie qui fu desguissee,* thus

INCLUSA

2265 In Mobrig[120] there was an excellent knight who in his
sleep saw a lady whom he fell in love with, and so he set out
to find her. The same night a lady in the kingdom of 'Hungry'
had seen her love in her sleep, but she did not know where he
lived. After having passed through many lands[121], the knight
and his squire[122] came to 'Vngary' and there in a city he saw
a lady sitting at a window whom he recognised at once as his
loved one; she saw him and knew he was the one she had seen
in her dream.

2291 The knight then went to the lady's husband who was the
king's steward[123], saying he had slain a knight in his own
country and could therefore no longer stay there, and offer-
ing to fight for the king and the steward. He was incorporated
into the king's guard and given board and lodging with a bur-
gess. He won great renown in battles, but always tried to
2315 find a way to get to the lady. He told the steward that he
could not sleep in a thatched house and asked for permission
to build a tower with a stone wall leaning against the ste-
ward's castle. His request was granted and he had a mason
make a secret passage to the lady's room, after she had
dropped him a love-letter[124]. Whenever the steward went out
he locked all the gates and took the keys with him, but the
knight got into the castle by means of his passage and he and
the lady became lovers[125]. In token of their love she gave

rendering it more credible that the lord should not recognise her; this article of clothing is not mentioned in D, where she is dressed in clothes her husband had never seen. In both K and D she puts on these clothes in her own room. In HF p. 144 the lady puts on, as in *BSS* 2421, clothes as worn in the knight's country. In HL p. 61 the knight just orders her to dress herself *vestimentis tuis preciosis*. In A the knight makes her put on *vne reube toute nueue fresce & nouele qui onques nauoit este vestue ne veue al pais. puis li fist afubler vne rice cape par deseure boutonee dessi a la boutine & li fist metre mlt rices aniaus en ses dois* (Ars.3152 and McCl.179 are practically identical, as are also Gg.6.28 and St.J.CII). In Gg.I.1 it is *une riche robe qil auoit de son pais aportee ... e vn mlt bele chape forree*. In CR she has new garments that no one in the country knows. In Br. he brings her down and makes her change into other clothes; in E, B and Ar it is a robe of his own country; in F *a robe of anodur ble, soch was non yn that contre*. In D* 2960 the idea of the second deception again originates with the lady. There is nothing about special clothes.

129. In HL p. 62 she changes back into her own clothes *upstairs*, which is consistent with the foregoing, likewise in HF p. 145. In K she takes off her clothes downstairs and after having reached her room she goes to her bed, where the lord finds her. In D she changes back into her normal clothes once she has reached her room, and afterwards feigns sleep. In A she changes back into her own clothes *downstairs*. In Br. she changes *downstairs* before she returns, as in CR.

130. *BSS* 2428 f. ... *him thocht baith be woce and taist It was his awne wyf werraly;* cf. HL p.61 *O sancta Maria, mulier ista in gestu, in loquendo, in facie, in omnibus aliis similis est uxori mee!*

130[a] *BSS* 2445. *Off body, colour, voce and cast Nor ȝit twa women lykast I trow for suth God never wrocht*; cf. HL p. 62 *numquam vidi mulierem nec aliquam creaturam tam similem tibi in gestu, in uoce, in loquela, in tantum ...;* HF p. 145 has once only *de parole, de manière et de faczon de dire, du vasage, des mains, de tout le corps*. A (BN 95) has ... *femes samblables de cors et de fachon et de chiere,* once only. K and D have no such enumerations, nor are these found in CR, Br. and D .

131. This is a rather tame conclusion, also found in K, D, A, CR; in D* he jumps from the tower and breaks his neck.

132. No musical catalogue occurs in K, D, A, L, CR, Br., D*. HL p. 69 has ... *XXIV tube eum diversis generibus musicorum ante eum cum omni melodya et honore;* HF p. 158 *Et tout devant furent vingt et quatre instruys a mener, jouer, et sonner de tous diverses instrumens a toute melodie et honnour, triumphe et jubilacion, et vindrent contre le palaix.* In the English versions (CR and Br.) the emperor goes to church first, then after mass he returns to the palace. In the H-versions the church is not mentioned at all. In *BSS* after 2527 it is not made clear that he goes back to the palace.

VATICINIUM

133. They (i.e. the father and son, for the mother does not accompany them in the other versions) go to visit a recluse in K and A; on the ship two *corneilles* alight; in D they go fishing and two *cornoiles* sit down on their ship. In the H-versions the parents are at table with the son when a nightingale appears; in HF p. 164 the father throws his son into the sea the following night, but not while sailing; in HL he throws him into the sea at once (p. 72); H shows further differences in specifying Egypt as the land which the son, called Alexandre, finally reaches and in which he attains such miraculous distinction. Also H combines VATICINIUM with AMICI, an early

him a ring that her husband had once given her. The knight
2369 slew the mason[126] who was the only person who knew of the
secret passage; thus the lovers could use it freely, he some-
times going to her, at other times she coming to him.

2375 One day at dinner the steward noticed the ring[127] on the
knight's finger; saying it was his own, he asked the knight
how he had come by it. The knight found an evading answer
and when the steward had gone to his castle the knight ran
through the secret passage, gave the lady her ring and was
gone. The steward came in hurriedly and asked his wife for
the ring and she, of course, was able to say 'Here it is!'
He then told her that he had seen a knight who had exactly
the same kind of ring, so that he had wondered whether it was
his own, but she said that she would guard the ring as her
own body!

2403 Some time afterwards the steward locked up his wife and
invited the knight to go hunting with him, but the knight
said that his love had come to marry him and that after the
marriage they would return to his country, since he had been
forgiven his crime. He asked the steward to dine with him to
meet his lady-love and later to give away the bride. The ste-
ward gladly granted this and went his way. The knight then
went to the lady and dressed her after the manner of his own
country with clothes he had brought with him, and when they
went in to dinner the lady sat at the head of the table with
her husband, who marvelled so much at her likeness to his
2433 wife[130] that he could hardly eat[128]. After dinner he hurried
to the castle; she took off the foreign dress, ran up to her
room, changed into her own clothes again[129], and was ready
for him when he came up. When he saw her he was greatly re-
lieved and told her that the foreign knight's fiancée had
come and that she was so like to her, his wife, that nobody
would be able to tell them apart[130a]. She answered him that
such things sometimes happened, and flattered him about his
generous attitude towards these foreigners when she heard
that he was going to give the bride away.

2459 The following morning the steward locked her in and went

version of the story of *Amis and Amiloun* (Campbell 1907, p. cxii). In D* father and son go to visit an island, when three ravens alight on their ship; in all the other ME versions father and son go sailing; in CR and E two ravens settle on the ship, in B and Ar there are two crows; in F they go sailing to a strange land and two rooks perch on their ship.

134. The son is twelve years old in *BSS*, the father is a rich man, similarly in K; D does not mention the boy's age, the father is a fisherman; in A the boy is twelve years old, the father is *.i. uauasor*; in H no age is mentioned, the father is *ung chevalier* and a *miles*; in CR the boy is fifteen winters, the father simply 'a man', as also in E, B and Ar; in F the boy's age is *vij yere*, the father is referred to as 'a man'; D* is differently conceived.

135. In K 4731 he lands on a rock where he stays for four days without food and drink, before a fisherman rescues him. In D p. 48 he finds a piece of wood to cling to, so that he arrives at a rock where he stays for three days without food and drink until merchants passing on a ship notice him and take him to their country. In HF p. 164 he swims to the other side of the water; on the fifth day he is rescued by a ship; in HL p. 72 he swims to a rock whence he is rescued by seamen after ten days. In A he reaches a rock and after three days he is rescued by a fisherman. In CR he swims to an island, where he stays for four days; then he is rescued by a fisherman; in Br. he comes to land on a rock, where after four days a fisherman finds him; in D* he climbs on to a rock whence he is rescued by a fisherman after two days and two nights.

136. This part of the story in the rhymed version K runs as follows:

4743. Il le mist dedens son *batel*
Puis l'enmena a un *chastel*,
Ki de grant maniere estoit *fors*,
A trente liues de che *pors*.

It is interesting to see that in many of the prose-versions traces of these rhymes are present:

BN 95 and Gg.6.28 ... *et maintenant le mist en son* batel *et lenmena a un* chastel *qui mout estoit* fors *qui fu .xxx. liues loing de la ou ses peres manoit;*

St.J.CII ... *maintenant le mist en son* batel *et le mena droit a un* chastel *qui moult estoit* fort, *xxx lieues loins du* port *la ou son pere le getta en la mer;*

Gg.I.1 ... *maintenant le mist en sun* batel *e lenmena tuit droit a vn* chastel *qi estoit mlt* fors *xxx luies estoit longe de cele* port *ou les peres le getta en mer;*

L (BN 2137) p. 99 *Meintenant le mist en son* batel *et l'enmena tout droit à .i.* chastel *qui estoit moult* fort. *.xxx. luies estoit loing de cel* port *où son pere le jeta en mer.*

No rhyme-elements are left in

Ars.3152 *lors le mist en son batel si li mena a sa maison .xx. lieues loing dou manoir son pere;*

McCl.179 *lors le mist en son batiel si lenmena en sa maison loing .xx. lieues en sus dou manoir son pere.*

D p. 48 has lost the rhyme-elements too: *Par la passèrent marchans en une nef qui l'enfant aperceurent au rochier, si l'accueillirent avec eulx et l'en ont porté en leur pays*, similarly HF p. 164: *Don les nautoniers vindrent a terre et mirent sus la navile cestuy filz qui leur sembla moult biau et tres gracieux. Et le menarent en ung pais bien loing et estrange.*

Cf. note 117 on the birth of Merlins in SAPIENTES, where traces of rhyme

to the church. He gave the bride to the groom with some fitting words and was asked to accompany them to their ship and to repeat the performance there, and so it was done. They sailed away and when he came home he found to what extent he had been beguiled[131].

2502 Concluding, Craton warned the emperor not to trust his wife and promised him again that the youth would speak the next morning and tell the whole truth. So the following day the sages went to the king's son, dressed him in precious clothes, and in a jubilant procession[132] brought him before the emperor. The youth fell on his knees before him and spoke, whereat the emperor wept for joy. Explanations followed and another tale, this time told by the youth (VATICINIUM), the story of the father who cast his son into the sea.

VATICINIUM

2563 A rich man passed over the sea on a pilgrimage[133] with
his wife and son[134]; a nightingale perched on the mast and
sang very sweetly, which caused the father to say that he
who could explain the nightingale's song would be very for-
tunate indeed. Then his son said that he could do this and
explained that the bird sang that he, the boy, would one
day be very highly placed and that his father would wash his
feet and his mother would hold the towel. The father was very
2593 angry as this and cast his son into the sea. The boy was
rescued at once by another ship[135] and later sold for twenty
marks to the steward of a castle[136] the ship came to. In
this steward's service he grew up to be a very lovable per-
son.

One day the king of that country summoned a parliament
and the steward went there, taking the youth with him. At
the parliament the king complained about three ravens which
were forever pestering him; he offered his daughter in mar-
riage and his kingdom in heritage to the man who could tell
the cause of the odd behaviour of the birds[137]. The youth
2648 then told the king that the two old ravens were the parents

are also referred to. Gaston Paris signalises similarity in rhymes between K and D, see *Deux réd.*, pp. vi f., and between A and K, see *ibid.*, pp. xviii f., but since he does not mention this case it seems useful to give it here, even though it is not relevant to the ME versions and *BSS*.

137. When the youth tells the steward that he can solve the problem the latter believes him at once, similarly in D* , Br. and H; differently in D, A, K, CR.

138. There were two old ravens and a young one; the mother left the father to look after the son in time of famine, as also in H; in other versions the three ravens are two males and one female. The older male having left the female in time of famine, the younger male has looked after her since; similarly in K, D, ars.3152, McCl.179, BN 95, Gg.6.28, Gg.I.1, D*, CR, B, E, F. *BSS* 2649 *ȝone twa ald ravinnis producit the thrid*, cf. HL p. 73 *Accidit quodam tempore, quando coruus masculus et femella tercium coruum produxerunt ambo inter se*, a striking similarity; none of the other versions uses the equivalent of *to produce*.

139. In *BSS* the king knows where his parents are living *(in sic a forest*, after having fallen *in gret purete)*.
HF p. 193 has *en son pais*, i.e. his former country; no mention is made of poverty; HL p. 88 *in longinquis partibus*; poverty is not mentioned.
D p. 49 *La maison du pére n'estoit pas loing*; he is poor and in need of help; K 4925 the parents are *au Plaseïs*; they have fallen into poverty; L does not have VATICINIUM. A (BN 2137) speaks of *Plesséiz*; the parents have fallen *en grant povreté* (L. de L., Appendix, p. 101); BN 95 says they have fallen into great poverty, have fled their country and have settled in that of the young king. They are now living at *Placeis*. Ars.3152 and McCl.179 say that they are poor and live *au plaisseis*, Gg.I.1 *au pleseiz*. In CR, having fallen into poverty, the parent have left their own country and have come to live in the town where their son resides as king. A vision informs the latter of their whereabouts. He sends two servants to *spir in stretes, vp and downe Efter a man of strange cuntre Newly cumen, hys whife and he*. In Br. there is no vision, the son just knows that they are in his own country after having become poor; in D* 3327 they are living now *in the toun of Plecie*, having become poor.

140. In most versions it is the father who is brought word of the coming of the young king, but in Ars.3152 it is the mother. Though on the whole McCl.179 is extremely near Ars.3152 they differ on this point, where McCl.179 agrees with the other versions.

141. No name is given for the father, neither in H, D, D*. In K he is *Gerart le fil Terri*, as also in A, e.g. *Girars le filz tierry*; BN 95 calls him *Garrain le fil Thieri*; cf. note 108 above. CR has *Gerard Nories son*, as also B and F; E has *Barnarde Norysshe sone*.

142. The statement in *BSS* 2718-20 has a clear parallel in the H-versions; in HF the story is told at much greater length but the young king towards the end says (p. 195) *Ce fut ... grant folie a vous de vouloir empechier la volenté de Dieu a la exaltacion de vostre filz*; HL pp. 89 f. ... *sed stultum vobis erat contra divinam voluntatem laborare*. K, D, A, L (BN 2137), CR, D*, Br. have nothing like H or *BSS*.

143. In HF the explanation of the incident between the queen and the prince is placed before the telling of VATICINIUM as also the revealing of the man posing as a lady-in-waiting (p.159); similarly in HL p. 69.

144. The lover disguised as a woman (*BSS* 2762) is found only in H-versions, cf. especially HL p. 69: *Pater, precipe ut coram omnibus spolietur et tunc apparebit sanctitas imperatricis et qualis puella in camera eius nutritur!* with *BSS* 2755 f.: ... *It sall opynly be previt Sa synfull lyf as scho has*

of the third[138]. In a famine the she-raven had flown away, leaving the male bird to look after the young one and see that it did not starve. Now, however, the she-raven was claiming her young again, on the ground that she had hatched it. The he-raven said that she did not deserve it, since she had left her starving young for him to bring up. They had come to the king for judgement and would not trouble him any-
2675 more once he had given it. The king then ruled that the bird who had saved the young one's life should have it, and the ravens flew away, never to be seen again.

Thus the youth got the king's daughter and ruled after the king's death. Then one day he thought of his father and longed to see his mother, so he sent out servants to find them[139] and tell them[140] that the king was coming to dine with them[141]. At his arrival his father knelt with the basin and his mother was on her knees with the towel, but the king made them rise and asked them if they did not know him. When they said that they only knew he was their king he declared himself to be the son who had been cast into the sea, and said that it was folly for man to go against God's disposition[142]. Afterwards he raised them to riches and dignity.

levit and with *BSS* 2768 ff.: ... *Tak this damysele, And spulȝe now that all may se Quhidder scho man or woman be, And quhat seruice wnder coloure He maid my fader the emprioure!* Botermans (p.15) says that among the Oriental versions of our story the Hebrew is the only one in which the disguised lover is found; cf. Hermann Varnhagen, *Eine italienische Prosaversion der sieben Weisen, nach einer Londoner Hs. herausgegeben,* Berlin, 1881, where he mentions a Middle Low German version which has the man in women's clothes, presumably an H-text. The motif is also found in Rolland's version which is derived from Wynkyn de Worde, whose source is an H-version. See Epstein, 1967, pp. 247 ff., where the tale IUVENIS FEMINA deals with this. In a note he says: 'In the conclusion of the *Historia* version of the *Seven Sages* the prince exposes the queen's intrigue with a youth who is disguised as one of her female slaves. Goedeke considers this incident as having been adapted from the story *Iuvenis Femina* [in *MiS.*,in] *Orient u. Occ.*, III (1866), 394. This view was upheld by Landau (op.cit., p. 48 f.). Campbell however feels (*A Study*, p. 16) that since this story appears in no other Western version, we can only infer that it was a late incorporation on the part of the *Historia* rather than a carry-over from the lost Western original.'

2722 The king's son then explained what had happened between the queen and himself[143] in her bedchamber and the emperor ordered her to be burned. But the young man asked for a pause; then he caused all the ladies-in-waiting of the queen to come to the assembly and showed that one of these was a man whom the queen had had as her lover[144]. The emperor decreed that the man should be drawn and the empress burned, and thus the youth was saved and became emperor after his father's death.

CONCLUSION

The preceding comparative study reveals that in *The Buke of the Sevyne Sagis* there are a number of striking similarities with the H-versions:

PROLOGUE 1. The consistent decrease of the number of years that each master needs to teach the prince, see note 3 above;

2. the fact that one of the sages is called Craton(e), note 4;

3. in the observation of the stars the moon is not mentioned, note 15;

4. the *Bois Saint Martin* is not mentioned, note 16.

ARBOR 5. The owner of the tree is criticised by his fellow-citizens, note 27.

CANIS 6. The day of the tournament is not specified, note 29;

7. the baby in his cradle is not taken to the foot of the wall; the fight between the dog and the snake takes place in the hall, not in the open air as in the other versions;

8. with *BSS* 482 compare HF, p. 78 *cogneu par certains signes que le levrier l'avoit mis a mort en deffendant l'enfant;* HL, p. 18 *per certa signa cognouit quod leporarius ob defensionem pueri serpentem occidit;*

9. with *BSS* 485 compare HF, p. 78 *et prist une lance par destresse et la frascha en troys parties, puis s'en ala en la terre sainte;* HL, p. 18 *Fregit lanceam suam in .iii. partes et nudis pedibus ad terram sanctam perrexit, vbi toto tempore vite sue vixit;* note 36;

10. after APER there is an allegorical explanation by the queen in *BSS* and H, not in A, &c.

MEDICUS 11. *BSS* 673 ff. is also found in H, see note 44;

12. *BSS* 679 is found in HL, p. 47 *Provideatis de alio medico!.* there is notning similar in HF or any other version;

13. with *BSS* 704 compare HF, p. 123, HL, p. 47; note 47;

14. Ypocras confesses having killed his nephew; this is not found in the versions A, L, K or D, see note 49.

GAZA 15. *BSS* 829 *Thar duelt twa knychtis* is in conformity with the H-versions; in other versions we find seven or two sages, see note 51. No wife is mentioned, see note 52.

PUTEUS 16. *BSS* 1035 *The dure he lokkit ilka day &c.*, see note 62;

17. *BSS* 1084 and H: she left the house, she says, because a messenger had come to fetch her to her mother, note 64;

18. *BSS* 1109: the mention of the testament is found only in *BSS* and H, note 65;

19. *BSS* 1146: the short shrift he gets from the guard and the wife is peculiar to *BSS* and H, note 66;

20. after PUTEUS mention is made of the empress's father in both *BSS* and H, note 67.

SENESCALCUS 21. In *BSS* and H the king is not accused of sodomy, note 70;

22. the wife resists because she is asked to commit a sin; note 75;

23. for the three attempts of the seneschal to induce the king to let the lady leave his bed see note 76.

TENTAMINA 24. No previous wives are mentioned, note 80;

25. HL also mentions the dry stick, note 82;

26. in H and *BSS* the dog jumps on to the bed. In all the other versions he either lies on her furs or hurts her when she is playing with him in her lap, note 85;

27. *BSS* 1499 ff.: there is a striking similarity with H on the point of the reminder that the wife was suckled by the mother, note 88;

28. *BSS* 1506: *I and thi fader to ...*, cf. HF p. 110: ... *la ou sera ton père et moy et les plus nobles de toute la cité*; HL p. 39: ... *in quo conuiuio pater tuus et ego erimus et omnes nobiliores civitatis romane*; no parallel to this is found in any of the other versions checked;

29. *BSS* 1586 *my lord alane*, cf. HF p. 113:... *car jamais aultre n'aymeray que mon mary*, and HL p. 41: *Numquam de cetero aliquem uolo diligere nisi dominum meum*, note 89.

VIRGILIUS 30. In *BSS* and H the story starts with the mention of the covetous emperor unlike the other versions which mention Virgil first;

31. the caption on the forehead of the statue speaks of revenge in both *BSS* and H to the exception of the other versions, note 93;
32. both *BSS* and H speak of a great number of statues, note 96;
33. in *BSS* and H there are three inimical kings; in all the other versions it is the king of Poyle who has evil designs on Rome, note 98;
34. both *BSS* and H have four knights and four barrels of gold, this in common only with K and D, see notes 99 and 100;
35. in the words said to the emperor who is about to be poured full of molten gold, in *BSS* as well as in H there is mention of drinking gold, which is found nowhere else, note 103;
36. see note 104.

AVIS

37. No candles are mentioned either in *BSS* or H; in the other versions these are used to imitate lightning, note 111;
38. see note 113; again *BSS* and H agree to the exception of all the other versions investigated.

SAPIENTES

39. In *BSS* and H it is Herod's wife who gives him good advice, as different from the other versions;
40. nothing is found in *BSS* or H about Merlin being born fatherless, see note 117.

INCLUSA

41. *BSS* 2334 *a luf letter*; in H we also find a letter, see note 124; in A-versions we often find an empty hollow reed, similarly in K.

VATICINIUM

42. See notes 138, 142, 144.

From the above it is clear that *BSS* and H must be related in some way, since they show a great number of points on which they agree to the exclusion of the other versions examined. The known H-versions have a different sequence of stories from that of *BSS* which conforms with the sequence of the A-versions, see Appendix VI, p. 446. Since Gaston Paris, *Deux réd.*, p. xxx f., has shown that the source of H must be some manuscript belonging to A, it seems probable that *BSS* is derived from an early H-version nearer to A than the known ones; the present text sometimes differs markedly from the versions of H extant, see e.g. notes 38, 107, 114, 127, 133, which makes the existence of an intermediate H/A-version even more probable, but of this possible H/A-version no manuscript has so far come to light.

Another possibility is that the author of *BSS* knew both versions A and H and made a new poem, allowing himself to be inspired by both, with an admixture from the *Disciplina Clericalis* in the stories PUTEUS and AVIS, which may have been his own contribution or may have figured in his model.

Whichever of these solutions is right, points 12 and 25 mentioned above, where *BSS* uses exactly the same wordings as HL, make it likely that the author of *BSS* knew a Latin H-version or a French one closely related to it (cf. note 103), or had one in front of him.

XIV. SOURCES AND ANALOGUES

The frame-story of the Seven Sages of Rome was one of the most popular romances[1] throughout Europe in the Middle Ages and also later as is testified by several extant eighteenth-century manuscript copies of medieval MSS (cf. Brunner[2], p. xiv, note 1: MSS. *e, ff, gg*), and by printed books of even later date; for a list of English printed versions see Campbell[3], pp. lx ff., and for American published forms ibid., p. xxi, n. 2.

Practically every European country has or had its version(s) of the *SSR*. C.Brunel (*Romania*, LXXVI, 1955, pp. 244-47) mentions versions in French, Provençal, English, Welsh, German, Latin, Italian, Spanish, Catalan, Danish, Swedish, Icelandic, Dutch, Hungarian, Russian, Armenian, Polish, Turkish and Greek. Campbell gives three versions that Brunel does not have: Bohemian, Bulgarian, Lithuanian[4], while he mentions the Scottish poem of 1578 by John Rolland of Dalkeith with the English versions[5]. Rolland himself called this book "The Seuin Seages, translatit out of prois in Scottis meter ...'[6]. Finally there is the subject of the present work, the Middle Scots *Buke of the Sevyne Sagis* in octosyllabic couplets of c. 1500.

Outside Europe there are versions in Persian, Arabic, Hebrew and Syriac, which together with a Greek and an Old Spanish version constitute the Oriental group, usually called *The Book of Sindbad*.

For a long time most of the scholars dealing with the subject assumed an Indian origin for this book about Sindbad and the Seven Wise Masters, the ultimate source of the story of the *Seven Sages of Rome*. In doing so they based themselves on a statement by a tenth-century Arab historian, Masᶜūdi, who in his chronicle *Meadows of Gold and Mines of Gems*, speaking of an Indian king Kurush, said: 'In his reign lived Sindbad, author of the Book of the Seven Wazirs, of the Teacher, the Young Man and the King's Wife. It is entitled *Kitab Sindbad*...'[7]

Authorities like Görres, Loiseleur Deslongchamps, Benfey, Goedeke, Comparetti, Landau, Clouston, Cassel, Botermans, Killis Campbell, Hilka and Schmidt all agree on an Indian origin for the story[8]. Although in 1884 Richard F.Burton, reviewing William A. Clouston's study *The Book of Sindibad* in *The Academy* (Vol. XXVI, p. 175), had already argued that 'the course of literature would be from Persia to India, not *vice versa*', there is no evidence that much attention was paid to his statement. In 1933 Jean Misrahi in his edition of MS. BN fr. 1553, the only complete MS of the *Roman des Sept Sages* in verse (the K-version, see Section XIII, pp. 131-32), states: ' ... *le* Livre de Sindbad *est nommé déjà par l'écrivain arabe Al-Ya*ᶜ*qoūbī vers 880, et Mas*ᶜ*oūdī (934-5) dans sa* Chronique *dit que Abân Lâhiquî (815-6) l'a mis en couplets rimés. Le prologue du texte grec dit que l'histoire vient d'une traduction syriaque d'un livre du Persan Moūsos. Donc, l'intermédiaire entre l'indien et l'arabe est définitivement inconnue, de même que la langue dont fut tiré le roman de Moūsos, probablement le pehlevi*'[9]. In 1956 in an article in *Medium AEvum* Jessie Crosland disputed the Indian theory[10] on the ground that there is nothing definitely Indian or Buddhistic about the story, and that no Indian original has been found, pointing out that the idea of Seven Sages of Rome may have been inspired by the Seven Sages of Greece.

In 1958 Morris Epstein submitted that the *Book of Sindibad* as we have it may have been of Hebraic origin[11]. 'Absorbed into the Persian stream of literature, it may have appeared in Pahlavi in the sixth or seventh century of our era. It had by then possibly, passed into Oriental Jewish tradition, whence it was translated into Arabic and embraced by the Arab world, as indeed the Torah was by the Koran. Cloaked in Arab garb, it made its way from one spellbound audience to another, until it reached the West.' In his edition of the *Mishle Sendebar*[12] Epstein mentions this point again; the agents of transmission may have been the Radanites (Persian *rah-dan* 'knowing the way'), 'the Jewish merchantmen who forged trade links in the ninth century by every available route between France and China, and the first Europeans, according to Louis Rabinowitz[13], to establish direct contact between East and West'. Epstein also cites contemporary evidence that these merchants spoke Arabic, Persian, Latin, the languages of the Franks, Andalusians, and Slavs, and that they went to India and China.

In 1960 Ben Edwin Perry in an extensive study adduced 'positive evidence that the Book of Sindbad originated in Persia or the Near

East'[14]. On p. 64 he gives a table showing the stemma of various versions, which differs considerably from the tables given by Clouston, Landau and Botermans. The latter's table has the advantage that it shows at a glance the approximate dates of the different versions. More recently Hans R.Runte, going over the same ground in his edition of one of the branches of the *SSR*[15], has given an excellent survey of the origins and transmission to Europe of this part of the 'matter of the Orient', going deeper into the matter than I have been doing here. Morris Epstein's edition mentioned in note 12 above, too, contains several very valuable chapters in connection with the *matière* of the *Seven Sages of Rome*.

Botermans' system, combined with data produced by Epstein, Perry, Runte and earlier scholars, results in the Table on pp. 186-87.

Perry also points out the existence in Persian of a *Book of Shimas* by a Greek author, which shows such close parallels with the *Book of Sindbad* 'that there can be no doubt that one of them influenced the composition of the other'[18]. He conjectures that the *Book of Shimas* dates from not long after the middle of the eighth century, that the *Book of Sindbad* is of a somewhat later date (around 800) than the *Book of Shimas* and that it has been influenced by the latter[19].

None of the versions mentioned in the table directly influenced the Western European versions with which we are concerned. In this respect, too, we can ignore the Spanish prose version *Libro de los Engaños* which belongs to the Eastern group, but which, though Spain at the time was a country occupied by the Arabs, is said to be nearer to the *Syntipas* and the Syrian *Sindban* than to the Arabic versions[20].

Summing up we may say that it is not known how the *Book of Sindbad* came to the West. Two obvious possibilities are usually postulated for works of this kind: by way of Byzantium, where many peoples were represented among the multifarious inhabitants and passing travellers, and by Arab channels issuing in Spain through the writings of Jewish translators and in Syria through stories told to the Crusaders. But cf. Epstein, 1967, p. 31, where it is stated that the Crusaders cannot have been the transmitters, 'for the *Seven Sages* was known in the West before the Crusades'.

Gaston Paris, who occupied himself intensely with the Seven

TABLE OF EASTERN AND WESTERN VERSIONS

The Eastern Versions[a]

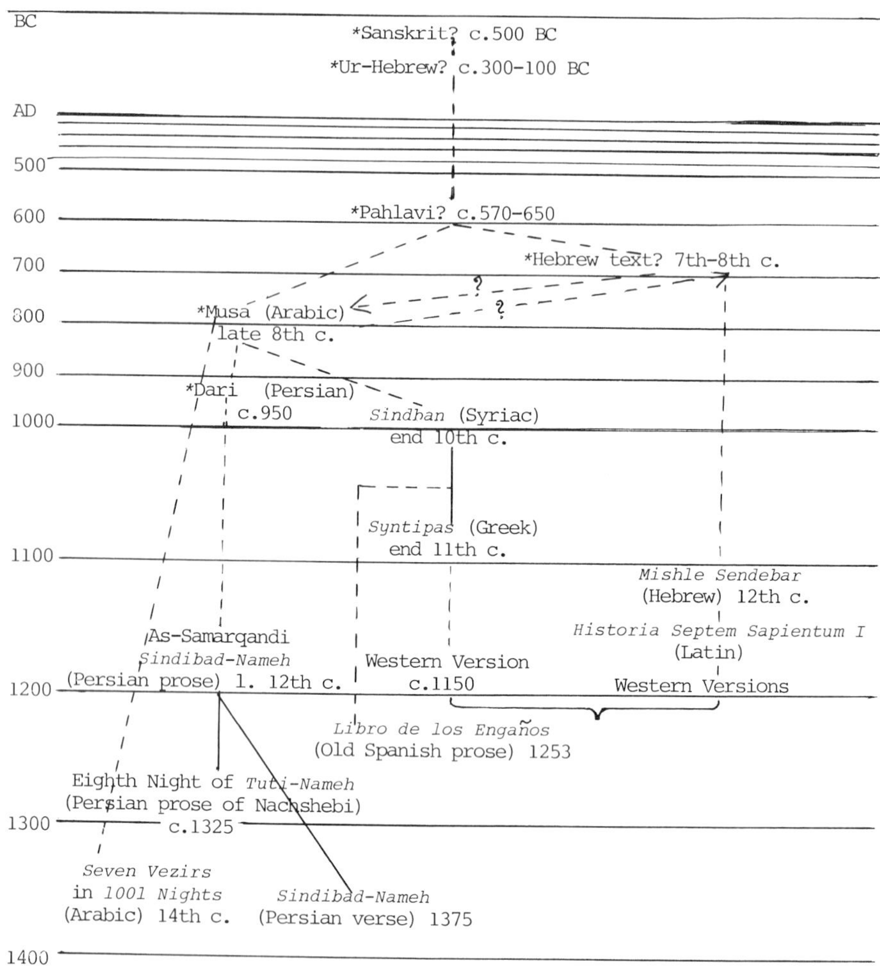

[a] The above names are explained on pp. 188-89.

TABLE OF EASTERN AND WESTERN VERSIONS

The Western Versions[b]

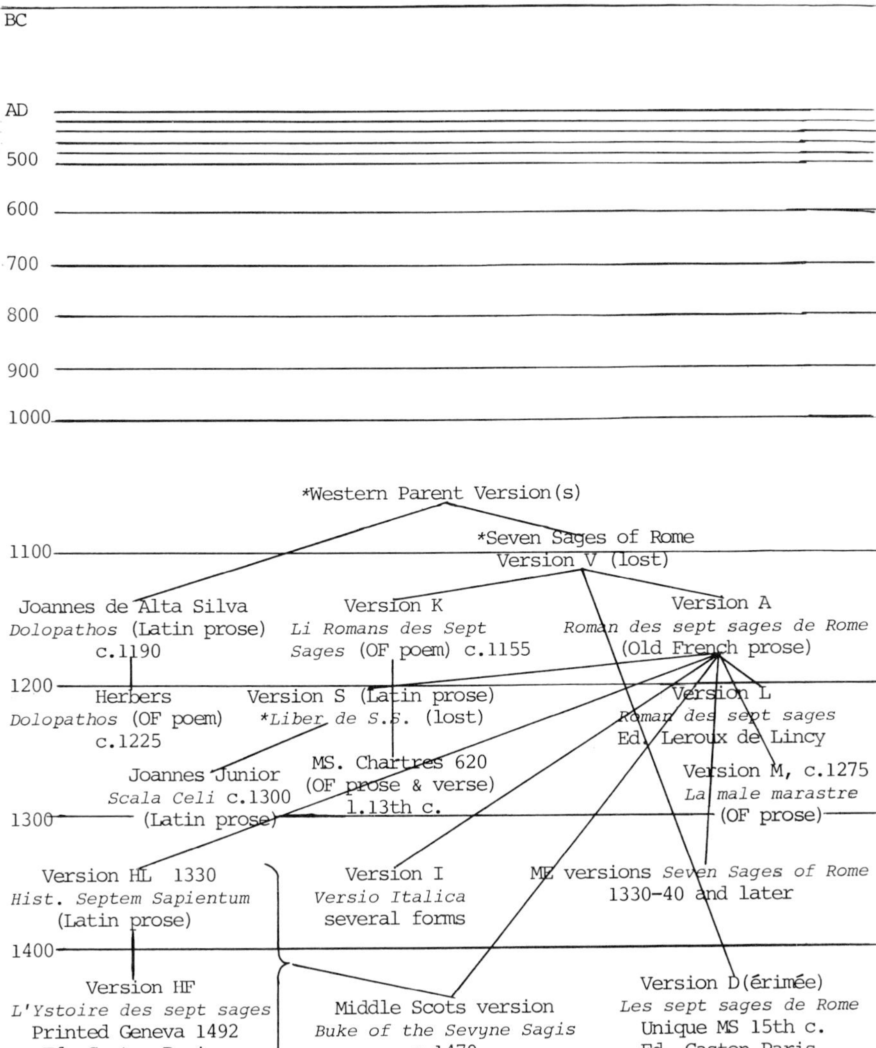

[b] The above sigla are explained on pp. 131-32.

Notes on titles used in Table of Eastern and Western Versions

*Musa[16]: Musa's translation of the Pahlavi *Sindbad* into Arabic, c. 800, parent version of a non-preserved Syriac form, which gave rise to the Syriac *Sindban*. According to the prologue of *Syntipas* (see below) the story had previously been written by 'Mousos (Musa), the Persian'.[17]

*Dari: the lost version of *Sindbad* in Dari (New Persian), mentioned by As-Samarqandi. He uses it as a primary source.

Sindban: the Syriac text published by Friedrich von Baethgen under the title *Sindban oder die sieben weisen Meister, syrisch und deutsch*, Leipzig, 1879. This text is preserved in a unique MS written before 1579.

Syntipas: the Greek *Book of Syntipas*, translated from the Syriac by Michael Andreopulos near Melitene on the borders of Syria in the last decade of the eleventh century; edited by J.F.Boissonade, Paris, 1828.

As-Samarqandi: the *Sindibad-Nameh* by Muhammad b. Ali az-Zahiri as-Samarqandi, c.1160.

Libro de los Engaños: the Old Spanish version, translated from the Arabic in 1253, first published by Domenico Comparetti in the Italian version, dated 1869, of his *Researches respecting the Book of Sindbad*, London, 1882, and more recently by John E.Keller, *El Libro de los Engaños*, Chapel Hill, North Carolina, 1953.

Tuti-Nameh: the eighth night of Nachshebi's *Tuti-Nameh*, derived from As-Samarqandi, c. 1325.

Sindibad-Nameh: poetical *Sindibad-Nameh*, 1375; contains nothing of the frame-story, and only one inserted story which is not also in As-Samarqandi, from which, in all probability, it was derived.

Mishle Sendebar: the Hebrew version *Mishle Sendebar* (The Parables of Sendebar), edited by Morris Epstein, *Tales of Sendebar, an Edition and Translation of the Hebrew Version of the SEVEN SAGES based on Unpublished Manuscripts*, The Jewish Publication Society of America, Philadelphia, 1967; see also his articles '*Mishle Sendebar*: New Light on the Transmission of

Folklore from East to West', *Proceedings of the American Academy for Jewish Research,* XXVII (1958), pp. 1-17, and 'The Manuscripts, Printed Editions, and Translation of *Mishle Sendebar', Bulletin of the New York Public Library,* 63 (1959), pp. 63-87.

Sages of Rome throughout his career, thought that the story first penetrated into the Byzantine world, then gained Italy and Rome. He suggested that it must have been in Rome towards the eleventh century that the story took a form not unlike the versions which have come down to us and that this form in its turn gave rise both by oral and written transmissions to two different versions: the *Sept Sages de Rome* and the *Dolopathos*[21].

In whatever way the matter of the Seven Sages travelled to the Occident, it changed considerably *en route*. In most of the Oriental versions the prince is educated by one master, not by seven as in the Western versions. In the Oriental group the seven wise men appear for the first time when the prince is going to be killed; then one by one they try to dissuade the king from executing the innocent creature and to impeach the woman, his accuser.

An exception to this is presented by the Hebrew version *Mishle Sendebar*[22], as hinted above, where one finds seven philosophers, mentioned by their names, the principal being Sendebar; in the other Eastern versions the wise men remain anonymous, whereas in most of the Western versions they have names. There are a few more features in *Mishle Sendebar* which connect it with *SSR*: the rivalry among the masters when it comes to the time needed to teach the prince; the fact that the prince is defended by the masters, not by the king's counsellors; and some details in the stories told, e.g. in APER the adversary of the wild boar is a man, not an ape as in some of the Oriental versions. Otherwise the *Parables of Sendebar* conform to the other versions of the Eastern group in that every wise man tells two stories, whereas in the Western versions every sage tells one story to counteract the poison dropped into the king's (emperor's) mind by each of his wife's tales. Campbell concludes from these and similar agreements that 'at best, they do no more ... than establish a slight probability in favor of the Hebrew version as the original of the Western group'[23]. But if we consider the popularity of the *Disciplina Clericalis*, of which it is known beyond doubt that it was the work of Petrus Alfonsi, a baptised Jewish author in Spain in the first decade of the twelfth century, it does not seem so unlikely after all that a Hebrew work like *Mishle Sendebar* should also have come West through similar channels (see Section XIII, AVIS, notes) and that here we have 'another case in which medieval Jewry conveyed the fruit of Eastern culture to the Christian world for the benefit of mankind as a whole'[24].

Generally speaking the Western versions show little affinity with the Oriental, except for the frame and a few of the tales. This is very aptly shown in a table by Landau[25]. Only four out of the fifteen to seventeen stories normally occurring in the Western versions of *SSR* are found in such Oriental versions as *Sindban*, *Syntipas*, *Mishle Sendebar*, *Sindibad-Nameh* and *Libro de los Engaños*, viz. CANIS, APER, SENESCALCUS and AVIS, and even then there are differences in details, like the ape/man divergence in APER just mentioned. Very appositely Mauricette Aïache observes[26] that the *Book of Sindbad* was *un lointain souvenir* by the time it reached the West.

On the continent of Europe the story of the Seven Sages of Rome in due course assumed a number of separate forms, of which the Western forms are mentioned in Section XIII. In connection with the present subject we can leave *Dolopathos* out of consideration, since its influence was very slight. There are two versions of this, a Latin prose text by Joannes de Alta Silva[27], probably dating from the end of the twelfth century[28], and a poem in Old French by Herbert[29], made from the Latin prose text about twenty-five years later. In *Dolopathos* as in the Oriental versions the prince has only one master; a feature peculiar to *Dolopathos* is the fact that it has only eight stories, as the queen does not tell any. Campbell thinks it reasonably certain that Joannes was in some way acquainted with some version of *SSR*, as *Dolopathos* has four tales in common with the latter, viz. CANIS, GAZA, PUTEUS and INCLUSA, whereas CANIS is the only tale which is also found in the *Book of Sindbad*[30]. In the present context we are mainly concerned with the French A-versions[31] because *BSS* in the Asloan MS. is largely an A-text, probably translated from French or Latin, see Section XIII, Conclusion. Of these French A-MSS a list is given below; for the sake of completeness and because of the inter-relationship of A and L the L-versions are included, following the list drawn up by Melle Aïache (op.cit., pp. ii ff.).

This list leaves out several items from Brunner's list (op.cit., pp. xiv f., note 1), viz. *e, ff* and *gg*, (presumably because these are eighteenth-century copies of items *d, bb* and *ee*), item *v* (eleven fragmentary leaves of the thirteenth-century MS BN nouv. acq. 1263, containing only three tales of *SSR*) and *xm* (Montpellier Bibl.Univ. 436). The latter is a *Dolopathos*-manuscript, however; see the P.S. in Gaston Paris's *compte-rendu* [32] of Hermann Oesterley's edition of *Dolopathos*, Strasbourg, 1873.

On the other hand several manuscripts are found in Melle Aïache's list which Brunner did not mention, viz. BN nouv.acq.fr. Nos. 12791 and 13521 which were acquired by the Bibliothèque Nationale between 1936 and 1952 and which Brunner therefore could not know about; item E, St.Etienne Bibl.Munic. No. 109 (anc. 965); item M, Mons Bibl.Publ. No. 330/215; item S^2, Berner Stadtbibl. No. 41; and item C, Cambridge Fitzwilliam Museum MS. MacClean 179 (see Section XIII, note 20).

LIST OF OLD FRENCH PROSE MANUSCRIPTS OF *RSS*

Brunner	Aïache		Date	Version
w	Ar	Arras, Bibl.Municipale 657	1278	A
i	B^1	Brussels, Bibl.Royale 10,171	13th c.	A
p	B^2	- - - 11,190	14th -	A/L
h	B^3	- - - 9,433	14th -	A
q	B^4	- - - 9,245	14th -	A/L
	C	Cambridge, Fitzw.Mus., MacCl.179	13th -	A
o	C^1	- Univ.Libr. Gg.I.1	14th -	A
s	C^2	- - - Gg.VI.28	e.15th c.	A/L
	E	St.Etienne, Bibl.Municipale 109	c.1300	A
x	F	Florence, Bibl.Laur., Ashb. 49	e.14th c.	A
u	Fr	Fribourg, Bibl.Munic. L 13	15th c.	A
k	L	London, Br.Libr. Harl. 3860	e.14th c.	A
	M	Mons, Bibl.Publique 330/215	13th c.	A
l	O	Oxford, St.John's Coll. 102	15th -	A
y	P	Philadelphia, Univ.Libr. 14	14th -	L
ee	S	Bern, Stadtbibliothek 354	14th -	L
t	S^1	- - - 388	c.1300	A
	S^2	- - - 41	13th c.	L

LIST OF OLD FRENCH PROSE MANUSCRIPTS OF *RSS* (continued)

Brunner	Aïache			Date	Version
	D	Paris, Bibl.nat.nouv.acq.fr.	13,521	end 13th	A
	G	- - - -	12,791	14th c.	A
g	H	- - - fds.franç.	93	1466	A
r	I	- - - -	95	13th c.	A/L
dd	K	- - - -	189	15th -	L
c	N	- - - -	1421	13th -	A
bb	Q	- - - -	1444	end 13th	L
a	R	- - - -	2137	13th -	A
n	T	- - - -	5586	15th -	A
aa	U	- - - -	19,166	13th -	L
b	V	- - - -	20,040	13th -	A
f	W	- - - -	22,548	13th -	A
hh	X	- - - -	22,933	13th -	L
cc	Y	- - - -	24,431	13th -	L
d	Z	- - - -	25,545	13th -	A
z	A^1	Paris, Bibl. de l'Arsenal	3516	1245	A/L
m	A^2	- - - -	3152	13th c.	A
u	A^3	- - - -	3354	15th -	L

The ME versions of *SSR*[33] have come down to us in eight manuscripts[34]; these are in chronological sequence:

1. A*: Auchinleck MS., in the National Library of Scotland, Edinburgh (pressmark Adv.MS. 19.2.1, No. 155), 1330-40[35]; dialect South-eastern English; edited by H. Weber[36] and by K. Brunner, op.cit.
2. R : MS. Rawlinson poet. 175, in the Bodleian Library, Oxford (Sum.Cat.No.14,667), middle of the fourteenth century; dialect Northern English (probably Yorkshire). Variants of this text on that of C* are given in footnotes by Campbell, op.cit.
3. D*: MS. Cambridge Dd.I.17, in Cambridge University Library, second half fourteenth century; dialect South East Midland with many Northern forms; edited by Thomas Wright, in the

Percy Society Publications, No. XVI, 1845.

4. C*: MS. Cotton Galba E IX, in the British Library; first third of the fifteenth century; dialect Northern English, probably Yorkshire; edited by K. Campbell, op.cit., pp. 1-145.

5. F : MS. Cambridge Ff.II.38, in Cambridge University Library, about 1450; dialect South Midland or Southern English, edited by Brunner, op.cit. The story AVIS from this MS was printed by Petras, op.cit., pp. 60 ff., and various shorter pieces are in Campbell's notes.

6. Ar: MS. Arundel 140, in the British Library, fifteenth century; East Midland dialect. Ll. 1-228 were printed by Campbell in his doctoral thesis[37] and in *PMLA*, XIV, 1899, pp. 1-107; edited by Brunner, op.cit.

7. E : MS. Egerton 1995, in the British Library, after 1469; London dialect; edited by Brunner, op.cit.

8. B : MS. Balliol Coll. 354, in the Library of Balliol College, Oxford, first half sixteenth century; Southern English dialect, perhaps Kentish; edited by Brunner, op.cit.

The investigations concerning these texts by Gaston Paris[38], Petras, Campbell and Brunner resulted in the conclusion that all the ME manuscripts were derived from an OF prose version of the A-type, because they contain the same number of stories in the same order, but that the problem as to which of the French manuscripts of the A-group had been the model must remain unsettled[39].

Brunner prints the following stemma of the English manuscripts[40]:

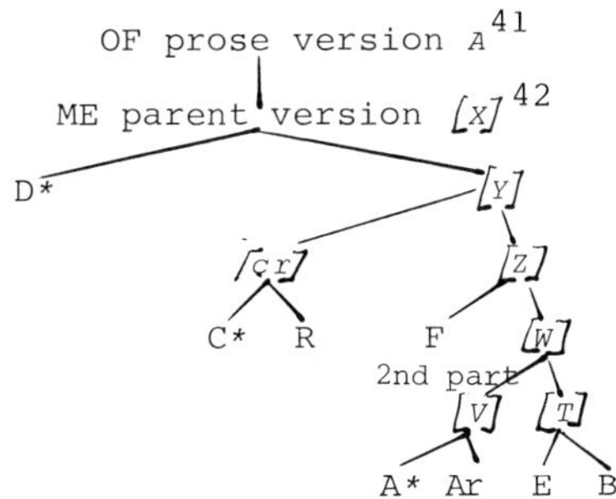

and suggests as an alternative that D* and *Y* might be derived straight from an OF prose version.

Campbell (p. xxxvi) and Brunner (p. v) agree that the Middle Scots *Buke of the Sevyne Sagis* has no connection with any of the ME manuscripts, and comparison of these with *BSS* shows that indeed the latter must have been created independently of the ME versions. Campbell does give some examples (pp. lvi f.) where *BSS* agrees closely with MS. C* and suggests that the agreement might be traced, as with MS. D*, to a development of *BSS* from [*X*], but he rejects this at once, judging that they are 'merely accidental agreements growing out of the sameness of the ME romancers' vocabulary'[43].

For my own opinion on the possible source(s) of *BSS* I may be allowed to refer the reader to the end of Section XIII.

Notes to Section XIV.

1. Objections might be raised to this denomination because the tales of *SSR* are more like *exempla* and *fabliaux* than romances, while the frame is not romance-like either, but since such authorities as J.E.Wells and Laura Hibbard classify *SSR* as a romance we may conform.
2. Karl Brunner, ed., *The Seven Sages of Rome (Southern Version)*, EETS OS 191, London, 1933.
3. Killis Campbell, ed., *The Seven Sages of Rome*, Boston USA, 1907.
4. Ibid., p. xxi.
5. This is the Scottish version referred to by Georg Buchner in his edition *Die Historia Septem Sapientum nach der Innsbrucker Handschrift v.J. 1342 nebst einer Untersuchung über die Quelle der Seuin Seages des Johne Rolland von Dalkeith*, Erlangen & Leipzig, 1889.
6. Ed. George F.Black, STS 3rd Ser., No. 3, Edinburgh, 1931.
7. Quoted by B.E.Perry, 'The Origin of the Book of Sindbad', *Fabula* III, pp. 1-94, Berlin, 1960, p. 3. See also p. 4 of the work mentioned in note 12 below.
8. For the titles of their works and many more on *SSR*, &c., see Bibliography, pp. 226-34.
9. Pp. x-xi.
10. Jessie Crosland, 'Dolopathos and the Seven Sages of Rome', *Medium Aevum*, XXV, 1956, pp. 1-12.
11. '*Mishle Sendebar*: New Light on the Transmission of Folklore from East to West', *Proceedings of the American Academy for Jewish Research*, XXVII, 1958, pp. 1-17.
12. *Tales of Sendebar*, p. 36. For fuller data on this title see note 22 below.
13. Louis Rabinowitz, *Jewish Merchant Adventurers*, London, 1948, p. 193, as mentioned by Epstein, op.cit., p. 386, n. 28.
14. B.E.Perry, op.cit., pp. 84 ff.
15. *Li Ystoire de la male marastre, Version M of the Roman des sept sages de Rome*, Tübingen, 1974, pp. xi-xiv. See also Section XIII, note 12.
16. The data in this list are for the most part derived from Epstein's article, see note 11, and from Perry's essay in *Fabula*, see note 7 above. Needless to say I do not know all the works

in the list at first hand as they do not directly concern *BSS*; I merely mention them for the sake of completeness.

17. Th.Nöldeke in *Zeitschr.d.d.morg.Gesellsch.*, XXXIII (1879), p. 521, previously suggested by Sylvestre de Sacy, *Notices et Extraits*, IX.405.
18. Op.cit., p. 93.
19. Op.cit., p. 94.
20. John Esten Keller, ed., *El Libro de los Engaños*, Univ. of North Carolina Studies in the Romance Languages and Literatures, No. 20, Chapel Hill, 1953; rev.edn, 1959.
21. Gaston Paris, *Revue de l'histoire des religions*, IV (1907), pp. 152 f. See also Jessie Crosland, op.cit. *Dolopathos* is referred to below.
22. Morris Epstein, ed., *Tales of Sendebar. Mishle Sendebar. An Edition and Translation of the Hebrew Version of the SEVEN SAGES Based on Unpublished Manuscripts*, Philadelphia, 1967.
23. Campbell, op.cit., p. xvii.
24. Morris Epstein, 'The Manuscripts, Printed Editions and Translations of *Mishle Sendebar*', *Bulletin of the New York Public Library*, 63, 1959, No. 2, (pp. 63-87), p. 65.
25. Marcus Landau, *Die Quellen des Dekameron*, 2. Edn, Stuttgart, 1884, opposite p. 340. See also Joseph Bédier, *Les Fabliaux*, 2e édn, Paris, 1895, opposite p. 136, and Comparetti, op.cit., p. 25.
26. Op.cit. (see Section XIII, note 6), p. 28.
27. *Joannis de Alta Silva Dolopathos, sive de Rege et Septem Sapientibus*, ed. Hermann Oesterley, Strassburg, 1873.
28. Gaston Paris, *Romania*, II, 1873, p. 501.
29. *Li Romans de Dolopathos*, ed. C. Brunet et A. de Montaiglon, Paris, 1856.
30. Campbell, op.cit., p. xx, but see Jessie Crosland, op.cit.
31. See Section XIII, p. 1.
32. *Romania*, II, 1873, p. 503.
33. This is the list promised in note 15 of Section XIII.
34. Cf. Paul Petras, *Uber die mittelenglischen Fassungen der Sage von den sieben weisen Meistern*, diss. Breslau, 1885; Killis Campbell, op. cit., pp. xxxvi ff.; Karl Brunner, op.cit., pp. ix ff.

35. Laura H.Loomis, 'The Auchinleck Manuscript and a possible London Bookshop of 1330-1340', *PMLA,* LVII, 1942, pp. 595-627.
36. Henry Weber, *Metrical Romances of the Thirteenth, Fourteenth and Fifteenth Centuries,* 3 vols, Edinburgh, 1810, vol. 3, pp. 8-108.
37. Killis Campbell, *A Study of the Romance of the Seven Sages with special reference to the Middle English Version,* diss. Baltimore, 1898.
38. Gaston Paris, *Deux rédactions du roman des sept sages de Rome,* Société des anciens textes français, Paris, 1876, p. xxvii.
39. Brunner, op.cit., p. xv.
40. Ibid., p. xxi.
41. The asterisks are mine, as explained in note 3 of Section XIII.
42. Hypothetical versions are in square brackets.
43. Campbell, op.cit., p. lvii.

XV. NOTE ON EDITORIAL METHOD

In the present edition the aim has been to present a diplomatic text of the *Buke of the Sevyne Sagis* which is more fully accessible than Craigie's in the STS-edition of the Asloan Manuscript, by introducing several changes. Craigie's treatment is entirely diplomatic; he printed as faithfully as possible the pages of the MS, even using a special type of large *a* where the MS had a letter which was different from the regular capital *A*. Scribal abbreviations were expanded in italics.

In this edition the following changes have been introduced. The use of capitals has been normalised, so as to conform to modern usage; each line now begins with a capital; capitals within the line have been changed to small letters where this accords with modern conventions, and proper names have been given capitals.

Punctuation, which is practically non-existent in the MS, has been introduced; it has been made to conform to modern usage and adapted to the lively style of the text; in the MS there are only occasional light slanting strokes, and these seem to have roughly the value of a modern comma, although sometimes they have no meaning whatever, as in line 1130 between the words *I* and *gar*, and in line 1498 between *of* and *lychtly*.

Hyphens have been introduced in words disjoined in the MS; independent words, joined in the MS contrary to modern usages, have been separated.

Abbreviations are expanded in italics in accordance with the spelling usual in the text when the word appears in full. Those of the present edition are generally the same as Craigie's, although there are a few to which a different value has been attached; a list of textual differences is presented in Section XIX. A full list of abbreviations with their expansions is given in Section XVI.

Other points in which the present edition differs from Craigie's are the following:

Flourished *r*, either r̓ or r͠, is not expanded; words in which they occur are also found written without the flourish, e.g. *augur(e)* 1701, 2641; *bair(e)* 524-5, 541, 545, and 532, 554, 567, 571. Flourished *d* (ð) is not expanded; it evidently need not mean *-de*, cf. ll. 165-6, *stude : gud*; 171-2 *besyde : aspyd*, where *gud* and *aspyd* end in flourished *d*. β is printed as *s* in agreement with the usage in *DOST*, except where it stands for *-is*: 1431 *pvni*ſβ. (In most MSS of the time we often find this combination of *s* and β to express plural or verbal forms: cf. Craigie's edition of the Asloan MS., Vol. I, p. 227, ll. 5 and 6 for the form *hou*ſβ 'houses' as against *hou*β 'house' in line 1 of the same page, and ibid., p. 232, l. 22, for *cau*ſβ 'causes'). β also stands for *ser-* (see Section XVI), and β*r* stands for *schir* 'sir'.

In cases where Craigie printed an *h* crossed like a *t* he meant to indicate a horizontal flourish over part of the syllable or word in which it occurred, e.g. 445-6 *sleuch : yneuch*, where both final *h*'s are written ħ. The same flourish is found in the case of final *n*, where the second minim is prolonged into a semi-circle: n̄, e.g. 119-20 *generacioun : confusioun*; 109-10 *ken : pen*. The flourish sometimes encircles the whole word, e.g. 195 *son*; 206, 207, 222 *on*. It has been disregarded in this edition.

Long *s* has been printed as *s*; *ff* at the beginning of a line is rendered by *F*; sometimes the MS has capital *F*, e.g. 550, 2494; *n* is occasionally indistinguishable from *u*, but this does not often present difficulties. The sign ⁊, used several times after the titles of the tales, is given as a full stop.

Scribal corrections and deletions, of which there are not many, are noted at the foot of the page concerned. Editorial insertions are enclosed in angular brackets.

Ornamental capitals are marked with an asterisk; there are only seven of these in *BSS*, the first seven; the others, not so marked, at the head of tales, were not supplied in the MS; their places were indicated by very small guide-letters, showing the scribe's intention of drawing them in later. Three capitals immediately following the first seven were probably taken from a parchment MS or document. They are red capitals *T* in lines 525, 821, and a capital *I*, also red, line 1883, cut out neatly and stuck on the paper of the MS (see Section I). The first letter of every page is usually slightly larger and more elaborate than the others, but not really ornamented.

The scribe does not distinguish between y < *þ (=th)* and *y (=y)*. Craigie uses for *th* a symbol y, very similar to the one used by the scribe, whereas for *y* in other functions modern typographical *y* is used. I employ *th* for Craigie's y as well as in those cases where *th* is spelled out in the MS.

ȝ as found in the MS has been preserved (usually standing for *y*, twice for *z*: 347 *citeȝouris*, 1019 *ceteȝener*), as also the *i* where modern usage has *j* in words like *iois, ioly*, &c., because the modern distinction between *i* and *j* had not arisen at the time of the execution of the MS. In DOST these words are to be found under J, but the actual *i*-spellings in the examples have been retained.

Accents have been placed on words like *cité, thé* 'thee', &c., in accordance with the usage in DOST in the headnotes.

The original foliation has been kept, as in Craigie's edition, but for greater convenience the text has been arranged into paragraphs in accordance with the tales and their introductions, and the Latin names of the tales commonly used in the literature dealing with SSR have been added in the margin and as running titles.

XVI. SCRIBAL ABBREVIATIONS AND THEIR EXPANSIONS

In *BSS* the following scribal abbreviations are used:

ↄ -*er* a back-curving loop or curl connected with the preceding letter serves as abbreviation in several cases. It stands for -*er* mostly at the end of a word but also within, e.g.

27 sou*er*ane	532 diu*er*s
33 deliu*er*, 399 deliu*er*ance	581 m*er*cy
79 chalm*er*	612 sist*er*
106, 1754 ȝist*er*day	685 w*er*itê
119 gen*er*acioun	1084 mod*er*
145, 153 lett*er*is	1110 pet*er*is
301 m*er*chandis	2014 ledd*er*
312 m*er*walous, 1063 m*er*walit	2140 m*er*lyng
338 bett*er*	2436 n*er*rest
402, 404-5 mast*er*	2536 reu*er*ens
412 wnd*er*tak	2571 w*er*ray
519 man*er*	2584 c*er*tanly

There are several cases where we find that a word, when written in full, has -*ir*, whereas the common abbreviation for -*er* is used elsewhere, e.g.*eftir* 15, 1195, 1335, 2403, and *eftirwart* 1017, beside eft*er* 317, 731, 839, and eft*er*wart 522, 722, 723, 744. Craigie expanded these words to eft*er* and eft*er*wart, the present edition to eft*ir*, eft*ir*wart.

-*er*/*ir*

Another example of this is found in eu*er* and neu*er* with their compounds, which, when written in full, are *evir* and *nevir*, except *never* in l. 1357. In the present edition *euer* and *neuer* represent the abbreviated forms and follow Craigie's convention.

Togiddir is written thus in six cases; it shows the abbreviated form once (1048), which therefore I have expanded to *togiddir*. *Hiddir* is written thus in three cases; once it is *hidder* (1946) and once it is abbreviated (677). *Quhidder* is spelled thus in 92, abbreviated in 2770, and written *quhiddir* in 1725. *Thiddir* is found only once in *BSS* (2605).

Oyↄ is found twice, as against the common form *vyↄ* thirteen times. Craigie expanded to *oyir* once (2443), because it is used in rhyme with *toyir*, and to *oyer* in 2610, where it occurs in the middle of a line. *Toyↄ* occurs in 833, 837 and 1560; the word is found as *toyir* in 732 and 2444. *Noyↄ* is found eight times as against *nothir* once (731), rhyming with *tothir*. From the above it appears that the author and/or the scribe could use either the *ir* or the *er* ending.Etymologically it is -*er* from such OE words as *hider*, *þider* and *hwider*, &c.

The back-curving loop used for -*er* and -*er*/-*ir* is found for -*ar* in *mark(is)*, n., and in *thar* and its compounds, like *thar-*
-*ar* *abone*, *tharfor*, *tharof*, *tharwith*, &c. Craigie expanded this to -*air*, but whenever the word is written in full it is spelled *thar*, &c.; consequently the present edition has adopted the spelling *thar* only.

In hon*or*ably 645, 1339 we find the same back-curving loop after the *n*. It cannot be decided whether to expand this
-*or*/ -*our* to -*or* or -*our*, because these are the only places in *BSS* where the word is found.

For -*ri*- we find more or less the same back-curving curl but
-*ri*- usually loose above the preceding letter and not attached to it as in the previously mentioned cases, e.g.

60, 110, 121, &c. emp*ri*our	1313 emp*ri*s
341 sup*ri*sit	1626 w*ri*ttin
414 p*ri*ce	1983 pilg*ri*mage
506 emp*ri*ce	

Craigie, and Skeat in his edition of the *Kingis Quair*, when expanding this abbreviation, italicised the *r* only, whereas in her edition of *Lancelot of the Laik* M.M. Gray italicised both *r* and *i*, which seems preferable.

The same loop, connected with the preceding letter, occurs for -*m*(-), e.g. in:

-*m*(-)

58, 250, 298 hi*m*	719 reme*m*berans
76, 148, &c. thai*m*	1616 su*m*
901, 1049, 1175 cu*m*	1694 da*m*mage
183 cu*m*myn	1740 ha*m*mer
575 cly*m*mis	1056, 1984 le*m*man

It is also found for -*n*(-), e.g. in:

-*n*(-)

57 cu*n*nyng	581 cu*n*tré
82, 211, 296, &c. i*n*	697 thi*n* 'thence'
99 walki*n*nit	853 thi*n* 'thine'
153 te*n*nour	960 samy*n*
201 quhe*n*	1061 dru*n*kin
208 mady*n*nis	1062 que*n*tis
251 torme*n*touris	1144, 1219 woma*n*
268, 899 wit*h*outi*n*	1202, 2707 tha*n*

A disconnected loop is found above the preceding letter e.g. in wo*n*nyt 3, 405 and in maso*n*nis 77.

Instead of an upward curl we find a curved line over the preceding two letters in: co*m*moun 1006, 1008, 2120; co*m*monly

-*m*-/-*n*- 834; co*m*mandit 2608, and in inco*n*tinent 2603.

A loop, first horizontal, then brought down backward to vertical, then usually rounded to horizontal again, is used

-*is* for -*is*:

42 ȝer*is*	251 torme*n*tou*ris*	1695 ba*r*rell*is*
59 pe*r*offer*is*	263 garr*is*	1895 kny*cht is*
78 midd*is*	400 ell*is*	2693 se*r*uand*is*
142, 230 ȝou*ris*		

The forms *scurgis* 253 and *spurris* 977 for *scurge* and *spur(e)* are perhaps due to the similarity of *e* and the abbreviation for -*is* in the manuscript copied by Asloan. The latter form was already corrected to *spur(e)* by Asloan himself; see also expl.note to line 253.

Com- and *con*- are often denoted by a sign resembling the letter *q* or an *o* with a downward long *s* attached, e.g. in c*om*myt

-*om*/-*on* 17, c*on*sentit 76, c*on*sauit 1154, c*on*sent 2738.

A mark resembling the figure 9 is found once, in man*us* 1116,

-*us* probably intended as slightly superscript.

A small *r*-like symbol above a word stands for -*ur* in:

-*ur*

25 empriou*r*	251 torme*n*tou*ris*
28 ȝou*r*	277 mu*r*nyt
49, 267 ou*r* 'our'	300 ou*r* 'over'
130 honou*r*	1250 hou*r*
142, 230 ȝouris	1258 cou*r*t, &c

Of modified letters we find the following in *BSS*:

The abbreviation for *per*- is variously realised, either by a horizontal stroke through the shaft of the *p*:

305 pe*r*chance	1559 pe*r*sauit
382 pe*r*rellis	1888 pe*r*fyte
419 pe*r*cas	2683 pe*r*saif

or by a cursively written form of *p*:

192 pe*r*rell	1679 pe*r*saif
556 pe*r*sauit	1886 prop*er*
1069 pe*r*fytlye.	

Once the crossed *p* is found where it stands for *pe* in

perofferis 59. *OED* affords only one example of *peroffer*, s.v. *proffer*: 1456 Sir G.Hay *Law Arms* (STS) 174 *And he peroffer resonable ranson*.

The two symbols used for *per* can also stand for *par*:

129, 1929 p*ar*amour 2177 p*ar* de
1686 p*ar*liament 2560 p*ar*t

ꞵ The symbol ꞵ which is normally used as a variant of *s* stands for *ser* in the cases of: 28 s*er*uis; 803, 1515, 1536 s*er*uit; 838, 1181 s*er*uice; 2693 s*er*uandis.

It is used in combination with superscript *r*, where it means *schir* 'sir' 353 and *passim*.

ƀ We find a *b* with a horizontal stroke through the shaft, standing for *bar*- in *barrellis* 1695.

An abbreviation of *vir*, represented by a *v* with a long-*s*-like symbol written through it at a slant, is found in *virgin(e)* 1332, 1656, and in *Virgilius* 1643, *Virgill* 1653, 1676. (Cf. A. Cappelli, *Dizionario di abbreviature latine ed italiane*, 6th edn, Milano, 1967, pp. 389 f.)

ꝗ *Quod*, whenever found in *BSS* (ten times), shows an abbreviated form, a letter *q* with an open sling at a slant through its descender toward the left (cf. Cappelli, op.cit., p. 302).

The following are abbreviations effected by means of superscript letters:

□ᵗ A *t* written above the line is used to represent -*cht*, e.g.

-*cht*

71 no*ch*t 596 bro*ch*t
95 my*ch*t 392, 405 kny*ch*t
293, 823, 1021 my*ch*ti 834, 2047 ny*ch*tbouris
133, 329 tho*ch*t

The same superscript *t* represents -*ith* in:

-*ith*

42 w*ith*outin 2007 cla*ith*
65, 216, 224 w*ith* 2466 cla*ith*is
73 owtw*ith* 2764 sca*ith*
344, 1674 ba*ith*

-*th* The same symbol again means -*th* in *hundreth* 1223, 1227, 1234, 1609, but *hundreith* is also found in Middle Scots manuscripts. There is no possibility of establishing the form in question in *BSS*.

-*at* We also find superscript *t* used in th*a*t 12, 68, 89, &c.

u/w Thro*u* 931, 2569 shows a kind of tilde or reduced *u* over the *o*, which Craigie expanded to *u*. In *BSS throw* is found eight times, *throwe* once, whereas *throu* is not found anywhere else in the text. It may, however, be an older form, wherefore it has been allowed to stand, especially since a distinct *w* written above the line is found e.g. in ȝow 70, 265.

lk, ll *lk* and *ll* written above the line are found e.g. in 404-5 q*uhi*lk, 575 qu*hi*lk, 2365 q*uhi*ll.

Strokes above words usually had become meaningless by the time the present manuscript was written. They are indicated in Craigie's edition and need not be discussed here.

XVII. BIBLIOGRAPHY

BIBLIOGRAPHIES, &C.

Aldis, H.G., *A List of Books Printed in Scotland before 1700*, Edinburgh, (1904) 1970.

Bald, Marjorie A., 'Vernacular books imported into Scotland, 1500-1625', *Scottish Historical Review*, 23, 1926, pp. 254-67.

Bennett, H.S., *English Books and Readers 1457-1557*, Cambridge University Press, 1952.

Bossuat, R., *Manuel bibliographique de la littérature française du moyen âge*, Melun, 1951.

Cabeen, D.C., *A Critical Bibliography of French Literature*, Vol. I, *The Medieval Period*, ed. U.T. Holmes Jr., Syracuse University Press, 1947.

Durkan, John, and Anthony Ross, *Early Scottish Libraries*, Glasgow, (1958) 1961.

Farrar, Clarissa P., and Austin P. Evans, *Bibliography of English Translations from Medieval Sources*, New York, 1946.

Ferguson, Joan P.S., *Scottish Family Histories held in Scottish Libraries*, Edinburgh, 1960.

Geddie, W.A., *A Bibliography of Middle Scots Poets*, STS 61, Edinburgh and London, 1912.

Hancock, P.D., *A Bibliography of Works Relating to Scotland, 1916-1950*, 2 vols, Edinburgh, 1959-60.

Ker, N.R., *Medieval Libraries in Great Britain*, London, (1941) 1964.

Mitchell, Sir Arthur, and C.G. Cash, *A Contribution to the Bibliography of Scottish Topography*, 2 vols, Scottish History Society, Edinburgh, 1917.

Reader's Guide to Scotland, a Bibliography, The National Book League, London, 1968.

Scottish Books, A Brief Bibliography for teachers and general readers, Saltire Society, Edinburgh, n.d.

Stuart, Margaret, and Sir James Balfour Paul, *Scottish Family History: A Guide to Works of Reference on the History and*

Genealogy of Scottish Families, Edinburgh, 1930.
Woledge, Brian, *Bibliographie des romans et nouvelles en prose française antérieurs à 1500*, Geneva-Lille, 1954.
Woledge, Brian and Clive, *Répertoire des plus anciens textes en prose française*, Geneva, 1964.
Woolley, J.S., *Bibliography for Scottish Linguistic Studies*, Edinburgh, 1954.

DICTIONARIES

Craigie, W.A., and A.J. Aitken, eds, *A Dictionary of the Older Scottish Tongue*, University of Chicago Press, in progress, 1937-
Dauzat, Albert, Jean Dubois et Henri Mitterand, *Nouveau dictionnaire étymologique*, Librairie Larousse, Paris, (1964) 1968.
Grandsaignes d'Hauterive, R., *Dictionnaire d'ancien français, moyen âge et renaissance*, Librairie Larousse, Paris, 1947.
Grant, W., and D.D. Murison, eds, *The Scottish National Dictionary*, Edinburgh, 1931-76.
Holthausen, F., *Altenglisches Etymologisches Wörterbuch*, Heidelberg, 1934.
Kurath, Hans, Sherman M. Kuhn and John Reidy, eds, *Middle English Dictionary*, Ann Arbor, Univ. of Michigan Press, in progress, 1952-
Murray, J.A.H., and others, eds, *A New English Dictionary on Historical Principles*, Oxford, 1888-1928.
Onions, C.T., *The Oxford Dictionary of English Etymology*, Oxford, 1966.
Sinclair, I.G., *The Thistle and Fleur de Lys: a Vocabulary of Franco-Scottish Words*, Edinburgh and London, 1904.
Skeat, W.W., *A Concise Etymological Dictionary of the English Language*, Oxford, (1882) 1951.
Stratmann, F.H., and H. Bradley, *A Middle English Dictionary*, Oxford, (1891) 1967.
Tilley, Morris P., *A Dictionary of the Proverbs in English in the Sixteenth and Seventeenth Centuries*, Ann Arbor, Univ. of Michigan Press, 1950.

Warrack, Alexander, ed., *Chambers's Scots Dictionary*, Edinburgh, (1911) 1959.

Zoega, G., *A Concise Dictionary of Old Icelandic*, Oxford, 1952.

EDITIONS OF MIDDLE ENGLISH TEXTS, &C.

Eliis, George, rev. J.O. Halliwell, *Specimens of Early Metrical Romances*, London, 1848.

Floris and Blauncheflur, a Middle English Romance, edited with Introduction, Notes and Glossary, by F.C. de Vries, diss. Utrecht, 1966.

Lydgate's Troy Book, ed. Henry Bergen, EETS E.S., 97, 103, 106, 126, London, 1906-35.

Prins, A.A., *The Booke of Common Prayer, 1549*, Amsterdam, 1933.

Sir Gawayne and the Grene Knyght, ed. Israel Gollancz, EETS O.S., 20, London, 1940.

Weber, Henry, *Metrical Romances of the Thirteenth, Fourteenth and Fifteenth Centuries*, Edinburgh, 1810, III, pp. 8-108.

Ywain and Gawain, eds Albert B. Friedman and Norman T. Harrington, EETS 254, London, 1964.

EDITIONS OF MIDDLE SCOTS TEXTS, &C.

The Asloan Manuscript, ed. W.A. Craigie, STS 2nd Ser. 14, 16, Edinburgh, 1923-25.

The Auchinleck Chronicle, Ane Schort Memoriale of the Scottis Corniklis for Addicioun, to which is added: A Short Chronicle of the Reign of James the Second King of Scots MCCCCXXXVI-MCCCCLX-I. Printed from the Asloan Manuscript in the Library at Auchinleck, Ayrshire, under the superintendence of Thomas Thomson, Advocate, Deputy-Clerk Register of Scotland, Edinburgh. Printed fro Private Circulation MDCCCXIX. With an introd. note by T.G.S(tevenson), Edinburgh, 1877.

The Bannatyne Manuscript, ed. W. Tod Ritchie, STS 2nd Ser. 22, 23, 26; 3rd Ser. 5, Edinburgh, 1927-32.

Barbour's Bruce, ed. W.W. Skeat, STS 1st Ser. 31, 32, 33, Edinburgh, 1893-94.

John Barbour's Bruce, ed. W. Mackay Mackenzie, London, 1909.

Barbour's ... Legendensammlung, nebst den Fragmenten seines Trojanerkrieges, ed. C. Horstmann, Heilbronn, 1881-82.

The Buik of Alexander, ed. R.L. Graeme Ritchie, STS 2nd Ser. 12, 17, 21, 25, Edinburgh, 1920-28.

The Buke of the Chess, ed. Sir Alexander Boswell, Frondes Caducae, Printed at the Auchinleck Press, Vol. VII, MDCCCXVIII. (See also Jac. da Cessole, under heading 'Seven Sages of Rome and related works', below.)

The Buke of the Howlat, in *The Asloan Manuscript* above, Vol. II, pp. 95-126.

The Buke of the Sevyne Sagis, ibid., pp. 1-88.

The Complaynt of Scotlande, ed. J.A.H. Murray, EETS E.S. 17, 18, London, 1872.

Devotional Pieces in Verse and Prose, ed. J.A.W. Bennett, STS 3rd Ser. 23, Edinburgh, 1949.

Diurnal of Remarkable Occurrents (1513-1575), ed. Thomas Thomson, Bannatyne and Maitland Clubs, Edinburgh, 1833.

Gavin Douglas, The Shorter Poems of, ed. Priscilla J. Bawcutt, STS 4th Ser. 3, 1958-59, Edinburgh, 1967.

Gavin Douglas, Virgil's Æneid, translated into Scottish Verse by --, ed. David F.C. Coldwell, STS 3rd Ser. 25, 27, 28, 30, Edinburgh, 1950-57.

William Dunbar, Poems of, ed. Jakob Schipper, Vienna, 1892.

- - - - , ed. W. Mackay Mackenzie, London, (1932) 1970.

Early Popular Poetry of Scotland, ed. David Laing (1822), re-arr. and revised W. Carew Hazlitt, London, 1895.

William Fowler, The Works of, ed. J. Craigie a.o., STS 2nd Ser. 6, 3rd Ser. 7, 13, Edinburgh, 1912, 1932, 1938.

Golagros and Gawane, in *Scottish Alliterative Poems*, ed. F.J. Amours, below.

Hary's Wallace, ed. Matthew P. McDiarmid, STS 4th Ser. 4, 5, Edinburgh, 1968-69.

Henry the Minstrel, Schir William Wallace, ed. James Moir, STS 1st Ser. 6, 7, 1884-85.

Henryson's Fables, ed. G. Gregory Smith, STS 1st Ser. 55, 58, 64, Edinburgh, 1906-14.

Robert Henryson, The Poems and Fables of, ed. H. Harvey Wood, Edinburgh and London, (1933) 1958.

Robert Henryson, Testament of Cresseid, ed. Denton Fox, Nelson's Medieval and Renaissance Library, London, 1968.

Holland's Buke of the Houlate, ... with studies in the Plot, Age, and Structure of the Poem, ed. Arthur Diebler, Chemnitz, 1893.

John Ireland, The Mirror of Wisdom, ed. Charles Macpherson, STS 2nd Ser. 19, 1926; Vol. II, ed. F. Quinn, STS 4th Ser. 2, 1958.

Quintin Kennedy (1520-1564) , Two Eucharistic Tracts, ed. Cornelis H. Kuipers, diss. Nijmegen, 1964.

King Hart, in *Gavin Douglas, The Shorter Poems of*, ed. Priscilla Bawcutt, above, pp. 139-70.

The Kingis Quair, ed. W.W. Skeat, STS 2nd Ser. 1, Edinburgh, 1911.

The Kingis Quair of James Stewart, ed. Matthew P. McDiarmid, London, 1973.

Lancelot of the Laik, ed. Margaret M. Gray, STS 2nd Ser. 2, Edinburgh, 1912.

'*The Lay of Sorrow* and *The Lufaris Complaynt*, an edition', Kenneth G. Wilson, *Speculum*, XXIX, 1954, pp. 708-26.

Legends of the Saints, ed. W.M. Metcalfe, STS 1st Ser. 13, 18, 23, 25, 35, 37, Edinburgh, 1887-96.

Liber Pluscardensis, ed. F.J.H. Skene, 2vols, Edinburgh, 1877-80.

The Quare of Jelusy, ed. Dr. J.T.T. Brown, STS 3rd Ser. 4, Miscellany Volume, 1932, pp. 191-212.

- - - - , eds John Norton Smith and Imogen Pravda, ed. fr. MS. Bodl. Arch. Selden B.24, Carl Winter, Heidelberg, 1976.

Ratis Raving and Other Early Scots Poems on Morals, ed. Ritchie Girvan, STS 3rd Ser. 11, Edinburgh, 1936-37.

Rauf Coilȝear, in *Scottish Alliterative Poems*, ed. F.J.Amours, below.

John Rolland's Court of Venus, ed. Walter Gregor, STS 1st Ser. 3, 1884.

John Rolland of Dalkeith, The Sevyn Sages in Scottish Metre, 1578, ed. David Laing, Bannatyne Club, Edinburgh, 1837.

John Rolland of Dalkeith, The Seuin Seages, translatit out of prois in Scottis meter, ed. George F. Black, STS 3rd Ser. 3, Edinburgh, 1932.

Ane Satyre of the Thrie Estaits by Sir David Lindsay, ed. James Kinsley, London, 1954.

Scottish Alliterative Poems, ed. F.J. Amours, STS 1st Ser. 27, 38, Edinburgh, 1891-97.

Scottish Troy Book Fragments, *Barbour's ... Legendensammlung, &c.*, ed. C. Horstmann, above.

Specimens of Middle Scots, ed. G. Gregory Smith, Edinburgh and London, 1902.

The Taill of Rauf Coilyear, ed. S.J.H. Herrtage, EETS E.S. 39, London, 1882.

The Thre Prestis of Peblis, ed. T.D. Robb, STS 2nd Ser. 8, Edinburgh, 1920.

Ane Tractat of a part of ye Ynglis Cronikle schawand of yar kings part of yar ewill & cursit gouernance and yar unhappie lynage, als weil fra autentik writ als fra yar awne fenȝeit Policronicon, ed. Sir Alexander Boswell, Frondes Caducae, Printed at the Auchinleck Press, Vol. VI, MDCCCXVIII.

Wallace, see *Hary's Wallace*, ed. Matthew P. McDiarmid, STS, above.

Andrew of Wyntoun, The Original Chronicle, ed. F.J. Amours, STS 1st Ser. 63, 50, 53, 54, 56, 57, Edinburgh, 1902-14.

HISTORY

Brown, Jennifer M., ed., *Scottish Society in the Fifteenth Century*, London, 1977.

Brunton, G., and D. Haig, *An Historical Account of the Senators of the College of Justice*, Edinburgh, 1832.

Buchanan, David, *The Treasure of Auchinleck, The Story of the Boswell Papers*, Heinemann, London, 1975.

Comrie, John D., *History of Scottish Medicine to 1860*, 2 vols, London, (1927) 1932.

Dickinson, William Croft, *Scotland from the Earliest Times to 1603*, London, 1961.

Donaldson, Gordon, *Scotland: James V- James VII*, The Edinburgh History of Scotland, Vol. III, Edinburgh, 1971.

- - and Robert S. Morpeth, *Who's Who in Scottish History*, Oxford, 1973.

- - - - - - , *A Dictionary of Scottish History*, Edinburgh, 1977.

Dunbar, Sir Archibald H., *Scottish Kings, A Revised Chronology of Scottish History, 1005-1625*, 2nd ed., Edinburgh, 1906.

Dunlop, Annie I., *Life and Times of James Kennedy, Bishop of St. Andrews*, Edinburgh, 1950.

Durkan, J., 'The Cultural Background in Sixteenth-Century Scotland', in *Essays on the Scottish Reformation*, ed. David McRoberts, Glasgow, 1962, pp. 274-331.

Innes, Cosmo, *Memoir of Thomas Thomson*, Bannatyne Club 99, Edinburgh, 1854.

Laing, David, 'Inquiries respecting some of the early historical writers of Scotland', *Proceedings of the Society of Antiquaries of Scotland*, XII, 1876-78, pp. 72-87.

Mackie, R.L., *King James IV of Scotland*, Edinburgh, 1958.

Marwick, Sir James D., *Edinburgh Guilds and Crafts*, Scottish Burgh Record Society, Edinburgh, 1909.

Meikle, H.W., *Scotland*, Edinburgh, 1947.

Nicholson, Ranald, *Scotland: The Later Middle Ages*, The Edinburgh History of Scotland, Vol. II, Edinburgh, 1974.

Paterson, James, *History of the County of Ayr*: with a Genealogical Account of the Families of Ayrshire, 2 vols, Ayr, 1847.

- - , *History of the Counties of Ayr and Wigton*, Vol. I, Part I, Edinburgh, 1863.

Robertson, W., *Ayrshire. Its History and Historic Families*, 2 vols, Kilmarnock and Ayr, 1908.

Stewart, Marion M., 'The Makars' Scotland; Some Facts from the Records', *Scottish Literary News*, 3, 1973, pp. 10-18.

LANGUAGE

Aitken, A.J., 'A Sixteenth Century Scottish Devotional Anthology' (Review of *Devotional Pieces in Prose and Verse*, ed. J.A.W. Bennett, STS, 1955), *Scottish Historical Review*, XXXVI, 1957, pp. 147-150.

- - - , 'Variation and variety in written Middle Scots', *Edinburgh Studies in English and Scots*, eds A.J. Aitken, Angus McIntosh and Hermann Pálsson, London, 1971, pp. 177-209.

- - - ed., *Lowland Scots*, Papers presented to an Edinburgh Conference, 1973.

- - - , 'How to Pronounce Older Scots', *Bards & Makars, Scottish Language and Literature, Medieval and Renaissance*, eds Adam J. Aitken, Matthew P. McDiarmid and Derick S. Thomson, Univ. of Glasgow Press, 1977, pp. 1-21.

Baildon, H.B., *On the Rimes in the Authentic Poems of William Dunbar*, diss. Freiburg, 1899.

Bald, Marjory A., 'The Anglicisation of Scottish Printing', *Scottish Historical Review*, XXIII, 1926, pp. 107-115.

- - - , 'The Pioneers of Anglicised Speech in Scotland', *Scottish Historical Review*, XXIV, 1927, pp. 179-193.

- - - , 'Contemporary References to the Scottish Speech of the Sixteenth Century', *Scottish Historical Review*, XXV, 1928, pp. 163-179.

Baugh, A.C., *A History of the English Language*, London, (1951) 1962.

Björkman, E., *Scandinavian Loanwords in Middle English*, Studien zur englischen Philologie, VII, Halle, 1900-02.

Bliss, A.J., 'Vowel-Quantity in Middle English Borrowings from Anglo-Norman', *Archivum Linguisticum*, IV, 1952, pp. 121-47; V, 1953, pp. 22-47.

Brown, Roger, and Albert Gilman, 'The Pronouns of Power and Solidarity', *Style in Language*, ed. T.A. Sebeok, New York and London, 1960, pp. 253-76.

Buss, Paul, *Sind die von Horstmann herausgegebenen schottischen Legenden ein Werk Barberes?*, diss. Göttingen, 1886; pp. 1-24 also in *Anglia*, IX, 1886, pp. 493-514.

Caldwell, Sarah J.G., *The Relative Pronoun in Early Scots, a Lexicographical and Syntactical Study*, Ph.D. Thesis (unpubl.), Edinburgh, 1967.

- - - - , *The Relative Pronoun in Early Scots*, Helsinki, 1974.

Campbell, A., *Old English Grammar*, Oxford, 1959.

Coldwell, D.F.C., ed., *Selections from Gavin Douglas*, Oxford, 1964.

Craigie, W.A., 'Older Scottish and English. A Study in Contrasts', *Transactions of the Philological Society*, London, 1935, pp. 1-15.

Davis, Norman, 'The *Litera Troili* and English Letters', *Review of English Studies*, XVI, 1965, pp. 233-44.

Dobson, E.J., *English Pronunciation 1500-1700*, 2 vols, Oxford, 1957.

Finkenstaedt, Thomas, *You and Thou: Studien zur Anrede im Englischen*, Berlin, 1963.

Gordon, E.V., *An Introduction to Old Norse*, Oxford, 1949.

Grant, W., and J.M. Dixon, *A Manual of Modern Scots*, Cambridge, 1921.

Heltveit, T., 'Dialect Words in "The Seven Sages"', *English Studies presented to R.W. Zandvoort on the occasion of his seventieth birthday*, a supplement to *English Studies*, Vol. XLV, Amsterdam, 1964, pp. 125-34.

Henschel, Friedrich H., *Darstellung der Flexionslehre in John Barbour's Bruce*, Leipzig, 1886.

Heuser, W., '*ai* und *ei* ... in der Cambridger Handschrift des Bruce', *Anglia*, XVII, 1895, pp. 91-105.

- - , 'Offenes und geschlossenes *EE* im Schottischen und Nordenglischen', *Anglia*, XVIII, 1896, pp. 114-28, and XIX, 1897, pp. 319-40.

- - , 'Die Lautveränderung von ā, ē, ī im Mittelschottischen, *Anglia*, XIX, 1897, pp. 405-408.

- - , 'Der Ursprung des unorganischen *i* in der mittelschottischen Schreibung', *Anglia*, XIX, 1897, pp. 409-412.

Heyne, H., *Die Sprache in Henry the Minstrel's Wallace, Laut- und Flexionslehre*, Kiel, 1910.

Hudnall, R.A., *A Presentation of the Grammatical Inflections in Androw of Wyntoun's 'Orygynale Cronykil of Scotland'*, diss. Leipzig, 1898.

Jespersen, O., *Growth and Structure of the English Language*, 9th ed., Oxford, 1948.

Johnson, Anne Carvey, 'The Pronoun of Direct Address in Seventeenth-Century English', *American Speech*, 41, 1966, pp. 261-69.

Jones, R.F., *The Triumph of the English Language*, London, 1953.

Jordan, Richard, *Handbuch der mittelenglischen Grammatik, Lautlehre*, Heidelberg, (1925) 1968.

Keller, W., *Skandinavischer Einfluss in der englischen Flexion*, Heidelberg, 1925.

Kellner, L., *Historical Outlines of English Syntax*, London, 1924.

Koeppel, E., 'Die Fragmente von Barbour's Trojanerkrieg', *Englische Studien*, X, 1887, pp. 373-82.

Kohler, K.J., 'Aspects of Middle Scots Phonemics and Graphemics. The Phonological Implications of the Sign <I>', *Transactions of the Philological Society*, Oxford, 1968, pp. 32-61.

Kolkwitz, Max, *Das Satzgefüge in Barber's Bruce und Henry's Wallace*, Halle, 1893.

Lenz, K., *Zur Lautlehre der französischen Elemente in den schottischen Dichtungen von 1500-1550* (G. Douglas, W. Dunbar, D. Lyndesay, *Clariodus*), Marburg, 1913.

Luick, Karl, *Historische Grammatik der englischen Sprache*, Vol. I, Parts I & II, Oxford, 1964.

McIntosh, Angus, 'The Analysis of Written Middle English', *Transactions of the Philological Society*, 1956, pp. 26-55.

- - , *Introduction to a Survey of Scottish Dialects*, Edinburgh, 1961.

- - , 'A New Approach to Middle English Dialectology', *English Studies*, XLIV, 1963, pp. 1-11.

- - , 'King Lear, Act I, Scene 1. A Stylistic Note', *Review of English Studies*, XVI, 1963, pp. 54-56.

- - , '"As You Like It": a grammatical clue to character' (1963) in M.A.K. Halliday & Angus McIntosh, eds,

Patterns of Language, Papers in General, Descriptive and Applied Linguistics, London, 1966, pp. 69-82.

Mossé, Fernand, *A Handbook of Middle English*, Baltimore, 1952.

Mühleisen, Fr. Wilhelm, *Textkritische, metrische und grammatische Untersuchungen von Barbour's Bruce*, Bonn, 1913.

Mullholland, J., '"Thou" and "You" in Shakespeare: a study in the second person', *English Studies*, 48, 1967, pp. 34-43.

Murison, David D., 'Linguistic Relationships in Medieval Scotland', in *The Scottish Tradition, Essays in Honour of Ronald Gordon Cant*, ed. G.W.S. Barrow, Edinburgh, 1974, pp. 71-83.

Murray, James A.H., *The Dialect of the Southern Counties of Scotland*, London, 1873.

Nathan, Norman, 'Pronouns of Address in the "Friar's Tale"', *Modern Language Quarterly*, XVII, 1956, pp. 39-42.

- - , 'Pronouns of Address in the "Canterbury Tales"', *Mediaeval Studies*, XXI, 1959, pp. 193-201.

Pope, Mildred K., *From Latin to Modern French with Especial Consideration of Anglo-Norman*, Manchester, (1934) 1952.

Preston, Priscilla, 'Did Gavin Douglas write *King Hart*?', *Medium Ævum*, 1959, pp. 31-47.

Prins, A.A., *French Influence in English Phrasing*, Leiden University Press, 1952.

- - - , *A Synopsis of the History of English Tonic Vowels*, Leiden University Press, 1966.

- - - , *A History of English Phonemes*, Leiden University Press, (1972) 1974.

Ridley, Florence H., 'Did Gawin Douglas write *King Hart*?', *Speculum*, 34, 1959, pp. 402-12.

Samuels, M.L., 'Some Applications of Middle English Dialectology', *English Studies*, XLIV, 1963, pp. 81-94.

Sheppard, E.A., *Studies in the Language of Bellenden's Boece*, Ph.D. Thesis (unpubl.), University of London, 1936.

Sisam, Kenneth, *Fourteenth Century Verse and Prose*, Oxford, (1921) 1950.

Smith, G.Gregory, *Specimens of Middle Scots*, Edinburgh, 1902.

Stidston, R.O., *The Use of 'Ye' in the Function of 'Thou' in Middle English Literature from MS. Auchinleck to MS. Vernon,* Stanford University, California, 1917.

Sundby, Bertil, 'Middle English overlapping of *v* and *w* and its phonemic significance', *Anglia,* 74, 1956, pp. 438-44.

Taylor, Rupert, 'Some Notes on the Use of CAN and COUTH as Preteritive Auxiliaries in Early and Middle Scottish Poetry', *Journal of English and Germanic Philology,* XVI, 1917, pp. 573-91.

Vachek, Joseph, *A Brief Survey of the Historical Development of English,* Part I: Old English; Part II: Middle English and Early Modern English, Leiden, 1969 (stencilled).

Walcutt, Charles Child, 'The Pronoun of Address in *Troilus and Criseyde*', *Philological Quarterly,* XIV, 1935, pp. 282-87.

Westergaard, Elisabeth, 'The Prepositions in Lowland Scotch', *Anglia,* XLI, 1917, pp. 444-55.

- - , 'Verbal Forms in Middle Scotch', *Anglia,* XLIII, 1919, 95-97.

- - , *Studies in Prefixes and Suffixes in Middle Scottish,* Oxford University Press, 1924.

Williams, O.T., 'The Development of *ai* and *ei* in Middle Scotch', *Transactions of the Philological Society,* 1907-10, pp. 285-87.

- - - , 'On OE *a*, *ā* and *æ* in the Rimes of Barbour's Brus and in Modern Scotch Dialects', *Transactions of the Philological Society,* 1911-16, pp. 7-26.

LITERATURE

Baugh, A.C., ed., *A Literary History of England,* London, (1948) 1967.

- - - , 'Improvisation in the Middle English Romances', *Proceedings of the American Philosophical Society,* 103, 1959, pp. 418-54.

Baxter, John Walker, *William Dunbar, a Biographical Study,* Edinburgh and London, 1952.

Bédier, Joseph, *Les Fabliaux,* Paris, (1893) 1925.

Brewer, D.S., ed., *Chaucer and Chaucerians*, London, 1966.

Brie, Friedrich, *Die nationale Literatur Schottlands von den Anfängen zur Renaissance*, Halle, 1937.

Chambers, R.W., *On the Continuity of English Prose from Alfred to More and his School*, EETS 191A, London, (1932) 1957.

Faral, Edmond, 'Le fabliau latin au moyen âge', *Romania*, I, 1872, pp. 321-85.

- - , *Recherches sur les sources latines des contes et romans courtois du moyen âge*, Paris, 1913.

Hart, Walter M., 'The fabliau and popular literature', *Publications of the Modern Language Association*, 23, 1908, pp. 330-74.

Henderson, T.F., *Scottish Vernacular Literature*, London, 1898.

Hibbard, Laura, *Medieval Romances in England*, New York, 1924.

Holmes, U.T., *A History of Old French Literature from the Origins to 1300*, New York, 1938.

Johnston, R.J., and D.D.R. Owen, eds, *Fabliaux*, 2nd ed., Oxford, 1965.

Ker, W.P., 'The History of the Ballads', *Proceedings of the British Academy*, London, 1909-10.

Kinghorn, A.M., 'The Minor Poems of Robert Henryson', *Studies in Scottish Literature*, III, 1965, pp. 30-40.

Kitchin, G., *A Survey of Burlesque and Parody in English*, Edinburgh, 1931.

Lewis, C.S., *English Literature in the Sixteenth Century Excluding Drama*, Oxford University Press, 1954.

Lindsay, Maurice, *History of Scottish Literature*, London, 1977.

Löhmann, Otto, *Die Rahmenerzählung des Decameron, Ihre Quellen und Nachwirkungen. Ein Beitrag zur Geschichte der Rahmenerzählung*, Halle, 1935.

Loiseleur Deslongchamps, A.L.A., *Essai sur les fables indiennes et sur leur introduction en Europe, suivi du Roman des sept sages de Rome en prose*, Paris, 1838.

Mackenzie, Agnes Mure, *An Historical Survey of Scottish Literature to 1714*, London, 1933.

McKnight, George H., *Middle English Humorous Tales in Verse*, Boston, 1913.

MacQueen, John, *Robert Henryson: A Study of the Major Narrative Poems*, Oxford University Press, 1967.

- - , 'The literature of fifteenth-century Scotland', in Jennifer M. Brown, ed., *Scottish Society in the Fifteenth Century*, London, 1977, pp. 184-208.

Millar, J.H., *A Literary History of Scotland*, London, 1903.

Montaiglon, Anatole de, et Gaston Raynaud, *Recueil général et complet des fabliaux des xiiie et xive siècles, imprimés ou inédits*, Paris, 6 vols, 1872-90.

Mosher, Joseph A., *The Exemplum in the Early Religious and Didactic Literature of England*, New York, Columbia University Press, 1911.

Neilson, George, *John Barbour, Poet and Translator*, London, 1900.

Nykrog, Per, *Les fabliaux: étude d'histoire littéraire et de stylistique médiévale*, (Copenhagen, 1957) Geneva, 1973.

Paris, Gaston, *Les contes orientaux dans la littérature française du moyen âge*, Paris, 1875.

- - , *La littérature française au moyen âge*, Paris, (1890) 1914.

Ritchie, R.L. Graeme, 'Chrétien de Troyes and Scotland', Zacharoff Lecture, Oxford, 1952.

Robbins, Rossell Hope, *The Hundred Tales* (*Les Cent Nouvelles Nouvelles*), New York, 1959.

Rogers, Katherine M., *The Troublesome Helpmate, A History of Misogyny in Literature*, Univ. of Washington Press, Seattle and London, 1966.

Rychner, Jean, *Contribution à l'étude des fabliaux*, Geneva, 1960.

Schlauch, Margaret, *English Medieval Literature and Its Social Foundations*, Warsaw, 1956.

- - , *Antecedents of the English Novel 1400-1600 (from Chaucer to Deloney)*, Warsaw, 1963.

Smith, G. Gregory, *The Transition Period*, Edinburgh, 1900.

- - - , *Scottish Literature: Character and Influence*, London, 1919.

Smith, Janet J., *The French Background of Middle Scots Literature*, Edinburgh, 1934.

Speirs, J., *The Scots Literary Tradition*, London, (1940) 1962.
Thomson, Stith, *The Folktale*, New York, 1946.
Utley, Francis Lee, *The Crooked Rib, an Analytical Index to the Argument about Women in English and Scots to the End of the Year 1568*, (Ohio State University, 1944) New York, 1970.
Vising, J., *Anglo-Norman Language and Literature*, London, 1923.
Wittig, Kurt, *The Scottish Tradition in Literature*, Edinburgh, 1958.

RECORD PUBLICATIONS

Livingstone, M., *A Guide to the Public Records of Scotland*, Edinburgh, 1905.
Thomson, Thomas, 'List of the Protocol Books of the City of Edinburgh, with Extracts', *Proceedings of the Society of Antiquaries of Scotland*, Vol. V, Edinburgh, 1865.

*****

Accounts of the Lord High Treasurers of Scotland, 1473-1566, ed. Thomas Dickson and Sir James Balfour Paul, 11 vols, 1877-1916.
Acts of the Lords of Council in Civil Causes, 1478-1495, ed. T. Thomson, Edinburgh, 1839.
Acts of the Lords of Council in Civil Causes, 1496-1501, with some *Acta Auditorum et Dominorum Concilii, 1469-1483*, ed. George Neilson and Henry Paton, Edinburgh, 1918.
Acts of the Lords of Council in Public Affairs, 1501-1554, ed. Robert Kerr Hannay, Edinburgh, 1932.
Acts of the Parliaments of Scotland, A.D. MCXXIV-MDCCVII, ed. Thomas Thomson and Cosmo Innes, 12 vols in 13, Edinburgh, 1814-75.
Calendar of Charters and other Original Documents preserved in H.M. Register House, Vol. 5, 1513-1550, Edinburgh.
Calendar of Writs preserved at Yester House, 1166-1625, compiled by C.C.H. Harvey and J. Macleod, Edinburgh, 1930.
City of Edinburgh Old Accounts, Vol. I, 1544-67, ed. Robert

Adam, Edinburgh, 1899.

Early Records of the University of St. Andrews: the Graduation Roll 1413-1597, and the Matriculation Roll, 1473-1597, ed. J. Maitland Anderson, Scottish History Society, Edinburgh, 1926.

Exchequer Rolls of Scotland, 1264-1600, eds Dr. J. Stuart, G. Burnett and others, 23 vols, Edinburgh, 1878-1908.

Extracts from the Records of the Burgh of Edinburgh, ed. J.D. Marwick, Scottish Burgh Records Society, Edinburgh, 1869.

The Lag Charters, 1400-1720, Sir Philip J. Hamilton-Grierson's Calendar, ed. Athol L. Murray, Scott. Record Soc. No. 88, Edinburgh, 1958.

Parliamentary Records of Scotland in the General Register House, Vol. I, ed. William Robertson, Edinburgh, 1804.

Pitcairn, Robert, ed., *Ancient Criminal Trials in Scotland from AD 1487-1624*, 3 vols in 4 (11 parts), Bannatyne and Maitland Clubs, 1829-33.

'Protocol Book (1541-1550) of Herbert Anderson, Notary in Dumfries', *Dumfriesshire and Galloway Natural History and Antiquarian Society Transactions*, 3.Ser.ii, Dumfries, 1914, pp. 176-224.

Protocol Book of John Foular, vols. I-III, eds Marguerite Wood and Walter Macleod, Scottish Record Society, nos. 64, 72, 75, Edinburgh, 1930, 1941, 1953.

Protocol Book of Henry Prestoun, ed. J. Fergusson, Ayrshire Archaeol. and Nat. Hist. Soc. Collections, 2nd Ser. III, 1950-54.

Protocol Book of Gavin Ros, eds John Anderson and Francis J. Grant, Scott. Rec. Soc., Edinburgh, 1907.

Protocol Book of James Young, 1485-1515, ed. Gordon Donaldson, Scott. Rec. Soc., Edinburgh, 1952.

Register of the Great Seal of Scotland, 1306-1668, ed. J.M. Thomson and others, 11 vols, Edinburgh, 1882-1914.

Register of the Privy Council of Scotland, First Ser., 1545-1625, ed. John Hill Burton and others, 14 vols, Edinburgh, 1877-98.

Registrum Cartarum Eccl. S. Egidii de Edinburgh, ed. David Laing, Bannatyne Club, Edinburgh, 1859.

Registrum Secreti Sigilli Regum Scotorum, Register of the Privy Seal of Scotland, 1488- , ed. M. Livingstone and others, Edinburgh, 1908- , in progress.

REFERENCE BOOKS

Album Studiosorum Academiae Lugduno Batavae MDCLXXV - MDCCCLXXV, Hagae Comitum, 1875.

Black, George F., *The Surnames of Scotland,* New York, 1946.

Bordman, Gerald, *Motif-Index of the English Metrical Romances,* FF Communications No. 190, ed. for the Folklore Fellows, Helsinki, 1963.

Boswelliana, The Commonplace Book of James Boswell, With a Memoir and Annotations by Charles Rogers, London, Grampian Club, 1876.

Briquet, C.M., *Les Filigranes, Dictionnaire Historique des Marques du Papier, 1282-1600,* 4 vols, Paris, 1907; and *A Facsimile of the 1907 Edition* with supplementary material contributed by a number of scholars, ed. Allan Stevenson, Amsterdam, 1968.

Burke's Peerage, Baronetage and Knightage, 104th edn, London, 1967.

Cheney, C.R., *Handbook of Dates for Students of English History,* Royal Historical Society, 1945.

Dickson, Robert, and J.P. Edmond, *Annals of Scottish Printing,* Cambridge, 1890.

Dictionary of National Biography, Oxford U.P., London, 1885-1904.

Doubleday, H.A., and Lord Howard de Walden, eds, *The Complete Peerage of England, Scotland, Ireland,* &c., 13 vols, London, 1910-59.

Flutre, Louis F., *Table des noms propres ... dans les romans du moyen âge ...,* Poitiers, 1962.

Heawood, E., *Historical Review of Watermarks,* Amsterdam, 1950.

Labarre, Emile J., *Dictionary and Encyclopaedia of Paper and Papermaking,* Amsterdam, 1952.

Langlois, Ernest, *Table des noms propres ... dans les chansons de geste*, Paris, 1904.

Leslie, Col. Charles, *Pedigree of the Family of Leslie of Balquhain*, Bakewell, 1861.

Loeber, E.G., *Supplement to Labarre's Dictionary*, Amsterdam, 1967.

Molhuysen, P.C., *Bronnen tot de Geschiedenis der Leidsche Universiteit*, Ve deel, 's Gravenhage, 1921.

Murray, David, *Legal Practice in Ayr and the West of Scotland in the Fifteenth and Sixteenth Centuries, A Study in Economic History*, Glasgow, 1910.

Paul, Sir James Balfour, ed., *The Scots Peerage, Founded on Wood's Edn of Sir Robert Douglas' Peerage of Scotland*, 9 vols, Edinburgh, 1904-14.

Peacock, Edward, *Index to English speaking Students who have graduated at Leyden University*, London, 1883.

Stair Society, *An Introductory Survey of the Sources and Literature of Scots Law*, Various contributors, Edinburgh, 1936.

Thompson, Stith, *Motif-Index of Folk Literature*, 5 vols and 1 vol. index, FF Communications Nos. 106-117, ed. for the Folklore Fellows, Helsinki, 1932-36.

Wells, J.E., *A Manual of the Writings in Middle English 1050-1400*, and supplements I-IX, New Haven, Conn., 1916-52.

Whiting, B.J., 'Proverbs and Proverbial Sayings from Scottish Writings before 1600', Part I, A-L, *Mediaeval Studies*, XI, 1949, pp. 123-205; Part II, M-Y, *Mediaeval Studies*, XIII, 1951, pp. 87-164.

SCRIBES AND HANDWRITINGS

van Buuren-Veenenbos, C.C., 'John Asloan, an Edinburgh Scribe', *English Studies*, XLVII, 1966, pp. 365-72.

Carr, Muriel B., 'Notes on an English Scribe's Methods', *University of Wisconsin Studies in Language and Literature*, 2, 1918, pp. 153-61.

Chalmers, G., Transcript of part of the Asloan Manuscript, University Library of Edinburgh, I. 521.

Chaytor, H.J., *From Script to Print, An Introduction to Medieval Vernacular Literature*, (Cambridge, 1945) London, 1966.

Cheney, C.R., *Notaries Public in England in the Thirteenth and Fourteenth Centuries*, Oxford, 1972.

Dell, Richard F., 'Some differences between Scottish and English archives', *Journal of the Society of Archivists*, III, 1965-68, pp. 386-97.

Denholm Young, N., *Handwriting in England and Wales*, Cardiff, (1954) 1964.

Francis, W. Nelson, 'Graphemic Analysis of Late Medieval English Manuscripts', *Speculum*, XXXVII, 1962, pp. 32-47.

Heawood, Edward, 'Sources of Early English Paper-supply', *The Library*, 4th ser., x, 1929-30, pp. 282-307, 427-54.

Hector, L.C., *The Handwriting of English Documents*, London, (1958) 1966.

McIntosh, Angus, 'The Analysis of Written Middle English', *Transactions of the Philological Society*, 1956, pp. 26-55.

McLaughlin, John C., *A Graphemic-Phonemic Study of a Middle English Manuscript*, The Hague, 1963.

Parkes, M.B., *English Cursive Book Hands, 1250-1500*, Oxford, 1969.

Poulle, Emmanuel, *Paléographie des Écritures Cursives en France du XVe au XVIIe siècle*, Geneva, 1966.

Simpson, Grant G., *Scottish Handwriting 1150-1650*, Edinburgh, 1973.

Stiennon, Jacques, *Paléographie du Moyen Age*, Paris, 1973.

Vinaver, Eugène, 'Principles of Textual Emendation', in *Studies in French Language and Medieval Literature Presented to Professor Mildred K. Pope*, Manchester, 1939, pp. 351-69.

Wright, C.E., *English Vernacular Hands from the Twelfth to the Fifteenth Centuries*, Oxford, 1960.

SEVEN SAGES OF ROME AND RELATED WORKS

Aïache, Mauricette, 'Les versions françaises en prose du roman des sept sages', dans *Positions des Thèses soutenues par les élèves de la promotion de 1966*, École des Chartres, Paris, 1966, pp. 9-13.

- -, *Les versions françaises en prose du roman des sept sages*, unpubl. thesis of the École des Chartres, Paris, 1966.

d'Ancona, Alessandro, ed., *Libro dei Sette Savi di Roma,* Collezione di antiche scritture italiane, IV, Pisa, 1864.

Baethgen, Friedrich von, *Sindban, oder die sieben weisen Meister,* Leipzig, 1879.

Benfey, Theodor, 'Beiträge zur Geschichte der Verbreitung der indischen Sammlungen von Fabeln und Erzählungen; ursprüngliche Grundlage der "Sieben weisen Meister"', *Orient und Occident,* III, 1866, pp. 171-80.

Bertoni, G., 'Un manuscrit du Roman des Sept Sages', *Zeitschrift für romanische Philologie,* 31, 1907, pp. 713-15.

Black, George F., ed., *The Seuin Seages by John Rolland of Dalkeith,* STS 3rd Ser. 3, 1932.

Boissonade, J.F., *Syntipas,* Paris, 1828.

Bond, D.F., 'Two Chap-Book Versions of "The Seven Sages of Rome"', *Modern Language Notes,* LII, 1937, pp. 494-98.

Botermans, Antonie J., *Die hystorie van die seven wijse mannen van romen* (ed. 1479), diss. Utrecht, 1898.

- - - , id. tekst; herdruk naar het eenig bekende exemplaar der editio princeps A^{o} 1479, berustende in de Bibl. Acad. Georgiae Augustae te Göttingen, Haarlem, 1898.

Brunel, C., 'Une version provençale des Sept Sages de Rome', *Romania,* LXXVI, 1955, pp. 244-47.

Brunner, Karl, ed., *The Seven Sages of Rome (Southern Version),* EETS O.S. 191, London, 1933.

Buchner, Georg, *Die Historia Septem Sapientum nach der Innsbrucker Handschrift v.J. 1342, nebst einer Untersuchung über die Quelle der Seuin Seages des Johne Rolland von Dalkeith,* Erlangen, 1889.

- - , 'Beiträge zur Geschichte der Sieben Weisen Meister', *Archiv für das Studium der neueren Sprachen und Literaturen,* Braunschweig, 1904, pp. 297-301.

Burton, Richard F., 'The Book of Sindibad ..., ed. by W.A. Clouston', *The Academy,* 26, 1884, pp. 175-76.

Campbell, Killis, *A Study of the Romance of the Seven Sages with special reference to the Middle English Version,* diss. Baltimore, 1898, and *PMLA,* XIV (1899), pp. 1-107.

Campbell, Killis, ed., *The Seven Sages of Rome*, Albion Series, Boston USA, 1907.

- - , 'The Source of the Story of "Sapientes"', *Modern Language Notes*, 23, 1908, pp. 202-04.

- - , 'A Note on "The Seven Sages of Rome"', *Modern Language Review*, XVII, 1922, p. 289.

Carmoly, Eliakim, *Les Paraboles de Sendabar, sur les ruses des femmes, traduites de l'hébreu*, Paris, 1849.

Cassel, Paulus, *Mischle Sindbad*, Berlin, 1888, repr. 1891.

Cesari, Augusto, ed., *L'Amabile di Continentia*, Collezione di opere inedite o rare dei primi tre secoli della lingua, Bologna, 1896.

Cessole, Jacopo da, *Das Schachzabelbuch des Jacobus de Cessolis, O.P. in mittelhochdeutscher Prosa-Übersetzung, nach den Handschriften herausgegeben* von Gerard F. Schmidt, Berlin, 1961.

- - -, *The Game of the Chess*, trsl. William Caxton, facsimile edition, Scolar Press, London, 1976, introd. N.F. Blake.

- - -, *The Buke of the Chess*, in *The Asloan Manuscript*, ed. W.A. Craigie, STS 2nd Ser. 14, Edinburgh, 1923, pp. 81-152.

Clouston, W.A., *The Book of Sindibâd*, Glasgow, 1884.

- - - , 'The Book of Sindibad', *The Athenaeum*, London, 12 Sept. 1891, pp. 355 f.

Comparetti, Domenico, *Researches respecting the Book of Sindibâd*, tr. Henry C. Coote, Folk-Lore Society, London, 1882.

- - , *Vergil in the Middle Ages*, tr. E.F.M. Benecke, London, (1895) 1966.

Cox, E.G., 'The Seven Sages of Rome, ed. by Killis Campbell', *Modern Language Notes*, 24, 1909, p. 153.

Crane, Thomas F., *The Exempla of Jacques de Vitry*, Folk-Lore Society, London, 1890.

Crosland, Jessie, 'Dolopathos and the Seven Sages of Rome', *Medium AEvum*, XXV, 1956, pp. 1-12.

Douce, Francis, *Illustrations of Shakespeare and of Ancient*

Manners, 'Dissertation on the *Gesta Romanorum*', London , 1839, pp. 516-75.

Eberhard, A., *In Joannis de Alta Silva Libro qui inscribitur Dolopathos emendationum spicilegium,* Magdeburg, 1875.

Ehret, Ph., *Der Verfasser des versificirten Romans des VII Sages und Herberz der Verfasser des altfranzösischen Dolopathos,* diss. Heidelberg, 1886.

Epstein, Morris, '*Mishle Sendebar*: New Light on the Transmission of Folklore from East to West', *Proceedings of the American Academy for Jewish Research,* XXVII, 1958, pp. 1-17.

\- - , 'A Medieval Jewish Tale', *Commentary,* XXV, 1958, pp. 528-31.

\- - , 'The Manuscripts, Printed Editions and Translations of *Mishle Sendebar*', *Bulletin of the New York Public Library,* 63, 1959, pp. 63-87.

\- - , 'Vatican Hebrew Codex 100 and the *Historia Septem Sapientum*', *Proceedings of the Fourth World Congress of Jewish Studies* (1965), Jerusalem, 1967.

\- - , *Tales of Sendebar. Mishle Sindbad, An Edition and Translation of the Hebrew Version of the SEVEN SAGES Based on Unpublished Manuscripts,* Philadelphia, The Jewish Publication Society of America, 1967.

Fischer, Hermann M.C., *Beiträge zur Literatur der sieben weisen Meister,* diss. Greifswald, 1902.

Gaster, Moses, *Die Geschichte des Kaisers Skinder, ein Rumänisch-Byzantinischer Roman. Beitrag zur Quellengeschichte der altfranzösischen 'Ystoire des sept sages de Rome'*, Athens, 1937.

Goedeke, Karl, ed., 'Liber de Septem Sapientibus', *Orient und Occident,* III, Göttingen, 1866, pp. 385-402.

\- - - , 'Scala Coeli', *Orient und Occident,* III, 1866, pp. 402-23.

Gollancz, Hermann, *The History of Sindban,* Folk-Lore Society VIII, London, 1897, pp. 99-130.

Gomme, George L., *The History of the Seven Wise Masters of Rome,* edition of a printed book of 1505 or 1520 (Wynkyn de Worde), Villon Society, London, 1885.

Hauteseille, Jean de, see Oesterley, *Dolopathos*.

Heinimann, Siegfried, 'Beiträge zur Kenntnis der altfranzösischen Handschriften der Berner Stadtbibliothek. Die drei Handschriften der "Roman des sept sages"', *Vox Romanica*, VI, 1941-42, pp. 365-67.

Herrtage, Sidney J.H., *The Early English Versions of the Gesta Romanorum*, EETS, 1879.

Hilka, Alfons, *Historia Septem Sapientum*: I. *Eine bisher unbekannte lateinische Übersetzung einer orientalischen Fassung der Sieben weisen Meister* (*Mischle Sendabar*); II. *Johannis de Alta Silva Dolopathos sive de Rege et Septem Sapientibus*, Sammlung mittellateinischer Texte, Nos. 4 & 5, Heidelberg, 1912-13.

- - , 'Historia Septem Sapientum. Die Fassung der *Scala Celi* des Johannes Gobii Junior'. *Festschrift für Alfred Hillebrandt*, Halle, 1912.

- - , 'Die Wanderung der Erzählung von der Inclusa aus dem Volksbuch der Sieben weisen Meister', *Mitt. d. schles. Ges. für Volkskunde*, XIX, Breslau, 1917, pp. 29-72.

- - & Werner Söderhjelm, *Die Disciplina Clericalis des Petrus Alfonsi, das älteste Novellenbuch des Mittelalters, nach allen bekannten Handschriften* (Kleine Ausgabe), Heidelberg, 1911.

- - - - - , eds, *Petri Alfonsi Disciplina Clericalis*, Acta Societatis Scientiarum Fennicae, Helsingfors, 1911, 1912, 1922.

Hulme, William H., 'A Valuable Middle English Manuscript', *Modern Philology*, IV, 1906, pp. 67-73.

- - - , 'A Middle English Addition to the Wager Cycle', *Modern Language Notes*, XXIV, 1909, pp. 218-22.

- - - , ed., *Peter Alphonse's Disciplina Clericalis from the Fifteenth-Century Worcester Cathedral Manuscript F. 172*, Cleveland, 1919.

Johannis de Alta Silva Dolopathos, see Oesterley.

Keller, Heinrich A. von, ed., *Li Romans des Sept Sages*, Tübingen, 1836.

Keller, (Heinrich) Adelbert, *Hans von Bühel's Dyocletian's Leben*, Quedlinburg u. Leipzig, 1841.

Keller, John Esten, *El Libro de los Engaños*, Chapel Hill, N. Carolina, (1953) 1959.

- - - , *The Book of the Wiles of Women*, Chapel Hill, N. Carolina, 1956.

Kittredge, G.L., ed., *Arthur and Gorlagon*, 'The Defence of the Child', Harvard Studies and Notes in Philol. & Lit., 8, 1903, pp. 222-45.

Kölbing, E., 'Collation of Wright's edition with MS. Cambr. U.L. Dd. I. 17', *Englische Studien*, VI, 1883, pp. 448-50.

- - , 'Collation of Auchinleck MS.', *Englische Studien*, VI, 1883, pp. 442-48.

- - , 'Vier Romanzen-Handschriften', *Englische Studien*, VII, 1884, pp. 177-91.

Krappe, A.H., 'Studies on the Seven Sages of Rome', *Archivum Romanicum*, Nos. 8, 9, 11, 16 and 19, 1924-35.

Landau, Marcus, *Die Quellen des Decameron*, Stuttgart, (1869)1884.

Le Roux de Lincy, A.J.V., ed., *Roman des sept sages en prose*, in A.L.A. Loiseleur Deslongchamps, *Essai sur les fables indiennes, &c.*, Paris, 1838.

Lumiansky, R.M., 'Thematic Antifeminism in the Middle English *Seven Sages of Rome*', *Tulane Studies in English*, VII, 1957, pp. 5-16.

Madden, Sir Frederic, ed., *Gesta Romanorum*, Roxburgh Club, 1838.

Massey, Isabella, *Text- und Quellenstudien zu dem anonymen mitteldeutschen Gedicht von den sieben weisen Meistern*, diss. Marburg, 1913.

Masudi, *El-Masudi's Historical Encyclopedia entitled Meadows of Gold and Mines of Gems*, tr. Alois Sprenger, London, 1841.

Meyer, Paul, 'Sur le MS 620 (ancien 261) de la bibliothèque de Chartres', *Bulletin de la Société des Anciens Textes franç.*, 1894.

Misrahi, Jean, ed., *Le Roman des Sept Sages*, Paris, 1933.

de Montaiglon, A., & Charles Brunet, eds, *Le roman de Dolopathos*, Paris, 1856.

Mussafia, Adolf, 'Ueber eine italienische Bearbeitung der Sieben Weisen Meister', *Jahrb. f. rom. u. engl. Litt.*, IV, 1862, pp. 166-75.

- - , 'Ueber die Quelle des altfranzösischen Dolopathos', *Sitzungsber. der kais. Akad. der Wissenschaften*, XLVIII, 1865, pp. 246-67.

- - , 'Beiträge zur Litteratur der Sieben Weisen Meister', *Sitzungsber. der. kais. Akad. der Wissenschaften*, Phil. Hist. Klasse, LVII, 1868, pp. 37-118.

Napier, Arthur S., 'A Hitherto Unnoticed Manuscript of the Seven Sages', (= Rawlinson Poet. 175), *Publ. of the Modern Lang. Assoc.*, XIV, 1899, pp. 459-64.

Nöldeke, Th., Review of F. Baethgen's *Sindban oder die Sieben Weisen Meister*, in *Zeitschr. der deutschen morgenländischen Gesellschaft*, 33, 1879, pp. 513-36.

Oesterley, Hermann, ed., *Gesta Romanorum*, Berlin, 1872.

- - , ed., *Johannis de Alta Silva Dolopathos sive De Rege et Septem Sapientibus*, Strasbourg, 1873.

Paris, A. Paulin, *Étude sur les différents textes, imprimés et manuscrits, du Roman des sept sages*, Paris, 1869.

Paris, Gaston, Review of Oesterley's *Dolopathos* edition, *Romania*, II, 1873, pp. 481-503.

- - , Study on story Roma, *Romania*, IV, 1875, pp. 125-29.

- - , *Deux rédactions du Roman des sept sages de Rome*, Société des Anciens Textes Français, Paris, 1876.

- - , Review of Johann Alton's edn *Le Roman de Marques de Rome*, *Romania*, 19, 1890, p. 493.

- - , Review of *Amabile di Continentia, romanzo morale del secolo XV*, edited by Augusto Cesare, *Romania*, XXVI, 1897, pp. 322-23.

- - , Review of the dissertations of Botermans and Plomp (*qq.vv.*), *Romania*, XXVIII, 1899, pp. 448-50.

- - , 'Le Conte du trésor du roi Rhampsinite', *Revue de l'histoire des religions*, 55, 1907, pp. 151-87, 267-316.

Paschke, P., *Ueber das anonyme mittelhochdeutsche Gedicht von den sieben weisen Meistern*, diss. Breslau, 1891.

Perry, Ben Edwin, 'The origin of the book of Sindbad', *Fabula*, III, 1960, pp. 1-94.

- - - , *Secundus the Silent Philosopher. The Greek Life of Secundus ... Edited ... With translations of the Greek and Oriental Texts ...*, American Philological Assoc., Monograph 22, Ithaca, New York, 1964.

Petras, Paul, *Ueber die mittelenglischen Fassungen der Sage von den sieben weisen Meistern*, diss. Breslau, 1885.

Plomp, Herman P.B., *De Middelnederlandsche bewerking van het gedicht van den VII Vroeden van binnen Rome*, diss. Utrecht, 1899.

Roloff, Volker, 'Motiv und Motivation des Schweigens in der Rahmenerzählung des *Roman des Sept Sages*', in *Reden und Schweigen: Zur Tradition eines mittelälterlichen Themas in der französischen Literatur*, München, 1973, pp. 78-85.

Runte, Hans R., 'L'Histoire de la male marastre - Nouvelles Recherches sur le *Roman des sept sages de Rome* , *Actes du XIIIe Congrès International de Linguistique et de Philologie romanes*, Quebec, 1971, pp. 213-19.

- - - , ed., *Li Ystoire de la male marastre*, *Beihefte zur Zeitschrift für romanische Philologie*, Band 141, Tübingen, 1974.

Schmidt, Michael, *Neue Beiträge zur Geschichte der Sieben Weisen Meister*, diss. Köln, 1928.

Schmitz, Jakob, *Die ältesten Fassungen des deutschen Romans von den Sieben Weisen Meistern*, diss. Greifswald, 1904.

Sengelmann, Heinrich, *Das Buch von den Sieben Weisen Meistern, aus dem Hebräischen ... Übersetzt*, Halle, 1842.

Smith, Hugh Allison, 'A Verse Version of the Sept Sages de Rome', *Romanic Review*, III, 1912, pp. 1-67.

Spargo, John Webster, *Virgil the Necromancer, Studies in Virgilian Legends*, Cambridge, Mass., 1934.

Stallaert, K.F., ed., *Van den VII Vroeden van binnen Rome, Een dichtwerk der XIVde eeuw*, Gent, 1889.

- - - , 'Van den VII Vroeden etc. Antwoord op de critiek van den heer F.A. Stoett', *Het Belfort*, Febr. 1890, pp. 173-90.

Stoett, F.A., 'Van den VII Vroeden van binnen Rome', *Noord en Zuid*, XII, 1889, pp. 511-39.

- - - , 'Van den VII Vroeden etc. Antwoord aan den heer K. Stallaert', *Het Belfort*, Maart 1890, pp. 313-24.

Swan, Charles, and W. Hooper, *Gesta Romanorum, translated from the Latin*, (London, 1876) Dover Publications Inc., New York, 1959.

Thorpe, Lewis, 'Paulin Paris and the French Sequels to the "Sept Sages de Rome"', *Scriptorium*, II, 1948, pp. 59-68.

Thorpe, Lewis, ed., *Le roman de Laurin*, 2 vols, Cambridge, 1950-58.

Tuttle, Edwin H., 'Notes on "The Seven Sages"', *Modern Language Review*, XVI, 1921, pp. 166-67.

Utley, Francis Lee, Review of Morris Epstein's *Tales of Sendebar*, *Journal of American Folklore*, 82, 1969, pp. 278-79.

Varnhagen, Hermann, 'Die handschriftliche Erwerbungen des British Museum auf dem Gebiete des Altromanischen in den Jahren von 1865 bis Mitte 1877', *Zeitschr.f.rom.Philol.*, I, 1877, pp. 541-55.

- - , 'Zu "Deux rẽdactions du Roman des sept sages de Rome, ed. G. Paris, 1876"', *Zeitschr.f.rom.Philol.*, I, 1877, p. 555.

- - , *Eine italienische Prosaversion der sieben weisen Meister, nach einer Londoner Hs. herausgegeben*, Berlin, 1881.

- - , Review of P. Petras' *Ueber die ME Fassungen der Sage von den sieben weisen Meistern*, *Englische Studien*, X, 1886, pp. 279-82.

- - , 'Ueber eine unbekannte schottische Bearbeitung der sieben Weisen', *Englische Studien*, XXV, 1898, pp. 321-25.

Wright, Thomas, ed., *The Seven Sages*, Percy Society Publications XVI.1, 1845.

Yohannan, J.D., *Joseph and Potiphar's Wife in World Literature*, New York, 1968.

TEXT

XVIII. THE TEXT OF *THE BUKE OF THE SEVYNE SAGIS*

*Heir begy*nn*is the buke of the sevyne sagis   Fol. 167r

*Ane empriour in tymes bygane
In Rome, callit Dioclesiane,
Wo*n*nyt in welth and hie emprys,
For he was witty, baith war and wys.
He had no barne bot ane in deid
That to the empyre micht succeid,
Ane sone baith fair and eligant,
And of his age richt till awant,
For he of eld was bot thré ȝeir
Quhen the empryce, his moder deir,
Throw det of natur this lyf left,
As all th*at* levis mon leif heir eft.
For hir the cité maide gret mane.
The barne hecht Dioclesiane
Eftir his fader, the empriour,
That than tuke study and gret dolour,
Quhom to he suld the child *comm*yt
To nurys, teche and leir him wit.
In Rome cité than was thar sevyne
Sagis, the wisest vnder hevyne,
For by the sternis thai couth sé how
Perellis appeir and tham eschewe.
Thai war brocht sone to the palace;
The first master thai callit Bantillas.
The empri*our* sone at him couth speir
Gif he wald tak his sone to leir.
He said: 'My sou*er*ane lord of prys,
This mony ȝeir in ȝ*our* servis
Wnder promyt of gud reward
. . . .

Fol. 167^{v}

I ask no mar to all my meid
Bot gif me the child to leir *and* feid;
Deliu*er* him in-to my cure
And sekerly I ȝow assure,
That I sall him all science leir
Within na mar space than sevyne ȝeir
That I haf and my fallous baith.'
Than rais the secound sage full raith,
Said: 'Lord, gif me the child and I
Sall teche him in astronomy
All hale the science liberale
Within sex ȝer*is* wi*th*outin fale.'
Quhen Amipullus had said thus,
Than rais the thrid sage, Lentalus,
Said: 'Lord, gif me the child to leir;
He sall be techit in five ȝer.'
Catone than thai callit the ferd;
He said: 'The child, lord, sall be lerd
Within four ȝeris *ou*r sciens all.'
The fyft sege Malcome men couth call;
He said, in thrē ȝer and na mair
He suld the child teche all thar lair.
Ampustinus thai callit the sext;
He askit bot twa ȝer*is* till his taxt.
The sevynt, that Cratone callit was,
Said, in a ȝer and na mair space
The child suld all the cu*n*nyng haf
That hi*m*-self had and all the laif.
Quhen thai thir peroffer*is* maid had.
The emp*ri*oure in hart was glad,
Thankit tham gretly of th*ar* gud will
. . . .

32. Craigie's edition prints *thi* instead of *the*; however, in the MS the *i* appears to have been corrected into *e*.

Fol. 168^{r}

To teche, to kepe, to leir sciens,
With all th*ar* witt*is* and deligens,
And thai w*ith* hed*is* bowit bair
Thankit the lord and bovnit to fair.
With thai*m* the child thai had away
And tuke counsall that ilka day,
Quhar thai the child suld leir *and* how.
Than Lentalus said: 'I counsall ȝow
He be no*ch*t techit in this cité
For dreid he walk in wanyté,
Bot erar owtw*ith* in a fair waist,
A grene, a myle of at the mast,
And thar to big ane hall of stane.'
Tharto co*n*sentit thai ilkane;
Thai semblit maso*n*nis than bedene
And in the midd*is* of a fair grene
Thai biggit the chalm*er* or thai wald blyn,
And on the wallis all w*ith*in
Thai pantit all the science sevyn,
And than i*n* mydd*is* of the chalm*er* evyn
The barnis bed thai haf set
And till his teching than but let
Thai did all cure that thai couth do;
Quhen ane was tyrit ane noth*er* ȝed to,
And gart him ythandly aye leir,
Quhill the ending of the sevyn ȝer.
Than said Cato, th*a*t noble clerk:
'I reid we sé gif all o*u*r werk
Into this child effect has tane
And quhidder he sciens has or nane.'
That it suld be sa thai all assentit
And ordanit him to be attempit,

69. Craigie: '*How* for *Quhat* or *Quhare*.' See expl. note.
82. Craigie: '*thai* is superfluous.' See expl. note.

That thai my*ch*t knaw how he was sped. Fol. 168v
Wnder ilk nuke of his bed
Ane edoke leif, th*a*t was wele thyn,
Quhen he was slepand thai stall in;
Bot quhen he walki*n*nit, also fast
His eyne wpwart aye couth he cast,
Quhill all his master*is* sperit quhy
He lukit wp sa ernistlye.
'I stud', he said, 'sumthing abasit,
For oder is the erd hiear rasit
Or hevyn declynit, I dar wele say,
Fer mar than it was ȝist*er*day.'
His master*is* leuch and knewe for-quhy:
He had yneugh of astronomy.
Thus leif I him science to ken
And to the emp*ri*our tornis my pen.

The wit of Rome, sa hie of prys,
Come to the emp*ri*our *with* awys,
Sayand: 'Lord, it is o*u*r desyr
For the successioun of ȝo*u*r empyr,
That ȝe wald wed a far lady
Of gret gentrys and this o*u*r quhy:
Ȝe haf nane vth*er* gottin bot ane,
And gif caise war th*a*t he war gane,
Than falȝeit ȝo*u*r gen*er*acioun;
Than war o*u*r haile confusioun.'
The emp*riou*r said: 'I am of age,
And a ȝoung wyf in hir barnage
My*ch*t be the caus to abrek my lyf.'
Thai said: 'Na lord, tak a wyf
And trast in God th*a*t kepis all,
And a fair madin get we sall,

Fol. 169^{r}

Ane king*is* dochter, ane madin bricht.'
Quhen scho was brocht in-till his sicht,
He lufit hir hartlie p*a*ramo*u*r
And marijt hir w*ith* gret hono*u*r.
Bot quhen scho hard he had a son,
With the sevyne sag*is* wit to cone,
Scho tho*ch*t allway to haf hi*m* deid
And hir sone air in-till his steid.
Ane day in the chalmer prevé
The emp*ri*our kist the gay ladye
And bad hir aske ane luf-asking
And scho said: 'Th*a*r is na thing
Bot that I wald ʒo*u*r sone fane sé.
Perchance ʒe will get nane of me;
Than wald I hald hi*m* for my awn
Alswele as ʒo*u*r*is*.' Bot all wnknawin
Was to the emp*riou*r hir wikit tho*ch*t.
For-thi he dowtit hir richt no*ch*t,
Bot gart direct his lett*er*is sone
To the sag*is* w*ith*outin hone.
He selit tham with his awne ryng,
Chargeand thai*m* his sone to bring
In the fest of the Trinité
Or ellis dreidles thai all suld dé.
The messinger thai haf resauit
With gret hono*u*r *and* syne consauit
Of thai lett*er*is the te*n*no*u*r richt.
For-thi thai ischit at mydnycht,
To sé by sternis and planet*is* all
Quhat of that passage suld befall,
And saw forsuth thai all togiddir,
At the set day the child come hiddir

Fol. 169^v

At the first word out of his hed
That evir he spak he suld be deid.
Of this thai war astonade sair:
The child suld dé *and* he come thar;
And he come no*ch*t, w*ith*out ma pled*is*
The sevyn sag*is* suld tyne th*a*r hed*is*.
Thai tald the barne than how it stude;
He bad thai*m* be of comfort gud
And said he wald dé him allane
Erar or thai suld ilkane.
Bot he wald gang the sternis to sé
Gif thar ony remeid my*ch*t be.
He sawe ane litill sterne besyde,
Quhar-throwe be science he aspyd,
And he my*ch*t dvm sevyn dayis be
The auchtand day than speke suld he
And all his enemys ourthrawe,
And this he gart his master*is* knawe,
And thai w*ith* grace th*a*t God wald send
Ilkane a day tuke to defend.
Than counsall gaf Bantillas,
That he allane w*ith* him wald pas
And ner-hand-by byde suld thai
And ilkane cum for th*a*r awne day.
Thus is the barne cu*m*myn to the palace,
With him his master Bantillas,
Resauit w*ith* the emp*ri*our
With mekle ioye and gret hono*u*r,
With cymbalis, organis *and* clarioun
And all menstraly in vnisoun.
Full courtasly inclynit he thar,
Bot a word les na mair

188. The MS has *vrisoun*, but cf. *vnisoun* in l. 2524.

Fol. 170[r]

He spak, becaus he knewe full wele
Be his science the gret p*er*rell.
The emp*riour* led him to the hall
And on a clath of silk *and* pall
Set him and said: 'My swet son, how
Art thow plesit of thi master*is* now?'
And he inclinit full courtasly,
Bot a word spak he no*ch*t for-thi.
The emp*riour* said to Bantillas:
'Has my son tynt his speche allace?
He spak full weile quhe*n* ȝe hi*m* tuke.'
Bantillas said: 'Schir, be this buke
And all the athis th*a*t may be sworne,
He spak full weile the day at morne.'
Of his come herd the empryce
And buskit hir on hir best wys
With crovne on hed and coronale,
Mady*n*nis w*ith* courche and w*ith* kell.
God wait gif scho was blyth to cum,
Quhen that scho herd th*a*t he was dvm.
With ladyis i*n* purpo*ur* *and* i*n* pall
Blythly come scho in the hall;
Scho said: 'My lord, is this ȝo*ur* child?'
'Ȝa,' he said, 'bot he is exild
Fra speche, th*a*t na word speke may he.'
Than said scho: 'He sall go w*ith* me
To chalmer; or we twa dissever
He sall speike anys and he speke eu*er*.'
Than by the hand scho couth him tak;
He wryth the face and drewe abak,
Quhill th*a*t his fader bad him rys,
Than hvmly on curtas wys

Fol. 170^{v}

To his fader he bowit and rais,
And sa w*ith* hir to chalm*er* he gais.
And sone be at thai come w*ith*in,
Scho bad wodas baith mar *and* myn
And all out of the chalm*er* ar gane
Quhill th*ar* was left bot thai*m* allane.
Than said scho thus: 'My swet hart deir,
All is ȝour*is* that I haf heir,
Body and hert; quhill I may lest,
Of all this warld I luf ȝow best.
It was no*ch*t w*ith* ȝour fader*is* age
I chesit to mak my mariage,
Bot fer mar to ȝo*ur* swet ȝouthhed,
That I haf kepit my madinhed
Quhill now; th*a*rfor ȝe tak it heir
W*ith* all my hart at ȝo*ur* pleseir.'
With that the barne scho wald haf kist;
He threwe the face and gart hir mist.
Than, quhe*n* scho saw it was na bute,
Than sodanely scho gat on fute
And w*ith* hir nalis raif hir face
And gaf a schout and cryit: 'Allace!'
With that the lord come hastely
And saw hir thusgat*is* drest bludy.
Than said scho: 'Lord, now schawis wele,
Ȝo*ur* callit son is bot a devill,
That schupe him thus me to deflour.'
The lord had slane hi*m* i*n* th*a*t hour
And gart four torme*n*tou*ris* him tak
And band his hand*is* behynd his bak,
Bad scurge him quhe*n* he was bundin fast,
Syne strik his hed of at the last.

226. The MS has *He*, but see note.
253. The MS has *scurgis*, but see note.

Fol. 171r

Bot than the worthy of the cité,
Quhen thai hard tell the child suld dé,
Gretlie for him can thai murn
And to the emp*ri*our but sudiorn
Thai come *and* said:'Leif lord, allace,
Quhar is ȝ*our* wit in-to this case,
That has bot a barne air to be,
And but iustice wald gar him dé?
Schir, gar*ris* kepe him quhill the morne,
That we, that ar ȝ*our* counsall sworne,
May ryplé counsall ȝ*ow* *and* reid,
Gif the child has maid caus of deid.
For and o*u*r enemys my*ch*t knawe
That ane suld dé w*ith*outin law,
Thai suld sclander the richt of Rome
In hethi*n*nes and in Cristindome.'
The emp*ri*our to th*ar* sawis tuk hed
And to the presound gart him leid,
Sayand, that nicht at the lest
The child suld leif at th*ar* request.
Thai thankit him w*ith* all th*ar* mane
And ilkane hamwart went agane.
The emprys m*u*rnyt and maid gret cair
And be the rut*is* raif hir hair.
He sperit quhy. 'Ȝe knawe full wele;
Ȝe hecht to revenge me of this devill
That schupe to fyle my woma*n*hed,
That he suld dé ane schamis deid,
And now ȝe haf th*a*t quyte forȝet.
Tharfor me think it war wele set
That to ȝou sic a chance betid
As till a burges of this tovne did.'

He prayit hir that to declair. Fol. 171^{v}
Scho said: 'I will, for ȝ*ou*r welfair.'

*The emprys tale of the pynetre ARBOR
And the gardyner.

*In-to this tovne was knawin wele
A burges duelt, callit Cornele,
Riche and myc*h*ti, blyth and glad,
And a fair orchard this burges had
Of frutfull treis of mony kynd.
Bot th*a*r was ane he had i*n* mynd
Our all the laif, a ioly pyne.
He callit his gardiner *and* bad hi*m* syne
Cure of the orchard he suld haf
And of the pyne o*u*r all the laif.
Syne passit the burges i*n* m*er*chandis;
The pyne grewe fair at all devys.
Quhen he come hame sone sperit he
Befor all thing: 'How dois my tré?'
The gardynar said: 'Go sé; p*er*chance
Tharof ȝe sall tak gret plesance!'
Quhen he it saw, so fair *and* hé,
Micht na man mar reiosit be.
To gud the tré than couth he bid
To gar it bere and so he did,
So plesand and so plentuos
Our all the laif, so m*er*walous,
Sa fair, sa fragrant and sa fyne,
That it was callit the pereles pyne.
The frut it bure had sic a grace,
That all the cité refreschit was.
Bot fra the rute sone eft*ir* syne
A pynule, a syon of this pyne,

310. On *he* see expl. note.

Grew wp and maid this burges blyth, Fol. 172^{r}
And he chargit his gardinar to kyth
All cure w*ith* erd that war birthy,
Till gar this pynull grow provdly
And sa it did, bot all barane
It was and frut bur neu*er* nane.
Tharof the burges was ill payd
And callit the gardinar *and* till hi*m* said:
'This pynule is lyk, as I consaif,
This ȝer na flour na frut till haf.'
'Schir', said the gardyner, 'tho*ch*t I be thra,
This litill prety pynula
Thar may na gudding it avalȝe,
This treis vmbre garr*is* it falȝe;
The branchis latt*is* it to get air.'
Than gart he hewe the bewes fair
Of the gret tré of sic revovne
That bure the frut on sic fussoun.
Quhe*n* all the branchis sa war sned
The ȝoung tré na bett*er* sped.
This noble tré stud all disgysit,
Nakit, hurt *and* ill sup*ris*it,
That it was peté for to se
Sa worthy frut suld perist be.
Ȝit quhe*n* the pynull wald no*ch*t growe
Than gart he tak ba*ith* ax *and* how
And hewe this gud tré by the rute,
That it my*ch*t neu*er* ber na frute.
The citeȝo*uris* maid richt gret dule,
That Cornele was sa gret a fule,
That had distroyit this noble tré
And wist no*ch*t quhat the plant wald be.

To the emp*riou*r than said the quene:
'Schir, wait ȝe quhat this tale may meyne?

This tré is ȝow, s*chir* emp*ri*our, Fol. 172v
Of micht, of riches and hono*u*r,
That comfort*is* mony seir cuntré
With frute of ȝo*u*r nobilité.
Ȝone devile, thi sone, the plant is evyn,
The fals gardinar the sag*is* sevyne
That will distroye thé quyte away.
Than sall all the barnage saye:
"Allace, we want o*u*r noble lord."'
Than said the emp*riour*: 'I stand ford,
For this ensample thow has schawin
My son sall be hangit *and* drawin.'
To presoun th*a*t ny*ch*t is he gane,
Bot on the morne, quhe*n* the sone schane,
He gart four torme*n*to*uris* him leid
Vnto the gallous to be deid,
And as he passit throw the streit
The tovne lord*is* that couth him meit
Grat for sorowe. Than at the last
Come the first sage prekand fast,
To sé gif he the child my*ch*t borowe;
Wit ȝe his hart was full of sorowe.
Than prekit he on withoutin baid
And salusyng to the emp*riou*r maide.
He said: 'Bantillas, neu*er* worth thé wele
That for my sone brocht me a devill,
Dwm and wald haf forsit my quene.'
'My lord,' said he, 'forsuth ȝestrene
He couth haf spokin; sa can he now,
War no*ch*t p*er*rellis he wald eschow,
That he knawis be experiens,
Apperand be his gret sciens;

After line 356 a line was deleted, see expl. note.

Fol. 173^{r}

And her att*our* full wele knaw ʒe
Be Romys lawis he suld no*ch*t dé,
Suppos he wald haf forsit the quene,
Bot gif th*a*t scho a madin had bene.
He may no*ch*t dé, schir, be the lawe,
And sla ʒe him for ʒo*ur* wyf*is* sawe,
Als gret mischance sall fall ʒe
As fell a kny*ch*t of this cité.'
*The emp*r*i*our* bad him tell but dreid.
He said: 'S*chi*r, quhat may th*a*t me speid,
The child th*a*t I deliu*er* wald
Gif he be deid or I haf tauld?
Bot gerr*is* the child be brocht ws till,
Syne heir my tale and gif gud skill;
Fra deid mak his deliu*er*ance,
Freth him or ell*is* do ʒo*ur* plesance.'
Than gart he bring the child agane.
Tharof his mast*er* was full fane
And said: 'S*chi*r, wald ʒe resoun knaw,
Ane suth sample I sall ʒow schawe.'

*Bantillas taile of the serpent th*a*t wald haf slane the barne and was helpit be the hound, q*uhi*lk was slane be his mast*er*.

CANIS

*Ther wo*n*nyt quhylis a gentill kny*ch*t,
Off hie worschipe, wys and wicht,
For our all vth*er* thing lufit he
Of armes gret nobilité,
Iusting and tor[na]ment*is* but let,
Tharon his hart allhale was set.
Gret cost th*a*ron wald he mak,
And gentill iornais wnd*er*tak,
Baith of ernist and of play
And oft the p*r*ice he bure away,

386. *nocht* had been forgotten and was inserted above the line between *suld* and *dé*.

So fer that of his gret renovne Fol. 173v
Thai spak in mony riche regioun,
That suthly as the story says
He had no peir in-till his dayis.
So happi*n*nit th*a*t he set *per* cas
Ane gret iornay wele ner his place.
To the set day come mony kny*ch*t,
And he him-self i*n* armes dicht
And to the feld him sped in haist.
His famelé folowit, sa th*a*t all waist
Left the castall. Baith mar *and* myn
Past to the feld that nane left in,
Saifand a barne, his aperand air,
In credill bundin lay slepand fair,
And a grewhound the lord best lufit,
That oft at hunting wele had prufit.
Nurys and all away was went.
Than in the hole was a serpent,
That saw all waist *and* set hir ȝarne
With all hir pith to sla this barne,
And to the credill schowit i*n* hy;
Bot the grewhound th*a*t lay th*ar*by
Baid hir batell for all hir bir.
Scho bait him sair, so did he hir;
Sa stifly thar in stowr thai stude
That the hous-flure was full of blud.
The barnis credill was cassyn owr,
Bot, as God wald, the torr*is* four
His face wele kepit fra the erd;
The barne lay slepand ȝit vnsterd,
Quhill the grewhound the edder sleuch
And lay to rest him wery yneuch

Fol. 174^{r}

Besyde the credill amang the blude
Of the edder; quhar it stude
The serpent*is* blud lay all about.
Sa come the nurys and gaf a schout,
Quhen scho the credill saw cassyn sa;
Scho wist no*ch*t quhat to do for wa,
Bot fled and schoutit and cryid: 'Allace!'
Than come the lady of the place
And sperit quhat gart th*a*t m*u*rnyng be.
Scho said: 'Full wa is me *and* thé;
We may no*ch*t falȝe to be forfarne:
The grewhound has slane thi a barne,
And ȝit is liand in his blud!'
Than cryit the lady as scho war wod;
Syne to the erd scho fell richt thar
And w*ith* hir hand*is* raif hir hair.
Sa come the lord *and* saw hir ly
Sa fer disgysit he sperit quhy.
'Full wa is ws,' scho said agane,
'Ȝo*u*r lufit grewhound ȝo*u*r son has slane!'
Than was he grevit and th*ar*-w*ith*-all
He sped him fast in-to the hall.
The grewhound, quhe*n* he saw the kny*ch*t,
Waikly rais as he best micht.
His lord full hartlie couth he fawne
And sone the kny*ch*t his swerd has drawin
And for his wyf*is* word, allake,
The grewgound he slewe at a straike,
That savit had his sone fra deid.
Quhen he had strikin of his hed,
Towart the credill than can he speir

Fol. 174v

And fand his ȝoung sone haile and feir,
And syne he fand this edder slane.
Than he misgaf him sair agane,
That he the gentill [grew]hound slewe,
For be the taki*n*nis weile he knew
The grewhound savit his so*n*nis lyf.
Than kest he fra him swerd *and* knyf
And brak his speir in part*is* four.
The ioye of armes th*ar* gaf he owr
And to the haly land wowit he,
For evir a pilgryme for to be.
And ȝit befor or he wald found,
Sa gret he for his gud grewhound,
And ba*n*nit the tyme th*a*t he drew swerd
Or slewe him for his wyf*is* word.

Quhen Bantillas had said that sawe,
To the emp*ri*our he knelit lawe
And said that he copy micht
How gret mischef come to this kny*ch*t,
That slewe the hound th*a*t savit the lyf
Of his ȝoung sone than for his wyf.
'Fer mair mischef sall cum to thé,
Gif that thow garr*is* thi awne sone dé
For word*is* of a fals woman.'
'Be my crovne!' said the emp*ri*our than,
'My son sall na way dé to-day!'
The clerk him thankit *and* ȝeid his way,
Bot wit ȝe weile, attour meso*u*r
The emprice on the emp*ri*our,
Quhen that scho hard of th*a*t delay,
Scho grat and cryit harmisay.

481. Craigie: '*hound* for *grewhound*(?)'.

APER

He askit quhy scho maid sic cheir. Fol. 175r
Sche said: 'I m*er*well quhy ȝe speir
The questioun; ȝe knawe full wele
How that ȝ*our* callit son, ȝone dele,
Sa fowlely wald haf forsit me,
Ȝe hecht I suld rewengit be,
Bot y*our* word stand*is* no*ch*t as king;
Tharfor I dreid att*our* all thing,
Als gret misavent*our* sall fall ȝe
As quhylom fell in this cu*n*tré.'
He bad hir tell the man*er* howe.
Sche said: 'Blythlie, and heir me now,
And luke ȝe prent it i*n* ȝ*our* hart,
For dreid ȝe rewe it eft*ir*wart.
Wald God th*at* ȝe me wnd*er*stud,
For all th*at* I tell is for ȝ*our* gud.'

The empryce tale of the baire
And the herd.

Than bly*n*nit the emprys of hir baile
And thus-way scho began hir tale:

In this cu*n*tré, no*ch*t fer heir west, APER
Sumtyme th*ar* stude a fair forest,
Of frute and tré lyke it was nane,
And wallit about w*ith* lyme *and* stane.
Mony diu*er*s kynd of best*is* war thar,
Bot our thai*m* all th*ar* was a bair,
And th*ar* was na man than sa wicht
Bot it was m*er*well, gif he micht
With lyf eschape fra he him knewe,
For gentill and sempill als he slewe;
Fra he thai*m* saw thai gat na grace.
It happi*n*nit swa i*n* litill space,

Ane pure herd that was thar by Fol. 175v
Come in the forest neir hastely.
Off him the baire sone gat a sicht;
The herd sawe that he chape no*ch*t micht
Nor that it was na bute to flé.
Nymly he clam wp in the tré;
Than, quhen the baire saw him abone,
To ryfe the rute than schupe he sone
And w*ith* his nalis and w*ith* his tusk*is*
Sa rudly at the rute he rusk*is*,
That all was lyke for to ga dovne.
For dreid the herd neir fell i*n* swoun;
Ane litill harting had he ȝit,
And w*ith* the froit th*a*t was so sweit,
He plukit and kest dovne gud scar.
Tharof wele plesit was the bair
And ete and leit the gnawyn be,
And when the herd p*er*sauit th*a*t he
Tuke the frute in sic plesans,
He kest him dovne sic haboundans
That he ete thai*m* so surfatly,
That he my*ch*t do na thing bot ly.
And quhen th*a*t he was sa lyand,
The herd wan till hi*m* w*ith* his hand,
And clawit him softly on the bak,
Syne on the wame, I wnd*er*tak,
That first he wynkit, syne fell on slepe.
Tharto the herd tuke grathly kepe,
And quhen sound slepand was the bair,
He drewe his knyf *and* slewe hi*m* thar.

'My lufit lord,' than said this quene,
'Ȝe wnd*er*stand wele quhat I meyne;

ȝe ar this bair,' scho said, 'for quhy Fol. 176r
All man obeys thi senȝeory.
The herd thi son is for to say,
That fordo thé wald ny*ch*t *and* day,
The qu*hi*lk th*ar*for cly*m*mis i*n* the tré
Of science and of subtilté,
And w*ith* the frut thi anger swag*is*,
That is the fair word*is* of the sag*is*,
That w*ith* th*ar* fals talis clawis thi bak,
Quhill that thai may thé slepand tak,
And than but m*er*cy put thé dovne
That thi fals sone may haf thi crovne.'
Thar was no*ch*t than bot on the morne
This child was iugit to be forlorne.
The torme*n*tou*ris* tuke him agane
And throw the tovne led to be slane,
That mekle dule than th*ar* was.
Sa come his mast*er* Maxillas
And prayit the torme*n*tou*ris* to tary,
For he trastit th*a*t tryst to wary,
And to the palace sped hi*m* sone
And halsit the emp*ri*ou*r* foroutin hone.
And he agane, full grevously,
Answerd and said full angerly:
'Wa worth ȝow in tyme to cum,
That has my son bro*ch*t to me dvm.'
'Schir,' said the mast*er*, 'God wait gif he
Be dvm and als wele wait [gif] we
Haf wyte th*ar*of or gif ȝo*ur* quene
Be sa lele as scho garr*is* ȝow wene.
Bot in wage dar I lay my hed:
Put ȝe ȝo*ur* son for hir to deid,
A mar mischance sall fall ȝe

587. Craigie: '*Than* for *That*, or *than* for *yare*(?)'; see expl. note.
598. *gif* inserted by Craigie.

MEDICUS

Than fell ane wysman in this cité.' Fol. 176v
He bad him tell. He said: 'Full fayne,
Sa ʒe gar bring the barne agane,
For litill bute to tell think me,
Or I haue tald, gif that he dé.
Bot ʒe sall lat me him replege,
Syne heir the resoun th*a*t I allege,
And gif ʒe can apply th*a*r-till,
Salf the child, ell*is* do ʒo*u*r will.'
The barne was sone brocht to presens;
Than thus he tald for his defence:

The taile of Maxillas of
Ypocras and his disciple.

MEDICUS

In this cité duelland th*a*r was
Ane famous clerk, hecht Ypocras,
Quhilk of phesik had sa gret fame
That throw the warld sprang his gud name,
For th*a*r was nane th*a*t tyme trewly
Sa expert in philosophy.
He had w*i*t*h* him his sist*er* son,
That able was all craft to con,
Bot he wald neu*er* leir hi*m* nane,
For dreid he of his rowme had tane.
Neu*er*theles the child was ay
Deligent i*n* all th*a*t he may,
And for to ken set all his tho*ch*t
The prattik*is* as his mast*er* wrocht,
Quhill th*a*t his eme p*er*savit i*n* deid
In subtelté he suld exceid.
So happi*n*nit sone i*n* litill space,
The king*is* sone tuke gret seknes.
Ane staitly message than maid was
On fra the king till Ypocras,

Fol. 177r

With promys of ful gret reward
And said na spending suld be sparde
To heile his son th*a*t to the crovne
Had apperand successioun.
Bot Ypocras no way wald wend,
Bot tho*ch*t he wald his newo send,
For he wald haue experiens
Gif he was subtell in sciens,
And he excusit his awne passing
And send his newo to the king.
The king resauit hi*m* hon*or*ably
And welcu*m*mit him, bot no*ch*t-for-thi
He had be fer in-to that case
Had his ald eme Ypocras.
This mediciner to chalm*er* ȝeid
And to the seike barne couth hi*m* speid.
His pous, his vryne sone he says
And his bodyis extremitéis,
And quhen he had thai*m* craftly sene
In secrete said he to the quene:
'Madame, gif ȝe desyr th*a*t I
Heile this child of malady,
To gar me sé it war na scaith
Ȝ*our* watter and the king*is* baith.'
Scho said th*a*t plesit hir hartfully,
And on the morne richt sone airly
Gart baith th*ar* watter*is* till hi*m* bring,
Of hir awne self *and* of the king.
He kest thai*m* i*n* his vrinale;
Quhat he th*ar* saw he wald no*ch*t tell,
Bot quhen he had thai*m* sene ilkane
He callit the quene by hir allane,

652. Craigie: *says* for *seys* = 'sees' (cf. *sene* 653, *se* 657).

Fol. 177v

And in gret counsall than he bad hir
Quha that was [the] carnale fader
Of hir seike son and quha hi*m* gat.
Scho said: 'Na questioun is th*a*rat;
The king my lord, wi*th*outin lane.'
'Na mair than I,' said he agane.
Scho said: 'Say ȝe that i*n* effek,
Thy hed sall gang than of thi nek!'
'Na hed haf I bot ane,' said he,
'And gret misfortoune happi*n*nit me
Gif I come hidd*ir* th*a*t hed to tyne.
Tharfor w*ith* Godd*is* blissing *and* myne,
Get ȝow ane nothe*r* mediciner,
For I will byde no langar heir.'
Than, quhen scho fastly had espyid
He bowned him and wald no*ch*t byid,
Sche prayit him full petuoslye
To heile counsall, and nakitlye
The w*er*ité scho suld declair,
And tharto was he oblist thar.
Quhen scho th*ar*on his faith had tane
Scho said: 'The ȝoung erle of Artane
With my lord herberit sekerly,
Sa ȝoung, sa fair *and* sa lufly!
His word*is* me tho*ch*t as hony swete;
I lufit him wele and sa he lete
He lufit me atto*ur* all wicht;
Ȝone child he gat on me th*a*t ny*ch*t.'
'Weile,' said he than, 'now sall I ȝarne
Kepe ȝo*ur* secret*is* *and* hele ȝo*ur* barne!'
He fed the child fra thi*n* w*ith* beif,
And watt*er* was his drinke mast leif.

668. Craigie: '*his* for *the*'.

Fol. 178^{r}

Tharwith in lytill tyme was he
Als hale as ony man my*ch*t be.
Gretlie reiosit than was the king,
And till his medicinar gart bring
Reward*is* th*a*t full worthy war.
The qwene i*n* secret gaf fer mar
And thus w*ith* worschipe *and* gret fame
Till his eme come his newo hame.
Sone sperit he gif the child was hale.
'Ȝa,' said his newo, 's*chi*r, but faile.'
He sperit quhat medicyne he gaf.
'Beif, watt*er*,' said he, 'our all the laif.'
Than said the wys clerk Ypocras:
'In hurdome than he gottin was.'
Fra th*a*t day furth his eme had dreid
That his newo suld him exceid
In craft and gar him lichtlyit be,
And studyet how he suld gar hi*m* de,
And noth*er* spair for syn nor schame
Or he tynt ocht of his gret fame.
This held he in reme*m*berans
With a fals fenȝeit countenans
For till vndo the innocent,
Quhilk eft*ir*wart sair he couth repent.
It happi*n*nit so heir eft*ir*wart
He passit to sport in the orchart,
And of ane herbe so medicinale
Ypocras said he feld but faile,
Sa fair, sa fragrant *and* sa soft,
That it w*ith* gold my*ch*t no*ch*t be coft.
He bad his newo draw it sone
And as he bad sone has he done.

Fol. 178v

Ane lytill eft*ir* he smellit ane nothir
And callit it bett*er* na the tothir;
Than wp he gart th*a*t herbe be tane.
Than war thai set dovne thai*m* allane
In the orchard wnder a trế,
And than agane he said th*a*t he
Had fundin the best of all but dowt,
And bad his newo laigh dovne lowte
And w*ith* the rute it hale wp tak.
Quhen he was lowtand, in-to the bak
With a lang knyf he straik him than
And slewe that saikles sib ȝoung man,
And slewe him-self in the maner.
For eft*ir*wart as ȝe sall heir
Sairlie for that gret trespas
God tuke wengeans on Ypocras
With sic ane schot in-till his wame,
That he had seiknes sair *and* schame,
That he couth stanche apon na mak
For spys or herbe that he couth tak.
Than all the master*is* th*a*t he had maide
Till him thai come w*ith*outin baid,
For stanche couth thai no*ch*t ilkane.
Tharfor thai m*u*rnyt and maid gret mane,
And quhen he saw all was i*n* wane,
A tvme toun gart tak i*n* plane
And boryt the bodome i*n* holis all.
Ane herbe i*n* it than leit he fall,
Syne fillit the twn w*ith* watt*er* fow,
Bot neu*er* a drope, I sover ȝow,
Wald ryn at all thai holis dovne,
The herbe maid sic restrictioun.

Fol. 179^{r}

Than said he to thai master*is* all:
'Be experiens now sé ȝe sall,
Ȝone herbe that gerr*is* the watter stop
At all ȝone holis, th*a*t neu*er* a drope
It latt*is* cum of ȝone borit tré,
War I stanchable it wald stanche me,
Bot God is grevit, it is full trewe,
Becaus that I my newo slewe
Bot for inwy of his science.
The wengeans of his innocens
Is on me fallyn now full feile.
War he liffand, he couth me heile,
Bot he is deid, th*ar*for allace!'
And tharwith deit Ypocras,
That in-to medicyne was so slé
That his renovne will neu*er* dé.

'My lord,' than said the clerk sa clene,
'Ȝe haue consauit quhat I mene.'
'Ȝa,' said the emp*riour*, 'at the best,
And has it in my hart degest.'
Than meikly answerd Ancillas:
'Quhat scaith had bene th*a*t Ypocras
Had lattin his newo liffand ga?
He my*ch*t had helit him *and* ma.
Be God, a war chance fall sall ȝe
And ȝe ȝo*ur* saikles son gar dé,
Or hurt or strik w*ith* knyf or sword
For ȝo*ur* fals wantoun wyf*is* word.'
'Ancillas,' than the lord can say,
'My son sall na way dé to-day!'
The sage thankit the empriour
And tuke his leif w*ith* gret honour

GAZA

Quhen he was respit on this wys, Fol. 179v
Wa was the hart of the emprys.
Scho held chalm*er* w*ith* lytill sang,
Gretand and m*u*rnand ay amang,
Quhill ny*ch*t come, that the emprio*ur*
In chalmer sperit of his dolo*ur*,
And scho answerd and stud nane awe:
'Allace that evir I ȝ*o*w saw,
For to my frend*is* ȝe s*er*uit feid,
For ȝe ar the hale caus of my deid.
Wald God I had bene borne on beir
That day till erd that I come heir.
Ȝe hecht I suld revengit be
Apon ȝo*ur* sone, bot now I sé
Ȝo*ur* word stand*is* no*ch*t as king;
My awne grevans I compt no thing,
Bot dowt*is* that thai sall put ȝ*o*w dovn,
And gif ȝone fals devill ȝo*ur* crovne.
Bot ȝe him sla, he will sla ȝow,
For it is lyke -- I mak a wowe --
That mair mischeif sall fall ȝe,
Than fell ane kny*ch*t i*n* this cité.'
'Tell on,' said he, 'how was the case?'
Scho said: 'God I beseike of grace,
That i*n* ȝo*ur* hart it tak effek,
Or nybill gif ȝow in the nek.'

The emprys tale of the kny*ch*t
that stall the empr*i*or*is* gold.

'This tale,' sayis scho, 'knawis mony ane.'

In the tyme of Octoviane, GAZA
That was ane my*ch*ti emp*r*i*o*ur

Fol. 180r

-- And lufit riches sa our mesour
That gold and silu*er* i*n* hurd had he
That vnes it my*ch*t novmerit be;
He gaderit moble sa our meso*u*r
That he a towr fillit of tresso*u*r --
Thar duelt twa kny*chtis* ner-hand the towne
Of richt vnlyke condicioun.
The tane was full of wretchidnes,
Aye sparand to spend mair or les.
The toth*er* wald spend to largely
And feist his ny*ch*tbour*is* co*m*monly.
Than in schort tyme for his largnes
This large kny*ch*t fell in-to distres.
The toth*er* for his sparing
Was tane in s*er*uice to the king
And sone eft*ir* maid governo*u*r,
To kepe the treso*u*r of the towr.
This large kny*ch*t fell so in det
That dedly mister w*ith* hi*m* met.
Than of na thing had he plesance,
Suppos he schewe fair countenans,
For bett*er* chos war for to dé
Than evir in det and mister be.
He callit his sone apon a day
And said: 'Deir sone, quhat sall I say?
I am so far in danger drawyn,
That I haf na thing of my awn,
Bot gif that I wald sell my land;
And sa war all mischef at hand,
For thow wald want thi*n* heretage,
Thy sister*is* want th*ar* mariage,
And I had lever to be deid.

Tharfor, deir son, gif me thi reid.' Fol. 180v
He said: 'Fader, quhat suld I say?
Quhat-evir ȝe will I will allway.'
Than said he: 'I sé na succour,
Bot gif we my*ch*t wyn i*n* the tovr,
Wnder the erd full prevely
With mattok*is* myne it subtelly.'
'Bot Fader, ȝit I dreid th*a*t we
Be tane, and th*a*rfor iugit be.'
He said: 'Na son, God will ws saif,
Becaus th*a*t we sic mist*er* haif.'
Than schupe thai for it w*ith* deligens;
Wnder the ny*ch*t*is* myrk scilens
Thai maid the myne and gat entré
And tuke of moble sic plenté,
That all his dett*is* he couth discharge,
And of his spens was als large
As of befor eu*er*ilk deile,
And marijt baith his douchter*is* wele,
And he sparit neu*er* for to spend,
Quhill of his gud*is* he maid ane end
And fell agane i*n* gret purté,
And tald his sone i*n* prevaté
That he wald, as he did befor,
Get gold or ell*is* his lyf forlor.
With baith th*a*r witt*is* than chesit thai
The towr agane for till assay,
Bot in the tyme than thai no*ch*t wist,
This kepand kny*ch*t the moble [m]ist,
And fande the hole quhar thai com in,
And thar devysit a subtell gyn
To lat that hole still opyn be,

884. Craigie: '*mist*; MS. *wist* from the preceding line.'

And vnd*er* it ane hole maid he, Fol. 181r
That quhasa-evir come throw the wall
In that depe hole behufit to fall,
And in a caldron full of pik
Neidforce thar behufit hi*m* stik.
Of this wist no*ch*t this large kny*ch*t,
Bot w*ith* his son apon the ny*ch*t
Past in, as he befor had done,
And in the caldron fell he sone.
Thar stak he still *and* my*ch*t no*ch*t steir,
And said: 'Allace th*a*t I come heir,
For I mon dé withouti*n* dowt;
I am quhar I may neu*er* get out.
Hald thé thar, son, cu*m* no*ch*t to me,
For bett*er* is ane na we baith dé.'
'Quhat will ȝe, Fader,' said he, 'I do?'
He said: 'Son, I sall tell thé, lo!
Strik of my hed *and* to thé draw;
My body than na man may knawe.
Sa may thow bruke thi heretage,
Of me gif th*ar* be na knawlege,
And o*u*r schame hid.' Than at th*a*t word
Swiftlie drewe the son his sword
And of his fader*is* hed strake he,
And kest it i*n*-till a foule prevé
That was ner-by of stynkand fen,
For dreid men my*ch*t it sé or ken.
He slewe his fader to chewe the schame,
To bruke wp all. Quhe*n* he come hame
He tald his sister*is* of the caise.
Thai grat w*ith* mony sair allace
And for th*ar* fader maid gret mane.

Fol. 181v

Thareft*ir*, be schort tyme was gane,
This kny*ch*t, the kepar of the towr,
Come to wesy the gret tresso*ur*,
And in the caldron fand he than
Ane hedles body of a man.
Of that tho*ch*t he a m*er*wale huge,
For th*ar* was neu*er* man couth iuge
The cors, na of it haf knawlege,
Becaus it wantit the wisage.
Bot alsa sone this kepand kny*ch*t
He vmbetho*ch*t him of a slicht
And at a hors tale thro*u* the streit
Gart drawe the body by the feit,
And quhar thai hard thai*m* m*u*rnyng mak,
Enter and all th*a*t houshald tak.
Bot quhe*n* the sister*is* th*ar* fader saw,
For deid na schame thai stude nane aw
To cry and schout as thai war wod,
And quhen the broth*er* saw how it stud,
He prayit his sister*is* to be in pes,
And quhen he saw thai wald no*ch*t ces,
With his awne knyf i*n*-to the thee
Weile neir the hip a wound maid he,
And sa haboudantly than can bleid,
That all the flure w*ith* blude can spreid.
Bot than the men that drewe the cors
In-to that hous thai come w*ith* fors,
And sperit quhat m*u*rnyng thai maid thar.
He said: 'My sister*is* gret*is* sa sair
Becaus I hurt me reklesly
And bled*is* thus sa haboundantly.
Thai trast my deid.' Thus he thai*m* wylit;

Fol. 182[r]

Thai trowit and sa past begy[lit].
This trat*ou*r sone did all this trane,
For first he has his fader slane
And cassyn his hed in-to the fen
He my*ch*t haf erdit w*ith* Cristin men,
Syne levit in lust and in delyte;
His fader he forȝet full tyte.

'Ȝe wnd*er*stand this', said the quene,
'This samy*n* sample beis on ȝow sene.
Ȝone devill, ȝ*ou*r son, bot ȝe put dovne,
He count*is* ȝow no*ch*t, haf he ȝ*ou*r crovne.
For-thi, allace, full wa is me.'
The emp*ri*our said: 'My son sall dé;
Tho*ch*t all the sag*is* sevyne had sworn,
He levis na langar than to-morne!'
'Do sa,' said scho, 'ȝe do wysly.
Ȝ*ou*r purpos God manteine for-thi.'
Than on the morne the emp*ri*our
Gart tak the child out of the towr
And bad the tormen*t*our*is* hi*m* hang.
Bot as he to the gallous couth gang,
Lentulus, his master deir,
Met thai*m* and hertlie can requer
That thai suld tary on the way,
To sé gif he couth schut the day.
His palfray strake he w*ith* his spur,
Syne lichtit *and* halsit the emp*ri*our,
Quhilk spak na word. Than Lentulus
Said: 'S*chi*r, I trowit no*ch*t to fynd it thus.'
The emp*ri*our said: 'Ȝe sall fynd all ewill,
That for my son brocht me a dewill,
Dwm and wald haf [forsi]t my quene;
For-thi ȝe all sall de b[edene].'

952. See expl. note. 977. Craigie: '*spure* corrected from *spurris*'; see expl.note.
984. *de* had been forgotten and was inserted from below the line with a caret. The last word is illegible except for the initial letter, owing to damage.

PUTEUS

Fol. 182v

Lentulus said: 'S*chi*r, I presome
Thar is na man this day i*n* Rome
Can speike bett*er* na ȝ*our* son can,
And it is lak till ony man (...)
Bot in prevé it is fer mair
To fische a caus heir or thar,
Na he schupe neu*er* ȝ*our* wyf to deir,
In tho*ch*t na deid, I dar wele swer.
To sla ȝ*our* sone and ȝe be sene
For fals relacioun of ȝ*our* quene,
Ȝ*our* misfortoun sall be als fell
As did a burges I herd tell
In this cité.' Than said he: 'How?'
Lentulus said: 'I sall tell ȝow,
Bot garr*is* ȝ*our* sone be brocht agane
Quhill I haf tauld, and heir remane
And syne th*ar*eft*ir* do may ȝe
Ȝ*our* awne plesans of him and me.'

Lentulus taile of the woman that
gart hir husband trowe th*a*t sche fell
in-to the well.

PUTEUS

Ane empriour in o*ur* eldar*is* dayis
Nocht lang bygane, as the story says,
Statut for the felicité
And commoun gud of this cité,
The ny*ch*t-walkar*is* for till expell,
That thai suld ryng a co*m*moun bell
Nichtly befor the cok*is* can crawe,
And th*ar*eft*ir* he maid ane law
That quha out of ane hous war fundin,
That thai suld takin be and bundin
And in preson (with/to sc)hame be done,

988. Craigie: 'Two or more lines appear to be missing here.'

Syne on the morn, quhill it war none,
On a pillar be done of bras
And thar thole schame for th*ar* trespas,
And eftir-wart, as it efferit,
Be iustifyet as the caus requerit.
Heir wy*n*nit quhylis ane ceteȝener
That in worschipe levit mony ȝer,
Weile lufit and myc*h*ti all his lyf,
Bot he wald neu*er* tak a wyf,
Quhill on a tyme his frend*is* haile
To mary gaif him sic counsall,
To haf successioun of his seid;
Ysak he hecht w*ith*outin dreid.
A fair ȝoung may Ianot was cald;
He marijt hir thoc*h*t he was ald,
And put hir in a hous of stane
He biggit, and thai duelt thai*m* allane
At th*ar* plesans liffand thar,
And all clething yneugh *and* mar,
Bot dure and wyndo was th*ar* nane
To enter na to luke furth bot ane.
The dure he lokkit ilka day,
And ilka nyc*h*t the keyis lay
Wnder his hed quhill that he slepit;
Thus in all way was Ianot kepit.
Than at th*a*t wyndo was all hir sport
To sit and sê and luke ourthort.
A fair ȝoung man a day p*er*cas
Happi*n*nit to luke wp to the place
And saw hir sit sa in a cage,
Sa lufly w*ith* gret corage.
He lukit mair *and* sa hartlye;
Scho lukit dovne sa amorusly,
That be th*ar* taky*n*nis thai knewe betwene

PUTEUS

Fol. 183v

Togidd*ir* fane thai wald haf bene,
Bot thai my*ch*t na way cu*m* th*a*rto,
So stratlie kepit in was scho.
Thai vsit this luking sa a quhile
Quhill at the last scho fand a wyle
And on ald Ysak birlit the wyne,
And quhen he was slepand syne,
The key scho staw and furth past scho
Till hir le*m*man, hir lust to do,
And than sic taki*n*nis scho hi*m* tald,
That he my*ch*t cu*m* quhe*n* eu*er* he wald
Befor ewyn mak till hir a syne,
That scho my*ch*t ald Ysak trane w*ith* wyne
And mak him dru*n*kin, and sa scho did
Lang tyme or hir que*n*tis was kid.
Bot Ysak m*er*walit at the last
Quhy scho birlit wyne sa fast
To mak hi*m* drunkin, (he) wist no*ch*t quhy.
He tho*ch*t the caus for till aspy
And sparit the wyne *and* fenȝeit slepe
And tho*ch*t to tak to hir gud kepe.
Richt sa he did sa p*er*fyt'lye
Quhill scho the keyis stall prewely
And past, hir lust for to fulfill,
And left ald Ysak lyand still.
Bot ȝit scho was begylit i*n* that;
Quhen scho was gane, on fut he gat,
The dure behynd hir lokit fast
And syne wp to the wyndo past
Hir (hame-)cu*m*myn for till haf sene,
And had knawlege quhar scho had bene.
Bot quhen scho come *and*fand all lokit
Meikly at the dure scho knokit,
And as he wist no*ch*t quha was thar,

1065. Craigie: '*sche* for *he*.'
1077. Craigie silently changed *Eme* into *hame*.

He spak and sperit quhay it war. Fol. 184r
Scho said: 'I, Ianot, and nane noth*er*;
Ane messinger fetchit me to my mod*er*,
And for to lat ȝow slepand ly,
I stall fra ȝow full prevely.'
'Thow leyis,' q*uod* he, 'as wele thow can;
Thow has bene at a ȝoung man,
And be the crovne of the emp*ri*our,
Thow sall byde thar the schamfull hour
And w*ith* the kepar*is* of the towne
This nyc*h*t be put in dungeoun.'
Scho said: 'My deir, quhy say ȝe sa?
My déand moder gart me ga.
Hald ȝe me heir, ȝe will me tyne.
Suthly, and all this warld war myne,
I wald it gif or I saw ȝow
In sic ane awentou*r* as I am now,
For richt now will thai ryng the bell,
And I had lever sla my-sell
Than now be fundyn on the gait.'
'Na,' said he, 'thow art o*ur*-hait
And thow will cule and thow stand thar;
Contrar suld be helit w*ith* contrar!'
'My sweit husband,' scho said, 'lat be
And lat me in or I sall dé.
Gif ȝe will noc*h*t w*ith* gud entent,
Richt heir I mak my testament:
To God allmyc*h*ti I leif my saull,
My body to Pet*er*is kirk *and* Paule,
And all my gud*is* I leif to ȝow,
For I will drovne my-self ewi*n* now.'
Fra this was said, no thing scho spak,
Bot a gret hewyn stane couth tak

Fol. 184v

And in the well scho leit it fall
And said: 'In man*us* tuas' th*a*r*w*it*h*all.
Quhen he the rusche herd i*n* the well,
He wend that scho had drownit hir-sell.
A waar man my*ch*t neu*er* be;
As he war wod than wpras he
And furth he past nakit *and* bair;
He wend scho had bene deid but mair.
Scho stude in hiddill*is* by the dure
And alsa sone as he furth fure,
In scho slaid and lokit fast
The dure and to the wyndo past
And spak furth w*ith* a sprete full stowt:
'Quhat devill is it mak*is* th*a*t dyn th*ar* owt?'
'Weile is me,' said he, 'thow art liffand!'
'That sall I gar thé wnd*er*stand!'
'Do opyn the dure and lat me in!'
'This hous,' q*uod* scho, 'thou may no*ch*t wyn,
And be the crovne of the emp*ri*our,
Thow sall byde thar the schamfull hour,
Presonit and pvnist to the deid.
Mycht no*ch*t serf thé my madinhed,
My ȝoung body to fald *and* fang,
Bot thow wald to the bordale gang.'
'Allace,' said he, 'quhy sayis thow sa?
Thow has gret syn me for to sla
And thow wait I am innocent.
Quhy suld thow gar me than be schent?
Thir forty ȝer*is*, sa God help me,
I lay w*ith* na woman bot thé!'
With that the bell rang sone on ane;
The chak-wache has Ysak tane.
Than was ald Ysak tane *and* bundyn

1131. Craigie reads *To*; see expl.note.

Fol. 185r

Becaus he was outwith foundyn,
And in-to presoun done that ny*ch*t,
And on the morne on pillar picht
And thar on him fer ma couth wounder
Na it of vth*er* had bene a hunder.

With that Bantillas knelit lawe
And said: 'S*ch*i*r*, ȝe haf *con*sauit my sawe.'
'Ȝa,' said the lord, 'effectuoslye.
That man was pvnist innocently
And our-falsly pvnist and tynt;
It was wele worthy scho had bene brynt.'
Bantillas said: 'War sall fall ȝow,
And ȝe ȝo*u*r awne son pvnis now.'
The emp*ri*our than till him can say:
'My son sall no*ch*t dé as this day.'
He thankit him gretly than of grace
And thus his leif tuke Bantillas.
The emprys herd that day delayd;
Atto*u*r mesour scho was ill-payd
And till hir chalm*er* scho hir sped,
In lango*u*r and in cair-bed,
And schortly scho wald byde na langar
For to leif in-to daly anger,
Bot till hir fader scho wald agane.
The emp*ri*our said: 'Ȝe sall remane
Quhill somer *and* I sall w*ith* ȝow ga;
Our hono*u*r best beis savit sa.'
Scho said: 'I dreid or somer cu*m*
Ȝe fordone be w*ith* ȝone devill*is* son.
Sla him and than sage be sage,
For I dar lay my hed in wage,
Mair mischeif fall sall ȝhe

1153. Craigie: '*bantillas* for *Lentulus*, and similarly in ll. 1159, 1164. The error is the author's, as shown by the rhyme with *grace* in the last instance.' 'Craigie' henceforward abbreviated to 'Cr.'

SENESCALCUS

Fol. 185v

Than fell the stewart of Eulope,
That in s*er*uice was nixt the king;
Bot it proffett*is*, I sé, na thing
Ony ensample for to say ȝow.'
'Tell on the man*er*,' said he, 'I pray ȝow.'
'To tell,' scho said, 'it dar na rak,
With-thi ȝe tak it in effek.'

The empryce tale of the king
that marijt his stewart*is* wyf.

SENESCALCUS

Off Apillis quhill King Oulumpus
He hatit women sa odious,
That he wald neu*er* ly w*ith* nane,
Quhill he w*ith* seiknes was o*u*r-tane
For falt of purgyn of his natur.
His wame was w*ith* sic inflature
And was sa rissyn, th*a*t nane mycht sé
The wand of his wirilité.
Eftir ane medicinar than he send
And sperit gif he couth hi*m* mend
For reward*is* hye, grete *and* newe.
The clerke, fra he the mater knew,
He said all hale he suld him mak,
Bot him behufit dyet to tak,
And he his lyf suld lay in wed
To mak him hele, *and* tha*n* hi*m* fed
With breid of beir, made of a gryst,
And dranke bot watt*er* quhen he had thrist;
And sa his heile he couth restore
Als hele as eu*er* he was befor,
And than this clerke said till hi*m* thus:
'Will thow thi hele hald, King Olimphus,

1180. Cr.: '*eulope*; called *oulumpus* in 1187 and *olimphus* in 1208.' See expl.note.
1192. Cr.: '*rissyn* is superfluous and written by anticipation of the following line.' It has been omitted here; it was placed between *was* and *with*.
1202, 1206. Cr.: '*hele* for *hale*.'

*Us women or ell*is* thow sall
Agane in-to thi seiknes fall.
Bot thow thi natur purge clenly,
Thow sall be inflat w*ith* mesalry.'
Than callit the king i*n* prevaté
His stewart that was his ane é,
And said that him behufit than
For hele haf deile w*ith* a woman,
And bad him get hi*m* ane ganand.
Bot he said: 'S*chi*r, I am dredand
That na woma*n* get may I,
For ȝe ar suspect of missalry.'
'Ȝeis,' said the king, 'for gret reward,
And sé na money now be spard.
A hundret*h* m*a*rk gif for a lair,
With-thi th*a*t scho be gud *and* fair.'
Bot than, allace, the gredy hart
Of this malicious instewart,
To hald the hundret*h* m*a*rk at hame,
His wyf, that was of full gud fame,
Wi*th* the king chargit for to ly
And haf the hunder m*a*rk for-thi.
Scho said: 'That syn I wald no*ch*t do,
Wald he his kinrik gif me to!'
'Nay, nay,' said he, 'lat be thi sonȝe;
Ane hundret*h* m*a*rk is mekle conȝe!
And tharto, and thow mak grutching,
For all the dayis of my liffing
In bed thow sall neu*er* negh me ner.'
Than answerd scho w*ith* sary cheir
And said: 'S*chi*r, I sall do ȝ*ou*r will,
Bot God I tak witnes me till,

Fol. 186v

That I had lever be far dé,
Or ell*is* be drownit in ʒone sé.
Bot I sall followe neu*er*theles
Ʒo*ur* will w*ith* alkyn sobirnes.'
That ny*ch*t than w*ith* the king scho lay
And on the morne, quhen it was day,
The stewart come fyll hastely
And bad hir rys, bot no*ch*t-for-thi
The kyng wald na waye lat hir ga.
Than taryit he ane ho*u*r or twa,
Syne come and bad hir rys i*n* hy;
Scho wald be schamed wtterly!
The kyng said: 'Na, it sall no*ch*t be;
Full hartfully scho plesis me!'
Than leit the stewart thai*m* allane,
Past furth and maid a sary mane
And grat full sair quhe*n* he wele saw
That all the co*u*rt his wyf wald knaw;
Syne come *and* said his sou*er*ane to:
'My lord, ʒe wait no*ch*t quhat ʒe do!
That is my awne wyf sekerly!'
The king than lukit crabitly
And bad him of his sicht than ga.
'It far*is* of thé as dois of ma;
Thy covatus hart has maid thé blynd.
In my kinrike sé nane thé fynd,
For byde thow th*ar*in dayis thré,
Be my crovne, thow sall hangit be,
That thi example mak vth*er* wys,
Sa for to fayne for covatis.'
Thus banist was the instewart
And all his lyf led in powert.

Fol. 187r

He liffit in seir cu*n*treis than.
The king marijt this worthy woman
For hir lawté w*ith* gret hono*ur*.

Than said scho to the emp*ri*our:
'Schir, ȝe wnd*er*stand weile my taile.'
'Ȝa,' q*uod* he, 'thi sentens all hale.'
Scho said: 'The king stude all i*n* quert
Fra he had ba*n*nist the instewart
And had this worthy woma*n* marijt.
For dreid or that ȝe be miscarijt,
Ȝe ba*n*nis all ȝone sag*is* sevyn
That schapis to fordo ȝowe ewyn,
And leif in lyking w*ith* me, ȝo*ur* wyf,
Or ell*is* schort quhile sall ȝe haf ȝo*ur* lyf.'
He said agane: 'Or th*a*t I dé,
To-morne my son sall hangit be!'
Scho said: 'Do sa but warians,
Than sall ȝe leif at all plesans.'
Than on the morne sone be sex hour*is*
The king gart call the tormento*ur**is*
And bad thai*m* tak the child agane
And sé but sudiorn he war slane,
And as thai passit throw the streit,
With the ferd master he couth meit,
Maucu*n*das, and quhen the barn hi*m* saw,
Till his master he lowtit law,
And he his hors w*ith* spurr*is* scharpe
Straike and tarijt no*ch*t to carpe,
Bot to the palace sped him than
And to the emp*riour* son he wan,
And halsit hi*m* full reuerently,
Bot he agane full grevously
Him gret *and* said: 'Neu*er* wele be thow

TENTAMINA

That for my son send me now   Fol. 187v
A dwm child that can bot luke
And couth speike wele quhe*n* ȝe hi*m* tuke,
That wald haf forsit my qwene.'
'Schir,' said the clerk, 'suth will be sene
As it will sone be eft*ir* this.
The child sall speike richt weile i-wis,
And sla ȝe ȝ*our* sone for the emp*r*is,
That w*ith* hir talis can ȝow tys,
Ȝe sall fall sic confusioun
As fell a lady in this tovne.'
'Tell on how,' said the emp*riou*r.
'Schir,' said he, 'garr*is* the child retour,
Syne heir my tale; than may ȝe do
Ȝ*our* will on him and me to.'
Than was the child reducit sone
And eft*ir*wart in presoun done.

Maucundas tale of the lady that
was lattyn blude.

Than thus began he for to tell:

TENTAMINA

In this cité couth quhilom duell
Ane kny*ch*t of riches and renovne,
And he to name hate Gedeon.
Weile passit was this lord i*n* age,
And mychti was of heretage;
He had na air that lynealy
Mycht bruke his land*is* lauchfully.
Compellit be his frend*is* syne
He has marijt a fair v*ir*gine
For to get barnis betuix thai*m* twa,
And scho was callit Pollema.
Sone eftir litill tyme gane by,

1316. Cr.: '*a lady*; MS *as lady*.'

Fol. 188r

This wyf rais in the morne airly
And to the kirk scho passit ȝar,
For to speike wi*th* hir moder thar.
Scho halsit hir full hon*or*ably
And scho at hir full tend*er*ly
Sperit how plesit scho hir lord.
'War,' scho said, 'na I can record!
Ȝone kny*ch*t is impotent trewlye!
Als leif th*ar*for war me to lye
By a stok of a widd*er*it tré!
Ane noth*er* luf I will ches me.'
Scho said: 'Na douchter, do no*ch*t sa,
Bot heir my counsall or th*o*w ga.
Sum vth*er* way first thow him gref,
For thusgat*is* best thow may hi*m* pref.
Gif he lichtly forgevis thé,
The hardear than may thow be.'
Scho said: 'Moder, th*a*t wald I do,
Wist I how to cu*m* th*ar*to.'
The mod*er* said: 'Thow may him taist
Be a tré th*a*t he luf*is* mast.
Hewe it, th*a*t it be never worth
And sé how he tak*is* it furth.'
Scho said: 'Ȝ*our* counsall sall be done.'
And sped hir hamewart full sone
And eft*ir* hir lord sperit hastely.
Thai answerd: 'W*ith* hound*is* i*n* wenary
And will be laite or he cu*m* heir.'
Than callit scho the gardyner,
And bad ane ax that he suld ta
And w*ith* hir i*n* the garding ga,
And to the lufit tré passit tyte
And bad the gardinar it dovne smyte,

TENTAMINA

Fol. 188v

For the wedd*er*, scho said, was cald,
'And my lord, as thow knawis, is auld;
It to distroye I think na harme;
Quhen he cu*m*mis hame it may hi*m* warme.'
He said: 'I will no*ch*t hew this tré
For all the gold in this cité!
Off it my lord has biddin me haf
Speciale luf o*ur* all the laif.'
'Gif me the ax,' than said scho sone,
'My will as now it sall be done!'
With hir awne hand*is* the tré couth hewe
And for the fyre maide brand*is* ynewe,
And in the chalm*er* kendillit syne.
The lord come hame fra the huntyne;
Than till his meting couth scho rys
And salust him on hir best wys,
His cloke tuke of and his atyre,
Syne set his chyar to the fyre,
And quhen the lord was warmed wele
He said: 'In-to this fyre I fele
The odo*ur* of a growand tré.'
'My lord,' said scho, 'becaus th*a*t ȝe
Was in sic cald, I tho*ch*t na lak
To get thir treis ȝo*ur* fyre to mak.'
'Gif God it ples,' than said he,
'I trast it be no*ch*t of my tré
That I sa lufit w*ith*outin peir!'
Than callit he the gardiner
And sperit, and he him tald trewly,
It was his awne tré sekerly.
'The lady reft fra me my bill,
And hewit it dovne agane my will.
Sche has it wtt*er*ly distroyit!'

TENTAMINA

Fol. 189^{Ir}

Than was the lord gretly anoyit
And said:'Ill woman, wa thé be,
Sa ill a deid has done to me!'
'My lord,' said scho, 'I wnd*er*stud
It that I did was for ȝo*ur* gud,
Bot now sen th*a*t ȝe movit ar
It that I did I rewe full sair.
Haf m*er*cy,' scho said, *and* th*a*r*wit*h*all
Scho grat and leit the ter*is* fall.
Than of hir had his hart peté
And bad hir lat hir greting be,
And hartly he forgaf hir thar,
Sa th*a*t scho did sic thing na mair.
Scho thankit him as scho couth best;
Than on the morne withoutin rest
More for hir moder than for the mes
To kirk scho went w*it*h this proces.
Scho tald hir moder halely
How scho forgevin was sa lichtly,
And said th*a*t scho wald luf on deid.
Hir moder said: 'Ȝit God forbeid!
Auld men,' scho said, 'ar full cruell
And quhylom will thai snyb full fell.
Ȝit tempe him anys or thow begyn
To luf or set thé for that syn.'
'How sall I do than?' couth scho speir.
Scho said: 'His dog th*a*t is him der,
And kepis his bed baith day *and* nyc*h*t,
Wald thow him sla in-till his sicht,
Gif he noc*h*t punisß thé na stryk*is*,
Than may thow luf quhom-evir th*o*w lyk*is*.
Of this ȝe heir na mair of me.'

TENTAMINA

Fol. 189^{Iv}

'Bot dowtles, dame, the dog sall dé.
That p*er*rell pertlie sall I prufe,
With-thi ʒe gif me leif to luf.'
Thus is scho past hame agane
And culʒeit hir lord wound*er* bane,
Bot scho was thinkand aye full thra,
How scho his lufit hound suld sla,
Quhill on a day, as the lord rais,
The hound lap wp on the bed-clathis,
Fawnand w*ith* the lord to playe.
Scho bad him downe i*n* the devill way
And th*arwith* straik him on the hed
And brak his harnis, sa was he deid.
Than was the lord richt sair aggrevit
And angrely has hir reprevit
That scho had done sa gret offens,
And sparit no*ch*t for his presens
To sla the hound that he lufit wele.
Scho said: 'Lat him ga to the devill!
Baith courting, cod, covering *and* schete
Of silk he fylis w*ith* his feit!
I wald all the dogg*is* of this cité
War deid or sic vnhonesté
War vsit, quhar I war quhill I levit!
Bot wa is me I sé ʒow grevit.'
He said: 'I haf gret caus *and* mair!'
Than fell scho to and grat richt sair.
He bad hir ces of hir greting.
Scho said: 'S*chi*r, grant me forgeving
This anys and neu*er* quhill I dé
Sall I ʒow greif.' 'I grant,' q*uod* he,
'With-thi that kepit be trewly,

TENTAMINA

Fol. 189^{2r}

All is forgevyn that is gane by.'
Scho thankit him th*ar*of full fane
And till hir moder past agane.
All hale the caus scho gart hir knawe,
Said, scho wald luf and stand nane awe,
For scho was chapit antar*is* twa.
Scho said: 'Deir doucht*er*, say no*ch*t sa!
Thy fader and I togiddir has bene,
And neu*er* ȝit ws twa betwene
Was nevir hard sic schrewit thing!'
Scho said: 'Douchter, leif for o*ur* blissing.'
Scho said: 'Moder, ȝe haue na consid*er*ans,
And ilkane marijt at plesans.
Ȝe had my fader in his ȝouthhed,
Ilkane vth*er*is madynhed,
Bot that is na thing lyke to me
And ane ald man dry as a tré!'
Hir moder said: 'Gif thow will no*ch*t let,
How schapis thow thi hart to set?'
Scho said: 'Ane prest, I will nane noth*er*!'
'Sanct Mary succo*ur*!' q*uod* the moder,
'Quhy a prest? Thi mynd is myrk!'
Scho sayd: 'He syng*is* sweit i*n* the kirk,
And has a fair hals to kis!'
Hir moder said: 'Thow chesis mys;
To luf it war fer honestar
Ane kny*ch*t or ell*is* a gaye sqwyar.'
'Na,' said scho, 'and lo my skill:
Of me thai wald haue sone th*ar* fill
And erar tak na gif reward;
The prest is bett*er* in regard
For ocht he has, it may be myne,
And he will no*ch*t leif of lychtly syne.'

Than said hir moder: 'Or thow tak the prest, Fol. 189[2v]
For the palpis apon my brest
Thow sowkit ȝoung, th*a*t bred thi banys,
Ȝit do my counsall and bot this anys,
For I sall neu*er* langar frist,
Bot that thow luf quhar-eu*er* thow list.'
'Quhat will ȝe,' said scho, 'that I do?'
Scho said: 'I and thi fader to,
With mony lord*is* of hono*u*r,
And his awne self, the senato*u*r,
At the dyner all hale will be
On Sondaye w*ith* thi lord and thé.
Thir lord*is* of worschipe ar eith to wit;
At the hie burd thai all sall sit,
And in the chyer of hono*u*r
Thy-self befor the senato*u*r.
Quhen all the mesis are se*r*uit *and* set,
Thy kist-keye in the claith thow plet,
Syne w*ith* a byr rys hastely,
That claith and meite cu*m* dovne halely,
And be that falt remittit thé,
Luf on, thow her*is* no mar of me!'
The chak scho tuke on hand to preif,
Syne at hir moder scho tuke hir leif.
The daye come of the ma*n*iory;
Quhen set was all the senȝeory,
The lady befor the senatour
Sat in a chyer of hie hono*u*r.
Quhen all thai danteis, th*a*t war deir,
War set, and blythest was th*a*r cheir,
Hir keye scho fessy*n*nit, as is forsaid,
Syne rais wp w*ith* a sudand braid,
Sayand scho had a knyf forȝet,

1526. *Sat* was originally omitted and therefore inserted in front of the line.

Fol. 190r

That claith and all that my*ch*ti mete
Halely of the burde come dovne
And maid a foull confusioun.
Hir lord th*ar*of he tho*ch*t gret schame
And said that scho had s*er*uit blame.
Scho said: 'I ȝeid to seike a knyf!'
The lord said: 'Lady, be my lyf,
I wald th*a*t knyf wnforgit had bene
Or we suld a schame syklyk sustene!'
The fylit clathis away thai drewe
And w*ith* clene napry cowerit newe,
Syne with danteis ynewe at all
Servit baith the burd and hall,
And sa w*ith* plenté, makand cheir,
Thai sat quhill th*a*t the ny*ch*t drewe neir.
Syne passit ilkane to thar herbery,
Bot Gedeon in the morn arlye
Gart fetche ane barbo*ur* till hi*m* tyte,
That in blude-latting was sa p*er*fyte,
And to the ladyis chalmer ȝeid
And bad hir rys, that scho my*ch*t bleid.
'Do heit ȝo*ur* arme *and* bynd it sone.'
And as he bad son was it done
And gart hir bleid aganis hir will,
A meso*ur* mekle mair na skill.
Scho changit colo*ur* and cryit m*er*cy;
Than gart he lous that arme i*n* hy,
For thai p*er*sauit scho worthit blynd.
The toth*er* arme than gart he bynd
And bad the barbo*ur* strike the vane,
That scho my*ch*t bleid alsmekle agane.

1550. Cr.: '*sa* is superfluous.' But cf. 1888 and 2621.

Fol. 190v

Sa did scho quhill scho falȝeit speche.
Than bad the lord hir lous and leche,
For he had done hir mekle gud
That menyst samekle of hir ill blud.
Than schupe the lord his way to ga
And left hir lyand in the stra,
All-mast lyfles, ill-farandly,
And past his way all crabitly.
Than for hir moder has scho send
And bad hir cum to sé hir end.
Hir moder than come on in hast
And fand hir douchter deid allmast
And said: 'Allace, my douchter, how
In-to sic perrell I fynd ȝow now?'
Scho said: 'Moder, full wa is me,
For I am deid, as ȝe may sé;
Na blud is in my body left,
Neir speche and sicht ar fra me reft,
My hart is haile out of my brest.'
Scho said: 'Will thow now luf a prest?'
'Na Moder, that I forsaike allway.
The forbot of God th*ar*on I· lay,
Prest or vth*er* that lyf has tane,
Quhill I leif bot my lord allane.'

Than said the mast*er*: 'Sc*hi*r, I trow
Ȝe haf consauit my menyng now.'
'Ȝa,' said the emp*riou*r, 'at the best.
Scho was pvnist tho*ch*t scho was frist.
Ane gud ensample *and* ald haf ȝe.'
He said: 'And ȝe ȝour sone gar dé
For the empris, ȝe sall fair wer

VIRGILIUS
Fol. 191r

Than did this kny*ch*t be mekle fer.'
He said: 'He sall no*ch*t dé this day.'
The master him thankit *and* raid his way.
Quhen the emp*ri*ce hard that delay,
Full bitt*er*ly scho grat all day,
Quhill at the emp*riour* come thar
And sperit quhy scho grat sa sair.
Scho said: 'I m*er*well of th*a*t saw,
To speir the question th*a*t ȝe knaw!
Of my dishono*ur* ȝe ken all how,
Bot I murn mekle mar for ȝow!
Ȝe trast samekle in ȝo*ur* sag*is*
That will sone put ȝow of ȝo*ur* stag*is*
And put ȝo*ur* dwm son to the crowne,
Quhilk sall be mair confusioun
To ȝow na was this hu*n*dret*h* ȝer
Of ane emp*ri*our that was heir,
And in four sag*is* trastit he:
Ane schamis deid thai gart hi*m* dé!'
He bad hir tell; scho said: 'Quhar-to?
At ȝow th*ar* may na sample do!
Ȝit will I tell *and* to God pray
That it may proffet ȝow su*m* way.'

The empryce tale of the
spekle of Rome.

VIRGILIUS

'Thar wo*n*nyt quhylis ane emp*ri*our,
Riche and covatus o*u*r mesour
Of gold *and* silu*er*; that tyme duelt heir
Virgile, th*a*t precious clerk but peir.
He maid a fyre birnand allway
To warme the pure folk ny*ch*t and day,

Fol. 191v

And maid a well for th*ar* drinkyn,
And th*ar*abone a me*r*walus thing:
Ane ymage w*ith* a (arow *and*) bow of bras
And in his forhed w*ri*ttin was:
"Quha stryk*is* me, trow weile th*a*t I
Sall me revenge richt hastely!"
To scule as the scolar*is* couth found
Ane scolar that hecht Edmound
Come by the well and red the tytill
And sayis to his fallows: "I rak bot litill
To strik this ymage for to sé
How that he may rewengit be!"
He liftit his hand *and* stud na aw
And to the ymag he gaf a blaw,
That furthw*ith* in the fyre it fell.
Than slokinnit the fyre *and* dryit the well.
Say ȝe no*ch*t this clerk ill hi*m* bure
That slokinnit the fyre that warmit the pure?'
The emp*riour* said: 'Gret syn did he,
And fer agane all cherité.'
Bot ȝit said scho: 'V*ir*gilius,
Quhen the fyre was slokinnit thus,
He biggit a towre w*ith*in the ȝet
And ten ymag*is* th*ar*in he set,
And ilkane had ane bell i*n* hand
To ryng quhe*n* it was tyme ganand.
Syne stude in mydd*is* of the towr
The farest ymage w*ith* a myrro*ur*
In hir richt hand, cler to behold,
In hir left hand ane aple of gold.
At V*ir*gill the wysest *and* the best
Sperit how lang that towre suld lest.

1625. See expl. note.

Fol. 192^{r}

He said it suld stand to that tyme
That a v*ir*gin but syn or cryme
Suld bere a son and suth said he:
It stude quhill Crist*is* natiuité.
Quhen God was of a madin born
The towr fell downe th*a*t ilka morn.
Thar duelt thré kyng*is* besyde Rome
That all th*ar* wit and th*ar* wisdome
Baith ny*ch*t and day was set th*ar*to,
How thai this cité my*ch*t vndo,
And oft attempit subtelly,
Bot thai wro*ch*t no*ch*t sa prevely
Bot all thai ymag*is* th*ar* bell*is* rang
And the myd ymage thai*m* amang
The myrou*r* schewe thai*m* opinly,
That the pepill my*ch*t knaw clerly
All that th*ar* enemys schupe to do,
How thai the cité my*ch*t fordo.
Thus w*ith* th*ar* ymag*is* warnit war thai
Of thar enemys, ba*ith* ny*ch*t *and* day,
That thai my*ch*t neu*er* do thai*m* ill
And all this wrocht this clerk V*ir*gill.
A counsall than thir king*is* has set,
How th*a*t thai suld the cité get.
Ane said: "My-self can no*ch*t p*er*saif,
Als lang as thai ȝone ymag*is* haf,
Bot all is in wane th*a*t we do may.
Sé how we sall get it away,
For quhill it lest*is* *and* ȝone ymage
Thar may na power do thai*m* da*m*mage."
Than rais four kny*ch*t*is* w*ith* ane consent
In mydd*is* of that hie p*ar*liament,

1661. MS has *duell*.

Fol. 192v

Sperand quhat gold and quhat tressour,
Thai wald gif to distroye that towr,
Bellis and ymagis and all,
And the myrr*ou*r gar brek *and* fall.
Thai answerd and bad ask *and* haif.
Thai askit gold and that thai gaf
Richt hartfully w*ith* all largenes;
Four barrel full thai tuke, na les.
Thai tursit thai b*a*rrell*is* weile at poynt
And past all four togiddir ioynt
To Rome vnto the emp*ri*our
And salust him w*ith* gret hon*ou*r.
Than sperit he sone of thar mistar;
Thai said: "S*chi*r, we ar men of lair
Off augure and diuinité,
For be o*u*r dremes fynd will we
Hid thing*is*, th*a*t the erd ar wnder,
Gold hurd*is* and thai war a hunder."
Bot or thai past the towne w*ith*in
Full prevely but noys or dyn,
As thai war wylye, war and witté,
Wnder ilk porte of the cité
At ilk port a hole thai maide,
And tharin a gold barell slaide
And cowerit tham all w*ith* erd abone,
Syne in the cité sped tham sone,
And did as nowe befor is said.
The covatus emp*riou*r was weile-payd
And said: "Than sall ȝe duell with me."
Thai said: "In cu*n*nand w*ith*-thi th*a*t ȝe
Gif ws the half of it we fynd,
To byde and dreme, s*chi*r, we ws bynd."

The emp*ri*our said: "That is all richt,
I grant ȝow!" Ane said: "This ny*ch*t
Of my dremyng the tyme begy*n*nis;
For-thi we will pas till o*u*r innes
And slepe in tyme and than I bynd
My lyf the gold to gar ȝow fynd,
Bot quhiddir that it be les or mar,
The half ȝe hecht ws till o*u*r scair."
Than to thar innes thai passit blyth
And maid gud cheir, syne slepit swyth.
Than on the morn thai come agane;
The emp*ri*our of thai*m* was full fayne,
For he was covatus and for-thi
He trowit tham all o*u*r-lichtly,
That gart him get w*ith*out remeid
Mekle magra and schamis deid.
The first dremar said: "S*chi*r, I sé
At the first port of this cité,
In a hole wnder the erd weile depe,
This ny*ch*t I haf sene in my slepe,
Thar lyis -- this I stand ford to ȝow ..
Ane ha*m*mer barrell of gold fowe."
"Now," said the emp*riou*r, "we sall ken
Thar-by gif ȝe be suthfast men."
Than to th*a*t port thai passit richt
With spaide and gavillok *and* mattok wicht;
Thai delvit quhill thai the barrall gat.
The emp*ri*our quhen he saw that
He trowit thai*m* alswele as hi*m*-sell,
Gaif tham the scair that to thai*m* fell.
Than said the secound: "S*chi*r, will ȝe

Fol. 193v

*I dreme this ny*ch*t?" "Hardely," said he.
The ny*ch*t he slepit, than on the morne
To the emp*ri*our has said *and* sworne:
"At the secound port fynd ȝe may
Alsmekle as ȝe did ȝist*er*day
Off gold in hurde wnder the erd."
Richtsa the thrid, richtsa the ferd
Dremyt and fand the barell*is* ay.
The emp*ri*our thus begylit thai
And syne thai all four at the last
With a voce ar till him past,
Said: "Lord, ȝe knaw th*a*t we haf art,
For we haf all four dremyt o*u*r part.
To schaw o*u*r sciens ȝit attour,
This ny*ch*t we schape to dreme all four,
To fynd sic fussoun we wald preif,
That all this cité my*ch*t releif."
The emp*ri*our said: "That wele I pleis!
God send ȝow grace to dreme at eis,
For lelar men ȝit neu*er* I saw,
For it ȝe tell in deid ȝe schaw!"
Than to thar innes all went thai;
Than on the morne, quhe*n* it was day,
To the emp*rio*ur thai come agane,
Sa blythlie th*a*t thai maide hi*m* fayne.
Thai said: "Lord, we haf gud tything,
For we all fowr has dremyt a thing,
That wnder the myro*u*r lyis wele lawe
Mair gold than all the hors will drawe
That is i*n* Rome w*i*t*h*outin dreid."
The emp*ri*our than said: "God forbeid

The myro*u*r be hurt in ony wys
That warnis ws of o*u*r enemys!"
Than said thai: "S*chi*r, we mene no*ch*t sa,
For quhar it lyis we can wele ga
And do na scaith to the myro*u*r,
Na to the ymage, na to th*a*t towr,
For the gold lyis in the flure."
"Cuth ȝe," q*uod* he, "with all ȝo*u*r cure
Get it *and* lat the myro*u*r stand?"
"Ȝa s*chi*r," q*uod* thai, "we tak on hand
And all o*u*r lyvis layis i*n* wage
To saif baith myrro*u*r *and* ymage.
Ȝe wait gif we be sumthing slé
And trast ȝe weile we wald no*ch*t dé."
"Do furth than," said the emp*ri*our,
"Bot our all thing, kepe the myrro*u*r!"
Than war thai blyth as bird on brer,
And all that ny*ch*t thai wro*ch*t but weir,
Quhill thai the foundement fand *and* brak
Quhar-on the myrro*u*r stude *and* stak,
And hastely *with* fyre of tunder
Ane gret mane fyre thai maide th*a*r-wnder.
Quhen this was done thai fled the tovne,
Bot thai maid ill conclusioun,
For fra the cité thai war no*ch*t gane
Twa leg*is* bot scantly ane,
Quhe*n* myrro*u*r, ymage, towr *and* all
In-to the fyre tuke sic ane fall,
That all was in-to powder brynt.
Thus was this iowell myrro*u*r tynt.

VIRGILIUS
Fol. 194^v

Than the gret heres of the towne,
Quhen at the myrro*ur* was sa put dovne,
Thai maid gret mayne, sighand full sair:
"Our wache is done for evir-mair!
Quha sall kep ws fra the suprys
Or warn ws of o*ur* enemys?"
Than to the emprio*ur* ar thai gane
And sone in hand*is* thai haf him tane,
And sperit quhy his gret covatis
Had spilt th*a*r iowell on sic a wys.
He said: "Ȝone sag*is* begylit me!"
Thai said: "Thow sall quyk erdit be
For thi cowatousnes; we think
Thow thristit gold and gold sall drink!"
Than quyk thai erdit him but let
And full of moltin gold hi*m* ȝet.
Thus dẽit the emp*ri*our miserably.

Ȝe consaif, *sch*ir,' scho said, 'trow I,
The ymage that stude abone the well
With bow and arrowe, it is thi-sell.
This fyre, it is thi*n* almous-deid
That luf*is* pure folk to cleith *and* feid.
The child that straik the ymag dovn
Is thi dwm son, will tak the crovne
And slokin the fyre of thi*n* almous.
The dremar*is* th*a*t war sa cawtelous,
Thai war the sag*is*, suth to saye,
That thẽ begylis ny*ch*t *and* day.
Thy-self may be the emp*ri*our
And I of warnyng the myrro*ur*.'

He said: 'In all that I can sé,
Ane gud ensample thow has tald me;
For-thi the morne for ony feid
Sone and sage all sall be deid.'
Scho said: 'Wald ʒe do as ʒe say,
Ʒo*ur*-self wald leif this mony day.'
Than als fast as the ny*ch*t was gane
The emp*ri*our gart his sone be tane
And w*ith* the torme*n*tour*is* led agane
Vnto the gallous to be slane.
The peple followit him but let,
With the fyft mast*er* quhill thai met,
Catoun was callit. Quhe*n* the child hi*m* saw,
Till his mast*er* he lowtit lawe,
And all the peple cryit ʒarne:
'Gud mast*er*, now defend thi barne!'
Than prekit Cato w*ith* all his pres
To the palace or he wald ces,
And halsit the emp*ri*our reu*er*ently
And he him gret full grevously,
Sayand: 'Trato*ur*, thow has na lair,
That sall dissaif me ony mair,
As did the dremar*is* of the hurd*is*.'
The master said: 'I ken thai word*is*!
Of his stepmoder that is the saw,
Bure no*ch*t ʒo*ur* son, bot ʒe sall knaw
The suth, I trast, w*ith*in thré dayis
And sé it end all vth*er*-wayis.
For heir I bynd me to the fyre
Befor the stat*is* of ʒo*ur* empyr,
And ʒe in hart be set sa thra

AVIS
Fol. 195v

For ȝ*our* fals wyf ȝ*our* son till sla,
Ane mair misawent*ur* sall fall ȝe,
Than fell a burges of this cité.'
'Tell how was that!' than said the king.
He said: 'The barne will ȝe gar bring
Agane, quhill I haf tald, but scaith;
Syne do ȝ*our* plesans of ws baith.'
The barne was brocht agane w*ith* that
And set in presoun quhar he eir sat.
Thar carpit Cato to the king,
Clerkly and w*ith* fair having.

The taile of Cato of the
pyote.

AVIS

*In this cité was a burges,
Wys, riche, cu*n*ning and courtas,
And held a michti hous at hame;
Annabill was his prop*er* name.
He had ane pyot forsuth i*n* deid,
Was sa p*er*fyte in Romane leid;
Fra he a day fra hame wald duell,
All that was done scho wald him tell
At his hame-come full opinly.
In danté held he hir for-thi.
His wyf lufit ane noth*er* kny*ch*t;
Quhen he fra hame was on a ny*ch*t
This kny*ch*t *is* cu*m*myn as of befor;
For-thi this pyot can scho schore,
Said: 'Leif thi talis th*a*t thou tellis,
Or thi lyf it sall cost thé ellis!'
Bot scho left noth*er* for schore nor schame
Bot tald him hale quhe*n* he come hame,

1893. Cr.: 'Some lines are probably missing here.' But this does not seem necessary.

Quhilk causit distance and mekle stryf Fol. 196^{r}
Betuix the burges and his wyf.
The burges for erand*is* to be done
Of m*er*chandis passit eft*ir* sone
Fra hame, and quhe*n* that saw the kny*ch*t,
Till hir he come th*a*t ilka ny*ch*t
And at the ȝet callit prevely.
Than gat scho wp full hastely
And welcu*m*mit him w*ith* hert *and* will.
He said: 'I dar no*ch*t cu*m* ȝou till,
Ȝone cursit pyot -- God gif hir cair --
Will tell that we do and mair.'
Scho said: 'Ȝe sall cu*m* in to-ny*ch*t,
For the pyot sall sé na licht;
Durr*is* and wyndois I sall steike
And huly vnd*er* ȝour voce ȝe speike,
And on the pyot trast wele th*a*t we
Sall eft*ir* this revengit be.'
He enterit than at hir counsall,
Bot the pyot p*er*sauit all hale
And said: 'Gud s*chi*r, for curtassy
Be curyale to my gay lady,
And defowle no*ch*t my lord*is* bed,
That weile has fosterit me *and* fed.
I sall him tell the man*er* how!'
The kny*ch*t said: 'Lady, I tald ȝow
Scho wald revele ws opinly.'
'Cum in,' q*uod* scho, 'set ȝe no*ch*t by.'
He ent*er*it than till his p*a*r*a*mour
And scantly had bene thar ane hour,
Quhen the lord callit at the ȝet.

Fol. 196^{v}

Wp fraitlye can the lady get
And left the kny*ch*t gretlie abasit,
Bot hir moder him wp has rasit
And gaf him i*n* hand ane nakit swerd
And bad him he suld speik na word,
Bot evyn before the dur stand still,
Quhill the lord ent*er*it at his will.
The lord ent*er*it and saw him stand
Sa with ane nakit swerd in hand.
He stettit sumthing and syne couth speir:
'Quhat art thow thus that stand*is* heir?'
Bot he spak na word mar nor myn.
Than said hir moder: 'Son, mak na dyn;
Thré kny*ch*t*is* to sla has chasit this man,
And for girth come he hidder than,
And we haf savit him as we may,
Quhill we trow thai be gane away.
Ȝongat*is* he stude, for he no*ch*t wist
Bot ȝe had bene thai th*at* him mist.
He dar no*ch*t ȝit steir for th*ar* feid
And thus he savit is ȝit fra deid.'
The lord said than: 'In all I sé
Ȝe haf done thar gret cherité,
And tharfor hartfully thank I ȝow
And I sall fande to kepe hi*m* now,
For w*ith* me sall he sit on ane,
Quhill he be seker his fais ar gane.'
And gart hi*m* sit w*ith* hi*m* ry*ch*t thar,
And maid gud cheir *and* mery fair.
The pyot that the man*er* knewe,
Scho sesit hir sang *and* maid na glewe.

The kny*ch*t ȝeid hame than at the last;
The burges till his pyot past,
Said: 'My deir bird, quhat alis thé,
That syng*is* no*ch*t quhe*n* thow seis me?'
Scho said: 'I sé thi scaith sa ryf;
Ȝone ald carling and thi awne wyf
Sa fowlely thai thé begyle,
That I may noth*er*ane syng nor smyle.'
The hale proces scho him tald,
How he him has maid cukkald,
Quhilk gretly grevit has Balaine,
And ma*n*nasing he maid thar than
Vnto his wyf, bot scho pertly
Denyit and swor opynly
That thai suld neu*er* be but baile
Quhill he trowit the pyot*is* tale,
Bot he suld sone knawe sekerly
The gret lesing*is* of that fals py.
Hir word*is* the burges sumthing trowit,
And sone eft*ir*, quhar he had wowit,
In pilg*ri*mage is passit Balan.
Than scho sone send for hir le*m*man
And maide him feist *and* mery cheir;
Thar was na danteis thai*m* to deir,
Bot gret blythnes and costly meit
And the pilgryme all quyte forȝet.
Neu*er*theles i*n* the mydd*is* of the fest,
Quhen at thai trowit all-thar-lest,
Balan at his awne ȝet couth call,
Bot than thai war astonait all.
The kny*ch*t was hid with litill dyn;

1970. Craigie left out *ane* but it does occur in the MS.
1984. Cr.: '*said* is deleted after *sone*.'

Fol. 197v

Syne was the burges lattin in.
He said: 'Gar grath my bed to ly
To rest, for trewly tyrit am I!'
Than witles was his wyf allmast.
Hir moder said: 'Douchter, haf na hast
To mak his bed, quhill he haf sene
His newe maid schet*is* ws twa betwene.'
Than of the scheit scho liftit ane nuke,
The doucht*er* wp ane noth*er* tuke,
And held befor the burges sicht,
Quhill quyte owt chapit was the kny*ch*t.
Thus clene begylit was Balan
And ȝit the wyf*is* he thankit than
That thai couth mak hi*m* sic a claith.
Bot than the moder swor ane aith:
'I haf maid ma of sic as this!'
The burges than thai*m* baith couth kis
And till his bed he went his way,
Bot his fals wyf, th*a*t ettillit ay
For till vndo this prety py,
Scho gat a ledd*er* prevely;
A madin than scho w*ith* hir gat,
And abone quhar the pyot sat
A hole thai made i*n*-to the thak,
And syne wp w*ith* thai*m* can thai tak
A ha*m*mer *and* small sandy stanys
To brek, and pik *and* ter (at) anys,
And a weschell of watter to.
Syne all togiddir temperit scho
And ȝet dovne on the pyot*is* heid
All ny*ch*t; be day scho was neir deid.

2015. Craigie suggested the change into *than* of MS *that*.
2020. Craigie added *at*.

Fol. 198^{r}

On morne this burges wald noc*h*t sit
Quhill he his pyot past to wit,
And sperit his deir how couth scho do.
'I am bot deid,' till him said scho,
'In me is noc*h*t ane vnhurt fedder,
With rane, fyreflaucht *and* all ill wedd*er*,
That neir the lyf is out of me,
And ʒit I am wepand for thé:
That thai begylit thé w*ith* a scheit
I wey fer mair than all my weit.'
Thar-at was Balan gretly movit,
Ʒit to the pyot th*a*t he lufit
He said: 'My bird, ʒit m*er*well I,
How that the rayne this nyc*h*t gane by
And how the ill wedder has thé o*ur*tane:
A farer nyc*h*t my-self saw nane,
Na ʒit a lownar as thoc*h*t me.'
Than said the wyf: 'S*chi*r, ʒe may sé
Hir falset, for this was bot feir;
It was the farest nyc*h*t was this ʒer!
Now may ʒe wit it was noc*h*t worth
To trow hir tale.' Than past he furth
And fra his ny*ch*tbour*is* he sperit the cais.
Thai answerd: 'Lovit be God of grace
This ʒer saw we sa fair ane nycht!'
Than spak the ald wyf all on hicht
All word*is* to gar the pyot dé.
Than said Balane: 'Pyot, I sé
With thi lesing*is* thow has maid stryf
Our-oft betuix me *and* my wyf,
Bot now sa sall thow do no mar!'
Than weryit he the bird richt thar.
Quhen he his iowall bird had slane

AVIS

Fol. 198v

Than lukit he wp agane,
And saw ane (hole) abone hir hed
And ane ledder wp for to leid.
He ferlyit and clam wp in hy
And fand the hole maid subtelly,
That all that sorow thai dropit dovn
Suld fall apon the pyot*is* crovne
With pik and ter that hir forfur.
Quhen he had sene that ill muxtur,
That my*ch*t no*ch*t drop in-to na place
Bot on the pyot, he said: 'Allace!'
-- For his fals wyf*is* fravde he knewe --
That he his iowell pyot slewe.
Than for his pyot grat he sair
And sone awaye his wyf gart car(e),
Sayand: 'Fair on, foull mot thé fall,
All-thar-werst woman of all!
With me thow sall na langar duell;
Pas on fra me and syne till hell!'
Sone eft*ir* he brak his sper in thré
And in the haly land wowit he.

Than said the clerk full courtasly:
'Schir, ȝe consaif quhat said haf I,
That the bird that tald the treuth
Scho gart him sla w*ith*outin reuth.
Sla ȝe ȝ*our* sone in siclyk wys
For the fals talis of the emprys,
Als mony sall ȝe fall mischef*is*.'
Than said the emp*ri*our: 'God ws levis,
Ane gud ensample ȝe haf said.
My so*n*nis dẹid sal be delayd
For thi example as this day.'
His mast*er* hi*m* thankit *and* went away,

2059. Craigie suggested *hole* instead of *ledder* as found in the MS.
2074. MS has *women*.

SAPIENTES

Bot quhen the emp*ri*ce hard of that, Fol. 199r
Gretand in-till hir bed scho sat,
And thar lay makand sair mayne,
Quhill the emp*rio*ur to bed is gane.
He sperit of hir diseis the quhy;
Scho said: 'Ȝe wait als wele as I!
Ȝo*u*r sone th*a*t schupe me to deflour
And to ʒo*u*r self (do) dishono*u*r.
Ȝe hecht I suld revengit be,
Bot it is lytill scaith to me,
For quhe*n* ʒo*u*r sag*is* has ʒow slane
My frend*is* may mary me agane.
Thai will sla ʒow bot ʒe thai*m* sla,
For that sall fall, I wnderta,
Of ʒow as of the sag*is* four
Fell to Herod the empriour.'
He bad hir tell the man*er* haile;
Scho said: 'Quhat mak*is* it avale?'
He said: 'Ȝis, sa may ʒe conclude
That ʒo*u*r ensample may ken ws gud,
And me fra pe*r*rell wele defend.'
Than said scho: 'It was wele kend.'

The emprys tale of the sevyne sag*is*
that dissauit the emp*ri*our be redyng
of dremes.

Ane emp*ri*our wo*n*nyt in this cité SAPIENTES
And Herod to name hecht he.
He had sevyne sag*is* *with* him ay
And be thar counsall he wrocht allway.
Ane conswetud thai maid but dreid,
That quha-sa had a dreme to reid
Suld bryng of gold a porcioun

2098. See expl.note.

Fol. 199v

To the sevyne sag*is* in co*m*moun,
And thai suld it interprit than;
Thus w*ith* th*a*r wylis sic gold thai wan.
Ȝit couth the king in-to thai*m* trow
As ȝe do in ȝour sag*is* now.
Herod baide aye in the cité;
Quhe*n* he passit furth he my*ch*t no*ch*t sé.
Ane ny*ch*t he menyt hi*m* to the quene;
Scho said: 'I trow it sall be sene
Of this thing, and ȝe be p*er*fyte,
That ȝour sevyne sag*is* has the wyte.'
Than has he callit thai*m* him till
And said in schort: 'It is my will
To tell the caus that I suth fynd,
Quhen I pas furth that I am blynd,
And seis quhe*n* w*ith*in I duell;
In pane of lyf*is* the caus ȝe tell.'
Thai askit awisit for to be
Of that mater and difficulté,
And than thai war avisit thus
To seike M*er*lyng, that m*er*walus,
And sa thai did and na ċost spard
Quhill thai him gat, *and* gret reward
Thai haf hecht and gret renovne
For to absolue the questioun.
He suld absolue it sudanlye;
The sag*is* war richt blyth for-thi,
And M*er*ling w*ith* thai*m* tuk thai than;
Ȝit by the gait thai met a man
With gold, that had a dreme to reid.
Than M*er*ling couth him forbed
His gold to gif the sag*is* sevyn;

Fol. 200r

He suld interprit it full evyne.
'That thow dremyt -- I ga no*ch*t wrang --
That a fair well on the grene sprang,
And grewe th*a*reft*ir* in a flude.
Of this thow sall haf mekle gud,
To mak thé riche *and* all thi kyn.'
The man past on or he wald blyn
And fande all suth th*a*t eu*er* he said.
Tharof he was full hartly payd;
Blyth war the sag*is* quhe*n* thai saw this,
That M*er*lyng na merk thing wald mys,
And had him to the emp*ri*our
On the set day w*it*h gret hono*ur*,
And said: 'Lo lord, this ȝoung child heir
Sall declar all th*a*t ȝe speir.'
The emp*ri*o*u*r was reiosit than
And said: 'Fair child, trow ȝe, ȝe can
Tell me quharfor I may no*ch*t sé
And I be out of this cité?'
'Ȝa,' said the child, 'i*n* pane of deid
I tell the caus *and* the remeid.
To chalm*er* w*it*h ȝow go will I
And gar ȝow wnd*er*stand clerly.'
Than at the king M*er*ling couth speir:
'Is this ȝo*ur* chalm*er*, s*chir*? Ly ȝe heir?'
'Ȝa," said the emp*ri*our, 'child, p*ar* dé.'
The barne said: 'S*chir*, than sall ȝe sé
The werité of ȝour myrk thing*is*;
Vnder ȝo*ur* bed (ar) sevyn well-spring*is*,
That buller*is and* playis ny*ch*t *and* day.
Thai ar the caus, I dar wele saye,

2179. Cr.: 'ȝ*our*; MS *your*, perhaps for *yir*', but the MS has a *y* corrected, rather ineffectively it is true, into ȝ.
2180. Cr.: '*at* for *ar*(?)'.

SAPIENTES

Fol. 200v

That thir sevyne rewar*is* cu*m*mis furth;
And to pref gif thir word*is* be worth,
Remuf ȝo*ur* bed and vnd*er* it evyne
(Thar) ȝe sall fynd the buller*is* sevyne,
In part ȝo*ur* questioun to declar.
Gif ȝe fynd this, ȝe will trow mar.'
Thai fitchit the bed *and* delfit the flur
And fand the buller*is*, I ȝow assur.
Than said the emp*r*iour: 'My deir hart,
In sciens I sē thow art expart.
Is ony remeid or medicyne
To get w*ith* ony gold of myne
Outw*ith* the ȝett*is* that I my*ch*t sē?'
'Ȝeis,' q*uod* the child, 'redy,' q*uod* he.
'Couth thir sevyn buller*is* sloki*n*nit be,
Outw*ith* as inw*ith*, ȝe suld wele sē.'
And quhen Me*r*ling this way had spokin,
The king sperit how he suld thai*m* slokin.
He said: 'Th*ar* was na thing thai*m* swagis,
Bot the hed*is* of ȝone sevyn sag*is*,
That garr*is* ȝow trow thai ar sa wys,
And rewlis ȝo*ur* land be covatis.
Strik of thar hed*is* and hiddir bring
And ilka hed sall stanche a spring;
And to be seker of this remeid,
Of the eldest strik of the hed,
And w*ith* that clerly sall ȝe sē
Quhat ry*ch*t of the laif sall be.'
The king gart strike his hed of tyte;
Than sloki*n*nit the first bullo*ur* quyte.
Than Me*r*ling said: 'Now may ȝe sē

2186. Cr.: '*That* for *Thar*.'

Quhat now of the laif will be.' Fol. 201^{r}
Than gart he hed thai*m* all bedene,
And all the bullo*ur*is slokin*n*it clene:
Thus war thai sag*is* fals fordone.
Than M*er*ling gart the king but hone
Leipe on his palfray *and* furth ryde,
And said that he wald be his gyde
Outw*ith* the ȝett*is* of the cité,
For till attempe gif he my*ch*t sé.
Quhen thai come furth, cler saw the king
And thar has ordanit M*er*ling
His stewart, and gaf him till his hyre
The governans of his hale empyr.

Than said the emp*r*ice: 'S*ch*ir, I weyne
Ȝe wnd*er*stand now quhat I mene;
That is: ȝo*ur* sag*is* wald put ȝ*o*w dovn,
And ȝo*ur* son, God*is* mawlisoun,
Thai will mak king in-to ȝo*ur* steid,
Bot ȝe be ordo*ur* gar thai*m* heid,
And M*er*ling*is* counsall tak *and* myne:
Sla thai*m* all sevyne, sa may ȝe syne ...'

The emp*ri*our said: 'For this th*a*t tald haf ȝe
Sall wyte the morne my son sall dé.'
Sone on the morne the emp*ri*our bad
To the gallhous his son be led
And throw the cité as thai past,
The vij master come prekand fast,
Prayit tham to tary *and* syne raid by,
And to the palace come in hy,
And on gud maner w*ith* hono*ur*
Mekly salust the emp*ri*our.

2234. Cr.: 'Here a considerable portion of the text is missing, containing the tale of the sixth sage and the empress's reply to it.' See expl.note.
2235. See expl.note.
2238. Cr.: '*led* does not rhyme with *bad*; the correct reading is no doubt *had*.'

INCLUSA

Bot he him answerd all w*ith* feid — Fol. 201v
And said that he had se*r*uit his deid.
He said: 'S*chi*r, we haue se*r*uit na cryme,
For ȝe sall sé to-morne be pryme
Ȝo*u*r son sall speike and all declar;
Forsuth, he may be dwm na mair.'
The emp*ri*our said: 'W*ith*outin weir
I wald be fane the suth to heir
Quha had of all this case the wrang,
For dome on thai*m* I sall gar gang
W*ith* the worthy of this cité.'
Than said Cratone: 'S*chi*r king, *and* ȝe
Sla ȝo*u*r sone for the emp*ri*ce,
Ȝe sall be comptit als wnwys
As he that in his wyf couth weyne,
Syne was begylit all bedene.'
The emp*ri*our said: 'That tale I ȝarne.'
The master bad bring agai*n* the barne
Quhill he haf tald, *and* sa has done
And he the tale began full sone.

The sevynt tale of Cratone
of the kny*ch*t qu*hi*lk gaf his wyf
fra him.

INCLUSA

In Mobrig was ane worthy kny*ch*t
And in armes baith wys *and* wicht;
For victory full oft had he.
Slepand in visioun couth he sé
Ane lady th*a*t he lufit best,
Bot in quhat cu*n*tré scho couth rest

2263. See expl.note.

He had na witt*er*ing mar nor les, Fol. 202r
Bot hir fig*ou*r and hir freschenes
He couth haue knawin, had he hir seyne,
Amang a thousand tho*ch*t scho had bene.
The samy*n* ny*ch*t ane fair lady
In the kinrik of Hungry
In slepe hir luf saw as scho tho*ch*t,
Bot quhar he duelt scho wist ry*ch*t no*ch*t.
This kny*ch*t was sa w*ith* luf o*u*rtane,
He tuke ane sqwyer *and* thai*m* allane
Past to seike fra land to land
Bot rest, quhill he this lady fand.
Throw mony cu*n*trê ar thai past,
Quhill in-till Vngary at the last
Thai come, *and* th*ar* a fair citê
Thai fand, w*ith* castall wallit hie,
And at a wyndow th*ar* he saw
His luf, and weile he couth hir knaw,
And be his fig*ou*r wele scho fand
That it was him scho saw slepand.
The kny*ch*t of na thing than had mynd,
Bot for to study in-to quhat kynd
That he my*ch*t speke w*ith* hir allane.
Than till hir husband is he gane,
That all th*a*t cu*n*trê had in cure,
And as stewart that office bure,
And swetly till him: 'S*chi*r,' said he,
'I am ane kny*ch*t of fer cu*n*trê;
At hame I happi*n*nit to sla ane kny*ch*t,
That th*ar* na langar duell I mi*ch*t,
And to this kynrik I come now,
To fecht baith for the king *and* ȝow

Fol. 202^{v}

Apon ȝo*u*r fais and strik thai*m* dovn.'
He welcu*m*mit him and bad hi*m* bovn
To be in-to the king*is* gard,
And he suld haf ane hie reward;
And syne to burde him fessy*n*nit he
With a burges of that cité.
Thar spendit he and was wele lufit
And oft in battell best he prufit.
The king*is* fais straike he dovn
And in armes wan gret renovne,
Bot eu*er* he studyit to fynd a gyn
How he my*ch*t to the lady wyn.
Than to the stewart he tho*ch*t best reid
To tell that he was wnd*er* feid,
And tald him he micht no*ch*t slepe
In a thak hous to ly *and* slepe.
Bot and he plesit he wald preif
To big, and he wald gif hi*m* leif,
Ane stark towr w*ith* ane stane wall
Till his castall in ane to-fall.
The stewart hi*m* grantit *and* was ry*ch*t blyth
And maso*n*nis he assemblit swyth;
Ane strait towr *and* a fair w*ith*-all
He biggit fast to the castall wall.
It happi*n*nit the kny*ch*t a day th*a*t he
Raid be the way his luf to sé,
And w*ith* the countenans th*a*t scho my*ch*t
Till him scho schewe plesans be sicht.
That maid him laith to pas fra hyne;
Than subtelly scho couth him syne
For to cum neir the castall wall,
And a luf lett*er* scho leit fall.

2317. Cr.: 'Either *slepe* is wrong, or some lines are missing.' See expl.note.

Fol. 203[r]

Quhen he it red, God wait gif he
Was blyth as ony man my*ch*t be,
For he fande wele he had hir luf;
Than kest he que*n*tans to contruf.
Wnder strait obligacoun
He discoverit him till a masoun,
And till him hecht gret reward,
And na expenses suld be spard,
W*ith* craft gif he wald wnd*er*tak
Ane prevé passage for to mak
Wnder the wall w*ith* ony gyn,
To the lady th*a*t he my*ch*t wyn.
The masoun wnd*er*tuke it tyte
And maide a passage wele p*er*fyte,
That na man wnd*er*stand it my*ch*t.
Thus in the castall wan the kny*ch*t,
Quhen lokit was all the ȝett*is* fast.
The stewart, as he was wont, out past
And all the keyis w*ith* him has tane
And left the lady hir allane.
The kny*ch*t fand hir i*n* chyar set;
Thai kist lyk lufar*is* quhe*n* thai met.
Of th*ar* deid I bid no*ch*t write
For thai had hartlie ioye p*er*fyte
Than na man wnd*er*stand it my*ch*t.
Thus in the castall wan the kny*ch*t
And w*ith* this lady had sic plesans,
Scho gaf the kny*ch*t i*n* acque*n*tans
Ane gold ryng th*a*t hir lord hir gaf,
To gar him oft i*n* mynd hir haf.
Thus blyth war thai q*uh*ill at the last

Fol. 203v

The kny*ch*t furth at the condit past,
For thar was nane that ke*n*nit th*a*t traide,
Saifand the masoun that it maid.
The kny*ch*t him slewe in haist or he
Micht discover his prevaté.
Than of the passage wist th*ar* nane
Bot the ladye and he allane,
And evir as thai micht wyn th*ar*to
Till vth*er* thai come, quhile he, quhile scho,
Quhill at the dynar a daye sittand
The stewart beheld the kny*ch*t*is* hand
And ke*n*nit the ryng *and* said: 'How now?
That is my ryng! Quha gaf it ȝow?'
The kny*ch*t said: 'S*ch*ir, certanlye
This ryng was neu*er* maid i*n* Vngry.'
Than to the castall he past to sé,
Bot at the condit in ȝeid he
And gaif the lady the ryng agane
And thar na langar wald remane,
Bot was furth, lang or he come in,
And closit the passage and the gyn.
Than come the stewart hastely
And askit the ryng at the lady.
Scho said: 'S*ch*ir, lo it redy heir!'
Than m*er*walit he on gret maner,
And said: 'Ȝone strange kny*ch*t i-wis,
He has the lykest ryng to this
That eu*er* in this warld was sene;
I wald haf trowit myn it had bene,
War no*ch*t now I sé it heir!'
Scho said: 'My lord, haf ȝe na weir,

Bot ȝo*ur* ryng and ȝo*ur* luf-drowry Fol. 204r
As my awne body kepe sall I!'
Off that scho maid na lesyng:
This kny*ch*t scho lufit o*ur* all thing
And ay redy till his plesans
Scho hantit at his governans.
The stewart past in-to hunting eftir,
The lady lokit at hame he left hir,
And prayit the kny*ch*t w*ith* him to ga.
He said: 'S*ch*i*r*, I may no*ch*t do sa;
My luf is cu*m*myn i*n* this cu*n*tré
For to be marijt now w*ith* me.
Syne will we hame w*ith*outin baide,
Scho tellis me my pece is maide.
Tharfor I pray ȝow w*ith* me to dyne
And sé ȝone le*m*man th*a*t is myne,
For quhe*n* I mak my wedding-band
I will resaif hir of ȝo*ur* hand.
Syne with worschipe hir wed will I.'
The stewart grantit him blythly
And passit furth to play him than.
The kny*ch*t wp to the lady wan
And till his hall he brocht hir dovn
And cled hir on a newe fassoun,
With clething of his awne cu*n*tré,
Quhilk th*a*t he brocht w*ith* him our sé.
The lady than began the dese
With hir awne husband at the mese,
And sic tent till hir has he tane
That he ete litill meit or nane,
Bot on hir me*r*walit all-thar-maist,
For him tho*ch*t baith be woce *and* taist

Fol. 204v

It was his awne wyf we*r*raly,
Bot of the castall sekerlye
He wist weile th*a*t scho micht no*ch*t wyn.
Full litill wist he of the gyn!
Quhen he had etyn he him sped
To the castell, and scho vncled
Swyth the clething th*a*t scho was in,
And wp the ne*r*rest gait can wyn,
And cled hir in hir awn clething,
As scho had wittin of na kyn thing.
Quhen he hir fand he changit cheir,
He wox blythar and said: 'My deir,
The kny*ch*t*is* luf is cu*m*my*n* hiddir,
And suthly, war ȝe to-giddir,
Thar is na clerk na ȝit nane oth*er*
That suld the tane knawe be the tothir
Off body, colo*u*r, voce and cast,
Nor ȝit twa women lykast
I trow forsuth God neu*er* wrocht.'
Scho said: 'S*chi*r, on (that) study no*ch*t,
For wome*n* oft-tymes has bene sene
And men has lyke till vth*er* bene
And tane for vth*er* in mony place.'
'Thai said the morne thai schape p*er*case
To mary, syne pas to thar land.
He wald I gaf hir of my hand
At the kirk-dure with all hono*u*r.'
'Schir,' said scho, 'be o*u*r saluio*u*r!
The worschip ȝe to strangear*is* do
Is ȝo*u*r hono*u*r and tha*ris* to!'
The stewart on the morne airly
Gat wp and maid hi*m* sone redy

2448. *that* was inserted by Craigie.

And to the kirk is prowdly past; Fol. 205r
The castall-dur*is* he lokit fast,
And w*ith* him has (the) keyis tane
And lokit his lady in allane.
Bot also sone as scho wprais,
The kny*ch*t gart cleth hir in his cla*ithis*,
Adornit as scho wald go to wed,
And sa furth to the kirk hir led.
The prest (was) redy all rewest,
And the stewart, as he my*ch*t best,
Befor thai*m* all that th*ar* couth stand,
Gaif wp his awne wyf be the hand
Vnto the kny*ch*t to hald for ay,
And said till hir: 'My derrast may,
For ony caise th*a*t eu*er* may fall,
Sé ȝe luf this man o*ur* thai*m* all.'
Quhen mes and mariage war maid,
Than buskit the kny*ch*t w*ith*outin baid,
And the stewart requyrit he
For to pas w*ith* him to the sé,
And gif agane, quhe*n* all was bovn,
His wyf and eike his benesoun.
Than to the schip thai passit on ane
And th*ar* befor thai*m* all ilkane
To the kny*ch*t he gaf his wyf,
And bad hir, quhill scho held hir lyf,
The kny*ch*t to luf atto*ur* all thing
And sa pas on w*ith* his blissing.
Than blythlie in the schip thai ȝud
And drewe wp saile -- the wynd was gud --
And w*ith* the lady fair *and* bricht
In his awn cu*n*tré come the kny*ch*t.
The stewart hamwart sone is past,

2463. See expl.note.
2469. *was* is a suggestion of Craigie's.

Fol. 205v

For dreid his lady to lang suld fast.
Bot quhen he fand scho was awaye,
He grat and had a dulefull day.
He said: 'Allace!' w*ith* hart full sair,
'My wyf*is* word*is* I trowit mair
Than it I saw w*ith* my awn eyne!
Now may I do bot murn *and* meyne
With scaith and lak and dishono*u*r.'

Than said Craton to the emp*ri*our:
'Trow no*ch*t ȝo*u*r wyf apon ȝo*u*r child,
For and ȝe do, ȝe ar begyld.
The morne the child sall speike but leis
And declar all the suthfastnes.'
The emp*ri*our said: 'That fane I wald,
And for the sample th*a*t thow has tauld
Quhill the morn-day girth I him gif.'
The clerk lowtit and tuke his leif.

Than on the morn be the son schane
Thir sag*is* come togiddir ilkane
And to the child in haist thai*m* sped.
In precious clething thai haf hi*m* cled,
Syne brocht him furth w*ith* gret hono*u*r
Lyk the son of ane emp*ri*our.
The baronis, quhen thai that couth sé,
And all the worthy of the cité,
Maid gret ioy, as the story tellis.
Thai blewe organis *and* rang the bellis,
With trumpe *and* talburn playit lowde,
Harpe, lute, gittern, clarschaw *and* crovde,
Psaltery, symphion *and* claroun,
All menstraly i*n* vnisoun,
Befor the barne all playit thai
For ioye that he suld speke th*a*t day.

The emp*ri*our*is* self to kirk he past Fol. 206r
And than the emprys at the last
Followit dulfully and full of dreid,
Full rad till heir hir awn misdeid.
All thus the sag*is* wi*th* all hono*u*r
The barne brocht to the emp*ri*our.
The child befor his fader fell
And than on knéis he spak his-sell
And with hie voce he bad scilens;
Syne halsit his fader wi*th* reu*e*rens.
The emp*ri*our than for hartlie ioye
He grat sa fast he my*ch*t no*ch*t hoye.
Than askit the child wi*th* all meiknes:
'Fader, I pray ȝ*o*w of forgifnes,
The caus that wi*th* me stud sa thrang,
That lettit me to speik sa lang,
That ȝo*u*r hienes sa fer has grevit;
For traist ȝe weile, *and* I had previt
Ane word to speike owt of my hed (...)
For-thi, Fader, forgif ȝo*u*r feid,
For first quhen that ȝe for me send
My master*is* and I to wesy wend
Quhat of my passage my*ch*t apper,
And we saw be the sternis cleir
Sevyn dayis my speche behovit be hid.
Bot do no*ch*t, Fader, as the man did
That kest his son in-to the sé
For caus he him schewe nakit lawté.'
'I pray thé, son, thow tell me how,
For thi lyf is defendit now
Be ensampillis that thi master*is* tald;
That thow tald now th*a*rfor I wald.'
The child said: 'Blythly, Fader deir,
And my awne pa*r*t I sall mak cleir,

2545. Cr.: 'Some lines are clearly wanting here.'

Fol. 206v

That vth*er*is ensample tak be me
And do the richt and falset flé.'

The child*is* tale of the fader th*a*t kest his son in the sé for the bird*is* sang.

VATICINIUM

'Ane man,' he said, 'was riche of gud;
Ane gud wyf had and thai*m* behude
Pas o*u*r the sey in pilg*ri*mage.
Thai had a son, tuelf ȝer*is* of age,
Full of sciens of sa lang space
And mekle couth of God*is* grace.
Than, as th*ar* schip the sé thro*u* past,
Ane ny*ch*ttingale lichtit on the mast
And sang sa w*er*ray dulce *and* sweit,
That neu*er* in all th*ar* dayis ȝet
Thai hard half sa sweit a sang,
That sa fer in th*ar* hart couth gang.
Than said this gud man till his wyf:
"Wele fortonyt war the man on lyf
That couth declair the knawlege clene,
The sweit sang of this philomeyne."
The child said: "Fader, that can I!
For me scho mak*is* this melody!"
"Swet son, how sa? Tell on! Lat sé!"
"Scho syng*is*, Fader, that I sall be
Put to sic worschip in ȝo*u*r dayis,
-- This c*er*tanly scho syng*is* *and* sayis --
That ȝe sall me the basyng hald,
And my moder the towall fald
W*ith* gret honour apon ȝo*u*r kné."
The fader th*ar*of said: "Thow sall lé!"
And crabitly, or his greif degest,

Fol. 207r

His son in-to the sé he kest.
The child in-to the sé couth fleyt
And cryit: "Me*r*cy, Ihesu sweit!"
Richtsa a schip come saland by;
The child thai succurit hastely,
And had him w*ith* thai*m* sovnde *and* hale,
Quhill thai come till a fair castale,
And to the stewart thai hi*m* sauld
For twenty m*ar*k*is* of pe*n*neis tald.
This child sa courtly *and* sa honest
He wox *and* bure him to the best,
Sa meike, sa sweit *and* sa lawly,
All man him lufit hartfully.
Than happi*n*nit the king inco*n*tinent
To set a gen*er*ale p*ar*liament.
The stewart thiddir couth hi*m* hy;
He tuke the child in company.
Quhen gadderit was all the confluens
The kyng co*m*mandit has scilens,
Syne said: "I haf ane douchtir fair
And na oth*er* to be my air.
Ane m*er*well movis me eu*er*mar;
Quha will the suth of it declar
My douchter I sall gif hi*m* fre
And all my land*is* eft*ir* me.
Thré ravy*n*nis ar eu*er* on me rolpand;
Etand, drynkand, slepand, walkand,
Thai follow me ay w*ith* sic clamo*ur*
That I may neu*er* slepe ane hour,
And sa vgsum me think th*ar* cry,
That of my lyf disparit am I;
And ony man war sa p*er*fyte

Fol. 207v

To tell the caus and sker thai*m* quyte
Fra me, that thai cu*m* neu*er* agane,
Heir I promit in p*ar*liament plane
That he sall haf my dochter fair
And of my kinrik sall be air."
The child, quhe*n* that the king said sa,
His master be the lap couth ta
And said: "Mast*er*, I tell ȝou this:
Will the king kepe his fair promis,
This mater sa sall I declair
That he sall heir ȝone ravi*n*nis no mair!"
Tharof the stewart was full blyth,
And to the king he said full swyth:
"Schir, will ȝe weile ȝo*u*r promis hald,
The treuth to ȝou sall wele be tald."
The king said: "Cert*is*, it sall be so,
I hecht in verbo regio!"
The stewart said: "Lo s*chi*r, this barne
Sall weile declar all th*a*t ȝe ȝarne,
For he of augur has cu*n*nyng,
In bird*is* voce and th*ar* syngyng."
The king said: "Barne, haf ȝe sic fele?"
The child said: "S*chi*r, th*a*t haf I wele.
Gar mak scilens, that all may heir,
For I sall mak this mater cleir."
Than for scilens he maid a pavs
And said: "My lord, this is the caus:
Ȝone twa ald ravi*n*nis producit the thrid
And happi*n*nit, quhe*n* scho was a bird,
For gret hunger in that cu*n*tré
The scho-ravyn away couth flé
To fende hir-self as scho my*ch*t best,

And left the ʒoung bird in the nest,
Redy to dé for falt of fude.
And quhe*n* the hie-ravyn vnd*er*stud
The scho-ravyn wald no*ch*t cu*m* agane,
He fed the ravyn w*ith* mekle pane
And brocht it wp quhill it couth flé,
And help the self alswele as he.
The scho-ravyn now cravis the bird
And sais scho aucht to be his hird,
For scho him of ane eg couth clek;
Of hir resoun this is the fek.
The hie-rawyn says scho aucht na scair,
For scho him left in mast mistair
In nest nakit redy to dé,
Quhill hi*m* w*ith* gret pane helpit he.
This causis all th*ar* argument.
Of ʒow, s*chi*r, thai wald haf iugement,
And followis ʒow baith day *and* ny*ch*t,
To wit quhilk to the bird has richt.
Gif furth ʒo*ur* dome, the caus declair,
And ʒe sall neu*er* heir thai*m* mair!:
The king said: "Suthly, I presome,
And wtterly I gif for dome:
The craw that savit the bird*is* lyf
Sall iois the bird but sturt or stryf."
Than rolpit the ravi*n*nis all w*ith* th*ar* mi*ch*t,
Syne sodanly thai tuke the flicht,
And flawe away as thai war fane,
And neu*er* thar was sene agane.
Than fra the king that can p*er*saif
His douchter to the child he gaf,
Quhilk was wele lufit w*ith* ilka man

Fol. 208v

Quhill the king levit and eft*ir* than
He was maid king *and* tuke the crovne
And wyslie governit his regioun.
Thus ryally as he couth ryng,
Apon his fader tho*ch*t the king
And langit his moder for to sé,
That than war fallyn i*n* gret pureté.
The king has callit his s*er*uand*is* than,
And said him thai suld fynd a man
In sic a forest and warne him syne
The king the morne w*ith* hi*m* wald dyne.
His s*er*uand*is* did as he thai*m* bad;
Tharof the ald ma*n* was full glad
And thankit God that sely hour,
That he my*ch*t sé his governo*ur*.
On the morn the king come hastely
And to the dyner schupe i*n* hy.
The fader the lawar sone couth get,
The moder the towall on knéis fet,
Bot than the king has gart thai*m* rys,
And chargit vth*er* to mak s*er*uis.
"Knaw ȝe no*ch*t me?" tha*n* said the king.
"Na s*chir*," said thai, "bot of a thing
We knawe: ȝe ar o*ur* king *and* lord."
"Ȝeis," said he, "*and* ȝe will remord
I am ȝo*ur* son the qu*h*ilk th*a*t ȝe
Forsuth kest in-to the sé.
Now it is sene as I couth tell."
Quhen thai that hard, to erd thai fell
And of that deid thai ask m*er*cy,
Bot he thai*m* rasit full tend*er*ly,
And bad thai*m* th*a*t thai suld no*ch*t dreid,

Fol. 209[r]

And said it was foly in deid
To man to hald opinioun
Aganis God*is* disposicioun.
Than eft*ir* tham awansit he
To riches and gret dignité.'

CONCLUSION

Than to the emp*riour* said his son:
'This hale empyr tho*ch*t I had won,
Ȝe suld haf (had) na noy of me
Mair than the child castin i*n* the sé
Did till his fader for his suprys.
Bot had the word*is* of the emprys
In hir malice gart ȝou sla me,
Ȝe suld haf levit i*n* mar purté,
And quhar scho plenȝeit on me th*a*t I
Wald hir haf forsit sa cruelly
God wait -- and him I gif the caus --
Gif th*a*t scho maide to me that paus
With all scho couth w*ith* hir to ly!
Bot God wait gif levir had I
Haf bene drawin *and* als torment,
And quhen sche saw I wald no*ch*t *con*sent,
With hir awne hand*is* scho raif hir face;
God is my witnes in this cais.'
Than said the emp*riour* hir till:
'Wikit woma*n*, fulfillit of ill,
Quhy art thow dum *and* answer*is* no*ch*t?'
Scho said agane: 'All ȝone I wrocht
To tempe thi sone allan*er*ly
And now tha*r*for I ask me*r*cy!'
The emp*riour* said: 'Full ill art th*o*w,
Thy awne mouth has *con*dampnit thé now,'
And to the fyre bad hir be harld

2725. *had* was inserted by Craigie.

Fol. 209v

To tak sic malice out of the warld.
Than prayit the child to mak a paus,
'And I sall schaw ȝow ane gretar caus
Befor ȝow all th*a*t scho suld dé,
Mair than ony caus of me,
For it sall opynly be previt
Sa synfull lyf as scho has levit.'
Than hastely he gart furth call
Of hir chalm*er* the madi*n*nis all
Agane hir will, for scho was rad
Hir to be discou*er*it for caus maid.
Amang hir madi*n*nis th*ar* was ane
A man th*a*t for a madin was tane
And Bribo*u*r callit was be name,
That for his syn gat sca*ith* *and* schame.
He lakit oft w*ith* the lady
Quhe*n*-eu*er* thai plesit, full prevely,
In woma*n*nis clething cled full wele.
The child bad: 'Tak this damysele
And spulȝe now, th*a*t all may sé,
Quhidd*ir* scho man or woman be,
And quhat s*er*uice wnd*er* colour
He maid my fader, the empriour!'
The lord*is* and the baro*n*nis than
Spulȝeit *and* fand it was a man.
Than gaf the emp*riour* be law
That thai to deid suld hi*m* draw.
The emprys, th*a*t hi*m* sa begyld,
He gart be brynt, *and* sa this child
Chapit *and* eft*ir* his fader*is* deces
He governit his land i*n* rest *and* peis,
Syne ȝeid till hevyn *and* sa do we.
Says all Amen for cherité.

Heir end*is* 'The Sevyn Sag*is*' p*er* M. Io. Asloan.

XIX. TEXTUAL NOTES

This is a list of textual differences between Craigie's and the present edition. It is to be remembered that Craigie worked from a transcription not executed by himself.

	Craigie	
13	made	maide
29	Vndir	Wnder
31	mor	mar
32	yi	ye (>the)
82	yai	yan (>than)
137	ask	aske
199	bautillas	Bantillas
201	ye	ȝe
250	Lord	lord
396	tald	tauld
428	credell	credill
482	knewe	knew
510	scho	sche
520	scho	sche
664	sawe	saw
683	scho	sche
684	nakitly	nakitlye
780	have	haue
789	stuk	strik
831	wretchednes	wretchidnes
878	son	sone
936	stud	stude
952	Thai tro(wit him) sa past	Thai trowit and sa past be-
betw.1002-3	scho be(gylit)	sche gy(lit)
1012	...	takin
1013	...	..hame
1019	an	ane
1076	syn	syne
1093	ye	ȝe
1131	To	Do
1223, 1227, 1230, 1234	merk	mark
1235	ȝow	yow (>thow)
1249	king	kyng
1380	maid	maide
1706	bot	but
1748	yaim (the 1st ex.)	yam (>tham)
1757	barrellis	barellis
1920	allhale	all hale
1951	ye	yar (>thar)
1974	yaim	yar (>thar)

2007 clath	claith
2282 bot	but
2415 worschip	worschipe
2427 yer	yar (>thar)
2466 clathis	claithis
2573 so	sa
2585 sal	sall
2598 m*er*kis	m*ar*kis
2608 king	kyng
2609 douchter	douchtir
2730 have	haf
2738 scho	sche
2764 scath	scaith
passim thair, yair	thar

Throughout Craigie italicises only the first *r* in words like *empriour, empris, emprice,* whereas the abbreviation is for both *r* and *i*, as also in *price* 414, *writtin* 1626.

Minor mistakes in Craigie's edition:

68 yat	y^{t}; *a* should be italicised
89 yat	idem
144 hir*e*	hir’
184 master*e*	master’
185 emp*r*iour*e*	emp*ri*our’
192, 1435, 1576, 2111 p*er*ell	p*er*rell
344 bath	ba*i*t*h*
382 p*er*ellis	p*er*rellis
394 ß*i*r	s*chi*r
462 hir*e*	hir’
621 sister	sist’, > sist*er*
703 yat	y^{t}, see 68 above
1011 war*e*	war’
1017 eftir’wart	eftirwart
1292 torme*n*tou*ris*	tormentou*ris*, *n* being written
1322 eftirwart	eft*ir*wart
1467 yairof	y’ of, > y*ar*of
1535 hir’	hir*e*
1609 hu*n*dreth	hu*n*dret*h*
1880 quhar*e*	quhar’
2039 wedder’	wedder*e*
2205 yar*e*	yar’
2269 yat	see 68 above
2333 neir*e*	neir’

XX. EXPLANATORY NOTES

Most of Craigie's notes to *BSS* are mentioned incidentally below.

2. The emperor's name occurs only here in this text, rhyming with *bygane*. His name appears in the ME *E* MS. as *Dioclician*, the son's as *Florentyne*; in MS. *B* as *Dyoclesyan*, the son's as *Fflorentyne*; in MS. *A** as *Dioclecian*, the son's as *Florentin*. The name of *Florentyne* is found only in the English versions, see Campbell's note to line 25. In the H-versions the emperor is usually called *Poncianus (Pontianus)* and the son *Dyoclecianus*. In versions A, L and S the emperor is *Dyoclesiyen*, &c., whereas the son has no name; only in the so-called continuations or sequels of *SSR* does it appear that the son is also called *Dyoclesiyen*, &c. (The first continuation is called *Le Roman de Marques de Rome*; the others are *Laurin*, *Cassidorus*, *Kanor*, *Peliarmenus*, and *Helcanus*. For their relationship see Hans R.Runte ed., *Li Ystoire de la male marastre*, Tübingen, 1974, p. xviii, and Lewis Thorpe, *Le roman de Laurin*, Vol. I, Ch. 5, pp. 89-117, 'Laurin and the other sequels to the "Sept Sages"') In version K the emperor is called *Vaspasianus*, the child has no name, and the place of the action is Constantinople. For the names in other versions compare Appendix VI. See also Section XIII. In the French redaction D the father is called *Marcomeris*; he is said to be the son of Priam, and emperor of Rome and Constantinople and king of France. The son again has no name.
9. The boy is *thre ȝeir* here; in most other versions he is said to be seven years old. This may be due to a misreading of .iii. for .vii.
12. *All that levis mon leif heir eft*, 'all who live must leave this world afterwards' or 'in the end'; *all that* occurs three times, cf. Glossary s.v. *all*; in each case it refers to a number of people.
14. The son is called *Dioclesiane* after his father, rhyming with *mane*; see note to line 2 above.
24. In the present version there are no personal descriptions of the sages as there are in the OF and ME versions. The combination of names for the sages given in *BSS* is not found in any other version, see Appendix VI.
30. The bottom of f. 167 is damaged so that lines 30 and 62 are lost. See Section I.
41. *the science liberale*: in the Middle Ages this term was often used for the seven sciences or arts, the studies comprised by the *Trivium* (grammar, logic and rhetoric) and the *Quadrivium* (arithmetic, astronomy, geometry and music).
43. *Amipullus* may be read as *Aunpullus*, which could be a corruption of *Aunxullus*, a form of *Aunxilles*, *Anxilles* or *Ancilles*, forms which appear in several other versions. This is the more likely because in the Asl. as in other MSc MSS *p* and *x* are easily confused. Although line 43 scans better with the form *Amipullus*, it can be made to scan with *Aunxullus* by placing the stress on the first syllable of the line. This is often done throughout the poem. The name of this second sage is, in fact, found as *Ancillas* rhyming with *Ypocras* (783), as *Maxillas* rhyming with *thar was* (588). For other forms of the name of this sage see Appendix VIa.
44. Cr.: '*Lentalus*, more correctly *Lentulus*, in l. 973, &c.'
50. Cr.: '*Malcome* = 1297 *Maucundas*, properly *Malquidras*.' The form *Malcome* may have arisen when the author or scribe found the name *Malcuidars* in his example, with *Malcui* at the end of a line and *dars* on the next (as is indeed the case in the Oxford MS. St.John's Coll. CII). He may then have taken

Malc + three minims for an abbreviated form of *Malcolm/Malcome*, especially if he was familiar with this Scottish name.

53. Cr.: '*Ampustinus* for *Maxentius*.' We have only this one mention of the name of the sixth sage, because his tale does not occur in the present version of the *Seven Sages*. In a number of A-versions the second sage is called *Augustus* instead of *Ancillas*. *Ampustinus* may be a variation of *Augustinus*, due to the form *Augustus*. (OF MS. St.John's Coll. CII has *Augustus* once for the second sage; OF MS. Cambridge Gg.I.1 calls him *Ancilles, Augustus* and *Anxilles*; the name *Augustus* is also found in the OF C-version (ed. Hugh A.Smith) for the second master.) In A-versions the sixth sage is usually called *Jesse, Gesse*, &c., in H-versions *Cleophas*, see Appendix VIa .

55. The name Craton is found in the *Hollands Volksboek* (ed. A.J.Botermans, *Die hystorie van die seuen wÿse mannen van romen, ed. 1479*, Utrecht, 1898), in the 1492 Geneva-version, ed. Gaston Paris, 1876, in Wynkyn de Worde's version and in Rolland's *Seven Sages*, all going back to H, where it is evidently an alternative form for the name of the third sage. The occurrence of the two forms *Cato* and *Craton* denoting different sages is unique in the Asloan MS.

62. Campbell 1907, p. xl, n.1, mentions 'a lacuna after l. 61, which Laing takes ... to involve the loss of an entire folio, but which probably amounts to less than ten lines.' It may be just one line, however, e.g. 'And the child than gaf tham till'.

69. Cr.: '*How* for *Quhat* or *Quhare*.' The first word of the line in the MS is *How*. Of Craigie's suggestions I prefer *Quhare*, because we have already been shown *what* the masters were going to teach the youth, and the following statement by Lentulus concerns the place *where* the teaching is going to take place.

74. *A grene, a myle of at the mast*. A mile seems a very short distance for the purpose intended, but in the English versions edited by Brunner we also find *a mile, a longe myle*; version CR l. 176 has *a myle fra toun bi a reuere*. OF MSS consulted have e.g.: St.John's MS. CII: *ung vergier hors de rome a une heure pres*; Gg.I.1:*on verger hors de rome a vne lieu pres*; BN.fr.19166, ed. Leroux de L.: *.i. vergier hors de rome a une liue pres de Rome*; BN.fr.95, ed. Plomp: *.i. biau lieu, a une lieue pres de Romme*.

In HL (ed. Buchner, p. 9) they take the boy to *quoddam viridarium Sancti Martini, ad duas leucas* from Rome. This is no doubt an echo of the *Bois Saint Martin* found in many of the A and L-version MSS, in K and also in the ME MSS, as the place where the masters later await their turns to defend their pupil.

82. In his notes Craigie says: '*thai* is superfluous'. This must be due to a mistake in the transcription he was working with. The MS has *than* as printed in the present edition.

86. *Quhen ane was tyrit ane nother ȝed to*, cf. CR 197 *When ane him left another him toke*; St.John CII *Et quant lun le lassoit lautre le reprenoit*, similarly Gg.I.1, BN.fr.19166, BN.fr. 95.

97. *edoke leif*, cf. Gaston Paris, *Deux rédactions*, p. 61: '...aux quatre boutz de son lit des feulles d'une herbe verde qui se nomme *edera*, laquelle monte au lung des murs ...' It seems possible that the author of the Scots poem, on seeing before him either a similar French text with this Latin word, or a Latin text with the form *ederae* or *edae*, made this into *edoke*, perhaps not knowing the right translation of *(h)edera* 'ivy'. The form *edae* is found in the *Scala Celi*, ed. Goedeke, *Or.u.Occ.*, III, 1866. HL has '*Ipso dormiente ponemus sub quolibet cornu lecti vnum folium edere et ante lectum eius stabimus, quousque a sompne excitatus fuerit*.' (ed. Buchner, p. 9)

In other texts various other kinds of leaves are used, e.g. *iubarb (iubark)* 'houseleek' in MSS. C and R; version K (BN.fr. 1553), ed. Misrahi: *fuelles de rue (= Ruta graveolens)*. In Rolland's and W. de Worde's versions olive-leaves are used.

109. With this and the following line cf. K 401 f. *Un poi vous lairons a ester / Au roi vous volrons retorner.*

117. *vyer (uther)* is the reading in the MS. It might be an error for *ayr* 'heir', cf. 1329, but also 2610.

123. *abrek.* Craigie in his note to this line, and *DOST* s.v. *abrege* v., take this to mean 'abridge', but cf. *MED* s.v. *abreken*: b. destroy, ruin (the health of).

137. *luf-asking,* cf. *luf-drowry* 2397.

157-60. '... and (they) saw truly, they all together, (that) at the appointed day (when) the youth (would) come hither, at the first word he might speak he would be killed.'

198. *nocht for-thi.* This expression here has a double purpose: it serves as a negative, and also *nocht for-thi* has its usual function of 'nevertheless'; maybe *bot* is to be looked upon as an adversative conjunction implying a negative, or we might conjecture *na word* instead of *a word.*

199. In the A-version it is not Bancillas who answers the emperor's question, saying: *Sire, il parloit ier toutes manieres de paroles,* but the emperor's *maistre despensier* (BN.fr.95). MS. Ars. 3152 has: *il parloit bien hier matin*; Gg.6.28: *il parloit hui matin toutes manere de paroles.* In St. John CII the master *qui estoit venus auesques lui* says: *Sire il parloit hui matin toutes manieres de parlemens.*

202. *be this buke.* This presumably implies that there is a Bible at hand somewhere.

204. *the day,* 'to-day' as in Modern Scots. This is a datable feature, see Section X.

220. *wryth.* The form one might expect here is *writhit,* taking it to be derived from OE *wrīþan.* Though the latter is a strong verb the present suggested form *writhit* would point to the tendency to reduce strong conjugations to weak, see G. Gregory Smith, *Specimens of Middle Scots,* Edinburgh, 1902, p. xxxvii. *Wryth* might also be interpreted as 3rd pers. sg. of *wry (OE wrigian).* The fact that we find a verb in the past tense in the same sentence need not invalidate this argument, since the practice occurs frequently in *BSS,* cf. e.g. ll. 223-4 and 226-7.

225. *sone be at thai come within,* 'soon after they entered'.

226. The MS has *He,* but it is clear from the context that this should be *Scho* or *Sche,* since the young man does not speak.
Scho bad wodas baith mar and myn. Craigie's note says: '*Wodas,* perh.=O.F. *voidez,* cf. *NED* s.v. *Voidee*'. It is, however, also possible to derive *wodas* from AN *voidaunce, NED* s.v. *voidance* n. 2, 'the action or fact of removing, clearing away, &c.', or interpret it as an aphetic form of 'avoidance', *NED* n. 5, 'the act of dismissing a person or bidding him quit'; 6. 'the action of quitting, withdrawal, departure'. The form *wodas* in the MS may be due to a misinterpreted abbreviation of *wodans* (with *n* reduced to a loop, see Section XVI). The diphthong /oi/ was levelled with /ō/ in MSc late in the fourteenth eentury (see Section VI); this would account for the form *wodans* for *woidans* (< *voidaunce*). Cf. also the W. de Worde-edition of the *Seven Wise Masters of Rome* (1520), ed. Gomme: *The empresse ... commaunded all other to auoyde & set hym by her.*

240. *He threwe the face.* Apart from the meaning given in the glossary: 'he turned his face aside (or to one side)', this might perhaps also imply: 'he pulled a wry face', cf. MoSc verb *thraw,* 'distort, twist, &c.'
mist may be a contracted form of *miss it* , although *mist* is also found as

an infinitive, see *NED* s.v. *mist* v.

250. *The lord had slane him in that hour,* the lord would have killed him ...

252. *band* if dependent on *gart* may be an infinitive, a form of the verb 'to band'. It can also be looked upon as a preterite, though in this case the syntax is not quite sound, unless we are given to understand that the emperor himself binds the youth's hands, which is unlikely. An error for *bind* is another possibility.

253. Craigie emends *scurge* for *scurgis* as found in the MS. *Scurgis* might be right, however, if we take it as an imperative, but the most obvious explanation seems that the final *-e* in copying was mistaken for the abbreviation for *-is*. Cf. F.J.Amours' edn of *Wyntoun's Chronicle,* Vol. II, pp. ix f.: "A more curious contraction - rare in the Wemyss, very common in the Cottonian - is a downward curl after a final 'g': it usually stands for 'is', the plural ending, but is commonly met with in nouns that are certainly in the singular. What is more difficult to explain is that the uncontracted ending 'gis' occurs at times in a singular form."

291. 'In this town (it) was well known (that there) dwelt a burgess ...'

310. It would seem, in connection with what follows, that *he* should be replaced by *it*. Possibly the scribe was led astray into writing *he did* by *he bid* in the preceding line.

350. '... and did not know what use (or good) the young tree would be.'

356. After this line the scribe has deleted a whole line, identical with l.350; the words *noble tre* and *nobilite* had evidently confused him while he was looking for the place where he had left off, or in copying his eyes may have passed from the end of line 356 to that of 349.

357. The lady switches from the polite forms (*ȝe, ȝow* and *ȝour)* to *thine* and *thé*; for usage here and later in the poem see 'A Note on the Use of *ȝe* and *thou*', Section IX, pp. 78-81.

364. *My son sall be hangit and drawin. Hangit be* would have given a better rhythm to the line.

380. *ȝestrene* here may mean 'yesterday' rather than 'yesterday evening'; cf. W.Grant and J.M.Dixon, *A Manual of Modern Scots,* Cambridge, 1921, p.134.

382. ... *War nocht perrellis ...,* 'if there were no dangers ...'

385 ff. Peculiar to *BSS,* though HF does mention the *loy publique escripte,* but not in connection with the queen being no virgin.

404. *Ane suth sample I sall ȝow schawe.* The line would read better if it had *ensample.*

404-05. It is *the barne* which is *helpit,* not *the serpent.*

409. *tornamentis.* The MS has *tormentis*; according to *NED torment* is sometimes written *tornament,* but the converse possibility is not mentioned.

425, 426. *left* 'remained'.

432. *in the hole; in a hole* would be better, cf. note to l. 544 below.

517. See note to l. 1471 below.

527. *nocht fer heir west.* If the emperor's wife is speaking in Rome there is not much land to the West. Campbell 1907, p. 159, remarks: 'Though this appears in all the ME MSS. except *Ar, D** and *F* ... there is nothing corresponding to it in any of the OF MSS. that have been published ... The phrase here is probably "merely formal"'. It may have been called forth by the need for a rhyme to *forest*; in the same way we find *west* as a rhyme-tag in G.L.Brook, *The Harley Lyrics,* Manchester U.P., (1956)1968, 5.37, 12.10 and 15.47.

528-30. Not quite regular unless l. 529 is taken as parenthetical. Perhaps ll. 530 and 529 should change places and read:

Sumtyme thar stude a fair forest,
Wallit about with lyme and stane;
Of frute and tre lyke it was nane.

544. *Nymly he clam wp in the tre: a tre* would have been better since a tree had not been mentioned before, cf. note to l. 432.
573. *The herd thi son is for to say,* 'the herdsman signifies your son'.
574. ... *That the fordo wald nycht and day* would give a better rhythm.
583. *Thar was nocht than bot ...,* 'there was nothing for it then but ...'
587. The MS has: *Than mekle dule than thar was.* Craigie suggests *That* for *Than,* or *thare* for *than,* but since *thar* occurs already, I prefer to change the first *Than* into *That,* meaning 'so that'.
588. *Maxillas,* see note to l. 43.
608. '... if he dies before I have told (my story)'.
616. *Ypocras,* i.e. Hippocrates, the well-known Greek physician, familiar to the Middle Ages.
640. The K-version gives a plausible reason for Ypocras not going in person: he is ill when summoned by the king and therefore sends his nephew.
646-7. *He had be fer ... had* 'he would much rather have had ...'; *be fer* may be a copyist's error for *lefer* 'rather', but cf. l. 1241.
651. It might perhaps be suggested that *says* could be an aphetic form of *assays,* cf. *NED say* v.2 'to test the nature &c. of, to try or examine for the sake of information', but the phonology points to 'sees', cf. Section VI, phoneme No. 2, pp.44-45.
668. *carnale fader.* This clearly implies here 'father of an adulterous child'. This meaning is also found in one of the examples adduced by *DOST, Reg. Privy Seal* 1542, where the 'dochter carnale' is later in the same item said to have 'deit bastart'. Cf. also 'filio carnale' in David Murray, *Legal Practice in Ayr and the West of Scotland in the Fifteenth and Sixteenth Centuries, A Study in Economic History,* Glasgow, 1910, p. 8, n. 4: '... In 1499 Richard Gibsoune designs himself "clericus Glasguensis dioceseos, pontifico, imperialique regali auctoritate notarius", Instrument of sasine in the lands of Borthwickshields, 22nd May, 1499, on charter by Walter Ker of Cessford, in favour of Mark Ker, his "filio carnali." ... The word "carnalis" here used, gave rise to a great deal of litigation between 1815 and 1822. In the result, the House of Lords held that the term was ambiguous and might imply either legitimacy or illegitimacy, and that the sense in which it was used in any deed may be established *aliunde.* "The use of the word," says Lord Eldon, "seems to have occurred between the fifteenth century and the sixteenth century. It seems to have been employed by conveyancers, many of whom, no doubt, were extremely ignorant."'
670. *Na question is tharat,* 'there is no room for dispute or doubt'.
688. *The ȝoung erle of Artane,* see note 45 of Section XIII (Summary).
692. *he lete ,* 'he behaved as if'.
679. *fra thin,* 'from that moment'.
706. The second *his* changed into *the* would perhaps be better.
726. *of ane herb ... he feld,* 'he smelled a herb'.
756. *in plane,* 'plainly, simply', a rhyme-tag.
784. *Quhat scaith ...,* 'What harm would it have done (him) if Ypocras had &c.'
805-6. *Wald God ... heir,* 'Had it only been God's wish that I was carried on a bier to the earth (to be buried) on the day that I came here.'
820. Craigie: '*nybill* is obscure'. The word has a figurative meaning: the empress wishes her story to give the emperor a shock. *Nybill* may be a rendering of modern *nibble,* n.: 'a sharp bite with a bird's beak or neb', see *SND*; or of *nevell* c.1500, 'a sharp blow with the fist, see *SND*. The scribe

may not have known this form and emended it to *nybill*. He may also have misread the *v* and made it a *b*.

822. The name of *Octavianus* is usually garbled in medieval texts.

876. *of his gudis he maid ane end*, 'he finished (used up) all his possessions'.

884. *This kepand knycht*. For *kepand DOST*, mentioning ll. 884 and 929 as sole examples, gives: 'retentive, sparing, miserly'. However, ll. 839-40 tell us that the niggardly knight was appointed '... *governour, To kepe the tresour of the towr*.' Therefore I think *kepand* here means: 'guarding, protecting, in charge of (the tower)'. Cf. also ll. 921, 1038 and 1091.

891. See Section XIII, note 54.

913. *of stynkand fen* depends on *a foule prevé*.

951. *Thai trast my deid*, 'they think I am going to die'.

952. The top and bottom of this leaf are damaged; ll. 952, 984, 1012 and 1013 have suffered slightly. I restore them as printed in the text. In l. 984 *de* in the MS is inserted from below the line with a caret; in l. 1013 the preposition before *(sc)hame* is completely lost; *to* and *with* suggest themselves. Only the parts between pointed brackets are illegible in the MS.

976. *To se gif he couth schut the day*. *NED* s.v. *shoot* v. 37: to avoid, escape; 1st ex. 1543 ... *shoting their dayes of meating*. In the context the fitting meaning is : cause to be postponed, delayed, cf. l. 1165: *The emprys herd that day delayd*. Mr D.D.Murison, editor of the *SND*, allowed me to consult his then unpublished material, which yielded *shoot by* 'to tide over' and *shoot the shower* 'avoid the shower'. The former especially seems to be very near to the meaning here.

977. Craigie: '*spure* corrected from *spurris*.' The scribe himself had done this.

984. See note to 952. I suggest *bedene* as the last word of this line, cf. 2260.

988. Craigie: 'Two or more lines appear to be missing here.'

990. *to fische a caus*, 'to seek or find, go to some trouble to contrive (an excuse), cf. Chaucer *Troilus and Criseyde*, III.1161: *as he that nedes most a cause fissche*.

1013. See note to 952.

1026-27. No names are given to the protagonists in other versions.

1032. Perhaps *all* is a misrepresentation of the verb *aw*, 'to own, possess'; this would give a better syntax, though no consistent use of tenses. In some contemporary scripts *w* and *ll* look very much alike, e.g. in Cambridge MS. Kk.5.30, and in Oxford MS. Douce 148 in the case of the second scribe (not Asloan); see my article on Asloan, *English Studies*, XLVII (1966), pp. 365-72. In this connection an interesting place is *Scottish Troy Book Fragments* 1717, where Asloan wrote *wallis* to rhyme with *schawis*; probably he miscopied his model and made a *w* into *ll* (see C.Horstmann, ed., *Barbour's ... Legendensammlung nebst den Fragmenten seines Trojanerkrieges*, Heilbronn, 1881, p. 276).

1055. *staw*, 'stole'.

1060. *ald* seems redundant metrically.

1061. *he*, the lover.

1078. *And had knawlege*, 'And (he then) knew &c.'

1098. See note to line 1471.

1116. *In manus tuas*, from the religious formula in St.Luke 23.46: *In manus tuas commendo spiritum meum*, also quoted in l. 228 of *The Lay of Havelok the Dane*, ed. W.W.Skeat, 2nd ed. rev. Kenneth Sisam, Oxford, (1915) 1963, in the *Reeve's Tale*, *Canterbury Tales*, I.4287, ed. F.N.Robinson, *The Works of Geoffrey Chaucer*, 2nd edn, Oxford U.P., 1966, p. 59, and elsewhere.

1131. *Do opyn the dure and lat me in*. Craigie reads *To opyn the dure* but this does not make sense. In the MS the letter in question appears quite certainly to be a *D*. For a parallel with the construction *Do open*, cf. 'Doe to the book, quench the candle, ring the bell', s.v. *BUIK* in the glossary of Sir David Lindsay's *Thrie Estaits,* ed. James Kinsley, London, 1954, p. 207. Parallels to both constructions *(Do to* 'close' and *do open)* are quite normal in present-day Dutch.

1153, 1159 & 1164. The third master is here called *Bantillas,* although when he appears before the emperor and at the beginning of the story his name is given as *Lentulus* (once rhyming with *thus*) in ll. 973, 979, 985, 998. Craigie comments: 'The error is the author's, as shown by the rhyme with *grace* in the last instance' (1164). If the author of the Scots text makes mistakes like these, it seems unlikely that he could have been translating or copying from another text, unless that text had the mistakes too.

1180. *Eulope*. Craigie says: '... called *Oulumpus* in 1187 and *olimphus* in 1208.' In 1180 it rhymes with *ȝhe*; the *eu* may be a copying mistake for *ou*, whereas the *o* may have resulted from the misinterpretation of a scribal abbreviation of *um* or *im*.

1185. *It dar na rak* is obscure to Craigie. I propose *dar* as a variant of *thar(f)* v. 'to need' (cf. *NED* and Stratmann & Bradley's *MED*), and *rak* as noun 'care, heed, consideration' (cf. *NED* s.v. *reck* n., 1st entry 1535 Lyndsay *Satyre* 210), so that the line might be translated as 'It needs no consideration to tell, it does not matter ...', or: 'there is no objection to telling'. Though the present text is older than Lyndsay's work the usage may have been current in colloquial speech much earlier. In the *Secunda Pastorum* of the Wakefield-cycle we find (l. 307): "... thou dar not reck of my long standyng', interpreted by the editor as 'You needn't care about keeping me standing so long', ed. A.C.Cawley, *The Wakefield Pageants in the Towneley Cycle,* Manchester U.P., (1958) 1971, p. 109, where *reck* is a verb. If we were to consider *rak* in 1185 as a verb it would imply that *na* is used as an adverb. In *BSS na/no* is found as adverb in connection with comparatives only. However, *DOST* shows several examples for this usage as from Barbour's *Bruce*, and its appearing only once in *BSS* is not an impossibility. If we adopt this solution the translation would be: 'It is not necessary to be troubled about telling', 'there is no need for reluctance to tell' or 'there is no harm in telling the story'. The meaning of the line, however interpreted, is sufficiently clear.

1187. *Apillis,* Apulia. For the names in other versions see Section XIII, note 69.

1188. The sin of sodomy is not mentioned in the Asloan version as in some of the English versions and in all of the French versions consulted. See Section XIII, note 70.

1195. The line does not scan; it would, however, if *medicinar* were replaced by *doctour,* but this word is not found in the present text; the first example of the required meaning of *doctour* given by *DOST* is from Henryson's *Testament of Cresseid.*

1202, 1206. Note Craigie: '*hele* for *hale*'. Cf. l. 1199 *hale.*

1214. *his ane ê,* equivalent to 'his right hand'.

1223. All the forms of *mark(is)* are abbreviated in the MS; they do not occur in rhyme; there seems to be no reason to assume *-er-* instead of *-ar-* as Craigie does. According to *DOST* ascertained instances of *merk* have not been found before the late sixteenth century.

1277. The line would scan if it ran: *Schir, wnderstand ȝe weile my taile?*

1302. *son,* 'soon'.

1314. *fall,* 'fall into, meet with'.

1320. *Ȝour will on him and me to.* The line would have a better rhythm if the preposition *on* were repeated between *and* and *me*.

1326. *Gedeon*. Other versions give no name to the knight nor to his wife (1334).

1386. *Chyar, chyer* (1513) is evidently disyllabic, as it is still in MoSc.

1410. *Scho grat and leit the teris fall*, a phrase reminiscent of the ballad-style, cf. Child, *English and Scottish Popular Ballads* (edn Sargent and Kittredge, London, 1904), 5A st. 7, 62A 18, 62E 11, 91A 28, 99A 18, to mention a few.

1434. *Dame* may as well mean 'lady' as 'mother', cf. *MED* s.v. *dame*, 4a.

1438. *culȝeit*. *DOST* gives as etymology: 'cf. e.m.E. *cully* 1576 & *cull* a.1564'. It seems, however, possible that *culȝeit* is an aphetic form related to OF *accueillir*, and that the meaning here is rather 'receive or entertain kindly' than 'caress, fondle' as suggested by *DOST*.

1441. In most of the known versions the lady kills the dog in the evening. In the present version *as the lord rais*, which seems to imply the morning, is perhaps occasioned by the author's wish to rhyme with *bed-clathis* (see next note).

1442. *clathis* rhymes with *rais*, cf. also ll. 2465-66. In l. 1541 it occurs within the line and there it is evidently monosyllabic too. Cf. MoSc *claes*. *Scho bad him downe*, 'she told the dog to go down, she gave him the command "Down"'; *in the devill way*, see Glossary, s.v. *devill*, *NED* s.v. *devil* 19, and cf. Skeat's note to stanza 56 in his edn of *The Kingis Quair*, STS, I.1, 1884, p. 72.

1471. *antaris*. In the other instance (l. 1098) the spelling is still *awentour*, as also in *misaventour* (l. 517), though the metre demands a contracted form in each case. In l. 1873 *misaventour* is pronounced as a four-syllabic word, however.

1503-4. *I sall neuer langar frist Bot that thow luf quhareuer thow list*, 'I shall no longer put anything in the way of your loving wherever (whomever) you like'.

1513. *chyer*, see note to l. 1386.

1516. *Thy kist-keye*, 'the key of your chest'.

1550. Craigie suggests that *sa* here is superfluous, but cf. l. 1888, where it also occurs in connection with *perfyte*, though 1889 f. can be looked upon as a following consequence clause (without *that*).

1554. *son*, 'soon'.

1591. *ane gud ensample and ald haf ȝe*. Instead of *and ald*, *tald* seems to make better sense. In the MS it appears as *& ald*.

1606. *stagis*. The plural is not necessary in this context but conditioned by the rhyme.

1611. *four sagis*. Actually they are four knights, cf. ll. 1685 ff., though in l. 1821 they are again referred to as *sagis*.

1616-17. *spekle*. The word does not figure in *NED* and occurs only once (this example) in the files of *DOST*.

1620. *Virgile, that precious clerk but peir*. As in so many other medieval writings Virgil is depicted as a magician; here he manufactures a magic fire, a magic fountain, a shooting statue, a statue with a magic mirror, &c. See Domenico Comparetti, *Vergil in the Middle Ages*, tr. E.F.M. Benecke, London, (1895) 1966.

1625. The MS has *Ane ymage with a arow and bow of bras*, where *arow and* are clearly metrically superfluous.

1630. *Edmound*. The English versions (ed. Brunner) have *a lombard*. See Section XIII, note 94.

1661. *duell* should be *duelt*. The scribe may have been misled by the word *fell* in the previous line.

1691. *Thai ... bad ask and haif*, 'they told them they would get whatever they asked.'

1708 ff. The word *port(e)* is used for 'gate' throughout this tale, whereas elsewhere in *BSS* the word *ȝet(tis)* is found, also for 'city-gates'.

1735 ff. The sequence of tenses may seem puzzling at first sight what with *I se ...* (1735) and *I haf sene ...* (1738); we may, however, explain l.1738 as a parenthetic clause which together with the one in the next line heightens the suspense.

1783. *we mene nocht sa,* 'we do not intend to do so'.

1805-6. *Fra the cité that war nocht gane Twa legis bot scantly ane.* Cf. examples from the ballads: Child, op.cit., 4H st. 4; 8A 3, 8, 10; 8B 2, 6, 8; 41A 3, 6; 41B 3; 52A 3; 76A 30; 79A 2, 3.

1833. *child* is used here to refer to the *scolar* of l. 1630, the *clerk* of l.1639.

1842. *for ony feid.* This phrase is not found in *DOST, MED* or *NED.* Its meaning is 'in despite of any hostility, in the face of any opposition, undeterred by anything, no matter what anybody says or does, assuredly'. It approximates *DOST* Fede *n.* 1 c (2).

1866. *Bure nocht ȝour son,* 'who did not bear your son, i.e. who is not his real mother'.

1886. On the name of the burgess in AVIS see Section XIII, note 105.

1912. The line would scan if e.g. *all* were inserted between *tell* and *that.*

1928. *set ȝe nocht by,* 'don't pay any attention'; cf. David Lindsay's *Thrie Estaits,* l. 2173: *Set thou nocht by,* 'think nothing of it' in the glossary of James Kinsley's edn; *in thar eild nane settis thaim by* in *Thewis off Gud Women,* l. 284, p. 100, and *Thai set nocht by this warldis gud* in *Foly of Fulys,* l. 273, p. 59 of *Ratis Raving,* STS, 3rd S. 11, 1937, ed. Ritchie Girvan, glossed 'hold of little account'.

1934-60, 1990-2012. The stories about the sword and the sheet, *De Gladio* and *De Lintheo,* Nos. xi and x of the *Disciplina Clericalis* by Petrus Alfonsi, have been incorporated into the story AVIS, as previously signalised by Hermann Varnhagen in his article in *Englische Studien,* XXV (1898), pp. 321 ff.

The *Disciplina Clericalis* is an early twelfth-century book of *exempla* with their applications, composed by Petrus Alfonsi, a Spanish Jew converted to Christianity and baptised on the first day of 1106. He was (1104-34) the court-physician of King Alfonso I of Aragon (d. 1134), 'einer der vielen jüdischen Intellektuellen die als Vermittler zwischen orientalischer und occidentalischer Bildung dienten, und deren Rolle in der mittelalterlichen Literatur- und Kulturgeschichte von höchster Bedeutung gewesen ist.' (Alfons Hilka and Werner Söderhjelm, eds, *Disciplina Clericalis* -Kleine Ausgabe-, Heidelberg, 1911, p. vii.)

The book is composed, as the author states in his Prologus, '... partim ex prouerbiis philosophorum et suis castigacionibus, partim ex prouerbiis et castigacionibus arabicis et fabulis et uersibus, partim ex animalium et uolucrum similitudinibus'. The collection was very popular throughout the Middle Ages and even later: many of its items are found in other frames and contexts. Many manuscripts have come down to us; in English libraries there are fifteen. In the just-mentioned small edition Hilka and Söderhjelm edit MS. Cambridge Peterhouse Coll. 252, dated beginning of the thirteenth century.

The tale of the sheet is also found in the *Gesta Romanorum,* where it is No. 123. The *Gesta Romanorum* is another collection of tales with morals, of miscellaneous origins and backgrounds, compiled in England around the end of the thirteenth century, of which there are also Dutch and German versions. See the Preface of *Gesta Romanorum,* translated and edited by Charles Swan and Wynnard Hooper, London, 1876, and *Gesta Romanorum,* ed.

Hermann Oesterley, Berlin, 1872. The date of the *Gesta Romanorum* is, however, later than that of the *Seven Sages of Rome*. The GLADIUS-motif is also found as a separate story in *Mishle Sindbad*, see ed. Morris Epstein, Philadelphia, 1967, pp. 219-27.

In none of the French, English, Dutch or Latin versions of the *SSR* which I have examined are these additions to be found, nor is there anywhere the mother-in-law these episodes postulate.

To allow of easy comparison, the Latin texts of *De Gladio* and *De Lintheo* are given in Appendix III.

2026\. *Quhill he his pyot past to wit*. The line might be better as follows: *Quhill to his pyot he past to wit*.

2030\. The lightning mentioned here by the bird could not be occasioned by any of the implements enumerated in ll. 2019 f., but see Section XIII, note 111.

2033-4. *That thai begylit thé with a scheit I wey fer mair than all my weit*, 'that they deceived you with a sheet I regard as much more important than the fact that I am all wet'.

2048-9. *Lovit be God of grace* (that) *This ȝer saw we sa fair ane nycht*.

2073\. *Fair on, foull mot thé fall*, 'off with you, may evil befall you'; cf. *Buik of Alexander* I.477: *Foule him befall That recryand will nocht me call*, and *Wallace* I.430: *Foule mot ȝow fall*.

2086\. *God ws levis*, '(As) *God ws lefe* (=dear) *is*.'

2098\. For the sake of sense and rhythm I think *do* should be inserted here between *ȝourself* and *dishonour*.

2105\. *the sagis four*. In the following story (SAPIENTES) there are really seven sages. This is perhaps a matter of mixing up SAPIENTES with VIRGILIUS, where there are indeed four 'knychtis' who deceive the emperor by dreams.

2105-6. *four* does not really rhyme with *empriour*, so this is an impure rhyme.

2112\. *It was wele kend*. This evidently links up with l. 2113, and points to the probability that the headings in an earlier copy were marginalia or not present at all.

2114\. The name *Herod* also figures in most of the English and French versions, see Section XIII, note 114.

2129\. *and ȝe be perfyte*, 'if you are fully informed'.

2135\. *seis* is disyllabic.

2145\. Presumably this is what Merlin said, cf. the gladness mentioned in the next line.

2183\. *rewaris*, 'rivers'. This unusual spelling is found also in Andrew of Wyntoun's *Original Chronicle*, Bk. IV, l. 1962 (Cotton MS.), ed. F.J.Amours, STS, I. 54, 1904, p.149.

2201\. The use of *was* occasions an imperfect transition from indirect to direct speech which can be amended, however, by emendation of *was* to *is*.

2234\. After l. 2234, which does not really end the queen's statement, there may be an omission. The scribe has not been conscious of this; he continues with the emperor's words that usually follow the stories told by the queen. It seems possible that the scribe (not necessarily Asloan, but perhaps a possible earlier copyist) in trying to find his place in the book he was copying took up the text at the wrong place, viz. after the thirteenth tale (ROMA), so that both this story and VIDUA were left out. For other solutions, see Section XIII, note 119.

2235\. On this line Craigie remarks that it is unmetrical and that it and the next line perhaps should read: *The empriour said: 'For this that ȝe / Haf tald, the morne my son sall de'*. I have a suggestion which implies a slighter change from the original text: *The empriour said: 'For this tale ȝe / Sall wyte the morne my son sall de'*. The somewhat unusual enjambment (pronoun subject/main verb) is also found in ll. 39 f.

2238. Craigie suggests *had* for *led*, since the latter does not rhyme with *bad* of the preceding line. Cf. l. 67.

2263. The MS has *sa has done*, but *sa was done* makes better sense.

2265. *Mobrig* is the name of a country, which in the English versions (ed.Brunner) figures as *Houngerye, Hungrye, Hongrye, Hongarye*. In MSS. *r, s, p* (see List of OF prose MSS in Section XIV,pp.193f.) and in the MDu poem it is *Montogier*, in MSS. *a, b, c, d, e, h, i, k, n, o: Monbergier*, in MSS. *f, g: Montuergier*, and in MS. *q: Monberengier*. *Mobrig* in the present text is evidently a name copied from an abbreviated form, perhaps *Monberg*, written as *mōbᵓg*, itself a corrupt form of *Monbergier*; the shortened form *Mobrig* fits well in the line as it stands.

2276. *Hungry* in the corresponding places in English MSS is sometimes *Poyle*, in MS. *Ar: Pletys*.

2317. Craigie says either *slepe* is wrong or some lines are missing. *Slepe* may be the kind of miscopying that occurs several times in the MS, see above note to 356 and footnote to 2059. If a change is to be suggested, I think the line makes sense if *slepe* is changed into reflexive *kepe*: *And tald him he micht nocht him kepe/In a thak hous to ly and slepe*. The addition of the reflexive *him* improves the rhythm of the line, moreover.

2323. *was rycht blyth* refers to the knight, not to the steward.

2334. *a luf letter scho leit fall*. This is more logical than what is found in many French versions where the lady drops a hollow reed with nothing inside. Cf. Section XIII, note 124.

2359-60. These lines are a practically identical repetition of ll. 2349-50. The mistake is evidently due to the final words *perfyte* in both ll. 2348 and 2358; cf. note to l. 356.

2428. *be woce and taist*; *taist* probably stands for *ca(i)st*, cf. l. 2445.

2442. The line would scan if *twa* were inserted between *ȝe* and *togidder*.

2463. The MS has ... *with him has he keyis tane*. Craigie suggested *the* for *he*.

2491. *fair and bricht* is a rhyme tag, often used to describe women throughout medieval literature.

2499. *It I saw*, cf. *It that I did* ll. 1406 and 1408.

2522. *crovde*. F.J.Amours,ed. *Scottish Alliterative Poems in Riming Stanzas*, STS I.27, 38, Edinburgh, 1897, remarks (p.310) in a note to l. 758 of the *Buke of the Howlat*: 'The *crowd* or *crwth*, a very old Celtic instrument, supposed to have been the "Chrotta Britanna" mentioned by Venantius Fortunatus. It had six strings and was played with a bow. Some specimens of this instrument are still in existence; see *Musical Instruments* by A.J. Hopkins, Edinburgh, 1888, p. 47.'

2535. *with hie voce*, a French phrase, see A.A.Prins, *French Influence in English Phrasing*, Leiden, 1952, pp. 104 and 154, and *NED* s.v. *voice*, I.l.c: 1422 tr. *Secr.Secr.*

2540-45. These lines seem somewhat confused. L. 2540 does not scan very well to begin with, and to let the three following *that*-clauses all be dependent on *the caus* seems inelegant and not in keeping with the style of the rest of the text, though all three do have the recurring *sa* + adj., and the author may have wished to express in this way that the young man was nervous. If *the caus* is dependent on *forgifnes*, a preposition might be expected to precede it; if *forgifnes* is to be followed by a semicolon, *the caus* has no verb but only three relative sub-clauses.

Ll. 2544 and 2545 belong together but they lack their logical sequence, and I agree with Craigie that some lines must be missing here. The rhyme *hed : feid* is not impure, it is true, but *hed* presumably might have rhymed with *ded* (cf. ll. 159-60), and *feid* might have corresponded with another rhyme-word in *-e(i)d*. In *BSS feid* rhymes three times with *deid* n., once with *reid* n. and once with *hed* n. How many lines are lost between 2545 and 2546 cannot be established; it might even be just two, cf. ll. 1595 ff. where the rhyme-sequence is *day:way:delay:way*, and ll. 2195-8 where we find *se:he:be:se*.

2567. *of sa lang space*, 'for that particular length of time, considering his age', cf. Chaucer, *Canterbury Tales, General Prologue*, l. 87.

2577. *the knawlege clene*. This would make better sense if *the* were changed into *be*, assuming a copying mistake. *clene* may be taken as either an adverb, meaning 'completely, entirely', for which there are parallels (ll. 2005 and 2216), or an adjective, meaning 'pure'. If one does not accept the suggestion of *be* instead of *the* , one might prefer the adverb 'completely'. In the other case the adjective 'pure' would perhaps be more satisfactory.

2588. *Thow sal lé* is conditioned by the rhyme. Its meaning is 'I shall show that you are a liar'.

2638. *in verbo regio*, 'with a king's word, with the royal promise'.

2649-50. *thrid:bird*. The form *brid* does not occur in this text, nor is it mentioned in *DOST*, so probably the original rhyme had *third*, but the scribe wrote down the form *thrid* that was familiar to him and which can be found in *BSS* and in the rest of the MS in non-rhyming positions.

2650 ff. Note that the young bird is referred to by *scho, it, his* and *him*.

2733. *caus* and *cas* are sometimes used indiscriminately, see *DOST*, s.v. *cause* n.; *him I gif the caus*, 'I hand over the case to Him' or 'for Him to judge'.

XXI. GLOSSARY

This glossary was composed with the help of *NED (OED)*, *MED*, *DOST* and unpublished material of the latter, beside a number of glossaries of STS and EETS-editions. It is an exhaustive record of the forms used in *BSS*, but not of all occurrences of each form. When a word is found three or fewer times in the text the lines in which it is used are all mentioned; when a word is found four times the first two occurrences are usually cited, followed by '&c.'; when three references are given, followed by '&c.', this means that the word is found at least five times in the text. Words with initial *u* (sometimes presented as *w*) and *v* are glossed together under *v*; ȝ (yogh) is alphabetised as *y*. For abbreviations see pp.viii f.

a, indef.art. a, an, 73, 74, 78, &c.; num. one, a single, 56, 74, 178, &c.; adj. only, 458. *ME a, OE ān*. See also ane.
abak, adv. back, drewe --, 220. *ME abak, OE on bæc*
abasit, ppl.a. dismayed, 103, 1933. *ME abaiss(e), AN abaiss-*
able, adj. capable, having ability or power to do something, 622. *ME, OF able*
abone, adv. above, on high, 545; on the surface, 1711; prep. above, directly over, in respect of place or position, 1829, 2016, 2059. *Contr.f. abuvin, OE onbufan, abufan*
about, adv. about, around, on every side, 449, 530. *ME ab(o)ute, OE onbūtan, abūtan*
abrek, v.tr. to ruin, shatter, 123. *OE abrecan*. See expl.note.
absolue, v.tr. to resolve, answer, 2144, 2145. (*OED* 1535) *L absolvere*
acquentans, n. acquaintance, intimacy, friendship; in --, in token of their intimacy, 2362. *ME acqueintaunce, OF acointance*
adornit, ppl.a. adorned, decorated, 2467. *ME adorne, OF adorner, L adornare*
agane, adv. again, back 276, 401, 606, &c.; once more, 480, 585, 593, &c.; in answer, 465, 672, 1287, 2744; again, 2262; agane, prep. against, contrary to, 1400, 1642, 2759. *NME again(e), ONhb ongean, ON igegn*
aganis, prep. against, contrary to, 1555, 2720. *ME aganys*
age, n. length of life, 8, 1327, 2566; advanced or old age, 121, 233. *ME, OF age*
aggrevit, ppl.a. annoyed, vexed, 1447. *ME agreved f. OF agrever*
air, n. heir (male), 134, 261, 427, &c.; (female), 2610. *ME air, OF (h)eir*
air, n. fresh air, breath, 333. *ME, OF air*
airly, arlye, adv. early, in the first part of the morning, 660, 1336, 1548, 2459. *NME arely, ONhb ārlīce, ON árliga*
aith, n. oath, solemn asseveration, 2008; pl. athis, 203. *NME ath(e), OE āþ*
ald, adj. old, advanced in years, 648, 1028, 1053, &c.; coming down from past times, 1591; as opposed to young, parent, 2649; auld, advanced in years, 1370, 1432. *NME a(u)ld, Ang ald*
alis, pr.3 s., ails, troubles, 1965. *ME aile, OE eġlan*
alkyn, adj. every kind of, 1244. *NME al kyn, OE ealra cynna*
all, adj. with sg.n. all, the whole of, 31, 35, 49, &c.; with pl.n. all, the whole number of, 80, 101, 155, &c.; every, 407, 516, 572, &c.; absol. all persons, 227, 532, 1844, &c.; all things, 125, 230, 433, &c.; with rel. that, all who, 12, 2471. *ME all, OE (e)all*
all, adv. altogether, entirely, quite, 142, 323, 339, &c.; at --, in every way, fully, 1543. *ME all, OE (e)all*
allace, interj. alas, 200, 244, 259, &c.; n. 918. *ME alace, OF alas*
allake, interj. alack, 473. *a* Ah! + *ME lak* loss
allane, adj. alone, solitary, unaccompanied, 180, 2293, 2372, 2464; preceded by pronouns like him, thaim, &c., 167, 666, 734, 2354; with lat or leif, 228, 1255, 2354. *NME al ān, OE (e)all + āne*

allanerly, adv. only, solely, merely, 2745. *all + anerly, a common variation of ānelī in ESc*
allege, pr.1 s. adduce, urge as reason, 610. *ME al(l)ege, L allegare, see OED, s.v. allege v.2*
allhale, adv. completely, wholly, 41, 410. *ME alhāl, OE (e)all + hāl*
all(-)mast, adv. almost, very nearly, 1569, 1574, 1997. *NME almaste, OE ealmǣst*
allmychti, adj. almighty, as an epithet of God, 1109. *ME almighty, OE ælmihtig*
all thar + superl. of all; -- lest, -- maist, -- werst, 1990, 2074, 2427. *ME alther, earlier aller, OE (e)allra, gen.pl. of (e)all*
all thus, adv. in this way, 2531. Cf. Du aldus; *MED* s.v. *al* adv.3. *OE (e)all + þus*
allway, adv. always, perpetually, 1621; on all occasions, 2116; altogether, entirely, 133, 858, 1583. *ME alway, allwaye*
almous, n. alms, charity, 1835. *NME almus, ON almusa*
almous-deid, n. charity, almsgiving, 1831. *NME almous dede*
als, adv. also, 536, 2737; as, equally, 1344, 2085; correl. with as, 391, 517, 700, &c. *ME als(e), reduced form of alsa*
alsa, adv. with sone, thereupon, at once, 929; -- sone as, as soon as, 1124. *ME al swa, ONhb allsuá, OE eall swá*. See also.
alsmekle, n. as much, as great a quantity, -- agane, 1562, -- as, 1754. *Prec. + ME mekill*
also, adv. as (-- sone as) 2465; -- fast, immediately, at once, 99. See alsa.
alswele, adv. as well (-- as) 142, 598, 1747, 2660. *als + wele*
am, see be.
amang, adv. ay --, every now and then, 798; prep. among, surrounded by, in the midst of, 447, 1668, 2274, 2761. *ME amang, OE onmang*
Amen, interj. Amen, 2782. *EME, OF, L amen*
amorusly, adv. in an amorous manner, lovingly, 1046. *ME, OF amorous + -ly*
and, conj. and, 3, 4, 7, &c.; often written &, 32, 69, 152, &c.; if, 163, 173, 218, &c.; written &, 162, 2256, 2544.*ME, OE and*
ane, num. a single pers. or thing, 5, 117, 296, &c.; in contrast to ane nother, 86; indef.pron. a certain pers., someone, 268, 1679, 1720; adj. one, a certain, 135, 1214, 1217, &c.; on ane, forthwith, straightway, 1145, 1957, 2483; indef.art. a, 1, 7, 75, &c. *NME ane, OE ān*. See also a.
anger, n. anger, passion, rage, 577; distress, anguish, 1170. *EME anger, ON angr*
angerly, angrely, adv. with anger or resentment, 594, 1448. *Prec. + -ly*
anoyit, ppl.a. annoyed, irritated, 1402. *ME anoye, OF anoier, anuier*
answerd, pt. answered, replied, 594, 783, 801, &c.; answeris, pr.2 s. reply to a question or remark, 2743. *ME answere, OE andswarian*
antaris, n.pl. perils, risks, 1471. *Reduced form of aventure, OF aventure.* See awentour.
anys, adv. once, one time only, 218, 1425; at anys, at one and the same time, together, 2020; n. once; this --, this time or occasion only, 1463, 1502. *NME anis, OE ānes*
aperand, apperand, ppl.a. apparent, obvious, 427, 638. *EME ap(p)ere, OF stem aper- of apareir, L apparēre*
aple, n. apple, ball resembling an apple, 1652. *ME ap(p)le, OE æppel, æple*
apon, prep. upon; in local position: on or above, 1500, 2064, 2587; revengit --, 808; in the direction of, against, 2303; above, more than, 2503;concerning, about, 2690; -- na mak, in or after no manner, 749; of time: on (a day, &c.), 847, 894. *ME apon, OE upp + on*
appeir, apper, v.intr. to appear to the mind or judgment, to be evident, 22, 2549; apperand, pr.p. appearing, becoming visible, 384. *EME apere, OF stem aper-*

apply, v.intr. to comply, consent to, 611. *ME applye, OF aplier, L applicare*
ar, are, see be.
argument, n. dispute, argumentation, 2669. *ME, F argument, L argumentum*
arlye, see airly
arme, n. arm (limb), 1553, 1558, 1560. *ME arm, OE (e)arm*
armes, n.pl.arms, weapons, 422; deeds or feats of arms, 408, 486, 2266, 2312. *EME armes, OF armes, L arma pl.*
arow, arrowe, n. arrow, 1625, 1830. *ME arow(e), OE arwe*
art, n. art, skill, learning, 1761. *EME art, OF art*
art, pr.s. see be.
as, adv. & conj. as, introd. explan. or confirm. clause, 327, 417, 744, &c.; with temp. force: when, while, 369, 972, 1295, &c.; with complementary cl., 730, 2697, 2713; before nouns: in the manner of, like, 809, 1797, 2398, &c.; in the capacity of, 2296; as if, introd. clause of compar., 460, 937, 1081, &c.; answering to als, sa, sic, 286, 600, 700, &c.; as well as, 2198; als wele --, 142, 1747, 2660; als gret --, 392; alsa sone --, 1124, 2465; as has restrictive force in as this day, this very day, for this one day, 1162, 2089; as now, at present, 1378; as of before, as before, 1895; in the manner that, 628. *Reduced form of* als.
ask(e), v.tr. to ask, 137, 1691; pr.1 s. ask, require, 31, 2746; 3 pl. 2715; askit, pt. requested, asked for a thing, 54, 1692, 2388; asked a question, 509, 2539; requested permission, 2137. *ME aske, ONhb ásciȝa, OE áscian, áxian*
asking, vbl.n. request, 137 (luf --). *ME asking*
aspy, v.tr. to discover by spying, *1066*; aspyd, pt.3 s. discovered, observed, 172. *EME aspie, OF espier, AN *aspier.* See also espyid.
assay, v.tr. to attack, assault, 882. *ME as(s)aye, OF as(s)ayer*
assemblit, pt.3 s. assembled, gathered, 2324. *ME assemble, OF assembler*
assentit, pt.3 pl. agreed, 93. *ME assent(e), OF assenter, L assentare*
assure, pr.1 s. inform positively or with confidence, 34, 2190. *ME assure, OF assurer*
astonade, astonait, ppl.a. astonished, 161, 1992. *ME astoneyd f. OF estoné*
astronomy, n.id. or astrology, 40, 108. *EME, OF astronomie, L astronomia*
at, enclitic following conjs., sone be --, 225; quhill --, 1599; quhen --, 1812, 1990. *NME at, ON at*
at, prep. of simple place, 931, 1039, 1080, &c.; of action, position, 430, 1509, 1512, &c.; of time, 154, 158, 204, &c.; of occasion, 159, 909, 2424; with absol. superl., -- the last, &c., 74, 254, 273, &c.; of relation to someone's will or disposition, 238, 274, 1031, &c.; of instrumentality, 302, 474; of state, condition, 1768; from (with vbs. of asking), 25, 1340, 1653, &c.; tuke leif --, 1522; to (of direction), 548, 1088; to (of mental aim), 1614; through, by (of direction), 761, 766, 2365, 2382; at hand, see hand; at hame, see hame; at all, in every way, 1543; at poynt, aptly, fitly, 1695. *ME at, OE æt*
athis, see aith.
attempe, v.tr. to attempt, endeavour, 2222; attempit, pt.3 pl. made an attempt, 1665; attempit, p.p. tried out, tested, 94. *OF attempter, L attemptare*
attour, adv. moreover, in addition, 1763; here --,385; prep. in respect of degree, quantity or number: above, beyond, more than, 505, 516, 693, &c. *at + our, ME at + over*
atyre, n. array, apparel, 1385. *ME atyre f. OF vb. atirer*
aucht, pt.3 s. possessed, had, 2665. *ME ahte, OE āht*
aucht, v.aux.pt.3 s. ought, deserved (to be), 2662. *See prec.*
auchtand, ord.num. eighth, 174. *NME aghten, aughtene, ON *ahtande, later áttande*
augur(e), n. prophetic skill, divination, 1701, 2641. *LME, OF augure*

auld, see ald.
avale, n. avail, profit, 2108. *ME avail f. vb.*
avalze, v.tr. to afford help, to benefit trans. 331. *Var. of avail, ME avail f. OF vaill-*
avisit, awisit, p.p. guided by consideration or reflection, counselled or advised, 2137, 2139. *ME avised f. OF aviser*
awansit, pt.3 s. raised, promoted, 2721. *ME ava(u)nce, OF avancer*
awant, v.tr. to praise, commend, of his age richt till --, very commendable for his age, 8. *ME ava(u)nte, OF ava(u)nter, ML vanitare*
away(e), adv. away, from a place, 67, 414, 1541, &c.; out of this life, 359; gone, 2495. *ME away(e), OE aweȝ*
aw(e), n. awe; to stand --, to be greatly afraid, 801, 936, 1470, 1635. *NME aw(e), ON age*
awentour, n. jeopardy, peril, 1098. *ME, OF aventure.* See antaris.
awn(e), adj. with poss.pron. preceding, to emphasise the poss. meaning, 147, 182, 500, &c.; absol. own, belonging to oneself, 141, 850. *NME awyn, OE āgen*
awys, n. counsel, advice, 112. *ME, OF avis*
ax, n. axe, too for hewing wood, trees, &c., 344, 1365, 1377. *ME, OE, ON ax*
ay(e), adv. always, ever, continually, 87, 100, 625, &c.; for --, for ever, 2473. *ME ay, ON ei*

bad, pt. of bid, v.tr. to request, command or order (a pers.) to do something, 137, 166, 221, &c.; usu. with inf., sometimes with that, or that implied, 297, 1365, 1936, 2727; baid, pt.3 s. offered, 437. *ME bid(de), OE biddan, early confused with OE bēodan.* See also bid.
baide, pt.3 s. stayed, remained, 2125. *ME bide(n), OE bīdan.*See also byde.
baid, n. delay, 375, 752, 2409, 2478. *NME, OE bād*
baile, n. grief, misery, 525, 1977. *ME bale, OE b(e)alu*
bair(e), a. bare, unclothed, 65, 1121. *ME bare, OE bær*
bair(e), n. boar, 524-5, 532, 541, &c. *NME bar(e), OE bar*
bait, pt.3 s. bit, injured with the teeth, 438. *ME bite(n), OE bītan, ON bíta*
baith, indef.pron. or adj., both, 874, 902, 1878, 2010; -- thar, gen. 661, 881; conj. in -- ... and, 4, 7, 226, &c.; referring to more than two objects, 1453; adv. as well, too, 37, 658. *NME ba(i)th, ON báðer*
bak, n. the back, 252, 563, 579, 740. *ME, ON bak, OE bæc*
band, n. agreement, bond; wedding --, 2413. *EME, ON band*
band, v.tr. to secure with a band or bands, 252. *Prec.* See expl.note.
bane, adv. promptly, readily, 1438. *ME bayn(e), bane, ON beinn,* straight, direct, ready to serve.
bannis, imperat. banish, expel, exile, 1283; ban(n)ist, p.p. banished, exiled, 1271, 1280. *ME ban(n)ysshe, OF baniss-*
bannit, pt.3 s. cursed, 491. *ME ban(ne), ON banna*
banys, n.pl. bones of the body, 1501. *NME ba(a)n, OE bān*
barane, adj. barren, without fruit or seed, said of a tree, 323. *ME barain, OF barai(g)ne*
barbour, n. barber (and surgeon), 1549, 1561. *ME, AF barbour*
barnage, n. nobles, lords, peerage, 360. *ME barnage, OF barnage, ML bar(o)nāgium*
barnage, n. childhood, youth, 122. *ME barnage, OE b(e)arn + -age*
barne, n. child, one's son or daughter, 5, 458, &c.; a very young boy, 14, 444, &c.; youth, young man, 165, 183, &c.; schoolboy, pupil, 1856; barnis, n.gen. 83, 441; barnis, n.pl. children, as one's offspring, 1333. *ME barn(e), OE bearn, ON barn*
baron(n)is, n.pl. barons, 2517, 2773. *ME baro(u)n, OF baron*

bar(r)ell, barrall, n. barrel, cask, 1710, 1740, 1745; pl. 1694; bar(r)ellis, n.pl. 1695, 1757. *ME barel(l), OF baril*
basyng, n. basin, 2585. *ME basin, OF bacin*
bat(t)ell, n. battle, combat, fight, 437, 2310. *ME bataile, OF bataille*
be, adv. when, 920, 2511; -- at, when, after, 225; prep. by the action or agency of (a pers.), 1331, 2561; by means of, by the use of (a thing), 172, 278, 383, &c.; in the name of, in forms of adjuration, 202, 502, 787, &c.; in accordance with, 386, 2116, 2232; in comparison with, 2444; along (the way), 2328; not later than (a specif.time), 1291, 2024, 2248; -- far (fer), by far, very much, 647, 1241; -- mekle fer, in a much greater degree, 1594; indicating succession of individuals of the same class, 1177. *(N)ME be, OE be, var. of bi.* See also by.
be, v. to be; am, pr.1 s. 121, 900, 1098, &c.; art, 2 s. 196, 1102, 1129, &c.; is, 3 s., 113, 138, 213, &c.; beis, with fut. sense, 960, 1174; ar, pl. 227, 264, 571, &c.; be, pr.subj. 71, 329, 396, &c.; war, pt.s. 321; was, 4, 9, 60, &c.; war, pt.pl. 23, 337, 531, &c.; was, 19, 1986; war, pt.subj. 118, 120, 284, &c.; be, imperat. 1922; bene, p.p. 388, 784, 805, &c. Used absol. to exist, live, 1119, 1883, 2029, &c.; with thar, 19, 138, 170, &c.; happen, take place, 455, 1253; become, 350, 2210, 2214; be the case or the fact, 382, 784, 2395; let --, let alone, cease, 555, 1105, 1233, &c.; used with adv. or prep.phr. stating where or how a thing is: to have or occupy a place somewhere, 260, 900, 1098, &c.; to sit, remain, &c. in a defined position, 93, 1181, 2637; to befall, with dat., e.g. wa is me, 456, 465, 963, &c.; used as copula, with adj. 173, 230, 902, &c.; with phr.= adj. 121, 166, 939, &c.; with noun connot. 123, 804, 1942, &c.; with noun, to exist as the thing known by a certain name, 261, 2176, &c.; to mean, to amount to, 1608; to signify, 353, 357, 573, &c.; used as aux. with p.p. in tr.vbs., forming the pass. 46, 48, 94, &c.; in intr.vbs. forming the perf., 227, 1760, 1817, &c.; with pr.p. with act.signif. 459, 774, 1805, &c. *ME be(n), OE bēon*
becaus, adv. & conj. because, 191, 770, 866, &c. *ME because, OE bi + OF cause*
bed, n. bed, 83, 96, 1237, &c. *ME bed(de), OE bed(d).* See also cair-bed.
bed-clathis, n.pl. bed-clothes, 1442. *ME bedclothes*
bedene, adv. forthwith, 77, 2215; all --, completely, 2260. *ME bedene, of uncertain origin*
befall, v.tr. to befall, happen, to become of, 156. *ME befalle(n), OE befeallan*
befor, adv. previously, earlier, 879, 895, 1206, 1713; conj. previous to the time when, 1009; -- or, 489; of --, formerly, 873, 1895; prep. in front of, 1937, 2003, &c.; in the presence of, 1514, 1525, &c.; earlier than, 304. *ME before, OE beforan*
begyle, pr.3 pl. beguile, deceive, 1969; begylis, pr.3 pl. 1838; begylit, p.p. deceived, 952, 1073, &c.; begyld, p.p. 2504; begylit, pt.pl. deceived, 1758, 1821, 2033; begyld, pt.sg. 2777. *ME begyle f. OF guiler*
begyn, pr.2 s.subj. begin, 1425; begynnis, pr.3 s. begins, bef. 1, 1721; began, pt.3 s. began, 526, 1323, 2264, 2423. *NME begin, OE beginnan*
beheld, pt.3 s. observed, looked at, 2376; behold, v.tr. to see, look upon, 1651. *ME behold, OE bihaldan*
behovit, pt.3 s. had to, must needs, 2551; behude, pt.3 s. impers. was necessary, 2564; behufit, pt.3 s. was under a necessity, had to, 890, 892; impers. 1200, 1215. *NME behufe, ME behoue, OE behōfian*
behynd, prep. behind, at the back of, 252, 1075. *ME behinde, OE behindan*
beif, n. beef, 697, 710. *ME befe, beef, AN bef, OF boef*
beir, n. barley, 1203. *ME, OE bere*
beir, n. bier, 805. *ME beer, ONhb bēr*

bell, n.bell, used for giving public notice, 1008, 1099, 1145, 1647; bellis, n.pl. bells, 1667, 1689, 2520. *ME bel(le), OE belle*

benesoun, n. blessing, benediction, 2482. *ME benesoun, OF beneisson*

bere, v.intr. to bear, produce fruit, 310; tr. to produce, 346, give birth to, 1657; born, p.p. brought forth, 1659; borne, p.p. carried, 805; bure, pt. 3 s. bore (fruit), 315, 324, 336; -- away, carried away as winner, 414; gave birth to, or bore for nine months, 1866; held (an office), 2296; refl. behaved, 1639, 2600. *ME bere, OE beran*

beseike, pr.1 s. beseech, entreat, 818. *ME beseke, OE besēcan*

best, adj. of the highest excellence, 206, 1384, 2315; absol. the best person(s) or thing(s), 737, 1653; adv. in the most excellent way, to the fullest extent, 232, 429, 470, &c.; at the --, in the best way, most excellently, 781, 1589; to the --, in the best way, 2600. *ME best, OE betst*

bestis, n.pl. animals, 531. *ME be(e)st(e), OF beste*

besyde, adv. near by, 171; prep. beside, close to, hard by, 447, 1661. *ME beside, OE be sīdan*

betid, pt.3 s. subj. befell, happened, 285. *ME betide(n), be + OE tīdan*

better, adj. more excellent, more profitable, 732, 845, 902, 1496; adv. in a better manner, 338, 987. *ME better, OE betera*

betuix, prep. between, with ref. to parentage, 1333; with ref. to dissension, difference, &c., 1902, 2054. *ME, OE betwix*

betwene, adv. between them, mutually, 1047; prep. between, with ref. to dissension, 1474; by the joint action of, 2000. *ME betwene, ONhb bitwēn*

bewes, n.pl. boughs, main branches, 334. *OE bogas, pl. of bōg, bōh*

bid, v.tr. to pray, give an order, 309; pr.1 s. offer, desire, 2357; biddin, p.p. ordered, 1375. *ME bid(de), OE biddan, mixed with bēodan.* See also bad.

big, v.tr. to build, 75, 2320; biggit, pt. built, 79, 1030, 1645, 2326. *ME big(ge), ON byggja*

bill, n. axe, 1399. *ME bill, OE bil*

bir, byr, n. force, might, 437; a strong rush of onward movement, 1517. *NME bir, byrre, ON byrr*

bird, n. bird, 1797, 1965, 2037, &c.; young bird, 2650, 2661, &c.; birdis, sg. gen. 2562-3, 2677; birdis, pl.gen. 2642. *ME bird, ONhb bird, OE brid*

birlit, pt.3 s. poured out for drinking (on a pers.), 1053, 1064. *ME birle, OE byrelian*

birnand, pr.p. burning, 1621. F. *ME birne, OE byrnan.* See also brynt.

birthy, adj. fertile, yielding produce, 321. (*NED* 1680). *F. ME birth(e), ON *byrðr, OIc burðr, + -y*

bitterly, adv. grievously, 1598. *ME bitterly, OE biterlīce*

blame, n. censure, reproof, 1536. *ME blame, OF bla(s)me*

blaw, n. blow, stroke, 1636. *NME blaw, of unknown origin*

bleid, v.intr. to bleed, lose blood from severe wounds, 943, 1552; tr. to be bled, 1555, 1562; bledis, pr.1 s. lose blood, 950. *ME blede, OE blēdan*

blewe, pt.3 pl. sounded a musical instrument by blowing, 2520. *F. NME blaw(e), OE blāwan*

blissing, n. benediction, 678, 2488; something that gives spiritual well-being or joy, 1476. *ME blissing, OE blētsung*

blud(e), n. blood, 440, 447, 449, &c. *NME blude, ME blode, OE blōd*

blude-latting, n. blood-letting, 1550. *ME blodlating*

bludy, adj. covered, stained with blood, 246. *NME bludy, ME blody, OE blōdig*

blyn, v.intr. to stop, desist, 79, 2158; blynnit, pt.3 s. desisted, 525. *ME blyn(e), OE blinnan*

blynd, adj. blind, 1265, 1559, 2134. *ME, OE blind*

blyth, **adj.** glad, pleased, 209, 319, 1727, &c.; gentle, 293; **blythar**, **adj.** more cheerful, 2440; **blythest**, **adj.** most pleasant, merriest, 1528. *ME blyth, OE blīþe*
blythly, **-lie**, **adv.** gladly, happily, 212, 520, 1774, &c. *ME blithly, OE blīþelīce*
blythnes, **n.** gaiety, good spirits, 1987. *ME blytheness, OE blīþnes*
bodome, **n.** bottom, 757. *ME bothom, OE botm*
body, **n.** human body, 231, 1137, &c.; dead body, 906, 924, &c.; **bodyis**, **gen.sg.** of the human body, 652. *ME body(e), OE bodig*
bordale, **n.** brothel, 1138. *ME, OF bordel*
borit, **ppl.a.** perforated, pierced, 767; **boryt**, **pt.3 s.** bored, pierced, 757. *ME bor(i)en, OE borian, ON bora*
born, **borne**, see **bere.**
borowe, **v.tr.** to ransom, rescue, 373. *ME borow(e), OE borgian*
bot, **adv.** only, no more than, 9, 54, 228, &c.; almost, 2028; **conj.** unless, 813, 961, 1211, &c.; except that, 583, 1681, 1950; -- **gif**, 388, 851, 860; but (in advers.sense), 73, 99, 131, &c.; -- **that**, 139, 1504; **bot**, **prep.** without, devoid of, 2043; except, other than, 5, 117, 560, &c.; **but**, **prep.** without, 84, 258, 262, &c. *NME bot, ME bote, bute, OE būtan*
bovn, **v.intr.** to get ready, prepare oneself, 2304; **bovnit**, **pt.3 pl.** got ready, prepared themselves, 66; **bowned**, **pt.3 s.** prepared himself, 682; **bovn**, **ppl.a.** made ready, put in order, 2481. *ME b(o)une, ON bún-, búenn, p.p. of búa*
bow, **n.** bow (weapon), 1625, 1830. *ME bow(e), OE boga*
bowit, **pt.3 s.** bowed in respect or submission, 223; **ppl.a.** inclined in reverence, 65. *ME bow(e), OE būgan*
bowned, see **bovnit.**
braid, **n.** quick movement, 1530. *ME braid, OE gebregd*
branchis, **n.pl.** branches of a tree, 333, 337. *ME branch(e), OF branche*
brandis, **n.pl.** pieces of fire-wood, 1380. *ME, OE brand*
bras, **n.** brass, 1015, 1625. *ME bras, OE bræs*
bred, **pt.3 pl.** nurtured, 1501. *F. ME brede, OE brēdan*
breid, **n.** bread, 1203. *ME brede, OE brēad*
brek, **v.tr.** to break, 1690, 2020; **brak**, **pt.3 s.** broke, 485, 2077; **pl.** 1799, shattered, 1446. *ME brek, OE brecan*
brer, **n.** briar, shrub, 1797. *ME breer(e), OE brēr, brǣr*
brest, **n.** breast, chest, 1500, 1581. *ME breest, brest(e), OE brēost*
bricht, **adj.** beautiful, fair (of women), 127, 2491. *ME bri(g)ht, OE briht, beorht*
bring, **v.tr.** to fetch, carry, convey, 148, 401, 606, &c.; **bryng**, **v.tr.** bring, come with, 2119; **bring**, **imperat.** bring, convey, 2205; **brocht**, **p.p.**, brought, conveyed, escorted, 23, 128, 397, &c.; **pt.** brought, escorted, 378, 982, 2419, &c.; -- **wp**, reared from childhood, 2659. *ME bring(e), OE bringan*
brother, **n.** brother, son of the same parents, 938. *ME brother, OE brōþor*
bruke, **v.tr.** to enjoy the use of, to use, possess, 907, 1330, -- **wp**, 916. *ME brouk(e), bruken, OE brūcan*
bryng, see **bring.**
brynt, **p.p.** burnt, consumed or destroyed by fire, 1158, 1809, 2778. *ME bryn(ne), ON brinna*. See **birnand.**
buke, **n.** book, bef. 1; a copy of the gospels, or other sacred writing, 202. *NME buk(e), OE bōc, ON bók*
bulleris, **pr.3 pl.** bubble up, 2181. *Cf. OF bullir, Ic bulla, to boil*
bullour, **n.** a boiling or bubbling up of water, 2212; **bulleris**, **bullouris**, **n.pl.** 2186, 2190, 2216. *F. vb.*
burd(e), **n.** table, 1512, 1533, 1544; daily meals in a pers.'s house, 2307. *NME burd(e), ME bord(e), OE bord*

bure, see bere.
burges, n. burgess, citizen, 286, 292, 294, &c.; gen. 2003. *ME burges,OF burgeis*
buskit, pt.3 s.refl. arrayed herself, 206; prepared himself, got ready, 2478. *F. NME busk, ON búask*
but, see bot.
bute, n. profit, help, 241, 543, 607. *NME bute, ME bote, OE, ON bót*
by, adv. near, close at hand, 181, 539; past a cert. point, also transf. to time, 1335, 1466, 2039, &c.; set ȝe nocht by, do not turn from your purpose, 1928; prep. of position: at the side or edge of, near, beside, 1123, 1345, 1631, 2148; -- hir allane, singly, in isolation, 666; of medium, by means of, 21, 155, 932; -- the hand scho couth him tak, 219; -- the feit, 932. *ME by, OE bi.* See also be, adv. & prep.
byde, v.intr. to wait, stay, remain, 181, 680, 1169, 1718; tr. await, 1090, 1134; byid, 682; byde, pr.2 subj. 1267. *ME byde(n), OE bīdan.* See also baide.
bygane, ppl.a. past, 1, 1004. *By + gane, p.p. of ga*
bynd, v.tr. to bind, tie, 1553, 1560; pr.1 pl.refl. oblige by a promise or vow, 1718; pr.1 s. 1723; pr.1 s.refl. 1869; bundin, bundyn, p.p. bound, made fast with bonds or fetters, 253, 1012, 1147; ppl.a. swaddled (of a child), 428. *ME bynde(n), OE bindan*
byr, see bir.

cage, n. cage, 1043. *ME, OF cage*
cair, n. lamentation, 277; sorrow, 1911. *ME care, OE caru*
cair-bed, n. sick-bed, 1168. *Cf. ON kǫr-beðr*
cais(e), case, n. an instance of the occurrence of a thing, fact, &c., 260, 647, 2740; event, occurrence, 817, 2253, 2475; the actual state or position of matters, the fact, 917, 2047; gif -- war that ..., if perchance ..., 118. (*NED* 1535). *ME cas(e), OF cas*
cald, adj. cold, of the weather, 1369; n. coldness of the body, 1391. *NME, Ang cald.*
cald, p.p. see call.
caldron, n. a large kettle, 891, 896, 923. *ME caldron, AN caud(e)ron*
call, v.tr. to call, name, 50; summon, 1292; -- furth, summon to come forward, 2757; intr. shout so as to be heard by those within, 1991; callit, ppl.a. so-called, 248, 512; p.p. named, 2, 55, 292, &c.; summoned, 2131, 2693; cald, p.p. called, named, 1027; callit, pt. called, named, 24, 47, 53, &c.; summoned, 298, 1213, &c.; bade to come, 666; termed, reckoned, 732; called so as to be let in, 1907, 1931. *ME cal(le(n), ON kalla*
can, aux.v. pr. can, 611, 1307, 1314, &c., with ell. of vb. 381, 987, 1087, 2579. See also couth, cuth, con(e). *ME can, OE can, inf. cunnan*
can, aux.v. pt. did, used to form a periphrastic pt., 257, 477, 791, &c., cf. Chaucer's use of gan. *Variant of gan, pt. of gin v.* See also couth.
car(e), v.tr. go, move, depart, 2072. *ME caire, ON keyra*
carling, n. old woman, crone, 1968. *NME, ON kerling*
carnale, adj. carnal, fleshly, 668. *LME carnall, L carnalis.* See expl.note.
carpe, v.intr. to talk, 1300; carpit, pt.3 s. talked, 1881. *ME carpe(n), ON karp n., Ic karpa*
case, see cais(e).
cassyn, see cast.
cast, v.tr. to cast, direct (the eyes), 100; castin, p.p. thrown, 2726; cassyn, p.p. cast, thrown, 441, 451, 955. *ME cast(e)n, ON kasta.* See also kest.
cast, n. shape, character, form, 2445. *ME cast, ON kast*
castall, castell, castale, n. castle, 425, 2286, 2322, &c.; 2434; 2596. *ME castel, ONF castel, ON kastali*

castall-duris, n.pl. castle-doors, 2462.
castall-wall, n. castle-wall, 2326, 2333.
caus, n. cause, that which produces an effect, 123, 1066, 2182, &c.; for -- (that), for the reason that, 2554; a person or other agent who brings about something or is to blame for mischief, 804; case, a matter before a court of decision, 1018, 2673, 2733; matter of concern, affair, business, 2541; adequate ground of action, 2752; make --, give reason for action, 266, 2760; to fische a caus 990, see expl.note. *ME, OF cause*
causis, pr.3 s. causes, brings about, 2669; causit, pt.3 s. brought about, 1901. *ME cause, OF causer*
cawtelous, adj. full of tricks, cunning, 1836. *ME cautelous*
certanly(e), adv. surely, without doubt, 2379, 2584. *ME certanli, adj. ME certan(e), OF certain*
certis, adv. certainly, assuredly, 2637. *ME certis, OF certes*
ces, v.intr. cease, stop, 940, 1858; absol. -- of, cease from, 1461. *ME cese, OF cesser.* See also sesit.
cetezener, n. citizen, 1019. *ME citezen, AN citezein, with suffix of burgh-er, forein-er.* See also citezouris.
chak, n. trick, device, 1521. *ME chak, chek, OF eschec, eschac*
chak-wache, n. patrol, watch. *ME chak, chek v., to check, inspect, arrest, + OE waecce*
chalmer, n. private room, 79, 82, 135, &c. *ME chaumer, chawmer, AF chaumbre, OF chambre*
chance, n. fortune, luck, lot, 787. *ME, OF chance*
changit, pt.3 s. underwent a change of, 1557, 2439. *ME change, AN chaunger, OF changer*
chape, v.intr. to escape, 542; chapit, p.p. got free or away from, 1471; got off unharmed, 2004; pt.3 s. got off unharmed, 2779. *ME chape, var. of achape, AN aschaper, OF eschaper*
chargeand, pr.p. ordering to do something, 148; chargit, pt.3 s. charged, ordered, 320, 1229, 2706. *ME charge, OF charger*
chasit, p.p. chased, pursued, 1945. *ME chas(e), OF chacier, chasser*
cheir, n. display of feeling, by rejoicing, 1528; id. by grieving, 509; face, mood, 1238; makand --, rejoicing, feasting, 1545, 1728, 1985; he changit --, changed countenance (with relief), 2439. *ME, OF chere*
cherité, n. charity, kindness, 1642, 1954; God's love to man, 2782. *ME cherité, early var. of ME, OF charité*
ches, v.tr. choose, select, 1346; chesis, pr.2 s. choose, 1490; chesit, pt. elected to do something, 234, 881. *ME chese, OE cēosan*
chewe, v.tr. avoid, escape, 915. *Reduced form of eschewe, OF eschever.* See eschewe.
child, n. young boy, 17, 32, 39, &c.; youth, 625, 2165, &c.; son, 213, 2503; schoolboy, student, 1833; childis, gen.sg. 2562-3. *ME child, OE cild*
chos, n. choice, 845. *ME, OF chois*
chyar, chyer, n. chair, 1386, 1513, 1526, 2355. *Var. of chear(e), ME cheiere, chaiere, OF chaiere*
cité, n. city, town, 13, 19, 71, &c. *ME, OF cité*
citezouris, n.pl. citizens, 347. *Irreg. var. of* cetezener, q.v.
claith, see clath.
clam, pt.3 s. climbed, 544, 2061. *F. ME clim, var. of climbe, OE climban.* See also clymmis.
clamour, n. clamour, loud vocal noise of birds, 2617. *ME, OF clamour*
clarioun, claroun, n. clarion, trumpet, 187, 2523. *ME clarioun, OF claron*

clarschaw, n. clairschach, Highland harp, 2522. *Gael. clàirseach*
clath, claith, n. covering for a bench, 194; table-cloth, 1516, 1518, 1532; woven fabric, 2007; **clathis, claithis**, n.pl. table-cloths, 1541; dress, raiment, 2466. *NME clath(e), OE clāþ*. See also **bed-clathis**.
clawis, pr.3 pl. scratch (gently), 579; **clawit**, pt.3 s. scratched, 563. *ME clawe(n), OE clawian*
cled, see **cleith**.
cleir, see **cler**.
cleith, v.tr. to clothe, provide with clothing, 1832; **cleth**, v.tr. to dress, 2466; **cled**, p.p. dressed, 2514, 2767; pt.3 s. dressed, 2420; refl. 2437. *ME clethe, OE clǣðan (rare), ON klæða*
clek, v.tr. to hatch from eggs, 2663. *NME clekke, ON klekja, to hatch*
clene, adj. clean, free from dirt, 1542; free from defect, perfect, 779; adv. completely, 2005, 2216, 2577. *ME clene, OE clǣne*
clenly, adv. completely, 1211. *Prec. + -ly*
cler, cleir, adj. clear, bright, brilliant, 1651, 2550; clear, fully intelligible, 2560, 2646; **cler**, adv. clearly, distinctly, 2223. *ME cler(e), OF cler*
clerk(e), n. clerk, man of book-learning, scholar, 89, 504, 616, &c.; pupil, student, 1639. *ME clerk(e), OE, OF clerc*
clerkly, adv. in clerkly fashion, scholarly, 1882. *Prec. + -ly*
clerly, adv. distincly, plainly, 1670, 2174, 2209. *ME cler(e) + -ly*
cleth, see **cleith**.
clething, n. clothing, apparel, 1032, 2421, 2435, &c. *ME clething*
cloke, n. cloak, 1385. *ME, OF cloke*
closit, pt.3 s. closed, shut, 2386. *F. ME close, OF clos-, stem of clore*
clymmis, pr.3 s. climbs, 575. *ME clim, climbe, OE climban*. See also **clam**.
cod, n. pillow, 1453. *NME cod, ON kodde*
coft, p.p. bought, 728. *MDu (ghe)coft, p.p. of copen, to buy*
cokis, n.pl. cocks (fowls), 1009. *ME cocke, cok, OE coc*
colour, n. colour of the face, 1557; complexion, 2445; pretence, pretext, in phr. **wnder --**, 2771. *ME, OF colour*
come, pt. see **cum**.
come, n. coming, arrival, 205. *ME com(e) f. come v.* See **hame-come**.
comfort, n. cheer, in phr. **to be of good --**, 166. *ME comfort, ME, OF confort*
comfortis, pr.3 s. comforts, ministers delight or pleasure to, 355. *ME comfort, conforte, OF conforter*
commandit, p.p. given order for, 2608. *ME commande, OF comander*
commonly, adv. usually, generally, 834. *ME comonly*
commoun, adj. common, public, 1006; belonging to, or owned by, the community, 1008. *ME commoun, OF comun*
commoun, n.; phr. **in --**, in joint use or possession, 2120. *Prec.*
commyt, v.tr. to commit, entrust, 17. *ME committe, -yt(te), L committere*
company, n; phr. **in --**, in his company, along with him, 2606. *ME company, AF compaynie, OF compa(i)gnie* *pellere*
compellit, p.p. urged irresistibly, 1331. *ME compell(e(, OF compeller, L com-*
compt, pr.1 s. count, regard, consider, 810; **comptit**, p.p. considered, 2258. *ME compte, OF compter, respelling of conter, after compte of L computare.* See also **countis**.
con(e), v.tr. to learn, 132, 622. *ME cunne, OE cunnan*
conclude, v.tr. to bring matters to a close, to finish a matter or subject, 2109. *ME conclude, L concludere*
conclusioun, n. end, finish, 1804. *ME conclusioun, OF conclusion, L conclusio*
condampnit, p.p. found guilty, convicted, 2748. *OF condam(p)ner, L dam(p)nare.*

condicioun, n. character, disposition, 830. *ME condicioun, OF condicion*
condit, n. underground passage, 2366, 2382. *ME condyt, OF conduit* *tia*
confluens, n. concourse (of people), crowd, 2607. *ME, OF confluence, L confluen-*
confusioun, n. discomfiture, ruin, 120, 1315, 1608; a state of disorder or chaos, 1534. *ME confusioun, OF confusion*
consaif, pr.s. perceive, understand, 327, 1828, 2080; consauit, p.p. 152, 780, 1154, 1588. *ME consaive, OF conceiv-, conceveir*
consent, n. agreement; phr.with ane --,unanimously, 1685. (*NED* 1580). *ME, OF consente*
consent, v.intr. to consent, comply, 2738; consentit, pt.3 pl. consented, agreed, 76. *ME consent, OF consentir* *siderantia*
considerans, n. consideration, 1477. *ME consideraunce, OF considerance, L con-*
consuetud, n. custom, observance, 2117. *ME, OF consuetude, L consuetudo*
contrar, n. opposite, 1104. *ME contra(i)re, OF contraire, L contrarius*
contruf, v.tr. to contrive, devise, 2338. *ME controve, OF controver*
conȝe, n. money, 1234. *OF cuigne, AN coigne*
copy, v.tr. to note, observe, 495. *ME copye, copie, OF copier, ML copiare*
corage, n. ardour, boldness, sexual desire, 1044. *ME, OF corage*
coronale, n. crown, coronet, garland, 207. *ME coronal f. OF coro(u)ne*
cors, n. dead body, 927, 945. *ME, OF cors*
cost, n. cost, expense, 411, 2141. *ME, OF cost*
cost, v.tr. to cost, necessitate the loss of (life), 1898. *ME cost(e), OF coster*
costly, adj. expensive, 1987. *ME costly*
counsall, n. counsel, advice, 68, 179, 1024, &c.; council, 264; assembly, 1677; in gret --, in the greatest confidentiality, 667; to heile --, to keep (someone's) secret, 684. *ME counsail, -sall, AN counseil, OF conseil*
counsall, v.tr. to counsel, advise, 265; counsall, pr.1 s. 70. *ME counsail(e), OF conseiller*
countenans, n. face, appearance, 720, 844; look, expression, 2329. *ME countenance, OF contenance*
countis, pr.3 s. reckons (at a cert. value), cares, 962. *ME count(en), AF counter, OF conter, cunter.* See also compt.
courche, n. kerchief, 208. *Reduced form of courchef f. OF couvre-chef*
court, n. court, royal entourage, 1258. *ME, OF court*
courtas, adj. courteous, gentle and polite, 1884; curtas, adj. 222. *ME courteis, curtas, OF curteis, corteis*
courtasly, adv. courteously, 189, 197, 2079. *Pre.+ -ly*
courting, n. bed-curtain, 1453. *ME courtyne, OF courtine*
courtly, adj. courtly, refined, 2599. *ME, OF court + -ly*
couth, aux.v.pt. could, 21, 85, 381, &c.; cuth, 1788. *OE cunnan, pt. cuþe*
couth, aux.v.pt. did, 25, 50, 100, &c. *Substitution analogous to* can *for* gan.
couth, pt.3 s. knew, 2568. *OE cunnan, pt. cuþe.* See also ken.
covatis, n. covetousness, inordinate desire for wealth, 1270, 1819, 2204. *ME covatise, OF coveitise.* See also cowatousnes.
covatus, adj. greedy, grasping, 1265, 1618, 1714, 1731. *ME covatus, OF coveitus*
covering, n. cover, cloth spread over a bed, 1453. *ME coveryng*
cowatousnes, n. covetousness, 1823. (*NED* 1526-34) *ME covatus + -nes.* See also covatus,
cowerit, pt.3 pl. covered, spread a cloth over, 1542; put someth. over ... with the effect of hiding it from view, 1711. *F. ME cover, OF covrir*
crabitly, adv. peevishly, sourly, 1262, 1570, 2589. *ME crabbedly, poss. f. OE crabba, crab*
craft, n. craft, skill, art, 622, 715, 2343. *ME craft(e), OE cræft*

craftly, adv. skilfully, cleverly, 653. *Prec. + -ly*
cravis, pr.3 s. ask for with insistence, 2661. *ME crave(n), OE crafian*
craw, n. crow, 2677. *NME crawe, OE crāwe*
crawe, v.intr. to utter the loud cry of a cock, 1009. *NME crawen, OE crāwan*
credill, n. cradle, 428, 435, &c. *ME credil(le), prob. OE *crædel, var. of cradel, cradol*
Cristin, adj. Christian, 956. *ME cristin(e), OE cristen*
Cristindome, n. the Christian world, 270. *ME cristendom(e), OE cristendōm*
crovde, n. crowd, fiddle, 2522. *ME croude, crowde, Welsh crwth*
crovne, n. crown, diadem (worn by monarch), 207; as a symbol of sovereignty, 502, 582, 2687, &c.; sovereignty, authority, 637, 1607, &c.; top part of the skull, by extension: the head, 2064 (*NED* 1594). *ME croun(e), shortened f. coroune, AN coroune, OF corune, -one*
cruell, adj. cruel, pitiless, 1423. *ME, OF cruel*
cruelly, adv. cruelly, fiercely, 2732. *Prec. + -ly*
cry, n. vocal utterance of birds, 2619. *ME cry(e), OF cri*
cry, v.intr. to utter the voice loudly under the influence of emotion, 937; cryit, cryid, pt. called out, tr. 244, 453, 508, 1855; tr. called in supplication, 1557, 2592; intr. uttered the voice loudly under the influence of emotion, 460. *ME cry(e), OF crier*
cryme, n. sin, offence, 1656; blame of having done wrong, 2247. *ME cryme, OF crime*
cukkald, n. cuckold, 1972. *NME cukewalde, ME cokewold, pointing to earlier OF *cucuald*
cule, v.intr. cool down, lose the heat of passion, 1103. *ME co(o)le, OE cōlian*
culȝeit, pt.3 s. received, entertained kindly, 1438. *OF accueillir*. See expl. note.
cum, v.intr. to come, present oneself, 182, 209, &c.; to approach, 2333; -- to, to befall, 499; -- in, to enter, 1913; -- agane, to return, 2657; -- of, issue from, 767; -- tharto, achieve it, 1049, 1354; in tyme to --, in the future, 595; imperat. -- to, approach, 901; -- in, enter hither, 1928; pr.3 s. subj. arrive, 1175, 1363; -- dovne, fall, 1518; -- agane, return, 2623; cummis, pr.3 s. -- hame, arrives home, 1372; 3 pl. -- furth, come into existence, 2183; cummyn, p.p. arrived, 183, 2407, 2441; presented oneself, 1895; com(e), pt. presented oneself, 112, 162, 163, &c.; moved, 158, 677, 1946; entered, 212, 225, 540, &c.; reached, 303, 706; arrived, 2512; arrived in due course, 799, 1523; happened, 496; with pr.p., 372, 2593; with inf. of purpose, 922; -- dovne, fell, dropped, 1533 (*NED* 1787); -- agane, returned, 1729, 1773; -- furth, came out, 2223; -- in, entered, 885, 2385. *ME cum(e), OE cuman*
cunnand, n. agreement; in -- that, on the condition that, 1716. *ME conand(e), reduced f. covenand, -ant*
cunnyng, adj. possessed of knowledge or skill, 1884. *ME cunnyng f. cunne, OE cunnan*
cunnyng, n. learning, knowledge, 57, 2641. *Prec.*
cuntré, n. region, district, 355; nation, land, 518, 527, &c.; with pers.pron.: country to which one belongs, 2421; cuntreis, n.pl. lands, 1273. *ME cuntré, OF cuntrée*
cure, n. care, attention, charge, 33, 85, 299, &c.; in --, in charge, 2296. *ME, OF cure*
cursit, ppl.a. cursed, damnable, 1911. *ME curse(n), OE cursian*
curtas, see courtas.
curtassy, n. courteousness, 1921. *ME curtasy, OF curtesie*

curyale, adj. courtly, 1922. *OF curial(e), L curialis*
cuth see couth.
cymbalis, n.pl. cymbals, 187. *ME cymbal, L cymbalum*

daly, adj. daily, occurring every day, 1170. *OE daeġlic*
dame, n. form of address, meaning either lady or woman, 1434. *ME, OF dame*
dammage, n. injury, harm, 1684. *ME, OF damage*
damysele, n. damsel, female attendant, 2768. *ME damisele, OF dami-, dameisele*
danger, n. obligation, debt, 849. *ME, OF danger*
danté, n. love, esteem, 1892; danteis, n.pl. delicacies, 1527, 1543, 1986. *ME daynté, OF dainté*
dar, aux.pr.s. dare, 105, 601, 992, &c., with inf. without to. *ME dar(e), ONhb darr*
dar, 1185, see expl.note.
day(e), n. day, the time of daylight, daybreak, 1246, 1772, 2024; often in nycht & day, day & nycht, 574, 1429, 1622, &c.; point or unit of time, on which anything happens or which fixes a date, 68, 158, 174, &c.; a(ne) day, on a certain day, 135, 2327, 2375; the day, to-day, 204; this day, to-day, 986, 1162, &c.; a specified or appointed day, 976, 1165; dayis, n.pl. days as space of time, 173, 1267, 1867, &c.; preceded by a poss.pron., lifetime, 418, 2572, 2583; period, time, 1003, 1236. *ME day(e), OE dæġ*
de, v.intr. to die, 150, 162, 167, &c.; of states, qualities: to come to an end, to pass out of memory, 778; tr. to die (a specif. death), 282, 1612; pr.sbj. 608, 902, 1287, 1463; deit, pt.3 s. died, ended his life, 766, 1827; deand, ppl.a. dying, at the point of death, 1094. *NME de, Ang *dēȝan*
deces, n. decease, death, 2779. *ME, OF deces*
declair, imperat. make known, unfold, 2673; declair, declar, v.tr. to make known, explain, relate, 287, 685, 2166. *ME declar, OF declarer, L declarare*
declynit, p.p. descended, 105. *ME declyne, OF decliner, L declinare*
dedly, adj. mortal, 842. *ME dedli, OE dēadlic*
defence, n. defence, protection, 614. *ME defence, OF defens(e)*
defend, imperat. defend, protect (by speech), 1856; v.intr. 178; tr. 2111; defendit p.p. 2566. *ME defende, OF defendre*
deflour, v.tr. to violate, 249, 2097. *ME defloure, OF desflourer*
defowle, imperat. outrage, defile by immorality, 1923. *Blend of ME foulen and OF defouler*
degest, pt.3 s. dispersed, dissolved, dissipated, 2589; p.p. considered, thought over, 782. *ME digest, OF digester, L digestus, p.p. of digerere*
deid, adj. dead (of persons) 775, 855, 1122, &c.; killed, 160, 368, &c.; (of dogs) 1446, 1456; to haf him --, to cause his death, to kill him, 133, cf. Chaucer *CT* VII.2901. *ME deed, ded(e), OE dēad*
deid, n. death, the act or fact of dying, 266, 282, 399, &c. *(N)ME deed, dede, var. of deth(e)*
deid, n. deed, action, 992, 1414, 2357, 2715; in --, 5, 1770, 1887, &c.; on --, indeed, 1421. *ME de(e)d(e), Ang dēd*
deile, n. dealing, intercourse, 1216; euerilk --, entirely, 873. *ME dele, deel, OE dǣl*
deir, adj. beloved, 10, 229, 848, &c.; expensive, 1527, 1986; der, adj. 1428. *ME der(e), OE deore*
deir, n. darling, dear one, 1093, 2027, 2440. *Prec.*
deir, v.tr. to harm, injure, 991. *ME dere, OE derian*
deit, see de.
delay, n. delay, putting off or deferring of an action, 507, 1597. *ME delay, OF delai*

delayd, p.p. deferred, postponed, 1165, 2088. *ME delaye, -laie, OF delaier, -layer*
dele, n. devil, mischievously wicked or troublesome fellow, 512. *Contracted form of* devil. See devill.
delfit, pt.3 pl. tr. dug up, 2189; delvit, pt.3 pl. intr. performed the act of digging, 1745. *ME delve(n), OE delfan*
deligens, n. diligence, industry, 64, 867. *ME, OF diligence*
deligent, adj. constant in application or work, 626. *ME, OF diligent*
deliuer, imperat. hand over, transfer, 33; v.tr. to rescue, 395. *ME delivere, OF delivrer*
deliuerance, n. deliverance, release, 399. *ME deliveraunce, OF delivrance*
delvit, see delfit
delyte, n. delight, pleasure, 957. *ME delyt(e), OF delit*
denyit, pt.3 s.intr. said 'no' to a statement, 1976. *ME deny(e), OF denier*
depe, adj. deep, 890, 1737. *ME depe, OE dēop*
der, see deir.
derrast, adj.superl. dearest, used in addressing a pers., 2474. *See* deir.
dese, n. dais, high table; began the --, presided at the feast, 2423. *ME des(e), OF deis*
desyr, n. desire, wish, request, 113. *ME desyre, OF desir*
desyr, pr.2 s. desire, have a strong wish for, 655. *ME desyre, OF desirer*
det, n. debt, that which is owed or due; -- of natur, the necessity of dying, death, 11; in --, under obligation to pay something, 841, 846; dettis, n.pl. debts, sums of money which one pers. owes to another, 871. *ME det(t(e), OF det(t)e*
devill, devile, n. devil, human being of diabolical character or qualities, 248, 357, 378, &c.; an evil spirit, demon, 1128; in the -- way, in the devil's name, 1444; ga to the --, go to ruin or perdition, 1452; devillis, n.gen. 1176; dewill, n. devil, fiend, 982. *ME devill, OE dēofol*. See also dele.
devys, n. device, way; at all --, in every way, in all respects, 302. *ME, OF devis*
devysit, pt.3 s. devised, invented, 886. *ME devyse, OF deviser*
dewill, see devill and dele.
dicht, pt.3 s. dressed, arrayed, 422. *ME dighte, OE dihtan*
did, see do.
difficulté, n. difficulty, perplexing question, 2138. *ME, OF difficulté*
dignité, n. dignity, high estate, 2722. *ME, OF dignité*
direct, v.tr. to address (a letter) to a pers. or persons, 145. *ME directe, L directus, p.p. of dirigere* *charger*
discharge, v.tr. to discharge, pay off (a debt), 871. *ME discharge, OF des-*
disciple, n. disciple, pupil, 614-5. *ME, OF disciple*
discover, v.tr. disclose, reveal, 2370; discouerit, p.p. found out, exposed, 2760; discoverit, pt.3 s.refl. revealed his secret, 2340. *ME discouer, OF descovrir*
diseis, n. disquiet, trouble, 2095. *ME disese, OF desaise* *desguiser*
disgysit, p.p. transformed, altered for the worse, 339, 464. *ME disgyse, OF*
dishonour, n. disgrace, ignominy, 1603, 2501. *ME dishonour, OF deshonor, -ur*
disparit, p.p. despairing, having given up hope, 2620. *ME dispaire, -spare, OF despeir-, tonic stem of desperer*
disposicioun, n. disposition, action of arranging or determining, 2720. *ME, OF disposicion*
dissaif, v.tr. to deceive, mislead, 1862; dissauit, pt.3 pl. misled, 2112-3. *ME dyssa(y)ve, OF deceiv-, tonic stem of deceveir*
dissever, pr.1 pl.subj. part, separate, 217. *ME dissever, OF disseverer*

distance, n. discord, disagreement, 1901. *ME, OF distance*
distres, n. distress, severe trouble, 836. *ME distresse, OF destresse*
distroye, v.tr. to destroy, 359, 1371, 1688; distroyit, p.p. destroyed, 349, 1401. *ME distroye, OF destruire*
diuers, adj. various, 531. *ME, OF divers(e), L diversus*
diuinité, n. the science of divine things, 1701. *ME, OF divinité*
do, v.tr. to do, perform, 85, 452, 560, &c.; with dat. of pers. affected by the act performed, 1675, 1684; v.intr. to act, 1427, 1845, 2055, &c.; to fare, 2027; to operate, be effective, 1614; imperat. perform, 400, 612, 1502, &c.; act, 967, 1289, 1347, &c.; causal use, with obj. + inf., to make or cause a pers. to do someth., 1553; pr. perform, 903, 1260, 1505, &c.; act, 967; with to (the pers. affected by the act performed) 2457; as subst. for vb. just used, 2124, 2504, 2781; pr.subj. 2562; did, pt. bestowed, gave, 85, 2727; exerted, used, 953; performed, 1406, 1408, 1414; committed, 1641; acted, 1713, 2697; subst. for vb. just used, 286, 310, 323, &c.; dois, pr.3 s. fares, 304; subst. for vb. just used, 1264; done, p.p. performed, 730, 1359, 1378, &c.; placed, 1013, 1015, 1149, 1322; finished, brought to an end, 1814; subst. for vb. just used, 895; with to or with dat., 1404, 1565. *ME do(n), OE dōn*
dochter, n. daughter, female child, 127, 2625; douchter, 1347, 1472, 1476, &c.; douchteris, pl. 874. *ME doghter, OE dohtor*
dog, n. dog, hound, 1428, 1434; doggis, pl. 1455. *ME dog, OE docga*
dois, see do.
dolour, n. grief, distress of mind, 16, 800. *ME, OF dolour*
dome, n. judgment (formally pronounced), 2254; to give --, 2673; to give for --, 2676. *ME dome, OE dōm*
done, see do.
douchter, see dochter.
dovn(e), downe, adv. down, in a descending direction, to the ground, from above, 549, 553, 738, &c.; to put --, destroy, 581, 811, 961, 1812; set --, seated, 734; down (to a dog), 1444. *ME doun(e), LOE dūne, for earlier of-dūne & ā-dūne*
dowt, n. doubt, 737, 899. *ME dowte, OF d(o)ute*
dowtis, pr.1 s. fear, 811; dowtit, pt. 3 sg. doubted, mistrusted, 144. *ME dowte, OF d(o)uter*
dowtles, adv. certainly, undoubtedly, 1434. *F.* n. *+ -les*
dranke, see drink.
draw(e), v.tr. to draw, pull out, 729; to drag (a criminal) at a horse's tail, 932; to pull anything after one, said of horses, 1778; to disembowel as a traitor or criminal, 2776; draw, imperat. pull, 905; drawin, drawyn, p.p. disembowelled, 364, 2737; pulled out of the sheath, 472; led or brought into a specified state or condition, 849; drew(e), pt. pulled out of the sheath, 491, 568, 910; pulled after them, 945; -- abak, moved back, 220; -- away, removed, 1541; -- neir, approached, 1546; -- wp, pulled up, hoisted, 2490. *ME drawe, OE draȝan, ON draga*
dredand, see dreid, v.
dreid, n. fear, 393, 550, 713, &c.; with obj.cl. 72, 914, 2494; doubt, 1026, 1779, 2117. *F. vb.*
dreid, v.intr. to be greatly afraid, 2717; pr.1 s. look forward to with terror or anxiety, with obj.cl. 516, 863, 1175; dredand, pr.p. fearing, with obj. cl., 1218. *ME drede(n), OE an-, ondrǣdan*
dreidles, adv. undoubtedly, 150. *Prec.*
dremar, n. dreamer, 1735; dremaris, n.pl. dreamers, visionaries, 1836, 1863. *F. vb.*

dreme, n. dream, vision during sleep, 2118, 2149; **dremes**, n.pl. dreams, visions, 1702, 2112-3. *ME dreme, a blend of OE drēam, joy, and ON draumr, dream*
dreme, v.intr. to dream, have visions in sleep, 1718, 1764, 1768; pr.1 s. see or imagine in sleep, 1750; **dremyt**, p.p. tr. dreamed, beheld in sleep, 1762, 1776; pt.s. dreamed, intr. 1757, tr. 2153. *ME dremen, answering in meaning to ON dreyma*
dremyng, n. dreaming, 1721. *F. vb.*
drest, p.p. treated, 246. *ME dresse, OF dresser*
drew(e), see **draw(e)**.
drink, v.tr. to drink, swallow down, 1824; **dranke**, pt.3 s. drank, 1204; **drynkand**, pr.p. drinking, partaking of liquid or liquor, 2616. *ME drinke, OE drincan*
drinke, n. drink, beverage, 698. *ME drink, OE drinc*
drinkyn, n. drinking, 1623. *F. vb.*
drop, v.intr. to fall vertically, to fall in drops, 2067; **dropit**, pt.3 pl. tr. caused to drip, 2063. *ME drop(pe), OE dropan*
drope, n. drop, globule of liquid, 760, 766. *ME drope, OE dropa*
drovne, v.refl. to drown, suffocate by submersion in water, 1112; **drownit**, p.p. drowned (herself), 1118; be --, to incur death by submersion, 1242. *ME drun(e), droun(e), pointing to OE *drūnian, rel. to ON drukna*
drowry, n. love-token, love-gift, 2397. *ME drowrye, OF druerie*
drunkin, adj. drunk, overcome by liquor, 1061, 1065. *F. vb.*
dry, adj. dry, parched, withered, 1482. *ME drye, OE drȳġe*
dryit, pt.3 s. dried, became dry, 1638. *ME drye, OE drȳġan*
drynkand, see **drink**.
duell, v.intr. to reside, 1324; to stay with a pers. 1715; to remain, 1889, 2075, 2300; pr.1 s. remain, 2135; **duelt**, pt. resided, 292, 1030, 1619, &c.; **duelland**, pr.p. residing, 615. *ME dwelle, OE dwellan*
dulce, adv. softly, melodiously, 2571. *L dulcis*
dule, n. mourning, lamentation, 347, 587. *ME dule, OF duel, dol.*
dulefull, adj. sorrowful, sad, 2496. *Prec.*
dulfully, adv. dismally, 2529. *Prec.*
dum, dvm, dwm, adj. dumb, unable to speak, persistently silent, 173, 210, 379, &c. *ME dumb(e), OE dumb*
dungeoun, n. dungeon, 1092. *ME dungeoun, OF donjon*
dur(e), n. door, 1033, 1035, 1075, &c.; **durris**, n.pl. doors, 1915. *ME dur(e), OE duru.* See also **castall-duris**, **kirk-dure**.
dyet, n. diet, prescribed course of food, esp. for medical reasons, 1200. *ME dyet, OF diete, ML dieta*
dyn, n. din, loud noise, 1128, 1706, 1944, 1993. *ME dyn(ne), OE dyn(e)*
dyne, v.intr. to take dinner, 2411, 2696. *ME dyne, OF di(s)ner*
dyner, dynar, n. dinner, repast, 1509, 2375, 2702. *Prec.*

e, n. eye, in fig. application of an especially trusted and valued servant, equivalent to: his right hand, 1214; **eyne**, n.pl. eyes, 100, 2499. *NME e, Ang ēġe, OE ēage*
edder, n. adder, 445, 448, 479. *ME edder, OE nǣdre*
edoke, n. water-lily, 97. *ME edokke, OE ēadocca*
effect, n. effect, result, 91, phr. to take --, to prove successful, to become operative; **effek**, n. effect, 819; in --, in fact, indeed, 673; tak it in --, take advantage of it, 1186. *ME, OF effect, L effectus.* See also **fek**.
effectuoslye, adv. effectually, with powerful effect, 1155. *ME effectuos, ML effectuosus + -lye*
efferit, pt.3 s. was right, fitting, 1017. *Var. of affer(e), vb. f. OF aferir, afferir.*

eft, adv. afterwards, 12. *ME, OE eft*
eftir, adv. afterwards, subsequently, 1335, 2403; sone --, -- sone, 317, 839, 1904, &c.; with the addition of than or syne, 317, 2686, 2721; ane lytill --, 731; prep. after; of time, 1311, 1918, 2779; about, concerning, 1361; after, named after, 15; in search of, 1195; in succession to, 2614. *ME efter, OE æfter, ON eptir*
eftirwart, adv. afterwards, 522, 722, 723, &c. *Normal Scots var. of efterward, OE æfterweard*
eg, n. egg, 2663. *ME, ON egg*
eike, adv. also, 2482. *ME eek(e), ONhb ēc, OE ēac*
eir, adv. before, a little while ago, 1880. *ME er(e), OE ǣr*. See also or, conj.[1]
eis, n. ease; at --, in comfort, unconstrained, 1768. *ME e(i)se, OF eise, aise*
eith, adj. easy, agreeable, 1511. *ME eth(e), OE ēaðe*
eld, n. age, with specification of the number of years, 9. *ME elde, Ang eldo*
eldaris, n.gen.pl. ancestors', 1003. *NME elderes, Ang eldran*
eldest, n. eldest person, 2208. *ME, Ang eldest*
eligant, adj. graceful, comely, 7. *(O)F élégant, L elegans*
ellis, adv. else, otherwise, 612; or --, expressing an alternative, 150, 400, 880, &c. *ME, OE elles*
eme, n. uncle, 629, 648, 706, 713. *ME eme, OE ēam*
empriour, n. emperor, 1, 15, 25, &c.; emprio(u)ris, n.gen. 820-21, 2527. *Var. of Emperour, OF empereor*
empryce, emprice, empris, emprys, n. empress, 10, 205, 277, &c.; used without ending as a possessive, 289, 524-5, 820-21, &c. *ME emprice, emperise, OF emperesse*
emprys, n. renown, distinction, 3. *ME, OF emprise*
empyr(e), n. empire, imperial rule or dignity, 6, 114, 1870, &c. *ME, OF empire*
end, n. end, termination of existence, death (of a person), 1572; phr. make an -- of, finish, 876. *ME end, OE ende*
ending, n. end, close of a period of time, 88. *ME ending, OE endung*
endis, pr.3 s. come to an end, after line 2782. *ME end, OE endian*
enemys, n.pl. enemies, foes, 175, 267, 1671, &c. *ME enemy, OF enemi*
ensample, n. example, illustrative instance, 363, 1183, 1591, &c.; phr. tak -- be, take as a practical warning, 2561; ensampillis, n.pl. examples, 2557. *ME, AN ensample*. See also example & sample.
entent, n. intention, phr. with gud --, with good intentions, 1107. *ME,OF entent*
enter, v.intr. to enter, go in, 934, 1034; enterit, pt.3 s. entered, 1919, 1929, &c. *ME enter, OF entrer*
entré, n. entry, opportunity of entering, 869. *ME entré, OF entrée*
erandis, n.pl. errands, 1903. *ME erand, OE ærende, ON erende, erindi*
erar, adv. sooner, rather, 73, 168; with contrasted vb.with na, 1495. *ME erer, OE ǣror*
erd, n. earth, ground as surface, 104, 443, 461, &c.; soil, 321, 1711. *(N)ME erd(e), OE eard*
erdit, p.p. buried, 956, 1822; pt.3 pl. 1825. *Prec.*
erle, n. earl, 688. *ME erl(e), OE eorl*
ernist, n. serious intention, earnest, 413. *ME ernest, OE eornost*
ernistlye, adv. seriously, 102. *Prec. + -lye*
eschape, v.intr. to get off safely, 535. *ME eschape, OF eschaper*
eschewe, eschow, v.tr. to avoid, keep clear of, 22, 382. *OF eschever, eschiwer, eschuer*. See also chewe.
espyid, p.p. espied, discovered, 681. *ME espye, OF espier*. See also aspy.
etand, see ete.

ete, pt.3 s. intr. ate, consumed food, 555; tr. consumed as food, 559, 2426; etand, pr.p. eating, partaking of food, 2616; etyn, p.p. intr. eaten, 2433. *ME ete, OE etan*
ettillit, pt.3 s. planned, intended to do something, 2012. *ME ettill, ON ætla*
etyn, see ete.
euer, adv. ever, at any time in the future, 218, 2475; at any time in the past, 1206, 2159, 2393; continually, 2313, 2615; evir, adv. ever, at all, 160, 802; constantly, always, 846; at any time, 858; -- as, whenever, 2373; for --, 488; for -- mair, for ever, 1814. *ME ever, evir, OE æfre.*
euerilk, adj. every, 873 (-- deile) *NME ever ilk, OE æfre + ilca*
euermar, adv. evermore, constantly, 2611. *NME evermare, OE æfre mā*
evyn(e), adv. even, exactly, 82, 2152, 2184; directly, 1937; indeed, truly, 357; ewin, ewyn, adv. even, quite, fully, 1284; -- now, right now, 1112. *ME evin, OE efne*
ewill, adj. evil, harmful, 981. *ME evyll, OE yfel*
ewin, ewyn, see evyn(e).
ewyn, n. evening, 1059. *ME evyn, OE ēfen, ǣfen*
example, n. example, guide to conduct, 1269; illustrative instance, 2089. *ME, OF example.* See also ensample & sample.
exceid, v.intr. to exceed, surpass, 630; tr. to outdo, 714. *ME excede, OF exceder, L excedere*
excusit, pt.3 s. offered an excuse for (some fault or failure), 643. *ME excuse, OF excuser, L excusare*
exild, p.p. debarred, deprived, 214. *ME exile, OF exil(i)er, L exiliare*
expart, adj. experienced, learned, 2192; expert, adj. 620. *ME, OF expert, L expertus*
expell, v.tr. to expel, 1007. *ME expelle, OF expeller, L expellere*
expenses, n.pl. expenses, spending of money, 2343. *ME, AN expense, LL expensa*
experiens, n. experience, actual observation of facts, considered as a source of knowledge, 383; proof by actual trial, 641, 764. *ME, OF experience, L experientia*
expert, see expart.
extremiteis, n.pl. extremities, uttermost parts (of the body), 652. *ME extremyté, OF extremité, L extremitas*
eyne, see e, n.

face, n. the face of a person, 220, 240, 243, &c. *ME, OF face*
fader, n. father, male parent, 15, 221, 223, &c.; faderis, gen.s. 233, 911, 2779. *ME fader, OE fæder*
faile, n. fail; but --, without fail, assuredly, 708, 726; fale, n. fail; withoutin --, 42. *ME faile, OF fail(l)e.* See also falȝe v.
fair, far, adj. fair, beautiful, good-looking; of persons, 7, 115, 690, &c.; of plants, trees, &c. 302, 307, 334, &c.; of tracts of land, forest, &c. 73, 78, 294; of a city, building, 2285, 2596; of words: pleasing at the first hearing, 578, 2630; of countenance: benignant, kindly, 844; of behaviour: gentle, 1882; of a well: clean, pure, 2154; of the weather: fine, not wet or stormy, 2049; fair, adv. fairly, quietly, 428; farer, adj. fairer, brighter, 2040; farest, adj. fairest, finest, 1650, 2044. *ME fair, OE fæġer*
fair, v.intr. to go, travel, 66; to fare, 'get on' (well or ill), 1593; fair, imperat., -- on, go away, 2073; faris, pr.3 s., -- of, happens to (a pers.), 1264; fure, pt.3 s. went, 1124. *ME fare, OE faran, p.t. fōr.* See also farandly.
fair, n. entertainment, cheer, 1960. *ME far(e), OE faru, fær*
fais, n.pl. enemies, 1958, 2303, 2311. *NME fa, OE ġefā*

faith, n. declaration of good faith, pledge to secrecy, 687. *ME faith, OF feit,*
fald, v.tr. to fold, 2586; to embrace, 1137. *NME fald, ONhb falda* *feid*
fale, see **faile**.
fall, v.intr. to fall, to drop from a high or rel. high position, 758, 890, 1115, &c.; to come down, 1690; -- **into**, to pass into some condition, 1210; to happen, occur, 2475; with **dat.** as **indir.obj.**, to happen, come to pass, 1159, 2073; -- **of**, happen to (a pers.), 2104; **tr.** to meet with, to fall into, 391, 517, 603, &c.; **fallyn**, **p.p.**, -- **in gret puretē**, 2692; -- **on** (a pers.) said of vengeance, 773; **fell**, **pt.3 s.** befell, happened, **absol.** 518; -- **to** (a pers.), 2106; met with, 392, 604, 816, &c.; **fell**, **pt. pers.** dropped down, 461, 896, 1637, &c.; -- **in(to)**, got into a certain state, 836, 841, 877; -- **to**, set to work, 1460; -- **to** (somebody), came as lot, portion or possession, 1748, 2106. *ME falle(n), OE feallan, fēoll, fallen*
fall, n. fall, a dropping down from a high position, 1808. *F. vb.*
fallous, **fallows**, n.pl. fellows, comrades, 37, 1632. *ME felow, OE fēolaȝa, ON félage*
fals, adj. false, mendacious, treacherous, 358, 501, 579, &c. *ME fals(e), LOE fals, OF fals*
falset, n. falseness, deceitfulness, 2043, 2562. *OF falset, ML falsatum*
falsly, adv. falsely, wrongfully, 1157. *F. adj.*
falt, n. default, offence, 1519; **for -- or**, through lack or want of, 1191, 2655. *OF falt, fau(l)te*
falȝe, v.tr. to fail, lose power or strength, 332; with **neg.**: to miss or avoid, **to -- + inf.**, 457; **falȝeit**, **pt.3 s.** would come to an end, become extinct, 119; lost, 1563. *OF faillir.* See also **fa(i)le n.**
fame, n. fame, renown, 617, 705, 718; character, reputation, 1228. *ME, OF fame*
famele, n. family, household, 424. *OF famille*
famous, adj. famous, renowned, 616. *ME, AN famous, L famosus*
fand(e) pt., see **fynd**.
fande, v.tr. with **to + inf.** to try or endeavour **to** do something, 1956. *ME fande, OE fandian*
fane, adj. & adv. see **fayne**, adj. & adv.
fang, v.tr. to clasp, embrace, 1137. *ME fang(e(n), replacing earlier fon, OE fōn, p.p. fangen, ON fanga*
far, adj., see **fair** adj.
far, adv. far; **so --**, to such a great degree, 849; **be --**, greatly, very much, 1241. *ME far, OE feorr.* See also **fer**.
farandly, adv. having a specified appearance, disposition: **ill --**, 1569. *F. No. pr.p. of faren*
farer, **farest**, see **fair adj.**
faris, see **fair v.**
fassoun, n. fashion, style, 2420. *ME fasoun, OF fasson*
fast, adv. closely, firmly fixed in its place, 1075, 1125, &c.; firmly tied, 253; firmly attached to something else, 2326; quickly, rapidly, 372, 468, 1064, &c.; vehemently, 2538; **also --**, immediately, 99; **als -- as**, as soon as, 1847. *ME fast, OE fæste, ON fast*
fast, v.intr. to fast, go without food, 2494. *ME fast, OE fæstan, ON fasta*
fastly, adv. definitely, 681. *ME fastely, OE faestlīce*
fawnand, see **fawne**.
fawne, v.tr. to fawn on, show delight or fondness to, 471; **fawnand**, **pr.p.** showing delight, 1443. *ME fawne, OE faȝenian*
fayne, adj. glad, well-pleased, 1774; with **of** (of the source of gladness) 1730; **fane**, **adj.** 402, 2681; with **to** (do or undergo someth.), 2252; **fayne**, **adv.** gladly, willingly, 605; **fane**, **adv.** 139, 1048, 2507; **full --**, 1467. *ME fayn(e), OE faeȝen, ON feginn*

fecht, v.intr. to fight, engage in fighting, 2302. *ME fehten, ONhb fehta*
fed, see feid, v.
fedder, n. feather, in the plumage of a bird, 2029. *ME fedder, OE feðer*
feid, n. feud, hatred, mortal enmity, ill-will, 803, 2245, &c.; wnder --, under a standing enmity, 2316; for ony --, 1843, see expl.note. *NME fede, OF fe(i)de*
feid, v.tr. to feed, supply with food, 32, 1832; fed, p.p. supplied with food, 1924; pt. 697, 1202, 2658. *ME feede, OE fēdan, p.p. fēdd*
feile, adj. much, great, 773. *ME feill(e), OE fela*
feir, adj. sound, unharmed: haile and --, 478. *EME fere, OE *fēre, ON fœrr*
feir, n. match, equal, 2043. *ME fere, OE gefēra*
feist, n. feast; without art. feasting, good cheer, 1985; fest, n. religious festivity, 149; sumptuous meal, 1989. *ME, OF feste, L festa*
feist, v.tr. to regale, entertain by feasting, 834. *ME feste, OF fester*
feit, n.pl. feet, of man or dog, 932, 1454. *ME pl. feete, OE fēt.* See also fut(e).
fek, n. effect, force, value, 2664. *Reduced form of* effect. See also effect.
feld, n. field, tilting ground, 423, 426. *ME feld(e), OE feld*
fele, n. mental feeling, perception, understanding, 2632. *F fele vb.*
fele, pr.1 s. perceive by smell, 1388; feld, pt. 3 s. -- of, 726. *ME fele, OE fēlan, pt. fēlde*
felicité, n. felicity, happiness, 1005. *ME, OF felicité, L felicitas*
fell, adj. severe, grievous, painful, 995; adv. fiercely, excessively, 1424. *ME fell(e), OF fel*
fell, pt. see fall, v.
fen, n. foul matter, filth, 913, 955. *ME fen, OE fen(n), ON fen*
fende, v.tr. to defend from want, maintain, refl. 2653. *Aphetic form of* defend.
fenȝeit, see fayne v.
fer, adj. far, remote, 527, 2298; adv. far, to a great degree or extent, 106, 235, 415, &c.; be --, be mekle --, by far, very much, 647, 1594. *ME fer(re), OE feor(r).* See also far.
ferd, ord.num. fourth, 47, 1296, 1756. *NME ferd, ONhb fēarða, OE fēorða*
ferlyit, pt.3 s. wondered, marvelled, 2061. *F. adj. ME ferly, ON ferlig-r, monstrous, dreadful*
fessynnit, pt.3 s. fastened, attached, 1529; to burde him -- he, he lodged him, 2307. *ME festnen, OE festnian, fæstnian*
fest, see feist.
fet, pt.3 s. fetched, brought, 2704. *ME fet(t), OE fetian*
fetche, v.tr.to fetch, go in quest of, and convey or conduct back, 1549; fetchit, pt.3 s., 1084. *ME fetch(e), OE fecc(e)an*
figour, n. figure, shape, appearance, 2272, 2289. *ME figour, OF figure*
fill, n. fill, enough to satisfy want of desire, 1494. *ME fill, OE fyllu*
fillit, pt.3 s. filled, made full, 759, 828. *ME fille(n), OE fyllan, ON fylla*
first, adj., ord.num. first, prior to all others, 159; first in order of succession, 24, 372, 1735, &c.; adv. first, before some other specified or implied thing, time, event, 565, 954, 1349, 2547. *ME first, OE fyrst*
fische, v.tr. to catch, get by artifice or patient effort: to -- a caus, 990. See expl.note. *ME fische, OE fiscian*
fitchit, pt.3 pl. removed, pulled aside, 2189. *Of obsc.orig.*
five, card.num. five, 46. *ME fif, five, OE fīf(e).* See also fyft.
flawe, see fle,
fle, v.intr. to fly, move through the air with wings, 2652, 2659; flawe, pt.3 pl. flew, 2681. *ME flie, pt. flaȝe, OE flē(o)ȝan*
fle, v.intr. to flee, take flight, 543; pr.3 pl.subj. tr. flee, avoid falling into, refrain from, 2562; fled, pt.3 s. intr. took flight, 453; pt. 3 pl.tr.

fled, ran away from, 1803. *ME fle(e), wk.pt. fled(de), ONhb flēa, OE flēon*
fleyt, v.intr. float (in water), 2591. *ME fleete, OE flēotan*
flicht, n. flight, the act of fleeing; tuke the --, 2680. *ME flight, OE flyht*
flour, n. flower, blossom, 328. *ME, OF flour*
flude, n. flood, river, stream, 2155. *ME flud(e), OE flōd*
flure, n. floor, 440, 944, 2189; ground, 1787. *ME fl(o)ure, OE flōr*
folk, n. people of a partic. class, indic. by adj., 1622, 1832. *ME folk, OE folc, ON folk*
followe, v.tr. to act in accordance with, 1243; follow, pr.3 pl. follow, come after, 2617; followis, pr.3 pl. id., 2671; fol(l)owit, pt.3 s. intr. followed, 424, 2529; pt.3 pl. tr., 1851. *ME follow(e), OE folȝian*
foly, n. folly, foolishness, 2718. *ME, OF folie*
for, conj. because, seeing that, since, 4, 9, 21, &c. *ME, OE for*
for, prep. on account of, by reason of, 72, 363, 371, &c.; with a view to, for the sake of, 13, 257, 490, &c.; on behalf of, to serve, defend, 114, 288, 1216, &c.; as, as being, in place of, 141, 378, 982, &c; in spite of, 437, 750, 1450, 2475; in return for, in payment of, 1197, 1221, 1223, &c.; (to continue) during (a cert. time), 488, 1236, 1814, 2473; to set oneself -- a sin, prepare to commit, 1426; to send -- somebody, 1571, 1984, 2547; -- quhy, wherefore, 107, 571; -- thi, therefore, 144, 154, 963, &c.; -- till with inf. 721, 882, 1007, &c.; -- to with inf. 341, 488, 549, &c. *ME, OE for*
forbed, v.tr. forbid, prohibit, 2150; forbeid, pr.3 s.subj. in deprecatory phr., absol. 1422; with clause as dir.obj. 1780. *ME forbede(n), OE forbēodan*
forbot, n. interdiction, prohibition, 1584. *ME forbot, ME, OE forbod*
ford, contr. of for it, in the phr. I stand ford, I guarantee, 362, 1739.
fordo, v.tr. destroy, kill, 574, 1284, 672; fordone, p.p. killed, ruined, 1176, 2217. *ME fordo, OE fordōn*
forest, n. forest of trees, 528, 540, 2695. *ME, OF forest, ML foresta*
forfarne, p.p. ruined, lost, 457; forfur, pt.3 pl. caused to perish, undid, 2065. *ME forfare(n), OE forfaran, pt. forfōr*
forgaf, pt.3 s. forgave, pardoned, 1413; forgevin, forgevyn, p.p. forgiven, 1420, 1466; forgevis, pr.3 s. forgives, 1351; forgif, imperat. give up, cease to harbour, 2546. *NME forgeve, Ang forgefan, OE forȝiefan*
forgeving, n. forgiveness, 1462. *Prec.*
forgifnes, n. forgiveness, pardon of a fault, 2540. *NME forgifnes, OE forȝifnes*
forhed, n. forehead, 1626. *ME forhed(e), OE forhēafod*
forlor, v.tr. lose, 880; forlorne, p.p. completely lost, destroyed, 584. *F. ME forlore, OE forlēosan, p.p. forloren*
foroutin, prep. without, 592. *OE forūtan, forūton*
fors, n. force, violence, 946. *ME, OF force*
forsaid, p.p. mentioned before, 1529. *ME forsaid, OE foresæȝd*
forsaike, pr.1 s. renounce, give up, 1583. *ME forsake, OE forsacan*
forsit, p.p. violated, ravished, 379, 387, 513, &c. *ME force, OF forcer*
forsuth, adv. truly, in truth, and used to introduce a statement, 157, 380, 1887, &c. *ME for soþe, OE forsōþ*
forthi, see thi
fortonyt, p.p. fortunate, favoured by fortune, lucky, 2576. *ME (wel) fortuned, OF fortuner*
forty, card.num. forty, 1143. *ME forti(e), OE fēowertiȝ*
forȝet, p.p. forgotten, lost remembrance of, 283, 1988; omitted to take, left behind inadvertently, 1531; pt.3 s. ceased to retain in one's memory, 958. *ME forȝete, OF forȝi(e)tan*
fosterit, p.p. fostered, nourished, 1924. *ME foster, ON fóstra*
foule, foull, adj. foul, loathsome, filthy, 912, 1534; absol. 2073 (see expl. note). *ME foul(e), OE fūl, ON fúll.* See also fowlely.
found, v.intr. to set out, start, 489; to betake oneself to, 1629. *ME found, OE fundian*

foundement, n. foundation or base of a building, 1799. *ME foundement, OF fondement*
foundyn, see fynd.
four, fowre, card.num. four, 49, 251, 367, &c. *ME four, fowr, OE fēower*
fow(e), adj. full (of something), 759, 1740. *Reduced form of ME & OE full.* See also full.
fowlely, adv. foully, shamefully, 513, 1969. See also foule.
fra, conj. from the time when, as soon as, 535, 537, 1113, &c. *F. prep.*
fra, prep. from, indicating departure from a place or pers., 1086, 1382, 1805, &c.; indic. distance, 443; indic. separation, deprivation, 215, 484, 1399, &c.; indic. deliverance, defence, 475, 1815, 1952, &c.; indic. absence, 1889, 1894; indic. the pers. or other source or origin of something, 317, 634; from, in respect of time, 697, 713. *NME fra, ON frá*
fragrant, adj. fragrant, sweet-smelling, 313, 727. *F fragrant, L fragrans*
fraitlye, adv. in alarm or fear, 1932. *P.p. of fray, ME fray, aphetic for affray, OE effraier*
fravde, n. fraud, deceitful conduct, 2069. *ME, OF fraude, L fraud-*
fre, adv. freely, with good will, 2613. *ME fre(e), OE frēo*
frendis, n.pl. kinsmen, relatives, 803, 1023, 1331, 2102. *ME frend(e), OE frēond*
freschenes, n. freshness, youthful appearance, 2272. *ME fresshnes, f. OF fresche, fem. + -nes*
freth, imperat. set free, grant safety, 400. *ME frethe, OE freoðian*
frist, v.intr. to make delay, 1503; p.p. tr. granted respite, 1590. *ME fryst, frest, ON fresta*
froit, n. fruit of a tree, 552; frut(e), n. id., 315, 324, 328, &c. *ME froite, fru(i)t, OF fruit*
frutfull, adj. bearing plenty of fruit, 295. *Prec. + -full*
fude, n. food, nourishment, 2655. *ME foode, fud(e), OE fōda*
fule, n. fool, one lacking wisdom, 347. *ME foul, fole, OF fol*
fulfill, v.tr. to satisfy, 1071; fulfillit, p.p. completely full of,2742. *ME fulfil(l), OE fulfyllan*
full, adj. full, 1694; -- of, filled with, containing abundance of, 374, 831, 891, &c.; covered with, 440. (*NED* 1563). *ME, OE ful(l)*
full, adv. very, exceedingly, with adj. 402, 635, 703, &c.; with adv. 38, 189, 191, &c.; -- sone, 1360; -- litill , 2432; fully, completely, 769. *Prec.* See also fow.
fundin, fundyn, see fynd.
fure, see fair v.
furth, adv. out from a place, 1034, 1055, 1121, &c.; away, 2366, 2385, 2417; onwards, of time, 713; afterwards, 1358; do --, go ahead, 1795; gif -- (dome), publish, pronounce, 2673. *ME furth, forth, OE forþ*
furthwith, adv. forthwith, at once, 1637. *Prec. + -with*
fussoun, n. abundance, 336, 1765. *ME fusoun, OF fu(i)son, var. of foison*
fut(e), n. foot; scho (he) gat on --, up, into a standing position, 242, 1074. *ME fote, fut, OE fōt.* See also feit.
fyft, ord.num. fifth, 50, 1852. *ME fift(e), OE fīfta.* See also five.
fyle, v.tr. to violate, defile, 281; fylis, pr.3 s. defiles, renders dirty, 1454; fylit, ppl.a. defiled, dirtied, 1541. *ME fyle, OE fȳlan f. fūl adj., foul.*
fynd, v.tr. to find, discover, come upon, obtain, 980, 1724; 1753, &c.; discover by experience or trial, 2313; pr.1 s. come upon in a cert. condition, 1576; perceive, 2133; pr.1 pl. discover, obtain, 1717; pr.subj. come across, meet with, 1266; discover, 2188; fand(e), pt. came upon in a cert.condition, 478, 479, 1079, 2355; discovered, 885, 923, 1757, &c.; discovered by ex-

perience or trial, 1052; discovered, by scrutiny, 2289; perceived, 2159; foundyn, p.p. found, discovered, 1148; fundin, fundyn, p.p. found, met with, 737, 1011, 1101. *ME find, OE findan, pt. fand, p.p. funden*

fyne, adj. fine, delicately beautiful (of a tree), 313. *ME fyne, OF fin, fem. fine*

fyre, n. fire, 1380, 1386, 1388, &c.; fig. fervour, 1835; torture or death by burning, 1869, 2749 (*NED* 1646). *ME fyr(e), OE fȳr*

fyreflaucht, n. lightning, 2030. *Prec. + ME flaght, ? OE *flaht, fleaht*

ga, v.intr. to leave, depart, 1094, 1249, 1263; move to, take one's way, 1452; -- with, to accompany, 1173, 1366, 2405; -- dovne, to be overthrown, to fall, 549; Y. had lattin his newo liffand --, Y. had allowed his nephew to depart alive, or go on living, 785; v.tr. to -- his way, with cogn.acc., to go one's way, to move away, depart, 1567; pr.1 s. take a specif. course, 2153; pr.2 s.subj. depart, 1348; gais, pr.3 s. takes his way, moves, 224; gane, p.p. departed, 227, 1074, 1805, &c.; dead, lost, 118; taken one's way to, 365, 1817, &c.; (of time) past, 920, 1847; -- away, departed, 1948; -- by (of time), past, 1335, 2038; -- by (of things), gone by, past, 1466. *NME ga, ONhb ga, OE gān.* See also gang & go.

gadderit, p.p. gathered, assembled, 2607; gaderit, pt.3 s. gathered, collected, amassed, 827. *ME gader, gaddren, OE gaderian*

gaf, gaif, see gif v.

gait, n. way, road, street, 1101; a partic. way, course, 2436; by the --, alongside the road, 2148. *ME gate, ON gata*

gallous, gallhous, n. gallows for hanging persons, 368, 972, 1850, 2238. *ME galewes, OE galȝan*

ganand, ppl.a. appropriate, suitable, 1217 (absol.), 1648. *NME gainand f. ON gegna*

gang, v.intr. to go, move, take one's way, foll. by an inf. with to, to express a purpose, 169; be carried, taken, 674, 972; -- in, go into, 2574; take one's way to, 1138; take its course, 2254. *NME gang(e), OE gangan, ON ganga.* See also ga and go.

gar, imperat.sg. cause, have (someth. done), 1995, pl. 2645; gar, inf. with obj. + act.inf., make, cause to, 262, 310, &c.; with obj. + pass.inf., 715, 1142; pr.subj. 606, 788, &c.; garris, imperat.pl. make, cause to, give instructions to (do or make someth.), with obj. + act.inf. 263; with obj. + pass. inf. 999, 1318; pr. with obj. + act.inf. 332, 500, &c.; gerris, imperat.pl. make, cause to, with obj. + pass.inf. 397; pr.3 s. with obj. + act.inf. 765; gart, p.p. made, caused to, with obj. + act.inf. 2705; pt. with obj. + act. inf. 87, 145, 176, &c.; with obj. + pass.inf. 1848, 2778. *Var. of ger, NME ger(r), ON gera*

gard, n. guard, body of soldiers, 2305. *ME, OF garde*

garding, n. garden, 1366. *ME, ONF gardin*

gardyner, gardiner, gardynar, gardinar, n. gardener, 290, 298, 305, &c. *ME gardiner, ONF *gardinier, ML gardinarius*

garris, gart, see gar.

gat, see get.

gavillok, n. an iron crowbar or lever, 1744. *ME gavilok, OE gafeluc*

gay(e), adj. gay, cheerful, handsome, 136, 1492, 1922. *ME gay(e), OF gai*

generacioun, n. lineage, progeny, 119. *ME, OF generacioun, L generatio*

generale, adj. general, established for the whole of a cert. territory, 2604. *ME generale, OF general, L generalis*

gentill, adj. noble, 405; appropriate to one of good birth, 412; of a good breed or kind, 481; absol.pl. gentle (persons), 536. *ME, OF gentil* gentrys, n. noble descent or rank, 116. *ME gent(e)rise, OF genterise*

gerris, see gar.

get, imperat. obtain, 679; v.tr. to obtain, 126, 140, 333, &c.; procreate, 1333; capture, 1678; -- ... away, succeed in destroying someth., 1682; -- out, succeed in coming or going out, 900; gat, pt. obtained, 537, 541, 869, &c.; begot, 669, 694; caused to come, 2015; sought out, 2142; -- on fut(e), rose, 242, 1074; -- wp, rose, 1908, 2460; gottin, p.p. obtained, begotten, 117, 712. *ME get, p.p. geten, goten, ON geta, pt. gat, p.p. getenn*

gif, conj. if, whether, 26, 90, 118, &c.; -- that, 500, 608; bot -- (that), unless, 388, 851, 860. *Var. of ME if, OE ȝif, by assim. to gif, vb.*

gif, imperat. give, commit, entrust, 32, 39, 45, &c.; offer, 398, 856; pay, 1223; hand over, 1377; -- furth, deliver, pronounce, 2673; gif, v.tr. to give, hand over, 812, 1097, 1232, &c.; bestow, 1495; pay, make over, 1688; give in marriage, 2481, 2613; -- leif, to permit, 2320; pr.subj. cause to have, 820, 1911; make over, 1717; deliver, 2676; hand over, 2733; grant, 1436, 2509; gaf, gaif, pt. gave, offered, 179, 1024, &c.; put forth: a shout, 244, 450, a blow, 1636; bestowed, 704; administered (medicine) 709; handed over, 1692, 1935, 2454; handed over as a present, 2362; handed over in marriage, 2485, 2684; awarded judgement, pronounced, 2775; -- agane, restored, 2383; -- owre, left off, abandoned, 486; -- wp, handed over, parted with, 2472. *ME gif, OE ȝifan, ON gefa*

girth, n. safety, refuge, 1946; to give --, to grant respite, 2509. *ME grith, OE griþ, ON grið*

gittern, n. kind of guitar, cithern, 2522. *ME giterne, OF guiterne*

glad, adj. happy, pleased, 60, 293; pleased or delighted with someth., 2698. *ME glad, OE glæd*

glewe, n. mirth, joyful music, 1962. *ME glew, OE glēow*

gnawyn, n. gnawing, 555. *ME gnawyng f. OE gnagan*

go, imperat. go, move (into a specif. direction), with simple inf. 305; v.intr. with inf. + to, 2467; -- with, to accompany, 216, 2173. *ME go.* See also ga & gang.

God, n. always in the Christian sense, 125, 177, 746, &c.; -- wait, 209, 597, 2335, &c.; as -- wald, 442; wald --, 523; be --, 787; gif -- it ples, 1393; -- gif hir cair, 1911; -- forbeid, 1422, 1780; God(d)is gen.s. 678, 2230, &c. *ME, OE god*

gold, n. gold, the most precious metal, 728, 825, 880, &c.; attrib. made of gold, 1704, 2363; filled with gold, 1710. *ME, OE gold*

gottin, see get.

governans, n. rule, control, command, 2226, 2402. *OE governance, OF gouvernance*

governit, pt.3 s. ruled with supreme authority, 2688, 2780. *ME governe, OF gover-ner*

governour, n. governor, officer in command of a fortress, 839; ruler, 2700. *ME governour, OF gouvernour, governeor*

grace, n. grace, favour, benevolence, 177, 818, &c.; pleasantness, 315; mercy, clemency, 537. *ME, OF grace*

grant, imperat. grant, allow, 1462; pr.1 s. grant, 1464, 1720; grantit, pt.3 s. granted, allowed, 2323, 2416. *ME grant, OF granter*

grat, see gret.

grath, v.tr. to prepare, put in order, 1995. *NME graith, ME greiðen, ON greiða*

grathly, adj. or adv. prompt(ly), careful(ly), 566. *ME grathli adj.,(N)ME graythely adv., ON greiðligr, adv. -liga*

gredy, adj. greedy, covetous, 1225. *ME gredi, OE grǣdig*

gref, pr.subj. grieve, provoke to anger, 1349; greif, v.tr. to grieve, cause sorrow, 1464; grevit, p.p. distressed, 467, 1458, 2543; angered, 769, 1973. *ME gref, greve, OF grever*

greif, n. grief, feeling of offence, anger, 2589. *ME greef, OF gr(i)ef*
grene, n. green, piece of grassy ground, 74, 78, 2154. *ME grene, OE grēne*
gret, adj. great, of qualities, emotions, conditions, actions or occurrences, 13, 16, 116, &c.; of dimensions: large, 335, 1114; gretar, adj. greater, more important, 2752. *ME grete, OE grēat*
gret, pt.3 s. greeted, saluted, 1305, 1860. *ME grete, OE grētan, grǣtan*
gret, pt.3 s. wept, 490; gretand, pr.p. crying, weeping, 798, 2092; gretis, pr.3 pl. weep, lament, 948; grat, pt. wept, shed tears, 371, 508, 918, &c. *(N)ME grete, Ang grētan*
gretar, see gret adj.
greting, n. weeping, lamentation, 1412, 1461. *F. vb.*
gretis, see gret, wept.
gretlie, gretly, adv. greatly, 61, 257, 701, &c. *F. adj.*
grevit, see gref v.
grevously, adv. grievously, sorrowfully, 593, 1304, 1860. *ME grevous, OF grev(o)us, + -ly*
grew(e), see grow.
grewhound, n. greyhound, 429, 436, 445, &c. *ME grewhounde, greyhound, Ang *grēghund*
grow(e), v.intr. to grow, increase in size, 322, 343; growand, ppl.a. still growing, fairly young, 1389; grew(e), pt.3 s. of vegetation: increased in size, 302; -- wp, sprang up, 319; increased in magnitude, 2155. *ME growe, OE grōwan, pt. grēow*
grutching, n. grumbling, reluctance, 1235. *ME gruching, f. OF gruchier*
gryst, n. corn after grinding, 1203. *ME gryst, OE grīst*
gud, adj. good, of persons, 1224, 2564, 2575; in addressing a pers., 1856, 1921; of material things, or animals, 29, 345, 490, 2490; with abstr.nouns, 61, 166, 398, &c.; of name, fame, 618, 1228; of quantity, 553. *NME gude, ME good, OE gōd*
gud, n. good, benefit, profit, 524, 1006, 1406, &c.; property, 2563; gudis, n.pl. goods, possessions, 876, 1111. *F. adj.*
gud, v.tr. to manure, 309. *ME goden, OE gōdian*
gudding, n. manure, manuring, 331. *Prec.*
gyde, n. guide, one who goes with others to show the way, 2220. *ME gyde, OF guide*
gyn, n. stratagem, trick, 886, 2313, &c. *ME gyn, reduced f. OF engin*

haboundans, n. abundance, a copious supply, 558. *OF habundance*
haboundantly, adv. abundantly, copiously, 943, 950. *F. prec. + -ly*
had, see haf.
haf, aux. inf. have, 239, 379, 381, &c.; pr. 83, 117, 151, &c.; subj. 396, 1000, 1999, &c.; haue, inf. have, 2273; pr. have, 780, 2247; subj.1 s. 608; has, pr. 91, 200, 363, &c.; had, pt. had, 43, 59, 349, &c.; would have, 250, 647, 965. *NME haf, OE habban*
haf, v.tr. to have, possess, 57, 582, 1680, &c.; get somebody into a specif. condition, 133; get, obtain, 328, 927, 1025, &c.; -- in mynd, remember, 2364; imperat. have (mercy, &c.), 1409, 1998, 2396, &c.; pr. ind. have, possess, 37, 230, 599, &c.; subj. 962; haif, v.tr. absol. to obtain, 1691; pr.1 pl. are subjected to, 866; haue, v.tr. have, get, 641, 1494; pr.2 s. have, show, 1477; has, pr. possess(e)s, 92, 261, 1489, &c.; in a weakened sense, 1140, 2130; had, pt.3 pl. took, led, 67 (-- away), 2163, 2595; pt.3 s. held, 1647; pt.1 s. in: -- lever, had rather, 855, 1100, 1241, 2736 (see also lever); pt. possessed, 5, 58, 108, &c.; was affected with, 713, 748, 1204; enjoyed, 843, 2358, 2361; suffered, 2496; entertained in the mind, 1411, 2291;

possessed in a weakened sense, -- with him, 621, 2115; -- in mynd, cherished, 296; had, p.p. consulted as physician, 647; experienced (2725). *NME haf(e), OE habban*

haif, see haf.

haile, see hale.

hair, n. hair (of the head), 278, 462. *NME hare, ON hār*

haist, n. haste; in -- , quickly, expeditiously, 423, 2369, 2513; hast, hurry, 1998; in --, quickly, 1573. *ME hast(e), OF haste.* See also hastely.

hait, adj. hot, excited with sexual desire, 1102. *NME hate, OE hāt*

hald, imperat. refl. remain, 901; v.tr. to hold, keep, 141, 1208, 1227; keep as one's own, 2473; hold in the hands, keep in position, 2585; observe, abide by, 2635; entertain, 2719; pr.subj. hold, detain, 1095; held, pt.3 s. kept (in memory), 719; remained in (a place), 797; maintained, 1885; regarded in a partic. way, 1892; kept in a partic. position, 2003; kept, escaped losing, 2486. *NME hald, ONhb halda, WS hēaldan, pt. hēold*

hale, adj. sound in body, in good health, 700, 707, 1199, 2595; whole, complete, 739, 804, 1971, &c.; haile, adj. safe, sound, 478; whole, entire, 120, 2107; with plur.n. all, 1023; hele, adj. hale, sound, well, 1202, 1206. *NME hal(e), OE hāl, ON heill*

hale, adv. fully, 1278, 1469, 1920, &c.; haile, adv. quite, entirely, 1581. *Prec.*

halely, adv. completely, wholly, 1419, 1518, 1533. *NME halely*

half, adv. qualifying an adv., 2573. *ME half, OE h(e)alf-*

half, n. half, one of two equal parts, 1717, 1726. *ME half, OE h(e)alf, ON hālfa*

hall, n. hall, residence, 75, 2419; large public room in a mansion, palace, 193, 468; company, assembled in a hall, 1544. *ME hall, OE h(e)all*

hals, n. neck, 1489. *ME hals, OE h(e)als, ON hals*

halsit, pt.3 s. saluted, greeted, 592, 978, 1303, &c. *LME halse, ME hailse, ON heilsa*

haly, adj. holy, 487. *NME haly, OE hālig*

halyland, n. Holy Land, 2078. *Prec.* + land

hame, adv. to one's home, house, 303, 706, 916, &c. *NME ham(e), OE hām*

hame, n. home, house, at (his) --, at his house, 1227, 1885, 2404; at --, in my country, 2299; fra --, away from his house, abroad, 1889, 1894, 1905. *Prec.*

hame-come, n. home-coming, 1891. See also come n.

hame-cummyn, n. home-coming, arrival at home, 1077. (MS has Eme cummyn)

ham(e)wart, adv. homeward, towards home, 276, 1360, 2493. *NME ham(w)ard(e), OE hāmweard*

hammer, n. hammer, instrument used for beating, breaking, &c., 2019. *ME hamer, OE hamor*

hammer, adj. var. of Hamburgh, in -- barrell, a kind of large barrel, 1740.

hand, n. hand, 219, 562, 1635, &c.; at --, near, close by, 852; in --, in the hand, 1647, 1935, 1940; tuke on --, undertook, set oneself to carry out, 1521, 1790; handis, n.pl. hands, 252, 462, 1379, &c.; in -- tane, taken into custody, 1818. *ME, OE hand*

hang, v.tr. to hang, put to death by hanging, 971; hangit, p.p. put to death by hanging, 364, 1268, &c. *ME hang, OE hangian, ON hanga*

hantit, pt.3 s. remained, 2402. *ME hante(n), OF hanter*

happinnit, pt.impers. 419, 538, 631, &c.; with indir. obj. 676, 2327; pers. had the hap or fortune, 1042, 2299, 2603. *ME happene, f. ON happ*

hard, pt. see heir, v.

hardéar, adj. more daring, 1352. *ME hardy, OF hardi*

hardely, adv. certainly, by all means, 1750. *ME hardely, OE heardlice*

harld, p.p. dragged forcibly or roughly, 2749. *Midl. & NME harle, of unknown origin*

harme, n. harm, damage, evil, 1371. *ME harm, OE hearm, ON harm-r*
harmisay, exclam. of grief and distress, 508. *App.* **harmis** *n.pl. and* **ay**, *adv.*
harnis, n.pl. brains, 1446. *NME harnes, ON hjarne*
harpe, n. harp, musical instrument, 2522. *ME harpe, OE hearpe, ON harpa*
hart, n. heart, mind, 60, 819, 1871; seat of emotions, 374, 796, 1411, &c.; will, desire, 410, 1484; seat of mental or intellectual faculties, 521; seat of life, 1581; intent, 1225, 1265; term of endearment, 229, 2191; **in my --**, inwardly, 782; **with all my --**, with great sincerity, with the utmost goodwill, 238; **hert**, n. heart, soul, the seat of one's inmost thoughts and secret feelings, 231; **with -- and will**, with pleasure and eagerness, 1909. *ME hart, ONhb hearta, OE heorte*
hartfully, adv. heartily, sincerely, 659, 1254, 1693, &c. *Prec. + -fully*
harting, n. heartening, encouragement, 551. *ME hartyng*
hartlie, adj. heartfelt, sincere, 2358, 2537. **hart** *n. + -lie*
hartlie, hartlye, adv. heartily, sincerely, 129, 471, 1045, &c.; **hertlie**, adv. heartily, earnestly, 974. *Prec.*
has, see **haf**.
hast, see **haist**.
hastely, adv. hurriedly, quickly, 235, 540, 1247, &c. *ME hastely*
hate, pt.3 s. was called, 1326. *NME hate, OE hātan, pt. hatte.* See also **hecht**.
hatit, pt.3 s. hated, detested, 1188. *ME hate, OE hatian*
haue, see **haf**.
having, n. behaviour, deportment, 1882. *ME having*
he, pers.pron. of man, 4, 5, 9, &c.; of dog, 438, 469, 470, &c.; of boar, 535, 536, 537, &c.; of bird, 2658, 2660, 2668; of **ymage**, 1634. *ME he, OE hē*
hē, adj., see **hie**.
hecht, p.p. promised, 2143; **pr.1 s.** promise, vow, 2638; **pt.s.** promised, 280, 514, 807, &c. *ME heghte, OE heht, pt. of hātan*
hecht, p.p. called, 616; **pt.3 s.** was called, 14, 1026, 1630, 2114. *ME heyghte, OE heht, pt. of hātan.* See also **hate**.
hed, v.tr. to behead, decapitate, 2215, 2232. *F. noun*
hed, heid, n. head, lit. sense, 159, 254, 674, &c.; a part essential to life, life, 601, 1178; of an animal, 1445, 2023, 2059; **hedis**, n.pl. 65, 164, 2202, 2205. *ME hed(e), heed, OE hēafod*
hed, n. heed, careful attention, 271. *ME hed(e), f. OE hēdan*
hedles, adj. headless, deprived of the head, 924. *ME he(e)dles, OE hēafodlēas*
heid, see **hed**.
heile, n. health, sound bodily condition, 1205; **hele**, n. health, freedom from sickness, 1208, 1216. *ME heele, OE hǣlu*
heile, v.tr. to heal, cure, free from disease, 637, 774; **pr.1 s. subj.** 656; **hele**, v.tr. cure, restore to health, 696; **helit**, p.p. cured, 786, 1104. *ME heel(e), OE hǣlan*
heile, v.tr. to keep secret, 684. *ME heele, OE hel(i)an*
heir, adv. here, in this place, bef. 1, 680, 1000, &c.; at this point, juncture, 237, 723, 1108, &c.; to this place, 806, 898; from this place, 527; this world, 12; in this world, 230; (he) who is here, 2165; **-- or thar**, in one place or in another, 990; **her**, **adv.**; phr. **-- attour**, furthermore, beside, 385. *ME her(e), heir, OE hēr*
heir, imperat. hear, 398, 520, 610, &c.; **v.tr.** to hear, perceive by ear, 744, 2252, 2632, 2674; listen to, 2530; **intr.absol.** to hear, 2645; **heir**, **pr.2 s.** hear, 1433; **heris**, **pr.2 s.** get to know, 1520; **hard**, **pt.** heard, received information, 131, 933, 1597, &c.; **-- tell**, 256; **-- of**, received information of, 507, 2091; **p.p.** perceived by ear, 1475; **herd**, **pt.3 s.** perceived by ear, 210, 1117; received information **of**, 205; got to know, with **acc. + p.p.**, 1165;

-- tell, 996. *ME here(n), Ang hēran*

heit, v.tr. to heat, raise the temperature of, 1553. *ME hete(n), OE hǣtan*

held, see hald,

hele adj. see hale adj.

hele v. see heile v.

hele n. see heile n.

helit, see heile v.

hell, n. hell, abode of the damned, 2076. *ME, OE hel(l)*

help, v.tr. refl. to maintain, support oneself, 2660; pr.3 s. subj. help, assist, 1143; helpit, p.p. rescued, succoured, 404-5; pt.3 s. helped, relieved the wants of, 2668. *ME helpe(n), OE helpan*

her, see heir adv.

herbe, n. herb, plant used for medicine, 725, 733, 750, &c. *ME, OF herbe*

herberit, pt.3 s. took shelter, lodged, stayed, 689. *See next*

herbery, n. lodging-place, 1547. *NME herbery, ON herbergi*

herd, n. herdsman, 524-5, 539, 542, &c.; hird, n. guardian, 2662. *ME herd, hird, OE hi(e)rde*

herd pt., see heir v.

heres, n.pl. lords, leaders, 1811. *NME here, OFris hêra, MLG & MDu hêre*

heretage, n. heritage, inheritance, 853, 907; heritable estate, 1328. *ME, OF heritage*

heris, see heir v.

hert, see hart.

hertlie, see hartlie adv.

hethinnes, n. the heathen world, 270. *ME hethenes(se), OE hǣðen(n)es*

hevyn(e), n. heaven, sky, 105; celestial abode of immortal beings, 2781; vnder --, on earth, chiefly rhyme-tag, 20. *ME hevyn, OE he(o)fon*

hew(e), imperat. hew, fell for destruction, 1357; v.tr. to hew, fell or cut wood either for destruction or use, 334, 1373, 1379; hew down, cut with an axe so as to bring down, 345; hewit, pt.3 s. -- dovne, cut down to the ground with an axe, 1400; hewyn, ppl.a. hewn, 1114. *ME hew(e), OE hēawan, pt. hēow, p.p. hēawen*

hicht, n. height; on --, aloud, 2050. *(N)ME hight, OE hīehþu, hēhþu*

hid, p.p. hidden, concealed, 1993, 2551; kept from the knowledge of others, 909; hid, ppl.a. hidden, secret, 1703. *ME hid, OE p.p. hȳded, hīdd*

hiddillis, n. hiding-place; in --, in hiding, 1123. *ME hid(d)els, OE hȳdels, f. hȳdan*

hiddir, hidder, adv. hither, to or towards this place, 158, 677, 1946, &c. *ME hid(d)er, OE hider*

hie, adj. high, of exalted rank, station, dignity or estimation, 3, 111, 406, &c.; of great amount, 2306; loud (of voice), 2535; hé, adj. high, tall, 307; hye, adj. high, of great amount, 1197. *NME he(e), OE hēge, hēage, infl.forms of hēh, hēah*

hie, adv. high, to a great extent upward, 2286. *Prec.*

hiear, adv. higher, more upwards, 104. *See* hie

hienes, n. highness, title of dignity given to princes, 2543. *See* hie

hie-ravyn, hie-rawyn, n. he-raven, male raven, 2656, 2665. *ME he + raven, OE hraefn, ON hrafn*

him, pers.pron.; dat. 18, 35, 221, &c.; acc. 25, 33, 40, &c.; him-self, him-sell, 58, 422, 743, 1747; him, with refl. meaning, 249, 423, 446, &c. *ME, OE him*

hip, n. hip-joint, 942. *ME hip, OE hype*

hir, pers.pron.; dat. 137, 287, 437, &c.; acc. 13, 129, 130, &c.; used for a serpent, 433, 437, 438; for a bird, 1892, 1911, 2065; with refl. meaning,

206, 433, 666, &c. *ME hir, OE hire*
hir, poss.pron. her, 122, 134, 143, &c.; for a serpent, 434, 437; for a bird, 1962, 2043, 2046, &c.; for an ymage, 1651, 1652. *ME hir, OE hire*
hird, see herd n.
hir-sell, see self.
his, poss.pron. his, 8, 10, 15, &c.; used for a boar, 547; for a dog, 1440, 1454; for a bird, 2662; for an ymage, 1626. *ME, OE his*
his-sell, see self.
hole, n. hole, a hollow place, cavity, 432, 1737; an aperture, opening, 885, 887, 2017, 2062; a pit, 888, 890, 1709; holis, n.pl. holes, perforations, 757, 761, 766. *ME hole, OE hol(a), ON hola*
hone, n. delay, tarrying, 146, 592, 2218. *NME hon(e), of obsc.origin*
honest, adj. respectable, worthy, held in honour, 2599; honestar, adj. more commendable, more befitting, 1491. *ME honest, OF honeste*
honorably, adv. honourably, in an honourable manner, 645, 1339. *ME, OF honorable, + -ly*
honour, n. honour, high respect, esteem or reverence, as required or shown, 130, 152, 186, &c.; exalted rank, 354, 1507; fame, good name, 1174; dignity, distinction, 1513, 1526. *ME, AN honour, OF honor, honur*
hony, n. honey, as an example of something sweet, 691. *ME hony, huny, OE hunig*
hors, n. horse, 1299; n.pl. 1778, gen.s. 931. *ME hors(e), OE hors*
hound, n. hound, dog generally, 404-05, 481, 497, &c.; houndis, n.pl. hounds, dogs used for the chase, 1362. *ME hound, OE hund*
hour, n. hour, a short or limited space of time, 1250, 1930, 2618; a definite time, occasion, 250, 1090, 1134, 2699; houris, n.pl. hours, (six) o'clock, 1291. *ME houre, AN houre, OF (h)ure, (h)ore*
hous, n. house, 946, 1011, 1029, &c.; household, 1885; gen.s. or in adj.use in hous-flure, 440. *ME hous(e), OE, ON hūs*
houshald, n. household, the inmates of a house collectively, 934. *NME houshald, cf. MDu huushoud, huysholt*
how(e), adv. how; in dir.questions, 195, 304, 817, &c.; in subord.clauses, 21, 69, 95, &c.; -- that, 512, 1634, 1678, 2038; -- sa? 2581; the maner --, 519, 1925; -- lang, 1654; n. the manner or way (in which), 1603 (*NED* 1551). *ME how, OE hū*
how, n. hoe, gardening instrument, 344. *ME howe, AN hoe, OF houe*
hoye, var. of ho, v.intr. to stop, desist, pause, 2538. *ME ho(o), f. ho, interj., OF ho*
huge, adj. huge, very great, 925. *ME huge, OF ahuge*
huly, adv. softly, 1916. *NME holy, huly, ON hóflega*
hunder, card.num.; adj. hundred, 1230; n. 1152, 1704. *Reduced form of* hundreth
hundreth, card.num. adj. hundred, 1223, 1227, 1234, 1609. *(N)ME hund(e)reth, ONhb hundra , -re , ON hundraþ*
hunger, n. hunger, famine, 2651. *ME h(o)unger, OE hungor, ON hungr*
hunting, vbl.n. the chase, venery, 430, 2403; huntyne, n. the chase, 1382. *ME huntinge, OE huntung*
hurd(e), n. treasury, 825, 1755; hurdis, n.pl. hidden or buried treasures, 1704, 1863. *NME hurd, ME ho(o)rd, OE hord*
hurdome, n. adultery, whoredom, 712. *ME hordom, ON hórdómr*
hurt, v.tr. to hurt, cause bodily injury to, 789; p.p. damaged, 1781; ppl.a. injured, damaged, 340; pt.1 s. wounded, injured, 949. *ME hurte, pt. hurte, OF hurter*
husband, n. husband, a man joined to a woman by marriage, 1002-3, 1105, &c. *ME housband, LOE hūsbonda, ON húsbóndi*
hvmly, adv. humbly, with humility, 222. *Reduced var. of Humily, f. OF humble + -ly*

hy, v.intr. to hurry, speed, 2605. *ME hy(e), OE hīġian*
hye, adj. see hie, adj.
hyne, adv. hence, from this place, 2331. *NME hien, hyne, hethen, ON heðan, with contraction, and vowel-assimilation to* syne, adv. *f. ON síðan*
hyre, n. pay, reward, 2225. *ME hyre, OE hȳr*

I, pers.pron. I, 31, 34, 35, &c. *ME I, OE ic*
ilk, adj. each, 96, 1708, 1709. *(N)ME ilk, OE(Merc) ylc*
ilka, adj. each, every, 1035, 1036, 2206, 2685. *(N)ME ilka*
ilka, adj. same, that --, 68, 1660, 1906. *Analogically substituted for* ilk,adj.
ilkane, pron. each one, 76, 168, 178, &c.; of two persons, 1478, 1480; in collocation with utheris, each ... the other's, 1480. *Pred. + ane*
ill, adj. bad, wicked, of a pers., 1403, 2747; harmful, of actions, 1404, 1804, of a substance, 2066, of weather, 2030, 2039; -- blud, enmity, animosity, 1566 (*NED* 1624). *(N)ME il(l), ON ill-r*
ill, adv. badly, unhappily, 340; wickedly, 1639; -- payd, displeased, 325, 1166; -- farandly, faring badly, 1569. *Prec.*
ill, n. evil, harm, 1675; depravity, sin, 2742. *Absol. use of the adj.*
impotent, adj. impotent, wholly lacking in sexual power, 1343 (*NED* 1615). *ME impotent, L impotens*
in, adv. in, of motion, 98, 885, 895, &c.; of position, 426, 1050, 2464. *ME, OE in(ne)*
in, prep. in, 1, 2, 3, &c.; -- deid, indeed, 5, 629, 1770, &c.; -- wane, in vain, 755, 1681; into, 212, 521, 540, &c.; on, 1626. *ME, OE in*
inclynit, inclinit, pt.3 s. inclined, bowed in token of respect, 189, 197. *ME incline, OF incliner*
incontinent, adv. at once, immediately, 2603. *ME, OF incontinent, LL in continenti (sc. tempore)*
inflat, p.p. inflated, 1212. *EMoE inflate, L inflatus*
inflature, n. inflation, swelling, 1192. *ML inflatura*
in manus tuas, 1116. See expl.note.
innes, n.pl. in sing.sense, lodging-place, 1722, 1727, 1771. *ME in(n), OE inn*
innocens, n. innocence, 772. *ME, OF innocence*
innocent, adj. not guilty, free from wrong or guilt, 1141. *ME, OF innocent*
innocent, n. innocent one, guiltless person, 721. *Prec.*
innocently, adv. in innocence, without having done harm, 1156. *Prec. + -ly*
instewart, n. steward of the inner part of the palace, i.e. of the king's private chambers, 1226, 1271, 1280. *NME instewart, OE stīw(e)ard*
interprit, v.tr. interpret, explain, expound the meaning of, 2121, 2152. *ME interprete, OF interpreter*
in-till, prep. in, 134, 418, 747, &c.; into, 128, 912. *ME intill*
in-to, prep. in a place, 291, 941, 1388, &c.; with abstr.nouns, 260, 777, 1170; into, so as to enter or be put in (a place, condition, charge, &c.), 33, 468, 740, &c. *ME, OE into*
in verbo regio, 2638. See expl.note.
inwith, adv. inside, within, 2198. *ME inwith*
inwy, n. envy, jealousy, 771. *LME invye*
iois, v.tr. to enjoy the possession of, 2678. *ME jois(s)en, OF joiss-, lengthened stem of joir*
ioly, adj. fine, handsome, 297. *ME iolie, joly, OF joli(f)*
iornay, n. day of tournament, 420; iornais, n.pl. contests in tournaments, 412. *ME jornay, OF jornee*
iowell, iowall, n. jewel, treasure, gem, 1820; used as adj., 1810, 2057, 2070. *ME iowel(le), OF jo(u)el*

ioy(e), n. joy, happiness, pleasure, 186, 2358, 2526, 2537; delight, 486; rejoicing, 2519. *ME ioy, ioie, OF joie, joye*
ioynt, p.p. joined, together, in one group, 1696. *ME joynt, OF joint(e)*
is, see be v.
ischit, pt.3 pl. issued, came out, 154. *LME issh, yssh, f. OF issir*
it, pers.pron. nom. 93, 106, 113, &c.; acc. 237, 307, 310, &c. *ME, OE hit*
iuge, v.tr. give sentence about, determine, 926; iugit, p.p. condemned, 584, 864. *ME iuge(n), AN juger, OF jugier*
iugement, n. judgement, formal or authoritative decision, as of an umpire or arbiter, 2670. *ME, OF jugement*
iugit, see iuge.
iustice, n. justice, judicial proceedings, 262. *ME iustice, OF justice*
iustifyet, p.p. executed, 1018. *ME justefy, F justifier*
iusting, n. jousting, tilting on horseback with a lance, 409. *F. ME iuste, OF juster*
i-wis, adv. surely, certainly, 1312, 2391. *ME iwis(se), OE gewis*

kell, n. a woman's hair-net, cap or head-dress, 208. *(N)ME kell(e), corresp. to ME calle, F cale*
ken, v.tr. to get to know, learn, find out, 109, 627, 1741; recognise, identify, 914; teach, direct, 2110; pr.1 s. recognised, 1864; pr.2 pl. are familiar with, 1603; kend, p.p. known, 2112; kennit, pt.3 s. knew of, was aware of, 2367; recognised, 2377. *ME ken(ne), pt. kend, kenned, p.p. kend, OE cennan, ON kenna*. See also couth.
kendillit, pt.3 s. kindled, lighted, 1381. *LME kendel, ME kindel, ON kynda*
kennit, see ken.
kepar, n. keeper, guardian, warden, 921; keparis, n.pl. guards, defenders, 1091. *F. vb.*
kep(e), v.tr. to keep, guard, 840, 2398; look after, look to the well-being of, 63; hold in custody, 263; protect, 1815; look after, keep safe, 1956; observe (a promise), 2630; keep (a secret), 696; kepe, imperat. preserve, save, 1796; kepis, pr.3 s. protects, guards, 125, 1429; kepand, ppl.a. guarding, custodian (adj.), 884, 929, see expl.note; kepit, p.p. preserved, 236; protected, 443; held captive, 1038; confined (within), 1050; observed, 1465. *ME kepe(n), p.p. kepte, OE cēpan*
kepe, n. care, heed, attention, 566, 1968. *F. vb.*
kest, pt.3 s. cast, threw, 484, 553, 558, &c.; put, placed, 663; revolved in his mind, 2338. See also cast.
key(e), n. key, 1055, 1516, 1529; keyis, n.pl. 1036, 1070, 2353, 2463. *ME key(e), OE cæg(e)*
kid, see kyth.
king, kyng, n. male sovereign, king, emperor, 515, 634, 644, &c.; kingis, gen. sg. 127, 632, 658, &c.; kingis, kyngis, nom.pl. 1661, 1677. *ME king, kyng, OE cyning, cyng*
kinrik(e), kynrik, n. kingdom, 1232, 1266, 2276, &c. *ME kinrik, OE cynerīce*
kirk, n. church (building), 1110, 1337, 1418, &c. *(N)ME, LOE kirke, ON kirkja*
kirk-dure, n. church-door, 2455. *Prec. + ME dur(e), OE duru*
kis, v.tr. to kiss, 1489, 2010; kist, pt.3 s. kissed, 136; pt.3 pl. intr. kissed, 2356; kist, p.p. tr. kissed, 239. *(N)ME kis(se), OE cyssan, ON kyssa*
kist, n. chest, large box or trunk used for safekeeping of things; -- keye, 1516. *(N)ME kist, ON kista*
knaw(e), v.tr. to know, have cognisance of someth. through observation, inquiry, or information, 95, 176, 267, 1670; understand, 403; recognise, 906, 1258, 2288; find out, 1866, 1979; be able to distinguish one thing from another, 2444; pr.pl. 385, 511, 1602, &c.; -- of, are assured of, 2709;

knawin, p.p. known, familiar to all, 291; recognised, 2273; knawis, pr.2, 3 sg. be familiar with by experience, 383; be conversant with, 821; be aware of, 1370; knew(e), pt. understood, 107; was conversant with (through study), 191; perceived (with the senses), 535; had learnt by study or practical experience, 1198, 1961, 2069. *(N)ME knaw(e), pt. knew, p.p. knawen, OE cnāwan*
knawlege, n. identification, recognition, 908, 927; acquaintance with a fact, 1078; acquaintance with a branch of learning, 2577. *(N)ME knawlag(e)*
kne, n. knee, 2587; kneis, n.pl. knees, 2534, 2704. *ME kne, OE cnēo, ON kné*
knelit, pt.3 s. knelt, 494, 1153. *ME knele(n), OE cneowlian*
knew(e), see knaw(e).
knokit, pt.3 s. knocked, rapped upon a door in order to gain admittance, 1080. *ME knok(k)e, OE cnocian, ON knoka*
knycht, n. knight, 392, 405, 421, &c.; knychtis, gen.s. 2376, 2441; nom.pl. 829, 1685, 1945. *ME knight, knyght, OE cniht*
knyf, n. knife, a weapon, 484, 568, 741, &c.; a cutting instrument, 1531, 1537, 1539. *ME knyf(e), LOE cnīf, ON knífr*
kyn, n. family, kinsfolk, 2157; sort, kind, 2438. *ME kyn(n), OE cynn, ON kyn*
kynd, n. sort, kind, 295, 531; manner, way, 2292. *ME kind, kynd, OE (ge)cynd(e)*
kyng, kyngis, see king.
kynrik, see kinrik(e).
kyth, v.tr.; phr. to -- all cure, to devote or give careful attendance, 320; kid, p.p. (made) known, 1062. *ME kythe, p.p. kid(de), OE cȳþan*

lady(e), n. lady, a woman of superior social position, 115, 1316, 2269, &c.; spouse of a man of rank, 136, 2765; female head of a household, 454, 1525; a mistress in relation to servants, 1399, 1922; wife, in address, 1538, 1926; ladyis, gen.s. 1551; n.pl. ladies-in-waiting, 211. *ME lady, ONhb hlāfdīa, OMerc hlāfdīe*
laif, n. rest, remainder, 58, 297, 300, &c. *OE lāf, ON leif*
laigh, adv. low, 738 (*NED* 1583 laich, adv.) *F. adj., NME lagh(e), lāh, ON lág-r.* See also law(e), adv.
lair, n. learning, knowledge, 52, 1700, 1861. *ME lar(e), OE lār*
lair, n. a lying with a man as a prostitute, 1223. *ME leir, lair, OE leġer*
laite, adj. late, after the customary time, 1363. *ME late, OE late, declensional forms of OE læt*
laith, adj. loath, reluctant, 2331. *(N)ME lath(e), OE lāþ*
lak, n. discredit, shame, 988, 2501; fault, offence, 1391. *ME lak, not recorded in OE, but cf. MLG lak, MDu lac, deficiency, lack, fault, disgrace*
lakit, pt.3 s. played, sported, in amorous sense, 2765. *NME laike,lake, ON leika.*
land, n. land, country, 487, 2204, 2281, &c.; landed property, 851; landis, n. pl. landed property, 1330, 2614. *ME, OE land*
lane, n. concealment, 671. *NME layn, lain, cf. ON leyni, leynd & vb. leyna*
lang, adj. long, having the length much greater than the breadth, 741; long (of a period of time), 1062, 2567. *NME, OE lang*
lang, adv. for or during a long time, 1004, 1654, 1680, &c. *Prec.*
langar, adv. longer (of time), 680, 966, 1169, &c. *Prec. + -ar*
langit, pt.3 s. longed, 2691. *NME lang, OE langian*
langour, n. distressed condition, affliction of spirit, 1168. *ME, OF langour, ML langor*
lap, n. fold of robe, 2628. *ME lappe, OE læppa*
lap, pt.3 s., see leipe.
large, adj. generous, 836, 841, 872, 893. *ME, OF large*
largely, adv. lavishly, 833. *Prec. + -ly*
largnes, largenes, n. largess, liberality, generosity, 835, 1693. *ME largenes*

last, adj. final; absol.in phr. at the --, in the end, finally, 254, 371, 1052, &c. *ME last, latst, OE latost*
lat, aux. inf. to permit, 609, 1249, 1789; allow, passing into: to cause, 887; imperat. permit, cause to, 1452; -- se , show (me), 2581; lattin, p.p. let, allowed, 785; lattis, pr.3 s. lets, permits, 767; leit, pt.3 s. aux., let, -- fall, let fall, dropped, 758, 1115, 2334; shed (tears), 1410; lat ... be, inf. to cease from, 1412; -- be, imperat. leave off, cease, 1105; -- be + acc., cease from, 1233; leit ... be, pt.3 s. ceased from, 555. *See next*
lat, v.tr., imperat., phr. -- me in, admit me, open the door to me, 1106, 1131; lattin, p.p., phr. -- in, admitted, 1994; lattyn, p.p. phr.--blud, let blood, bled, 1322-23; leit, pt.3 s. phr. -- ... allane, left ... by themselves, 1255; let, v.intr. to leave off, desist, 1483; lete, pt.3 s. behaved as if, pretended, 692. *ME lat, lete(n), pt. let(e), ONhb lēta, OE lǣtan, pt. lēt, ON láta, pt. lét*
lattis, pr.3 pl. prevent, hinder, 333; lettit, pt.3 s.with obj. + inf. + to, prevented, hindered, 2542. *ME lat(t), OE lettan*
lauchfully, adv. legally, in accordance with law, 1330. *NME lagh(ful), OE lagu, lah- in combinations*
law(e), adv. deeply, in obeisance, 494, 1153, 1298, 1854; under the ground, far down, 1777. *NME law(e), f. ON lágr.* See also laigh.
law(e), n. law, rule that must be obeyed, 1010; action of courts of law, 268; system of rules recognised by a people, 389; individual rule of a system, 2775; lawis, n.pl. laws, rules recognised as binding by state or community, 386. *ME lawe, LOE lagu, ON *lagu, ON lǫg*
lawar, n. ewer, vessel to hold water for washing, 2703. *ME lavo(u)r, OF laveoir*
lawis, see law(e) n.
lawly, adj. humble in spirit or disposition, 2601. *See* law(e) adv.
lawtē, n. loyalty, fidelity, 1275; truth, 2554. *ME lauté, var. of, and early supplanting leaute(e) f. OF leaute, lealte*
lay, v.tr. phr. -- in wage, -- in wed, to stake,wager, 601, 1178, 1201; pr.1 s. impose (an embargo, &c.) on, 1584; layis, pr.1 pl., -- in wage, 1791. *ME lay, OE lecg(e)an*
lay, pt. see ly(e).
le, v.intr. to lie, speak falsely, utter falsehood, 2588; leyis, pr.2 s. tell lies, 1087. *ME leȝe, lee, OE lēoȝan, OMerc lēgan*
leche, v.tr. to cure, heal a wounded or injured person, 1564. *ME læchen, leche, f. n. OE lǣce, ONhb lēce*
led, see leid, v.tr.
ledder, n. ladder, 2014, 2059, 2060. *EME leddre, OE hlǣd(d)er*
left, adj. left, as opposed to right, 1652. *NME left(e)*
left, p.p. &c., see leif, v.intr.
legis, n.pl. leagues (measures of distance), 1806. *LME lege, ML leuga* , &c.
leid, v.tr. to bring or take a pers. to a place, 272, 367; intr. to lead in a cert. direction, 2060; led, p.p. tr. conducted to a place, 1849, 2238; pt. tr. passed (one's life), 1272; conducted (a pers.) to, 193, 2468; -- throw, led through (the town), 586. *ME lede(n), pt. ledde, p.p. led(d), OE lǣdan, pt. lǣdde, p.p. lǣd(ed)*
leid, n. language, speech, 1888. *ME lede, OE lēoden*
leif, adj. dear, beloved, 259; agreeable, 698; agreeable, acceptable, in phr. als -- war me, 1344. *NME leif, OE lēof*
leif, v.intr. to leave; -- of, to cease doing something, 1498; imperat. cease, desist, 1476; tr. leave, go away from, 12; desist from, 1897; pr.1 s. tr. drop, cease speaking of, allow a pers. to do someth. without interference, 109; bequeathe, 1109. 1111; left, p.p. left, allowed to remain, 228, 1579;

pt.3 s. tr. left, went away from, 1072, 1933, 2354, &c.; parted with, lost, 11; relinquished, forsook, 2654, 2666; pt. intr. remained, 425, 426; ceased, desisted, 1899. *ME lefe, p.p. left, OE lǣfan, p.p. lǣfed*

leif, v.intr. to live, continue in life, 274, 1846; to pass life in a specif. fashion, 1170, 1290; imperat. id., 1285; pr.1 s. continue in life, 1586; levis, pr.3 s. lives, continues in life, 12, 966; levit, p.p. passed life in a specif. fashion, 2730; lived, quasi-trans. with cognate obj. 2756; pt. passed life in a specif. fashion, 957, 1020; was alive, 1457, 2686; liffand, pres.p. living, alive, 774, 785, 1129; passing life in a specif. manner, 1031; liffit, pt.3 s. lived, dwelled, 1273. *MSc var.:leif, leve, lif, ME live(n), NME lif, OE lifian (beside libban)*

leif, n. leave, permission, 1436, 2320; permission to depart, 794, 1164, &c. *NME lefe, OE lēaf*

leif, n. leaf of a plant, 97 (edoke --). *ME lefe, OE lēaf*

leipe, v.intr. leap, jump; mount on one's horse, 2219; lap, pt.3 s. leapt, jumped, 1442. *ME lepe, pt. lep, OE hlēapan, pt. hlēop*

leir, v.tr. to teach, instruct a pers., 18, 26, 32, &c.; intr. to learn, acquire knowledge, 87; lerd,p.p. taught, 48. *ME lere, p.p. lered, OE lǣran*

leis, n. lying, falsehood, 2505 . *ME lees, OE lēas*

leit, see lat, aux. and lat, v.tr.

lele, adj. loyal, honest, 600; lelar, adj. more loyal, more truthful, 1769. *ME lel(e), OF leel*

lemman, n. lover, unlawful lover, 1056, 1984; sweetheart, 2412. *ME lem(m)an, earlier leofmon*

lerd, see leir.

les, adj. absol., less, a less amount, 1694; mair or --, 832; mar nor --, 2271; -- na mair, 190; -- or mar, 1725. *ME lesse, OE lǣssa*

lesingis, n.pl. lies, slanders, 1980, 2053; lesyng, n. lie, falsehood, 2399. *ME lesing, OE lēasung*

lest, v.intr. to last, continue in life, endure, 231, 1654; lestis, pr.3 s. lasts, endures, 1683. *ME leste(n), OE lǣstan*

lest, adj.; absol. at the --, at least, at any rate, 273; adv. in the least degree, 1990. *ME lest, OE lǣst*

lesyng, see lesingis.

let, lete, see lat, v.tr.

lettit, see lattis.

let, n. delay; but --, without delay, at once, 84, 409, 1825, 1851. *F. vb.*

letter, n. letter, a written communication sent from one pers. to another, 2334; letteris, n.pl. 145, 153. *ME letter, OF lettre*

leuch, pt.3 pl. laughed, 107. *ME lough, OE hlōh*

lever, levir, adv. rather, more willingly, more gladly, had --, 855, 1100, 1241, 2736. *ME lever, OE lēofre*

levis, 2086, see explan.note.

levis, lives, & levit, see leif, to live.

leyis, see le.

liand, see ly)e.

liberale, adj. liberal (sciences), 41, see expl.note. *ME, OF liberal*

licht, n. light, 1914. *ME light, OE lēoht, Ang lēht*

lichtit, pt.3 s. intr. descended from a horse, 978; settled on (of a bird), 2570. *ME lighte, OE līhtan*

lichtly, adv. easily, 1351, 1420, 1732; lychtly, adv. easily, 1498. *ME lightly, OE lēohtlīce*

lichtlyit, p.p. despised, disdained, 715. *F.* lichtly *adj.*

liffand, see leif, to live.

liffing, n. life, life-time, 1236. *NME lyfyng, lifing*

liffit, see leif, to live.
liftit, pt.3 s. lifted, raised to a higher position, 2001; raised (his hand) to strike, 1635. *ME lift(e), ON lypta*
list, pr.2 s. wish, desire, choose, 1504. *ME list, OE lystan*
litill, lytill, adj. little, small in size, 171, 330; small in degree, 551, 607, 2100; short (of time), 538, 631, 699, 1335; barely any, 797, 1993, 2426; absol. not much, 1632, 2432; n. a little, a short time, 731. *ME litil, lytyll, OE lytel, ONhb lytill, ON lítell*
lo, interj. see here, look, 904, 1493, &c. *Shortened form of* luke, *imperat.*
lokit, p.p. locked, closed with lock and key, 1079, 2351; shut up, put under lock and key, 2404, 2464; lokkit, lokit, pt.3 s. fastened with lock and key, 1035, 1075, 1125, 2462. *ME locke, loke, ON loka*
lord, n. lord; indicating a prince, sovereign, 27, 66, 361, &c.; a knight, 429, 463, 1327, &c.; a husband, 213, 671, 1341, &c.; a burgess, 1931, 1938, 1939, &c.; a master (of a dog), 471; a master (of a gardener), 1375; lordis, gen.s. lord's (of the master of a magpie) 1923; lordis, n.pl. lords, men of exalted position, 370, 1507, 1511, 2773. *ME lord(e), lowerd, OE hlāford*
lous, v.tr. to release, 1558, 1564. *ME lowse, louse, cf. ON leysa f. lauss*
lovit, p.p. praised, 2048. *(N)ME love(n), OE lofian, ON lofa*
lowde, adv. loudly, 2521. *ME loud(e), lowd(e), OE hlūde*
lownar, adj. quieter, calmer, 2041. *F. ON logn n., calm weather*
lowtand, pr.p. bowing, stooping, 740; lowte, v.intr. to bow, bend, stoop, 738; lowtit, pt.3 s. bowed, 1298, 1854, 2510. *ME lout(e), lowt(e), OE lūtan, ON lúta*
luf, v.intr. to love, to be in love, take a lover, 1421, 1426, 1436, 1470; tr. to bear love to, to hold dear, 1432, 1491, 1582, 2487; imperat. absol. be in love, take a lover, 1520; pr. hold dear, 232, 2476; subj. take a lover, 1504 (see expl.note); lufis, pr.3 s. is fond of, has a strong liking for, 1356, 1832; lufit, pt. loved, held dear, 129, 407, 429, &c.; ppl.a. 466, 569, 1021, &c. *NME lufe, pt. lufde, OE lufian*
luf, n. love, sweetheart, 1346, 2277, 2288, &c.; warm affection, 2279, 2337; loving care, 1376; -- asking, love-request, 137; -- drowry, love-token, 2397; -- letter, love-letter, 2334. *ME luf(e), OE lufu*
lufaris, n.pl. lovers (enamoured with opposite sex), 2356. *ME luf(f)er*
lufis, lufit, see luf v.
lufly, adj. lovely, lovable, attractive, 690, 1044. *ME lufly, OE luflic*
luke, v.intr. to see, exercise the faculty of vision, 1307; -- ourethort, to look across, 1040; -- furth, to look out, 1034; -- wp, to look up, 1042; imperat. make sure, 521; lukit, pt.3 s. gave his eyes a certain direction, 1045; had a cert. look or appearance, 1262; -- wp, looked up, 102, 2058; -- dovne, looked down, 1046. *NME luk(e), OE lōcian*
luking, n. (the action of) looking, 1051. *ME lokinge*
lust, n. pleasure, desire, 957, 1056, 1071. *ME, OE lust*
lute, n. lute (musical instrument), 2522. *ME lute, OF leüt, MF lut*
ly(e), v.intr. to be in a prostrate or recumbent position, 463, 560, 1085; to assume a prostrate position, 1995; to have sexual intercourse with, 1189, 1229, 2735; to be in bed, 1344; to lie for the purpose of sleeping, 2318; pr.2 s. be in bed for the purpose of sleeping, 2176; liand, lyand, pr.p. recumbent, prostrate, 459, 561, 1072, 1568; lyis, pr.3 s. be deposited, remain in a specif. place, 1739, 1777, 1784, 1787; lay, pt. was in a prostrate or recumbent position, 428, 436, 446, &c.; was (placed) on the ground, 449; had a specif. position, 1036; had sexual intercourse with, 1144, 1245. *ME ly(en), pt. lay, OE licgan, læȝ*
lychtly, see lichtly.
lyf, n. life, animate existence, opposed to death, 11, 123, 484, &c.; lifetime, 1021, 1272; partic. manner or course of living, 2756; on --, alive, 2576;

with --, alive, 535; be my --, 1538; lyfis, n.pl. in pane of --, 2136; lyvis, n.pl. lives, as opposed to death, 1791. *ME lyf, OE līf*

lyfles, adj. lifeless, dead, 1569. *ME lyfles, OE līflēas*

lyk, adj. likely (to), 327, 549; probable, 814; similar, alike, 1481, 2450; lykast, lykest, adj. most similar, 2392, 2446. *ME lyke, OE (ge)līc, ON lík-r*

lyk(e), adv. quasi-prep. like, in or after the manner of, 529, 2356, 2516. *Prec.*

lyking, n. happiness, enjoyment, 1285. *ME lyking, OE līcung*

lykis, pr.2 s. like, take pleasure in, 1432. *ME lyke(n), OE līcian, ON líka*

lyme, n. lime, mortar, used in building, 530. *ME lym(e), OE, ON līm*

lynealy, adv. by lineal descent, 1329. *LME lynealy, F linéal, L linealis, + -ly*

lytill, see litill.

lyvis, see lyf.

ma, adj. more, greater in number, 163; n. more, a greater number of people, 786, 1151, 1264; an additional number, 2009. *NME ma, OE mā*. See also mair, mar, more.

madame, n. madam, a form of respectful address in speaking to a lady of high rank, 655. *ME madam(e), OF ma dame*

made, see mak.

madin, n. maiden, virgin, 126, 127, 388, &c.; maid-servant, 2015; girl, young woman, 2762; madinnis, madynnis, n.pl. maidens, female attendants, 208, 2758, 2761. *ME maiden, OE mǣȝden, mǣden*

madinhed, madynhed, n. maidenhead, virginity, 236, 1136, 1480. *ME maidenhede, (OE mæȝdenhād)*

magra, n. the state of being regarded with ill-will, 1734. *ME maugre, OF maugré, malgré*

maid(e), see mak.

mair, adj. greater in importance, 499, 989, 1608, &c.; greater (length of time), 51, 56; greater in quantity, 1778; les na --, (not) at all, 190; n. but --, without anything further, without more ado, 1122; something else in addition, na --, 1433, ony --, 1862; ... and --, used to indicate an indef. or unspecif. addition to what has been mentioned, 1459, 1912. *NME mar(e), OE māra*. See also ma and mar.

mair, adv. longer, again, 1045; to a greater degree, 2034, 2498; na --, just as little, 672; no longer, 2250; never again, 1414; for evir --, for ever, 1814; neuer --, never again, 2674; -- or les, in a greater or less degree, 832. *Prec.*See also mar and more.

maist, see mast.

mak, v.tr. to bring into existence, produce, bring about, 2007, 2344, 2645, &c.; to cause a pers. to be or become (what is denoted by the complement), 1061, 1065, 1199, &c.; to put together materials for (a fire) and set them alight, 1392; to prepare (a bed) for sleeping in, 1999; to create by election, 2231; to conclude, enter into, 234; to incur, 411; to offer, render, 2706; imperat. create, 1944; bring about, 399; pr.s. draw up(a testament), 1108; entertain or manifest, 1235; cause a pers. to be (wise), 1269; bring into existence, produce by action, 2413; -- a vow, 814; makis, pr.3 s. produces, 1128, 2580; signifies, 2108; makand, pr.p. entertaining or manifesting, 1545; producing, 2093; made, p.p. produced (an article of food) by culinary operations, 1203; pt.3 pl. produced (a hole), 2017; maid(e), p.p. offered, presented, rendered, 59, 266, 633, &c.; caused a pers. to be or become (what is denoted by the complement), 751, 1265, 1972, &c.; created by election, &c., 839, 2687; produced by action, 2053; constructed, fashioned, 2009, 2062, 2380; brought about, 2410; concluded, 2477; ppl.a. fashioned, 2000; pt. entertained, manifested, 277, 347, 509, &c.; offered, presented, 376, 2734, 2772; caused to be, 319, 1774, 2331; brought about, 762, 1534, 2647; produced, 869, 888, 942, &c.; enacted (a law), 1010; put together materials for (a fire) and set them alight, 1621, 1802; constructed, 1623; prepared, provided, 1985; established, 2117; told (a lie), 2399. *ME make(n), makie(n), OE macian*

mak, n. manner, fashion, 749. *F. vb.*

makis, see mak v.

malady, n. disease, sickness, 656. *ME, OF maladie*

malice, n. malice, wickedness, 2729, 2750. *ME, OF malice*

malicious, adj. malicious, wicked, 1226. *ME, OF malicius*

man, n. person, 308, 533, 572, &c.; male person, 742, 1041, 1482, &c.; adult male pers., 924, 1156, 2476, &c.; used indef. without art., 926, 2719; gud --, husband, 2575; men, pl. men, male persons, 1423, 1742, &c.; servants, soldiers, 945; -- of lair, men of learning, 1700; used indef. without art., 50, 914. *ME, OE man(n), pl. men(n)*

mane, adj. very large, powerful, 1802. *ME main, ON meginn, megn, OE mæġen-*

mane, n. might, power, 275. *ME main, OE mæġen, ON magn*, &c.

mane, mayne, n. moan, lamentation, 13, 754, 919, &c. *NME man, OE *mǣn*. See also meyne.

maner, n. manner, the way in which something is done, or takes place, mode of procedure, 519, 743, 1184, &c. *ME maner, AN manere*

maniory, n. feast, banquet, 1523. *ME mangeri, OF mangerie*

mannasing, n. menace, threatening, 1974. *ME manasing, OF manace*

manteine, pr.3 s. subj. maintain, assist, 968. *ME ma(i)nte(i)n(e), OF maintenir*

mar, adj. greater (of space of time), 36; greater in degree, extent, 603, 2730; absol. as n. a greater amount, 704; less or --, a smaller or greater quantity, 1725; -- or myn, of greater or smaller importance, 1943; -- nor less, (not) at all, 2271; more, something else in addition to what is specif., 31, 1520; ... and --, used to indicate an addition to what is mentioned, 1032; n.pl. -- and myn, persons of all ranks, 226, 425. *NME mar(e), OE māra*. See also ma, mair.

mar, adv. to a greater extent, 106, 235, 308, &c.; no --, not again, 2055. *Prec.* See also mair, more.

mariage, n. marriage, matrimonial alliance, 234; dowry, 854; ceremony by which two pers. are made husband and wife, 2477. *ME, OF mariage*

mark, n. mark, amount of money, 1223, 1227, &c.; markis, n.pl. marks, 2598. *ME mark, LOE marc, ON mǫrk*. See expl.note to l. 1223.

mary, v.intr. to take a husband or wife, contract matrimony, 1024, 2453; tr. to give in marriage, 2102; marijt, p.p. taken in marriage, 1281, 1332; intr. having taken a husband or wife, 1478; joined in wedlock, 2408; pt.3 s. tr. took in marriage, 874. *ME mary, OF marier*

masoun, n. mason, a builder and worker in stone, 2340, 2347, 2368; masonnis, n.pl. masons, 77, 2324. *ME maso(u)n, OF masson*

mast, adj. greatest, 2666; n. the largest admissible (distance), 74. *NME mast, ONhb māst*

mast, maist, adv. to the greatest extent, most, 698, 1356, 2427. *Prec.*

mast, n. mast, long pole set up upon the keel of a ship to support the sails, 2570. *ME mast, OE mæst*

master, n. master, teacher, 24, 184, 402, &c.; owner of a living creature, dog, 404-05; one who employs another in his service, 2628, 2629; masteris, n.pl. teachers, 101, 107, 176, &c.; men of approved learning, 751, 763. *ME maister, OE mæġester, maġister, OF maistre*

mater, n. matter, state of things, 1198, 2631, 2646; question, 2138. *ME mater, OF matere*

mattok, n. mattock, pick, 1744; mattokis, n.pl. 862. *ME mattok, OE mattuc*

mawlisoun, n. curse, malediction, 2230. *ME maliso(u)n, OF maleis(s)on* may, aux. pr. can, may; micht, mycht, pt. could, might; expressing ability or power: pr. 215, 331, 900, &c.; pt. 346, 560, 786, &c.; expr. objective possibility, opportunity or absence of prohib. conditions: pr. 203, 231, 265, &c.; pt. 6, 95, 170, &c.; with pass.inf., pt. 728; expr. permission or sanction: pr. 389, 1001, 1132, &c.; expr. subjective possibility, with inf., pr. 2101; pt. 123; with ell. of inf., pr. 626, 1947; pt. 470, 2329, 2470, 2653. *ME may, pt. might, OE mæȝ, pt. mihte, meahte*

may, n. maiden, virgin, 1027, 2474. *ME may, OE mǣġ*

mayne, see mane, moan

me, pers.pron. me; acc., as dir.obj., 249, 280, 513, &c.; dat., as indir.obj., 32, 378, 394, &c.; dat. with impers.vb., 284, 607, 691, &c.; governed by a prep., 140, 216, 596, &c.; refl., 949, 1628, 1869. *ME me, OE mē*

medicinale, adj. medicinal, having healing properties, 725. *ME medicynall, F médicinal, L medicinalis*

mediciner, medicinar, n. physician, 649, 679, 702, 1195. *Cf. OF medecineur*

medicyne, n. medicine, medicament, 709, 2193; knowledge of healing, 777. *ME, OF medicine, L medicina*

meid, n. reward, wages, recompense, 31. *ME mede, OE mēd*

meik, adj. meek, gentle, courteous, 2601. *ME meke, EME meoc, mec, ON mjúk-r*

meikly, mekly, adv. meekly, in a meek or humble manner, 783, 1080, 2244. *Prec.*

meiknes, n. meekness, humility, 2539. *See* meik, adj.

meit, v.tr. to meet, come face to face with, 370, 1296; met, pt. 974, 1852, &c.; lighted upon, 842. *ME mete, meet, OE mētan*

meit(e), mete, n. food, 1518, 1532, 1987, 2426. *ME mete, meet, OE mete*

mekle, adj. great, much, 186, 587, 1234, &c.; n. much, a great quantity, 2568; be -- far, in a much greater degree, 1594. *ME mekil(l), ON mikell*

mekle, adv. greatly, 1556, 1604. *Prec.*

mekly, see meikly.

melody, n. song, sweet music, 2580. *ME, OF melodie, ML melodia*

men, see man.

mend, v.tr. to restore to health, cure, 1196. *ME mende(n), AN mender, aphetic f. OF amender*

mene, see meyne, to mean.

menstraly, n. minstrelsy, music, 188, 2524. *Cf. OF memstralsie, ME mynstralsy*

menyng, n. meaning, intended sense of (a person's) words, 1588. *ME mening, f. OE mǣnan, cf. OHG meinunga, MDu mēninge.* See also meyne, mene.

menyst, pt.3 s. reduces, withdrew (a portion of something), 1566. *ME mynys, menuse, OF menu(i)sier, Vulg.L *minutiare*

menyt, see meyne, to moan.

merchandis, n. the action or business of buying and selling goods for profit, 301, 1904. *ME mercha(u)ndis(e), OF marchandise*

mercy, n. mercy, forbearance and compassion shown by one pers. to another, 581, 1409, &c.; God's pitiful forbearance tow. His creatures and forgiveness of their offences, 2592; scho cryit --, begged for pardon or forgiveness, 1557. *ME mercy, OF merci*

merk, adj., see myrk.

merwale, see merwell, n.

merwalit, see merwell, v.

merwalous, merwalus, adj. marvellous, astonishing, 312, 1624, 2140. *ME mervailouse, OF merveillos*

merwell, merwale, n. marvel, miracle, 534, 925, 2611. *ME merwal(e), OF merveille*

merwell, pr.1 s. wonder, with interr.cl., 510, 2037; with of, 1601; merwalit, pt.3 s. asked himself wonderingly, with interr.cl., 1063; was filled with wonder, absol. 2390; id. with on, 2427. *ME mervail, OF merveillier*

mery, adj. merry, pleasing, agreeable, 1960, 1985. *ME mery, OE mer(i)ȝe*
mes, n. mass, celebration of the Eucharist, 1417, 2477. *ME mes(s), OE mæsse, ON messa*
mesalry, missalry, n. leprosy, 1212, 1220. *ME meselrie, OF mesel(l)erie*
mese, n. company of persons eating together at a banquet, 2424; mesis, n.pl. dishes, 1515. *ME, OF mes*
mesour, n. moderation, measure; attour --, our --, excessively, 505, 824, 827, &c.; a quantity (of something), 1556. *ME mesour, OF mesure*
message, n. message, oral or written communication sent from one person to another, 633. *ME, OF message*
messinger, n. messenger, one who carries a message or goes on an errand, 151, 1084. *ME messengere, OF messager*
met, see meit v.
mete, see meit(e) n.
meting, n. meeting, the action of coming together or into the presence of each other, 1383. *ME meting f. vb.*
meyne, v.intr. to moan, lament, 2500; menyt, pt.3 s. moaned, lamented, 2127. *ME mene(n), pt. NME menit, OE mǣnan.* See also mane, mayne.
meyne, v.tr. to mean, signify, 352; pr.1 s. intend to indicate, 570; mene, id., 780, 2228; pr.1 pl. purpose, 1783. *ME mene(n), OE mǣnan.* see also menyng.
micht, pt., see may, aux.
micht, n. might, power, 354, 2679. *ME might, OE miht*
michti, mychti, a. powerful, mighty, strong, 293, 823, 1021, &c.; very great in amount, 1532. *ME myghty, OE mihtiġ*
middis, n. middle, 78; myddis, n. middle, midst, middle part or point, 82, 1649, 1686, 1989. *ME in middes, OE in middan; alteration due to the analogy of to middes, gen.*
misaventour, misawentur, n. misfortune, 517, 1873. *ME misaventour, OF mesaventure*
miscarijt, p.p. brought to discomfiture or harm, 1282. *ME miscarie, OF meskarier*
mischance, n. piece of bad luck, disaster, 391, 603. *ME mischance, OF meschance*
mischef, mischeif, n. misfortune, distress, 496, 499, 815, &c.; mischefis, n.pl. misfortunes, troubles, 2085. *ME misch(i)ef, OF meschief*
misdeid, n. offence, evil deed, 2530. *ME misdede, OE misdǣd*
miserably, adv. miserably, in misery, in extreme unhappiness, 1827. *EMoE myserable, F misérable, L miserabilis + -ly*
misfortoun(e), n. misfortune, (piece of) bad luck, 676, 995. *EMoE misfortune*
misgaf, pt.3 s. refl. had misgivings, 480 (*NED* 1641). *Cf. EMoE misgive*
missalry, see mesalry.
mist, v.tr. miss, fail to hit (something aimed at), or contr. form of mis it, 240; pt. discovered the absence of, 884; failed to get, failed to capture, 1950 (*NED* 1596); mys, v.tr. fail to see, 2162. *ME mis(se), OE missan*
mistar, n. profession, business, 1699; mister, mistair, n. need, a state of difficulty or distress, 842, 846, 866, 2666. *ME mister(e), AN mester, OF mestier*
mixtur, n. mixture, a product of mixing, 2066. *EMoE mixture, L mixtura*
moble, n. moveables, property, wealth, 827, 870, 884. *ME moble*
moder, n. mother, 10, 1084, 1094, &c. *ME moder, OE mōdor*
moltin, adj. molten, liquified by heating, 1826. *ME molten, p.p. of melte(n), OE meltan*
mon, aux. pr.s. must, 12, 899. *ME mon, ON mun, mon*
money, n. money, coin considered in reference to its value or purchasing power, 1222. *ME money(e), OF moneie*
mony, adj. many; with sg.n. without art., 28, 295, 355, &c.; with pl. 1507, 2085; -- ane, many a person, 821. *(N)ME mony, OE maniġ, moniġ*

more, adv. rather, 1417. *ME more, OE māra*. See also **mair** and **mar**.
morn-day, n. morrow, next day, 2509. *See next*
morn(e), n. morning, 204, 366, 583, &c.; next morning, 2025; **the --**, to-morrow, 263, 1843, 2236, &c.; **to --**, to-morrow, 966. *ME morn(e), OE morgen, ON morn-*
mot, aux. pr.3 s. may (used to express a wish), 2073. *ME mote, OE mōt*
mouth, n. mouth, 2748. *ME mouth, OE mūþ*
movis, pr.3 s. moves, affects with emotion, 2611; **movit**, p.p. provoked to anger, 1407; affected with emotion, 2035. *ME move(n), AN mover, OF moveir*
murn, v.intr. mourn, lament, 257, 2500; pr.1 s. mourn, grieve, 1604; **murnand**, pres.p. mourning, lamenting, 798; **murnyt**, pt. lamented, 277, 754. *ME murne(n), OE murnan*
murnyng, n. mourning, lamentation, 455, 933, 947. *F. prec.*
my, poss.pron. my, 27, 31, 33, &c.; **-- self**, subject 2040, dir.obj. 1112. *ME my, OE mīn*. See also **sell** s.v. **self**.
mycht, see **may**, aux.
mychti, see **michti**.
myd, adj. middle, occupying a central position, 1668. *ME mid, OE midd*
myddis, see **middis**.
mydnycht, n. midnight, 154. *ME mydnyght, OE midhiht*
myle, n. mile, 74. *ME myl(e), OE mīl*
myn, adj. less, 1943; n. low ones, people of low estate, **mar and --**, 226, 425. *ME minne, ON minne, compar. of lítill*
mynd, n. purpose, 1487; **have in --**, keep one's attention fixed on, 296, remember, 2364; **had -- of**, thought of, 2291. *ME mynd(e), OE gemynd*
myne, v.tr. to mine, make a subterranean passage, 862. *ME myne, OF miner*
myne, n. mine, subterranean passage, 869. *ME myne, OF mine*
myne, poss.pron. absol. mine, belonging to me, my property, 1096, 1497, 2194, &c.; **ellipt.** 678, 2233. *ME myn, OE mīn*
myrk, adj. dark, 868; obscure, hard to understand, 1487, 2179; **merk**, id., 2162. *ME myrk, merk(e), OE mirce, ON myrk-r*
myr(r)our, n. mirror (with magic properties), 1650, 1669, 1690, &c.; **fig. used** of a person, 1840. *ME myrrour, OF mirour*
mys, adv. wrongly, 1490. *ME mys, cf. ON á mis*
mys, v., see **mist**.
my-sell, see **self**.

na, adj. no, not any, 138, 215, 241, &c; **-- thing**, 1481; **-- waye**, 1249; **no**, adj. id., 5, 418; **-- thing**, 810, 113; **-- way**, 639. *NME na, reduced f. OE nān*
na, adv. no, not any, not at all, with **comp.**, 36, 51, 56, &c.; with **vb.** 1185; **no**, adv. with **comp.**, 31, 680, 1520, &c. *Prec.*
na, conj. nor, 190, 927, 936, &c.; than, 732, 902, 987, &c.; **na ... na**, neither ... nor, 328; **na ... neuer**, that ... never, 991. *NME na, OE nā*
na, interj. no, 124, 865, 1102, &c. *Prec.* See also **nay**.
nakit, adj. naked; bare, destitute, 340; unclothed, 1121; unsheathed, 1935, 1940; plain, straightforward, 2554; without any feathers as yet, 2667. *ME nakit, OE nacod*
nakitlye, adv. plainly, openly, 684. *Prec. + -lye*
nalis, n.pl. (a woman's) nails, 243; hooves (of a boar), 547. *ME nail, OE naeġel*
name, n. name, the individual designation of a person, 1326, 1886, &c.; repute, fame, 618. *ME name, OE nama*
nane, adj. no, none, not any, **-- awe**, 801, 936, 1470; **-- vther, othir, nother**, 117, 1083, 1485, 2443. *NME nane, OE nān*
nane, pron. none, no one, not any, 140, 324, 426, &c.; **ellipt.** not any such thing as previously ment., 92, 623, 2436. *Prec.*

napry, n. napery, table linen, 1542. *ME naprye, obs. F nap(p)erie*

natiuité, n. nativity, birth, 1658. *ME, OF natiuité, L nativitas*

natur, n. nature, 11 (see s.v. det); semen, 1191, 1211. *ME, OF nature*

nay, interj. no, negative answer to a statement, doubled for emphasis, 1233. *ME nay, ON nei.* See also na, interj.

negh, v.tr. to approach, go near to a person, 1237. *ME neghen, f. adv. OE nēah, nēh*

neidforce, adv. perforce, of necessity, 892. *ME ned(e), OE nēd + OF force*

neir, adv. near, 540, 1546; almost, 550, 1580, &c.; ner by, adv. nearby, close by, 913; ner hand, adv. near, close at hand, 181. *ME nere, OE nēar, ON nær*

neir, prep. near, close to, 942, 2333; ner, prep. id., 420, 1237; ner hand, prep. near, 829. *Prec.*

nek, n. neck, the narrow part below or behind the head, 674, 820. *ME nek, OE hnecca*

ner, see neir, adv. & prep.

nerrest, adj. shortest, 2436. *See* neir.

nest, n. bird's nest, 2654, 2667. *ME nest(e), OE nest*

neuer, adv. never, at no time, 324, 346, 377, &c.; in no way, 760, 926, &c.; nevir, adv. 1357, 1475. *ME neuer, OE nǣfre*

neuertheles, adv. nevertheless, 625, 1243, 1989. *ME neuer the les(se), OE nǣfre + þȳ lǣs*

nevir, see neuer.

newe, adj. new, not previously known, 1197, 2420. *ME new(e), OE nīwe, nēowe*

newe, adv. anew, afresh, 1542; newly, recently, 2000. *Prec.*

newo, n. nephew, sister's son, 640, 644, 706, &c. *ME nevow, ONF nevo, OF neveu*

nicht, see nycht.

nichtly, adv. nightly, happening or occurring every night, 1009. *LME neghtly, OE nihtlīċ*

nixt, adj. in pred.use, nearest in respect of intimacy or other such relationship, 1181. *ME next, OE nēhst*

no, adj. & adv., see na.

nobilité, n. nobleness of mind or character, 356; quality of being noble in respect of excellence, value or importance, 408. *ME nobilite(e), OF nobilité*

noble, adj. noble, illustrious, 89, 361; admirable, splendid, 339, 349. *ME, OF noble, L nobilis*

nocht, adv. not, 71, 163, 233, &c.; richt (rycht) --, not at all, in no way, 144, 2278; -- for thi, nevertheless, 198, 646, 1248. *ME noght, EME nowiht, OE nōht, nōwiht*

none, n. noon, midday, 1014. *ME non(e), OE nōn, ON nón*

nor, conj. nor, continuing the force of a neg., 543, 1943, 2446; correl. to nother, 717, 1899, 1970. *ME nor, prob. a contraction of nother*

nother, adj. other, 679, 1893; nother, nothir, pron. used with ane and nane, 86, 731, 1083, &c. *ME nother, var. of other*

nother, adv. neither, -- ... nor, 717, 1899, 1970. *ME nother, OE noðer, nowðer, contracted f. nōhwæðer*

notherane, adv. (conj.), neither, 1970. *nother + ane*

novmerit, p.p. counted, measured, 826. *LME nowmer, OF nombrer, L numerare*

now, adv. now, at the present moment or time, 196, 247, 283, &c.; nowe, id. 1713; quhill now, until now, 237; richt --, 1099; ewin --, right now, 1112; as --, just now, at this time, 1378; how --?, what is this? 2377. *ME now, OE nū*

noy, n. annoyance, trouble, 2725. *ME noy, aphetic form of anoy, OF anoi, anui*

noyse, n. noise, loud sound, 1706. *ME noys(e), OF noise, noyse*

nuke, n. corner of a square or angular thing, 96, 2001. *NME nok(e), of obscure origin*

nurys, n. nurse, 431, 450. *ME nurice, OF nurise*
nurys, v.tr. to bring up, rear, 18. *ME norys, nuris, OF nuris(s)-, lengthened stem of nurir*
nybill, n. 820, see expl.note.
nycht, n. night, the time between evening and morning, 365, 1036, 1092, &c.; nicht, id., 273; nychtis, gen.seg. 868; the --, during the night, 1751; apon the --, during the night, 894; with adj. denoting the kind of weather prevailing, 2044, 2049. *ME nyht, OE niht*
nychtbouris, n.pl. neighbours, persons living near, 834, 2047. *ME neghtboure, OE nēhhebūr*
nychttingale, n. nightingale, 2570. *ME nyhtingale, nihtegale, OE nihtegale*
nycht-walkaris, n.pl. night-walkers, people who walk about by night, esp. with criminal intentions, 1007. *EMoE nyghtwalker, OE niht + wealcan vb.*
nymly, adv. nimbly, quickly, in an agile manner, 544. *ME nem(e)ly, OE numol, *nimol + -ly*

obeys, pr. obey, submit to, 572. *LME obeisse, OF obeiss-, lengthened stem of obéir*
obligacoun, n. obligation, an agreement whereby one pers. is bound to another, 2339. *ME obligacioun, OF obligacion, L obligatio*
oblist, p.p. bound by an oath, 686. *Scots form, ME oblisht, f. OF obliger*
ocht, pron. anything, aught, 718, 1497. *ME ocht, OE ōht, ōwiht*
oder, conj. either (-- ... or), 104. *ME other, of uncert.origin, ? contr.form of OE ōhwæðer*
odious, adv. odiously, with great aversion, 1188. *ME, AN odious, OF odieus, L odiosus*
odour, n. scent, fragrance, 1389. *ME, AN odour, OF odor, odur, L odor*
of, adv. off, expressing separation, 254, 476, 905, &c.; distant, 74. *ME, OE of*
of, prep. off, from, 674, 1263, 1520, &c. *Prec.*
of, off, prep. from, out of, of; of motion, direction, distance, 767, 2298, 2414; of liberation and privation, with blin 525, ces, 1461, heile 656, revenge, 280; of origin or source: expressing descent, 140, 318, 669, &c.; local origin, 2421; (born) of, 1659, 2663; with to take, 624, 870, to tyne, 718; of the source or starting point of an action, emotion, 408, 486, 2725; with to thank, 61, 1163; with fayne, adj., 1730; haf gud --, 2156; indic. agent or doer, 11, 1584; indic. means or instrument, 1840; with full, fullit, fulfillit, 374, 440, 828, &c.; indic. the material or substance of which anything is made or consists, 75, 194, 1015, &c.; forming gen. of definition, 149, 2276; after a quantitative word, 2598; indic. the subj.-matter of thought, feeling or action: concerning, with regard to, about, 843, 1002, 1601, &c.; esp. after intr.vbs. of learning, knowing, thinking, 893, 908, 925, &c.; with to hear, 205, 507, &c.; after to become, befall, &c., 156, 1264, 2105, &c.; after to have mercy, pity, 1411, 2715; objective gen. 29, 635, 725, &c.; after an agent-n. 921, 1091; in respect of, 8, 872; esp. in -- age, -- eld, 9, 2566; forming gen. of quality or description, 27, 116, 354, &c.; partit. gen., 108, 1152, &c.; foll. by a poss. case or an absol. poss.pron., 850, 2194; preceded by a superl. 232, 737, 2074; belonging to a thing, 78, 88, 96, &c.; belonging to a place as king, citizen, &c., 111, 255, 688, &c.; belonging to a thing as someth. related in a way, defined or implied by its nature, e.g. cause, effect, &c., 1603, 2095, 2179, &c.; following a n. of time, and indic. a qualif. word, 1236, 1523, 1721; indic. a circumstantial position, 166; found in, contained by, 153; as to, 529; for, 266, 804; -- age, of advanced or old age, 121; -- before, 873, 1895, where of has little meaning; for falt --, 2655; nereby --, 913; in pane --, 2136, 2171. *ME, OE of*

offens, n. offence, sin, wrong, 1449. *ME, OF offens, L offensus* cium
office, n. office, a position of trust, authority, 2296. *ME, OF office, L offi-*
oft, adv. often, many times, frequently, 414, 430, 1665, &c. *ME, OE oft*
oft-tymes, adv. often, 2449. *Prec. + tymes*
on, adv. onward, forward, 375, 634; towards something, approaching, 1573; onward in time, luf --, 1520; tell--, continue to tell, 817, 1317, 2581; with vbs of going: onward, away, 2073, 2076, 2158, &c. *ME, OE on*
on, prep. on, upon (of position), 207, 805, 1797, &c.; indic. the part of the body which supports one, 242, 1074, 2534, 2704; indic. time, 366, 1023, 1441, &c.; indic. manner, 206, 336, 2243, &c.; indic. state, condition, action, 565, 2576; of motion or direction towards a position: onto, 80, 194, 1015, &c.; indic. the pers. to which action, feeling, &c. is directed, 506, 773, 2615; indic. a pers. or thing to which hostile action is directed: against, 1320, 2731; with respect to, 960, 1151, 2427, 2448; used with words expr. vengeance, &c., 746, 1917, 2254; with to (be)get, 694; -- ane, at once, 1145, 1957, 2483; -- hicht, with a loud voice, 2050; equivalent to in, to tak on hand, 1521, 1790. *Prec.*
ony, adj. any, 170, 700, 988, &c.; adv. -- mair, in any degree, 1862. *ME ony, any, OE ǣniġ*
opinioun, n. opinion, view, notion, 2719. *ME, OF opinion, L opinio*
opinly, opynly, adv. openly, clearly, 1669, 2755; unreservedly, 1927, 1976; without concealment, 1891. *ME open, opyn, OE open + -ly*
opyn, adj. open, not covered or closed, 887. *See prec.*
opyn, v.tr. to open, move or turn (a door) from its closed position, so as to admit of passage, 1131. *NME op(p)yn, OE op(e)nian*
or, conj.[1] before, 79, 168, 217, &c.; -- that, before, 1287. *NME ar(e), or, ON ár.* See also eir.
or, conj.[2] or, 92, 492, 599, &c.; oder ... --, 105; -- ellis, 150, 400, 880, &c.; otherwise, 1106. *ME or, reduc.var. of Other, conj.*
orchard, orchart, n. orchard, a garden for herbs and fruit trees, 294, 299, 724, 735. *ME orchard, OE orceard*
ordanit, pt. planned, devised, with inf. 94; appointed to an office, 2224. *ME ordain(e), pt. ordayned, OF ordeiner*
ordour, n. order, command, 2232. *ME ordour, OF ordre*
organis, n.pl. organs (musical instruments), 187, 2520. *ME, OF organe, L organum*
other, see vther.
our, poss.pron. our, 49, 90, 113, &c. *ME our, OE ūre*
our, prefix, over-, excessively, 1102, 1157, 1732, 2054. *See next.*
our, prep. over, above, more than, 297, 300, 312, &c.; above (in power), 532; above (in degree), 824, 827, 1618, &c.; across, 2422, 2565. *Scots form corresp. to ME over, OE ofer.* See also owr.
ourtane, p.p. seized, caught, surprised, 1190, 2039; captivated, 2279. *Prec. + p.p. of ta(k)*
ourthort, adv. across, 1040. *NME ourthuert, over + ME þwert adv., ON þvert, neuter of þverr, transverse*
ourthrawe, v.tr. to overthrow, defeat, 175. *Scots form, corresp. to ME overthrowe*
out, owt, adv. out, from within, 900, 2004; from within doors, 2352; -- of, from within, 159, 227, 970, &c.; outside, 1011, 2170; thar --, outside, 1127. *ME out, OE ūt*
outwith, owtwith, adv. outside, 73, 1148, 2198. *ME outwith*
outwith, prep. outside of, without, 2195, 2221. *Prec.*
owr, adv. over, (turned) upside down, 441; gaf --, left off, abandoned, 486. *See* our, prep.

palace, n. palace, official residence of an emperor or king, 23, 183, 591, &c. *ME palayce, OF palais*
palfray, n. palfrey, saddle-horse, 977, 2219. *ME palfray, OF palefrai*
pall, n. rich cloth, spread over someth., a coverlet, 194; used for the robes of persons of high rank, 211. *ME pall, OE pæll, L pallium*
palpis, n.pl. nipples or breasts of a woman, 1500. *ME pap(pe), app. f. Scand.*
pane, n. pain; penalty, punishment, 2136, 2176; trouble, toil, 2658, 2668. *ME pain(e), OF peine*
pantit, pt.3 pl. tr. painted, 81. *ME paint, OF peint, p.p. of peindre*
paramour, adv. to love --, to be in love with, to love by way of (sexual) love, 129. *ME paramour, OF par amour*
paramour, n. lover, sweetheart, 1929. *Prec.*
par de, interj. by God, indeed, 2177. *ME parde(e), OF pardé, used merely to signify: indeed*
parliament, n. id., assembly, council, 1686, 2604, 2624. *ME parliament, Anglo-L parl(i)amentum*
part, n. portion, share, 1762, 2560; in --, partly, 2187; partis, n.pl. fragments, pieces, 485. *ME, OF part, L part-*
pas, v.intr. to pass, go, proceed, 180, 1722, 2331, &c.; -- on, to proceed on one's way, 2488; pr.1 s. -- furth, go out, 2134; passit, past, pt. went, proceeded, 301, 369, 426, &c.; -- furth, went out, 1055, 2126, 2417, &c.; with other adv.: in, 895; on, 2158; out, 2352; with acc. he -- his way, 1570; pas, imperat. pass, go; -- on, go away, 2076; past, passit, p.p. gone, 1760, 1983, 2283, &c.; -- hame, 1437; -- hamwart, 2493; passit, ppl.a. advanced (in age), 1327. *ME pas(se), OF passer*
passage, n. journey, movement from one place to another, 156, 2549; passage, entrance, channel, 2344, 2348, &c. *ME, OF passage*
passing, n. going, 643. *F. vb.*
paus, pavs, n. pause, an act of stopping or ceasing for a short time in a course of action, esp. in speaking, 2647, 2751; to mak a -- to (another), to cause him to stop in astonishment, 2734. *LME pawse, F pause, L pausa*
payd, p.p. pleased, content; ill --, 325, 1166; weile --, 1714; hartly --, 2160. *ME pay, OF payer*
pece, n. peace, reconciliation, 2410; peis, n. freedom from disturbance, 2780; pes n. quiet, silence, 939. *ME pais, peis, pece, OF pais*
peir, n. peer, equal, 418, 1395, 1620. *ME per(e), AN, OF per, peer*
peis, see pece.
pen, n. pen, writing tool, 110.*ME, OF penne*
penneis, n.pl. pennies, coins, 2598. *ME penies, OE pen(n)ingas, pennigas*
pepill, peple, n. people, a body of persons composing a community, 1670; the persons constituting a partic. concourse, 1851, 1855. *ME pepill, peple, AN poeple*
per, prep. by, after line 2782.
per cas, percas, percase, adv. by chance, by accident, 419, 1041; as it may happen, 2452. *ME, AN per-, par cas*
perchance, adv. perhaps, 140, 305. *ME, AN per-, par chance*
pereles, adj. peerless, matchless, 314. *ME pereles*
perfyte, adj. perfect; thoroughly skilled, 1550, 2621; fully accomplished, 1888; faultless, 2348; complete, 2358; completely informed, perfectly sure, 2129. *ME perfyte, OF parfit*
perfytlye, adv. in a perfect or faultless way, 1069. *Prec. + -lye*
perist, p.p., -- be, perish, suffer destruction, 342. *ME peris(se), OF periss-, lengthened stem of perir*

perofferis, n.pl. offers, proposals, 59. *F. OF poroffrir*
perrell, n. danger, peril, 192, 1435, &c.; **perrellis**, n.pl. 22, 382. *ME peril, perell, OF peril*
persaif, v.tr. to perceive, understand, 1679, 2683; **persauit**, **persavit**, pt. perceived, understood, 556, 629, 1559, 1920. *ME persayue, OF *perceiv-re*
pertlie, **pertly**, adv. openly, cleverly, promptly, 1435, 1975. *ME pert, aphetic f. apert, OF apert + -lie, -ly*
pes, see **pece**
peté, n. pity, compassion; **had --**, felt pity, 1411; a ground or cause for pity, 341. *ME pite, pete, OF pité*
petuoslye, adv. piteously, 683. *ME, AN pitous, OF pitos, piteus, + -lye*
phesik, n. medicine, medical science, 617. *ME fisike, OF fisique, L physica*
philomeyne, n. nightingale, 2578. *ME philomene, F philomèle, ML philomena, see* C.T.Onions, *ODEE, s.v. Philomel*
philosophy, n. id., 620. *ME philosophye, OF philosophie*
picht, p.p. fixed (on a pole), 1150. *ME pight. Of obsc. orig. & history, ? OE *picc(e)an, pt. *pihte?*
pik, n. pitch, residue from the distillation of tar, 891, 2020, 2065. *ME pik, OE pic, L pix, picem*
pilgrimage, n. id., journey undertaken for some pious purpose, 1983, 2565. *ME pelrimage, OF peligrinage*
pilgryme, n. pilgrim, 488, 1988. *EME pilegrim, repr. OF *pelegrin*
pillar, n. stand on which people publicly appeared as a penance, 1015, 1150. *ME pillar(e), pyllar, OF piler, ML pilarium*
pith, n. strength, might, 434. *ME pith, OE piþa*
place, n. id., residence, house, 420, 454; a partic. part or spot, 1042, 2067; locality, situation, 2451. *ME, OF place*
plane, adj. full, complete, esp. of a council, assembly, 2624. *ME, OF plein, plain, L plenus*
plane, adj. used as n.; **in --**, plainly, 756. *ME pla(i)ne, OF plain, L planus*
planetis, n.pl. planets, heavenly bodies, 155. *ME, OF planete, ML planeta*
plant, n. plant, young tree, 350, 357. *ME plant(e), OE plante, OF plante, L planta*
play, n. play, fun, sport, 413. *ME play, OE plega, plæġa*
play(e), v.intr. to play, frolic, 1443; **refl.** to amuse or disport oneself, 2417; **playis**, pr.3 pl. bubble and roll about as a boiling liquid, 2181; **playit**, pt.3 pl. performed instrumental music, 2521, 2525. *ME play(e), OE pleġan, plæġian*
pledis, n.pl. pleadings, 163. *Scots form of ME, OF plaid*
pleis, pr.1 s. tr. take pleasure in, like, 1767; **plesis**, pr.3 s. pleases, delights, 1254; **plesit**, pt. delighted, 659, 1341; **intr. he, thai --**, it pleased him, them, 2319, 2766; **p.p.** pleased, contented, 196, 554; **ples**, pr.3 s.subj. please, 1393; **plesand**, ppl.a. pleasant, agreeable, 311. *ME pleise, OF plais-ir*
plenté, n. abundance, 870, 1545. *ME, OF plenté*
plentuos, adj. plenteous, abundant, 311. *ME plentuous, OF plentivous*
plenzeit, pt.3 s. made complaint, 2731. *ME plenȝe, OF plaign-*
ples, &c., see **pleis**.
plesance, **plesans**, n. pleasure, 306, 557, 843, &c.; desire, 2330, 2401; will, 400, 1002. *ME plesance, OF plaisance*
plesand, see **pleis**.
plesans, see **plesance**.
pleseir, n. pleasure; **at ȝour --**, as you please, 238. *ME, OF plesir, plaisir*
plesis, **plesit**, see **pleis**.

plet, imperat. plait, twist, 1516. *Scots form of ME playt, OF pleit-*
plukit, pt.3 s. plucked, pulled off from where it grew, 553. *ME pluk(e), OE pluccian, ON plukka*
porcioun, n. amount, 2119. *ME porcioun, OF porcion, L portio*
port(e), n. gate, gateway of a city or walled town, 1708, 1709, &c. *ME, OF porte, L porta*
pous, n. pulse, 651. *ME pous, pouce, OF pous, L pulsus*
powder, n. powder, dust, ashes, 1809. *ME powder, OF poudre*
power, n. power, force, 1684. *ME power, OF poër*
powert, n. poverty, 1272. *ME powert(e), OF poverté.* See also pureté.
poynt, n. point, part; at --, aptly, suitably, 1695. *ME poynt, OF point*
prattikis, n.pl. practices, professional work, 628. *OF practike, prat(t)ique*
pray, v.tr. pray, beseech, 1615; pr.1 s. 1184, 2411, 2540, 2555; prayit, pt.3 s. prayed, requested, 287, 589, 683, &c. *ME pray, OF preier*
precious, adj. precious, costly, 2514; held in high esteem, 1620. *ME, OF precios, L preciosus*
pref, preif, v.tr. try, test, find out, 1350, 1521, 1765, 2184, 2319; previt, p.p. tried, 2544; previt, p.p. proved, given demonstration or proof of by action, 2755. *ME preuen, OF prover*
prekand, pr.p. riding (fast), 372, 2240; prekit, pt.3 s. rode, 375, 1857. *ME prike, OE prician*
prent, pr.2 s. impress (a story) upon the heart, 521. *ME prente, printe, OF preinte, fem.form of preint, p.p. of preind-re*
pres, n. haste, 1857. *ME press, OF presse*
presens, n. presence, ceremonious attendance upon the emperor, 613; for his --, himself being present, 1450. *ME presense, OF presence*
presome, pr.1 s. presume, assume or take for granted, 985, 2675. *ME presum, OF presumer*
preson, presoun, n. prison, 272, 365, 1013, &c. *ME preso(u)n, OF prisun, preson*
presonit, p.p. imprisoned, 1135. *Prec.*
prest, n. priest, a member of the clerical profession, 1485, 1487, 1496, &c. *ME preste, preest, OE prēost, ON prest-r*
prety, adj. excellent, admirable, 330, 2013. *ME prety, OE praettiġ*
prevaté, n. privacy, secrecy, 878, 1213; secret matter, personal affairs, 2370. *ME prevatee, OF priveté, privité*
prevé, adj. private (of appartment in royal residence), 135; secret, hidden, 2344; in --, 989. *ME preve, OF privé*
prevé, n. privy, latrine, 912. *F.adj.*
prevely, prewely, adv. secretly, stealthily, 861, 1070, 1086, &c. *Adj. + -ly*
previt, see pref.
price, n. prize, trophy or symbol of victory, 414; prys, n. excellence, of --, worthy, excellent, 27; esteemed, honourable, 111. *ME pris, price, OF pris*
proces, n. story, tale, 1418, 1971. *ME, OF proces, L processus*
producit, pt.3 pl. produced, brought forth, 2649. *L producere*
proffet, v.tr. to be of advantage, do good to, 1616; proffettis, pr.3 s. intr. is of advantage, 1182. *ME prof(f)et, OF profiter*
promis, promys, n. promise, declaration made to another person as to the giving of some specif. thing, 635, 2630, 2635. *L promissum*
promit, pr.1 s. promise, 2624. *ME promit, L promittere*
promyt, n. promise, 29. *F. vb.*
proper, adj. proper, used to designate a partic. person, -- name, 1886. *ME, OF propre, L proprius*
provdly, prowdly, adv. splendidly, 322; in dignified fashion, 2461. *ME proud, LOE prūd, ON prúð-r, both prob. f. OF prud*

prufe, v.tr. to put to the test, 1435;prufit, p.p.-- wele, shown himself to be good, 430; pt.3 s. showed himself to be, 2310. *ME profe, OE profian, succeeded by OF prover.* See also pref.

pryme, n. prime, the first hour of the day, 2248. *ME prime, OE prīm, L prima*

prys, see price.

psaltery, n. psaltery (medieval stringed instrument), 2523. *OF psalterie, L psalterium*

pure, adj. poor, having few possessions, 539; -- folk, the poor as a clas, 1622, 1832. *ME poore, pour, OF poure*

pure, n. poor people as a class, paupers, 1640. *Prec.*

pur(e)té, n. poverty, destitution, 877, 2692, 2730. *ME, OF poureté.* See also powert.

purge, pr.2 s. subj. purge, empty (the stomach, bowels, &c.), 1211. *ME purge, OF purger*

purgyn, n. purgation, discharge of waste matter from the body, 1191. *F. vb.*

purpos, n. purpose, intention, resolution, 968. *ME, OF purpos*

purpour, n. purple cloth, purple robe, 211. *ME purpour, OE purpure, ON purpuri, L purpura*

put, v.tr. to put; -- of ..., remove from, 1606; -- ... to, promote ... to, 1607; -- dovn(e), kill or dethrone, 581, 811, 2229; pr.2 s. subj. -- to deid, -- dovne, put to death, kill, 602, 961; pt.3 s. placed, 1029; p.p. promoted, exalted, 2583; -- dovne, ruined, demolished, 1812. *ME put(t), OE *putian*

pvnis, pvniss, pr.s. subj. punish, cause to suffer for an offence, 1160, 1431; pvnist, p.p. punished, 1135, 1156, &c. *ME punyse, OF puniss-, extended stem of punir*

py, n. magpie, 1980, 2013. *ME py, OF pie*

pyne, n. pine-tree, 297, 300, 302, &c. *ME pine, pyne, OE pīn, L pinus*

pynetré, n.pine-tree, 289. *ME pyne tre, OE pīn trēo*

pynula, pynule, pynull, n. young pine-tree, 318, 322, 327, 330. *ML pinula*

pyot(e), n. magpie, 1882-3, 1887, 1896, &c.; pyotis, n.gen.s. 1978, 2023, 2064. *ME piot, f. pie n. + -ot*

quene, n. queen, the wife of a king, 654, 666; the wife of an emperor, 351, 379, 387, &c.; qwene, n. queen, empress, 704, 1309. *ME quene, OE cwēn*

quentans, n. acquaintance, 2338. *ME queyntance, aphetic form of acquaintance, OF acointance*

quentis, n. device, stratagem, cunning, 1062. *ME qua(y)ntyse, OF cointise, quen-tise*

quert, n. health, sound condition, 1279. *App. f. ON *kwert (*kwerr-r)*

question, questioun, n. question, inquiry, 511, 1602; problem, 2144, 2187; na -- is tharat, there is not room for doubt, 670. *ME questio(u)n, AN questiun, OF question, L quaestion-*

quha, interr.pron. who, 1815, 2378; in a dependent question, or cl. of similar meaning, 668, 669, 1081, &.; rel.pron. whoever, without correl., 1011, 1627, 2612; quhay, 1082. *NME wha, OE hwā*

quhar, adv. where, in direct question, 260; in depend.cl. 2278; in or at the (or a) place in or at which, 448, 900, 933, &c.; introd. a cl., as obj. of a vb. or prep. 1078, 2016; simple rel. 885;in advers. sense: whereas, 2731. *NME hware, OE hwār, hwǣr*

quhar-euer, adv. rel. wherever, 1504.

quharfor, adv. wherefore, for what cause or reason, why, 2169.

quhar-on, adv.rel. on which, whereon, 1800.

quhar-throwe, adv.rel. whereby, by means of which, 172.

quar-to, adv. to what end, whereto, 1613.
quha-sa, rel.pron. whoever, any(one) who, 2118.
quhasa-evir, rel.pron. whoever, 889.
quhat, exclam.adj. what; -- scaith, 784. *NME quat, OE hwæt*
quhat, interr.adj. what, what kind of, 1128; in indir.question and dep.cl. of sim. meaning, 709, 1687, 2270, &c. *prec.*
quhat, interr.pron. what, 394, 848, 857, &c.; of a pers., in pred. use, equiv. to who, 1942; in indir.question, or cl. of sim. meaning, 156, 455, 2549, &c. *Prec.*
quhat-evir, rel.pron. whatever, anything that, 858.
quhay, see quha.
quhen, adv. when, at the time that, in ref. to a def. actual occurrence in the past, 10, 43, 59, &c.; in ref. to a fut. time, 1372; with the notion of time modif. or merged in that of mere connexion, 1966, 2126, &c., -- that, 210, 507, 2547; -- at, 1812, 1990. *ME hwenne, whan, OE hwænne*
quhen-euer, adv. whenever, at any time when, 1058, 2766.
quhidder, conj. if, whether, 92, 2770; quhiddir that, id., 1725. *ME whydyr, OE hwæþer, hweþer*
quhile, n. while, a portion of time, considered with respect to its duration, 1051; with adj. expressing length, 1286. *ME whyle, quile, OE hwīle*
quhile ... quhile, correl.conj., now ... now, at one time ... at another time, 2374. *Prec.*
quhilk, rel.pron. who, which, 617, 979, 2264-5, 2685; referring to a fact, circumstance, or statement, 722, 1608, 1901, 1973; introd. a continuative cl., 404-5; -- that, 2422;interr.pron., which, 2672; the --, 575, 2711. *ME whilke, quilke, OE hwilc*
quhill, adv. once, at one time, 1187. *See* quhile n.
quhill, conj. until, up to the time that, 101, 228, 799, &c.; -- that, 221, 580, 629; -- at, 1599; conj. while, during the time that, 231, 445, 1457, &c.; -- that, 1037. *Prec.*
quhill, prep. until, 237, 263, 1173, &c. *Prec.*
quhilom, adv. once, some time ago, 1324; quhylom, id., 518; at times, 1424. *ME whilom, quilum, OE hwīlum*
quhom, rel.pron.whom, in dep.question or cl. of sim. meaning, as object of a prep. 17. *ME whom, OE hwām*
quhom-evir, compound rel.pron. whomever, any(one) whom, 1432.
quhy, adv. why, wherefore, (in dir.question), 1093, 1139, 1142, &c.; in indir. question or a dep.cl. of sim. meaning, 101, 279, 509, &c.; for --, as indir.interr., for what reason, why, 107; for which cause, wherefore, 571. *ME why, OE hwī*
quhy, n. reason, cause, 116, 2095. *Prec.*
quhylis, adv. once, formerly, 405, 1019, 1617. *ME whyles, OE -hwīles*
quhylom, see quhilom.
quod, pt.3 s. quoth, said, 1087, 1132, 1278, &c. *ME quoth, quod, OE cwæð, ON kvað*
quyk, adv. alive, 1822, 1825. *ME quick, OE cwic*
quyte, adv. quite, completely, 283, 359, 1988, &c. *ME quyte, OF quite*

rad, adj. afraid, 2530, 2759. *ME radd, rade, ON hrædd-r*
raid, see ryde.
raif, see ryfe.
rais, see rys.
raith, adv. quickly, without delay, 38. *ME rathe, OE hraðe, hræðe*

rak, pr.1 s. with to + inf. care, am reluctant, feel aversion, 1632. *ME rek, OE reccan, ON rœkja*
rak, n. care, heed, consideration, 1185. *F. vb.* See expl.note.
rane, rayne, n. rain, 2030, 2038. *ME rayn, raine, OE reġn, rēn*
rang, see ryng, to ring.
rasit, p.p. raised, elevated, 104; lifted (a pers.) and placed in a standing position, 1934; pt.3 s. assisted (one) to rise, 2716. *ME rais, ON reisa*
ravyn, n. raven (bird), 2658; ravinnis, ravynnis, n.pl. ravens, 2615, 2632, &c. *ME ravyn, OE hræfn, ON hrafn.* See also hie-ravyn, scho-ravyn.
record, v.tr. to relate in words, 1342. *OF recorder*
red, see reid, v.tr.
reducit, p.p. brought back, 1321. *L reducere*
redy, adj. ready, 2401, 2460, 2469; available, 2389; with to + inf., prepared, 2655, 2667. *ME redy, EME ræ̣diġ, OE rǣde*
redy, adv. without difficulty, 2196. *Prec.*
redyng, vbl.n. reading, the act of interpreting or expounding,2112-3. *ME redyng, OE rǣding*
refreschit, p.p. refreshed, provided with refreshment, 316. *OF refresch(i)er*
reft, p.p. taken away, 1580; pt.3 s. took away from another for oneself, 1399. *ME pt. refde, p.p. reued, OE rēafod(e), inf. rēafian*
regard, n., in --, in comparison, 1496. *OF regard*
regioun, n. region, country, 416; kingdom, 2688. *ME regioun, AN regiun, L region-*
reid, v.tr. to advise, 265; to read, expound, declare, 2118, 2149; pr.1 s. advise, 90, red, pt.3 s. read, looked over someth. written with understanding of what is meant, 1631, 2335.*ME rede, redde, OE rǣdan, rǣdde*
reid, n. advice, 856; phr. to think gude &c. --, to think advisable, 2315. *ME rede, OE rǣd*
reiosit, ppl.a. made glad, delighted, 308, 701, 2167. *ME reioisen, OF rejoiss-, lengthened stem of rejoir*
reklesly, adv. accidentally, through carelessness, 949. *ME rekkeles, OE recceleās + -ly*
relacioun, n. narration, account, 994. *ME relacioun, OF relation, L relation-*
releif, v.tr. to relieve, help in poverty or necessity, 1766.*NME releef, OF relever*
remane, v.intr. to remain, stay, 1000, 1172, 2384. *ME rema(y)ne, AN remayn-, OF remanoir*
remeid, n. remedy, 170, 1733, 2172, &c. *ME, OF remede*
rememberans, n. remembrance, recollection, 719. *ME rememberans, OF remembrance*
remittit, p.p. pardoned, forgiven, 1519. *ME remitte, L remittere*
remord, v.tr. to recall to mind with remorse, 2710. *ME remord(e), OF remordre*
remuf, imperat. remove, shift from the place occupied, 2185. *ME remoue, OF remo(u)v-*
renovne, n. renown, celebrity, fame, 335, 415, 778, &c. *ME renoun(e), AN ren(o)un, OF renon*
repent, v.tr. to repent, feel regret, sorrow or contrition for, 722. *ME repent, OF repentir*
replege, v.tr. to withdraw a person from the jurisdiction of another court to one's own upon pledge that justice shall be done, to redeem, 609. (*NED* 1536). *OF repleger, ML replegiare*
reprevit, p.p. reproved, chided, 1448. *ME repreve, AN repreov-, OF repreuv-*
requer, v.tr. to entreat, request, 974; requerit, pt.3 s. required, demanded as necessary, 1018; requyrit, pt.3 s. requested, begged, 2479. *ME requer, OF requer-, stem of requerre*
request, n. request, expression of one's desire or wish, 274. *ME, OF requeste*

requyrit, see requer.
resaif, v.tr. to receive, accept in a specif. manner, 2414; resauit, pt.3 s. received, greeted (a pers.) in a specif. manner, 645; p.p. received, welcomed, 151, 185. *ME resaive, ONF receivre*
resoun, n. reason, grounds for an argument or case, 610; the act of reasoning, 2664; to knaw --, to take a reasonable view of the matter, 403. *ME resoun, OF res(o)un*
respit, p.p. granted a respite, 795. *ME p.p. respit, OF respiter*
rest, v.intr. to stay, dwell, 2270; rest, v.refl. to take repose by lying down, 446. *ME rest, OE restan, ræstan*
rest, n. rest, sleep, 1996; quiet, freedom from aggression or distress, 2780; withoutin --, without delay, 1416; bot --, without intermission, 2282. *ME rest, OE rest, ræst*
restore, v.tr. to restore, give back, 1205. *OF restorer*
restrictioun, n. constriction, 762 (*NED* 1758). *OF restriction, ML restriction-*
retour, v.intr. to return to a place, 1318. *F. OF n. retour*
reuth, n. pity, 2082. *EME reuþe. OE hrēow with addit. -th, suggested by ON hryggþ*
revele, v.tr. to betray, 1927. (*NED* 1640). *ME reuele, OF reveler*
revenge, v.tr. to avenge, 280; refl. to avenge oneself, 1628; revengit, p.p. avenged, 807, 1918, 2099; rewengit, p.p. id., 514, 1634. *OF revenger*
reuerens, n. reverence, respect shown towards a pers., 2536. *ME reuerence, OF reverence, L reverentia*
reuerently, adv. in a reverent manner, 1303, 1859. *ME, OF reverent, L reverent- + -ly*
reward, n. reward, 29, 635, 1221, &c.; rewardis, n.pl. rewards, 703, 1197. *ME, ONF reward*
rewaris, n.pl. rivers, 2183. *ME revere, AN river(e), OF reviere*
rewe, pr.s. regret, repent of, 522, 1408. *ME rewe, OE hrēowan*
rewengit, see revenge.
rewest, p.p. arrayed in ecclesiastical vestments, 2469. *ME reuest f. OF revestir, LL revestire*
rewlis, pr.3 s. rule, guide, 2204. *ME rewle, OF riuler, reuler*
riche, adj. rich, having large possessions, 293, 416, 1618, &c. *ME riche, OF rice*
riches, n. riches, wealth, 354, 824, &c. *ME riches, OF richesse*
richt, rycht, adj. right, as opposed to left, 1651; fitting, appropriate, 1719 (see expl.note), 2210, *ME right, OE riht*
richt, rycht, adv. right(ly), precisely, 153; -- heir, -- thar, 461, 1108, 1959, 2056; -- now, 1099; -- nocht, not at all, 144, 2278; of motion, straight, 1743; very, extremely, with adv. and adj. 8, 347, 660, &c. *Prec.*
richt, n. law, justice, 269; the right thing, 2562; justifiable claim, 2672. *ME right, OE riht*
richtsa, richt sa, adv. right so, in the same way, 1069, 1756; at that moment, 2593.
rissyn, see rys.
rolpand, pres.p. crying, croaking, 2615; rolpit, pt.3 pl. cried, croaked, 2679. *OE hrōpan, ON raupa*
Romane, adj. Latin, 1888. *ME, OF romain*
rowme, n. position, 624. *ME rown(e), OE rūm*
rudlye, adv. roughly, violently, 548. *ME rud(e)li(e), f. OF ru(i)de*
rusche, n. a rushing sound, sudden violent movement, 1117. *ME ruschen, AN russher*
ruskis, pr.3 s. tears, tugs at, 548. *ME rusk(e(n), Scand: Icel, Fær, Norw, MSw ruska, Da ruske*

rute, n. root, part of a plant below the surface, 317, 345, 546, &c.; rutis, n.pl. roots of the hair, 278. *ME root, LOE rōt, ON rót*
ryally, adv. royally, in a manner befitting a king, 2689. *ME rial + -ly, OF rial, var. of real, roial*
ryde, v.intr. to ride, move about on horseback, 2219; raid, pt.3 s. rode, 1596, 2241, 2328. *ME ride, pt. NME rade, OE rīdan, rād*
ryf, adj. rife, widespread, abundant, 1967. *ME ryf(e), ON ríf-r*
ryfe, v.tr. to tear apart, 546; raif, pt.3 s. lacerated with the hands, 243, 2739; tore apart, 278, 462. *ME ryfe, pt. NME rafe, ON rífa, pt. reif*
ryn, v.intr. to run, flow, 761. *OE rinnan, ON rinna* *OF regner*
ryng, v.intr. to reign, rule or govern as king, 2689. *Scots form of ME reigne,*
ryng, v.tr. to ring, cause (a bell) to give forth sound, 1008, 1099, 1648; rang, pt. intr. (of bells), rang, 1145; tr. caused (a bell) to give forth sound, 1667, 2520. *ME ryng, pt. NME rang, OE hringan*
ryng, n. ring, used as a seal, 147; used as a token, 2363, 2377, 2378, &c. *ME ryng, OE hring*
ryplé, adv. ripely, with ripe or mature consideration, 265. *ME rype, OE rīpe + -lé*
rys, imperat. rise, get up, 1517; v.intr. to get up from sitting, kneeling or lying posture, 221, 1248, 1251, &c.; rais, pt. got up, 38, 44, 223, &c.; got up from sleep, 1336, 1441; -- wp, 1530; rissyn, p.p. risen, swollen, 1193. *ME rise, pt. NME rase, OE rīsan, pt. rās*

sa, so, swa, adv. & conj. so, in the way or manner described, indic. or suggested, 337, 451, 561, &c.; with vbs. like do, say, &c., 1093, 2055, &c.; used as pred. with the vb. be, 93, 2637; in ell. use How sa? 2581; used to confirm or strengthen a previous statement, 310, 323, 1061, &c.; denoting similarity between two facts, actions, &c., 381, 438, 692, 2263; consequently, 852, 907, 952, &c.; then, thereupon, 224, 419, 450, &c.; to that extent, in that degree, 102, 111, 313, &c.; in affirm.cl., tending to become a mere intensitive without compar. force, with adj. followed by a, 348, 1404; with vb., intensitive, 1395; in adjuration, 1143; sa ... as, to the same extent, in the same degree as, 600; sa that, denoting result or logical consequence, 424; sa (so) ... that, in such a way, to such an extent that, with adj. & adv., 311, 415, 439, &c.; with vb., 824, 2631; with but, 533; with omission of that, 2279, 2538, 2601; provided that, 606, 1414; as follows, with ell. of that, 538 (swa), 723 (so). *ME so, NME swa, sa, OE swā*
sage, n. sage, a man of profound wisdom, 38, 44, 372, &c.; sagis, n.pl. 20, 132, 146, &c.; sege, n. sage, 50. *ME, OF sage*
said, see say(e).
saif, v.tr. to save, protect from someth. unwelcome, 865; to guard from damage, 1792; savit, pt.3 s. saved, rescued from death, 483, 497, 2677; p.p. id., 475, 1952; guarded from loss, 1174; protected, 1947. *NME saf(e), saw(e), AN sa(u)ver, OF salver.* See also salf.
saifand, prep. except, 427, 2368. *Prec.*
saikles, adj. guiltless, innocent, 742, 788. *ME sakles, LOE saclēas, perh.after ON sak-lauss*
saile, n. sail, sails collectively, 2490. *ME saile, OE segel.* See also saland.
sair, adj. of sickness: severe, 748; of manifestations of grief: bitter, 918, 2093; afflicted with sorrow, distressed, 2497. *NME sa(i)r, OE sār*
sair, adv. sorely; of biting: violently, severely, 438; with vbs. of grieving, annoying, &c.: deeply, intensely, 480, 1447; with vbs.of lamenting, 948, 1460, 1600, &c.; with vbs. of repenting, 722, 1408; with vbs. of astonishment, 161. *Prec.*

sairlie, adv. severely, 745. *Sair, adj. + -lie*
sais, see say.
saland, pr.p. sailing, moving or travelling on water by means of sails, 2593. *ME sa(i)le, OE segl(i)an.* See also saile.
salbe = sall be, 2088.
salf, imperat. save, rescue from death, 612. *ME salve, sauf, OF salver, L salvare.* See also saif.
sall, aux.v. pr., with inf. without to; must, 609, 1106; indic. what is appointed or settled to take place, is to, 2678; in commands or instructions, in the 2nd pers., equivalent to an imperat., 1172; expressing the speaker's intention to bring about some action, event or state of things, 216, 218, 364, &c.; in questions introd. by an interr.pron. or adv., 848, 1427, 1682; as an aux. of the future, 404, 695, 744, &c.; of prophecy, 360, 1290, 1593, &c.; of promise, 35, 40, 46, &c.; of threat, 391, 499, 603, &c.; thow -- lē, conditioned by the rhyme, 2588, see expl.note; suld, pt. should, used in indir. reported utterance, or other statements relating to past time, where sall would be used if the time referred to were present, 52, 57, 93, &c.; in commands, &c., 181, 269, 342, &c.; in hypoth. & final cl., 1540, 2198; in noun-cl. dep. on expressions of willing, desiring, requesting, &c., 299, 975, &c.; in statements of propriety, 1104, 2753; in the apodosis of a hypoth. proposition, indic. that the supposition is unreal, 269, 2444, &c.; in a cl. expressing the obj. of fear, 714, 2494. *ME s(ch) all, OE sceal; ME pt.s(ch)ulde, OE sceolde*
saluiour, n. Saviour, 2456. *ME saveour, OF sauveour*
salust, pt. saluted, 1384, 1698, 2244. *NME salusid, salust, f. OF n. saluz, salus*
salusyng, vbl.n. salute, greeting, 376. *Prec.*
samekle, n. so large a quantity, 1566; adv. in such a degree, 1605. *See* sa & mekle
sample, n. example, a story which serves to illustrate some statement, 404, 960, 1614, 2508. *ME sa(u)mple, aphetic f.AN assample, OF essample.* See also ensample & example.
samyn, adj. same, 960, 2275. *Poss. f. OE *samen, ON saman*
sanct, adj. saint, holy, 1486. *OE sanct, L sanctus*
sandy, adj. sandy, composed of or containing a large proportion of sand, 2019. *ME sandy, OE sandiġ*
sang, n. song, vocal music, 797; the musical utterance of certain birds, 1962, 2562-3, &c. *NME, OE sang*
sang, pt. see syng.
sary, adj. sorrowful, distressed, 1238, 1256. *NME sary, OE sārig*
sat, see sit.
sauld, see sell.
saull, n. soul, the spiritual part of man regarded as surviving after death, 1109. *NME saull, OE sawol*
savit, see saif.
saw(e), see se vb.
saw(e), n. speech, story, tale, 390, 493, 1154, 1601, 1865; sawis, n.pl. words, 271. *ME saw(e), OE *sagu*
say(e), v.tr. to say, utter specif. words, 360, 791, 1161; to tell, 1183; with obj. a pron.: to declare, state, 848, 857; suth to --, 1837; I dar wele --, 105, 2182; pr.2 pl. subj. declare, state, 673; absol. 1093, 1845; utter or pronounce specif. words with ell. of that, 1639; sais, pr.3 s. says, declares in words, 2662; says, pr.3 s. tells, 417; declares, with obj.cl. with ell. of that, 2665; sayis, pr.s. utters specif. words, 821, 1632;

declares, 1004, 2584; absol. with sa, 1139; said, sayd, pt. uttered, declared, spoke, 27, 39, 45, &c.; say, imperat. 1472; says, imperat.pl. utter, pronounce, 2782; sayand, pres.p. declaring, 113, 273, 1531, &c.; said, p.p. 43, 1713, 1752; uttered, 2087; with pron. 1113, 2080; with cogn.obj. 493. *ME sayn, seyn, pt. seyde, p.p. seyd, OE secgan, sæġde, sæġd*

says, see say(e), & se vb.

scair, see scar.

scaith, n. harm, damage, 657, 1785, 1877, &c.; matter for sorrow or regret, 784. *ME skathe, ON skaþe*

scantly, adv. hardly, scarcely, 1806, 1930. *ME skant, ON skamt + -ly*

scar, scair, n. share, portion, 553, 1726, 1748, 2665. *ME share, schar, OE scearu, with /sk/ due to Scand*

schame, n. shame, disgrace, 717, 748, 909, &c.; tharof he thocht gret --, was ... ashamed, 1535; schamis, gen.s., ane -- deid, a shameful death, 282, 1612, 1734. *ME shame, OE sceamu*

schamed, p.p. disgraced, 1252. *ME shame(n), OE sceamian*

schamfull, adj. shameful, degrading, 1090, 1134. *ME shameful, OE sceamful*

schane, pt.3 s. shone, shed beams of bright light, 366, 2511. *NME s(c)hane, OE scān, pt. of scīnan*

schape, pr.pl. devise, plan, with inf. as obj., 1764, 2452; schapis, pr. id., 1284, 1484; schupe, pt. devised, planned, 281, 546, 867, &c.; refl. set himself, 249. *ME shap(p)e, pt. shope, OE sc(i)eppan, pt. scōp*

scharpe, adj. sharp, having a keen edge or point, 1299. *ME s(c)harpe, OE scearp*

schaw(e), v.tr. to show by telling, 404; to display (a quality) by one's action, 1763; to reveal, 2752; pr.2 pl. show, put in overt act, 1770; schawis, pr.s., intr. impers. is seen, shown, evident, 247; schawin, p.p. shown, told, 363; schewe, pt.3 s. showed, displayed, 844, 1669, 2330; pointed out, made known, 2554. *NME schaw(e), pt. schew(e), p.p. schawen, OE sceāwian*

sche, pers.pron. 510, 520, 683, 1002-3, 1401, 2738. *ME sche, OE sēo.* See also scho.

scheit, schete, n. sheet, article of bedding, 1453, 2001, 2033; schetis, n.pl. sheets, 2000. *ME s(c)hete, NME scheit, Ang scēte*

schent, p.p. ruined, disgraced, 1142. *ME schent, p.p., f. OE scendan*

schewe, see schaw.

schip, n. ship, sea-going vessel, 2483, 2489, &c. *ME s(c)hip, OE scip*

schir, n. sir, in address, 202, 263, 329, &c. *ME sir, OF sire*

scho, pers.pron. she, 128, 131, 133, &c. *NME scho, OE sēo.* See also sche.

scho-ravyn, n. she-raven, 2652, 2657, 2661. *See* scho & ravyn.

schore, v.tr. to threaten, 1896. *F. the (chiefly Scots) adj. schore, precipitous, rugged, ultim. cogn. with schere v., OE sceran, p.p. scoren*

schore, n. threat, menace, 1899. *Prec.*

schort, adj. short, brief, of time, 835, 920, 1286; quasi-n.: in --, briefly, concisely, 2132. *ME schort, OE sceort*

schortly, adv. shortly, soon, 1169. *ME schortly, OE sceortlīce*

schot, n. discharge, flux, 747. *NE schot, OE sc(e)ot*

schout, n. shout, a loud, vehement cry, 244, 450. *Corresponds formally to ON skúta, skúti, a taunt; prob. derived from root of shoot, vb., OE sceotan*

schout, v.intr. to shout, make a loud outcry, 937; schoutit, pt.3 s. shouted, 453. *Prec.*

schowit, pt.3 s. shoved, pushed its way forward, 435. *ME schovede f. OE scūfan*

schrewit, adj. depraved, wicked, 1475. *ME schrewed*

schupe, see schape.

schut, v.tr. to avoid, escape, 976. *OE scēotan.* See expl.note.

science, sciens, n. knowledge, the arts, 35, 41, 49, &c. *ME, OF science*
scilens, n. silence, absence of all sound or noise, 868, 2535, 2608, &c. *ME, OF silence*
sclander, v.tr. to slander, defame, speak evil of, 269. *ME sclander, OF esclandre*
scolar, n. scholar, pupil, one who is taught in school, 1630; **scolaris**, n.pl. 1629. *ME scoler, -ar(e), OF escoler, OE scolere, LL scholaris*
scule, n. school, non-fig., 1629. *ME schole, OE scōl, OF escole*
scurge, v.tr. to scourge, whip, flog, 253. *ME scurge, f. AN n. escurge.* See expl.note.
se, v.tr. to see, perceive by sight, 764, 914, 1193; to perceive mentally, 1841, 2178; to ascertain by inspection, 21, 373, 976, &c.; to ascertain by experiment, 1633; contemplate, examine, 169, 657; to meet and converse with, 139, 2412, 2691, 2700; look at, contemplate, 341; to ensure, 1294; to witness, 1572, 1868; to behold in a dream, 2268; **intr.** to look, 305, 1040; to perceive objects by sight, 2126, 2195, &c.; **lat --**, show (me), 2581; **pr.1 s.** perceive with the eyes, 1458, 1953, 1967, &c.; perceive mentally, 808, 859, 1182, &c.; ascertain by inspection, 90; **seis, pr.s.** perceive with the eyes, 1966; perceive objects by sight, have the faculty of seeing, 2135; **says**, for **seys**, **pr.3 s.** sees, examines, 651; **saw(e), pt.** perceived by sight, 157, 171, 241, &c.; met, 802; met with in the course of one's experience, 1769, 2040, 2049; ascertained by inspection, 938, 2550; witnessed, 1097; beheld in a dream, 2277; perceived objects by sight, 2223; **se, imperat.** ensure, 1222, 1266, 2476; make sure by inspection, 1358, 1682; **sene, seyne, p.p.** perceived by sight, 960, 993, 1077, &c.; examined, 653, 2066; beheld in a dream, 1738; looked at, scrutinised, 1999; **pass. to be sene**, to appear, 1310, 2128, 2713. *ME se(e), pt. saw(e), p.p. se(i)ne, OE sēon*
se, n. sea, 1242, 2422, 2480, &c.; **sey**, id., 2565. *ME se(e), OE sǣ*
secound, ord.num. second, 38, 1749, 1753. *ME seco(u)nd, OF second*
secret(e), n. secret; **in --**, in private, secretly, 654, 704; **secretis**, n.pl. secrets, 696. *ME, OF secret*
sege, see **sage**.
seid, n. seed, semen, generation, 1025. *ME sede, seed, OE sǣd*
seike, adj. sick, ailing, 650, 669. *ME seke, OE sēoc*
seike, v.tr. to seek, go in search of, look for, 1537, 2140; **intr.** to make search, 2281. *NME seke, OE sēcan*
seiknes, seknes, n. sickness, illness, 632, 748, 1190, 1210. *ME sek(e)nes(se), OE sēocnes*
seir, adj. various, 355, 1273. *ME ser(e), ON sér*
seis, see **se** vb.
seker, adj. sure, fully assured or convinced, 1958, 2207. *ME siker, OE sicor*
sekerly(e), adv. certainly, 1261, 1398, 1979; with full certainty or conviction, 2430; positively, 34; safely, 689. *Prec. + -ly(e)*
self, n. self, in **compound pers.pron.**, 58, 422, 743, &c.; **his, hir awne --**, 662, 1508; **the empriouris --**, 2527; **the --**, itself, 2660; **sell**, n. self, in **compound pers.pron.** 1118, 1747, 1830, 2534. *ME, OE self*
selit, pt.3 s. sealed, placed a seal on, 147. *ME sele, OF seeler*
sell, v.tr. to sell, give up for money, 851; **sauld**, pt.3 pl. sold, handed over to another pers. for money, 2597. *ME sell, pt. NME sald, OE sellan, Ang salde*
sell, n. see **self**.
sely, adj. happy, blissful, 2699. *ME sely, OE sǣliġ*
semblit, pt.3 pl. assembled, brought together (persons) into one place or company, 77. *ME semble, OF (a)sembler*

sempill, adj. absol. pl. humble (persons), 536. *ME simpil, OF simple*
sen, conj. since, -- that, 1407. *Contr. form of ME sethen*
senatour, n. senator, a member of a senate, 1508, 1514, 1525. *ME senatour, OF senateur, L senator*
send, v.tr. to send, order to go, 640; of God: to cause to happen or come into existence, 177; pr.subj. send, give (of God), 1768; pt.3 s. ordered to go, 644; induced to go, 1306; -- for, -- eftir, sent for, 1195, 1984, 2547; p.p. sent for, 1571. *ME send(e), OE sendan*
sene, seyne, see se vb.
sentens, n. meaning, 1278. *ME sentens(e), OF sentence, L sententia*
senȝeory, n. sovereignty, dominion, 572; a body of 'seigniors' or lords, 1524. *ME se(i)gno(u)ry, OF seignorie*
serf, v.tr. to serve, suffice (a pers.) in regard to some need or requirement, 1136; seruit, servit, pt. served, supplied with food, 1544; supplied, furnished, 803; seruit, p.p. served, dished up, brought in, 1515; deserved, merited, 1536, 2246, 2247 (*poss. aphetic f. OF deservir*). *ME serf, serve, OF servir*
serpent, n. snake, 404-5, 432; serpentis, gen.s. 449. *ME, OF serpent, L serpent-*
seruandis, n.pl. servants, personal or domestic attendants, 2693, 2697. *ME servand, OF servant*
seruice, seruis, n. service, the condition of being a servant of a partic. master, performance of the duties of a servant, 28, 838, 1181, 2706, 2771. *ME servis(e), OF servise, -vice*
seruit, servit, see serf.
sesit, pt.3 s. ceased, stopped, 1962. *ME ses(e), OF cesser*. See also ces.
set, ppl.a. appointed, fixed (of a point of time), 158, 421, 2164. *See next*
set, v.tr. to place, cause to dwell, 1484; to arrange, appoint a day for, cause to sit, 2604; refl. to set oneself for something, decide upon, prepare for, 1426; pt.3 s. placed, set 195, 419, 433, &c.; imperat. -- ȝe nocht by, 1928, see expl.note; p.p. set, placed, 83, 410, 1515, &c.; arranged, disposed, 284; seated, 734, 1524, 2355. *ME set, OE settan*
sevyn(e), card.num. seven, 19, 36, 81, &c. *ME sevin, sevyne, OE seofon*
sevynt, ord.num. seventh, 55, 2264-5; written vij, 2240. *NME sevynte, Ang seofunda*
sex, card.num. six, 42, 1291. *ME, OE sex*
sext, ord.num. sixth, 53. *ME sext, OE sexta*
sey, see se n.
seyne, see se vb.
sib, adj. related by blood, 742. *ME, OE sib(b)*
sic, adj. such; in ordin. attrib. use, 335, 336, 509, &c.; foll. by a or ane, 285, 315, 747, &c.; absol. such things, 2009. *Reduced form of ME swik, swilk*
sicht, n. sight, a view, glimpse of something, 541; field of vision, 1263, 2003; eyesight, 1580; the act of seeing or looking, 2330; in till his --, before his eyes, 128, 1430. *ME sight, OE siht*
siclyk, adj. similar, 2083; syklyk, adj.such, of such kind, 1540. See sic, + *-lyk*
sighand, pr.p. sighing, heaving a sigh, 1813. *ME sih(en), sigh(en), OE sīcan*
silk, n. silk, cloth or textile fabric made of silk, 194, 1454. *ME silk, ON silki*
siluer, n. silver, the metal regarded as a valuable possession, 825, 1619. *ME siluer, ON silfr*
sister, n.gen.s. sister's, 621; sisteris, n.pl. 854, 917, 935, &c. *NME sister, ON systir*
sit, v.intr. to sit, be seated, 1040, 1043, 1959; to have one's seat, 1512; to sit down, 2025; to abide, remain, 1957; sat, pt. was seated, 1526, 2092; remained seated, 1546; dwelled, 1880; perched, 2016; sittand, pr.p. sitting, engaged in eating, 2375. *ME sitte, pt. sat, OE sittan, pt. sǣt*

sker, v.tr. to scare, frighten away, 2622. *ME skerre, ON skirra*
skill, n. reason, argument, 1493; discriminating attention, 398; that which is reasonable or right, 1556. *ME skill, ON skil*
sla, v.tr. to kill, 434, 813, 1100, &c.; to execute, 993, 1872; pr.subj. kill, put to death, 390, 813, 1313, &c.; **sleuch**, pt.3 s. killed, 445; **slewe**, pt.s. killed, 474, 481, 492, &c.; **sla**, imperat. kill, put to death, 1177, 2234; **slane**, p.p. killed, put to death, 250, 404-5, 458, &c. *NME sla, pt. slew, p.p. slane, NOE slān, ON slá*
slaid(e), pt.intr. moved stealthily, 1125; tr. introduced quietly or dexterously, 1710. *NME pt. slaid, OE slād, inf. slīdan*
slane, see **sla**.
sle, adj. wise, skilful, clever, 777, 1793. *ME slēȝ, ON slœgr*
slepe, n. sleep, 1067, 1738, 2277. *ME sle(e)p, Ang slēp*
slepe, v.intr. to take repose, sleep, 1723, 2317, 2318, 2618; **slepit**, pt. slept, 1037, 1728, 1751; **slepand**, pr.p.sleeping, taking repose, 98, 428, 444, &c. *ME slepe, Ang slēpan*
sleuch, **slewe**, see **sla**.
slicht, n. trick, stratagem, 930. *ME slight, ON slœgð*
slokin, v.tr. extinguish, 1835, 2200; **slokinnit**, pt.intr. died down, went out, 1638; ceased, subsided, 2212, 2216; tr. extinguished, 1640; p.p.tr. extinguished, 1644, 2197. *ME sloknin, ON slokkva, to extinguish. ON slokna, to be extinguished*
small, adj. small, 2019. *ME smal, OE smæl, ON smal-r*
smellit, pt.3 s. tr. smelled, 731. *ME smelle*
smyle, v.intr. to smile, 1970. *ME smile, Scand smila*
smyte, v.tr. to knock or strike down, 1368. *ME smite, OE smītan*
sned, p.p. cut off, lopped off, 337. *OE snǣdan, p.p. snǣdd*
snyb, v.intr. to rebuke, reprimand, 1424. *Scand; cf. older Da snibbe*
so, see **sa**.
sobirnes, n. soberness, patience, 1244. *ME sobrenesse, OF sobre + -nes*
sodan(e)ly, adv. suddenly, all at once, 242; forthwith, without delay, 2680. *ME sodeinly, f. AN sodein, OF soudain + -ly.* See also **sudanlye**.
soft, adj. soft, pleasing (in taste, smell or to the eye), 727. *ME soft(e), OE sōft(e)*
softly, adv. softly, gently, 563. *Prec. + -ly*
somer, n. summer, 1173, 1175. *ME somer, OE sumer, -mor*
son(e), n. son, male child in relation to either or to both of his parents, 7, 26, 131, &c.; son-in-law, in address, 1944 (*NED* 1533); **sonnis**, n.gen.s. son's, 483, 2088. *ME son(e), OE sunu, ON sun-r, son-r*
son(e), adv. soon, within a short time, without delay, 23, 25, 145, &c.; early, betimes, 660, 1291, 2237; preceded or foll. by **efter**, 317, 839, 1904, &c. *ME son(e), OE sōna.* See **alsa**.
son(e), n. sun, 366, 2511. *ME son(ne), OE sunne*
sondaye, n. Sunday, first day of the week, 1510. *ME sondaye, OE sunnandæġ*
sonȝe, n. excuse, plea, 1233. *ME soigne, OF (es)soigne (Chaucer essoyne, MoSc sonyie)*
sorow(e), n. sorrow, grief, 371, 374; mischief, harm, 2063. *ME sorowe, OE sorg, infl. sorge*
souerane, adj. sovereign, supreme, as a qualification of **lord**, 27. *ME sovereyn(e), OF soverain*
souerane, n. sovereign, monarch, 1259. *Prec.*
sound, adv. soundly, -- **slepand**, 567. *ME sound, OE (ge)sund*
sovnde, adj. sound, safe, uninjured, -- **and hale**, 2595. *Prec.*
sover, pr.1 s. assure, 760. *Aphetic form f. OF assoürer*
sowkit, pt.2 s. sucked, drew milk from with the mouth, 1501. *ME souke, OE sūcan*

space, n. space, time, lapse or extent of time between two definite points, 36, 56, 538, &c. *ME space, OF espace*
spaide, n. spade, tool for digging, 1744. *ME spade, OE spadu*
spair, v.absol. to exercise or show mercy, forbearance, or leniency, 717; sparand, pr.p.tr. abstaining, refraining (from), -- to + inf. 832; spard, pt.3 pl. spared, avoided incurring (expense), 2141; spard(e), p.p. spared, saved, 636, 1222, 2342; sparit, pt.3 s. abstained (from), 1067; -- (for) to + inf. 875, 1450. *ME spare, OE sparian, ON spara*
spak, see speike.
sparing, n. parsimony, economising, 837. *See* spair
speche, n. speech, the faculty or power of speaking, 200, 215, 1563, &c. *ME speche, OE spæc, spec*
speciale, adj. special, exceptional in character, 1376. *ME speciale, OF especial, L specialis*
sped, see speid vb.
speid, v.intr. to hurry, go with speed, refl. 650; sped, pt. hurried, 423, 468, 591, &c. *ME spede, OE spēdan*
speid, v.tr. to prosper, benefit, 394; sped, pt.3 s. intr. prospered, thrived, 338; p.p. prospered, succeeded, fared, with how, 95. *Prec.*
speik(e), speke, v.intr. to speak, 174, 218, 987, &c.; to converse, 1338; tr. to utter (a word or words), 215, 1936, 2545; pr.subj. use the faculty of speech, 218; speak, converse, 1916; spak, pt. intr. 201, 416, 1082, &c.; tr. 160, 191, 198, &c.; spokin, p.p. spoken, pronounced words, 381; expressed his thoughts by words, 2199. *ME speke, pt. spac, p.p. spoken, OE sprecan, specan*
speir, sper, n. spear, thrusting weapon, 485, 2077. *ME, OE spere*
speir, v.tr. to ask, enquire, 25, 1427, 1602, &c.; to enquire one's way, to make one's way, proceed or go to a place, 477; speir, pr.2 pl. ask, with cogn.obj., 510; sperit, pt. asked, enquired, 279, 303, 464, &c.; with obj.cl. 101, 455, 707, &c.; -- of, 800, 1699; -- efter, 1361; sperand, pr.p. asking, with obj.cl.,1687. *ME spere, OE spyrian, ON spyrja, cf. OFris spera*
speke, see speik(e).
spekle, n. mirror, 1616-7. *L speculum.* This form not in *NED.*
spend, v.tr. absol. to spend, make or incur expenditure of money, 832, 833, 875; spendit, pt.3 s. spent, ate freely, 2309. *ME spend, OE *spendan, L expendere*
spending, n. expenditure, 636. *Prec.*
spens, n. expense, expenditure, 872. *ME spens, AN expense, OF espense*
spilt, p.p. destroyed, wrecked, 1820. *ME spill, OE spillan, ON spilla*
spokin, see speik(e).
sport, n. amusement, diversion, 1039. *Next*
sport, v.intr. to amuse or divert oneself, 724. *ME sport, aphetic form of disport, AN desporter*
sprang, pt.3 s., of fame: spread, 618; of water: rose in a stream out of the ground, 2154. *ME, OE sprang, pt. OE springan*
spreid, v.intr. to be covered with, 944. *ME sprede, OE sprǣdan.* This usage not in *NED.*
sprete, n. spirit, courage, self-assertion, 1127. *ME sprete, AN spirit(e), OF esprit*
spring, n. spring, a flow of water rising or issuing naturally out of the earth, 2206; springis, n.pl. 2180 (well --). *ME, OE spring*
spulȝe, v.tr. absol. to despoil or strip a person, 2769; spulȝeit, pt.3 pl. stripped, 2774. *OF espoillier, L spoliare.* The use without obj. not in *NED.*
spur, n. spur, goading instrument on a rider's heel, 977; spurris, n.pl. 1299. *ME spur, OE spura, ON spori*
spys, n. spice, aromatic substance used for medicine, 750. *ME spice, OF espice*

sqwyar, sqwyer, n. squire, a young man of good birth, attendant upon a knight, 2280; one ranking next to a knight, 1491. *ME sqwyer, OF escuier, esquier*
stagis, n.pl.in sing. meaning, place, position, 1606. *ME stage, OF estage*
staitly, adj. stately, impressive, 633. *ME statly, OF estat + -ly*
stak, see stik.
stall, pt.s. stole, took away dishonestly, 820-21, 1070; -- in, put in secretly, 98; -- fra ʒow, departed, left you secretly, 1086; staw, pt.3 s. stole, took away stealthily, 1055. *ME stall, OE stæl, pt. of stelan*
stanchable, adj.staunchable; war I --, if my diarrhoea could be stopped, 768. *Next*
stanche, v.tr. to stop the flow of, 2206; to arrest the progress of, 749; to stop the diarrhoea of (a pers.), 753, 768. *ME stanche, OF estanchier*
stand, v.intr. to remain firm, upright, 1655, 1789; to maintain an erect attitude on one's feet, 1939; to remain erect on one's feet in a specif. place, position, condition, &c., 1937, 2471; pr.2 s. remain in a place, 1103; I -- ford, I warrant, 362, 1739; standis, pr.2 s. stand, support yourself erect on your feet, 1942; of a king's word: remains firm, 515, 809; stud(e), pt. was in a specif. condition, 103, 165, 339, &c.; was placed, 448; grew erect, 528; remained erect and entire, resisted destruction or decay, 1658; was set firmly, 1800; was set, placed, 1829; remained erect on his feet in a place, 1949; stood (caus.), placed, 1649; tr. to -- ... aw(e), to be greatly afraid, 801, 936, 1470, 1635. *ME stand, pt. stode, OE standan, pt. stōd*
stane, n. stone, as building material, 75, 530, 1029; piece of stone, 1114; attrib.: made of stone, 2321; stanys, n.pl.stones, pieces of rock of a small size, 2019. *NME stane, OE stān*
stark, adj. strong, powerful, 2321. *ME stark, OE stearc, ON sterk-r*
statis, n.pl. estates of a realm, 1870. *ME state, OF estat*
statut, pt.3 s. decreed, ordained, with cl. as obj., 1005. *L statut-*
staw, see stall.
steid, n. stead, place; in-till his --, in-to ʒour --, as a successor in his, your place, 134, 2231. *ME, OE stede* *can*
steike, v.tr. to fasten, shut (a door, window, &c.), 1915. *EME steken, OE *ste-*
steir, v.intr. to stir, make any movement, 897, 1951. *NME steer, OE styrian, cf.*
stepmoder, n. stepmother, 1865. *ME stepmoder, OE steōpmōdor* *OFris -stēra*
sterne, n. star, in astrolog. use, 171; sternis, n.pl. stars, 21, 155, 169, 2550. *NME sterne, ON stjarna*
stettit, pt.3 s. intr. started, made a sudden involuntary movement of surprise, 1941. *ME stette, pt. of stete, OE *stīetan, cf. OFris steta*
stewart, n. steward, officer of the royal household, 1180, 1214; magistrate appointed by the king to administer a country, governor, 2225, 2296, 2597, 2605; stewartis, n. gen.s. steward's, 1186-7. *ME steward, OE stīw(e)ard*
stifly, adv. stubbornly, stoutly, hard, 439. *ME stiff, OE stīf, + -ly*
stik, v.intr. to be set fast or entangled in sand, clay, mud or the like, 892; stak, pt.3 s. was set fast or entangled, 897; was fixed in or as in a socket, 1800. *ME stik, pt. stak, OE stician*
still, adv. motionless, 897, 1937; at rest, 1072; still, indic. the continuance of a previous action or condition, 887. *ME, OE stille*
stok, n. trunk or stem of a tree, 1345. *ME stok(ke), OE stoc(c), ON stokk-r*
stop, v.tr. to stop, prevent the passage of ... by blocking the channel or outlet, 765. *ME stopp, OE *stoppian*
story, n. story, narrative, 417, 1004, 2519. *ME story, AN estorie*
stowr, n. battle, combat, 439. *ME stowr, stour, OF estour*
stowt, adj. haughty, defiant, 1127. *ME stowt, stout, OF estout*

stra, n. straw, as filling for bedding, bed, 1568. *NME stra, ON strá*
straike, n. stroke, blow; at a --, with a single blow, 474. *NME strake, OE *strāc*
straik(e), pt., see strik(e).
strait, adj. narrow, 2325; stringent, strict, allowing no evasion, 2339. *ME strait, AN estreit.* See also stratlie.
strake, see strik(e).
strange, adj. foreign, 2391. *ME straunge, OF estrange*
strangearis, n.pl. foreigners, 2457. *ME straunger, OF estrangier*
stratlie, adv. closely, strictly, 1050. *ME stratly.* See also strait.
streit, n. street, road, 369, 931, 1295. *ME strete, OE strǣt*
strik(e), v.tr. to deal a blow, 1633; to hit with an implement, 1561; to hit with a weapon, 789; -- of, to cut off with a stroke of a sword, axe, &c., 254, 2211; -- dovn, to conquer, 2303; straik(e), strake, pt.3 s. dealt a blow, 741, 1445; hit with spur(s), 977, 1300; -- dovn, felled to the ground with a blow, conquered, 1833, 2311; -- of, cut off with a stroke of a sword, 911; strik, imperat. -- of, 905, 2205, 2208; strikin, p.p. -- of, 476; strykis, pr.3 s. deals a blow, 1431, 1627. *ME strike, strak, striken, OE strican, strac, stricen*
stryf, n. strife, contention, quarrel, 1901, 2053, 2678. *ME stryf, OF estrif f. ON stríf*
strykis, see strik(e).
stud(e), see stand.
study, n. thought or meditation, directed to the accomplishment of a purpose, 16. *ME study, OF estudie, L studium*
study, v.tr. to reflect, debate with oneself, 2292; studyet, studyit, pt.3 s. meditated, considered, 716, 2313; study, imperat. reflect, think intently on, 2448. *ME studie, OF estudier, ML studiare*
sturt, n. contention, violent quarrelling, 2678. *ME strutt, OE *strut*
stynkand, adj. stinking, offensively smelling, 913. *ME stink, OE stincan*
subtell, adj. subtle, clever, expert, 642; ingenious, cleverly designed, 886. *ME subtille, OF sutil, F subtil, L subtilis*
subtelly, adv. skilfully, dexterously, 862, 2062; artfully, cunningly, 1665, 2332. *Prec. + -ly*
subtelté, subtilté, n. subtlety, sagacity, 576, 630. *ME subtilte(e), sutilte, OF s(o)utilté, L subtilitas*
succeid, v.intr. to succeed, be the immediate successor in an office, &c., 6. *OF succeder, L succedere*
successioun, n. succession, the act of a pers. or thing following or succeeding to the place of another, 114; the process by which one pers. succeeds another in the occupation of a throne or the like, 638; progeny, issue, 1025. *ME successioun, OF succession, L succession-*
succour, n. help, 859, 1486. *ME succour, OF sucurs*
succurit, pt.3 pl. assisted, saved, 2594. *ME succur, OF succurre, L succurrere*
sudand, adj. sudden, happening or coming without warning, 1530. *ME suddayn, sud(d)an(e), AN sudein, sodein, OF soudain*
sudanlye, adv. suddenly, immediately, 2145. *Prec. + -lye.* See also sodan(e)ly.
sudiorn, n. delay; but --, without delay, 258, 1294. *ME soio(u)rn(e), OF su(r)-jurn*
suld, see sall.
sum, adj., with sing.n. some, one or other, undetermined, unspecified, 1349, 1616. *ME, OE sum*
sumthing, adv. in some degree, to some extent, 103, 1793, 1941, 1981. *ME sumþing*
sumtyme, adv. in former times, at a certain time, 528. *ME sumtyme*

suppos, adv. although, 387, 844. *F. OF supposer*
suprisit, ppl.a. overcome, outraged, 340. *OF supris-e f. surprendre*
suprys, n. unexpected attack, 1815; wrong, outrage, 2727. *OF suprise, var. of surprise*
surfatly, adv. immoderately, 559. *OF surfet, -fait, + -ly*
suspect, p.p. suspected, regarded with suspicion or distrust, 1220. *ME suspect, L suspectus*
sustene, v.tr. to undergo, suffer, experience, 1540. *ME suste(i)ne, AN sustein, OF so(u)stein-, tonic stem of so(u)stenir*
suth, adj. true, in accordance with truth, 404, 2133, 2159. *Next*
suth, n. truth; without art., 1310, 1657, 1837; with art., 1867, 2252, 2612. *NME suth, OE sōð*
suthfast, adj. true, speaking or adhering to the truth, 1742. *ME sothfast, OE sōðfæst*
suthfastnes, n. truth, 2506. *Prec. + -nes*
suthly, adv. truly, really, 417, 1096, &c. *ME soth(e)ly, OE sōðlīce*
swa, see sa.
swagis, pr.3 s. assuages, appeases, 577, 2201. *ME suage, AN suag(i)er, swag(i)er*
sweit, adj. sweet; pleasing to the ear, 2573, 2578; beloved, 1105, 2592; charming, 2601; pleasing to the taste, 552; swet(e), adj. dear, beloved, 195, 2581; lovely, 235; pleasing to the taste, fig. 691; adv. sweetly, with a sweet voice or sound, 1488, 2571. *ME swete, OE swēte*. See also swetly.
swer, v.tr. to swear, affirm, assert by oath, 992; swor, pt.3 s. swore, affirmed emphatically, 1976; declared with an oath, 2008; sworn(e), p.p. taken or uttered (oaths), 203; made oaths, 965; asserted with an oath, 1752; ppl.a. sworn, appointed or admitted with a formal oath to some office or function, 264. *ME swer, pt. swor, p.p. sworn(e), OE swerian, pt. swōr, p.p. sworen*
swerd, n. sword, a weapon for cutting and thrusting, 472, 484, 491, &c.; sword, id., 789, 910. *ME swerd, sworde, OE sweord, ON sverð*
swet(e), see sweit, adj.
swetly, adv. sweetly, graciously, 2297. *ME swetely*. See also sweit, adv.
swiftlie, adv. swiftly, with great speed, without delay, 910. *ME swiftly, OE swyftlīce*
swor, see swer.
sword, see swerd.
sworn(e), see swer.
swoun, n. swoon, fainting fit, 550. *ME swoune, f. OE (ā)swōgan, p.p. -swogen*
swyth, adv. quickly, swiftly, 1728, 2324, &c. *ME swyðe, OE swīðe*
syklyk, see siclyk.
symphion, n. musical instrument, 2523. *OF simphoine, f. L symphonia*
syn, n. sin, violation of divine law, 717, 1140, 1426, &c. *ME sin(n), OE syn(n)*
syn(e), adv. then,thereupon, immediately afterwards, 152, 254, 298, &c. *Contr. form of OE siþþan, ON síðan*
syne, n. sign, gesture or motion of the hand, head, &c., serving to convey an intimation or to communicate some idea, 1059. *ME sign, OF signe*
syne, v.tr. to intimate, convey, by a sign, 2332. *ME signe, f. OF signer*
synfull, adj. sinful, wicked, 2756. *ME synful*
syng, v.intr. of a bird: to produce tuneful or musical sounds, warble, 1970; pr.s intr. produces tuneful sounds, 1966; chants, intones, says mass, 1488; tr. declares in song, 2582, 2584; sang, pt.3 s. sang, produced tuneful sounds, 2571. *ME syng, pt. sang, OE singan, sang*
syngyng, vbl.n. singing, bird-song, 2642. *ME syngyng*
syon, n. shoot or twig of a tree, 318. *ME syon, OF cion, sion*

ta, v.tr. to take (an implement), 1365; to grasp (be the lap), 2628; tak, to take (an implement), 344, 756, 2018; to take prisoner, 251, 934, 1293, &c.; to get hold of, 1114; to grasp (by the hand), 219; to receive charge of, 26; to enter into the enjoyment of, 306; to catch (with pr.p.), 580; to eat or drink, 750; to carry, convey, 970; to adopt, use, 1200; to receive, accept, 1495; to take, in ref. to marriage, 1022; -- kepe, to have heed to, watch, 1068; -- out of, to remove from within, 2750; -- wp, to lift, pick up, 739; tak, pres. bring into some relation to oneself (here as witness), 1240; -- on hand, undertake, 1790; pr.subj. seize, enter into possession or use of something, 237; take as a lover, 1499; receive, get (advice), 2233; take (example), 2561; derive (effect), 819, 1186; takis furth, pr.3 s. receives with the mind, 1358; takin, p.p. seized, captured, 1012; tak, imperat. take, in ref. to marriage, 124; tane, p.p. taken, received, 687, 1585; received into some relation to oneself, 838; seized, captured, 864, 1146, &c.; conveyed, 2353, 2463; took over (another's position), 624; had (effect), 91; -- for, supposed to be, 2451, 2762; -- in handis, seized as prisoner, 1818; -- tent, paid heed, attention, 2425; -- wp, lifted, 733; tuk(e), pt. took, caused to go with one, 201, 1308, &c.; carried with one, 1694; took prisoner, 585; appropriated, 870; selected, 178; ate, 557; -- study, pondered, 16; -- hed, -- kepe, paid attention, 271, 566; -- seknes, contracted, fell into, 632; exacted (vengeance), 746; accepted or assumed (the crown), 2687; took (flight), 2680; -- counsall, deliberated, 68; -- on hand, undertook, 1521; -- leif, obtained permission to depart, 794, 1164, &c.; -- of, removed, 1385; -- wp, lifted, 2002. *ME take, pt. took, p.p. taken, ON taka, tók, tekinn*

taile, see tale.

taist, v.tr. to test, put to the proof, 1355. *ME taste, OF taster*

taist, n. touch, 2428. *ME, OF tast*

tak, see ta.

takinnis, takynnis, n.pl. tokens, signs, indication, 482, 1047, 1057. *ME taken, OE tācn*

talburn, n. tabour, small drum, 2521. *ME taburn(e), OF tab(o)ur, ML taburna*

tald, see tell.

tale, n. tail of a horse, 931. *ME tail(e), OE tæg(e)l, ON tagl*

tale, taile, n. tale, relation of a series of events, 289, 352, 398, &c.; idle or mischievous gossip, 1978, 2046; talis, n.pl. tales, falsehoods, 579, 1314, &c. *ME tale, OE talu, ON tala*

tane, n. (the) one, 831, 2444. *EME þe tān for earlier þat ān*

tane, p.p. see ta.

tary, v.intr. to tarry, wait before doing something, 589, 975, 2241; taryit, tarijt, pt.3 s. tarried, lingered in expectation of a pers. or occurrence, 1250; with inf. delayed to do something, 1300. *ME tarien of obsc. origin*

tauld, see tell.

taxt, n. task, work assigned to one as a definite duty, 54. *For task, ME taxe, ONF tasque, by metathesis for taxa, L taxare*

teche, v.tr. to teach, impart knowledge, 18, 40, 52, 63; techit, p.p. taught, given instruction, 46, 71. *ME teche, OE tæc(e)an*

teching, n. teaching, instruction, 84. *Prec.*

tell, v.tr. to tell, relate, narrate, 519, 2107, &c.; with indir.obj., 998, 1890, 1925; with obj.cl. 256, 664, 1912, &c.; absol. 393, 605, 607, &c.; pr. 524, 1770, 2172, &c.; tellis, pr.s. 1897, 2410, 2519; tald, pt. 165, 614, 878, &c.; tell, imperat. tell, relate, 817, 1184, 1317, &c.; tald, tauld, p.p. told, given an account, 396, 608, 1000, &c.; related, 1842, 2235, 2508, 2636; counted, 2598. *ME tell, NME pt., p.p. tald, OE tellan, Ang pt. talde, p.p. tald*

tempe, imperat. test, put to the proof, 1425; inf. 2745. *ME tempt, OF tempter, L temptare*

temperit, pt.3 s. mixed, mingled, 2022. *ME tempre, OE temprian, L temperare*
ten, card.num. ten, 1646. *ME tenn, Ang tēn(e)*
tenderly, adv. tenderly, kindly, 1340, 2716. *ME tenderly, OF tendre + -ly*
tennour, n. tenor, purport, 153. *ME tennour, OF teno(u)r, L tenōr-em*
tent, n. attention, heed, 2425. *Aphetic for attent*
ter, n. tar, 2020, 2065. *ME ter, OE te(o)ru, ON tjara*
teris, n.pl. tears (visible feature of weeping), 1410. *ME tere, OE tēar, tǣr, ON tár*
testament, n. testament, last will, 1108. *ME testament, L testamentum*
thai, dem.adj. those, 153, 761, 763, &c.; dem.pron. those, 1950. *NME tha, OE þā*
thai, pers.pron. they, 21, 23, 59, &c.; used indef. 24, 47, 53, &c. *ME thai, thei, ON þei-r*
thaim, tham, pers.pron. them, 22, 61, 67, &c.; themselves, 734, 1030, 1712, &c.; to them, 166, 1293, 1669, &c. *ME theim, thaim, tham(e), ON þeim, ONhb þām*
thak, n. roof, 2017; adj.thatched, 2318. *ME thak, ON þak*
tham, see thaim.
than, conj.particle used after a compar.adj.or adv. than, 36, 106, 604, &c. *ME than, OE þan(ne)*
than, adv. then, after that, 38, 44, 70, &c.; at that time, 19, 432, 533, &c.; therefore, 16, 77, 165, &c.; in that case, 119, 120, 141, &c.; so, 583, 835, 969, &c.; thereupon, 2150; bot --, but then, 255, 945, 1225, &c.; sometimes used merely for the sake of metre or rhyme, 47, 498, 587, 1215. *ME than, OE þanne*
thank, pr.1 s. thank, give thanks to, 1955; thankit, pt. thanked, 61, 66, 275, &c. *ME thank, OE þancian*
thar, poss.pron. their, 52, 61, 64, &c. *ME their(e), ON þeir(r)a, ONhb þara*
thar, adv. there, in that place, 75, 162, 189, &c.; there, unemphatic, 19, 138, 170, &c.; heir or --, in one place or another, 990; ther, adv. there, used unemphat. to introd. a sentence, 405. *NME thar, OE þǣr, ONhb þār, ON þar*
tharabone, adv. above or on the top of that, 1624
tharat, adv. in connection with that, 670; because of that, 2035.
tharby, adv. beside that, 436; by means of that, 1742.
thareftir, adv. thereafter, after that in time, 920, 1001, &c.
tharfor, adv. therefore, for that reason, because of that, 237, 289, 516, &c.
tharin, adv. therein, in that place, 1267, 1646, 1710.
tharis, poss.pron.absol. theirs, 2458.
tharof, adv. thereof, of that, 306, 325, 402, &c.
tharon, adv. thereon, on that, 410, 411, &c.
thartill, adv. thereto, 611.
tharto, adv. to that, 76, 566, 686, &c.; moreover, 1235.
tharwith, adv. thereupon, 776, 1445; by means of that, 699.
tharwithall, adv. therewith, thereat, 467, 1116; that being said, 1409.
tharwnder, adv. thereunder, below that, 1802.
that, conj. that, introd. a dep.n.cl., as subj., obj., or other element of the princip. cl., or as complement of a n. or adj., or in appos. with a n. therein, 35, 268, 714, &c.; following a cl. of the form it is + adv. or adv.phr., 236, 285, 815; introd. an exclam.cl. expr. some emotion (Allace), 802, 898, 2070; introd. a cl. expr. the cause, ground, reason, of what is stated in the princip.cl., 348, 481, 1449; introd. a cl. expr. purpose, end, aim or desire, with subjunct., 93, 115, 180, &c.; introd. a cl. expr. the result or conseq. of what is stated in the princip. cl., with indicative: with antec. sa, so or sic, 314, 316, 440, &c.; without antec., 'so that', 95, 264, 282, &c.; added to rel. or dep.interrog., 668, 2293, 2422; enclit. after: becaus, 770, 866, 1390; bot, 139; bot gif, 388, 851; gif, 500, 608, 2734; how, 512, 1634, &c.; or, 1282, 1287; quhen, 210, 507, 561, &c.; quhidder, 1725;

quhill, 221, 580, 629, &c.;sen, 1407; with thi, 1224, 1716. *ME that, OE þæt*

that, dem.pron. that, denoting a thing or pers. pointed out or present, or that has just been mentioned: a thing, 1481, 1692, 2378, &c.; a person, 1261; a fact, statement, occurrence, &c., 283, 287, 394, &c.; referring to a precise time just mentioned, with --, 239, 245, 1145, &c.; -- is, namely, 2229. *ME that, OE þæt*

that, dem.adj. that, simple dem. to indic. a pers. or thing pointed out or present, mentioned before, 156, 250, 273, &c.; indic. a pers. or thing assumed to be known, in contexts of censure, recommendation, &c., 89, 742, 1128, &c.; -- ilka ..., that same ..., 68, 1660, 1906; qualif. a n., which is the antec. to a relative (expressed or understood), 806, 1231, 1655, 2699. *Prec.*

that, rel.pron. that, 6, 37, 58, &c.; who, 16, 55, 125, &c. *Prec.*

the, def.art. referring to an object already known, 6, 10, 13, &c.; -- quhilk, 575, 2711; the tane ... the tother, 831-33, 2444; before a word denoting a specif. point in time, 158, 883, 894, &c.; -- day, to-day, 204;-- morne, to-morrow, 263, 1843, 2236, &c.; before the name of a unique obj. or one so considered, 366, 618, 2511, &c.; with names of natural phenomena, seasons, &c., 21, 169, 1369, &c.; with parts of the body, 219, 220, 240, &c.; before self, itself, 2660; marking an obj. not mentioned before, defined by a rel.cl., 404-5, 491, 610, &c.; used with a n. particularised by a foll. phr. with prep.,esp. of, 88, 114, 149, &c.; with a n. particul. by an inf.phr. with to, 123; with a n. particul. by an adj., 41, 442, 487, &c.; with a n. partic. by a superl., 1650, 2044; by an ord.num., 24, 38, 44, &c.; the also stands before the same adjs. when used absol.: superl. 74, 254, 371, &c.; ord.num. 47, 53, 55, &c.; bef. an adj. or participle having a pl. application, 20, 1640, &c. *ME the, LOE ðe*

the, adv. preceding an adj. in the comp. the, 1352. *ME the, OE þē*

thé, pers.pron. thee, 359, 499, 574, &c.; thyself, 901, 1426; to thee, 377, 456, 904, &c. *ME the(e), OE ðē.* See 'Note on the Use of ȜE and THOU', pp. 78-81.

thee, n. thigh, 941. *ME the(e), OE þēoh, Ang þēh*

ther, see thar, adv.

thi in the phr. for --, therefore, for this reason, 144, 154, 198, &c. *ME forthi, OE forþȳ, forþī*

thi, see thy.

thiddir, adv. thither, to that place, 2605. *ME thidder, OE ðiðer*

thin, poss.pron. thine, 853, 1831, 1835, before h or vowel. *ME thin(e), OE ðīn, ON þín.* See also thy.

thin, adv. thence, from that moment, preceded by redundant fra, 697. *ME thine, app. reduced f. thethen, ON þeðan*

thing, n. thing, deed, act, 407, 1414; event, circumstance, 1475; matter, 2162, 2438, 2708; object, 1624; subject, 1776; sum --, somewhat, 103; na --, nothing, 138, 560, 843, &c.; na (no) --, not at all, 810, 1182, 1481; all --, everything, 304, 516, 1796, &c.; thingis, n.pl. things, objects, 1703; matters, 2179. *ME thing, OE þing*

think, pr. impers., seems, appears, 284, 607, 2619; pr. think, 1371, 1823; thinkand, pr.p. thinking, considering, with indir. question, 1439; thocht, pt.s. thought, designed, planned, 133, 640, 1066, 1068; considered .. to be, 1391, 2315; imagined, 2277; -- of, 925, 1535; -- apon, called to mind, 2690; impers. seemed, 691, 2041, 2428. *ME think, pt. thoght, OE þencean, þōhte; þyncean, þūhte*

thir, dem.adj. these, 59, 1143, 1392, &c. *NME thir, origin obscure*

this, dem.adj. this, 11, 28, 71, &c. *ME this, OE þis*

this, dem.pron. 161, 176, &c.; contr. of this is, 116; -- anys, this once, 1463, 1502. *Prec.*

thi-sell, see self.
thocht, adv. although, 329, 965, 1028, &c. *ME þŏh, ON *þōh, (prehist. form of ON þó) + excrescent t*
thocht, n. thought, intention, 143; attention, 627; imagination, 992. *ME thoghte, OE þoht*
thocht, pt. see think.
thole, v.tr. to suffer, have to bear, 1016. *ME thole, OE þolian, ON þola*
thou, pers.pron. thou, 1132, 1897; thow, id., 196, 363, 500, &c. *ME thou, OE þū.* See 'Note on the Use of ȜE and THOU', pp. 78-81.
thousand, card.num., n. thousand, 2274. *ME thousand, OE þusend*
thra, adj. keen, zealous, 329; fierce, violent, 1871. *ME thra, ON þrá-r*
thra, adv. eagerly, fiercely, 1439. *Prec.*
thrang, adj. pressing, 2541. *ME thrange*
thre, card.num. three, 9, 51, 1267, &c.; ellipt. for three parts, 2077. *ME thre(e), OE þrēo, þrī*
threwe, pt.3 s. turned, twisted aside, phr. he -- the face, 240. *ME threwe pt., OE þrāwan, pt. þrēow.* See expl.note.
thrid, ord.num. third, 44; with n. understood, 1756, 2649. *ME thridd, OE þridda, ON þriðe*
thrist, n. thirst, physical condition resulting from want of drink, 1204. *ME thrist, OE þirst, þurst*
thristit, pt.2 s. thirsted, desired vehemently, 1824. *ME thrist-, OE þyrstan, ON þyrsta*
throu, prep. through, along within, 931; over along, 2569; throw(e), prep. through, 369, 586, 1295; from one side, one end, to another, 889, 2239, 2283; by reason of, 11; throughout, 618. *ME thrughe, throw, OE ðurh*
thus, adv. thus, in this way, 43, 249, 705, &c.; as follows, 229, 614, 1207, 1323; and so, 109, 1271; accordingly, 1437. *ME thus, OE þus*
thusgatis, adv. so, in this way, 246, 1350. *ME þusgates*
thus-way, adv. thus, in this way, 526.
thy, poss.pron. thy, 674, 854, 1265, &c.; -- self, 1514, 1839; thi, poss.pron. thy, 196, 357, 458, &c. *ME thi. See also* thin, poss.pron.
thyn, adj. thin, of little thickness, 97. *ME thinn(e), OE þynne*
till, particle with inf. to, 8, 322, 328, &c. *ME till, ONhb til, ON til.* See also to.
till, prep. to; local: 397, 562, 661, &c.; dative: 54, 84, 286, &c. *Prec.*
time, see tyme.
to, adv. too, in excess, overmuch, 833, 1986, 2494; also, too, in addition, 1320, 1506, 2021, 2458; to ga or fall --, to set to, set about doing something, 86, 1460. *ME to, OE tō*
to, particle with inf., to, 18, 26, 32, &c. *Prec.* See also till.
to, prep. to; of motion, direction, 23, 112, 146, &c.; of motion, fig., 6, 110, 271, &c.; of time: until, 1655; of purpose, intention, 1613, 1996, &c.; indic. outcome, 31, 602, 1135, 2776; -- the best, 2600; for the behoof of, to serve, 235; indic. the obj. of a right, 2672; attached, joined to, 2326; -- (as or for) name, 1326, 2114; supplying the place of the dat., 1785, 2098, 2719, &c.; indic. a pers. addressed, 351, 654, 763, &c.; indic. the recipient of anything given, 1232, 1636, &c.; indic. the pers. upon whom an event acts, 17, 285, 838, &c.; indic. the pers. towards whom an action is directed, 223, 376, 803, &c.; expr. relation of an adj. to a n., 143, 1481, 2392. *ME to, OE tō*
to-day, adv. to-day, on this very day, 503, 792. *ME to day, OE tō dæg*
to-fall, n. lean-to, annex, 2322.

togiddir, adv. together, 157, 1696, 2022, &c.; of two pers. 1048, 1473, 2442. *ME togider, OE tōgædre*
to-morne, adv. to-morrow, 966, 1288, 2248. *ME tomorn, OE tō morġen*
to-nycht, adv. to-night, 1913. *ME to night, OE tō niht*
torment, p.p. tormented, inflicted torture upon, 2737. *ME torment(ed), OF tormenter, ML tormentare*
tormentouris, n.pl. official torturers, executioners, 251, 367, 585, &c. *ME, AN tormentour*
tor(na)mentis, n.pl. tournaments, 409. *ME tor(ne)ment, AN tornement*
tornis, pr.1 s. turn, direct (towards), 110. *ME turn, OE turnian, tyrnan, OF torner, L tornare*
torris, see **tovr**. *with initial t the result of wrong division*
tother, **tothir**, n. (the) other, 732, 833, 837, &c. *ME other, OE oþer,*
toun, **twn**, n. tun, large cask or barrel, 756, 759. *ME t(o)un, OE tunne*
tovne, **towne**, n. town, city (of Rome), 286, 291, 370, &c. *ME toun(e), towne, OE tūn*
tovr, **towr(e)**, n. tower, stronghold, tall building, 828, 840, 860, &c.; **torris**, n.pl. towers, the four posts of a cradle, 442. *ME tour(e), towr, LOE tūr, AN, OF to(u)r, L turris*
towall, n. towel, cloth, esp. for wiping the hands, face, &c. after washing, 2586, 2704. *ME towall, OF toaille*
towart, prep. towards, in the direction of, 477. *ME toward, OE tōweard*
towne, see **tovne**.
towr(e), see **tovr**.
traide, n. course, way, path, 2367. *App. introd. into Engl. in the 14th cent. f. Hanseatic MLG trade*
traist, see **trast**.
trane, n. treachery, deceit, 953. *NME trane, OF traïne, f. OF traïr*
trane, v.tr. to deceive, lead astray, 1060. *F. prec.*
trast, **pres.** trust, 1394; expect with confidence, 951; -- **in**, have confidence in, 1605; **absol.** 1867; **trast**, **traist**, **imperat.** trust, 1794, 1917; **absol.**(?) 2544 ; -- **in**, 125; **trastit**, **pt.3 s.** trusted, 590; -- **in**, 1611. *ME tra(i)st, ON treysta*
tratour, n. traitor, 953, 1861. *ME traitour, OF traitor*
tre, n. tree, 304, 309, 335, &c.; piece of wood, 1482; wood as material of a barrel, 767; **treis**, **n.pl.** trees, 295; logs, 1392; **gen.s.** 332. *ME tre(e), OE trēo, ON tré*
tresour, **tressour**, n. treasure, wealth or riches stored or accumulated, 828, 840, 922, 1687. *ME treso(u)r, tressour, OF tresor*
trespas, n. trespass, offence, sin, 745, 1016. *ME, OF trespas*
treuth, n. truth, true statement or account, 2081, 2636. *ME treuth(e), OE trēowþ*
trewe, adj. true, consistent with fact, 769. *ME trewe, OE trēowe*
trewly(e), adv. truly, really, 1343, 1996; indeed, 619; faithfully, 1397, 1465. *ME trewly, OE trēowlīce*
trinité, n. Trinity (the fest of the --) 149. *ME trinite(e), OF trinité*
trow(e), v.tr. to believe (someth. to be true), 1002-3, 2046, 2188, 2203; -- **in-to**, to trust (a pers.), 2123; **trow**, **pres.** believe (someth. to be true), 1587, 1828, 1948, &c.; **trowit**, **pt.** trusted (a pers.), 1723, 1747; believed (someth. to be true), 1978, 1981, 2498; **absol.** 952; expected, 1990; **p.p.** believed, 2394. *ME trowe, OE trūwian, ON trúa*
trumpe, n. trumpet, 2521. *ME trumpe, OF trompe*
tryst, n. tryst, arrangement, 590. *OF triste*
tuelf, **card.num.** twelve, 2566. *ME, OE twelf*
tuk(e), see **ta**.

tunder, n. tinder, dry inflammable material, 1801. *ME tunder, ON tundr*
tursit, pt.3 pl. trussed, packed, 1695. *ME trus, OF tr(o)usser, tourser*
tuskis, n.pl. tusks, long pointed teeth, 547. *ME tuske, OE tusc, tux*
tvme, adj. toom, empty, 756. *ME tome, tume, OE tōm, ON tómr*
twa, card.num. two, 54, 829, 1471, &c.; absol. with ell. of n. 217, 1333, &c.; ane ... or --, an indef. small number of, 1250. *ME twa, OE twā*
twenty, card.num. twenty, 2598. *ME twenti, OE twentiġ*
twn, see toun.
tyme, n. time; moment, a point of time, 491, 1655; a favourable point of time for doing someth., 1721, (spelled time 1648); period, length of time, 699, 835, 920, &c.; lifetime, 822; that --, then, 619, 1619; in --, not too late, 1723; in the --, at that time, 883; in -- to cum, in future time, 595; tymes, n.pl. times, a period in the existence or history of the world, 1. *ME tyme, OE tīma, ON tími*
tyne, v.tr. to lose, 164, 677, 1095; tynt, pt.3 s. lost, should lose, 718; p.p. lost, 200; ruined, destroyed, 1157, 1810. *ME tyne, pt., p.p. tynt, ON týna*
tyrit, ppl.a. tired, fatigued, 86, 1996. *ME terid, tyred, f. OE tēorian, tȳrian*
tys, v.tr. to entice, incite, 1314. *ME tyse, poss. f. OF (a)-tiser*
tyte, adv. soon, quickly, 958, 1367, 1549, &c. *ME tyte, ON títt, nt. of tíðr*
tything, n. news, piece of news, 1775. *ME tything, OE tēoðung, Ang tiġeðing*
tytill, n. title, inscription placed on or over an object, 1631. *ME tityll, OF title, L titulus*

U, see V.

vane, n. vein, bloodvessel, 1561. *ME vayne, OF vaine, veine, L vena*
va-, ve-, see wa-, we-.
vgsum, adj. horrible, loathsome, 2619. *ON ugg- + -sum*
victory, n. victory, triumph, 2267. *ME victory, AN victorie, L victoria*
virgin(e), n. virgin, unmarried or chaste maiden or woman, 1332, 1656. *ME virgin(e), OF virgine*
visioun, n. vision, revelation, 2268. *ME visio(u)n, OF vision, L vision-*
vmbethocht, pt.3 s. bethought (-- him), 930. *ME vmbithoght, pt. of umbethink, OE ymbeþencean*
vmbre, n. shade, 332. *ME vmbre, OF vmbre, L umbra*
vncled, pt.3 s. undressed, took off (clothes), non-refl., 2434. *See* cleith.
vnder, wnder, prep. beneath or below, 20, 96, 888, &c.; below (the ground), under (the surface of the earth), 861, 1703, 1708, &c.; beneath the cover or shelter of, 735, 868; with words denoting or implying subjection to, or being the subject of: consideration, trial or notice, 29, 2316, 2339; -- ȝour voce, in a low voice, in a whisper, 1916; -- colour, under pretext, pretence, 2771. *ME, OE under*
wnderstand, v.tr. to understand, apprehend the meaning of, 1130, 2174, &c.; pr.2 pl. 570, 959, &c.; wnderstud, pt. understood, 523; believed, with obj. cl. 1405; vnderstud, pt.3 s. realised, with obj.cl. 2656. *ME understonde(n), pt. -stood, OE understandan, -stōd*
wnderta, see wndertak.
wndertak, v.tr. to undertake, take upon oneself, 412, 2343; wnderta, wndertak, pr.1 s. in parenthetic cl., I declare, venture to assert, 564, 2104; wndertuke, pt.3 s.undertook, took in hand, 2347. *ME undertake, pt. -took, under- + ON taka*
vndo, v.tr. to undo, destroy, ruin, 721, 1664, 2013. *ME vndo, OE undōn*
vnes, adv. hardly, not easily, 826. *ME uneth, OE unēaðes*

wnforgit, p.p. unforged (of a knife), 1539. *ME vnforged, un- + OF forger*
vnhonesté, n. unpleasantness, indecency, filth, 1456. *un- + OF (h)onesté*
vnhurt, adj. unhurt, 2029. *ME unhurt, un- + OF hurter*
vnisoun, n. unison, union or combination of concordant sounds, 188, 2524. *OF unison, ML unisonus*
wnknawin, adj.unknown, strange, unfamiliar, 142. *NME unknawen, OE un(ge)cnawen*
vnlyke, adj. unlike, dissimilar, different, 830. *ME unlyke, OE un(ge)līc*
vnsterd, ppl.a. unstirred, undisturbed, 444. *ME vnstird, un- + OE styrian*
vnto, prep. to (of direction), 368, 1697, 1850; to, denoting the recipient of a gift, 2473; against, in respect of opposition or hostility, 1975. *On the analogy of until, prep., by substitution of to for No. til*
wnwys, adj. unwise, foolish, 2258. *ME unwise, OE unwīs*
voce, woce, n. voice, the human voice, sound of speech, 2428, 2445; vocal sound of a bird, 2642; with a --, unanimously, 1760; with hie --, in a loud voice, 2535; vnder ȝour --, under your breath, in a low voice, 1916. *NME voce, OF vois, L voc-em*
wp, adv. up, denoting movement, to a point overhead, 102, 1042, 2058; to a point higher than another, 544, 2061; to a higher position, 2002, 2490; from out of the soil, 319, 733, 739; from a sitting to a standing position, 1530, 1908, 1932; to a standing posture, 1934; upwards, 2018, 2060, 2418; out of bed, 2460; with preps. to and on, from below, 1076, 1442; with vbs.: bruke --, 916; gaif --, 2472; brocht --, 2659. *ME, OE up*
wp, prep. up, from a lower to a higher point on or along (an ascent), 2436. *Prec.*
wprais, wpras, pt.3 s. rose to his feet, assumed a standing posture, 1120; got up from bed, 2465. *ME vpras, OE uprīsan, pt. -rās*
wpwart, adv. upward, from a lower to a loftier level, 100. *ME vpward, OE up-weard*
vrinale, n. urinal, a glass vessel employed to receive urine for medical examination, 663. *ME vrinal, OF, L urinal*
vryne, n. urine, 651. *ME vryne, OF urine, L urina*
vs, imperat. use, have sexual intercourse with, 1209; vsit, p.p. used, usual, customary, 1457; pt.3 pl., used, carried on, 1051. *ME vse, OF user*
ws, pers.pron. us; acc. 865, 1782, 1815, &c.; acc.refl. 1718; dat. 465, 1717, 1726, &c.; obj. of a prep. 397, 1474, &c. *ME us, OE ūs*
vther, adj. other, remaining, 407; different, 1349. *ME other, OE ōþer*
vther, n., sg. another person, 117, 1585; pl. 1152, 1269, 2706; each other, 2374, 2450, 2451; vtheris, pron. gen.sg. the other's, 1480; pl. others, 2561; other, n. another person, 2443, 2610. *Prec.* See also nother, adj.
vtherwayis, adv. otherwise, 1868. *ME oferweies*
wtterly, adv. utterly, to an extreme degree, 1252; entirely, 1401; plainly, straightway, 2676. *ME vtterly, (OE ūtorlīc), ON útarliga*

wa, adj. sad, wretched, 456, 465, 796, &c.; waar, adj. more woeful, grieved, 1119. *NME wa, OE wā*
wa, n. woe, distress, misery, 452; -- worth ȝow, -- thé be, -- is me, 595, 1403, 1458. *Prec.*
waar, see wa, adj.
wache, n. watch, an object that watches for purposes of guarding and protecting a town, 1814. *ME wache, OE wæcce*
wage, n. pledge, wager, in --, 601, 1178, 1791. *ME, AN, OF wage*
waikly, adv. weakly, with little strength, 470. *NME waykly, weikly, ON veik-r + -ly*
waist, adj. deserted, empty, unoccupied, 424, 433. *ME, OF wast*

waist, n. uninhabited country, a piece of land not cultivated or used for any purpose, 73. *ME wast, OF wast(e)*
wait, pres. know(s), with dep.cl. 209, 352, 1141, &c. *NME wait, OE (witan), wāt*
wald, see will.
walk, pr.3 s.subj. walk, be, live in a cert. condition, 72. *ME walk, OE wealcan*
walkand, pr.p. waking, being awake, 2616. Inverted spelling for wauk. *NME walk, OE wacan, wacian*
walkinnit, pt.3 s. wakened, woke up, 99. *ME wakin, OE wæcnan, ON vakna*
wall, n. wall, an enclosing structure, composed of bricks, stones, &c.; each of the sides of a building, 889, 2321, 2326, &c.; wallis, n.pl. the interior walls of an apartment, 80. *ME, OE wall*
wallit, ppl.a. surrounded with a wall, -- about, 530; provided with fortified walls, -- hie, 2286. *ME walled, f. OE *weallian*
wame, n. belly, abdomen, 564, 747, 1192. *ME, OE wamb*
wan, see wyn.
wand, n. rod, staff, 1194. *ME wand, ON vǫnd-r (*vandu-r)*
wane, adj. vain; in --, to no effect or purpose, 755, 1681. *ME vain, wain, OF vain, vein, L vanus*
want, v.tr. to want, desire, wish for, 853, 854; pr.1 pl. 361; wantit, pt.3 s. lacked, had not, 928. *ME wante, ON vanta*
wantoun, adj.wanton, lascivious, 790. *ME wantoun, wantowen, wan- + OE togen, p.p. of tēon*
wanyté, n. vanity, 72. *ME vanite(e), OF vanité, L vanitas*
war, adj. prudent, sagacious, 4, 1707. *ME war, OE wær, ON var-r*
war, adj. worse, 787; absol. worse (fate), 1159. *NME war, ON verre*. See also werst.
war, adv. worse, 1342; wer, id., 1593. *Prec.*
war, pt. see be, vb.
warians, n. variance, deviation, inconstancy in persons, 1289. *ME, OF variance*
warld, n. world, the entire earth, universe, the whole of mankind, 232, 618, 1096, 2393, 2750. *NME warld, OE worold*
warme, v.tr. to warm, impart warmth to a person or persons suffering from cold, 1372, 1622; warmit, pt.3 s. warmed, made warm, 1640; warmed, p.p. made warm, 1387. *ME warme, OE wearmian*
warn(e), v.tr. to warn, give timely notice to (a pers.) of impending danger, 1816; to inform, notify, 2695; warnis, pr.3 s. warns of impending danger, 1782; warnit, p.p. warned of impending danger, 1673. *ME warn(e), OE w(e)arnian*
warnyng, n. warning, previous intimation of impending evil or danger, 1840. *ME warnyng, OE war(e)nung*
wary, v.tr. to cause to change or alter, 590. *ME vary, OF varier, L variare*
was, pt. see be, vb.
watter, n. water, liquid of seas, springs, rivers, rain, &c., 759, 765, 2021; as a drink, satisfying thirst, 698, 710, 1204; urine, 658; watteris, n.pl. urine, 661. *ME water, OE wæter*
way(e), n. way, manner, 1349, 1616, 2199; na (no) --, in no manner, not at all, 503, 639, &c.; in all --, in every way, 1038; in the devill --, in the devil's name, 1444; ȝeid, &c., his --, went away, retired, 504, 1567, 1570, &c.; be the --, along the road, 2328; on the --, on the road, in the course of the journey, 975. *ME way(e), OE weġ*
we, pers.pron. we, 90, 126, 217, &c.; used by a sovereign to denote himself, 1741. *ME we, OE wē*
wed, v.tr. to marry someone, 115, 2415; intr. to get married, 2467. *ME wed, OE weddian, ON veðja*

wed, n. wager, pledge; in --, as a pledge, 1201. *ME wedd, OE wed(d), ON veð*

wedder, n. weather, 1369, 2030, 2039. *ME, OE weder*

wedding-band, n. wedding-bond, 2413. *ME wedding + band, OE weddung + ON band*

weile, see wele.

weile-payd, ppl.a. highly pleased or satisfied, 1714. *ME well paide*

weir, n. doubt, 2251; fear, 1798, 2396. *ME (chiefly No) were, prob. cogn. with ME werre 'war';cf. ON vari 'caution'*

weit, n. moisture, wetness, 2034. *ME wete, OE wǣt*

welcummit, pt.3 s. welcomed, received (a guest) gladly and hospitably, 646, 1909, 2304. *ME welcome, OE wilcumian*

wele, weile, adj. well,used pred. to denote a state of good fortune, &c., with dat. of the pers.prons., 377, 1129, 1305. *ME wele, OE wel(l)*

wele, weile, adv. very, fully, considerably, as an intensitive with adj., adv., &c., 97, 420, 942, &c.; carefully, 1924; faithfully, 2635, 2636; properly, 284; certainly, indeed, 2644; readily, 105, 992; without difficulty, easily, 1784, 2198; effectively, 443, 2111; to a high degree, 554, 692, &c.; definitely, without any doubt, 191; in a skilful manner, expertly, 201, 204, 247, &c.; in a satisfact. manner, 430, 874, 1387; elegantly, 2767; to introduce a remark or statement, 695. *Prec.*

welfair, n. welfare, happiness, 288. *ME welfare, OE wel- + faru*

well, n. well, a pit dug in the ground to obtain a supply of spring-water, 1002-3, 1115, 1117, &c.; a spring of water rising to the surface of the earth and forming a small pool or flowing in a stream, 2154, 2180. *ME well, Ang wælle, welle*

welth, n. wealth, well-being, prosperity, 3. *ME welthe*

wenary, n. hunting, the chase, 1362. *ME venerye, OF venerie, L venari 'to hunt'*

wend, v.intr. to go, travel, proceed, 639; went, pt. went, proceeded, 276, 1418, 1771, &c.; p.p. gone, 431. *ME wend, OE wendan, ON venda*

wend, pt. see wene.

wene, v.tr. to think, believe, 600; wend, pt. thought, 1118, 1122, 2548; weyne, v.tr. to believe, trust, 2259; pr.l s. believe, think, 2227. *ME wene, OE wē-nan*

wengeans, n. revenge, punishment, 746, 772. *ME vengeans, OF vengeance*

went, see wend, to go.

wepand, pr.p. weeping, shedding tears, 2032. *ME wepe, OE wēpan*

wer, see war 'worse' adv.

werité, n. truth, 685, 2179. *ME verite, OF verité, L veritas*

werk, n. work, doing, 90. *ME werke, OE we(o)rc, ON verk*

werraly, adv. truly, really, 2429. *NME verraly, OF verrai + -ly*

werray, adv. truly, 2571. *Prec.*

werst, adj. worst, 2074. *ME werst, Ang wersta, ON verstr.* See also war.

wery, adj. weary, tired, 446. *ME wery, OE wērig*

weryit, pt.3 s. strangled, killed by compressing the throat, 2056. *ME wery, wirien, OE wyrgan*

weschell, n. vessel, receptacle for a liquid, 2021. *ME vessele, wessele, AN vessele, OF vaissele, L vascella*

west, adv. westwards, 527. *ME, OE west*

wesy, v.tr. to examine, inspect, 922, 2548. *ONF viseer, L visere*

wey, pr.l s. value, estimate, regard, 2034. *ME wey(e), OE wegan, wegen*

weyne, see wene.

wicht, adj. strong, brave, valiant, 406, 533, 2266; strongly built or constructed, 1744. *ME wighte, ON vígt, nt. of vígr*

wicht, n. person, creature, 693. *ME wyght, OE wiht*

widderit, ppl.a. withered, shrivelled, 1345. *ME widder, OE widrian*

wikit, adj. wicked, malicious, 143, 2742. *ME wicked, wikked f. OE wicca* will, n. will, desire, wish, 612, 1239, 1244, &c.; intention, 61; eagerness, 1909; agane (aganis) my, hir, --, 1400, 1555, 2759; at his --, according to his volition or choice, 1938. *ME will, OE willa*

will, aux.v., pres. will, with dep. inf. without to; desire, wish to, 1483, 2414; consent to, 1876; have the habit of, 1424; expr. potentiality or capacity, 1778, 2612; futurity, intention, 359, 680, 813, &c.; with neg.: am determined not to, 1373; mere futurity, 140, 778, 865, &c.; contingent event, result to be expected, 1095, 1310, 1311, 2710; with ell. of act. vb., 288, 1107; wald, aux.v., pt. would, with dep. inf. without to; wished, intended to, 79, 180, 239, &c.; would be willing to, 26, 115, 177, &c.; would like to, 139, 141, 167, &c.; used to, was accustomed to, 411, 833; was capable of, could, 761, 768, 1889, 1890; in indir. reports, implying intention, 169, 640, 1927, 2220; with neg., commonly denoting refusal, 343; aux. of anterior fut., in dep. cl. of virtual reported speech, 350, 2162, 2670; should be willing to, 1097, 1231; possibility or contingency in the supposed case, 853, 1252, 1258, &c.; chose or were willing to, 403; in a hypoth. cl., were to, 1232, 1845. *ME wille, NME pt. wald, OE *willan, Ang walde*

will, v.tr., pres. wish, desire; with simple obj., 858, 1485, 1505; with obj. cl., 858, 1749; with ell. of vb. of motion, 2409; wald, pt.s. with simple obj., 2507; with obj. cl., 523, 1455, 1539, &c.; absol. 442; with ell. of vb. of motion, 1171. *Prec.*

wirilité, n. virility, capacity for sexual intercourse, 1194.(*NED* 1586). *OF virilitè, L virilitas*

wisage, n. face, front part of the head, 928. *ME, OF visage*

wisdome, n. wisdom, knowledge, learning, 1662. *ME wisdome, OE wīsdōm*

wisest, see wysest.

wist, see wit, vb.

wit, n. knowledge, sense, learning, 18, 132, 260, 1662; in collect. sense, wise men, 111; wittis, n.pl. senses, wits, intellectual powers, 64, 881. *ME witt, OE wit(t)*

wit, v.tr. to know, 1511, 2045, 2672; to find out, 2026; wist, pt. knew, 1065; with obj. cl. 350, 452, 883, &c.; -- of, 893, 2371, 2432; wit, imperat. know, be assured, 374, 505; wittin, p.p. known, 2438; wyte, v.tr. know, 2236. *ME wyt(e), witte, pt. wiste, OE witan, wiste*

with, prep.; denoting opposition: against, with vb. to meet, 842, 1296, 1852; denoting pers. relation, agreement, association, &c., with vb. to speak, 1338, 2293; upon, to, 2541; expr. simultaneous occurrence, foll. by that, 239, 245, 1145, &c.; following vb. to marry, 233, 2408; indic. association or participation in some act, 1443; with such vbs. as take, come, go, 180, 216, 2018, &c.; in the company, society, or presence of, 956, 1144, 1285, &c.; at the house of, 132, 689, 2308; bringing (someth. meterial or non-material), 67, 112, 211, &c.; accompanied by, 621, 1362; having, possessing, 187, 2286, &c.; indic. a quality or attribute of the action spoken of, 238, 275, 434, &c.; indic. a feeling, purpose, or other mental state accompanying the action spoken of, 64, 130, 207, &c.; still having, without loss of, 535; indic. an accomp. or attendant circumstance, 65, 720, 797, &c.; indic. the means or instrument: by means of, 147, 177, 243, &c.; used in cases where by is now the usual const., 1176; after words of furnishing, filling, covering, &c., 759, 944, 2053, &c.; indic. the cause or reason: in consequence of, because of, through, 1192, 1212, 2030; after a pass. vb. or partic., indic. the princip. agent, 185, 1091, 1104, &c. *ME with, OE wiþ*

with-all, adv. besides, as well, 2325.

within, adv. within, inside, 80, 225, 2135. *ME within, OE wiþinnan*

within, prep. within; of time, 36, 42, &c.; of place, 1645, 1705. *Prec.*

without, prep. without, with absence of, 163, 1733. *ME withoute, OE wiþūtan*
withoutin, prep. without, not having with it or with one, 42, 146, 268,&c.*Prec.*
with-thi, conj. provided that, on the condition that, 1186, 1224, 1436, &c. *OE wið + ðȳ*
witles, adj. deprived of reason, crazy, 1997. *ME witles, OE witlēas*
witnes, n. witness, in asseverative formula in which God is invoked, 1240, 2740. *ME, OE witnes*
witté, see witty.
wittering, n. information, cognisance, 2271. *NME witering, ON vitr, vitring*
wittin, wittis, see wit vb. & n.
witty, witté, adj. wise, clever, cunning, 4, 1707. *ME witty, OE wit(t)ig*
wnder(-) &c., see vnder(-) &c.
wn- &c., see vn- &c.
woce, see voce.
wod, adj. mad, 460, 937, 1120. *ME wod, OE wōd*
wodas, n. voidance, sending away persons, 226, see expl.note. *AN voidaunce, OE vuidance*
woman, n. woman, an adult female human being, 501, 1002-3, 1144; without art. 2770; mode of address, 1403, 2074; womannis, gen.sg. woman's, 2767; women, n.pl. women, 2446; without art., in gen. use, 1188, 1209, 2449. *ME woman, OE wīfman(n)*
womanhed, n. womanhood, the state or conditon of being a woman, 281. *Prec. + ME hēd(e), repr. OE *hǣdu*
won, see wyn.
wonnyt, pt.3 s. lived, dwelled, 3, 405, 1617, 2113. *ME wonne, OE wunian.* See also wynnit.
wont, p.p. accustomed, 2352. *ME wont, OE (ge)wunod*
word, n. word, speech, utterance, 159, 190, 198, &c.; promise, 515, 809; wordis, n.pl. words, 501, 578, 691, &c. *ME, OE word*
worschip(e), n. honour, distinction, 705; high degree, 1511, 2583; respect, honour shown to a pers., 2415, 2457; renown, good name, 406, 1020. *ME worship, OE w(e)orðscipe*
worth, adj. of value, of use, 1357; of merit, deserving, 2184; worth while, 2045. *ME worth, OE w(e)orþ, wurþ*
worth, pr.subj. may (it) be, become, expr. a wish for someth. to happen to one, with dat. of pers., 377, 595; worthit, pt.3 s. became, 1559. *ME worthe, OE weorðan*
worthy, adj. worthy, excellent, 342, 703, 1281, &c.; appropriate, 703, 1158. *ME worthy, n. worth + -y*
worthy, n.pl. worthy ones, distinguised or eminent persons, 255, 2255, 2518.
wound, n. wound, external injury, 942. *ME wound, OE wund* *Prec.*
wounder, adv. wonderfully, exceedingly, 1438. *ME wonder, OE wundor*
wounder, v.intr. to wonder, marvel, 1151. *ME wonder, OE wundrian*
wowe, n. vow, a solemn promise, 814. *ME vowe, AN vou, OF vo(u)*
wowit, pt.3 s. vowed, bound himself by a vow, 487, 2078; p.p. promised solemnly, 1982. *ME vow(e), OF vouer, vower*
wox, pt.3 s. grew, 2600; became, with adj. complement, 2440. *NME wox, (OE weaxan), ONhb pt. wōx*
wp, &c., see vp, &c.
wrang, adv. wrong; I ga nocht --, I do not make a mistake, I am right, 2153. *NME wrang, OE wrang, ON *wrang-r, rang-r*
wrang, n. wrong, the position of acting unjustly or indefensibly, 2253. *Prec.*
wretchidnes, n. wretchedness, meanness, 831. *ME wrecched + -nes*
writtin, see wryte.

wrocht, pt.tr. wrought, did, made, 628, 1676, 2447, 2744; intr. proceeded, acted, 1666, 2116; worked, 1798. *ME wroght, OE (wyrcan), pt. wroht*

wryte , v.intr. to write, perform the action of composing and putting on paper, with of, 2357; writtin, p.p. written, stated in writing, 1626. *ME wryte, p.p. written, OE wrītan, p.p. writen*

wryth, pt.3 s. averted, turned aside, 220. *OE wrīþan or OE wrigian, see expl. note.*

ws, see under v.

wtterly, see under v.

wyf, n. wife, a woman joined to a man by marriage, 122, 124, 498, &c.; woman, 2050; wyfis, gen.sg. wife's, 390, 473, 492, &c.; n.pl. women, 2006. *ME wyf, OE wīf*

wyle, n. wile, a crafty, deceitful trick, 1052; wylis, n.pl. wiles, tricks, 2122. *EME wīl, perh. Scand *wihl-, ON vél*

wylit, pt.3 s. beguiled, deluded, 951. *Aphetic f. biwile (be- + wile vb.) or f. prec.*

wylye, adj. cunning, crafty, 1707. *ME wyly, f. n. + -ye*

wyn, v.intr. to come, get, make one's way; -- in, get into, 860; -- to, get to, reach, 2314, 2346; -- tharto, attain it, 2373; -- of, get out of, 2431; v.tr. enter, 1132; wan, pt. intr., made his way, till, to, in, wp to, 562, 1302, 2360, 2418; tr. obtained, 2122, 2312; won, p.p. tr. won, obtained, 2724. *ME winne, pt. wan, p.p. won, OE winnan, wan, gewunnen*

wynd, n. wind, current of air, 2490. *ME wynd, OE wind*

wyndo(w), n. window, opening in a wall, 1033, 1039, 2287, &c.; wyndois, n.pl. windows, 1915. *ME windowe, -doȝe, ON vindauga*

wyne, n. wine, 1053, 1060, &c. *ME wyne, OE wīn*

wynkit, pt.3 s. winked, closed his eyes, 565. *ME wynk, OE wincian*

wynnit, pt.3 s. dwelt, resided, 1019. Var. of won(nyt), q.v.

wys, adj. wise, learned, having sound judgement, 4, 406, 711, &c. *ME wys, OE wīs*

wys, n. way, manner, 206, 222, 795, &c. *ME wyse, OE wīse*

wysest, n.pl. wisest men, most learned men, 1653; wisest, adj. wisest, cleverest, most learned, 20. *See* wys, adj.

wyslie, wysly, adv. wisely, with wisdom, 967, 2688. *ME wysly, OE wīslīce*

wysman, n. wise man, scholar, sage, 604. *ME wysman, OE wīse mann*

wyte, see wit vb.

wyte, n. blame, reproach, 599, 2130. *ME wyte, OE wīte*

ȝa, interj.yes, simple affirmation, 214, 708, 781, &c. *ME ȝa, OE ġēa, ġeā, ON já.* See also ȝeis & ȝis.

ȝar, adv. quickly, without delay, 1337. *ME ȝar, OE ġearu, -o*

ȝarne, adv. diligently, 433, 695, 1855. *ME ȝarn, ȝerne, OE ġeorne, ON gjarna*

ȝarne, pres. desire earnestly, 2261, 2640. *ME ȝarne, ONhb ġiorna*

ȝe, pers.pron. you; used in addressing a number of persons in the nom. 201, 374, 505, &c.; used in addressing a single pers. 115, 117, 140, &c.; sg. with vb. fall, meet with, cf. *DOST*, s.v.fall 6 c, 391, 517, 603, &c.; ȝhe, pers.pron. dat.sg. you, 1179. *ME ȝe, NME ȝhe, OE ġē̆.* See also ȝow, & ȝow(e), and 'Note on the Use of ȜE and THOU, pp.78-81.

ȝed, pt.3 s. went, 86; ȝeid, pt.s. went, 504, 649, 1537, &c.; ȝud, pt.3 pl. went, 2489. *ME ȝed, ȝeide, ȝode, OE ġe-ēode*

ȝeir, ȝer, n.sg. and pl. year(s), 9, 28, 36, &c.; ȝeris, n.pl. years, 42, 49, 54, &c. *ME ȝer, yeir, Ang ġēr*

ȝeis, interj. yes, in answer to a question involving a neg., 1221; in answer to a question not involving a neg., 2196, 2710; ȝis, interj. yes, 2109. *ME ȝe(i)s, ȝis, OE ġese, ġise.* See also ȝa.

ȝestrene, adv. last night, yesterday evening, 380. *ME ȝystrewin f. ȝystir + ewin.* See also ȝisterday.
ȝet, adv. yet, with neg., never till now, 2572; ȝit, adv. yet, still, 343, 444, 459, &c.; neuer --, -- neuer, 1474, 1769; nocht --, 1951; na --, 2041, 2443; nor --, 2446. *ME ȝet, ȝit, OE ġet, ġit*
ȝet, n. gate, 1645, 1907, 1931, 1991; ȝettis, n.pl. gates, 2195, 2221, 2351. *ME ȝet, ONhb ġēt*
ȝet, pt. poured, 1826, 2023. *ME ȝet(e), OE ġeotan, pt. ġēat*
ȝhe, see ȝe.
ȝis, see ȝeis.
ȝisterday, adv. yesterday, 106, 1754. *ME ȝisterday, OE ġiestran dæġ*
ȝit, see ȝet, adv.
ymag(e), n. image, statue, 1625, 1633, 1636, &c.; ymagis, n.pl. 1646, 1667, 1673, &c. *ME ymag(e), OF image*
yneuch, adv. enough, fully, quite, 446; yneugh, adj. enough, in sg. concord, 1032; yneugh, n.absol. in sg. enough, as much as is requisite or desired, 108; ynewe, adj. enough, sufficient in quantity, in pl. concord, 1380, 1543. *ME ynough, ynew, NME yneuch, OE ġenōh, ġenōg*
ȝone, dem.adj. yon, that, 357, 512, 694, &c.; dem.pron. that, all --, 2744. *ME ȝone, OE ġeon*
ȝongatis, adv. thus, in that way, 1949. *Prec. + -gatis, ON gata*
ȝou, pers.pron. you; obj. to a prep. 285, 1910, 2636; indir.obj. 2629; dir.obj. 2729; ȝow(e), pers.pron. you; as pl. used in addressing a number of persons: indir.obj. 1720, 1768, 1955; in appos. with a noun, num., &c., 2753; as sg. used in addr. one pers.: indir.obj. 34, 70, 265, &c.; dir.obj. 232, 600, 802, &c.; refl., yourself, 679; as obj. of a prep.960, 1086, 1111, &c.; this tre is --, 353. *ME you, ȝow(e), OE ēow*
ȝoung, adj. young, of persons, 122, 478, 688, &c.; of a tree, 338; of a body, 1137; of a bird, 2654.*ME ȝong, ȝung, OE ġeong, ġiung*
ȝour, poss.adj. your, of one pers., 28, 114, 119, &c.; of more persons, 1788, 2303. *ME ȝour, OE ēower*
ȝouris, pron. used predic. 142, 230. *ME ȝouris, OE ēowres*
ȝouthhed, n.youth, youngness, 235; adolescence, 1479. *ME ȝouthhede, OE ġeoguð + -hed*
ȝow(e), see ȝou.
ythandly, adv. constantly, 87. *NME iþenli, ON iðinn + -ly*
ȝud, see ȝed.

XXII. LIST OF PROPER NAMES AND PLACE-NAMES, fully exhaustive. Most of these are commented on in the relevant explanatory notes.

Amipullus, the second sage, 43; his name is also found as Maxillas and Ancillas
Ampustinus, the sixth sage, 53.
Ancillas, the second sage, 783, 791, see also Amipullus and Maxillas.
Annabill, one of the forms of the name of the burgess in AVIS, 1886. See also Balaine.
Apillis, name of a country in SENESCALCUS, 1187.
Artane, name of a county in MEDICUS, 688.
Balaine, Balan(e), the burgess in AVIS, 1973, 1983, 1991, 2005, 2035, 2052. See also Annabill.
Bantillas, the first sage, 24, 179, 184, 199, 202, 377, bef. 405, 493, 1153 (should be Lentulus), 1159 (id.), 1164 (id.).
Bribour, the man in women's clothing, 2763.
Cato, Catone, Catoun, the fourth sage, 47, 89, 1853, 1857, 1881, 1882-3.
Cornele, the burgess in ARBOR, 292, 348.
Craton(e), the seventh sage, 55, 2256, 2264-5, 2502.
Cristis, gen. Christ's, 1658.
Dioclesiane, the emperor, 2; his son, 14.
Edmound, the scholar in VIRGILIUS, 1630.
Eulope, name of the king in SENESCALCUS, 1180, see also Olimphus and Oulumpus.
Gedeon, the burgess in TENTAMINA, 1326, 1548.
God, God, always in the Christian sense, 125, 177, 209, 442, 523, 597, 746, 769, 787, 805, 818, 865, 968, 1109, 1143, 1240, 1393, 1422, 1584, 1615, 1659,1768, 1780, 1911, 2086, 2335, 2447, 2699, 2733, 2736, 2740; God(d)is, gen. God's, 678, 2230, 2568, 2720.
Herod, the king in SAPIENTES, 2106, 2114, 2125.
Hungry, name of the country in INCLUSA, 2276. See also Vngary.
Ianot, the wife in PUTEUS, 1027, 1038, 1083.
Ihesu, Jesus, 2592.
Io / Asloan, the scribe of the MS, after 2782. See Section II.
Lentalus, Lentulus, the third sage, 44, 70, 973, 979, 985, 998, 1002-3.
Malcome, the fifth sage, 50; see also Maucundas.
Mary, Sanct --, 1486.
Maucundas, the fifth sage, 1296, 1322-3; see also Malcome.
Maxillas, the second sage, 588, 614-5; see also Amipullus and Ancillas.
Merling, Merlyng, the young man who rids Herod of his sages in SAPIENTES, 2140, 2147, 2150, 2162, 2175, 2199, 2213, 2218, 2224; Merlingis, gen. 2233.
Mobrig, the name of the knight's country in INCLUSA, 2265.
Octoviane, the emperor in GAZA, 822.
Olimphus, Oulumpus, the king in SENESCALCUS, 1187, 1208. See also Eulope.
Paule, St.Paul, 1110.
Peteris, St.Peter's, 1110.
Pollema, the wife in TENTAMINA, 1334.
Romane, a. Latin, 1888. *OF Romain*
Rome, (the city of) Rome, 2, 19, 111, 269, 986, 1616-7, 1661, 1697, 1779; Romys, gen. Rome's, 386.
Vngary, Vngry, 2284, 2380; see also Hungry.

APPENDIX I
THE TABLES OF CONTENTS IN THE ASLOAN MANUSCRIPT

The first Table of Contents is in the hand of Alexander Boswell, the later Lord Auchinleck; it is here printed with the original punctuation. The numbers of the folios have been added later, very probably in the same hand. The numbers preceding the items are editorial. For descriptions of the items see the preface of Craigie's STS edition, and G.Gregory Smith, *Specimens of Middle Scots,* Edinburgh and London, 1902, p. lxx.

The Contents

1. Some treatises upon divinity, upon the passion of Christ, the sacraments, penance, confession &c.
2. The Book of the Chess in verse f. 41
3. The Division of all the warld called the Cart shortly drawn f 77
4. The vertues of Nobleness. f. 86.
5. The Scott's Original. f. 93.
6. A part of the English Cronicle showing of the part of their Kings their evil government. f. 99
7. Memorial of the Scott's Chronicle for Addition. f. 109 } [1]
8. A tractat drawn out of the Scotts Chronicle beginning at the third age of y[e] warld. f. 124 }
9. The spectacle of Love or delectation of Love of Women. f. 137.
10. An Extract of the Bible of the six work days according to the six ages. f. 151

In verse

11. The Buke of the sevyn sages f. 167[2]
    The Empress s tale of the prentice & the Gairdiner f v. 170.
    Pantillas[3] tale of the serpent that wald have slain the barnis as was helpit be the Hound whilk was slain be his Master f 172.
    The Emperors[4] tale of the baire and the Herd f 174
    The tale of Maxillas of Yppocras and his disciple f v 175
    The Empress s tale of the Knight who stall the Emperors gold f. v 178
    Lentalus tale of the woman that gart her husband trow she fell in the well f v 181
    The Empress s tale of the King that maryt the Stewarts wife f. 184. v.
    Maucundas tale of the Lady that was lattin blude f. v 186
    The Emprices tale of the spekle of Rome f 191
    The tale of Cato & the pyote f. 195. v
    The Emprices tale of the seven sages who deceived the Emperor by reading dreams f 199.
    The tale of the Knight who gave his Wife frae him. f 201
    The Childs tale of the fader who kist[5] his son[6] for the birds sang f. v 206
12. The Justs between the Tailȝeour & the Soutar f 210
13. Of the feignd false ffryar of Tungland f. v 211
14. The Buke of the Howlat. f 213.

Verso.

15. The Talis of the fyve bestis[7]
    The (Horsis Tale)[7]) Imperfect[7]
    The (Hartis Tale)[7] f. 230)

The Unicorns tale f. 231
The Baris tale f.v 233
The Wolfs tale f v. 234
16. The Tale of the uplands mouse & the borowstoun mouse[7] f 236
17. The manner of the crying ane play f. 240 (imperfect)[7]
18. The buke of Orpheus & Euridices his Queen f. 247
19. The buke of the three preists of Peblis how they tald their tales f. 257
The tale of Master John of three Questions f 258[8]
20. The contemplation of sinnaris for ilk day of the week f 263
21. The Passion of Jesus f.v. 290
22. Ane Ballat of our Lady f. 292
23. The desport of Chaucer f. 293
24. Divers[9] Ballats of our Lady f v 300 to y[e] end.[7]
Fragment of "ane ballat of luf" f 243[7]

Notes to Appendix I.

1. In the list items 7 and 8 change places, a small 1 and 2 having been placed before them.
2. Boswell's list says erroneously f. 166.
3. Craigie prints *Gautillas*. Boswell perhaps knew Rolland's *Seuin Seages* where the name figures as Pantyllas, Pantillas.
4. This should be *Empress's*.
5. Corrected in pencil to *cast*.
6. *in the Sea* inserted in pencil between *son* and *for*.
7. In pencil in a later hand.
8. This is part of the preceding item.
9. Three in number, a, b, c.

The second Table of Contents was written by John Asloan and shows the original component parts of the manuscript. The numbers preceding the items are editorial.

Heir begynis (the contentis of the)[1]
buke follow(and)[1]

1) In the later hand (Alexander Boswell's)
2) Omitted

23.	Itm a ballat of steidfastnes	xxxiij
24.	Itm a ballat of recompence	xxxiiij
25.	Itm a ballat of our lady of pete	xxxv
26.	Itm a ballat of disputacoun betuix ye body & saull	xxxvj
27.	Itm a ballat of ye devillis Inquest	xxxvij
28.	Itm a ballat of our lady	xxxviij
29.	Itm ye buke of colkelby	xxxix
30.	Itm ye buke of ye otter and ye ele	xl
31.	Itm ye flyting betuix kennyde & dunbar	xlj
32.	Itm ye fablis of Esope And first of the paddok and ye mous	xlij
33.	Itm ye preching of ye swallow	xliij
34.	Itm ye lyoun and ye mous	xliiij
35.	Itm of chanticler and ye fox	xlv
36.	Itm of ye tod and ye wolf	xlvj
37.	Itm ye parliament of bestis	xlvij
38.	Itm By a palace as I couth pas	xlviij
39.	Itm a ballat of treuth	xlix
40.	Itm ye buke of ye howlat	l
41.	Itm ye talis of ye fyve bestis	lj
42.	Itm ye wplandis mous & borowstovnis	lij
43.	Itm ye manner of ye crying of a play	liij
43^{a}.	Itm ane ballat of luf	liiij[3]
44.	Itm ye buke of schir orpheus & erudices	lv
45.	Itm ye talis of ye thre prestis of peblis	lvj
46.	Itm ye buke of ye contemplacoun of synnaris	lvij
47.	Itm ane ballat of ye passioun	lviij
48.	Itm ane ballat of our lady	lix
49.	Itm ye maying & disport of chaucer	lx
50.	Itm ane ballat of our lady	lxj
51.	Itm ane ballat of our lady	lxij
52.	Itm ane ballat of our lady	lxiij
53.	Itm ye buke of ralf colȝear	lxiiij
54.	The buke of schir gologrus & schir gawane	lxv
55.	Itm ye disputacoun betuix ye merle & ye nychttingale	lxvj
56.	Itm Dunbarris Derige of Edinburgh & strivling	lxvij
57.	Itm ane ballat of all officeris	lxviij
58.	Itm ane ballat of making of	lxix
59.	Itm ane ballat of pacience	lxx
60.	Itm ane ballat of wardlie plesance	lxxj

Items 14-39 and 53-60 are not found in the manuscript in its present form and must have been lost before it received the shape in which it came to Alexander Boswell in 1730.

Item 43^{a} is ff. 243-46 which were misplaced and really form part of item 49, 'The maying and disport of Chaucer' (cf.pp.11-2), so this misplacement had occurred already in Asloan's time.

3) 43^{a} is part of 49.

APPENDIX II.
DATES OF THE ITEMS IN THE ASLOAN MANUSCRIPT.

PROSE (except item 2)

1. *Theological treatises.* Asloan's index attributes these to John of Ireland, whose work is generally dated c.1490. He was confessor to James IV. For his career see *The Meroure of Wysdome*, eds Charles MacPherson and F. Quinn, 2 vols., STS, 2nd ser. 19, 1926, and 4th ser. 2, 1965 (for 1957-58). Quinn is inclined to doubt Ireland's authorship of the present item, op.cit., pp. xxx f.
2. *The Buke of the Chess* is in decasyllabic couplets, based on the Latin original by Jacobus de Cessolis, a Lombardic Dominican, who wrote it c.1275[1]. *DOST* dates the present text *a.* 1500[2].
3. *The Divisioun of all the Warld* contains various chapters of Trevisa's translation of Higden's *Polychronicon,* which was completed in 1387.
4. *The Wertuis of Nobleness,* a Scots version of the poem *Le bréviaire des nobles* by Alain Chartier (c.1385-c.1429), cf. William Beattie, *The Chepman and Myllar Prints,* Edinburgh Bibliographical Society, 1950.
5. *The Scottis Originale,* see Section V.
6. *A Part of the Ynglis Cronikle* ends with an occurrence in the eighteenth year of Henry VI (1422-61), but it is incomplete and is followed by a blank folio in the manuscript.
7. *Memoriale of the Scottis Corniklis for Addicioun*; its latest entry is of 1460, but again the end of this item is missing.
8. *Ane tractat drawin owt of the Scottis Cronikle,* see Section V.
9. *The Spektakle of Luf* was written in 1492, as stated in the text, p. 297, line 8.
10. *Ane extract of the bibill,* not dated.

VERSE

11. *The Buke of the Sevyne Sagis, a.* 1500[2].
12. *The Iustis betuix the Talȝeour & the Sowtar,* by Dunbar, who was writing between c.1500 and c.1512.
13. *Off the fenȝeit fals frer of Tungland,* Dunbar, c.1500-c.1512.
14. *The Buke of the Howlat,* by Sir Richard Holland, is dated c.1450-52[2].
15. *The Talis of the fyve bestes* is c.1500[2].
16. *The Tale of the wplandis mous and the borowstoun mous* is by Robert Henryson, whose work is dated *a.* 1500[2].
17. *The maner of the crying of ane playe,* sometimes attributed to Dunbar, but not definitely so, is c.1500[2].
18. *The tale of Orpheus and Erudices his Quene,* Robert Henryson, *a.*1500.
19. *The Thre Prestis of Peblis* is dated 1484-88 by T.D.Robb in his STS-edition[3]; Robb dates *BSS* as probably earlier than *The Thre Prestis*[4].
20. *The contemplacioun of synnaris* is *a.*1499, when the anglicised text was printed by Wynkyn de Worde.
21. *The Passioun of Ihesu,* Dunbar, c.1500-c.1512.
22. *Ane ballat of our Lady,* no known author, no date.
23. *The Mayng and Disport of Chauceir* is by John Lydgate (1370?-1451?); Asloan probably copied this from the Chepman and Myllar prints of 1508.

24. *Ane ballat of our Lady,* no known author, no date.
25. *Ane ballat of our Lady,* by Walter Kennedy (1460?-1508?)
26. *Ane ballat of our Lady,* by Dunbar, c.1500-c.1512.

[1] *Das Schachzabelbuch des Jacobus de Cessolis, O.P.,* ed. Gerard F.Schmidt, Berlin, 1961. It was very popular in the Middle Ages; we still have hundreds of Latin MSS and hundreds of MSS in other languages.

[2] See *DOST,* Combined Register of Works Quoted.

[3] STS, New Series, No. 8, 1920, p.xiv.

[4] Ibid., p.xxii.

APPENDIX III
Petrus Alfonsi, *DISCIPLINA CLERICALIS*[1].

Exemplum XI: De gladio (pp. 16-17) *BSS* ll. 1934-60 AVIS

Relatum est, inquit, iterum quod quidam proficiscens peregre commisit coniugem suam socrui sue seruandam. Vxor autem clam iuuenem quendam amauit, quod sue matri protinus indicauit. Illa uero amori consensit paratoque conuiuio asciuit iuuenem. Quibus epulantibus dominus ueniens ianuam pulsauit. Surrexit itaque uxor et dimisit maritum intrare. Sed mater cum amasio filie remanens, quia locus ubi absconderetur non erat, quid faceret dubitauit. Sed dum filia sua aperiret hostium marito, arripuit uetula nudum gladium et commisit amasio iussitque ut ante hostium in introitu mariti filie sue stricto gladio staret, et si aliquid ei maritus loqueretur, nichil responderet. Fecit ut iusserat. Hostioque aperto ut illum maritus sic stare uidit, substitit et: Quis, inquit, tu es? Quo non respondente, cum primum obstupuisset, tunc magis extimuit. Respondit intus uetula: Care gener, tace, ne aliquis te audiat! Ad hec ille magis mirans: Quid hoc est, inquit, cara domina? Tunc mulier: Bone fili, venerant huc tres persequentes istum, et nos aperto hostio hunc cum suo gladio intrare permisimus, donec discederent qui illum interficere uolebant. Qui nunc timens te aliquem ex illis esse stupefactus nichil tibi respondit. Et ait maritus: Bene habeas, domina, que hoc modo hunc liberasti a morte. Et introiens aduocauit amasium uxoris sue et secum sedere fecit. Sicque dulcibus alloquiis delinitum circa noctem exire dimisit.

Exemplum X: De lintheo (pp. 15-16) *BSS* ll. 1983-2009 AVIS

Dictum est de quodam qui peregre proficiscens commisit uxorem suam sue socrui. Vxor autem sua alium quendam adamauit et matri hoc indicauit. Que commota pro filia fauit amori et conuocans procum eundem cepit cum illo et filia epulari. Epulantibus illis superuenit maritus et hostium pulsauit. Et consurgens mulier procum abscondit et hostium postea domino aperuit. Qui postquam intrauit, ut lectus sibi pararetur precepit; nam quiescere uolebat quia lassus erat. Turbata mulier dubitauit quid faceret. Quod uidens mater: Ne festines, inquit, filia, lectum parare, donec monstremus marito tuo lintheum quod fecimus. Et extrahens lintheum uetula quantum potuit unum cornu illius sustulit et alterum filie subleuandum dedit. Sicque lintheo extenso delusus est maritus, quousque qui latuerat egrederetur amicus. Tunc ait mulier filie sue: Extende lintheum super lectum mariti tui, quia manibus tuis et meis est contextum. Cui maritus: Et tu, domina, scis tale lintheum parare? Et illa: O fili, multa huiusmodi paraui.

Exemplum XIV: De puteo (pp. 20-21) *BSS* ll. 1003-1152 PUTEUS

Quidam iuuenis fuit, qui totam intencionem suam et totum sensum suum et adhuc totum tempus suum ad hoc misit ut sciret omnimodam artem mulieris, et hoc facto uoluit ducere uxorem. Sed primitus perrexit querere consilium et sapienciorem illius regionis adiit hominem et qualiter custodire posset quam ducere uolebat quesiuit uxorem. Sapiens uero hoc audiens dedit sibi consilium quod construeret domum altis parietibus lapideis poneretque intus mulierem daretque sibi satis ad comedendum et non superflua indumenta, faceretque ita domum quod non esset in ea nisi solum hostium solaque fenestra per quam uideret, et tali altitudine et tali composicione per quam nemo intrare posset uel exire. Iuuenis uero audito consilio sapientis, sicuti ei iusserat egit. Mane uero quando iuuenis de domo exibat, hostium domus firmabat, et similiter quando intrabat; quando autem dormiebat, sub capite suo claues domus abscondebat. Hoc autem longo tempore egit. Quadam uero die dum iuuenis ad forum iret, mulier sua, ut erat solita facere, ascendit fenestram et euntes et regredientes intente aspexit. Hec una die cum ad fenestram staret, uidit quendam iuuenem formosum corpore atque facie. Quo uiso statim illius amore succensa fuit. Mulier hec amore iuuenis succensa et ut supradictum est custodita cepit cogitare quomodo et qua arte posset loqui cum adamato iuuene. At ipsa plena ingenio ac dolositatis arte cogitauit quod claues domini sui furaretur dum dormiret. Et ita egit. Hec uero assueta erat dominum suum unaquaque nocte uino inebriare, ut securius ad amicum suum posset exire et suam uoluntatem explere. Dominus uero illius philosophicis iam edoctus monitis sine dolo nullos esse muliebres actus cepit excogitare quid sua coniunx strueret frequenti et cotidiana potacione. Quod ut sub oculo poneret, se finxit ebrium esse. Cuius rei mulier inscia de lecto nocte consurgens perrexit ad hostium domus et aperto hostio exiuit ad amicum. Vir autem suus in silencio noctis suauiter consurgens uenit ad hostium et apertum clausit et firmauit et fenestram ascendit stetitque ibi donec in camisia sua mulierem suam nudam reuertentem uidit. Que domum rediens hostium clausum inuenit; unde animo multum condeluit et tamen hostium pulsauit. Vir mulierem suam audiens et uidens ac si nesciret interrogauit quis esset. At ipsa culpe ueniam petens et nunquam amplius se hoc facturam promittens nichil profecit, sed uir iratus ait quod eam intrare non permitteret, sed esse suum suis parentibus ostenderet. At ipsa magis ac magis clamans dixit quod nisi hostium domus recluderet, in puteum qui iuxta domum erat saliret et ita uitam finiret, sicque de morte sua amicis et propinquis racionem reddere deceret. Spretis minis dominus sue mulieris intrare non permisit. Mulier uero plena arte et calliditate sumpsit lapidem, quem proiecit in puteum hac intencione ut uir suus audito sonitu lapidis in puteum ruentis putaret sese in puteum cecidisse. Et hoc peracto mulier post puteum se abscondit. Vir simplex atque insipiens audito sonitu lapidis in puteum ruentis mox et absque mora de domo egrediens celeri cursu ad puteum uenit, putans uerum esse quod mulierem audisset cecidisse. Mulier uero uidens hostium domus apertum et non oblita sue artis intrauit domum firmatoque hostio ascendit fenestram. Ille autem uidens se esse deceptum inquit: O mulier fallax et plena arte diaboli, permitte me intrare et quicquid michi forisfecisti me condonaturum tibi crede! At illa eum increpans introitumque domus omnimodo facto atque sacramento denegans ait: O seductor, tuum esse atque tuum facinus parentibus tuis ostendam, quia unaquaque nocte es solitus ita furtim a me exire et meretrices adire. Et ita egit. Parentes uero hec audientes atque uerum esse existimantes increpauerunt eum. Et ita mulier illa liberata arte sua flagicium quod meruerat in uirum retrusit. Cui nichil profuit, immo obfuit mulierem custodisse: nam iste eciam accidit cumulus miserie quod existimacione plurimorum quod paciebatur meruisse crederetur. Vnde quidem bonis compluribus pulsus, dignitatibus exutus, existimacione fedatus ob uxoris maliloquium incestitatis tulit supplicium.

[1] *Die Disciplina Clericalis des Petrus Alfonsi (das älteste Novellenbuch des Mittelalters) nach allen bekannten Handschriften herausgegeben* von Alfons Hilka und Werner Söderhjelm (Kleine Ausgabe), Heidelberg, 1911.

APPENDIX IV
FULL LISTS OF WORDS WITH ORIGINAL TONIC /ā/, /ai/, /ē/, /ei/, AND *u* REPRESENGING PHON. 7 (ESc /ō/ > MSc /ū/)

/a/, /ai/ spellings:

/ā/ spelled *a* only:

a
able
age
-age
allace
allake
amen
ane
anys
banys
blame
cage
chape
chasit
cravis
(ma)dame
eschape
face

fais *n.pl.*
fame
fra
ga
grace
haly
hame
hate
hatit
having
lady(e)
ma
medicinale
nakit
name
nane
napry
natur

organis
place
ravyn
sa, swa
sage
salust
samyn
schame *n., v.*
schane *pret.*
schape *pret.*
sla, slane
space
stagis
stane
stra
swagis
ta 'take'
takinnis

tary
thar 'there'
thra
twa
wa
wage
wame
wanyté
warians
wary
ȝa
ȝar

/ā/ spelled *ai* only:

baid *pret.*
baid *n.*
baile
bair(e) *a.*
bair(e) 'boar'
bait *pret.*
baith
cair
fair *n.*
forsaike
hait 'hot'
laif
laigh

lair *(OE lār)*
laite 'late'
laith
raid
raif
raith
scaith
slaid(e)
spaide
taist *v., n.*
traide
waist
wait
welfair

/ai/ spelled *ai, ay* only:

air
assay
aye
braid
delay(d)
day
fraitlye
gay
hair
lair
lay
may *v.*
may *n.*

palfray
payd
play *n., v.*
pray
say(e)
thai 'they'
waikly
way(e)
werray

/ai/ spelled *a* only:

abasit
aganis
avale (avalȝe)
bane *(ON ei)*
barane
contrar
danté
daly (day)
ganand

grath(ly)
lakit *(ON ei)*
lane *(ON ey)*
madin
mane *a., n.*
(OE mægen)
nalis
ordanit *(AN ei)*
palace

pane 'pain'
pantit 'painted'
plane
rasit *(ON ei)*
remane
Romane
sodan(e)ly
souerane
surfatly

tale 'tail'
trane *(OF aï)*
tratour *(OF ai)*
vane
wane *(OF ai)*
werraly (werray)

/ā/ spelled *a, ai, ay*:		/ai/ spelled *a, ai, ay*:
airly, arlye	ma(y)ne 'moan'	consaif, -sauit, also with prefixes dis-, per-, re-
aith, athis	ma(i)r	fa(i)le *n.*
ca(i)s(e)	ma(i)st	fa(y)ne
cla(i)th(is)	na(y)	ra(y)ne
decla(i)r	quha(y)	sale, sailand
faris, fair *v.*	(wp)ra(i)s	strait, stratlie
ga(i)f	saif, savit	tha(i)m
gait, þusgatis, ȝongatis	sair, sary	tra(i)st
ha(i)f	sca(i)r	
ha(i)le	sca(i)th	
ha(i)st	spair, sparand, sparing	
ma(i)de *pret.*	stra(i)ke *pret.*	
	ta(i)le 'tale'	

It is to be noted that very often an adverb shows a spelling different from that of its head-word, e.g. day/daly, sodan(e)ly, statis/staitly, strait/stratlie, surfatly, werray/werraly.

Summary of *a/ai/ay* spellings:

before *d* mad(e), maide;
f ga(i)f, ha(i)f, saif/savit, con-, dis-, per-, re- saif/sauit;
k strake, straik(e);
l fa(i)le, ha(i)le, ta(i)le, sale/sailand;
m tha(i)m;
n fa(y)ne, ma(y)ne, ra(y)ne;
r arlye/airly, faris/fair *v.*, decla(i)r, ma(i)r, sary/sair, sca(i)r, spair/sparand/sparing;
s ca(i)s(e), rais/(wp)ra(i)s;
st ha(i)st, ma(i)st, tra(i)st;
t gait/gatis, statis/staitly, strait/stratlie;
th cla(i)th, sca(i)th;
# na(y);

ai is replaced by *ay* before *n* and *#*. Note also *sais/sayis, said/sayd,* and *aye, way(e), payd.*
Various etymological sources do not variously influence the phenomenon: examples are from both Germanic and Romance derivations. Rhyme-words do not obviously influence the spellings, e.g.: *haf:laif; haif:gaf; rad:maid; payd:said; haile:counsall; thar:hair; declar:mair; allake:straike.*

/ē/, /ei/ spellings:

/ē/ spelled *e* only:

aggrevit	eme	gret *pret.* 'saluted'	prest
allege	entré	grevously	prevé
be *v.*	erd	hed 'heed'	quene
bedene	ete, etand, etyne	-hed suffix	replege
bere *v.*	evyn, ewin, ewyn	heres	revele
betwene	feld	kepar, kepe	selit
brek	fele *n., v.*	kne	sely
brer	ferd	knelit	sle
brest	fle 'fly'	leche *v.*	slepe *n., v.*
ces, sesit	fle 'flee'	legis	speche
ches	fre	lele	-té suffix
clene, clenly	frendis	lerd	teche
cuntré	freth *v.*	lesingis	teris *n.pl.*
deces	gredy	lever	thé *pers.pron.*
dele 'devil'	grene	levis 'grants'	thee *n.*
depe	gret *a.*,gretly	me	thré
dreme *n., v.,* dremyng	gret(is), gretand 'weep'	mese, mesis	tré
edoke		negh *v.*	we
efferit		-er suffix *(nomen agentis)*	wepand
			wery
			ȝé

/ē/ spelled *ei* only:

beif	feir *n.*	remeid
beir 'barley'	feit	seid *n.*
beir 'bier'	fleyt 'float'	seike *v.*
beseike	heile *v.* 'hide'	seir
breid 'bread'	heit *v.* 'to heat'	speid *v.*
cheir	leid *v.*	spreid
deid *a.* (dedly)	leid *n.* 'language'	steid
deid *n.* 'death'	leif *a.* 'dear'	steike
deid *n.* 'deed'	leif *v., n.* 'leave'	steir
deile	leif *n.* 'leaf'	streit
deir *v.* (OE *derian*)	leip	succeid
eike *adv.*	leir	weir
eir *adv.*	leis	weit
eith *a.*	leit *pret.* 'let' aux.	ȝeis
exceid	meid	
feid *n.* 'feud'	neidforce	
feid *v.*	reid *n.*	
feile 'many'	releif	
feir *a.*		

/ei/ spelled *ei, ey* only:	/ei/ spelled *e* only:
eis, diseis	de
key	dese
obeys	sustene
wey	

/ē/ spelled *e, ei, ey*:

aper(and), appeir
bleid, bledis
cle(i)th, clething
cle(i)r, clerly
deid *a.*, dedly
deir, der(rast)
dreid, dreidles, dredand
fe(i)st
forbe(i)d
gre(i)f
he(i)d, hedis 'head'
he(i)le *n.*, *v.*
he(i)r *adv.*
heir, heris *v.*
leif, levis, levit 'live'
leit, lete *pret.* 'left'
meik, -nes, meikly, mekly
meit *n.*, meting
meit(e), mete 'food'

me(y)ne 'mean'
meyne, menyt 'moan'
mische(i)f
ne(i)r
peir, pereles
pre(i)f
reid, redyng
requer(it), requyrit(!)
schete, scheit
se *v.*, sene, seyne
se *n.*, sey
seike *a.*, se(i)knes
speik(e), speke
spe(i)r *n.*
speir, sperit, sperand
sweit, swet(e) *a.*, swetly
we(i)le *a.*, *adv.*
we(y)ne
ȝe(i)d
ȝe(i)r
Note he-, hie-ravyn
he, hie, hye 'high'
requer(it), requyrit

/ei/ spelled *e, ei, ey*:

e, eyne
le, leyis
pece, peis, pes
pleis, plesis, pleseir

Summary of *e/ei/ey* spellings:

before *d* bleid/bledis, deid/dedly, dreid/dredand, forbe(i)d, he(i)d, reid/redyng, ȝe(i)d;
f/v gre(i)f, leif/levis/levit, mische(i)f, pre(i)f;
k meik/mekly, seike/se(i)knes, spe(i)ke;
l he(i)le, we(i)le;
n e/eyne, me(y)ne, meyne/menyt, se(y)ne, we(y)ne;
r aper/appeir, cle(i)r, de(i)r, he(i)r, ne(i)r, peir/ pereles, spe(i)r *n.*, speir/sperit/sperand; ȝe(i)r;
s pe(i)s/pece, pleis/plesis;
st fe(i)st;
t lete/leit, meit/meting, mete/meit(e), schete/scheit, sweit/swet(e);
th cle(i)th;
# le/leyis, se/sey *n.*

ei is replaced by *ey* before *n* and *#*.

PHONEME 7

u spellings:

behude, behufit/behovit
blude
buke
burd(e)
bure *pret.*
bute
cule
dure
flude
flure
fude
fure
fut(e)
gud
hurdome
luf(it)
luke
nuke
rute
schupe
schut
scule
stude
suth
tuke
tvme
vther
ȝud
assure
augure
conclude
contruf
(conȝe)
cure
curyale
conswetude
dule
excusit
frute
fule
fussoun
huge
iuge
lute
mixtur
(movis/-it)
nature
(presome)
prufe
pvnis(s)
pure
remuf
rudlye
scurgis
(sonȝe)
spulȝe
study
vs

o spellings:

abone
brother
do
dome
done
hone
lo
moder
nother
other
scho
sone
to
wisdome
wod

APPENDIX V. /a/ and /ai/-rhymes in Early and Middle Scots poetry

		Number of lines checked	Rhymes in /ai/ with						
			thay (*þai*)	other final /ai/	/aid/	/aif/	/ail/	/ailit/	/ain/ (*slane*)
Rhyming in couplets									
Bruce	1375	2785	27	49	1	1	11	5	23 (10)
Leg.Saints	a.1400	2782	10	80	-	-	5	-	4 (1)
Sc.Troy Bk	c.1400	2782	13	35	1	-	7	-	19 (4)
Wyntoun	c.1420	2786	6	23	-	-	4	-	5 (1)
Bk Alex.	a.1400 or 1438	2785	1	40	1	-	16	-	23 (4)
Wallace	c.1475	2782	5	18	-	-	10	-	43 (22)
Thre Pr.	a.1500	1342 (x 2.07)	2	43	2	-	-	-	12 (2)
Lanc.Laik	a.1500	2782	6	52	3	1	5	-	15 (1)
Bk Chess	a.1500	2191 (x 1.27)	-	4	1	-	-	-	33 (13)
Ratis Ravyng	c.1420	1815 (x 1.53)	3	57	-	-	3	1.5	3 (-)
BSS	a.1500	2782	6	33	6	-	1	-	23 (8)
Alliterative stanzas									
Bk Howlat	c.1450-2	1000 (x 2.78)	-	53	3	-	-	-	11 (-)
Gol.& Gaw.	a.1500	1362 (x 2.04)	2	59	-	-	9	-	32 (1)
Rauf Coilȝ.	a.1500	972 (x 2.86)	9	94	14	-	4	-	19 (-)
Stanzas									
King Hart	a.1500	960 (x 2.9)	-	38	-	-	3	-	23 (3)
Kingis Qu.	c.1436 MS. c.1490	1379 (x 2.0)	-	36	11	-	8	2	43 (-)
Various metres									
Henryson	a.1500	1391 (x 2.0)	2	42	2	-	2	4	16 (4)
Dunbar	c.1500- c.1512	1391 (x 2.0)	4	28	-	-	2	3	46 (4)
Gavin Douglas	1501	2169 (x 1.28)	-	19	10	-	6	4	28 (6)
Gavin Douglas	1513	1391 (x 2.0)	4	32	-	-	-	-	14 (-)

Rhymes in /ai/ continued

/ainis/	/ains/	/aint/	/air/	/ais/	/ait/ -*ayit*	/aivit/
-	1	-	3	2	2	1
-	-	-	1	-	-	-
5	-	-	2	1	-	-
-	-	-	15	5	-	-
-	-	-	-	1	1	-
-	-	-	6	1	-	-
-	-	4	2	-	-	-
-	-	1	4	1	4	-
-	-	-	5	4	-	-
-	-	1.5	12	5	-	-
-	-	-	5	4	-	1
-	-	-	-	-	-	-
-	-	-	-	3	-	-
-	-	-	4	6	-	-
-	-	-	-	3	3	-
-	-	-	8	4	-	-
-	-	-	2	2	-	-
4	-	-	2	3	13	-
-	-	-	12	5	3	-
-	-	-	2	2	-	-

Impure rhymes in /ai/,/a:/

	final /ai/	/aid/	/aif/ -*aue*, -*awe*, -*awit*	/ail, ailis/	/ain, anis/	/air/	/ais/ -*aist* -*aisit*	total	
Rhyming in couplets									
Bruce	2	-	-	-	3	-	-	5	
Leg.Saints	-	-	-	-	-	1	-	1	
Sc.Troy Bk	-	-	1	-	1	-	2	4	
Wyntoun	1	-	-	2	-	-	3	6	
Bk Alex.	2	-	-	-	7	1	1	11	
Wallace	-	1	2	6	2	24	-	35	
Thre Pr.	-	-	-	6	17	21	4	48	
Lanc.Laik	-	3	5	1	5	14	2	30	
Bk Chess	2	9	5	5	1	1	1	24	
Ratis Ravyng	3	-	-	-	-	1	-	4	
BSS	-	-	3	2	1	1	-	7	
Alliterat.stanzas									
Bk Howlat	3	-	-	17	35	18	-	73	
Gol. & Gaw.	-	-	-	-	-	-	2	2	
Rauf Coilȝ.	-	-	-	7	6	-	-	13	
Stanzas									
King Hart	-	-	-	12	-	3	-	15	
Kingis Qu.	-	-	-	-	1	-	-	1	
Various metres									
Henryson	2	-	-	-	4	-	-	6	
Dunbar	-	-	-	2	18	6	-	26	
Gav.Douglas 1501	-	4	2	6	4	17	3	39	(+ 3 /ait/)
Gav.Douglas 1513	10	12	-	6	20	6	-	62	(+ 8 /ait/)

Rhymes in /a:/

final /a:/	-a(is)	-able	-ade	-afe	-age	-ake	-ale	-ame	-ane	-anis
53	5	1	30	1	14	-	4	1	32	1
29	-	4	51	4	-	-	6	9	36	-
23	2	3	27	4	3	-	-	9	4	-
51	1	-	12	1	-	-	-	9	12	1
36	5	-	12	1	-	2	4	1	27	1
21	-	-	29	14	-	-	2	4	29	-
21	2	2	-	-	6	-	8	15	10	-
1	2	-	6	1	-	-	-	9	-	-
5	1	-	7	10	-	3	1	5	4	-
12	-	-	-	11	1.5	4.5	1.5	8	5	3
19	3	-	7	7	12	1	4	10	37	2
8	-	21	6	11	-	6	9	-	11	-
22	-	8	22	3	6	-	26	4	10	2
21	6	-	31	6	-	-	-	9	41	14
29	-	-	15	3	9	-	-	-	12	3
-	-	10	6	-	7	13	7	10	-	-
5	-	18	2	-	6	-	-	4	8	2
2	-	12	-	4	4	-	-	26	26	2
15	-	12	-	1	14	9	-	3	5	2
16	2	2	4	-	18	4	2	10	10	6

Rhymes in /a:/ continued

	-are	*-ary*	*-ase, -ace, -as*	*-asit*	*-a(i)st*	*-ate*	*-atis*	*-a(i)th*
Rhyming in couplets								
Bruce	57	-	2	-	-	6	3	4
Leg.Saints	64	-	-	-	-	6	-	13
Sc.Troy Bk	39	-	-	-	-	6	-	3
Wyntoun	31	-	15	-	-	11	-	2
Bk Alex.	44	-	-	-	-	4	-	11
Wallace	55	-	26	-	1	7	-	-
Thre Pr.	17	-	23	-	15	2	-	4
Lanc.Laik	15	-	11	-	-	7	-	-
Bk Chess	19	-	15	-	3	14	-	1
Ratis Ravyng	34	-	12	-	14	5	-	5
BSS	38	1	3	2	6	1	-	4
Alliterat.stanzas								
Bk Howlat	26	-	33	-	-	10	-	-
Gol. & Gaw.	33	-	25	2	-	9	-	-
Rauf Coilȝ.	57	-	7	-	11	6	-	4
Stanzas								
King Hart	9	-	3	-	6	9	-	3
Kingis Qu.	2	2	34	-	-	11	-	-
Various metres								
Henryson	28	2	14	-	-	26	-	-
Dunbar	18	4	10	-	-	5	2	-
Gav.Douglas 1501	12	4	12	-	-	35	-	-
Gav.Douglas 1513	30	6	18	-	-	16	-	12

Rhymes in /a:/ continued

-ave	-avit	-awe	-awin	-awis	-ape
5	-	11	2	2	-
-	-	4	-	-	3
2	-	-	-	-	-
-	-	9	2	2	-
2	-	5	1	-	-
3	-	23	-	-	-
8	-	4	-	-	-
1	-	-	-	-	-
-	-	3	-	-	-
-	-	9	4.5	-	-
-	1	21	4	-	-
-	-	3	11	7	8
-	-	28	5	-	-
-	-	-	10	-	-
-	-	6	-	-	-
-	-	12	-	-	-
2	-	8	-	-	-
4	-	-	-	5	-
4	-	14	-	-	4
4	-	8	-	2	2

/a/,/e/-variation

	-ft	*-ge*	*-k*	*-l*	*-n*	*-ns*	*-r*	*-rt*	*-s*	*-st*	*-xt*
Rhyming in couplets											
Bruce	–	–	–	–	–	–	7	–	6	–	–
Leg.Saints	1(*-f*)	–	–	–	–	–	1	–	16	–	–
Sc.Troy Bk	–	–	–	–	–	–	7	–	12	–	–
Wyntoun	–	2	–	1	–	–	4	5	12	–	–
Bk Alex.	–	–	–	–	1	–	1	–	–	–	–
Wallace	–	–	–	–	–	–	–	–	3	–	–
Thre Pr.	2	–	–	–	–	–	4	–	2	–	–
Lanc.Laik	–	–	2	–	–	1	2	–	–	1	–
Bk Chess	–	–	–	–	–	3	–	1	10	–	–
Ratis Ravyng	–	5	–	–	–	–	3	–	3	1.5	–
BSS	–	2	1	2	–	–	1	2	2	–	1
Alliterat.stanzas											
Bk Howlat	–	–	–	–	1	–	–	–	13	10	–
Gol. & Gaw.	–	–	–	–	–	–	–	2	3	2	–
Rauf Coilȝ.	–	–	–	–	1	–	–	1	–	–	–
Stanzas											
King Hart	–	–	–	–	–	–	–	–	3	6	–
Kingis Qu.	–	–	–	–	–	–	–	–	–	–	–
Various metres											
Henryson	–	–	–	–	–	–	–	6	–	–	–
Dunbar	–	–	–	–	–	–	–	2	–	–	–
Gav.Douglas 1501	–	–	–	–	–	–	–	1	3	–	–
Gav.Douglas 1513	–	–	–	–	–	–	–	2	2	–	–

Rhymes in /a/

-acht	*-ad*	*-adder* *-ad hir* *-ader*	*-af*	*-aggit*	*-ak*	*-ald*	*-all*	*-als*	*-alt*	*-an*
-	-	-	-	-	7	6	16	-	-	4
1	-	-	-	-	12	5	17	1	-	30
-	-	-	-	-	4	1	12	1	-	12
-	-	-	-	-	3	4	21	2	-	9
-	-	-	-	-	2	7	20	2	-	7
-	-	-	-	-	3	7	9	1	-	10
2	10	2	-	2	8	8	15	2	2	23
-	-	-	-	-	20	2	9	-	-	4
-	-	-	-	-	14	10	12	-	-	32
-	1.5	-	-	-	1.5	6	26	1.5	-	15
-	5	1	-	-	14	10	22	-	-	19
4	8	-	-	-	-	18	19	-	-	21
4	-	-	-	-	6	15	9	-	-	7
-	-	-	-	-	-	14	37	-	-	27
-	-	-	-	-	9	9	20	-	-	6
-	7	-	-	-	-	-	35	-	-	7
-	2	-	-	-	16	6	22	-	-	3
-	3	-	-	-	10	5	17	-	-	5
1	-	-	-	-	3	11	14	-	-	-
-	2	-	-	-	6	12	26	2	-	8

Rhymes in /a/ continued

Rhyming in couplets	*-and -andis*	*-ang*	*-ank*	*-ans -ance*	*-ant -antis*	*-anȝe*	*-ap -appit*	*-ard*
Bruce	38	2	-	4	-	1	-	-
Leg.Saints	35	5	1	3	-	1	-	1
Sc.Troy Bk	53	1	-	2	-	-	-	-
Wyntoun	49	1	-	-	-	-	1	3
Bk Alex.	40	7	-	1	-	-	-	-
Wallace	43	32	-	-	-	-	-	-
Thre Pr.	19	2	-	8	-	-	2	2
Lanc.Laik	4	-	-	-	-	-	-	1
Bk Chess	66	12	-	-	1	-	-	-
Ratis Ravyng	21	-	-	3	-	-	-	-
BSS	14	8	-	9	1	-	-	7
Alliterat.stanzas								
Bk Howlat	28	8	-	3	-	-	-	4
Gol. & Gaw.	52	22	-	10	-	-	-	2
Rauf Coilȝ.	64	-	-	6	-	-	-	6
Stanzas								
King Hart	9	32	-	17	-	-	3	6
Kingis Qu.	8	9	-	54	5	-	2	-
Various metres								
Henryson	6	4	-	10	-	-	-	-
Dunbar	12	6	-	25	-	-	-	-
Gav.Douglas 1501	19	19	-	24	17	-	5	-
Gav.Douglas 1513	20	-	-	4	6	-	4	-

Rhymes in /a/ continued

-arge	*-ark*	*-arld*	*-arm*	*-armys*	*-arn*	*-arp*	*-art*	*-as*	*-ast*	*-at*
-	-	-	-	-	1	-	-	34	8	-
-	-	-	-	-	5	-	1	46	13	2
-	-	-	-	-	-	-	2	65	11	-
-	-	-	-	-	-	-	1	13	11	10
-	-	-	-	-	1	-	1	36	6	3
-	-	-	-	2	-	-	1	20	36	-
2	4	-	-	-	2	-	6	2	2	-
-	-	-	-	1	-	-	13	5	3	1
-	-	-	1	-	-	-	-	3	1	3
-	-	-	-	-	-	-	9	4.5	3	1.5
1	-	1	1	-	6	1	5	29	17	6
-	-	-	-	1	-	-	13	21	-	-
-	-	-	-	-	-	-	2	-	-	-
-	-	-	-	-	-	-	1	-	-	-
6	-	-	-	-	-	-	6	3	29	-
4	-	-	-	-	-	-	16	-	2	-
-	-	-	-	-	-	-	6	12	2	2
4	4	-	-	-	-	-	2	-	5	-
1	-	-	-	3	-	-	12	11	7	-
-	-	-	-	2	-	2	2	-	6	-

Rhyming in couplets		Number of lines checked	Some other interesting rhymes: *-yne/ -ing*	*sere*	*certane*	Anglic. in rh.	Asso- nance	*self sell*
Bruce	1375	2785	-	2	-	1	1	-
Leg.Saints	a.1400	2782	7	14	-	1	6	-
Sc.Troy Bk	c.1400	2782	1	7	12	freq.	-	-
Wyntoun	c.1420	2786	-	13	-	1	-	-
Bk Alex.	a.1400 or 1438	2785	7	3	2	-	1	-
Wallace	c.1475	2782	-	1	-	13	-	1
Thre Pr.	a.1500	1342 (x 2.07)	-	-	-	-	4	-
Lanc.Laik	a.1500	2782	-	8	-	freq.	rare	-
Bk Chess	a.1500	2191 (x 1.27)	-	-	-	freq.	-	-
Ratis Ravyng	c.1420	1815 (x 1.53)	4.5	15	-	-	1.5	-
BSS	a.1500	2782	2	-	-	2	4	5
Alliterative stanzas								
Bk Howlat	c.1450-2	1000 (x 2.78)	-	4	1	11	-	-
Gol.& Gaw.	a.1500	1362 (x 2.04)	-	2	4	9	-	-
Rauf Coilȝ.	a.1500	972 (x 2.86)	-	4	-	-	3	-
Stanzas								
King Hart	a.1500	960 (x 2.9)	-	3	-	15	-	-
Kingis Qu.	c.1436 MS. c.1490	1379 (x 2.0)	-	-	1	freq.	-	-
Various metres								
Henryson	a.1500	1391 (x 2.0)	-	-	-	freq.	-	-
Dunbar	c.1500-c.1512	1391 (x 2.0)	-	-	-	6	-	-
Gavin Douglas	1501	2169 (x 1.28)	-	3	1	freq.	-	-
Gavin Douglas	1513	1391 (x 2.0)	-	8	-	some	-	-

APPENDIX VI

TABLE OF VERSIONS OF THE *SEVEN SAGES OF ROME* AND OF THE PRINCIPAL CHARACTERS IN A NUMBER OF VERSIONS AND MANUSCRIPTS

Dolopathos (Dol.)	*Scala Celi* (S) Latin prose, 13th c.	Vienna MS. 13538 Joh. Gobii Junior 1320-30
CANIS	ARBOR	
GAZA	CANIS	Vancilles
SENES	APER	
CREDITOR	MEDICUS	Anxilles
VIDUAE FILIUS	GAZA	
LATRONIS FILIUS	TENTAMINA	Lentulles
CYGNI EQUES	SENESCALCUS	
INCLUSA+PUTEUS	PUTEUS	Malquidas
	VIRGILIUS	
	AVIS	Caton
	VII SAPIENTES	
	VIDUA	Joce
	FILIA	
	NOVERCA	Marrons
	VATICINIUM	
	The stepmother is burnt after the duel (Aïache, p. 38), not in Goedeke's edn.	

King: Dolopathos of Sicily
Son: Lucinus; mother: Auguste
One teacher: Virgil
Seven councillors: no names
Stepmother: no name, tells no stories
Virgil tells the eighth story

1. Latin text, prose, by Joannes de Alta Silva, c.1190.
   Ed. H. Oesterley, Strassburg, 1873;
   and Le Roux de Lincy in *Essai sur les fables indiennes* by A.Loiseleur Deslongchamps, Paris, 1838.
2. Old French text, approx. 13,000 lines in octosyllabic couplets, by Herbers 1223-26, eds Brunet & de Montaiglon, Paris, 1856.

King: Dyocletianus
Son: no name; stepmother no name
Sages: no names in Goedeke's edn.

S is based on a lost *Liber de Septem Sapientibus,* not later than c.1250 (Campb. 1907, p.xxiii).

Goedeke, *Or.u.Occ.*1866, ed. impression Lübeck 1476.
There is a MS of the final redaction in Bruges, Bibl.de la Ville, no. 494 (Aïache) and in Vienna Codex *Summa Recreatorum,* 15th c. (Mussafia), which differs slightly from Goedeke's text. Substitution of FILIA and NOVERCA for ROMA and INCLUSA is found elsewhere only in L and A/L.
Campb. 1907, p.xxiv: it is not probable that S was based on L, rather that L was influenced by S.

Buchner, *Beiträge,* 1904, gives the sequence of Cod.Lat.3855 (Bibl.Mazarine) and says that the story GAZA which he prints is common to the Innsbr.MS.310 (an HL-version). I notice that the sequence is that of S, and that the tale is almost literally identical with the S-GAZA as printed by Goedeke, see above, and not at all with Innsbr.310.

/ē/, /ei/ spellings:

/ē/ spelled *e* only:

aggrevit
allege
be *v.*
bedene
bere *v.*
betwene
brek
brer
brest
ces, sesit
ches
clene, clenly
cuntré
deces
dele 'devil'
depe
dreme *n., v.*, dremyng
edoke
efferit
eme
entré
erd
ete, etand,
ethyne
evyn, ewin, ewyn
feld
fele *n., v.*
ferd
fle 'fly'
fle 'flee'
fre
frendis
freth *v.*
gredy
grene
gret *a.*, gretly
gret(is), gretand 'weep'
gret *pret.* 'saluted'
grevously
hed 'heed'
-hede suffix
here
kepar, kepe
kne
knelit
leche *v.*
legis
lele
lerd
lesingis
lever
levis 'grants'
me
mese, mesis
negh *v.*
-er suffix (*nomen agentis*)
prest
prevé
quene
replege
sete
sele
sely
sle
slepe *n., v.*
speche
-té suffix
teche
teris *n.pl.*
the *pers.pron.*
thee *n.*
thre
tré
we
wepand
wery
zé

/ē/ spelled *ei* only:

beif
beir 'barley'
beir 'bier'
beseike
breid 'bread'
cheir
deid *a.* (dedly)
deid *n.* 'death'
deid *n.* 'deed'
deill
deir *v.* (OE derian)
eike *adv.*
eir *adv.*
eith *a.*
ekeid
feid *n.* 'feud'
feid *v.*
feile 'many'
feir *a.*
feir *n.*
feit
fleyt 'float'
heile *v.* 'hide'
heit *v.* 'to heat'
leid *v.*
leid *n.* 'language'
leif *a.* 'dear'
leif *v.*
leif *n.* 'leaf'
leip
leir
leis
leit *pret.*
meid
neidforce
reid *n.*
releif
remeid
seid *n.*
seike *v.*
seir
speid *v.*
spreid
steid
streit
succeid
weir
weit

/ei/ spelled *ei, ey* only:

eis, diseis
key
obeys
wey

/ei/ spelled *e* only:

de
dese
sustene

K (OF verse) c.1155	MS. BN fr 1553 AD 1284	C (OF prose and verse)	MS. Chartres 620 late 13th c.
ARBOR	Ba(n)cillas	ARBOR	Baucillas
CANIS		CANIS	
SENESCALCUS		APER	
MEDICUS	Dammas, Ausire(s), Anchilles	MEDICUS	Augustus
APER		GAZA	
PUTEUS	Malquidas, Malkidas	PUTEUS	(Lentulius)
ROMA		SENESCALCUS	
TENTAMINA	Lentulus, Gentulus, Gentillus	TENTAMINA	(Malcuidas)
GAZA		ROMA	
AVIS	Cathon(s)	AVIS	Cathon
SAPIENTES		SAPIENTES	
VIDUA	Jessé(s), Gesses	VIDUA	Jesse
VIRGILIUS		VIRGILIUS	5
INCLUSA	Berous	INCLUSA	(Merous) Berous?
VATICINIUM		VATICINIUM	

The stepmother is burnt alive.

King: Vespasian, son of Methusaleh
Son: no name

Sequence of sages' stories as in A
In the stories VIDUA, ROMA, INCLUSA, and VATICINIUM K shows a very close, at times even verbal agreement with A

Sequence of sages' stories as in A
The verse begins only at TENTAMINA

Ed. H.A.Keller, Tübingen, 1836
- Jean Misrahi, Paris, 1933

Ed. Hugh Allison Smith, 'A Verse Version of the *SSR*', *Romanic Review*, III (1912), pp. 1-67

/ē/ spelled *e, ei, ey*:

aper(and), appeir
bleid, bledis
cle(i)th, clething
cle(i)r, clerly
deid *a.*, dedly
deir, der(rast)
dreid, dreidles,
dredand
fe(i)st
forbe(i)d
gre(i)f
he(i)d, hedis
'head'
he(i)le *n.*, *v.*
he(i)r *adv.*
heir, heris *v.*
leif, levis,
levit 'live'
leit, lete *pret.*
'left'
meik, -nes, meikly,
mekly
meit *n.*, meting
meit(e), mete
'food'

me(y)ne 'mean'
meyne, menyt 'moan'
mischè(i)f
ne(i)r
peir, pereles
pre(i)f
reid, redyng
requer(it), requyrit
schete, scheit
se *v.*, sene, seyne
se *n.*, sey
seike *a.*, se(i)knes
speik(e), speke
spe(i)r *n.*
speir, sperit, sperand
sweit, swet(e) *a.*,
swetly
we(i)le *a.*, *adv.*
we(y)ne
ʒe(i)d
ʒe(i)r
Note he-, hie-ravyn
he, hie, hye 'high'
requer(it), requyrit

/ei/ spelled *e, ei, ey*:

e, eyne
le, leyis
pece, peis, pes
pleis, plesis,
pleseir

D (OF prose) late 13th c.	MS. BN fr 5036 15th c.	A (OF prose) 13th-15th c.	MS. McCl.179 13th c.
ARBOR		ARBOR	
CANIS	Bencillas, Baucillas	CANIS	Bancillas
SENESCALCUS		APER	
MEDICUS	Aussire, Ancille	MEDICUS	Anxilles
APER		GAZA	
PUTEUS	Mauquidas	PUTEUS	Lentilus, Lentulus
SAPIENTES		SENESCALCUS	
TENTAMINA	Lentulus	TENTAMINA	Malquidans
ROMA		VIRGILIUS	
AVIS	Cathon	AVIS	Catons
GAZA		SAPIENTES	
VIDUA	Gesse, Jesse	VIDUA	Iesse
VIRGILIUS		ROMA	
INCLUSA	Meros, Meras	INCLUSA	Martins

Summary of *e/ei/ey* spellings:

before *d* bleid/bledis, deid/dedly, dreid/dredand, forbe(i)d, he(i)d, reid/redyng, ʒe(i)d;
f/v gre(i)f, leif/levis/levit, mischè(i)f, pre(i)f;
k meik/mekly, seike/se(i)knes, spe(i)ke;
l he(i)le, we(i)le;
n e/eyne, me(y)ne, meyne/menyt, se(y)ne, we(y)ne;
r aper/appeir, cle(i)r, de(i)r, he(i)r, ne(i)r, peir/ pereles, spe(i)r *n.*, speir/sperit/sperand; ʒe(i)r;
s pe(i)s/pece, pleis/plesis;
st fe(i)st;
t lete/leit, meit/meting, mete/meit(e), schete/scheit, sweit/swet(e);
th cle(i)th;
# le/leyis, se/sey *n.*

ei is replaced by *ey* before *n* and *#*.

L (OF prose) 13 tales 13th-15th c.	MS. BN fr 22,933 14 tales (VATIC. added)	A/L (OF prose) 16 tales 13th-15th c. (FILIA instead of ROMA)	MS. Ars. 3156 AD 1245
ARBOR		ARBOR	
CANIS	Bauxillas	CANIS	Baucillas
APER		APER	
MEDICUS	Ancilles	MEDICUS	Anxilles
GAZA		GAZA	
PUTEUS	Lentulles	PUTEUS	Lentulus
SENESCALCUS		SENESCALCUS	
TENTAMINA	Malqudas	TENTAMINA	Malquidars li Tors
VIRGILIUS		VIRGILIUS	
AVIS	Caton	AVIS	Caton
SAPIENTES		SAPIENTES	
NOVERCA	Jessé	VIDUA	Jessé
FILIA + DUEL		FILIA	
		INCLUSA	Maras
		VATICINIUM	
		NOVERCA	

Emperor: Diocliciens
Son: no name, wife no name

It has the duel; the empress is burnt

Ed. Le Roux de Lincy (see under Dol.)
MS. BN fr 19,166 with variations from MS. BN fr 2137
- Mauricette Aïache, unpubl., 1966, MS. BN fr 19,166

See Gaston Paris, *Deux réd.*, pp. xx ff.

A/L (OF prose) 16 tales (NOVERCA added)	MS. Bruss. KB 9245 14th c.	A/L (OF prose) 17 tales (FILIA & NOVERCA added)	MS. BN fr 95 13th c.
ARBOR		ARBOR	
CANIS		CANIS	Bancillas
APER		APER	
MEDICUS		MEDICUS	Anxilles
GAZA		GAZA	
PUTEUS		PUTEUS	Lentullus
SENESCALCUS		SENESCALCUS	
TENTAMINA		TENTAMINA	Malquidars li roux
VIRGILIUS		VIRGILIUS	
AVIS		AVIS	Catons de Rome
SAPIENTES		SAPIENTES	
VIDUA		VIDUA	Iesse
ROMA		FILIA	
INCLUSA		INCLUSA	Mauras
VATICINIUM		ROMA	
NOVERCA		VATICINIUM	
		NOVERCA	

Emperor: Dyoclesiens
Son: no name

It has the duel

Gaston Paris, *Romania*, XXVIII, p.449: '... *BN fr 95 (auquel le MS. Gg.6.28 de Cambridge est à peu près identique) offre le texte le plus voisin du poême néerlandais ...*'

Ed. H.P.B.Plomp, *De Middelnederlandsche bewerking van het gedicht van den VII Vroeden van binnen Rome*, Utrecht, 1899, pp. 1* ff.

Rhymes in /a:/ continued

	-are	*-ary*	*-ase, -ace, -as*	*-asit*	*-a(i)st*	*-ate*	*-atis*	*-a(i)th*
Rhyming in couplets								
Bruce	57	-	2	-	-	6	3	4
Leg.Saints	64	-	-	-	-	6	-	13
Sc.Troy Bk	39	-	-	-	-	6	-	3
Wyntoun	31	-	15	-	-	11	-	2
Bk Alex.	44	-	-	-	-	4	-	11
Wallace	55	-	26	-	1	7	-	-
Thre Pr.	17	-	23	-	15	2	-	4
Lanc.Laik	15	-	11	-	-	7	-	-
Bk Chess	19	-	15	-	3	14	-	1
Ratis Ravyng	34	-	12	-	14	5	-	5
BSS	38	1	3	2	6	1	-	4
Alliterat.stanzas								
Bk Howlat	26	-	33	-	-	10	-	-
Gol. & Gaw.	33	-	25	2	-	9	-	-
Rauf Coilȝ.	57	-	7	-	11	6	-	4
Stanzas								
King Hart	9	-	3	-	6	9	-	3
Kingis Qu.	2	2	34	-	-	11	-	-
Various metres								
Henryson	28	2	14	-	-	26	-	-
Dunbar	18	4	10	-	-	5	2	-
Gav.Douglas 1501	12	4	12	-	-	35	-	-
Gav.Douglas 1513	30	6	18	-	-	16	-	12

Rhymes in /a:/ continued

-ave *-avit* *-awe* *-awin* *-awis* *-ape*

5 - 11 2 2 -
BUKE OF THE SEVYNE SAGIS
(MiddleScots verse) c.1515
4 - - 3

ARBOR 2 - - - - -
CANIS Bantillas
APER - 9 2 2 -
MEDICUS Amipullus, Maxillas,
GAZA 2 - 5 1 Ancillas -
PUTEUS Lentalus, Lentulus
SENESCALCUS 3 - 23 - - -
TENTAMINA Malcome, Maucundas
VIRGILIUS 8 - 4 - - -
AVIS Cato(ne), Catoun
SAPIENTES 1 - - - - -

--- - 3 Ampustinus, --- -

INCLUSA - 9 Craton(e) 4.5 - -
VATICINIUM
- 1 21 4 - -

Emperor: Dioclesiane 3 11 7 8
Son: Dioclesiane
Mother: no name 28 5 - -
Stepmother: no name
- - - 10 - -
Ed. W.A.Craigie, 1925, STS
Ed. C.C.van Buuren-Veenenbos, 1982

- - 6 - - -

- - 12 - - -

2 - 8 - - -

4 - - - 5 -

4 - 14 - - 4

4 - 8 - 2 2

HL (Latin prose)	MS. Innsbr.Cod.Lat. 310 AD 1342	HF (French prose)	Genève, 1492 Printed
ARBOR		ARBOR	
CANIS	Bantillas, Bancillas	CANIS	Pancillas
APER		APER	
PUTEUS	Lentul(l)us	PUTEUS	Lentulus
GAZA		GAZA	
AVIS	Katho, C(h)ato	AVIS	Craton
SAPIENTES		SAPIENTES	
TENTAMINA	Malquidrac	TENTAMINA	Malquedrac
VIRGILIUS		VIRGILIUS	
MEDICUS	Josephus	MEDICUS	Josephus
SENESC. + ROMA		SENESCALCUS + ROMA	
AMATORES	Cleophas	AMATORES	Cleophas
INCLUSA		INCLUSA	
VIDUA	Joachim	VIDUA	Joachim
VATIC. + AMICI		VATICINIUM + AMICI	

HL	HF
Emperor: Poncianus Son: Dyoclecyanus	Emperor: Poncianus Son: Dyoclecianus
Source, according to Gaston Paris, some manuscript belonging to A	
Ed. Georg Buchner, 1889	Ed. Gaston Paris, *Deux réd.*, pp. 55 ff.

APPENDIX VIa
NAMES OF SAGES IN OTHER MANUSCRIPTS

FRENCH A MSS

BN fr 1421	BN fr 2137	BN fr 20,040	BN fr 22,548
Bencillas, Bansillas, Bensillas	Bancillas, Ancilles	Baucillas	Baucillas
Ancilles, Augustes	Augustes	Augustes	Aucilles
Lentillus, Lencullus, Lencillus, Lentullus	Lentillus, Lantillus	Lentulle	Lentulus
Malcuidas, Malquidars li Rouz, Roux, Rox	Malcuidars li Rous	Malquidars li Rouz	Maucuidas li Tors
Chatons	Caton(s)	Chaton	Caton
Iessé	Jessé, Iosse	Jessé	Jessé
Martins, Mercon	Martine, Meron	Malqus	Mereneus

Cambr. Gg.I.1	BN nouv.acq.fr 13,521	Ars 3152	BN fr 25,545
Bancillas	Bancillas	Bancillas	Baucillas
Ancilles, Augustus, Anxilles	Ausilles, Augustes	Anxilles	Anxilles
Lentul(l)us, Lentillus	Tulles	Lentulles	Lentulus
Man-, Malquidras li Rouge, Mauquidanz	Malquildas li rous, Mauquidarz	Malquidans, Mauquidans	Maucuidas li Tors
Catoun de li roys rome, Catons,-touns	Chaton(s) de Rome	--- loss of a quire	Cathons
Iesse, Jesse	Gesse	---	Jessé
Mar(c)ius, Meron	Marcius, Meron	Martins	Mereus

Harl. 3860	Oxf.St.J.Coll.CII	BN fr 5586	BN fr 93
Baucillas	Ban-, Bencillas	Baucillas	Baucillas
Augustes	Banxilles, A(u)-gustus	Auxilles	Ancilles
Lentulus	Lentul(l)us	Lentilles	Lentulles
Mauquidras	Malcuidars, Mal-quidars	Melcuidras le Roux	Manonidas li Tors
Cathons	Caton(s)	Cathon	Catons
Iesse	Gesse	Jessé	Jessé
Anchilles	Maraus	Merous	Mereneus

ME A MSS

Auch.	D*	CR	F	Ar
Bancillas	Baucillas	Ban-, Bau-, Bawcyllas	Han-, Ban-, Ancyllas	---
Ancilles	Ancillees	Anxilles	Han-, Ancyllas	---
Lentilioun	Lentulus	Lentilio(u)n, -own(e)	Lentylyon	Lentilioun
Malquidras	Maladas	Malquidras	Malquydras	---
Katoun, Catoun	Caton(e)	Caton(n), -toun, -town	Caton of Rome	---
Sexte maister	Jess	Iesse	Jesse	---
---	Marcius	Maxencius	Maxencius, -yus	Maxione

E	B
Bancillas	Bancyllas
Anxulles	Ancyllas
Lentyllous, -iloun	Lentilius
Malquydras	Malendryas
Catoune of Rome	Caton
Gesse	Jesse
Maxious, Maxencyon	Maxius

A MS

MDu verse, MS.Bruss.KB II.1171
Bau-, Ban-xillas
Anxilles
Tin-, Ten-tillus
Mael-, Male-quidart
Cat(h)oen
Iesse
Mauras

L MSS

BN fr 19,166	BN fr 24,431	BN fr 1444	BN fr 189	Ars 3354
Baucil(l)as	Baucillas	Baucillas	Baucillas	Bazille
Anx-, Auxilles, Augustes	Auxilles	Augustes	Ancilles	Anxilles
Lantul(l)es	Lantulus	Tulles	Lentulle	Lentulus
Malquidras li Tors	Malquidars li Tors	Malcuidars li Tors	Maulcuidars	Malcuidas li Tors
Chaton(s) de Rome	Caton	Caton	Caton	Caton
Jessé, Iesse	Jessé	Jessé	Jessé	Jessé
Merons	---	---	---	---

A/L MSS		M MSS		
Ars 3516	Cambr.Gg.6.28	BN fr 573	Ars 2998	Ars 2999
Baucillas	Bancillas	Baucillas	Baucillas	Baucillas
Anxilles	Lentulus	Anxilles	Anxilles	Anxilles
Lentulus	Anxilles	Caton	Caton.	Caton
Malquidars li Tors	Malquidas	Lentulus	Lentulus	Lentulus
Caton	Catons	Jessé	Jessé	Jessé
Jessé	Iesse	Martins	Lentulus	Lentullus
Maras	Moras	Markes de Rome	Marques	Marques

HL MS	HF MS	HF MS
MDu prose	W.de Worde	Rolland
Bancillas	Pantyllas	Pantyllas, Pantillas
Lentulus	Lentulus	Lentalus, Lentulus
Craton	Craton	Craton
Malquedrac Waldag	Malquydrac	Malquydrak
Josephus	Josephus	Iosephus
Cleophas	Cleophas	Cleophas
Joachim	---	---

ADDENDA TO BIBLIOGRAPHY

Abercrombie, David, *Elements of General Phonetics*, Edinburgh University Press, 1967

Abercrombie, David, 'Some functions of silent stress', *Edinburgh Studies in English and Scots*, eds A.J.Aitken, Angus McIntosh and Hermann Pálsson, Longman, London, 1971, pp. 147-56

Burke's Genealogical and Heraldic History of the Landed Gentry, founded 1836 by John Burke and (John) Bernard Burke, ed. L.G.Pine, 17th edn, London, 1952

Cappelli, Adriano, *Dizionario di abbreviature latine ed italiane*, 6th edn, Milano, 1967

Craigie, James, ed., *The Poems of James VI of Scotland*, Vol. I, STS 3.22, Edinburgh, 1955 (for 1948); Vol. II, STS 3.26, Edinburgh, 1958 (for 1952)

Ellenberger, Bengt, *The Latin Element in the Vocabulary of the Earlier Makars, Henryson and Dunbar*, Lund Studies in English, 51, 1977

Kolinsky, Muriel, 'Pronouns of Address and the Status of Pilgrims in the *Canterbury Tales*', *Papers in Language and Literature*, 3 (1967), pp. 40-48

Latham, R.E., *Revised Medieval Latin Word-List from British and Irish Sources*, London, Published for The British Academy by The Oxford University Press, (1965) 1973

Murison, David, *The Guid Scots Tongue*, William Blackwood, Edinburgh, (1977) 1978

Roloff, Volker, *Reden und Schweigen. Zur Tradition und Gestaltung eines mittelalterlichen Themas in der französischen Literatur*, Wilhelm Fink Verlag, München, 1973

Stevenson, Allan, *The Problem of the Missale Speciale*, London, The Bibliographical Society, 1967

INDEX

ADDENDA